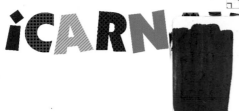

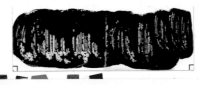

Carnaval!

D0567781

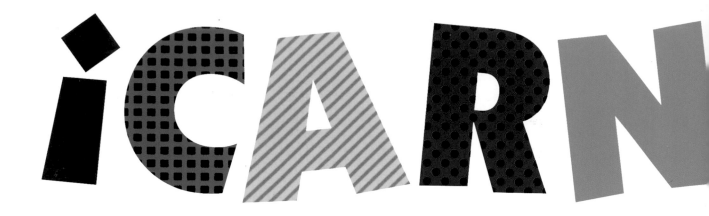

MUSEUM OF INTERNATIONAL FOLK ART *Santa Fe*

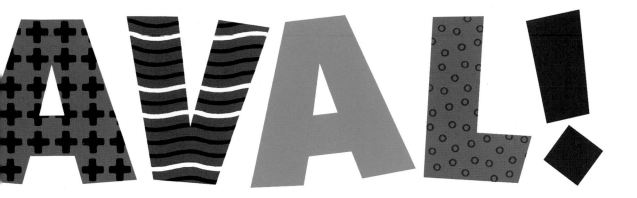

EDITED BY BARBARA MAULDIN

UNIVERSITY OF WASHINGTON PRESS *Seattle*

This book is published in conjunction with an exhibition
of the same name, produced by the Museum of International
Folk Art in collaboration with the UCLA Fowler Museum
of Cultural History.

Edited by Jane Kepp
Designed by Audrey Meyer and Ashley Saleeba
Maps by Deborah Reade

University of Washington Press
PO Box 50096, Seattle, WA 98145
www.washington.edu/uwpress

Library of Congress Cataloging-in-Publication Data

Carnaval! / edited by Barbara Mauldin
        p.   cm.
Includes bibliographical references and index.
ISBN 0-295-98426-0 (cloth : alk. paper)
ISBN 0-295-98427-9 (pbk. : alk. paper)

1. Carnival. I. Mauldin, Barbara, 1949–
GT4180.C26   2004
394.25–dc22   2004041958

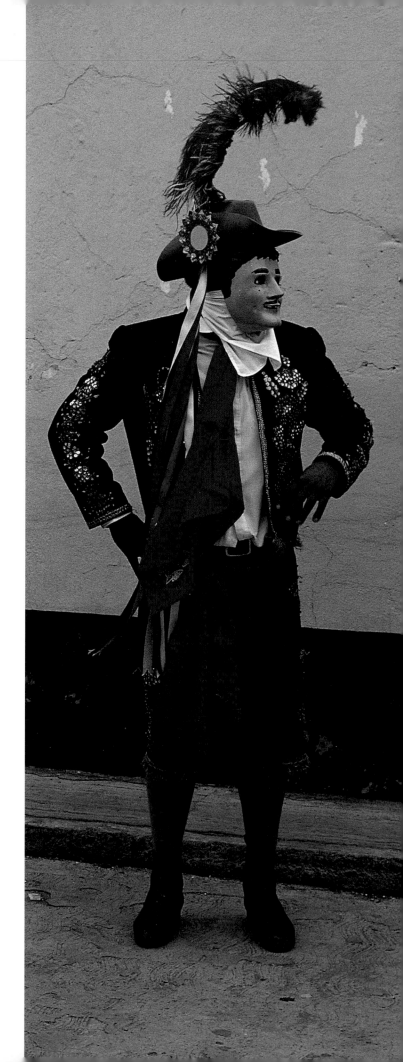

Español masquerader in Tepeyanco, Tlaxcala. *Photograph
by Barbara Mauldin, 2002.*

CONTENTS

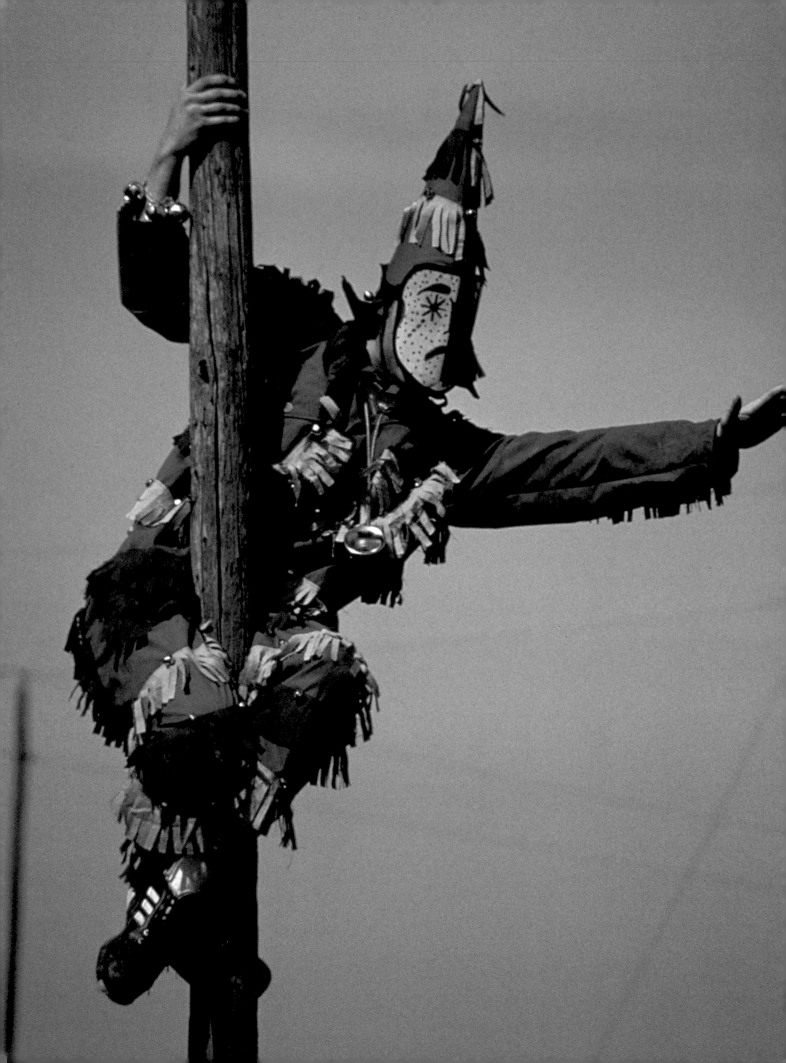

FOREWORD

FESTIVALS AS CULTURAL phenomena never fail to intrigue and captivate us as human beings, whether we are casual observers, researchers, or participants. The power of a seasonal observance such as Carnival rests in its conflation of the usual boundaries and categories that mark daily life, time, and space. The diversity of peoples and cultures all celebrating the same festival, old and yet ever new, makes for a range of playful complexities, continuity mixed with innovation, and endless varieties of human behavior.

For more than fifty years, the Museum of International Folk Art (MOIFA) has been documenting, presenting, and preserving the artistic traditions of the world's cultures. The study of festivals provides rich possibilities for examining an interrelated set of concepts and traditional practices such as cultural identity, foodways, costumes, ritual, play, dance, and music. The publication of this volume on Carnival fulfills another aspect of the museum's mission, which is to promote a greater understanding of these traditions through their documentation.

Like the boisterous festival depicted in the exhibi-

Sauvage Shane Lavergne scales a telephone pole during Mardi Gras in Basile, Louisiana. *Photograph by Maida Owens, 1992.*

tion mounted at MOIFA in conjunction with this book, the ¡CARNAVAL! project has taken on a larger-than-life quality for the Museum of International Folk Art. It began simply enough as an idea to organize a major exhibition and publication focusing on a single festival across cultures. I well remember curators Barbara Mauldin, from the Museum of International Folk Art, and John Nunley, of the Saint Louis Art Museum, sitting in the living room of then MOIFA director Charlene Cerny's home in Santa Fe, talking about the possibilities for such a project. Soon Doran Ross, then director of the UCLA Fowler Museum of Cultural History, was enlisted, and several planning meetings were organized, with participants representing all three museums.

On that evening in the mid-1990s, none of us could have predicted the many unexpected turns this project took along its path. Staff retirements, changes in leadership, and a vastly different economic and cultural climate required adjustments in the initial division of responsibilities. Yet despite these challenges, the essence of the project as it was sketched that night has endured, taking shape through the efforts of an international team of artists, dancers, researchers, photographers, videographers, curators, and scholars from many disciplines, working across three continents and eleven field sites and encompassing multiple cultures, languages, climates, and seasons.

Field research has been an important component of the ¡CARNAVAL! project as an investigation into the significance of this festival within communities. Identifying and interviewing community leaders, organizers, and participants in Carnival activities, as well as scholars who have studied this field, has ensured that multiple perspectives from within and outside a culture are represented by the diverse voices. The research consistently points up the nature of Carnival as a cyclical event that entails year-round preparations, each year beginning again shortly after the previous Carnival season concludes—still another indicator of Carnival's importance within a community context.

The driving force behind the project from the very beginning has been Barbara Mauldin, curator of Latin American folk art at MOIFA. Her unwavering dedica-tion to the field research, exhibition, and publication has been as impressive as her focus and organizational skills. Her vision for ¡CARNAVAL! has guided the project through every phase of its development. Barbara's hard work as curator, editor, and project director is evident in the exhibition and publication resulting from these efforts.

The essays in this book take us on a detailed and nuanced exploration of the fascinating dimensions of Carnival as the authors analyze the historical and present-day expressions of this festival of play and renewal.

Joyce Ice, Director
Museum of International Folk Art

ACKNOWLEDGMENTS

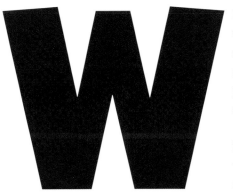

WHEN I BEGAN thinking about the ¡CARNAVAL! project in the spring of 1995, I never imagined the vast amount of time and work that such an undertaking would involve. Perhaps I was too ambitious in my desire to investigate and present a study of one type of celebration in a number of different communities in Europe and the Americas. However, I persevered and along the way enlisted the assistance of many people and the support of various institutions that helped bring the project to a successful conclusion.

This publication was made possible in part by a grant from the National Endowment for the Humanities, which is dedicated to expanding American understanding of human experience and cultural heritage. Generous funding was also provided by the Rockefeller Foundation, the Neutrogena Corporation, the International Folk Art Foundation, the Museum of New Mexico Foundation, the B. F. Foundation, the Eugene McDermott Foundation, the Margie E. Murdy Foundation, and individual donors such as Connie Thrasher Jaquith.

I want to thank John Nunley, Morton D. May Curator of the Arts of Africa, Oceania, and the Americas at the Saint Louis Art Museum, and Doran Ross, retired director at the UCLA Fowler Museum of Cultural History, who served as co-curators in the initial phase of the project. They helped to conceptualize the approach, select the sites to be included, and identify scholars for us to work with. Nunley and Ross also conducted fieldwork at some of the sites, and Nunley read many of the essays submitted for the book and provided valuable commentary.

I am grateful to all of the consultants and contributors to the publication, who embraced the project and made an effort to bring new ideas to the topic of Carnival. Among these were Samuel Kinser (European Carnival historian), Mariana Regalado, Antonio Muñoz Carrion, and Antonio Regalado (Laza, Spain), Valeria Fol (Bulgaria), Alessandro Falassi (Venice, Italy), Peter Tokofsky and Stefen Ospel (Basel, Switzerland), Carl Lindahl (Basile, USA), Cynthia LeCount Samaké, Peter McFarren, and Ryan Taylor (Oruro, Bolivia), Katarina Real (Recife and Olinda, Brazil), John Nunley, John Cupid, and Jerry and Alice Besson (Port of Spain, Trinidad and Tobago), Donald Cosentino (Haiti), and Jason Berry, William Fagaly, and Phoebe Ferguson (New Orleans, USA). In the notes to the essays, the individual authors have acknowledged others who assisted them with their research.

The prints and photographs in this book add another important level of information to our understanding of the various Carnival celebrations. Again

I want to thank the authors, who provided many outstanding photographs. Several institutions and other photographers must be acknowledged as well. Reproductions and permission to use historic prints and photographs came from the Kunsthistorisches Museum, Vienna, Austria; National Library, Paris, France; Fundación del Banco Central and Servicio Gráfico Quipus, La Paz, Bolivia; Paria Archive and Publishing Company, Port of Spain, Trinidad and Tobago; New York Public Library, Prints Collection, New York; LSU Libraries, Baton Rouge; and the UCLA Fowler Museum of Cultural History, Los Angeles.

I am indebted to many photographers who have devoted much of their careers to photographing Carnival at various sites and who spent time going through their slides to select images for use in the book. These include Shirley and David Rowen, Robert Jerome, Syndey Byrd, Gianni Vecchiato, Ruth Lechuga, Helga Ancona, George Ancona, Phyllis Galembo, Doran Ross, Michael P. Smith, and Susan Leavines. I also want to thank photographers Peter McFarren, Marilyn Houlberg, Gabriel Alatriste Montoto, Rossen Kolev, Pietro Rosai, Luca Betti, Helena Putnam, Heather Bohannan, Maida Owens, Mary Caroline Ancelet, Cornelia Palmer, and Sally Campbell who provided valuable images.

I am grateful to members of the Fowler Museum publication staff—Lynne Kostman, editor, and Daniel Brauer, press director and designer—for their assistance in getting the book started. The staff of the University of Washington Press have been a joy to work with, and I appreciate their enthusiasm for the book and their professional skill in seeing it through production. Many thanks to Pat Soden, director, Marilyn Trueblood, managing editor, Audrey Meyer, art director, John Stevenson, production manager, and Ashley Saleeba, designer. I am also indebted to Jane Kepp, editor on the project, who skillfully smoothed out the wrinkles in the text. Credit must go to Bonnie Bishop, the graphic designer who created the lively ¡CARNAVAL! logo that established the graphic style for the publication and rest of the project. In addition, I thank Deborah Reade for designing the maps and Dan Nerren for creating the index.

I would never have survived the final phase of preparing the manuscript for the press without the assistance of my intern, Micaela Seidel, whose skills in proofing and manipulating computer files were invaluable. Assistance from other members of the Museum of International Folk Art staff was also greatly appreciated. Joyce Ice, director, provided moral support and guidance throughout the project and helped with proofing the final copy. Ree Mobley, librarian and archivist, tracked down obscure references and acquired some of the historic images from other institutions. Jacqueline Duke, assistant director, skillfully oversaw the complex budget, and Frank Cordero, financial specialist, and Leslie Evans, of the Museum of New Mexico Foundation, processed hundreds of payments. Blair Clark, photographer for the Museum of New Mexico, provided studio photos for some of the prints and other images. I want to thank all of the other members of the MOIFA staff, several close friends, and my family for their support and patience while I was busy focusing my time and attention on the ¡CARNAVAL! project.

Most importantly, I want to acknowledge the people living in the eleven communities featured in this publication, who have kept their Carnival traditions alive. Many of them have dedicated much of their lives to planning, creating, practicing, and carrying out the various events involved in the festivities. As they bring a sense of renewal to themselves and their communities, they help the rest of us gain a better understanding of the importance and function of Carnival play.

Barbara Mauldin
Santa Fe, January 2004

¡CARNAVAL!

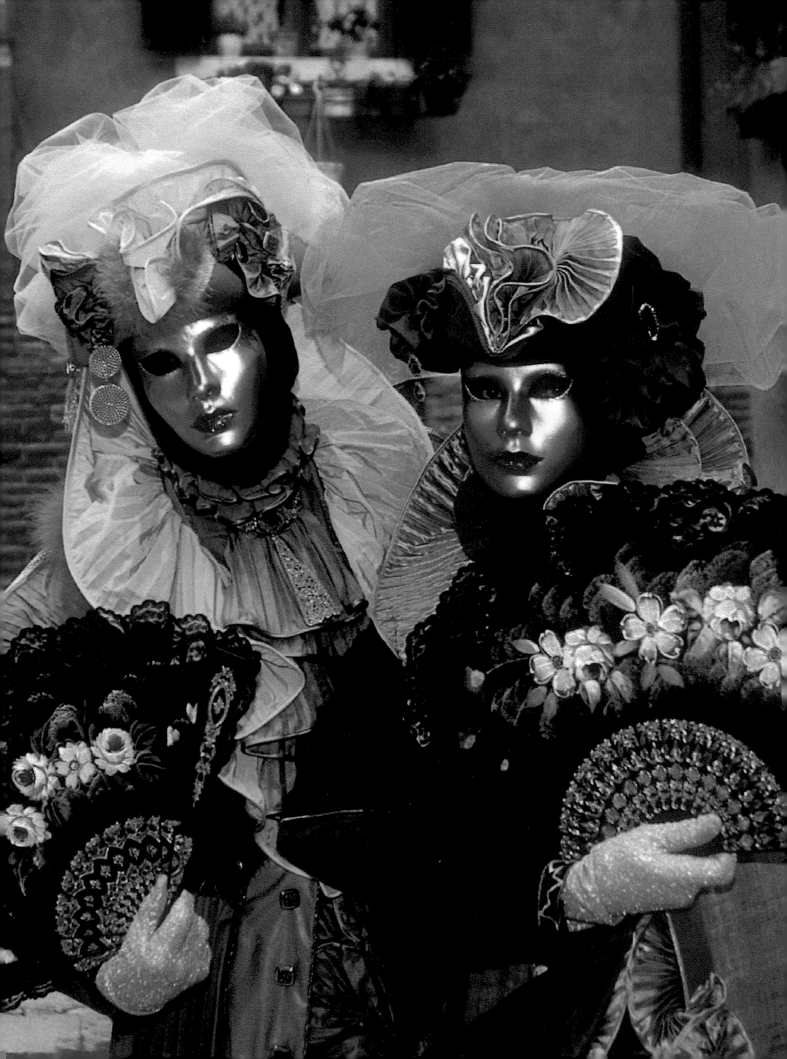

1 Introduction

CARNIVAL IN EUROPE AND THE AMERICAS

BARBARA MAULDIN

ASTER, WHICH MARKED the death and resurrection of Jesus, was one of the most important feasts of the early Catholic Church. To properly prepare for this day, Christians were asked to observe a few days of fasting. By the end of the fourth century the fast had been extended to several weeks, and the period became known as Lent. In the older Catholic calendar this fast lasted thirty-six days (not including Sundays), beginning on Monday six weeks before Easter Sunday. In the eleventh century the fast was extended to forty days, beginning on Ash Wednesday. Besides cutting back on the number of meals and certain kinds of foods, the Church insisted upon abstinence from sin and vice.[1]

The first written description of a celebration occurring just before the beginning of the Lenten fast is found in a Roman text dating from the early twelfth century. The pope and other Roman citizens watched a parade through the city, which was followed by the killing of steers and other animals.[2] The Roman pre-Lenten festival continued to be observed and grew in popularity over the next few centuries, gradually spreading to other European cities as well. The Latin term *carnem-levare,* meaning "to remove [oneself] (*levare*) from flesh or meat (*carnem*)," came to be associated with the celebration. Eventually the Italians shortened the name to *carnevale* (flesh farewell).

By the fourteenth century the celebration had become a rowdy tradition featuring boisterous games and bodily self-indulgence, having absorbed activities from other late winter and early spring festivals with pre-Christian roots.[3] Carnival was a secular event that marked the approach of Catholic Lent and the seasonal change from winter to spring. Through ritual, masquerade, and play, which exaggerate and invert everyday behavior, the celebration led people through this time with irony, disguise, laughter, and revelry, helping to ensure a proper renewal and growth for themselves and their communities.[4]

From the beginning Carnival was dynamic, absorbing other festival traditions in each of the countries and regions where it was celebrated. The Italian name for the festival, *carnevale,* was translated into languages such as Spanish and Portuguese as *carnaval,* into English as Carnival or Shrove Tide (fasting season), into French as *Mardi Gras* (fat Tuesday), and into German as *Karneval* or *Fasching* (fasting). Sometimes local names were used to refer to the celebration, such as *entrudo* or *entroido* (the opening) in parts of Portugal and northwestern Spain.[5]

Despite the regional differences, by the fifteenth and sixteen centuries some basic characteristics were

1.1 Carnival masqueraders in Venice, Italy. *Photograph by Shirley and David Rowen, 2000.*

prevalent in Carnivals throughout Europe. The season for the festival generally began in January with preparations and events that grew in intensity and excitement as the time drew closer to Lent. For the elite members of society in the larger cities and royal courts, the celebrations generally consisted of raucous masked balls, comical theatrical performances, and sponsorship of various forms of public competition. For the rest of the population in the cities and rural communities, Carnival was made up of a set of loosely structured events organized by groups of friends, clubs, fraternities, and guilds, primarily consisting of young men.[6]

A prominent activity in the rural celebrations, known as charivari, featured groups of merrymakers traveling from house to house singing songs or ballads that criticized or made fun of the occupants. Charivari was sometimes accompanied by loud, rough music, such as the playing of pots and pans. In return for the mock serenade, the homeowner would often douse the troupe with a bucket of water or ashes (fig. 1.2).[7] A related activity carried out in other communities was known as mumming, in which wandering groups performed a begging ritual in exchange for food and other items.[8] Many rural carnivals also featured one or more men dressed in animal skins or other, more elaborate costumes, with bells hung from belts around their waists. As part of their performance, the ringing of the bells was said not only to announce their presence in the community but also to be a sign of rebirth, of coming out of the darkness of winter.[9]

In the larger towns and urban centers, Carnival groups often carried out processions, with costumed people singing and dancing in the streets or riding on floats. The masquerades portrayed a variety of themes, many of which poked fun at historical or contemporary members of society. Other characters were derived from the popular Italian comical theater known as the commedia dell'arte. This was also a time to break down class distinctions and play a social "rite of reversal," which included men dressing as women and women dressing as men. An important public event was the recitation of satirical poetry or the performance of a comical play, either of which provided social and political commentary. Another type of entertainment featured a debate or battle between Carnival and Lent (fig. 1.3).

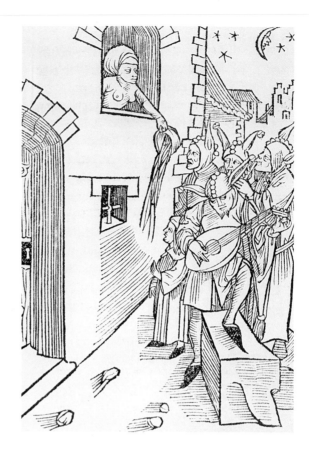

1.2 Carnival charivari troupe in Dijon, France, 1749. Woodcut print by J. B. Lucotte DuTilliot. *Photograph courtesy of the National Library, Paris, France, Department of Prints.*

In both rural and urban areas, some kind of competition often took place, as well as a hunt, traditionally aimed at capturing a bear, bull, or cock to use as the sacrificial victim of the Carnival feast. Less formally structured activities, such as gambling, aggressive assaults with buckets of water and other substances, and a variety of promiscuous acts, went on intermittently. There was massive eating of meat and other special foods, and people consumed alcohol as if they might never drink again. All of these activities ceased on the morning of Ash Wednesday, when the revelers went to church to receive the blessing of ash on their foreheads and begin their Lenten fast.[10] In some areas Church officials followed the old Catholic calendar, with Lent beginning on Monday, so the celebration was allowed to continue through Sunday night.[11]

For the most part, the pre-Lenten festivals in Europe continued to evolve throughout the seventeenth and eighteenth centuries, although the Catholic Church, which had always been critical of Carnival festivities, developed an even stronger opposition to the events' sinful conduct and vulgar disorder. In some European cities, Church authorities successfully subdued or abolished Carnival altogether.

The democratic and industrial revolutions of the nineteenth century had a different effect on Carnival celebrations in Europe. With the development of a new class structure and the blossoming of the bourgeoisie, the Carnivals that had survived began to be organized differently and take on new meanings. The emerging middle class saw Carnivals as civic events that helped to mold the identity of their cities and towns. Carnival balls and parties were now open to a larger segment of the population, and the street parades became more organized. Groups from different neighborhoods or workers' leagues competed with one another for the best performances, costumes, dancing, and music. Carnival was still a time to express social and political criticism, generally through public readings of satirical poetry, ballads, or testaments.[12]

During the late sixteenth and seventeenth centuries, Spain, Portugal, and France began colonizing parts of the Americas. The colonists carried their Catholic religion and associated festival traditions with them. By the eighteenth century, Carnival celebrations were being held in some colonial communities in what is now the southern United States, Mexico, Central and South America, and the Caribbean. The festivities took a variety of forms, including fancy dress balls, house-to-house visitations, informal street processions, and rowdy antics.[13] Local Indian groups and the enslaved Africans who were brought to work for the colonists may have observed these activities, but with a few exceptions they would not have been allowed to join in.[14]

1.3 *Combat of Carnival against Lent, 1559*. Painting by Pieter Brueghel. *Photograph courtesy of the Kunsthistorisches Museum, Vienna, Austria.*

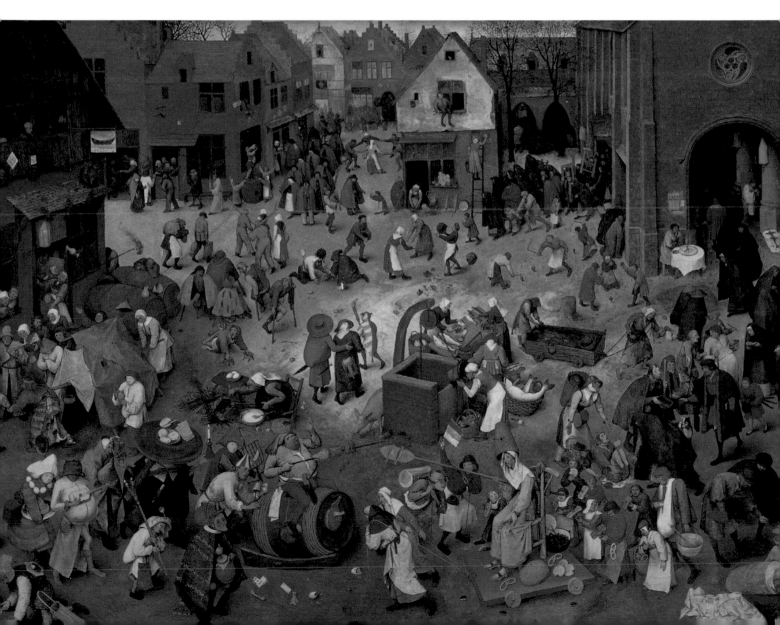

The nineteenth century saw a major shift in politics and class structure in the Americas as nations liberated themselves from their European overlords. The upper- and middle-class citizens of the newly formed states, however, wanted to model their lives after those of Europeans, and as part of this effort, Carnival celebrations gained popularity. These celebrations often took the form of fancy balls and more organized street parades.[15] At the same time, lower-class indigenous peoples became freer and African slaves were emancipated. Each of these groups had its own festival traditions, which had been suppressed under colonial rule; now they could conduct their rituals and celebrations more openly. By the mid- to late nineteenth century, Indians and African descendents were regularly participating in Carnival, either in their own communities or as part of a larger urban celebration.[16]

During the twentieth century in many urban centers of Europe and the Americas, the focus on fancy Carnival balls decreased, except among the upper class. In contrast, civic parades continued to grow in popularity, with groups choosing different themes for their masquerades and competing with other troupes as they marched or danced down the streets or rode on floats. The themes for the costumes drew from a variety of sources, ranging from ancient history and world events to local issues and traditions and fantasy creations. By the second half of the century, women were taking a much more active role in the groups, and city officials were organizing processions and other events specifically for children and families, so everyone in the community could feel part of the celebrations.[17]

In parts of Europe and the Americas, Carnivals also continued to be carried out in rural communities. There the activities often reflected a more medieval form of ritual and play. In some cases this featured one group of revelers going from house to house during the course of a day to perform or make fun of the occupants and to collect food, or both, afterwards joining with everyone in the town center for a community celebration.[18] In other cases, many people took part in a series of semistructured events held over several days in the center of town.[19] In both forms, the activities and the interchange among the villagers were often rowdy and full of local satire.

1.4 *Peliqueiros* in Laza, Spain, act as authority figures to encourage revelry and keep order during the *entroido* festivities. *Photograph by Aurelia Gomez, 1999.*

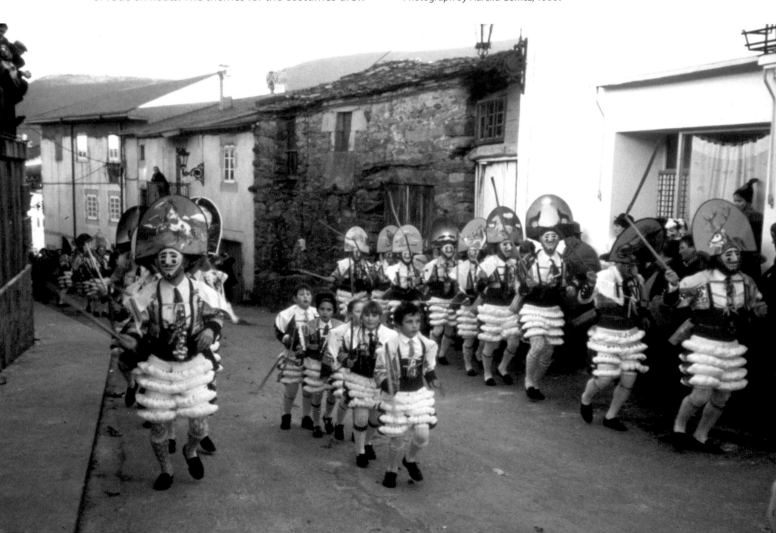

As we move into the twenty-first century, Carnival persists as an important celebration in many urban and rural communities in central and southern Europe and in the southern United States, Mexico, Central and South America, and the Caribbean. In many cases, participants' cultural traditions are annually reinvented. Topics relating to current social and political issues may also be added, allowing the festivals to be relevant to the communities. Groups begin preparing months ahead of time. In many locations, Carnival events start in January, and anticipation continues to build during the weeks leading up to the actual celebration.[20]

Carnival in Eleven Communities

Each of the essays in this book offers a window into a cultural region and community in Europe or the Americas where Carnival is an important part of the annual cycle of activities. The various names used to refer to the pre-Lenten festival reflect the different languages spoken by the participants, and their diverse masquerades and performances represent the history and evolution of traditions in each region, city, or town.[21]

LAZA, SPAIN

The small rural community of Laza is located in the northwest corner of Spain in a region known as Galicia. Because of its geography, the area has always been somewhat isolated from the rest of Spain and is often viewed as "poor and backward" by the rest of the country—but Galicians take great pride in their cultural heritage and their way of life. Their Carnival, known regionally as *entroido,* has roots in medieval festival traditions, though it is still a vibrant part of village life today. The play is acted out through music, dance, and feasting but also involves ritualized aggression such as participants whipping spectators and throwing ashes, flour, water, and dirt filled with ants on one another. Social and political commentary is provided through makeshift floats and the public reading of a testament. The primary masked characters are the *peliqueiros,* who wear elaborate costumes with large bells around their waists and act as authority figures in both encouraging revelry and keeping order in the festival (fig. 1.4).

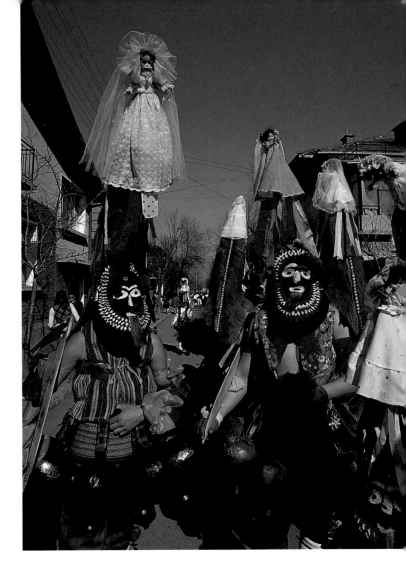

1.5 Kouker masqueraders in Pavel Banja, Bulgaria, play a lead role in the ritual drama carried out during the pre-Lenten celebration. *Photograph by Shirley and David Rowen, 1998.*

RURAL BULGARIA

From ancient times the rolling hillsides of Bulgaria in southeastern Europe have been occupied by a series of ethnic groups and political powers, first the ancient Thracians, Greeks, and Romans and later Slavs, Bulgars, Turks, and Russians. Despite years of oppression under the Soviet government, most Bulgarians remained members of the Eastern Orthodox Church and continued to observe Lent and the Carnival celebration that precedes it. In many areas they call this festival Kouker's Day, referring to the primary male masquerader—the Kouker—who wears a costume made of goatskins and bells around his waist (fig. 1.5). This tradition is particularly well preserved in villages of the Strandzha

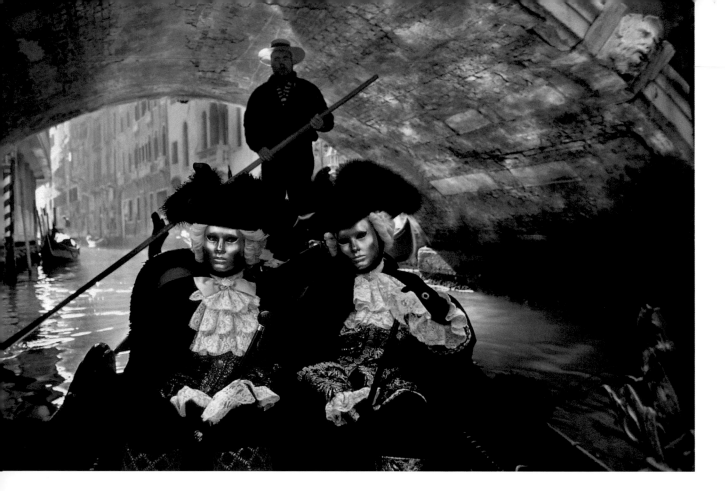

Mountain region in southeastern Bulgaria. As part of the Carnival play, the Kouker and other masqueraders carry out rituals to encourage fertility in the coming agricultural season. These include visiting each house in the community to collect special foods and a ritual plowing in the center of town.

VENICE, ITALY

The *carnevale* of Venice, Italy, began in the Middle Ages, when the great squares of the city were turned over to aristocratic pageantry, public sports competitions, and performances by roving minstrels and actors. The excesses of the festival were heavily criticized by government and religious reformers of the eighteenth and nineteenth centuries, and by the early twentieth century Venice's Carnival had stopped being celebrated altogether. Its revival in the 1980s was a reincarnation of the aristocratic festival as it was known in the Renaissance era. Today Venice's *carnevale* is open to everyone, and participants come from many countries and a range of social backgrounds to take on the identities of classical personages and fantasy characters (figs. 1.1, 1.6). The costumed revelers slowly make their way through the narrow streets of

1.6 *Carnevale* in Venice, Italy, is open to anyone who wants to participate. Many choose to wear beautiful masks and elaborate, seventeenth-century court costumes. *Photograph by Shirley and David Rowen, 1998.*

Venice and across bridges wrapped in a thin layer of fog, while others ride through the canals in gondolas decorated for the festive occasion.

BASEL, SWITZERLAND

Basel, located in northern Switzerland bordering Germany and France, spreads out on both sides of the Rhine River, a strategic location that allowed it to become an important production and trade center as early as the fifteenth century. Basel's Carnival, known by the Swiss-German name *Fasnacht* (night before fasting), dates from the Middle Ages. Then, villagers put on costumes and masks and roamed the streets, participating in spontaneous, rowdy affairs. After the Reformation in the sixteenth century, many of the townspeople became Protestants, and the date of the celebration was moved to the week after the beginning of Lent. By the nineteenth century the structure of the celebration had become more formalized, with members of work guilds joining together into fife and drum troupes that paraded through the streets. This form continues today, and the themes of costumes, painted lanterns, and oral presentations are focused on conveying social and political criticism (fig. 1.7).

BASILE, USA

The Cajun *courir de Mardi gras* (run of Mardi Gras) of rural southwestern Louisiana reflects French traditions transported from Europe into Nova Scotia and carried from there to Louisiana by Acadian immigrants in the latter part of the eighteenth century. The celebration has antecedents in medieval European mumming, or ceremonial begging, a tradition that merged with influences from the diverse cultures that came together on the Louisiana prairies. Today, Cajun Mardi Gras troupes are made up primarily of rural white men and women who masquerade as *sauvages* (wild men) and go from house to house in their communities performing songs and other acts in exchange for a chicken and other types of food (fig. 1.8). The food eventually goes into the gumbo that everyone in town shares at an evening dance party.

TLAXCALA, MEXICO

The Tlaxcala area of south-central Mexico has long been inhabited by Nahuatl-speaking peoples, who came under Spanish rule in the early sixteenth century. Wealthy Spanish and French landowners forced the Indians to labor on their plantations, and Catholic priests worked to convert them to Christianity. Since the late nineteenth century the Indians of this region have regained much of their freedom, but they still consider themselves Catholics and observe Lent and the *carnaval* celebration that precedes it. Groups in communities throughout the region go from house to house in their neighborhoods and perform French quadrilles, or square dances. Much of the masquerading and play is oriented toward making fun of the Europeans who once controlled the region (fig. 1.9), but underlying this practice are petitions for rain, fertility, and well-being for the community in the coming spring and agricultural season.

ORURO, BOLIVIA

Oruro, a mining town located in the high plateau region of the Bolivian Andes, 12,144 feet above sea level, was founded by Spaniards in 1606 as a base for exploiting rich mineral deposits in the surrounding hills. The Aymara and Quechua peoples of this area were already working the local mines and subsequently became laborers for the Europeans. Enslaved Africans were also brought here to work, but the high altitude and cold climate made it difficult for them to survive. The *carnaval* celebration and costumes worn in Oruro have evolved over time to incorporate diverse aspects of the region's cultural history (fig. 1.10). Because of Oruro's location in the Southern Hemisphere, its pre-Lenten festival takes place in

1.7 Each year the *Fasnacht* clubs in Basel, Switzerland, select themes to portray in their costumes and painted lanterns. This one pokes fun at a local museum. *Photograph by Robert Jerome, 1999.*

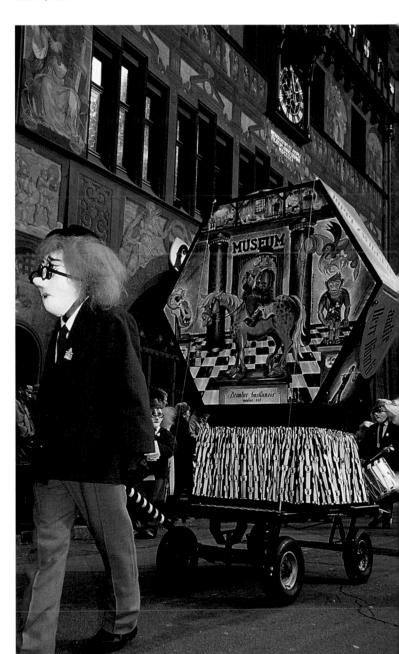

the fall, traditionally a time to make offerings to the Andean gods. Some of these rituals have been incorporated into the Carnival activities, along with a strong devotion to the Catholic Virgin Mary. The festival features many different groups who perform tightly choreographed dances in a procession that winds through the streets of the town.

RECIFE AND OLINDA, BRAZIL

Recife and its neighboring city of Olinda grew up in the sixteenth and seventeenth centuries as commercial harbors for the rich sugar plantations established by Portuguese colonists in northeastern Brazil, just south of the equator. During the conquest, most of the local Indian population was destroyed or forced into the interior of the country, and African slaves were brought to work in the fields. Since their emancipation in the late nineteenth century, Afro-Brazilians have been able to join in the *carnaval* celebrations, and today Carnival is a dynamic event with over a million participants from different social classes. The transition from winter to spring is far from the minds of the residents of Recife and Olinda, thanks to a year-round tropical climate and the fact that Lent and Easter actually take place in their late summer. However, the organizational structure of the celebration follows the European urban model, with distinct clubs coming out of trade guilds, religious organizations, and neighborhood associations. They compete with one another through performances that feature costumes, rhythms, and choreography drawing from European, African, and mythic Brazilian Indian traditions (fig. 1.11).

PORT OF SPAIN, TRINIDAD AND TOBAGO

The small, two-island nation of Trinidad and Tobago lies in the green, tropical West Indies just north of the equator in the Caribbean. Carnival was first introduced there by Spaniards in the early eighteenth century and later celebrated by British colonizers and French plantation owners who settled on the islands in the late eighteenth century. The African slaves who worked on the plantations were emancipated in the early nineteenth century and soon embraced the festival as a symbolic rite of liberation. Chinese and East Indian indentured laborers and later American navy men added to the personality of the celebration. Known as *mas* (an abbreviation for mask or masquerade),

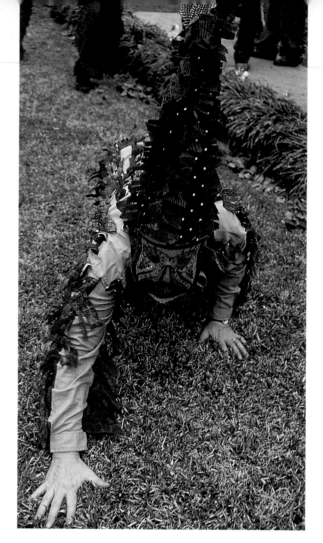

1.8 A Mardi Gras reveler in the rural community of Basile, Louisiana, stalks a chicken during a stop at a home where the troupe "begs" for food. *Photograph by Helena Putnam, 1994.*

Carnival in Port of Spain has evolved into a huge celebration in which thousands of revelers come together from all ethnic groups and social classes to join Carnival troupes and dance through the streets of town. The themes of their masquerades draw from the history of the island, the Americas, and the world, as well as conveying contemporary aesthetic expressions (fig. 1.12).

HAITI

Carnival was introduced into the Caribbean nation of Haiti by French colonists who established the colony of St. Domingue in 1697. Revelers brought with them their Breton and Norman traditions, which were said to be among the most raucous in Europe at that time. From the beginning, Mardi Gras celebrations in Haiti

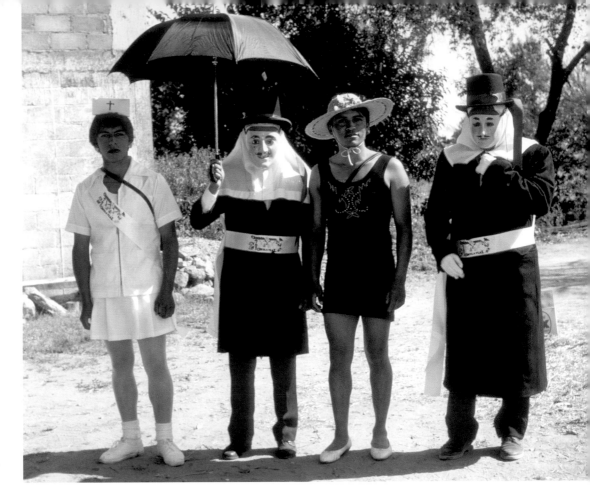

1.9 Young men in the rural village of Contla in Tlaxcala, Mexico, wear *carnaval* masquerades that impersonate and make fun of the French dandies who once lived in this region. Their "female" dance partners are played by other young men, who enjoy dressing up and acting as women. *Photograph by Barbara Mauldin, 1999.*

were deeply politicized, with Carnival troupes making fun of French royalty and local officials. During the years of the Haitian Revolution (1791–1804), revelers supported and provoked political change, a trend that continued into the following century. As elsewhere in the Americas, African slaves had been brought to the island to work on the plantations, and with emancipation in the early nineteenth century, they, too, joined in the Carnival festivities. Today, the Afro-Caribbean residents of Haiti dominate politics and Carnival festivities (fig. 1.13). As in the past, Mardi Gras revelers use the festive occasion to criticize the government and military officials, and they have been successful in bringing about political changes.

NEW ORLEANS, USA

The Carnival celebration in the southern US city of New Orleans is also known as Mardi Gras, because the festival is historically associated with French groups who settled there in the early eighteenth century. It was not until the mid-nineteenth century, however, with the influx of Anglo, Native American, Afro-American, Afro-Caribbean, and Creole people, that the celebration we know today began to emerge. Fol-

lowing nineteenth-century urban models, societies known as "krewes" were organized to participate in elaborate balls and public parades, many of which included the use of large floats. The Carnival organizations in New Orleans were formed along social and racial lines, a situation that has continued to the present time. These organizations range from all-white male secret societies of the upper class to flamboyant gay groups, the white-collar Afro-American Zulu club, and the working-class, Afro-American "Indians," whose costumes are the most elaborate of all (fig. 1.14).

Broad View and Comparisons

Each of these regions, cities, and towns has developed its own distinct form of Carnival, but a broad view provides some interesting comparisons.

As might be expected, Carnival celebrations in the four rural areas—Laza, Spain, southeastern Bulgaria, Basile, USA, and Tlaxcala, Mexico—all have close ties to the spring seasonal cycle, and participants carry out festival activities that have customarily corresponded to this season. Much of the Carnival play in Laza relates to the boisterous charivari tradition,

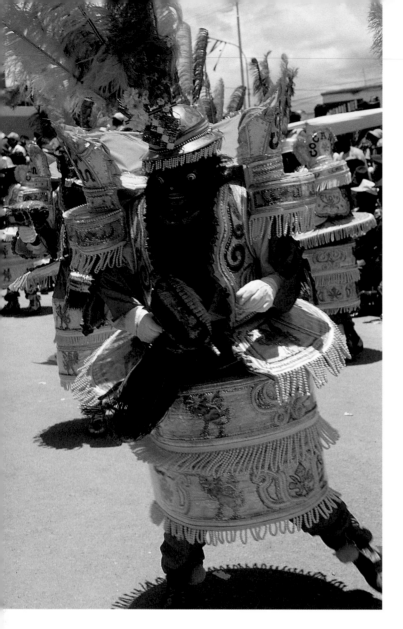

1.10 *Moreno* masqueraders in the *carnaval* procession in Oruro, Bolivia, portray Africans who once worked as slaves alongside Andean Indians in mines and on lowland plantations. *Photograph by Barbara Mauldin, 2000.*

whereas activities in Bulgaria and Basile take the form of ceremonial begging, or mumming. The main characters in Laza and Bulgaria are individuals or groups of masqueraders who wear bells tied around their waists; these create a distinctive sound related to Carnival and to the awakening of spring. The Nahuatl Indian people of Tlaxcala, Mexico, have developed a Carnival that draws from both European and indigenous traditions, with dancers performing for other members of their barrio, or neighborhood. An underlying goal of the activities is to bring fertility and prosperity to the whole community.

The revived Carnival celebration carried out in Venice, Italy, today reflects the medieval and Renaissance model of an elite urban celebration, with individuals or small groups masquerading for their own enjoyment. In contrast, the festival in Basel, Switzerland, exemplifies the civic urban model that developed in the nineteenth century. That is, large, organized troupes that derive from workers' guilds, social clubs, and neighborhoods wear masquerades with specific themes and compete with one another in musical parades. In general, this is the model found in the urban Carnivals of Oruro, Bolivia; Recife and Olinda, Brazil; Port of Spain, Trinidad and Tobago; Port-au-Prince, Haiti; and New Orleans, USA.

An interesting aspect found in the last four cities is the strong heritage from former African slaves, who struggled to position themselves in lower-class society once they were emancipated. Many Carnival groups grew out of neighborhood gangs that fought one another violently to establish their seniority. Eventually this fighting was transformed into competition through Carnival costumes and performances, a mode of rivalry that encouraged the poor and suppressed to find greater resiliency by redefining themselves. Some of the most spectacular and ingenious masquerades found in Carnival celebrations in these cities today are created in lower-class neighborhoods, where residents often embrace the annual festival as a means of bringing about social change.

Religion led to the creation of the Carnival celebration, for it grew out of the desire to play and indulge oneself before the beginning of the Catholic Lenten fast. Most members of European and American communities, however, view it as a secular festival, and many people who participate in Carnival activities today are not devout Catholics. Indeed, Carnival activities in many of the towns and cities featured in this book continue after Lent begins, and *Fasnacht* in Basel does not start until the Monday after Ash Wednesday, partially because of Protestants' defiance of the strict rules of the Catholic Church.

Religion does play a role in some community celebrations in which residents have layered Christianity with older beliefs and practices. This is seen in Carnival activities carried out in the rural villages of southeastern Bulgaria, where masqueraders perform ancient ritual dramas intended to bring fertility to the community. In the rural villages of Tlaxcala, Mexico, and the mining town of Oruro, Bolivia, indigenous people adopted elements of Catholicism and integrated them with their own pre-Hispanic religions. All aspects of their lives have spiritual significance, and rowdy festivals are no exception. Indeed, Carnival season was traditionally a time to pay tribute to their gods, and many Carnival participants in both places visit the local Catholic church and pray to the saints as part of their activities. In Oruro, many residents also make offerings to Andean deities on specific days during the celebrations. Some of the Carnival troupes in Recife and Olinda, Brazil, and in Port-au-Prince, Haiti, come directly out of Xango and Vodou temples, which serve as community and religious centers for devotees of African-derived religion. As in the temples, the dancers may go into trance during their Carnival performance.

Among the eleven regions and communities covered in this book, a wide variety of characters and themes is portrayed in the masquerades. Some of those seen in Venice and among the old guard in New Orleans represent ancient Greek and Roman gods. Another popular group of masquerades found in Venice, Basel, Recife, and New Orleans is derived from the Italian commedia dell'arte, which had become an important part of European Carnival by the late sixteenth century. Among these, the characters Harlequin and Pierrot are the most prevalent.

Many masquerades are taken from local history and culture. For example, the *peliqueiros* in Laza, Spain, are said to derive from sixteenth-century tax collectors. The *diablos,* or devil masqueraders, that play a prominent role in Oruro's Carnival honor the Andean god of the underworld, Supay, whom Catholic priests viewed as diabolical and on whose images they put horns to further their point. Some of the most elegant costumes worn by Afro-Brazilians in the *carnaval* of Recife and Olinda represent kings and queens from the Portuguese royal court, a tradition that began on the colonial sugar plantations when wealthy owners dressed their slaves in such costumes for Christmas pageants. The sailor costumes worn by Afro-Trinidadians in Carnival processions in Port of Spain imitate the distinctive clothing of British and American seamen who have been stationed on the island. A different type of example is found in Port-au-Prince, where young

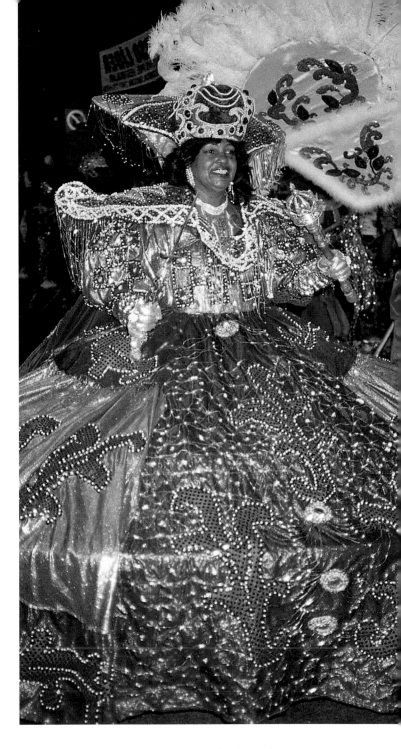

1.11 Among the most impressive groups performing in the *carnaval* celebration in Recife and Olinda in Pernambuco, Brazil, are the *maracatu* nations. Their costumes portray a king and queen and their royal court. *Photograph by Katarina Real, 1996.*

Afro-Haitian men masquerade as the Vodou trickster god, Gede.

In some cases, masquerades drawn from local history are worn as a means of criticizing and making fun of certain individuals or whole groups. An example is found in Basel, where a popular masquerade known

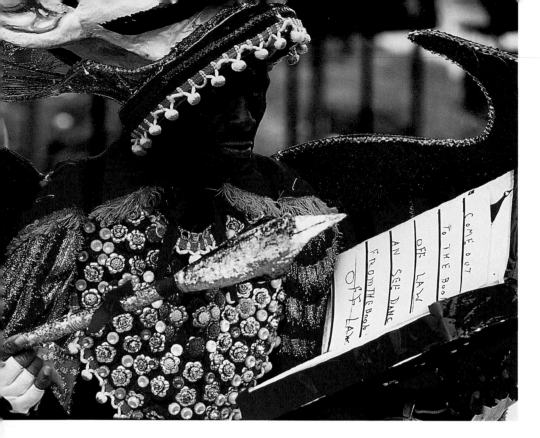

1.12 One of the traditional masked characters appearing in *mas* performances in Port of Spain, Trinidad and Tobago, is a devil known as the Bookman. He carries a large pen so he can write what he sees into the "Book of Law." *Photograph by Robert Jerome, 2001.*

as *Waggis* portrays the unruly French farmers from the neighboring region of Alsace who used to come into Basel and sell their produce in the street markets. Many young Indian men in the rural villages of Tlaxcala wear elaborate costumes and beautiful pink-skin masks that impersonate and make fun of the wealthy Spanish and French ranchers and dandies who once controlled the political and economic life of their region. Some Mardi Gras revelers in Port-au-Prince even go so far as to dress themselves as past dictators or their henchmen, people who made Haitians' lives so miserable. Giant puppet masqueraders in Olinda often portray prominent politicians and other local celebrities in humorous ways. On the streets of the French Quarter in New Orleans, people masquerade in a variety of creative costumes, including some that make fun of national leaders such as President George W. Bush.

Other types of costumes and Carnival activities are focused on broader social and political issues, either within the community or the region or on the larger world scene. The "testament of the donkey" read in Laza on the last day of *entroido* provides a satirical accounting of the scandals and other interesting events that have taken place in this small community during the past year. The large *Fasnacht* groups in Basel annually chose a theme for their costumes and painted lanterns that criticizes a specific local or inter-

national issue, such as packs of wild dogs running loose on the city streets or the war in Iraq. Other groups go from tavern to tavern in Basel, reading a form of poetry that cleverly conveys similar types of critical commentary. Some of the themes chosen by the large Carnival groups in Port of Spain have dealt with environmental issues in the islands. In Haiti, Carnival songs have retold scandals of politicians' lives and served as rallying cries for citizens to rise up against rulers.

Role reversal has been an aspect of Carnival masquerading since medieval times, especially the exchange of men dressing as women. This tradition remains popular today, and some form of it is found in each of the eleven communities featured here. Most of this cross-dressing is carried out by heterosexual men who enjoy the chance to dress up in a feminine outfit and burlesque the antics of women. In Bulgaria, men traditionally dress as women to carry out part of the ritual drama connected with the Carnival festivities. Until recently in Tlaxcala, conservative attitudes did not allow girls and young women to participate in Carnival performances, so young men wearing dresses and feminine masks took the role of female dance partners. In several of the eleven communities, individuals or small groups of gay men dress up as women and join in the festivities. This is particularly true in New Orleans, where a large number of gay men have formed their own Mardi Gras societies, each sponsoring a fancy ball in which members wear elaborate gowns and wigs and gorgeous makeup. They also participate in a costume competition in the French Quarter, where more flamboyant outfits can be seen.

In some cities and towns, such as Venice, Basel, Basile, Oruro, and New Orleans, women enjoy dressing as men and playing out masculine roles under the guise of their masquerade. In many communities, however, women's participation in rowdy Carnival performances was minimal until the mid-twentieth century, and once they achieved the status of participants, they chose to play up the feminine side of their costuming and movements.

Another interesting type of role reversal is found in cities in the Americas where indigenous people and African slaves were brought together under colonial rulers. Over time, masquerades and performances were developed that featured one ethnic group consciously portraying and playing with the cultural expressions of the other. In Oruro, Andeans created the *morenada* groups, whose rich costumes and performances portray a mythical rendition of the African slaves who once lived and worked alongside native people in the mines and on lowland plantations. In Recife-Olinda, Port of Spain, Haiti, and New Orleans we find descendants of African slaves wearing elaborate costumes and giving performances that imitate and identify with the Indians who had been a part of their history in the Americas.

In Port of Spain and New Orleans we also find African Americans playing with their African identity. Over the years, some Carnival groups in Trinidad have utilized African fabrics, patterns, and iconography in their costumes to emphasize and identify with their cultural heritage. The Zulu Carnival society, made up of middle-class African American men in New Orleans, takes this practice one step further; its members wear blackface and grass skirts, carry spears, and throw coconuts as a statement against the stereotyping of black people in American society.

Other types of masquerades are also found in Carnival celebrations, ranging from animals and birds to different kinds of foods, musical instruments, and even aliens from outer space. Many costumes and masks worn in Venice, Port of Spain, and New Orleans are

purely fantasy and exhibit superb aesthetic design. Some of the more exotic or one-of-a-kind masquerades might be made by the persons who wear them. But for the most part, Carnival costumes and masks worn in the eleven communities are made in small workshops run by mask makers and seamstresses or by the organizers of a Carnival troupe. When participants are part of a large group with a new theme each year, their costumes are annually purchased, whereas

1.13 A giant papier-mâché puppet in the costume of a *vodouisant* (devotee of Vodou) moves through the crowd during the Carnival of Hope in Port-au-Prince, Haiti. *Photograph by Donald Cosentino, 1995.*

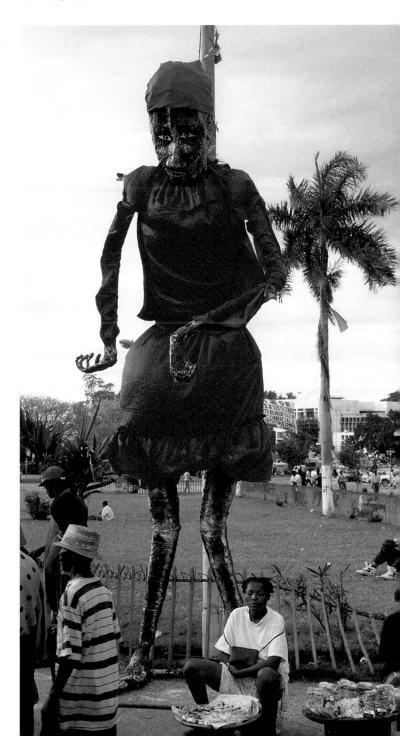

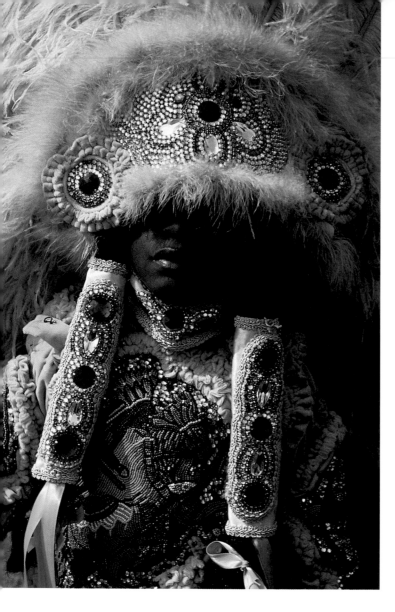

1.14 A young Mardi Gras Indian in New Orleans, USA, is dressed in an elaborate bead and feather costume of the sort that has become traditional costuming for the black "tribes." *Photograph by Syndey Byrd, 1989.*

in cases in which the same types of masquerades are worn year after year, they are reused or rented for a day or two.

In some communities, such as Laza, Tlaxcala, Oruro, and Recife-Olinda, and among the Mardi Gras Indians in New Orleans, children wear miniature versions of adult costumes and perform alongside older partici-pants in the main events. In other places, such as Basel, Basile, Port of Spain, and mainstream New Orleans, Car-nival officials organize special parades or other events for the children, who are dressed in costumes that are traditional to their community or entirely fanciful.

Floats are another component of some Carnival processions. They range from the makeshift carts con-veying social criticism found in Laza to the elaborately decorated cars that honor the Virgin Mary in Oruro and the huge vehicles ornamented with fiberglass sculptures that carry krewe members in New Orleans. In Port of Spain and Recife, large trucks carry musi-cians playing live music or huge speakers blasting taped music into the streets.

Music and dancing are prominent activities in most of the eleven sites, but again styles vary from one cultural area to another. Bagpipes are the tradi-tional instrument for Carnival music in both Laza, Spain, and southeastern Bulgaria, reflecting the wide-spread use this ancient instrument once had in rural festivals across Europe. Venice is known for its classical music, and in some settings Carnival participants might dance the waltz. In Basel, movement takes the form of marching as *Fasnacht* revelers play the fife and drum. The distinctive Cajun music of Basile features the vio-lin, and residents crowd into the town hall to listen to local bands and dance a country two-step. Tlaxcalan masqueraders perform square dances in the streets and plazas of their villages while small groups of musicians play European-derived music on brass horns and drums. Many of the groups in the Oruro Carnival parade practice for months to be able to perform highly choreographed dance steps to various types of European brass and drum marching music. Others dance to Andean tunes played on panpipes.

As might be expected, Carnival music in Recife-Olinda, Port-au-Prince, Port of Spain, and New Orleans is infused with lively percussion rhythms introduced from Africa. In each location, these rhythms were com-bined with European musical traditions, and out of the amalgam evolved unique styles of music and dance. Two of the distinctive types of music found in Recife-Olinda are known as *maracatu* and *frevo*, the latter also being the name for the popular Carnival dance. Port of Spain has its steel drum, calypso, and *soca* music, and Carnival revelers "chip," "wine," and "jump up" as they make their way down the street. The local innovation in Haitian music is called "roots," and the lively dance steps that go along with it can be described as "bump and grind." Mardi Gras in New Orleans features musi-cal forms including Dixieland, jazz, and the marching chants of the Mardi Gras Indians. The lively dance performances in the street parades are often referred to as "the second line."

Along with music and dance is the eating of special foods and drinks that might be served in private homes and local restaurants or provided as a community meal. In some places, vendors set up makeshift kitchens and tables along the streets to catch Carnival revelers and performers as they pass by. Carnival foods in Laza include various forms of pork, cake (known as *bica*), and locally made wine and liquors. Following the Eastern Orthodox tradition, Bulgarians begin a partial fast in the week leading up to Lent, so the festival foods are pita bread, cheese, eggs, and wine. Residents of Basel crowd into local taverns to eat flour soup and onion tarts, washed down with beer and wine, whereas chicken gumbo and beer are the ultimate delicacies at the community Mardi Gras party in Basile, Louisiana. In the cold, high-altitude climate of Oruro, Carnival participants favor pork, chicken, and potato soups and warm alcoholic drinks prepared by street vendors. Food and drink booths also line the streets of Port of Spain, but there the preference is for a type of curry and potato wrap known as *roti,* roasted corn, fresh coconut milk, and rum. The restaurants of New Orleans offer barbecue, boiled shrimp, and a variety of other southern dishes and beer, but the distinctive Mardi Gras food is "king cake," which is served at parties in homes and clubhouses.

Aggressive throwing is another Carnival activity that dates back to medieval festivals and is still popular today in many communities. In Laza this custom follows the traditional mode of dumping buckets of water or ashes from second-story windows onto unsuspecting people standing or walking below. People in Laza also have street battles in which they use muddy rags, handfuls of dirt filled with ants, and prickly branches. Residents of Basel love to throw confetti, and the streets quickly fill up with the colorful flecks of paper. In Oruro the preferred weapons of attack are large squirt guns, water balloons, and, in recent years, aerosol cans filled with foam. In the hot climate of Recife and Olinda, many people wait to be sprayed with a garden hose, whereas in Port of Spain one might expect to be doused with baby powder carried by a masquerade sailor. Throwing in New Orleans

has become extremely formalized as society members riding on floats throw strings of plastic beads, doubloons, and cups to the eager crowd waiting below.

For all participants—rich or poor, young or old—Carnival offers the possibility of imagining alternatives to the status quo. As in medieval times, laughter and play are the key underlying elements of the celebration. Risk and improvisation may be aspects of this play, but fundamental rules and regulations allow these to happen. Overall it is important that all members of a group or larger community take part in the festivities, in order to bring everyone to a common level of exhilaration, exhaustion, and renewal.[22]

NOTES

I want to thank Samuel Kinser, a noted scholar of early modern European history and popular culture, for serving as a consultant for the ¡CARNAVAL! project and helping me gain a better understanding of the origin and evolution of European Carnival. I am also indebted to John Nunley, a collaborator on this project, for his thoughts on the history of Carnival and the significance of the festival in the communities represented in this book.

1. William James O'Shea et al., "Lent," in *New Catholic Encyclopedia* (Detroit: Gale, 2003), 7: 468–469.

2. Louis Duchesne, ed., *Liber pontificalis* (Paris, 1889), 2: 172–173; Samuel Kinser, *Carnival American Style: Mardi Gras at New Orleans and Mobile* (Chicago: University of Chicago Press, 1990), 3 and 326 n. 2.

3. Kinser, *Carnival American Style,* 3–8 and 326 n. 3. As Kinser aptly states, many scholars have mistakenly suggested that Carnival originated in ancient times in the form of winter-spring celebrations carried out in Rome or in rural communities in broader Europe. However, as Kinser points out, the Carnival celebration began in the Middle Ages as an urban and courtly reaction to Lenten rules of the Catholic Church and gradually spread to rural areas. Along the way, a variety of social and agricultural festive practices that had originally been celebrated at different points in late winter and early spring were incorporated into the Carnival activities. Many of the practices were very old, reflecting pre-Christian forms of play and ritual that had gone through adaptation and transformation for at least a thousand years by the time they were associated with the pre-Lenten festival. One example of rituals carried out during pre-Lenten celebrations that seem to have close ties to ancient cult practices is found in Bulgaria, as discussed by Valeria Fol in chapter 3. Much of the misguided scholarship has hailed the Roman urban festival of Saturnalia, which took place in mid-December, as the true birthplace of Carnival, but as E. K. Chambers points out (*The Mediaeval Stage* [London: Oxford University Press, 1925], 1: 244–45), little was

heard about Saturnalia in Christian times. However, the Roman New Year celebration, known as Kalends, continued to be popular in every region of the former Roman empire, where it was condemned by Church authorities over several centuries. Aspects of the playful antics carried out in the New Year festivities described in the Church records and summarized by Chambers (258–264) are similar to those found in European Carnivals from the late fifteen to the eighteenth century, as reported by Peter Burke (*Popular Culture in Early Modern Europe* [New York: New York University Press, 1978], 178–204).

4. Mikhail Bakhtin, *Rabelais and His World,* trans. Helène Iswolsky (Bloomington: Indiana University Press, 1984), 5–13, 71–103, 218–220, 235–248, 273–277; Burke, *Popular Culture,* 178–204.

5. The various names used for Carnival and the history and development of this pre-Lenten festival in different parts of Europe are discussed in chapters 2 through 5.

6. Burke, *Popular Culture,* 182–183.

7. Ibid., 198.

8. Chambers, *Mediaeval Stage,* 205–227. As Chambers points out, this type of Carnival activity grew out of comical plays performed at Christmas time in England and central Europe.

9. Julio Caro Baroja, *El Carnaval* (Madrid: Taurus Ediciones, 1986), 196–200, 216–234, 269–280; Bakhtin, *Rabelais,* 214–215.

10. Burke, *Popular Culture,* 182–204.

11. Kinser, *Carnival American Style,* 8 and 327 n. 8. This practice is still found in parts of Germany and Switzerland (see chapter 5) and in Bolivia (see chapter 8).

12. Kinser, *Carnival American Style,* 7–9; Elaine Glovka Spencer, "Regimenting Revelry: Rhenish Carnival in the Early Nineteenth Century," *Central European History* 28, no. 4 (1995): 457–481. A good example of the evolution of Carnival into a more organized civic event, with a number of troupes coming out of working guilds, is found in Basel, Switzerland (chapter 5).

13. Examples of eighteenth-century Carnival celebrations are found in Mexico (chapter 7), Bolivia (chapter 8), Brazil (chapter 9), Trinidad (chapter 10), Haiti (chapter 11), and New Orleans in the southern United States (chapter 12).

14. This was true in Mexico (chapter 7), Brazil (chapter 9), Trinidad (chapter 10), and Haiti (chapter 11). Apparently, Native people and freed African slaves participated in some aspects of Carnival festivities in Bolivia (chapter 8) and New Orleans (chapter 12).

15. Examples of this are found in Oruro, Bolivia (chapter 8),

Recife, Brazil (chapter 9), Port of Spain, Trinidad (chapter 10), and New Orleans (chapter 12).

16. Examples of this are found in Tlaxcala, Mexico (chapter 7), Oruro, Bolivia (chapter 8), Recife, Brazil (chapter 9), Port of Spain, Trinidad (chapter 10), Haiti (chapter 11) and New Orleans, USA (chapter 12).

17. Examples of this are found in Basel, Switzerland (chapter 5), Oruro, Bolivia (chapter 8), Recife, Brazil (chapter 9), Port of Spain, Trinidad (chapter 10), and New Orleans, USA (chapter 12).

18. Examples of this type of activity are found in rural Bulgaria (chapter 3) and the Cajun region of Louisiana, USA (chapter 6).

19. This is found in Laza, Spain (chapter 2).

20. This is evident in the discussions and associated references in the different Carnival celebrations featured in this book. Other publications that provide good information and visual overviews of recent Carnival celebrations in various communities in Europe are Françoise Giroux, *Carnavals et fêtes d'hiver* (Paris: Centre Georges Pompidou, 1984); Michel Revelard, *Musée International du Carnaval et du Masque* (Binche: Crédit Communal, n.d.); and Cesare Poppi, "The Other Within: Masks and Masquerades in Europe," in *Masks and the Art of Expression,* ed. John Mack (New York: Abrams, 1994), 190–215. Another book, Alexander Orloff's *Carnival: Myth and Cult* (Wörgl, Austria: Perlinger Verlag, 1981), provides beautiful photographs of Carnival celebrations in various parts of Europe and the Americas.

21. The following summaries and comparative overview are taken from the essays in this book.

22. Further discussion and analysis of the role of play, order and disorder, and community bonding in contemporary Carnival celebrations can be found in Roger D. Abrahams and Richard Bauman, "Ranges of Festival Behavior," in *The Reversible World: Symbolic Inversion in Art and Society,* ed. Barbara A. Babcock (Ithaca, NY: Cornell University Press, 1978), 193–208; Victor Turner, *Process, Performance and Pilgrimage: A Study in Comparative Symbology* (New Delhi: Concept Publishing, 1979); Daniel J. Crowley, "Carnival as Secular Ritual: A Pan-Portuguese Perspective," in *Folklore and Historical Process,* eds. Dunja Rihtman-Auguštin and Maja Povrzanovif (Zagreb: Institute of Folklore Research, 1989), 143–148; and Max Harris, *Carnival and Other Christian Festivals, Folk Theology, and Folk Performance* (Austin: University of Texas Press, 2003).

1.15 Many of the rural *maracatu* Carnival groups in Pernambuco, Brazil, have a standard as well as a king and queen and their attendants. *Photograph by Barbara Mauldin, 1998.*

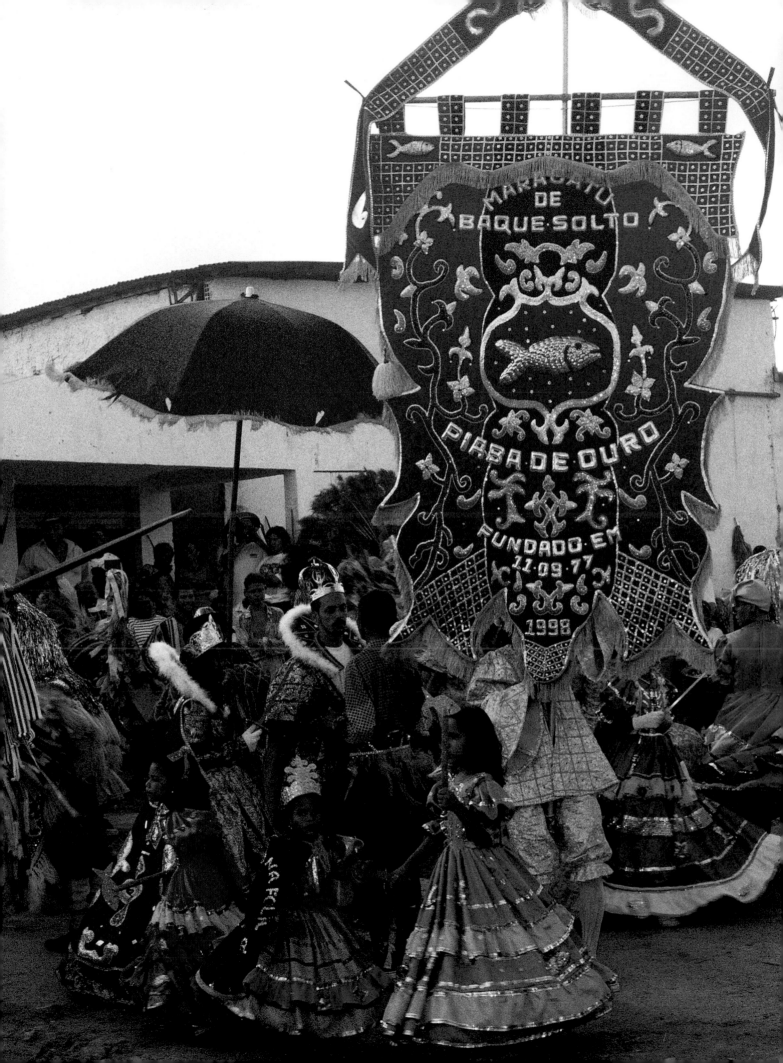

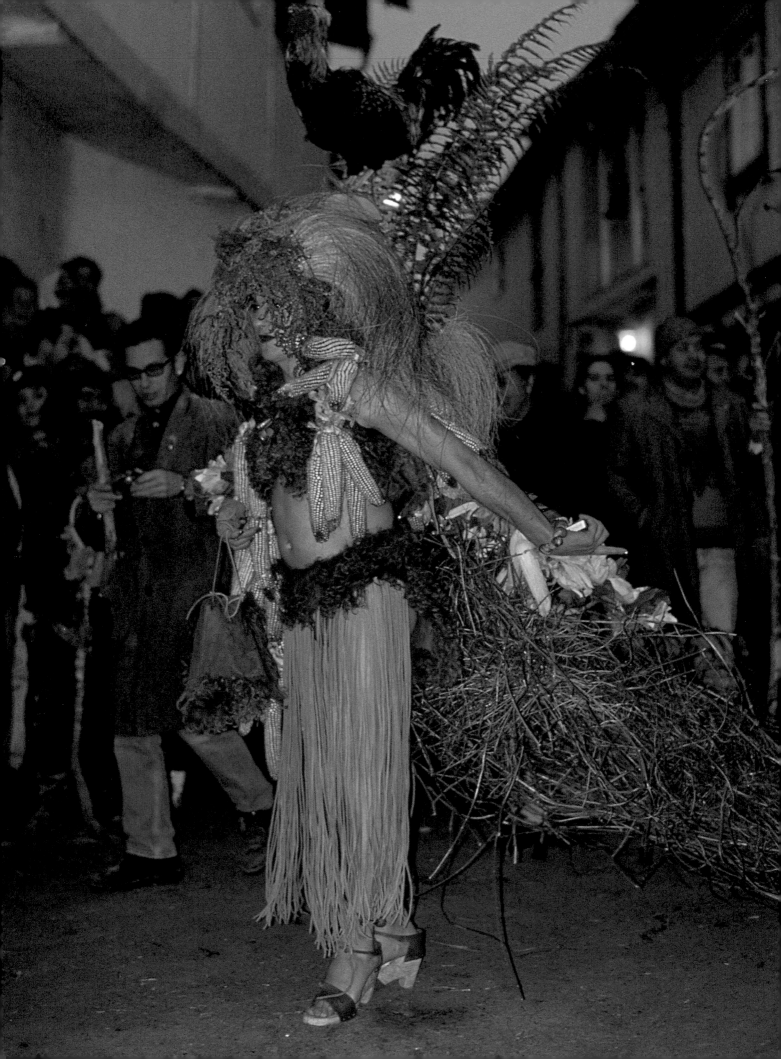

2 *Entroido* in Laza, Spain

A CONTINUING RURAL CARNIVAL TRADITION

MARIANA REGALADO

With contributions by Antonio Muñoz Carrión

T IS FRIDAY NIGHT BEFORE LENT. A farmer's cart bearing a barrel of burning tires makes its way up a dark, narrow street, leaving a trail of noxious black smoke. The wooden wheels turning on their wooden axles squeal over the chugging of the tractor that pulls the cart. Moving forward with it is a procession of neighbors and friends in old, dirty coats and hats or scarves, their faces lit by the torches of burning straw they carry. They stop to drink at every café and roust out neighbors along the way. A small but hardy core of revelers keeps on all night, while others stay behind talking to friends, children are taken home, and the less stalwart make their way to the local disco.

The procession has a haphazard, improvised feel to it. This is no decorous parade but a highly uncivilized procession.[1] It's dirty, it's noisy, it's rude, it's hilarious—almost a mob scene, but filled with laughter and singing. Everyone here, from the youngest to the oldest, is banging pots or tooting horns, walking, talking, laughing, and singing. Two little girls run by, throwing flour at everyone as they pass. Women and children wear *chocos,* large cowbells, belted to their waists—clang clang. From behind can be heard the wail of a bagpipe

over the sound of a big drum—boom, boom, boom, boom.

Some boys run into a garden and pull up long stalks of *grelos* (winter kale). "Hey, it's time to gather the crops!" they shout as they rejoin the crowd, waving the leafy *grelos* like flags. As the procession passes a certain crossroads, watch out! An old woman comes out on her balcony and douses the passing crowd with ashes. It's the *folión*—the noisy, stinking procession that makes its way through the streets of Laza and its outlying hamlets throughout Friday night, heralding the coming Carnival and warning that the new rules of social interaction and behavior that characterize this festival will soon be in force (fig. 2.2).[2]

Laza is a rural village in the province of Ourense, in the larger region known as Galicia in northwestern Spain (fig. 2.3). Because of a rugged mountain range, Galicia has traditionally been isolated from the rest of the Iberian Peninsula, though it has an extensive western coastline along the Atlantic and the Bay of Biscay to the north. This region is characterized by heavy rainfall and year-round greenery, but in general the soil is poor for agriculture. Galicia is known for its seafood and as a center of smuggling, and mining is an economic mainstay in the mountainous interior. This region is also recognized for a variety of folk traditions and festivals with roots going back to early times. The Galician language spoken here is closely related to Portuguese.[3]

A town of about nine hundred inhabitants, Laza sits

2.1 A young man is dressed as a goddess from the farm, with a rooster perched on his head. *Photograph by Antonio Muñoz Carrión, 2000.*

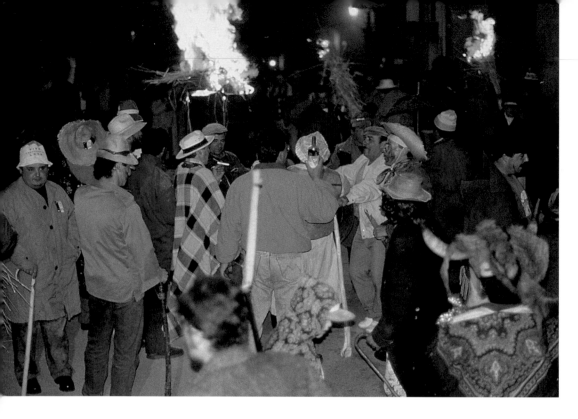

2.2 The *folión*, the rowdy procession in which the people of Laza announce the coming of *entroido* on Friday night. *Photograph by Antonio Muñoz Carrión, 1991.*

at the junction of two small rivers at the head of a narrow green valley surrounded by bleak mountains. It is a distinctly rural community in which most families have at least a few small fields under cultivation (fig. 2.4). Although many now work in construction, local banks, or forestry service, the rhythm of life in the town is that of the farm. Cows and hay carts are driven through the streets morning and evening, and in winter there is little to do. It is an old village growing into a town with five or six central streets, where old stone houses stand by homes built of concrete blocks and even a few three-story apartment buildings (fig. 2.5). As elsewhere in Galicia, the residents of Laza have retained many rural folk traditions, but they are particularly noted for their Carnival celebration,[4] known in the Galician language as the *entroido* or *antroido,* a term thought to derive from the Latin *introitus,* "beginning" or "entrance."[5]

History of the Region and Evolution of Carnival

People lived in this area long before the Romans conquered the Iberian Peninsula around 140 B.C. Although these inhabitants were related to Celtic groups who settled in the central and western parts of the peninsula, the physical isolation of Galicia led to the development of a culture with ethnic traditions somewhat distinct from those of the rest of Spain. It is known that in ancient times, large family groups lived together. Bread made from acorn flour was a food staple, and people also kept a few goats and pigs and practiced rudimentary agriculture. Ancient religious life focused on local gods who were honored with annual festivals. These early celebrations included foot races and mock battles, music played on pipes and trumpets, and dancing that emphasized squatting and jumping steps. In what might be viewed as an early festive practice, wild berries were gathered in the mountains and made into a liquor that was drunk as part of the events, as is still true at festivals in Galicia today.

When Romans began exploring the Iberian Peninsula, they identified different ethnic areas and named them after local groups or leaders. Thus, they named the province Gallaecia after Gallaeci, a prominent figure in the northwestern region.[6] Despite Roman mining interests in the mountains of Gallaecia, the rugged terrain and poor soil did not attract colonization, and thus the imprint of Roman civilization on the local people was less marked than in other parts of the peninsula. The Romans allowed the ancient Galicians to continue their local religious and cultural practices, which included soothsaying and making herbal medicines.[7] Indeed, the Galicians retained many aspects of their early Iron Age culture until as late as the eighth century.[8]

Even after the Romans introduced Christianity, they tolerated local cults, a policy that continued under subsequent Christian conquerors of the Iberian Peninsula: the Goths, Sueves, and Franks. By the sixth and seventh centuries the Christian Church had a stronger presence on the peninsula, and Church authorities began to condemn non-Christian beliefs and rituals. In 561 a bishop admitted that "pagan" practices were widespread in Galicia and that people living in the remoter parts of the region had little or no knowledge of the "true" teaching. Christians and non-Christians in many parts of the peninsula continued to celebrate Kalends, the old Roman New Year festival. The revelry included dressing in the skins of animals or, for men, in women's clothing, drinking and feasting, miming, dancing, and singing in mixed choirs of men and women, which led Iberian Church officials to try to prohibit these celebrations in the early seventh century.[9]

Syrian Muslims invaded the Iberian Peninsula in 711, and they and other Islamic peoples controlled most of it for the next five hundred years. Christian

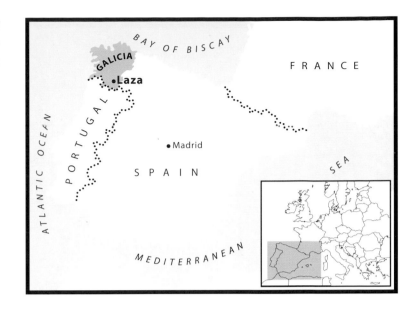

2.3 Location of Laza in the Galicia region of Spain.

2.4 Looking down at Laza from one of the many garden plots that surround the village, where families cultivate potatoes, winter kale, corn, and other crops for their own use. *Photograph by Antonio Muñoz Carrión, 1995.*

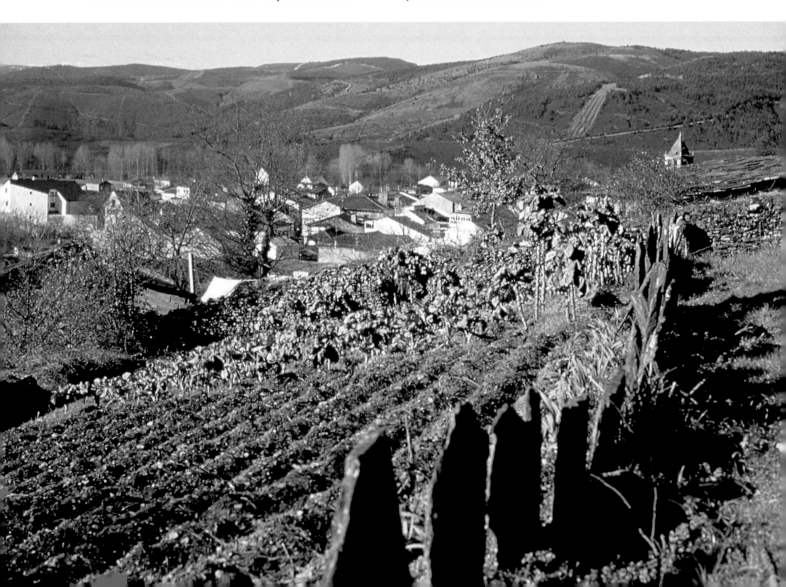

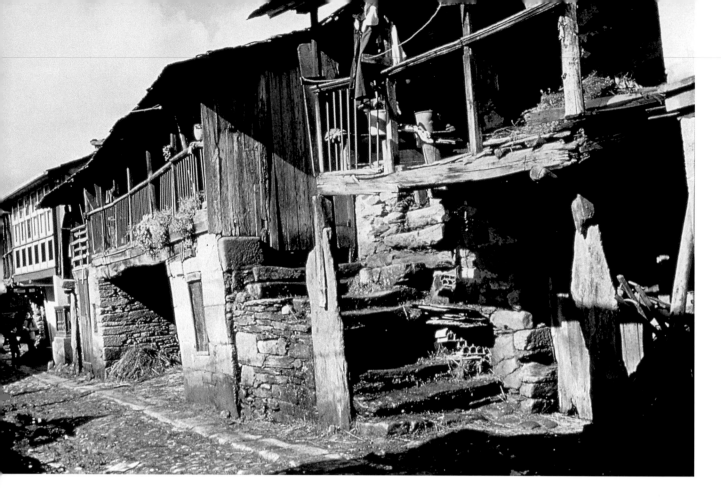

2.5 Older houses in Laza have an area underneath where animals are kept along with hay, ears of corn, and farming tools. *Photograph by Antonio Muñoz Carrión, 1977.*

rulers living in the northern part of the territory resisted, however, and eventually their small kingdoms joined forces to fight the Islamic chieftains. By the mid-thirteenth century the Spanish Christian kings had successfully reclaimed close to 80 percent of the peninsula. In the late fifteenth century the last Islamic stronghold in the southern part of the region was defeated, resulting in the peninsula's unification as one Spanish kingdom ruled by Isabel of Castile and Ferdinand of Aragon.

During the early phases of the Christian reconquest, in the eleventh and twelfth centuries, the Christian Church reestablished itself in the northern kingdoms. It introduced the types of Christian devotional practices that were common in Italy and other parts of Europe at that time. These practices expanded as Muslims were gradually forced out of the peninsula and Christianity came to dominate the entire region under the rulership of Isabel and Ferdinand.[10]

Once Christianity was reestablished in Spain, the observance of Lent became an important part of the Christian devotional calendar, and it secured the place of Carnival as the culmination of winter merrymaking. Even the Spanish kings recognized Carnival, as recorded in thirteenth-century court documents and in *The Chronicles of the Christian Kings* in the fourteenth century.[11] The Spanish Hapsburg kings, especially during the reigns of Philip V (1621–1665) and his son Charles II (1665–1700), celebrated Carnival with improvised dramatic representations at the royal palace that included obscene and grotesque scenes. The royal families even engaged in Carnivalesque merriment such as battles with decorated eggs filled with cologne.[12]

Carnival was also an important and enduring source of inspiration in Spanish literature. One of the most brilliant literary versions of the contrast between Carnival and Lent is the poem "Batalla entre don Carnal y doña Cuaresma" (Battle between Sir Carnival and Lady Lent), by the Spanish author Juan Ruiz, archpriest of Hita (1284?–1351?). During the Renaissance, the Carnival spirit inspired an inexhaustible universe of masks, masquerades, and inversions in the first modern European novel, *Don Quixote,* by Miguel de Cervantes (1547–1616). In seventeenth-century Spanish theater, Carnival appears as an essential motif in *entremeses* (one-act farces), notably in *Las Carnestolendas* by Pedro Calderón de la Barca (1600–1681), in which the characters eat, drink, and make merry in the "crazy time" of Carnival. Carnival also provided a means for criticizing authority, as is seen in the allegorical philosophical novel *El Criticón* (The Critic, 1651) by Baltasar Gracián (1601–1658). Later, in the nineteenth century, Carnival became the bitter backdrop for the moral miseries of the urban bourgeoisie in the satires of Mariano José de Larra (1809–1837).[13]

Carnival's emphasis on satire and the mocking of authority (fig. 2.6) led to repeated government prohibitions of its celebration from the sixteenth through the early nineteenth century. Spanish legislation restricting Carnival focused on the festival's tendency to disrupt public order and especially on the wearing of masks, because the anonymity they provided was seen as incentive to crime and riot.[14] To a certain degree, legal and ecclesiastical prohibitions weakened the urban celebrations of the festival, yet they persisted. In the seventeenth and eighteenth centuries Spanish urban Carnivals included roving maskers, dances, processions, and bullfights.[15] In the eighteenth century, rationalist ideas began to enter Spain along with the French Bourbon dynasty. As these ideas deepened the schism between high culture and the popular class, traditional Carnival practices were thought to be in bad taste or even immoral. Carnival in urban areas increasingly became entertainment to be watched.[16] The participatory nature of the urban festival was further diluted in the eighteenth and nineteenth centuries as new European modes of celebration incorporated great balls, cavalcades, and processions of floats and carriages that attracted spectators rather than participants (fig. 2.7).[17]

2.6 The *peliqueiros* of Laza wear elaborate costumes said to be derived from clothing worn by sixteenth-century tax collectors. Their masks have grimacing smiles, and each headdress is painted with an animal or other symbol. *Photograph by Antonio Muñoz Carrión, 1997.*

2.7. (overleaf) *Entrada y entierro del carnabal en Barcelana* (The entrance and burial of carnival in Barcelona). Detail from a printed broadside, late nineteenth century, offering a glimpse of the types of masquerades and floats that once appeared in the Barcelona Carnival procession. Collection of the San Antonio Museum of Art. Photograph by Blair Clark.

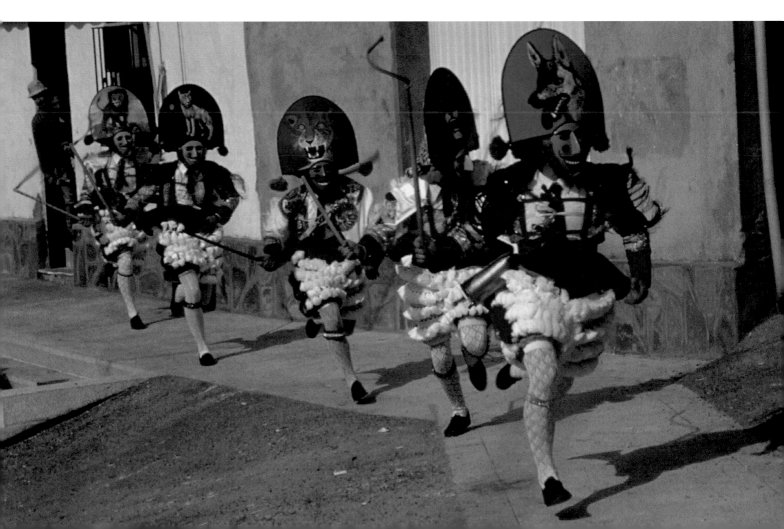

Entrada y entierro del carna...

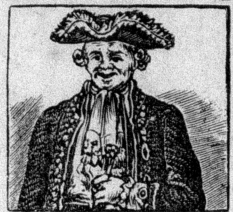

1. Aunque es mi nombre ideal,
hoy todo el Crbe me aclama
por señor del Carnaval.

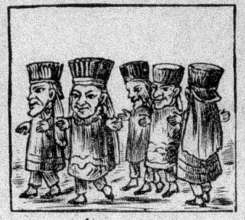

2. A tan alto personage,
los enanos le tributan
el mas completo homenage.

3. Con mucha gracia y meneo,
haciendo mil contorsiones
van bailando el

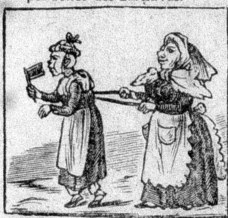

7. Alegre doña Neomisa,
á un niño de cuarenta años
vá sirviendo de nodriza.

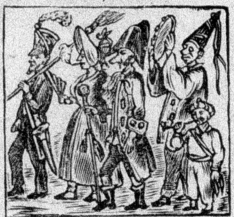

8. Siguen grandes reuniones
con trages de mil hechuras
vestidos de mascarones.

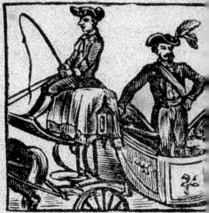

9. En carroza muy formal,
va un insigne limpiabotas
vestido de general.

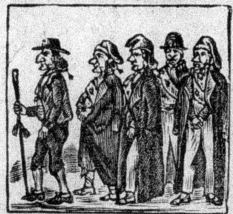

13. Un rural Ayunta-miento,
al señor Carnestolendas
vá á obsequiar muy contento.

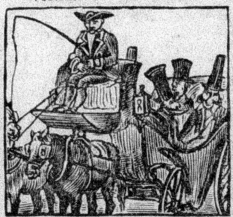

14. Con trages semi-estratégicos,
sigue, en carroza montada
la comitiva de obsequios.

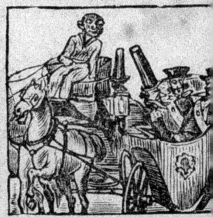

15. La autoridad con-paten...
al señor Carnestolendas
obsequia reverente.

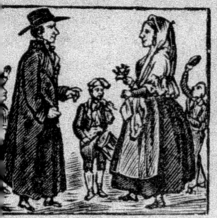

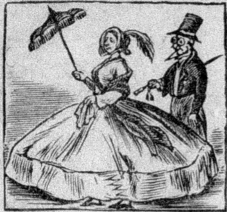

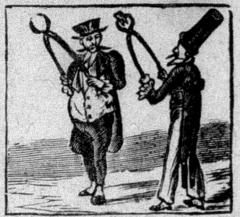

Los gigantes van danzando,
y con su garbo y donaire
la concurrencia animando.

5. La dama del miriñaque,
es servida y obsequiada
por ese quidam del fraque.

6. Dos estupendos dentistas,
para arrancar las quijadas,
tienen las tenazas listas.

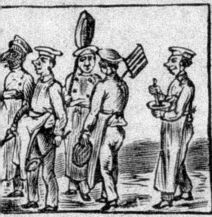

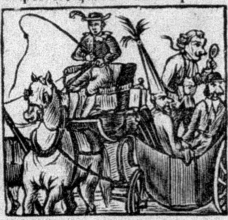

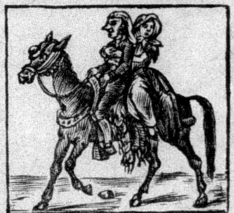

. Comparsas de cocineros,
con los trastes de cocina,
caminan muy placenteros.

11. Elegante gente moza,
con diversidad de trages
ocupan esta carroza.

12. Desde los montes de Ordal
bajaron estos payeses
para ver al Carnaval.

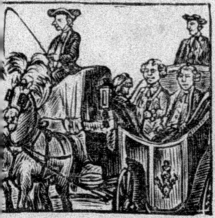

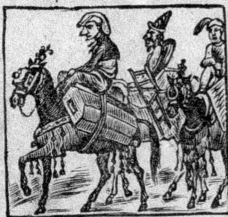

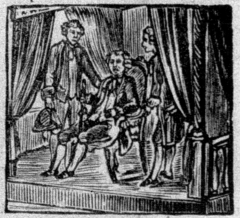

6. Entra en la ciudad Condal,
el insigne, bullicioso
y esperado Carnaval.

17. Los mulos con atalaje,
por arrieros servidos
entran su grande equipage.

18. Vista la ciudad despacio,
tiene la satisfaccion
de sentarse en su palacio.

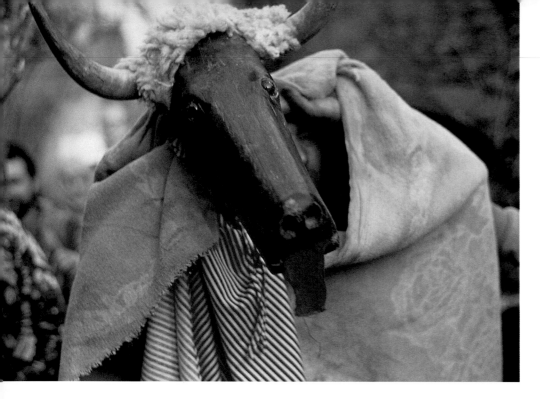

2.8 The *morena,* or cow, masquerader holds his mask on a pole so that he can manipulate it in aggressive gestures as he makes his way through the crowd. *Photograph by Antonio Muñoz Carrión, 1992.*

In contrast, Carnival celebrations in the rural communities of northern Spain continued to be carried out in a traditional, participatory manner. Although the earliest dates for pre-Lenten Carnival in this region are unknown, it probably began sometime in the twelfth and thirteenth centuries, when the Christian Church was reestablishing itself there. As elsewhere in Europe, people living in these rural communities would have incorporated activities from their traditional pre-Christian festivals into the rowdy secular event. This was a time to celebrate the end of winter and the coming of spring; the impositions of Lent made it even more important to rejoice while they could. As Spain gradually strengthened its ties to the rest of Europe, the northern communities were probably exposed to other types of festival activities that were popular in provincial villages of neighboring countries. By the early twentieth century, when scholars began documenting the rural festivals of northern Spain, they found a variety of celebratory practices that were common to the whole region.[18]

General Francisco Franco prohibited Carnival throughout Spain in 1937, during the Spanish Civil War, and then continued to ban masquerading and festivals in the first decades of his dictatorship. By the 1950s, however, Franco's administration had begun to loosen these restrictions, and some of the rural celebrations began to be revived, although masks continued to be prohibited. After Spain returned to democratic leadership in the 1980s, Carnival and masquerading could again be openly carried out, but the tradition had faded away across much of the Iberian Peninsula. Important revivals of the festival took place in some provinces of Andalusia (notably in the city of Cádiz) and in the provinces of Valencia and the Canary Islands (notably in the city of Santa Cruz de Tenerife).[19] It also saw a resurgence in the rural communities of northern Spain, where the tradition had not entirely died out. Many of the Carnival activities seen in this region today are similar to those recorded in the early twentieth century.

One important tradition is known as the *cencerrada,* a riotous noise made with large cowbells (*cencerros*). It serves as an announcement of the coming festival, as a rude noise during the activities, and even as a special music associated only with Carnival.[20] In rural towns across northern Spain, *cencerros* are usually worn by specific masked characters, with costumes ranging from crude animal skins to elaborate jackets and pants similar to those worn in theatrical farces. A large headdress often accompanies the latter style of costume (see fig. 2.6). From town to town the masqueraders are referred to by different names, and they exhibit local patterns of running or dancing to create a particular sound with the bells. Most portray aggressive behavior and carry sticks or bladders with which to hit or beat people, though generally in fun.[21]

Other masqueraders also appear in the rural Carni-

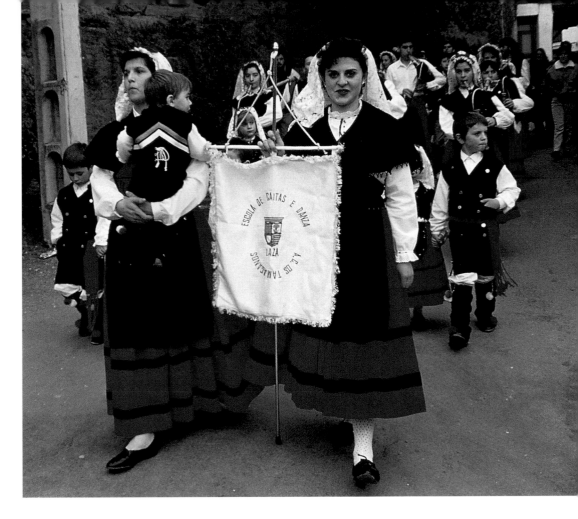

2.9 A procession of men, women, and children playing bagpipes makes its way through Laza wearing the traditional Galician costume. *Photograph by Antonio Muñoz Carrión, 1978.*

2.10 Men in Laza take great delight in dressing as women and comically impersonating feminine gestures. *Photograph by Antonio Muñoz Carrión, 1998.*

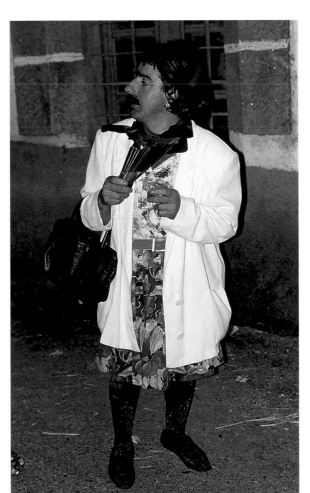

val celebrations of northern Spain, although less consistently than those wearing *cencerros.* One of these is the *ziripot,* a foolish fat rascal dressed in potato sacks stuffed with dry grasses who hits passersby with an inflated bladder. Another is the *zaldico,* or hobbyhorse, which is worn around the waist of a young man so that the horse's head projects out in front and its tail behind.[22] In Laza, as I describe later, a man carries a pole with a wooden cow's head attached to the end and hides his own body under a blanket (fig. 2.8).[23]

It is also traditional throughout the communities for men, young and old, to dress up as women (figs. 2.1, 2.10). The act of putting on a feminine costume and emerging into the streets with a new and temporary identity is a basic experience of Carnival play.[24] Another widespread custom is to perform acts of mockery or criticism that highlight the behavior of individuals or groups (fig. 2.11). These acts appear in a number of satirical modes, notably as witty insults, gossip made public, and symbolic trials and burials. In the Galicia region this tradition is often seen in mocking sermons or testaments.[25] Much of the Carnival play in these rural communities is also quite aggressive. The aggression is not limited to specific characters; all participants may throw materials such as flour, ashes, muddy rags, water, eggs, and fruit at one another.[26]

Music and dancing are also part of the celebration. The bagpipe and drum are characteristic of traditional Galician music, but bands playing trumpets, amplified guitars, and drum sets are also popular in rural communities.[27] Finally, the celebration of Carnival is nourished with rich food and excessive drink. The former includes pancakes and other pastries, all products of pork, and other types of meat. In general, wine is the drink of choice, though local specialties are brought out to be shared.[28]

Entroido in Laza

Laza's Carnival, or *entroido,* is the measure of a new year and one of the focal points around which the townspeople organize their lives. They often describe

it as a time when they are "completely free" and can "do whatever they want." Yet it is more than a disordered time and a break from daily routine. The apparently wild and chaotic world of *entroido* is in fact a carefully regulated one in which the value and importance of the everyday is reiterated and intensified through its distortion.[29] Broad participation, in which everyone has a role to play, is also fundamental. Laza's Carnival is an experience inescapably shared in the streets and at home by old people, sedate middle-aged farm couples, babies, and youths alike.[30]

In Laza, the masqueraders who wear the *cencerros,* or bells, are known as *peliqueiros.* They function as authority figures during the scheduled events of Carnival, as well as sporadically running through the streets clanking their bells and stopping to whip bystanders as a reminder that it is time to play by *entroido* rules (figs. 2.6, 2.12). *Peliqueiros,* who are generally young men and occasionally young women, wear elaborate costumes that take more than an hour and the help of two or three dressers to put on. The costume consists of a cropped red and gold jacket lavishly trimmed with gold braid and worn over a white

2.11 A *carroza,* or float, criticizes the lack of emergency medical services in Laza. *Photograph by Antonio Muñoz Carrión, 1990.*

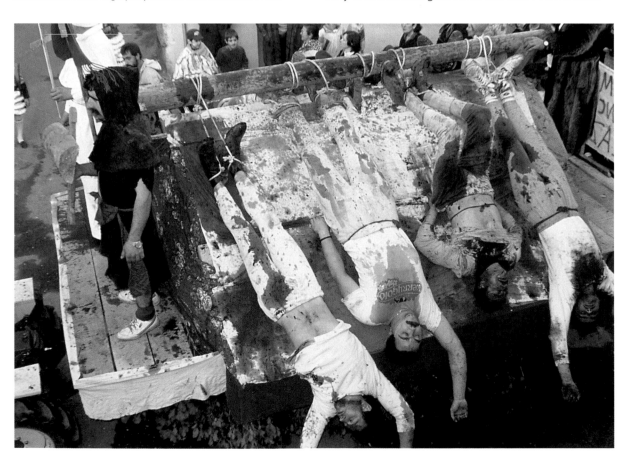

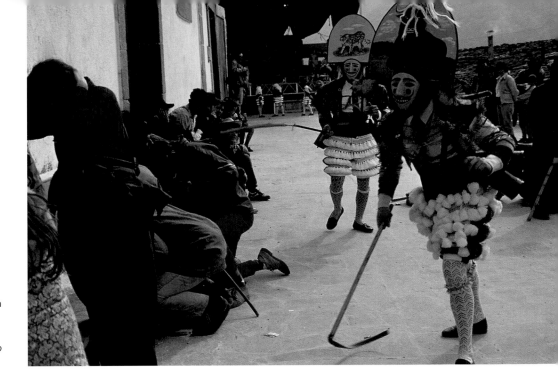

2.12 *Peliqueiros* appear on Sunday morning and begin whipping everyone in sight to remind them that it is time to play. *Photograph by Antonio Muñoz Carrión, 1992.*

dress shirt and tie. Over the shoulders of the jacket is pinned a large kerchief, traditionally lent by a sweetheart. The pants are knee-length white knickers decorated with four horizontal rows of white pom-poms front and back, with red and green pom-poms running down each side. A long, wide sash of red or blue wool is wound tightly around the midriff to prevent rubbing from the six cowbells, or *chocos,* each weighing more than two pounds, that are strapped around the waist on a leather belt. White crocheted stockings over colorful tights cover the lower legs, and the finishing touches are garters and black shoes.

A distinctive feature of the *peliqueiro* costume is its mask, carved from a block of wood, which sports a prominent hooked nose and a beard of rabbit fur. Each mask is painted with a mustache and an identical smiling and somewhat foolish grin. Attached above the mask is a broad headpiece shaped like a wide, single-peaked miter, with large pom-poms dangling from the lower corners. The front is made of a sheet of tin on which is usually painted an animal, which can be anything from a familiar creature such as a cat, dog, or horse to a more exotic one such as a tiger, eagle, or even an ostrich. Hanging from the top of the mask is a "tail" of horsehair. The back of the headpiece is made of fur, traditionally a rabbit's or cat's hide complete with the tail hanging down the back, but now cut from synthetic furlike material. This hide, the *pelica,* may be the source of the term *peliqueiro.*[31] The exact origin of the costume and mask is unknown, but some scholars

have compared them to the ornate clothing and comical masks worn in theatrical farces.[32] Local legend states that the *peliqueiros'* outfit and mannerisms derive from the fifteenth and sixteenth centuries, when the feudal rulers of the local kingdom sent men dressed in such costumes to the villages to collect taxes. They carried whips and wore masks with grimacing smiles to intimidate the townspeople.[33]

Another traditional masquerade that appears briefly during the *entroido* in Laza is the *morena,* or cow. Its carved wooden mask with horns is attached to one end of a long pole, with a cornhusk or horsehair tail fastened to the other end. A man covers his own head and back with a blanket or thatched raincoat and holds the pole in front of his face. This way he can manipulate the mask in aggressive gestures as he makes his way through the crowd.[34]

At some moments, particularly on Sunday, men and women wearing Galician costumes appear carrying bagpipes and drums and playing traditional music of the region. For women the costume consists of a long-sleeved white blouse, a long red skirt, and an embroidered black shawl that ties around the bodice. Men wear white shirts, black vests and pants, and red sashes around their waists (fig. 2.9).[35]

Other costuming in Laza's *entroido* provides an opportunity for members of the community to play with and highlight familiar elements of ordinary life. A burly farmer dressed in a gauzy blue sundress coyly flirts; a married man dressed as a priest reads solemnly from *Playboy;* a fisherman sits in a bar fishing with a mouse as bait and a cat in his creel. Male-to-female cross-dressing is the most notable and common Carnival costuming and is sometimes presented as a performance (fig. 2.10). A man in a woman's wig and a bathrobe runs into the plaza groaning that he's about to deliver a child and finally "gives birth" to a dog. These individual performances are often spontaneous: the "priest" reading *Playboy* meets a devil quoting scripture and they promptly clasp hands and skip away together. Those who have not made up a specific costume wear the standard *entroido* outfit, a dirty old coat and hat worn year after year and never cleaned.[36]

Another important feature of Laza's Carnival is its *carrozas* (carts), or floats, which pass one by one through the main square (known as the *picota*) during the afternoons of *entroido.* These are mobile tableaux, always satirical and often vulgar, that derive their themes from social life, religion, or politics in Laza, Spain, or the world. Never the same from one year to the next, they can represent a collective social experience of gossip made public.[37] Frustration over the lack of emergency medical services in Laza, for example, was highlighted in a *carroza* bearing eight men hanging by their ankles, wearing only loincloths and covered in blood—an apparent slaughterhouse (fig. 2.11). An executioner masked with a goat's skull stood on the cart, and on the back of the cart a sign read, "Now we really have emergencies in Laza." Some *carrozas*

highlight social norms through scenes that represent inversions or violations of them. One cart trespassed the most sacred religious and sexual boundaries by showing "Jesus" lying naked on a cross with a man dressed as a woman at his side (the Virgin? Mary Magdalene?), apparently about to perform fellatio. *Carrozas* such as this one provoke embarrassment and laughter from the crowd, but although mothers may shake their heads, they do not prevent their children from seeing these scandalous depictions. It is understood that such scenes represent what cannot be true the rest of the year. Furthermore, things that happen in Carnival are *cousas do entroido* (*entroido* things) and must be taken as such, rather than censured as they might be out of Carnival time.[38]

Mockery or criticism in Laza's Carnival is also carried out in an official reading known as the *testamento do burro* (testament of the donkey), a satirical recounting of the scandalous events that occurred in Laza during the previous year.[39] It is followed by the "death and burial" of *entroido,* which parodies Catholic rituals.[40] Ritualized aggression, such as the throwing of ashes, dirt, flour, and muddy rags at passersby, is also an important element in Laza's Carnival (fig. 2.13).[41]

While the public activities of *entroido* are its most distinctive component, mundane events such as visiting, eating, and talking are exaggerated throughout the festival. Largely unseen by outsiders, families and groups of friends visit one another, sharing favorite *entroido* foods, especially *bica* (heavy pound cake)

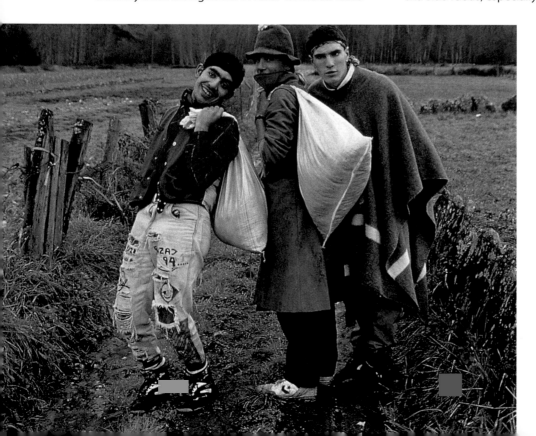

2.13 Young men go to the hillsides to collect dirt full of ants, which they bring into Laza to throw at other villagers as part of *entroido. Photograph by Antonio Muñoz Carrión, 1994.*

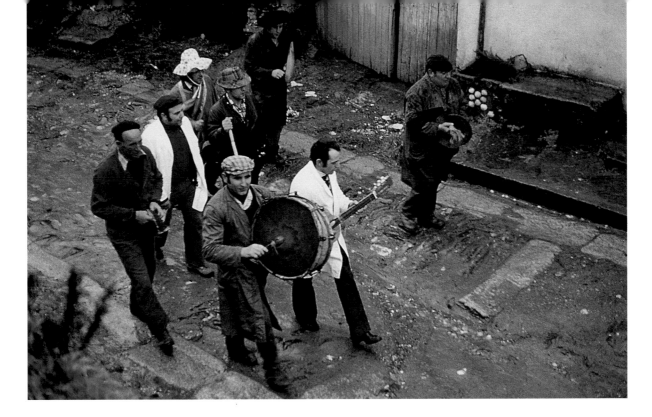

2.14 Small groups of musicians wander through the streets of Laza on Sunday morning, loudly playing music to announce the beginning of the *entroido,* or Carnival. *Photograph by Antonio Muñoz Carrión, 1977.*

but also *chorizo* (paprika-flavored sausage), *torradas* (bread fried in batter), fruit, and plenty of *licor* (fruit liqueur). When visitors come—groups of revelers, even outsiders—they are plied with a selection of home-made *licor, bica,* and talk. Each household shows hospitality to visitors. Traditionally, groups of young men went from house to house either begging for food or stealing it for a picnic in the plaza. Widespread visiting, not to mention pilfering, is quite particular to Entroido, for normally only very close family and friends go to one another's homes. Such visiting goes on throughout Carnival, day and night.[42]

Social conversation, another staple of daily life, is also distorted and exaggerated during Entroido through considerable lewd and sexual talk. When directed at the bearded farmer teetering around on high heels in a tight dress, it can be quite vulgar. Young men and women banter about sneaking off for "a roll in the hay." In modern, more permissive times such notions are less shocking or exciting than they must have been in the past. Much of the gossiping and talk that goes on among older men and women involves recollection of the days of their own youth, and men in particular banter freely about sexual activity.[43]

The Sequence and Excitement of Entroido

The first sign of *entroido* in January nowadays is the sound of the clanging *chocos,* or cowbells, worn by young and sometimes not-so-young men who run the streets of Laza late in the evening, building endurance for their role as *peliqueiros.* The sounds of the *chocos* in January is also an invitation to less formal water and flour throwing, running, and prank playing.[44] Carnival becomes the predominant topic of conversation. Recollection of *entroidos* past and contemplation of the one coming up add an emotional backdrop to the physical and practical preparations made for running the *peliqueiro,* for costumes and *carrozas,* and for the specific events of the festival. Posting of the predictable calendar of Carnival events heightens anticipation. The schedule provides intense focal points for all festive activity, a structure that allows for improvisation and creativity.[45]

FRIDAY

The *folión* (rumpus), described at the beginning of this essay, marks the climactic moment of excited anticipation for the coming festivities. Villagers taking part in the noisy, stinking procession that is *o folión* make their way through the streets of Laza and its outlying hamlets throughout the Friday night before Lent (see fig. 2.2). The *folión* heralds the coming festival and warns that the new rules of social behavior that characterize Carnival will soon be in force. It announces the end of pre-Carnival time and the imminent arrival of *entroido* itself.[46]

SATURDAY

Saturday morning dawns sleepy and slow. The last of the all-night revelers make their way through streets littered with evidence of the *folión*—ashes, *grelos,* burnt bits of tire and straw, discarded horns and hats. *Entroido* is upon the town. People are tired and hung over, but more importantly they are excited and eager for Carnival to begin. Today is the last day to rest and prepare for the festival. Perhaps the most important preparation is the readying of the *peliqueiro* costumes, which are brushed and hung out to air. *Chocos* are washed and set aside, and their clanging noise is noticeably absent—a lull before the storm.[47]

Saturday is also a day of food preparation—baking *bica,* the ubiquitous *entroido* cake, roasting *cabrito,* or baby goat, and boiling *cachuchas,* or pigs' heads, a local delicacy that is something of an acquired taste. These foods will be shared during Carnival in both private acts of hospitality and communion and public acts of hospitality and excess consumption. The appetite for *entroido* itself is whetted on Saturday night when the roasted *cabrito* is eaten at events called *cabritadas.* A typical festival eve dinner, the *cabritada* is unusual in that it is eaten with gathered friends rather than family and takes place in a barn or hayloft, a spot usually reserved for animals or farming activities.[48] Traditionally the *cabritada* was a dinner among men, but in recent times young women have made their own, too.[49]

Although Laza's *entroido* is famous for maintaining traditional folkways, the festival continues to evolve in the context of modern trends and activities. The greater public role of women in the festival reflects the changing role of women in Spanish society generally. Other signs of modernization include the introduction of amplified dance music in the main square, the use of tractors to pull *carrozas,* and the appearance of store-bought costumes. The innovation that has had the greatest effect on the celebration and experience of Carnival is the single disco bar in town. Built in the early 1980s by an enterprising returning emigrant, it has become the scene of most late-night *entroido*

activity for young men and women. It has necessarily brought about a decrease in more traditional forms of entertainment, notably singing. Although *cabritadas* are still characterized by the singing of traditional songs, they nevertheless break up earlier than they did in the past, and the disco starts to fill up around one or two in the morning.[50]

SUNDAY

Clang, clang, clang. It's *entroido* Sunday. The first *peliqueiros* are out running in the streets, and the distinctive sound of their bells says, "Get up, come out, Entroido has begun!" In groups of two to five, they begin to "run the *peliqueiro*" around eight or nine in the morning. In previous weeks, *chocos* could be heard as young men built up endurance for running, but the clanging of the bells on Sunday morning is different. Now they are worn only by the *peliqueiros,* the symbolic embodiment of Carnival, and the charac-

2.15 This woman has embellished her *entroido* outfit with packaged foods and cooking utensils, which symbolize her domestic life. *Photograph by Antonio Muñoz Carrión, 1999.*

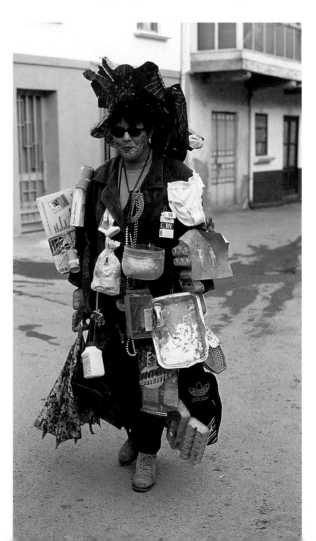

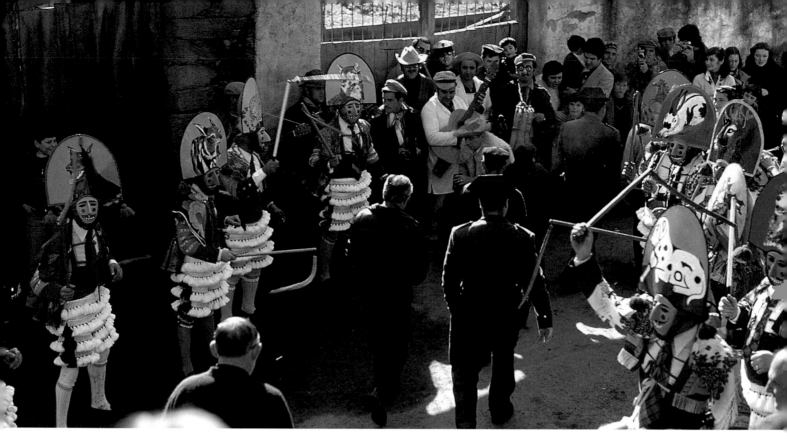

2.16 The *peliqueiros* stand outside the church on Sunday morning and lightly whip those who have attended mass, reminding them that regular behavior such as churchgoing is prohibited during *entroido. Photograph by Antonio Muñoz Carrión, 1978.*

teristic "accent" of the bells comes from their wearers' particular prancing jump. For those who have experienced *entroido* before, the sound of the ringing *chocos* on Sunday morning is exhilarating and heart-stirring.[51]

Any sleepy revelers not awakened by the running *peliqueiros* will soon be roused on Sunday morning by two musical bands that rove about the town. The *farandula,* usually one or two bagpipers with a drummer, always plays regional music.[52] A small band also marches around the streets (fig. 2.14) and even into the houses of band members' neighbors and friends— with any luck to find a lay-a-bed to roust out. These bands and any *peliqueiros* or other neighbors who stop in are treated to *bica* and some fortifying homemade *licor* before they head out into the streets again.

By ten o'clock, the main square and the bars around it are filled with revelers joking, drinking, and playing pranks. Today is the day when most people come down to the square from the surrounding hamlets, and the bars in the plaza are full of jolly talk. Watch out! The *peliqueiros* flail their whips as they run, and avoiding a whipping can be tricky. The first costumes

appear now, too (figs. 2.1, 2.15). Look, there's a fat shopkeeper, his thick hairy legs showing under a dress that matches his hat. And here come two little "bears," their pacifiers pinned to their sleeves. Out in the plaza, young folk lie and sit in the middle of the square, teasing one another, painting one another's faces, drinking. They are excited and ready.

Around eleven-thirty, there is a sudden rush of *peliqueiros* to the entrance of the churchyard, about fifty feet up a narrow street from the square. There they form an aisle, shaking their hips so their *chocos* ring out. Through this cacophonous aisle must pass all those leaving mass. As the laughing churchgoers walk between the lines of *peliqueiros,* they are lightly whipped (fig. 2.16). This is the *saludo dos peliqueiros* (salutation of the *peliqueiros*), the opening ceremony of *entroido.* In Laza the whipping is generally understood to be in punishment for going to church. The *peliqueiros* exert their authority to show that not only is permission granted to behave in *entroido* ways but regular behavior is prohibited. The rules of Carnival are in place, and the normal rules of social life have been suspended. Despite the overtones of punishment, the mood is festive, and everyone is excited to see the *peliqueiros* and get *entroido* under way.

After the *saludo,* everyone returns to the main square for the public *distribución da bica* (distribution

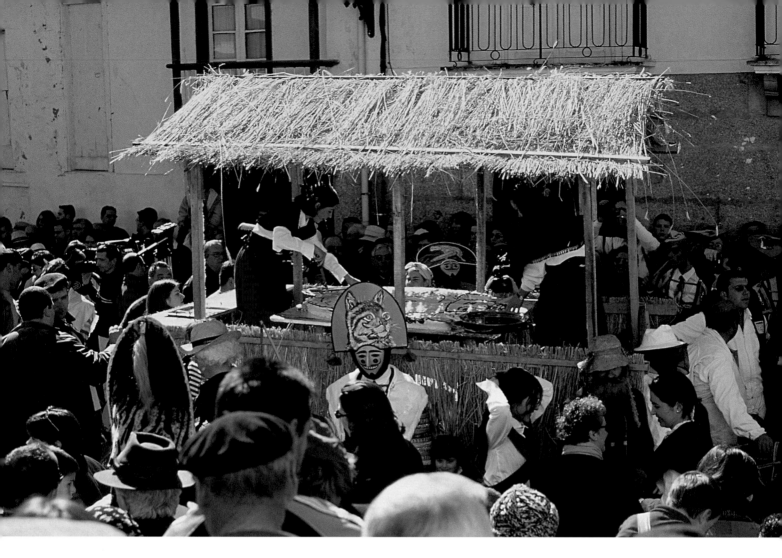

2.17 On Sunday afternoon, young women dressed in traditional Galician costumes distribute *bica* (cake) to everyone in town. *Photograph by Antonio Muñoz Carrión, 2000.*

of cake). There is a tremendous clanging of *chocos* as the *peliqueiros* prance slowly into the square in two long lines, clearing the way for a farmer's cart drawn by a pack of wild men dressed in burlap sacks and fur. The cart that carries the *bica* pulls to a stop in the middle of the square, where the *peliqueiros* make room and keep the boisterous, unpredictable *entroideiros* at bay. From the cart, young women dressed in traditional Galician shawls and red skirts pass cake out to the crowd (fig. 2.17). An instance of unusual public eating, the *distribución da bica* is also a collective extension of the hospitality and food sharing that goes on in private homes. It is a point of some importance that there be *bica* for everyone, including people not from Laza.

The theme of eating is never far from the events of Entroido. After the *distribución,* people mill about, socializing and drinking with friends, family, and neighbors until one-thirty or two in the afternoon. In the Spanish tradition, the midday meal is the most important one of the day, and soon the plaza empties out as people head home or to someone else's house to eat. It is a point of pride for some not to return home during the three days of *entroido,* so getting invited for lunch and dinner is important and a source of ongoing negotiation. *Vamos,* come to eat!

In the afternoon people return to the main square for more drinking, laughing, and singing. There are no official acts on Sunday afternoon, but more costumes appear and—best of all—many *carrozas* come through (fig. 2.18). Here comes one now—a tractor pulling a cart with, why yes, it's the prime minister sitting on a toilet wiping himself with the constitution! And there's a man in an "airplane," running through the square spewing flour on everyone, "putting out forest fires." Everyone's attention is drawn at once, and after each *carroza* passes, people return to their conversations.

On Sunday evening after dinner there is a *verbena*—

dancing into the night in the main square. An amplified band plays both popular and traditional Galician music until early morning. All Spanish festivals have a *verbena,* and Laza's Entroido is no exception. Someone gets a fire started in the plaza to make a *queimada,* a traditional drink in Galicia made with distilled alcohol mixed with sugar, fruit, and coffee beans. The mixture is then lit and allowed to burn while the sugar dissolves. The *queimada* is particularly welcome to all-night merrymakers when temperatures drop to near freezing.[53]

MONDAY

It's Monday, the "dirty" and "wild" day of entroido. A small cavalcade of "Gypsies" on donkeys roams the streets of Laza. In the late morning people are talking and drinking in the bars and out in the square as usual. Almost no one is in costume, though many wear overalls and capes, and their heads and necks are well covered. There are few *peliqueiros* around. Many faces peer out from the doorways of the bars or from windows above the square in hope of watching the young and foolhardy "do the *farrapada*" without being drawn in themselves.

The *farrapada* (ragging) begins when one *entroideiro* surreptitiously lobs a soaking muddy rag at someone whose attention has been distracted. The idea of the *farrapada* is to "rag" the victim with a good muddy wallop, without being seen. Of course the "victim" then takes possession of the rag and either lights out after the perpetrator or tries to get his or her own opportunity to surprise someone. Once the first rag is thrown, more rags—usually strips of burlap, but anything will do—come out. Only the most alert and agile may avoid getting splashed and slapped with mud themselves. Soon, so many people are running and throwing rags that it is hard to see where the next muddy assault will originate.

The *farrapada* quickly escalates into an all-out mud war lasting more than two hours, in which anyone entering the plaza is bound to get caught. To the dismay of local homeowners, the carefully whitewashed houses lining the square are inevitably covered with big splotches of mud by the time it is over. However, the muddy prints left on the buildings for weeks after *entroido* are contemplated with much satisfaction by everyone else. Before the streets were paved, mud was a disagreeable fact of life in this rainy region, and the *farrapada* was a much muddier event. Nowadays, when paved streets keep the town cleaner, a wheelbarrow full of earth and a bucket of water are brought in to make the mud. Sometimes manure is thrown into the mix as well. To the surprise of villagers, the *farrapada,* which had been dying out, has become a popular event

2.18 A *carroza,* or makeshift float, satirizes some corrupt Spanish politicians and bankers who have gone to prison. *Photograph by Antonio Muñoz Carrión, 1995.*

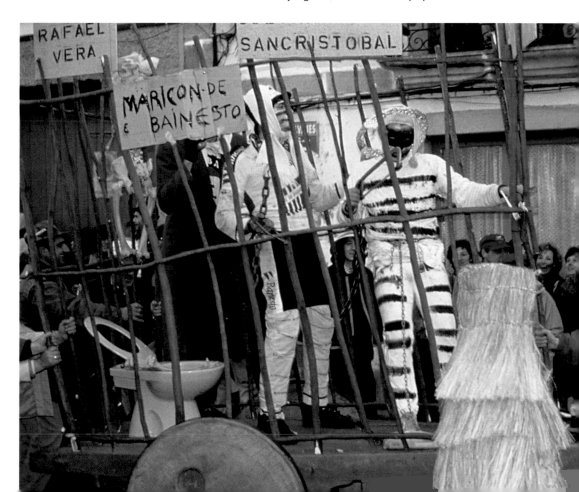

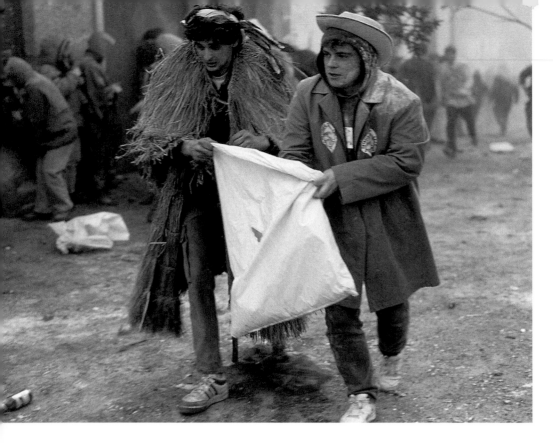

2.19 Young men carrying large sacks of dirt filled with ants are about to start throwing it onto the crowd on Monday afternoon during the event known as *formigas* (the ants). *Photograph by Antonio Muñoz Carrión, 1995.*

for young Spanish tourists. In recent years it has grown rapidly, with over a hundred people reveling in the filthy battle, whereas a decade earlier a few dozen participants had kept it going. The *farrapada* ends only when people begin to leave the plaza, headed home to eat. The mud and rag throwing do not leave the plaza, so watch out! You're likely to get a muddy jolt in the back if you do not pay attention as you walk away.

On Monday afternoon, after the long midday meal, everyone heads back to the main square for the most chaotic moment in the festival. The plaza and the bars are filling up, there is a buzz of people talking and singing, the band is playing and couples dance, there is a real feeling of fiesta. New costumes and floats appear this afternoon. The *peliqueiros* hit harder than they did on Sunday; the square is crowded and they have to whip hard to clear a path for themselves. People are tired and dirty, excited and happy—they are in the thick of *entroido,* with plenty of time still to go.

As dusk approaches, people begin glancing toward the churchyard increasingly often. There is a jumpiness to the crowd, though everyone continues dancing and talking as usual. Then, without warning, the *formigas* (ants) arrive. Three or four dozen men and women dressed only in loincloths or covered head to toe in burlap or scarves suddenly pour into the square carrying large sacks of dirt filled with ants (fig. 2.19). As they enter the square, they spread out, flinging dirt and ants by the handful into the air, into peoples' faces, or, in the "ace shot," right down the back of someone's neck to give him a good dose of ants inside his clothes. Others in this invasion carry long branches of *toxo,* a kind of prickly, thistly tree, which they swing around behind them, bumping and scratching people as they rush away from the flying ants, cowering futilely against a wall (fig. 2.20). The *formigas* are accompanied by a threshing machine pulled haphazardly around the plaza on a groaning wooden cart, spewing clouds of tiny bits of straw everywhere and making an immense racket. There is nowhere to turn; the air is full of ants, dirt, prickly branches, and chaff.

Ducking in and out between the *toxos* and the laughing, running people is the *morena,* perhaps the most important element of the *formigas* event after the ants themselves, and dear to the hearts of *entroideiros.* The *morena* character acts like a mad cow loose in the square, butting people, lifting women's skirts, and adding to the sense of chaos (fig. 2.21). And then, as suddenly as it started, the *formigas* is over, the noise stops, the dust, dirt, and ants settle, and the *morena* is gone.[54]

Both the *formigas* and the *morena* came down from Cimadevila, a small neighborhood of Laza about a half mile from the center of town. The ants were carefully dug out of anthills in the countryside and then given bread and doused with vinegar to wake them up[55]—and, as locals will roar at you if you ask, "to make them hungry!"

In the plaza, while some shake ants out of their hair and clothes, others come out of the bars and houses where they have been hiding to survey the scene, which looks like the aftermath of a dirty battle indeed. People laugh and recount their own versions of what happened: "Did you see the *morena?*" Excited boys and girls run around scooping up ants and dirt and throwing them at each other. Anyone who didn't get ants in his hair or down his shirt before is likely to get them now.

After the *formigas* event, the *peliqueiros* return, clearing the way with their cacophony of bells for a cart pulled by wild men and filled with *cachuchas* (boiled pigs' heads). The *cachuchas* are distributed to one and all. It makes quite a scene: dirty, excited people munching on cooked snouts and jaws, with prancing, skipping *peliqueiros* and ants crawling every-where. It seems truly a feast of fools, but it is also a convivial moment of community and sharing. The rest of Monday is filled with happy chatter, *carrozas,* and dancing into the night.[56]

TUESDAY

It is Tuesday. The festive mood is tinged with sadness and urgency, for it is the last day of *entroido.* Tuesday is a late-rising day for many of the young people, but in the morning older men come out to run as *peliqueiros veteranos* (veterans). This gives them an opportunity to demonstrate their endurance as well as to exhibit older styles of running the *peliqueiro,* highlighting cultural and stylistic changes in *entroido.* Continuity of tradition in the context of an evolving and changing Carnival is taken seriously in Laza.[57] Participants see themselves as maintaining traditions from time immemorial yet evolving during their own lifetimes. Throughout the festival, older *entroideiros* carefully watch the activities of the young men and women, recalling how it used to be and providing suggestions or criticisms. While the older folk usually talk about how good it was when they were young, younger people generally declare that *this* is the best *entroido* ever. This intergenerational conversation is a subtle and important element in reaffirming community identity.

On Tuesday afternoon people again gather in the main square for the two climactic acts of Carnival: the *testamento do burro* and the *entierro do entroido* (death and burial of Entroido). By dusk, the plaza is filled with people of every age who have come to hear the *testamento.* Even those who do not participate in the rest

2.20 This man is carrying the branch of a prickly tree, which he swings around to bump and scratch people as they run by. *Photograph by Antonio Muñoz Carrión, 1996.*

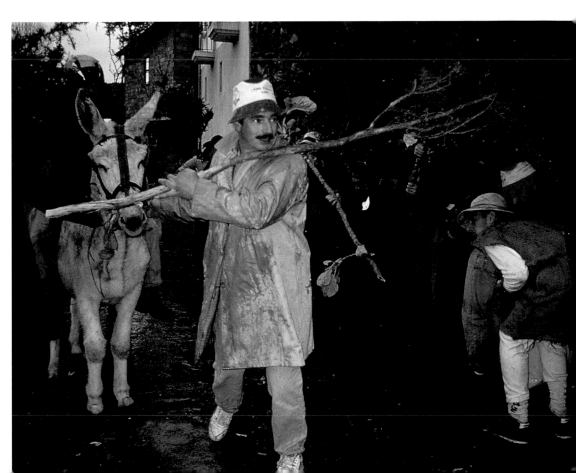

of the festival want to hear what the *testamento* will say about them and their neighbors. The crowd buzzes with expectation. The rhythmic clanging of the bells is heard well before a double column of at least twenty *peliqueiros* appears, opening a passage through the crowd. Many of the *peliqueiros* now wear black bands on their headdresses, a sign of mourning for the death of *entroido*. Following them into the square comes the *testamenteiro,* the creator and reader of the testament. Riding (sometimes backward) on a donkey led by masked associates, he holds the white scroll he is about to read conspicuously in his hand. Both the *testamenteiro* and his associates wear *corozas* (thatched raincoats) and assorted horned or thatched headgear (fig. 2.22).[58]

Prepared and read by the *testamenteiro*—always the same man from Laza in recent years—the *testamento* is a rhymed verse composition in the Galician language. It is a satirical and mocking recounting of events in Laza during the last year, gossip made public, the revelation of "truths not known."[59] Its main elements are set in a framing fiction, the verbal "distribution" of the body parts of a donkey given to the people of the town in symbolic recognition of their

actions from the past year. In the *testamento,* individuals and events are criticized and appreciated through the retelling of actual events or the telling of made-up stories. Social norms are acknowledged and reinforced through satire and criticism.

As is true throughout the rest of the festival, the structure and contours of the *testamento* have a long tradition and follow the same form year to year, but the specific events and stories are unique. In some sense the *testamento* is predictable, because everyone knows what has gone on in the past year. However, it is also highly unpredictable, because no one knows how the *testamenteiro* will spin the story, except that he will make it vulgar or satirical. Each piece of the donkey is used to represent an explicitly evaluative and symbolic assessment, and each year the donkey's body parts are given new symbolic meaning. For example, one year the *testamenteiro* teased the old people in the town for being miserly by giving them the filet mignon of the donkey, so they could taste an expensive cut of meat. Another year a man who had lost his pig from the back of his truck on his way to market received the eyes of the donkey so that he might keep better track of his animals in the future. One time the donkey's eyes were given to the Portuguese women who worked in or had married into the town, so that they might see that they were well loved by the people of Laza. Along with the distribution of the donkey,

2.21 The *morena,* or cow, masquerader runs through the crowd, hitting people and lifting women's skirts, adding to the sense of chaos. *Photograph by Antonio Muñoz Carrión, 1996.*

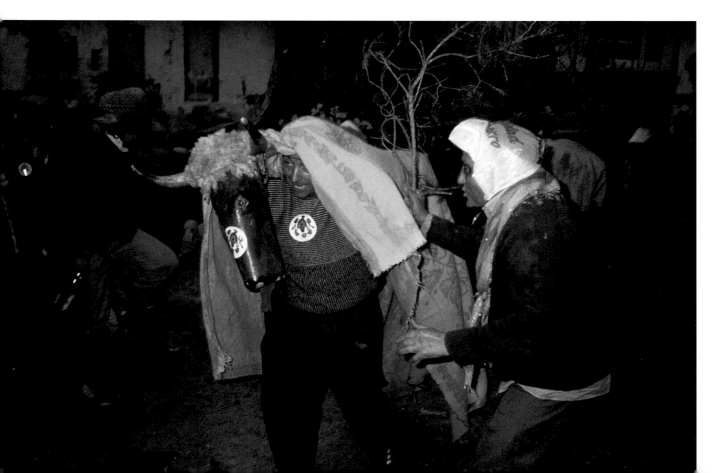

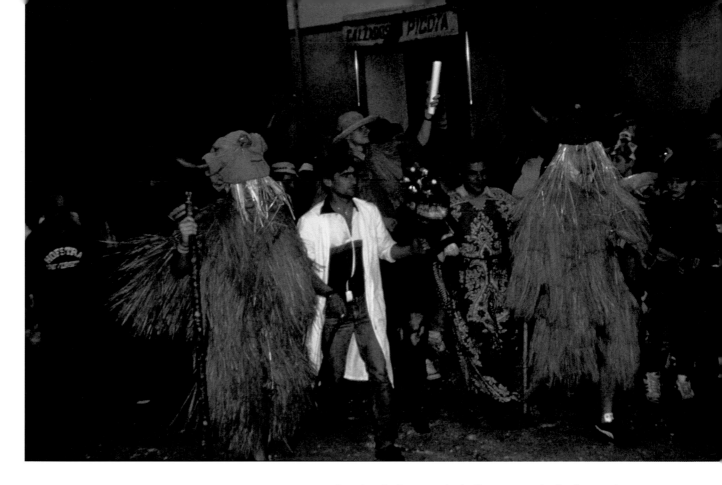

2.22 The man who will read the "testament of the donkey" on Tuesday evening enters the main square on the back of a donkey. He is accompanied by men wearing thatched raincoats and horned headgear. *Photograph by Antonio Muñoz Carrión, 1987.*

the *testamenteiro* uses obscenity and sexual suggestiveness, and he exaggerates the personality traits and behavior of individuals to evaluate and pass judgment on Laza. It is central to the *testamento* that despite its hilarious criticism of people, they are still represented as integral members of the community.

Although the *testamento* is now read in the main square over a sound system, it is actually a very local, almost private affair, because to follow it one needs to understand the Galician language and to know the people being talked about. Although the ultimate responsibility for the assignment of donkey parts, the stories told, and the judgments made belongs to the *testamenteiro,* he carefully includes the voices of the townsfolk, reflecting their opinions and feelings. In this way social identity, both of the collectivity and of individuals, is reiterated and reaffirmed, and the social and cosmic order of Laza's everyday world is validated. The *testamento* is a source of intense speculation before-

hand and of a great deal of interest and talk afterward, because it serves as a powerful recapitulation and performance of the year's gossip. It is truly the climactic moment of Laza's Carnival.[60]

Entroido is almost over. After the *testamento* comes the *entierro,* which usually represents Carnival in the form of a man or doll who "dies," is mourned, and then comes to life again. Like all the seasons, Carnival must end, but it will return.[61] Though the manner of the death and burial varies from year to year, it most often parodies Catholic rituals, with a mass and procession, the burning of a heretic or a witch, or a crucifixion. One particularly elaborate *entierro* involved a forty-minute drunken "mass," including a "bishop" who "blessed" everyone with the finger. At the end of the mass the bishop intoned, "Arise, Arise," at which time the twenty-four-inch-long penis of *entroido*'s "corpse" rose, shaking, above the coffin in which the corpse lay. Then the whole procession left the square, Entroido clearly alive and well, ready to return the following year. The death of *entroido* marks the beginning of the return to normal life. After Carnival "there is a gladness in turning again" to ordinary life; "a little of the [*entroido*'s] brightness is carried over, and the world is no longer the same."[62]

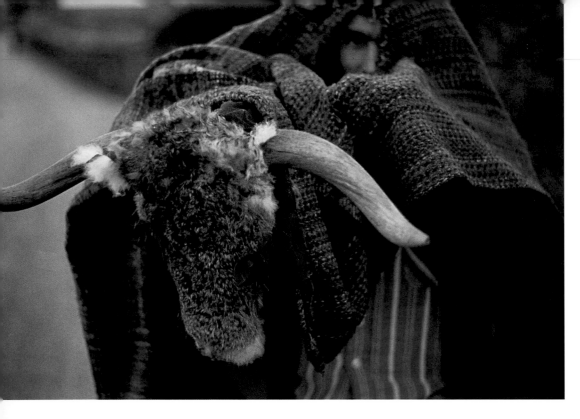

2.23. A young man from Laza carries a pole with a *morena*, or cow's head, attached to one end while he hides his own body under a blanket. *Photograph by Antonio Muñoz Carrión, 1997.*

Conclusion

Entroido in Laza is exciting and fun because it is such a brief departure from the usual. It must be experienced completely, not a moment wasted. The constant reminders of ordinary, everyday life and the short, intense experience of Carnival provide a sense of assurance that the world will return to its normal ways. The world upside-down can be enjoyed to the fullest only if it is clear that the world will right itself again.

The essential attribute of Carnival is that it is a time apart from ordinary life, a wild time of exuberant, uncontrolled, licentious behavior in which chaos reigns and order seems to disappear.[63] But the festival establishes its own order, through which it invokes and reaffirms the social values and relationships in existence the rest of the year. In *entroido* the community of Laza finds renewal, not in any particular artifact or moment of the festival but in the collective participation of all the people.

NOTES

Many thanks are due to Antonio Muñoz Carrión, who began his studies of Laza in the 1970s, for introducing me to the community. I also thank and acknowledge all the *entroideiros* of Laza for their help and interest in my study of their marvelous festival.

1. Personal observations during the Carnival season in Laza, 1988–1996; Susan Davis, *Parades and Power: Street Theatre in Nineteenth-Century Philadelphia* (Philadelphia: Temple University Press, 1986), 159–161.

2. Personal observations during the Carnival season in Laza, 1988–1996; Xesús Taboada Chivite, "La Cencerrada en Galicia," in *Ritos y creencias gallegas* (A Coruna: Salvora, 1980 [1969]), 214.

3. Carmelo Lisón Tolsana, *Antropología cultural de Galicia* (Madrid: Akal Universitaria, 1983), 15–16; Eric Solsten and Sandra W. Meditz, *Spain: A Country Study* (Washington, DC: Library of Congress, 1990), 69–77, 161, 168.

4. Personal observations during the Carnival season in Laza, 1988–1996; Xesús Blanco Conde, *Laza: O Entroido enxebre* (Ourense: Diputación Provincial de Ourense, 2000), 15–16; Taboada Chivite, *Etnografía galega* (Vigo: Editorial Galaxia, 1972), 429–431.

5. Julio Caro Baroja, *El Carnaval* (Madrid: Taurus Ediciones, 1986), 40; Federico Cocho, *O Carnaval en Galicia* (Vigo: Ediciónes Xerais de Galicia, 1992), 33.

6. Julio Caro Baroja, *España primitiva y romana* (Barcelona: Editorial Seix Barral, 1957), 65–69, 73–77.

7. Ibid., 77, 101–102.

8. Roger Collins, *Early Medieval Spain: Unity and Diversity, 400–1000* (New York: St. Martin's, 1983), 7–9.

9. Caro Baroja, *Carnaval,* 43, 169; E. A. Thompson, *The Goths in Spain* (Oxford: Clarendon, 1969), 1–3, 55–56, 90, 309.

10. Stanley G. Payne, *Spanish Catholicism: An Historical Overview* (Madison: University of Wisconsin Press, 1984), 3–9, 14–16, 30–31; J. N. Hillgarth, *The Spanish Kingdoms, 1250–1516* (Oxford: Clarendon, 1978), 2: 352, 367–388, 393.

11. Caro Baroja, *Carnaval,* 36–38.

12. Catalina Buezo, *El Carnaval y otras procesiones burlescas del viejo Madrid* (Madrid: Lavapiés, 1992), 21–25.

13. Juan Ruiz, archpriest of Hita, *El libro de buen amor* (Madrid: Editorial Castalia, 1985), 197–209; Miguel de Cervantes Saavedra, *The History of the Ingenious Gentleman, Don Quijote de la Mancha* (New York: Norton, 1995); Baltasar Gracián y Morales, *El Criticón* (Madrid: Espasa-Calpe, 1971); Mariano José de Larra y Sanchez de Castro, "Todo el mundo es máscaras, Todo el año es carnaval," *El Pobrecito Hablador* (March 14, 1833).

14. Caro Baroja, *Carnaval,* 154–155 ; Buezo, *Carnaval y otras procesiones,* 45.

15. Buezo, *Carnaval y otras procesiones,* 45.

16. Antonio Bonet Correa, "La Fiesta como metáfora," in *España festejante: El Siglo XVIII* (Málaga: Centro de Ediciones de la Diputación de Málaga, 2000), 13–14.

17. Ibid., 14; Buezo, *Carnaval y otras procesiones,* 117.

18. Caro Baroja, *Carnaval,* 146–157, 178–234, 357–367.

19. David Gilmore, *Carnival and Culture: Sex, Symbol, and Status in Spain* (New Haven: Yale University Press, 1998), 12–13.

20. Taboada Chivite, "La Cencerrada en Galicia," 213.

21. Caro Baroja, *Carnaval,* 196–200, 216–234, 357–367.

22. Ibid., 205–210.

23. Personal observations during the Carnival season in Laza, 1988–1996; Caro Baroja, *Carnaval,* 61–62; Xerardo Dasairas, *O Entroido en terras de Monterrei* (Vilaboa, Pontevedra: Ediciónes do Cumio, 1990) 54–55; Josefina Roma Riu, *Aragón y el carnaval* (Zaragoza: Guara Editorial, 1980), 79, 87–88.

24. Gilmore, *Carnival and Culture,* 19–23; José Manuel González Reboredo and José Mariño Ferro, *Entroido: Aproximación a la fiesta del carnaval en Galicia* (La Coruña: Editorial Diputación Provincial, 1987), 174.

25. Lisón Tolsana, *Antropología cultural,* 150; Mariana Regalado, "Ounhas Couces do Nabizo" (a few kicks from the donkey): Evaluation in the Performance of the Testament of the Donkey" (master's thesis, New York University, 1992).

26. Caro Baroja, *Carnaval,* 67–71, 91, 95; Gilmore, *Carnival and Culture,* 14.

27. Personal observations during the Carnival season in Laza, 1988–1996; Cocho, *Carnaval en Galicia,* 354–356.

28. Cocho, *Carnaval en Galicia,* 307–311; Dasairas, *O Entroido,* 58–59; Lisón Tolsana, *Antropología cultural,* 147–148.

29. Personal observations during the Carnival season in Laza, 1988–1996; Jane Cowan, "Women, Men, and Pre-Lenten Carnival in Northern Greece: An Anthropological Exploration of Gender Transformation in Symbol and Practice," *Rural History* 5, no. 2 (1994): 195–210.

30. Personal observations during the Carnival season in Laza, 1988–1996.

31. Blanco Conde, *Laza,* 94–95, 97–111.

32. Caro Baroja, *Carnaval,* 229.

33. Blanco Conde, *Laza,* 99–100.

34. Ibid., 118–122.

35. Personal observations during the Carnival season in Laza, 1988–1996.

36. Personal communication from Antonio Muñoz Carrión, and personal observations during the Carnival season in Laza, 1988–1996; Antonio Muñoz Carrión, "Elementos comunicacionales en la parodia grotesca: Introducción metodológica," *Revista Internacional de Sociología* 44 (1) (1986): 81–92.

37. Blanco Conde, *Laza,* 115–117.

38. Ibid., 93–94; personal observations during the Carnival season in Laza, 1988–1996.

39. Regalado, "Ounhas couces do nabizo."

40. Taboada Chivite, "La Cencerrada en Galicia," 52.

41. Blanco Conde, *Laza,* 92–94, 121.

42. Lisón Tolsana, *Antropología cultural,* 148–149; Cocho, *Carnaval en Galicia,* 302.

43. Personal observations during the Carnival season in Laza, 1988–1996.

44. Vicente Risco, "Notas sobre las fiestas de carnaval en Galicia," *Revista de Dialectología y Tradiciones Populares* 4, no. 2 (1948): 164.

45. Personal observations during the Carnival season in Laza, 1988–1996.

46. Taboada Chivite, "La Cencerrada en Galicia," 214.

47. Personal observations during the Carnival season in Laza, 1988–1996.

48. Lisón Tolsana, *Antropología cultural,* 148.

49. Blanco Conde, *Laza,* 89.

50. Personal observations during the Carnival season in Laza, 1988–1996.

51. Ibid.

52. Dasairas, *O Entroido,* 92.

53. Personal observations during the Carnival season in Laza, 1988–1996.

54. Ibid.

55. Blanco Conde, *Laza,* 92–94.

56. Personal observations during the Carnival season in Laza, 1988–1996.

57. Blanco Conde, *Laza,* 122–123.

58. Personal observations during the Carnival season in Laza, 1988–1996.

59. Ibid.; Caro Baroja, *Carnaval,* 121.

60. Regalado, "Ounhas couces do nabizo."

61. Xesús Taboada Chivite, "El Entierro de la Sardina: Ritualidad del carnaval gallego," in *Ritos y creencias gallegas* (A Coruna: Salvora, 1980), 52.

62. Personal observations during the Carnival season in Laza, 1988–1996; Isabel Knox, "Towards a Philosophy of Humor," *Journal of Philosophy* 48, no. 18 (1951): 546.

63. Octavio Paz, *The Labyrinth of Solitude* (New York: Grove Press, 1961), 50; Mikhail Bakhtin, *Rabelais and His World* (Bloomington: Indiana University Press, 1984), 7.

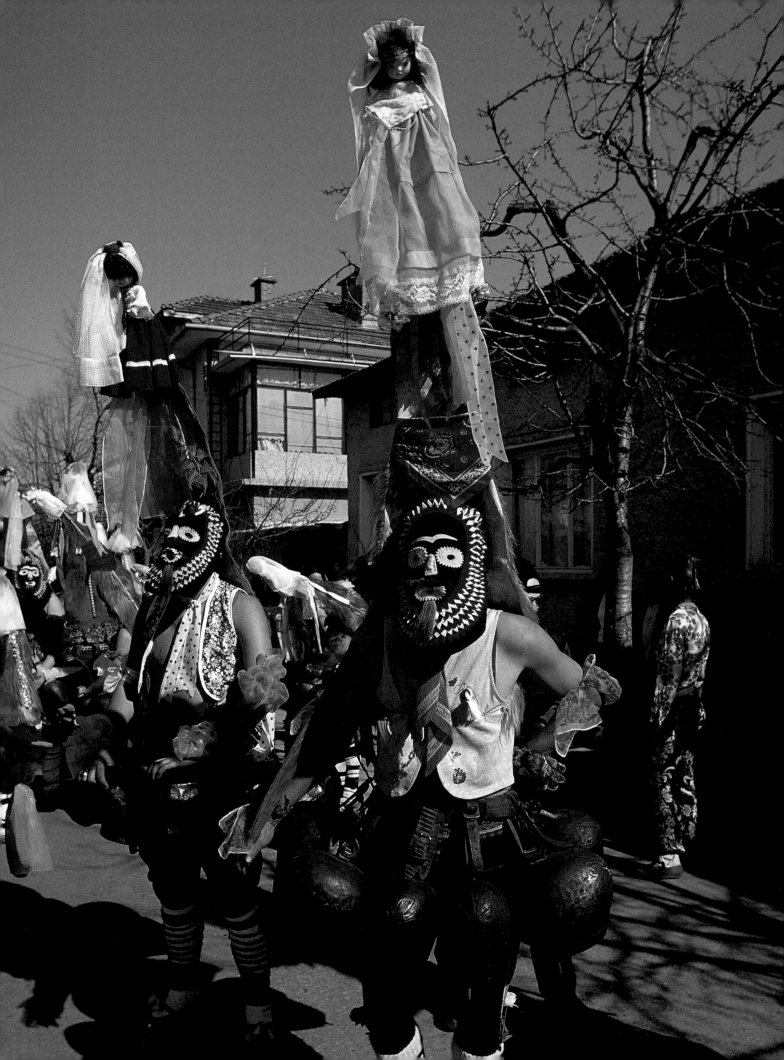

3 Mask and Masquerade

FROM MYSTERIOUS INITIATION TO CARNIVAL IN BULGARIA

VALERIA FOL

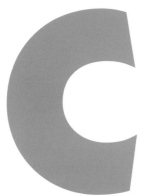

ARNIVAL MASQUERADES and performances in contemporary Bulgaria are derived in part from cults and rites that developed in the second millennium BC among Thracian peoples in the southeastern Balkan Peninsula. As an alternative to the religion of the ancient Greeks on the Olympic Peninsula, the Thracians adhered to a faith now called "nonliterary Orphism,"[1] in which people believed they could reach immortality after death through rituals carried out during New Year festival initiations, which took place in the spring. The Thracian Orphic practitioners believed that through masquerade and the sacrifice of horses, bulls, rams, or goats, Dionysus, son of the Great Mother Goddess, would return from death and be reborn. The Orphic followers thought they could bring the Godson into themselves while in a state of trance, and the mask then guided Dionysus and the followers through the underworld back to life on earth. This performance went through a cycle of the Orphic Godson's conception, birth, death, and rebirth, and in this way the people approached immortality. Nonliterary Orphism

was carried out at two levels, one among the aristocrats and the other among the general population.[2]

In the contemporary culture of southeastern Europe, including Bulgaria, many Orphic rites that originated in the ancient faith of the general populace are still preserved. For many Bulgarians, these form the roots of the rituals carried out in present-day pre-Lenten ceremonies, commonly known as the Kouker festival or Kouker's Day, after the main character or characters in the activities (fig. 3.1).[3]

The date for Easter, and thus for the beginning of Lent, in the Eastern Orthodox Church follows the original Julian calendar, which varies slightly from the Gregorian calendar adopted by Roman Catholics in AD 1582.[4] Lent, known as Meat-Fast Shrovetide, begins in the sixth week before Easter, but Eastern Orthodox Catholics also begin a semi-fast during the week preceding this. At this time they give up meat but can still eat eggs and dairy products. The Bulgarian Carnival, or Kouker festival, most frequently takes place on the Monday of this week, known as Cheese-Fast Shrovetide.[5]

An example of a Kouker celebration was recorded by John Nunley in the village of Pavel Banja in south-central Bulgaria on Monday, March 1, 1998:

Early that morning, celebrants pinned little red and white figures of humans and animals to their clothing in order to appease the old hag, Baba Marta (or Granny March), lest she become irritated and punish her followers by extending the harsh winter season and threatening the birth of

3.1 Koukers in Pavel Banja wear masks made of felt and large headdresses with dolls attached to the top as symbols of fertility. *Photograph by Shirley and David Rowen, 1998.*

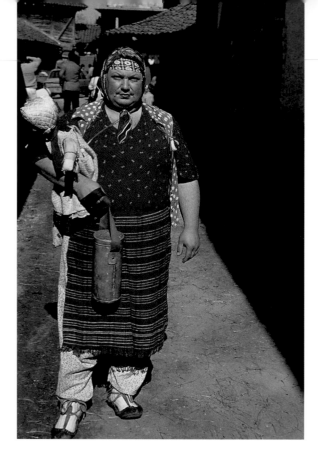

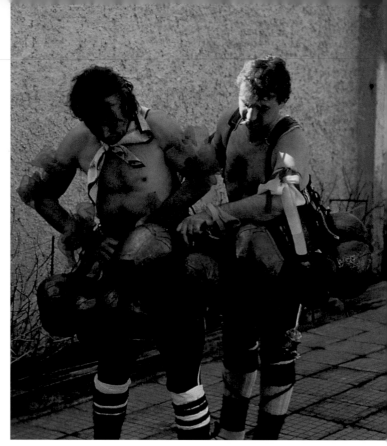

3.2 Man wearing the masquerade for the character of Babba, the old woman, as part of the Kouker festival in Pavel Banja. *Photograph by John Nunley, 1998.*

3.3 Young men from Pavel Banja getting dressed in Kouker costumes, each tying the characteristic large bells to a belt around his waist. *Photograph by John Nunley, 1998.*

spring [fig. 3.2].[7] By seven o'clock, young men throughout the village were being dressed in the elaborate Kouker masquerades [fig. 3.3]. Solemnly and carefully the leggings and bells were attached to the men's bodies, shirts were fitted and ribbons tied, and finally masks were placed over their heads. In Pavel Banja the Koukers wear masks made from fabric and tall, animal-hide headdresses with dolls attached to the top as a symbol of fertility for the community and the agricultural season.

In the meantime, prospective audiences, including women, children, visitors, and tourists, gathered at the local pubs for drinks and food, waiting for the house-to-house processions of the Koukers. As the maskers assembled in the streets, bagpipe and clarinet music played by Gypsies began to energize the group, and suddenly they were off to the first house. The owner of this residence peered through the slightly opened door and then invited the Koukers inside. They danced before the seated household members, bestowing upon them the blessings of fertility and health. In return, the host offered the performers wine, bread, cheese, stuffed grape leaves, and various dried meats and nuts that were on a table festooned with the yellow-blossomed branches of the sacred cornelian cherry tree (*Cornus mas*), known for its fertility powers.

Afterward, the Koukers returned to the streets. Smoke bombs were set off, creating a surreal battlefield on which

chaotic maskers, armed with staffs, threatened each other as well as onlookers. The house-to-house visitations continued through the late afternoon as the Koukers paraded through all the neighborhoods of the village. Occasionally, performers rested along the streets while talking with friends and adjusting costumes that had become disheveled in the highly athletic dancing [fig. 3.4].

As the sun crossed the sky toward the western horizon, villagers and Koukers proceeded to the village square, where ritual plowing and symbolic sacrifice of the Kouker were performed. The plow was attached by a rope to one of the Koukers, who appeared to be unaware of what was happening. Next, some of the performers pulled the line to which the Kouker was attached, and in response he fell down as if dead. As the music resumed he suddenly came back to life and completed the symbolic plowing. In the background loomed the complex building projects constructed during the communist era. Gypsies, Turks, Bulgarians, and tourists cheered the rebirth of the dead Kouker and the eventual return of spring and new life.[6]

A Historical Sketch of Bulgaria

How have such complex ritual events evolved in Bulgaria into contemporary times? The answer to this question lies in the equally complex history of the region (fig. 3.5). The earliest inhabits of the Balkan region were the Thracians, who originated there as Indo-European peoples. They introduced the Orphic and Dionysian religions, whose primary goals included the achievement of immortality and general fecundity through human and animal sacrifice. The Great Mother Goddess was and remains the primary spiritual force.[8]

The Thracians created one of the most powerful and famous kingdoms in antiquity, extending over a large part of the southeastern Balkans. Because of this location and their power, the Thracians had a great impact on ancient cultures in Asia Minor. The Romans conducted wars for two and a half centuries, from the end of the second century BC until AD 106, before finally conquering the last Thracian kingdom. They retained the power and privileges of the Thracian aristocracy and, in keeping with their methods of colonization, did not intrude in local religious life, under the condition that the people honor the official Roman pantheon and, above all, the divine emperor.

The Thracian provinces of the Roman Empire resisted the attacks of the "barbaric tribes" until the fifth century AD and even of Attila's Huns in the late fifth century. About the same time, Slavs from the Baltic region migrated southward across the Danube River and settled. They were primarily agriculturalists who maintained a decentralized form of government. By the early seventh century AD the Proto-Bulgarians, from central Asia, had entered the region, and together with the Slavic tribes they united the country against the Byzantine Empire. In 681, the emperor of Byzantium concluded a peace treaty with Asparuh, the leader of this new coalition, thus marking the formation of the Bulgarian state. In 865, Boris I adopted the Byzantine form of Christianity, although it is likely that rural people adapted the state religion to their own seasonal and agricultural rituals, which were based in part on the old cults.[9]

For many centuries the country enjoyed peace and prosperity, and the different cultures fused into a single sense of identity. This period of tranquillity ended with the Ottoman conquest in 1396, and for the next five hundred years Bulgarians were second-class subjects ruled and taxed by the new Islamic state. The country finally regained its freedom in 1878 as a result of Russia's victory in the Russo-Turkish War. Sofia became the nation's capital, and Eastern Orthodoxy was officially reinstated. After the Second World War, Bulgarian land came under the sphere of the commu-

3.4 Koukers and other masqueraders in the performance troupe assemble in the central square in Pavel Banja. *Photograph by Shirley and David Rowen, 1998.*

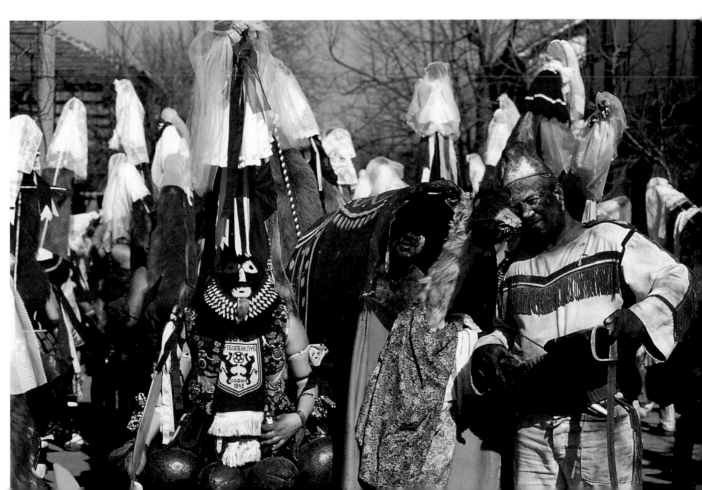

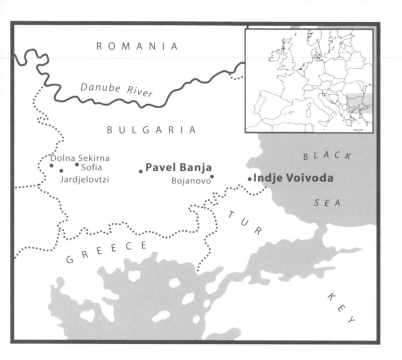

3.5 Southeastern Europe, showing Bulgarian regions and towns mentioned in chapter 3.

nistic bloc. Russians reappeared with the rise of the Soviet Union, and during that era Christianity was downplayed and the rural masquerades were encouraged as the communists sought greater control of the country at the expense of the Church.[10] With the collapse of the Soviet Union, a new democratic Bulgarian government encouraged private initiative in business and agriculture. The resulting changes led to an economic crisis, and local farmers have had to retain their traditional, preindustrial technology, which includes relying on ox- and horse-drawn wooden carts.

History of Festival Traditions and the Christian Church

The ancient masquerade festivals of the Thracians in southeastern Europe were focused on the Great Mother Goddess and her son, Dionysus. Versions of the myth of his conception, birth, and resurrection were "retold" in the language of mask ritualism in order to ensure the renovation of the cosmos and society. Much of the performance had sexual overtones played out by men and women sometimes dressed in each other's clothing. The ceremonies took place at the beginning of the ancient New Year, which occurred in early spring, and at specified times in the fall and winter.[11]

Eastern Orthodox Church records indicate that a variety of non-Christian festivals and rituals were still being carried out in communities throughout southeastern Europe from late antiquity to the late Middle Ages. Origen, a Christian apologist and philosopher who lived in the second and third centuries AD, mentioned masquerading and burlesquing in association with Dionysian rites.[12] The Ankyrria Parochial Council (AD 314) condemned not only sorcery but also pagan customs (Canon 24).[13] Two rules formulated in the decisions of the Parochial Council of Carthage (AD 419, Canons 71 and 72) condemned the shameful games and words that disgraced the honor of mothers and families.[14]

In 678, Church officials attending the Sixth Ecumenical Council (the Council of Trullo) developed the earlier prohibitions in even greater detail; these were coded in Canons 61, 62, and 65 of the final documents. Canon 65 described "men jumping over open fires in accordance with some old custom" (a ritual that is still performed in many villages in southeastern Europe in the Kouker's games held during Cheese-Fast Shrovetide). Canon 62 condemned "the dressing of men in women's clothes, as well as of women in men's clothes, the wearing of masks, the calling out of the name of Dionysus, and the jokes and madness." Canon 61 condemned the custom of leading bears and other animals.[15]

Despite such prohibitions, the masquerade ritual tradition was so deeply rooted in the festival calendar of southeastern European people that it continued to be practiced. The interpreters of the canons of the Sixth Ecumenical Council, writing in the twelfth century, not only elucidated the prohibitions but gave even more details about local customs. They wrote that men disguised themselves as monks and quadruped animals, wore swords, and ridiculed Church officials and institutions. They also painted their cheeks and performed indecent acts that were characteristic of women, to provoke laughter among the spectators. One of the twelfth-century Church officials asked the participants who continued to carry out the rituals why they dared to do so. He was told that "it was done according to an old tradition." An appendix to Canon 61, which addressed the leading of bears and other animals, stated that the animals were actually men dressed in fur clothes who wore fur masks on their faces.[16]

In the fourteenth century another writer described masquerade festivals that took place in Bulgaria in January and March. During these feasts men dressed up in women's clothes and women in men's, they "changed their faces," and their games had features of fornication. The writer also mentioned that some celebrants led bears, and he defined the ritual as "Dionysiac and Hellenic."[17]

One valuable source concerning masquerade games performed by people living around the lower Danube during late antiquity and the early Middle Ages is the anonymous life story of the Thracian Dazius, a Christian martyr slain in AD 303 for his refusal to dress up in royal clothes and take part in a celebration of the god Cronos.[18] The story was narrated by a medieval analyst at the end of the fifth century and beginning of the sixth. He commented that during the feast, participants wrapped themselves in goatskins, and by changing their faces, "they give up goodness and enter the evil."[19]

The Eastern Orthodox Church is still an enemy of the masquerade ritual tradition that is carried on in Bulgaria today, which the Church defines as "fiendish" and "diabolic." After the Second World War, however, the secular authorities of the Balkan states did not prohibit the festivals and even allocated money for sponsoring national and international events at which ritual performances were presented. Residents of many rural communities continue to carry out ritual masquerading at certain times of the autumn and winter.[20]

The winter masquerade ritual, most frequently called Sourvaki,[21] is performed during the days between Christmas (December 25) and Epiphany (January 6), but usually on the day of the Holy Circumcision (Basil's Day, January 1). It is related to the winter solstice and marks the beginning of the astronomical year. However, the period in question was not adopted in a religious sense by folk Christians in Bulgaria, so these days were called "unclean" (unbaptized) days. The winter masquerade is carried out in communities west and southwest of the city of Sofia (around the towns of Blagoevgrad, Kyustendil, and Gevgeli in present-day Macedonia), in south-central and northern Bulgaria (around the towns of Plovdiv, Pleven, Ruse, Lovech, and Razgrad), and in certain villages of the western Rhodope Mountains.

Bachelors and recently married men take part in

the ritual. They dress in costumes that portray animals (resembling a ram or he-goat), birds, and a wedding couple. In some villages, two of the men are dressed as a bear and bear trainer or as a camel and camel driver. The main performers of the ritual dress in furs and carry many bells around their waists, sometimes attached to several bands worn one above the other. Their masks are made of fur, horns, and feathers, and they are armed with short, heavy clubs, wooden weights, and swords. The party chooses a leader who conducts the ritual ceremonies, including the blessing for health, fertility, and a happy new year.

One of the most important parts of the winter (New Year's) masquerade is a tour around the houses in the village. The homeowners meet and present gifts to the party of ritually initiated men. If a host does not want to let the masked sourvakari into his house, they have the right to break in. The masked group also carries out other rituals such as mock weddings, mock plowing in the center of town, followed by mock sowing, and making the "bear" or "camel" dance. When a wedding couple is part of the group, they often simulate sexual intercourse during their tour around the village, encouraged by both masked and unmasked observers. The "camel" is openly involved in phallic games while the bear, often dressed like a bride, dances and wallows on the ground.

The autumn masquerade is performed either during or just after threshing. It is observed in areas around the towns of Razgrad and Shumen in northeastern Bulgaria and is similar to the winter masquerade just described.

The Kouker Festival

The most widespread masquerade tradition is the spring one—the New Year's masquerade tradition of antiquity—known as Kouker's Day. Festival traditions similar to the Bulgarian Kouker's Day have been documented for the European part of Turkey (before Bulgarians and Greeks were expelled from there in the late nineteenth and early twentieth centuries), for Serbia, and for Thessalonica in northern Greece. Researchers who have studied these festivals agree that the characters and activities found in the masquerades and performances seem to be derived from ancient Orphic cults of Thrace and that they focus

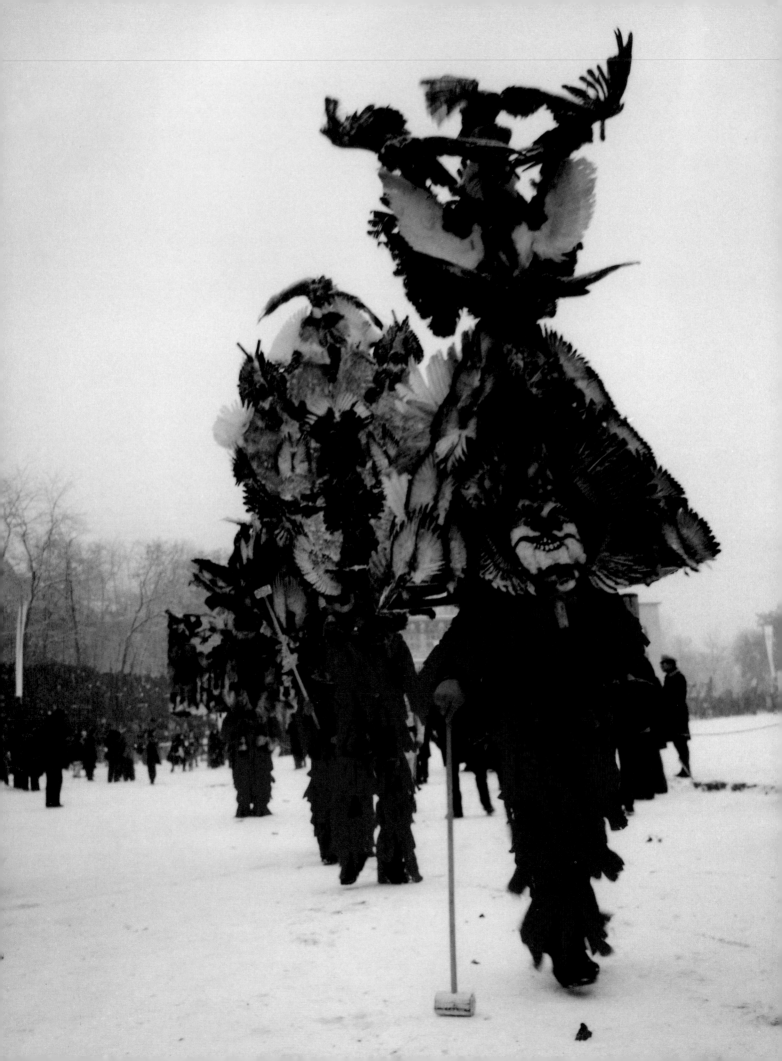

on the death and resurrection of Dionysus, the son of the Great Mother Goddess.[22]

In Bulgaria, the Kouker festival is carried out in villages from the ridge of Stara Planina on the shore of the Black Sea in the northeast all the way to the western side of the country around the towns of Straldzha and Yambol. The largest concentration of towns that celebrate Kouker's Day, however, is in the southern part of Bulgaria, particularly in the southeast.[23] As described earlier for the town of Pavel Banja, many of these festivals feature several Koukers, whose costumes include masks and elaborate headdresses. Examples are found in the villages of Jardjelovtzi and Dolna Sekirna in the district of Pernik in southwestern Bulgaria (figs. 3.6, 3.7), in the town of Bojanovo in the south-central part of the country (fig. 3.8), and in Shiroka Laka in the Rhodope Mountains (fig. 3.9).

The appearance of multiple Koukers with ornate costumes has evolved out of the traditional ritual, in which only one Kouker takes part and wears animal

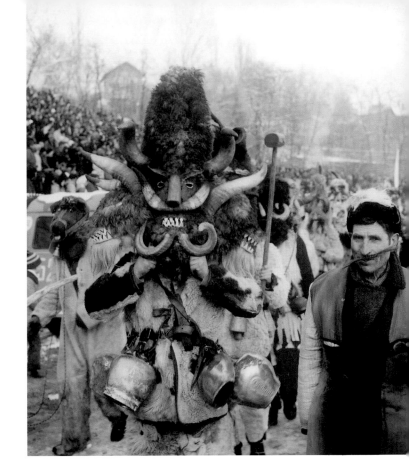

3.6 Kouker masqueraders in the village of Jardjelovtzi in southwestern Bulgaria. *Photograph by Rossen Kolev, 1981.*

3.7 Kouker masqueraders in the village of Dolna Sekirna in southwestern Bulgaria. *Photograph by Rossen Kolev, 1981.*

3.8 Kouker masqueraders in the village of Bojanovo in south-central Bulgaria. *Photograph by Rossen Kolev, 1981.*

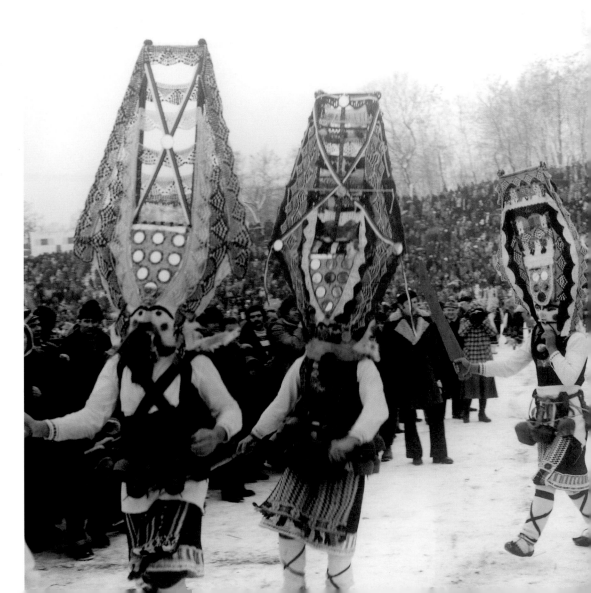

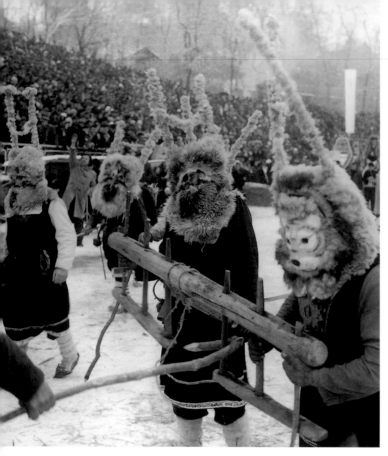

skins without a formal mask or headdress. This change may have occurred after World War II, when government-sponsored national and international events featured the masqueraders, encouraging them to look more striking and to compete in their costuming with other villagers. Tourists have shown increasing interest and now attend annual Carnival festivals in some of the less remote villages. The appearance of several Koukers wearing elaborate costumes and headdresses draws larger crowds.[24]

The more traditional form of the Kouker festival has been preserved in rural villages of the Strandzha

3.9 Kouker masqueraders near the town of Smoljan in the Rhodope Mountains of Bulgaria. *Photograph by Rossen Kolev, 1981.*

3.10 The single Kouker masquerader in the village of Indje Voivoda wears goatskins, and instead of covering his face with a mask, he wears it blackened with shoe polish. *Photograph by Valeria Fol, 1984.*

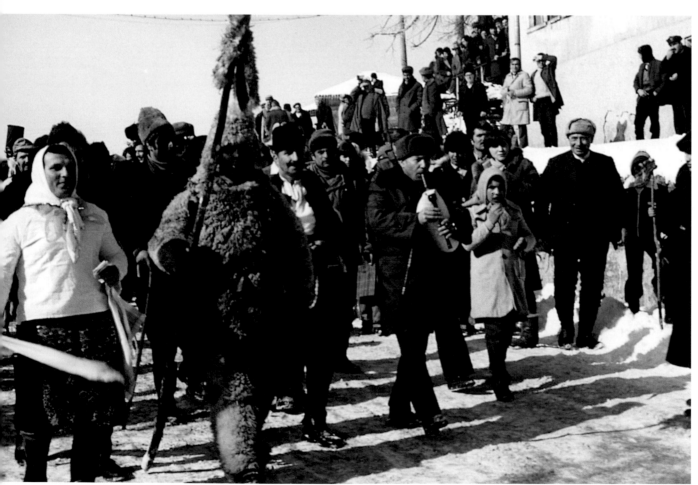

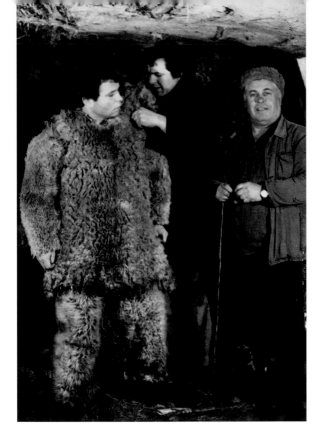

3.11 The Kouker masquerader is dressed in a barn by the elders of Indje Voivoda, who piece together sections of goat hide and sew them with hemp thread. *Photograph by Valeria Fol, 1984.*

Mountains that were first researched by scholars in the nineteenth century.[25] Subsequent research has uncovered written evidence that villagers in Strandzha region have performed these masquerade rituals since ancient Thracian times, throughout the Middle Ages, and into the present.[26] Here the rituals revolve around a single, or *mono,* Kouker, who is sacrificed and born anew. In order to better understand the historical as well as the present significance of this ritual, it is important to learn about the main characters that take part in the modern-day celebration. The following descriptions are based on my twenty years of observations in all the villages in the Strandzha Mountains in which Kouker's Day is celebrated.[27]

THE KOUKER

The major character of the performance is the Kouker, and rather than wearing a formal mask, his face is covered with soot from rye straw mixed with oil. Recently this mixture has been replaced by black shoe cream. The Kouker's wrists and palms are also blackened, suggesting that he is essentially a black animal. He is dressed in seven sheep or goat hides supplied by the

headmen of seven households in the village. One hide is worn on each arm, one on each leg, one on the chest, and one on the back. The seventh is sewn as a hood with a pointed top (*pylos*), which the Kouker wears over his head. The character's blackened skin and the bull and buffalo bells he wears suspended around his waist may make reference to the sacrificial bulls of the ancient cults. A large wooden phallus, painted red, hangs in front of the Kouker among the bells (fig. 3.10).

The requirements for the man who plays the Kouker are that he be married, Christian, and poor. He is dressed by elders early in the morning in a closed space, often a barn or a tavern. The hides are sewn together directly on his body with hemp thread (fig. 3.11). Sometimes small horns are placed on top of the pointed hood, near the ears that are left on the hide of the lamb or kid to enhance the realistic portrayal of the animal. After the ritual dressing is completed, the Kouker begins to jump, thus announcing his own birth by the chiming of his bells. At this moment, the crowd gathering outside shouts "Houy!" (a vernacular word for phallus in Bulgarian). The Kouker's party and all the people in the village, who are both participants in the ritual and audience, shout this word throughout the day. The sound of the bells and the cry "Houy!" proclaim the approach of the Kouker during the house-to-house tour. The Kouker himself does not speak or cry out—he is a mime—but does his best to sustain the loud sound of the bells in all directions throughout the day.

The Kouker carries a thyrsus, or scepter, a pole about two meters long with a piece of leather or a cloth attached to its upper end; the thyrsus is never taken into an enclosed space. With this phallic device the Kouker strikes both the ground and the spectators— especially women, for it is believed that they will conceive faster and more easily after being hit with it (fig. 3.12). Often the Kouker performs indecent acts toward other men with the wooden phallus hanging from his waist; these acts are called *koukering.* The Kouker is not allowed to take in his hands any of the gifts that households are obligated to give to his party, so they are collected and carried by other members of his troupe. At the very end of the celebration, the seven hides in which the Kouker was dressed are buried in farmland in seven different places outside the village, in order to promote fertility. Similarly, the wooden

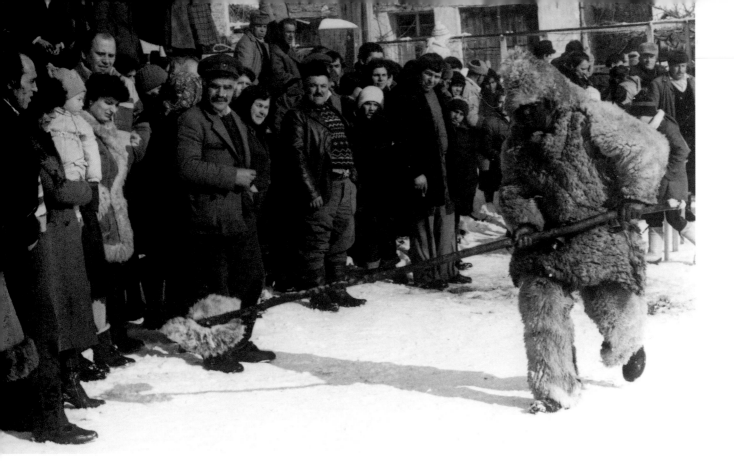

3.12 The Kouker strikes spectators in Indje Voivoda with his phallic scepter to bring them fertility and prosperity. *Photograph by Valeria Fol, 1984.*

phallus that hung from his waist is secretly placed in the bag of a man whose wife has apparently been unable to conceive.

OTHER RITUAL PERFORMERS

Babba, or the old woman, is another central character in Kouker's Day performances in the Strandzha Mountains. This role must be played by a married man whose children are all living, a rule still strictly observed in certain villages. He wears the traditional clothing of an elderly woman: a dark-colored dress belted by an apron, and a black kerchief on the head. The Babba is necessarily hunchbacked, and her kerchief is decorated with a garlic clove and a coin, like that of a woman who has just had a baby. Her painted black face is highlighted by a large mushroom that is placed in her mouth and painted with big teeth (fig. 3.13). She appears as the hag, the humble side of the Great Mother Goddess, and she carries a spindle, a distaff, and a bag or basket holding a puppy or a kitten. The

baby doll that the Babba also carries is dressed like a girl but has a phallus under its skirt. The hermaphroditic element of this doll may be derived from the ancient Mother Goddess, who, with attributes of both sexes, was able to self-conceive. Babba spins continuously during the entire performance in order to produce yarn that she might use to make clothing for her "children," who include the Kouker and all of the masked men.

Babba's attendant is a character known as Dyaddo (elderly man, grandfather), who must be played by a married man. He is dressed in the dark clothing traditional for men of this region, and his face is blackened with soot. Two of his major duties are to protect Babba from the sexual attempts of both peasants and other masqueraders and to play at having "sexual intercourse" with her himself. He also helps her to "deliver" her baby and to harness the young men who play the role of Guards to a plow for a ritual plowing.

The Tsar (king), or Krustnik (godfather), is a ritual character whose impersonator is chosen for his merits. He is acknowledged to be the best farmer and stockbreeder in the village, and his wife is raising many children. The Tsar dresses in his best clothes, and there is nothing comical or indecent in his appearance or behavior. Like the Kouker, he is not allowed to take any of the gifts that households give to the traveling party.

The Tsaritsa (queen) is the wife of the man who has been chosen to play the Tsar. Her ritual obligation is to make the Kouker's specially kneaded round bread (pita bread). She does not take a direct part in the ritual, but her qualities, such as being a good house-keeper, should supplement those of her husband's that qualify him to enact the Tsar.

The next two characters, Momma (the maid) and Ergen (the bachelor), are a betrothed version of Babba and Dyaddo, symbolizing the transition of youths from one social status to another. The young man who plays the Momma is heavily made up and is "armed" with a kerchief with a stone or onion tied to the corner, which

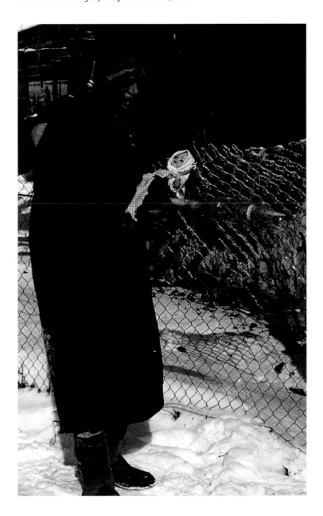

3.13 A man masquerades as the old woman known as Babba, another central character in Kouker's Day performances in Indje Voivoda. *Photograph by Valeria Fol, 1984*

the character uses to defend herself from the bachelor's aspirations. The Momma leads the ritual *horo* (ring dance) and walks in front of the cart in which the Kouker brings the Tsar to the center of town for the ritual plowing, sowing, and predicting. The Ergen is not made up, nor is his face blackened, but he carries a wooden sword and beats the wooers of the Momma.

The Guards are played by young unmarried men. They are divided into two groups, one dressed in good clothes and with unpainted faces, the other dressed in ragged clothes and with blackened faces. The Guards of both groups wear red kerchiefs around their necks, similar to those worn at weddings. They are belted with red girdles and in some villages wear red mantles as well. They are armed with wooden swords, the blades of which are either entirely painted red or are decorated with wavelike red lines. Their basic function is to guard the Kouker, the Babba, and the Momma, but they are also harnessed to the cart that delivers the Tsar and to the plow for the ritual plowing. The two kinds of Guards have different names in different villages, but they always suggest warriors' functions. With their wooden swords the Guards hit the villagers who stand on the sidelines of the performance, thus bestowing upon them the ability to have many children.

The characters Tsiganin (he-Gypsy) and Tsiganka (she-Gypsy) appear in the Kouker's suite in only some villages. Married men with blackened faces, dressed in ragged clothes, play the ritual couple. The Tsiganin carries both smithing and tinworking tools while the Tsiganka carries a bag of cinders that she sprinkles on everyone around. These personages are not considered to represent true Gypsies but rather to parody the "deities of fire," for they represent the pure infernal energy in the new creation of the world through these ritual actions.

A character who is always present in the Kouker's troupe is the Barber. A married man, he is outfitted in a way that provokes laughter. His face is not blackened, but he carries barber's tools and a tripod chair with a nail projecting up on the seat (fig. 3.14). A mirror hangs on his behind. He "works" nonstop, symbolically shaving the men and styling the women's hair. Each person to be groomed must pretend to sit on his chair with its phallic nail, a performance associated with the sexual act and again called *koukering*. The shaving of the men is a parody of the sacred shaving of males in Mediterranean funeral practices in which the cut hair is considered an offering to the spirits. This offering brings the worlds of men and the gods together in ritual action.

The Healer is a character that probably came from ancient and medieval games that mimicked sexual intercourse in order to bring about fertility and the rebirth of the pagan god.[28] The Healer's part in the Kouker ritual is to show his inability to bring the killed Kouker back to life.

The Pop (Eastern Orthodox priest) is a parodic personage that probably appeared during the early Christian era,[29] replacing the ancient priest who originally conducted the ritual. Today, a married man dressed as an Orthodox priest plays the character. He carries a small cauldron filled with ivy and a bunch of basil to sprinkle on those who participate in the festival, thereby blessing them (fig. 3.15). In some villages the Pop carries a doll that is dressed like him but has a big movable phallus, another symbol of fertility.

The Shoeshine character can be played by either a married man or a bachelor. He is dressed in old clothes, and his face is painted black. He carries shoeshine tools and stains everything around him, creating chaos.

The role of the Ranger, or tax collector, is usually entrusted to a married man. He is dressed in the typical clothing of his profession and is armed with a gun. As part of the ritual drama, he continuously collects money from the villagers watching the performance. It is thought that this character appeared in the Kouker's troupe in early medieval times, when his presence in the mimic games in Byzantium was noted.[30]

Finally, because the Kouker and the Tsar are not allowed to take the gifts presented to them by households during the tour around the village, bachelors called Magaretas (donkeys or carriers) dress in rags and carry bags in which to put gifts such as flour, eggs, cheese, cereals, money, and wine.

THE KOUKER PERFORMANCE

The Kouker Carnival celebration is a one-day event structured around various actions, performances, and

3.14 The Barber is another character who is always part of the Kouker's troupe in Indje Voivoda. He carries barber's tools and a small tripod chair with a nail projecting from the top that serves as a phallic symbol. *Photograph by Valeria Fol, 1984*

3.15 The masquerader known as Pop impersonates an Eastern Orthodox priest in Indje Voivoda. He carries a small cauldron filled with ivy and basil that he sprinkles on villagers as a form of blessing. *Photograph by Valeria Fol, 1984.*

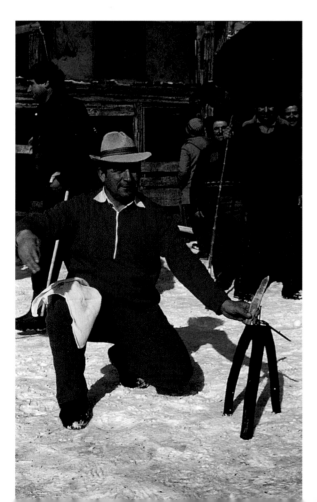

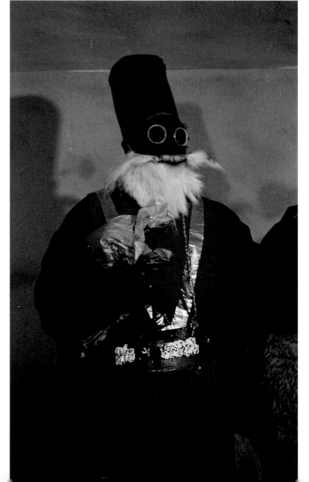

rituals. The Kouker and his entourage repeat some actions and perform others only once, at fixed times and in specific places.

First thing in the morning, most of the households in the village "clarify" their dogs in the "healing of the dogs" ritual. The men take their animals to a small pond where a rope is tied to a pole on either side of the water. One by one the dogs are attached to the ropes, which are twisted around each other into a central line (fig. 3.16). The dog is swung out over the water, and gradually the ropes start to unwind. Before long the animal is spinning wildly in space, and eventually it falls into the water. This action is supposed to prevent the dogs from ever contracting rabies.[31]

The day also begins with the ritual participants dressing at their homes while the Kouker is prepared in an isolated room. The Kouker's appearance in the village square is announced by the sound of his bells, and he is greeted by villagers who await him enthusiastically. After receiving permission from the town's mayor to begin the performance, the Kouker and his troupe start their ritual tour of the houses in the village. In the past, the village elders granted this right. The permission is given only after the masked party promises "not to do a lot of mischief." The Kouker and his group appear to be in continuous conflict with people without masks during the house-to-house procession. The entourage represents a threat, in the form of chaos, to the order symbolized by the village houses and, by extension, families. As part of the activities, villagers try to kidnap Babba and Momma, who are protected by the Guards. The actions of these spectators and their indecent words and phrases convey a strong sense of sexual aggression. Babba and Dyaddo frequently mimic sexual intercourse, encouraged by the cheers of the crowd. Meanwhile, the Kouker "sharpens" his wooden phallus on the wheels of his cart, which has been overturned, and uses it to perform mock sexual acts on both men and women.

The Kouker and his troupe visit each house in the village, starting in an easterly direction and then turning north, moving opposite to the direction of the sun. Usually householders meet the party in their yard, where a table is set with pita bread, cheese, eggs, and wine. The masked group dance *horo,* usually led by the Momma, performing the dance three times around each house, again moving opposite to the sun's path.

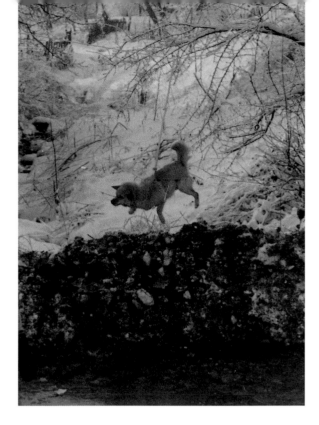

3.16 As part of the Kouker's Day rituals, dogs in Indje Voivoda are tied to ropes and swung over a pond, into which they eventually fall. The act is intended to protect the animals from rabies. *Photograph by Valeria Fol, 1984.*

The Kouker breaks the pita, eats a mouthful of it, and drinks from the wine pitcher; then the rest of the masked party eats and drinks. While they drink the wine provided by the master of the house, he in turn drinks the wine the troupe has brought. When the guests are invited inside the house, the Kouker enters first and rolls on the floor for "health and fertility." The contact of the Kouker's body with the floor is thought to bring fertility to the earth, to the farm's livestock, and to the women of the house. The raking-over of the cinders in the hearth by the Momma or the Babba is another necessary rite, assuring fire and warmth for the New Year. If there is a small child in the house, it is briefly given to the Babba or the Momma to be carried "for health." All the other personages do their usual work—the Shoeshine "cleans" shoes, the Tsiganin "mends" metal vessels, and the Pop "blesses." The owners of the household present the masked party with money, eggs, flour, and cheese, which are taken by the Magareta.

In some cases the Kouker singles out unwanted families who should leave the village because of their antisocial behavior. He uses his thyrsus to inscribe a

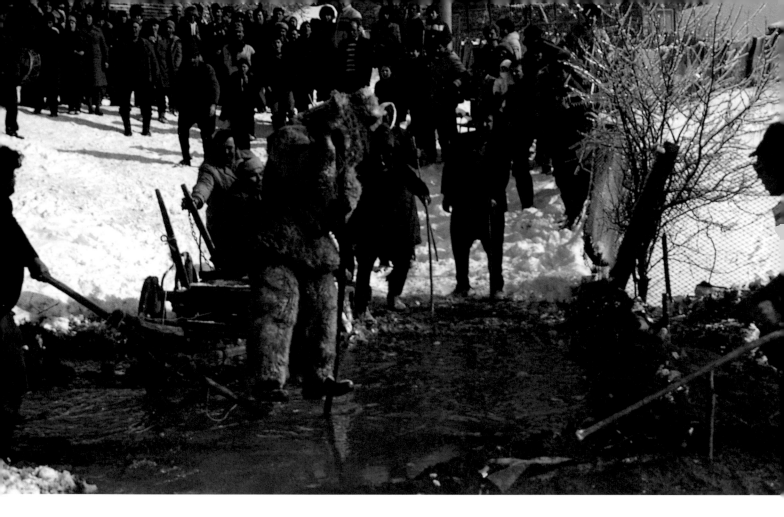

3.17 The Kouker and his troupe stop at a pond in Indje Voivoda to perform one of the day's rituals, the "bathing of the godfather"—that is, bathing him with the primordial mud of Creation. *Photograph by Valeria Fol, 1984.*

cross over the windows and the doors of the family's house. Thus identified, the family is eventually forced to move from the village. If certain families do not let the masked party into their yard, the troupe has the right to break in and cause damage. The Kouker and his party never violate the hosts or their home territory once they are allowed to enter.

The ritual chaos provoked by the masked performers is finally overcome at the end of the day when everyone, performers and spectators alike, gather in the village square, where the Kouker and his troupe carry out the concluding rituals with the enthusiastic approval of the crowd (fig. 3.17).

Dyaddo and Ergen, the bachelor, take the wheeled cart to the square. Ergen and the Guards are harnessed to it, while the Kouker climbs in and stands in the back, resting on the thyrsus. Momma then leads the cart, followed by all the other masked performers,

toward the home of the Tsar. The latter has to be brought ceremonially to the square together with the pita bread baked by his wife, the Tsaritsa. The wine, cheese, and eggs that have been given to the Kouker are also put in the cart, along with a bag or a half-bushel of seeds. The Tsar is seated in the cart next to the standing Kouker, and they are pulled into the square, where they are met by the crowd with a mighty cry of "Houy!"

Suddenly, Babba lies down on the ground and begins to cry, explaining that she is in labor. The "child" she gives birth to is symbolized by a puppy or kitten that she carries in a bag. Traditionally, the Babba may perform this ritual birth on a bridge over the river, in a tree, on a staircase, or on the roof of a pigsty. It is a parody of the Great Mother Goddess, who gave birth to her self-conceived son in his zoomorphic image of a wolf or its equivalent, a dog. The action is debased even further when Babba takes a kitten from under her skirts.

During the tour around the village, the masked party held mock battles, and the characters who were defeated and killed were "brought back to life" by the

Healer. Now, in the square, the last fight is between the Kouker and someone from his suite (fig. 3.18). Suddenly the Kouker drops dead (in a more modern variant, death comes to him after the sound of a gunshot), and the Healer is helpless. Only Babba can bring the Kouker back to life, and she lifts his head toward her groin, perhaps symbolizing sexual intercourse and more certainly his rebirth.

For the next part of the performance, Dyaddo and the Guards bring a wooden plow onto the square (fig. 3.19). They carry out a ritual plowing, which is always done in a circle. Dyaddo plays the plowman while Babba leads the oxen, played by the harnessed Guards (fig. 3.20). Moving from west to east—opposite to the sun's daily path—the party makes three circular furrows.

After the "plowing," the Tsar performs the sowing with the bag of seeds, followed by the Kouker and all the masked men (fig. 3.21). The Tsar says blessings for good crops and the birth of many children. When he is finished, he throws the empty bag (or the half-bushel vessel) into the air, and by observing where and how it falls to the ground, he foretells how fruitful the new year will be.

Then a table with the Kouker's pita bread, cheese, wine, and eggs is set up in the square. As the Kouker eats, the other masqueraders and villagers tie him to the plow. When the Kouker has taken his third bite of bread, they begin to pull the plow, and he immediately falls down. The crowd then drags him along

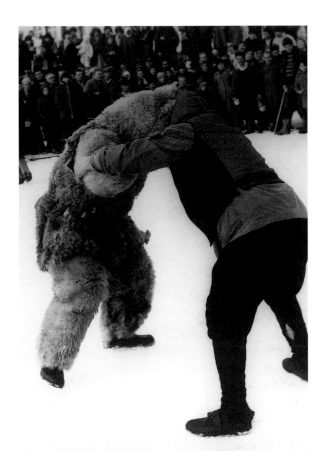

3.18 The Kouker holds a mock wrestling match with one of the other masqueraders in his troupe in Indje Voivoda. *Photograph by Valeria Fol, 1984.*

3.19 The Guards, now dressed in animal masquerades, pull the sacred plow into the central square of Indje Voivoda. *Photograph by Valeria Fol, 1984.*

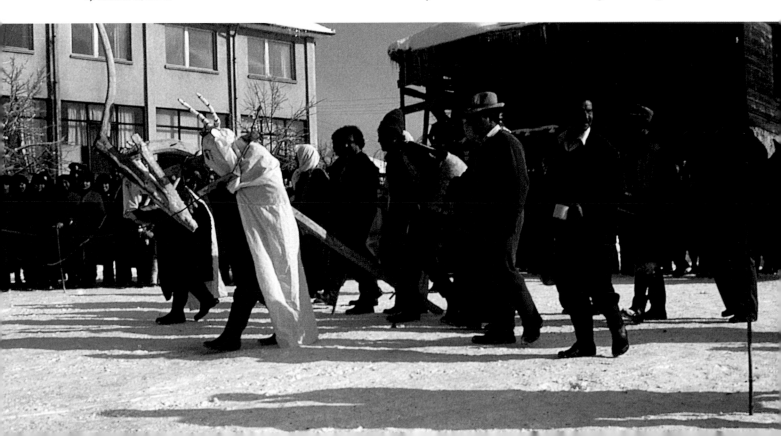

the "plowed" and "sown" furrows, "to cover the sown seeds with earth by means of his own body." In this way he performs the Great Mother Goddess-Son mystery-initiation. The Kouker is born anew immediately afterward, and as at the beginning of the day, he jumps to his feet and starts to make noise with the cowbells. All the housewives rush to gather seeds that had been cast on the square, in order to place them in the food of both animals and birds. In a final act the elders take off the Kouker's seven hides and throw them onto the village lands where they were originally obtained. The wooden phallus is given to a childless couple in hope of conception. Alas, Kouker's Day is done and the sun has set—but another year of survival is assured. Long live the Kouker! His thyrsus is preserved for a whole year in the village bakery, a practice of magical ritualism for promoting fertility.

The Cosmological Framework

The Kouker performance of masked personages is meant to create continuous conflict with the rest of the members of the community. The manner in which the troupe walks around the houses looking for a way to gain entrance demonstrates its willingness to break down the borders between the world of chaos and order. The threat of chaos is implied all day by collisions between the masked and those without masks. The world is overturned, nasty words are spoken, mock sexual acts are performed publicly, obscene suggestions and gestures are made. Everything in these ritual episodes speaks to the cyclical destruction and creation of the universe. The chaos is a guarantee of future fertility. Reintegration occurs simultaneously during the ritual when the performers are invited into people's homes and when the Kouker is killed and rises from the dead.

Like many other ancient springtime rituals, the Kouker Carnival celebration is of an initiatory nature. The masked and disguised or parodied young men suffer a ritual death in order to be born again into another social status—ready for married life.[32] In this manner the masks (or blackened faces) in this region have retained their most ancient meanings and purposes in the ritual context; they are used as a means for obtaining transition from one world into another,

3.20 The Babba leads the sacred plowing, which is always done in a circle around the central square in Indje Voivoda. *Photograph by Valeria Fol, 1984.*

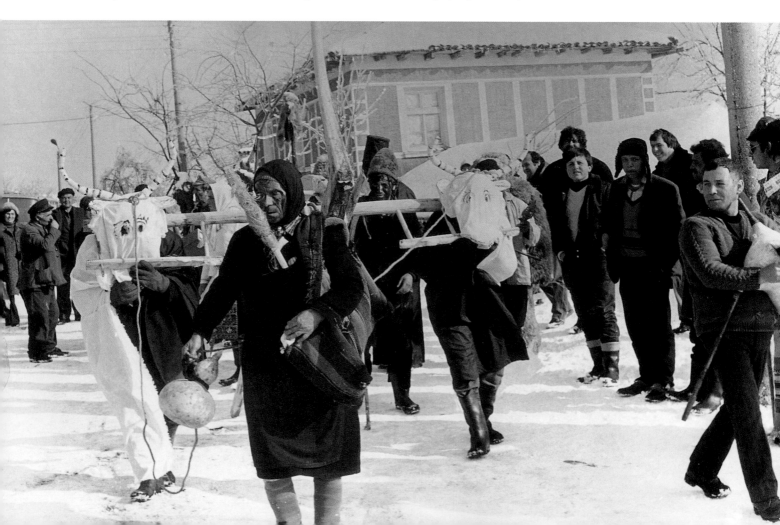

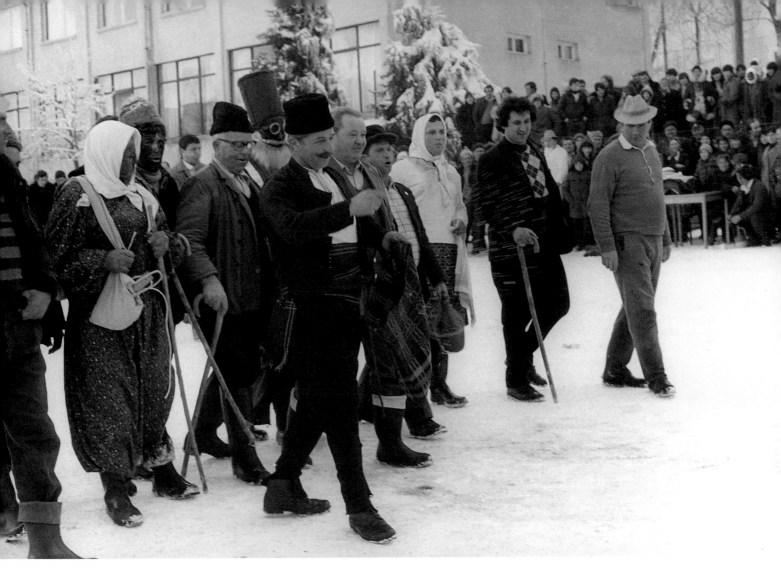

3.21 The Tsar scatters seeds in the plowed tracks as a form of sacred sowing in Indje Voivoda. *Photograph by Valeria Fol, 1984.*

a transition often fraught with danger. The full circle of life-death-rebirth is acted out during Kouker's Day. Its magic guarantees the renewal of spring and the promise of the harvest and long life. This Carnival restores order in an otherwise chaotic world.

NOTES

My special thanks to Barbara Mauldin and to John Nunley for the invitation to present mask ritualism in Bulgaria in this book. I also thank Rosen Kolev, John Nunley, and Shirley and David Rowen for many of the photographs reproduced with this essay.

1. The literary-philosophical Orphism connected with Pythagoreanism originated from nonliterary Orphism. See M. L. West, *The Orphic Poems* (Oxford: Clarendon, 1983). The latest summary of nonliterary Orphism in southeastern Europe, with a text-critical analysis of the written sources and overview of the preceding literature, is found in Alexander Fol, *The Thracian Dionysos,* Book 3, *Naming and Faith* (in Bulgarian, with abstract in English; Sofia: Sofia University Press, 2002).

2. The Orphism professed in closed aristocratic male societies was esoteric in character. In these societies, believers traversed the path to immortality through individual mysterial initiations that had in mind their elevation to the status of god. See Fol, *Thracian Dionysos,* Book 3.

3. Valeria Fol, "The Kouker without Mask: The Masquerade Feasts in Southeastern Europe," *Orpheus: Journal of Indoeuropean and Thracian Studies* 7 (1997): 83–99. For an account of the Orphic cult rituals and their presence in the Kouker masquerades, see James George Frazer, *The Golden Bough: A Study in Magic and Religion,* Part 5 (New York: St. Martin's Press, 1990 [1890]), 1: 1–34, 2: 331–335. The etymology of the word *kouker* is unclear. Linguists see the root *kouk-* as coming both from *koukla* (doll) and from "phallus," because *kouk* in some Bulgarian dialects, as well as *maskara* (mask, masked man in Arabic), means phallus. See D. Arnaudov, *Studies in the Bulgarian Rituals and Legends* (in Bulgarian; Sofia: Publishing House of the Bulgarian Academy of Sciences, 1972), 2: 105–112. Phallic dolls with moving limbs are known from ancient times and are connected with the Dionysian ritual tradition. The different manifestations of Dionysos in the Thracian faith and ritualism are

developed by Alexander Fol, *The Thracian Dionysos,* Book 1, *Zagreus* (in German; Sofia: Sofia University Press, 1993), and *The Thracian Dionysos,* Book 2, *Sabazius* (in Bulgarian, with abstract in English; Sofia: Sofia University Press, 1994).

4. "Calendar," in *The New Encyclopedia Britannica,* 15th ed. (Chicago: Encyclopedia Britannica, 1974), 3: 600–603.

5. S. Raychevski and Valeria Fol, *The Kouker without Mask* (in Bulgarian; Sofia: Sofia University Press, 1993), 7–40. This work also provides an overview of and commentary on all preceding literature.

6. I thank John Nunley for providing this brief description of the Kouker celebration in Pavel Banja. Maya Avramova, curator at the National History Museum of Bulgaria, arranged for his visit to the festival. To his description I would add that the fusion of Kouker ritualism with the rite of decorating clothing with small figures for health on March 1 is caused by the official holidays during this time in Bulgaria.

7. Mercia MacDermot, *Bulgarian Folk Customs* (London: Jessica Kingsley, 1998), 190–192.

8. Alexander Fol, *The Thracian Orphism* (in Bulgarian, with abstracts in Russian and English; Sofia: Sofia University Press, 1986).

9. A. G. Poulter, *Nicopolis ad Istrum: A Roman to Early Byzantium City* (London: Leicester University Press, 1999), 6, 13–15, 20–21, 24. For the syncretism of the mysterial and masquerade ritualism in this early period of Bulgarian history and for the acceptance of Christianity, see Ivan Venedikov, *The Copper Threshing Floor of the Proto-Bulgarians* (in Bulgarian; Sofia: Nauka I Izkustvo Press, 1983), 123–147, 253–266.

10. Poulter, *Nicopolis ad Istrum,* 28–31; Venedikov, *Copper Threshing Floor,* 123–147, 253–266.

11. Fol, *Thracian Orphism,* 38–45.

12. Orig. *Contra Cels* 3: 22–23 Borret.

13. *Rules of the Sacred Orthodox Church* (in Bulgarian; Sofia: Union of the Priests' Fraternities in Bulgaria, 1936), 234.

14. Ibid., 301.

15. Ibid., 196–197.

16. See the 64th chapter of the 123d novel in Rudolf Schoell and Wilhelm Kroll, eds., *The Novels (Novellae consitutiones post codicem) of Justinian* (Justinian I, *Novellae*), *Corpus Iuris Civilis,* vol. 3., 2d ed. (Berlin, 1928).

17. S. Karakostov, *Bulgarian Theater: Middle Ages, Renaissance, Enlightenment* (in Bulgarian; Sofia: Publishing House of the Bulgarian Academy of Sciences, 1972), 44.

18. Translation and commentary by V. Tupkova-Zaimova, "Information about Mediaeval Kouker's Games in the Silistra Region," in *Lingual-Ethnographic Studies in Memory of Acad. Stoyan Romanski* (in Bulgarian; Sofia: Publishing House of the Bulgarian Academy of Sciences, 1960), 705–710.

19. Ibid., 707.

20. Personal observation in Bulgaria and Greece.

21. The term *sourvaki* comes from a New Year's blessing that masked persons pronounce and accompany with strokes with a *sourvachka* on the recipient's back. A *sourvachka* is a bough of the cornel tree that is adorned with dried fruits, nuts, and woolen threads.

22. G. M. Vizyinos, "The Kalogeroi and the Cult of Dionysos in Thrace" (in Greek), *Hebdomax* 5 (1888): 32–35; R. M. Dawkins, "The Modern Carnival in Thrace and the Cult of Dionysus," *Journal of Hellenic Studies* 26 (1906): 191–206; Frazer, *Golden Bough,* part 5, 1: 1–34, 2: 331–335; K. Kakouri, *Dionysiaka: Aspects of the Popular Thracian Religion of To-day* (Athens: G. C. Eleftheroudakis, 1965; Greek edition, 1963); W. Puchner, "Die thrakische Karnevalsszene und die Ursprungstrheorien zum altgriechischen Drama: Ein Beitrag zur wissenschafts-geschichtlichen Rezeptionsforsforschung," *Balkan Studies* 24, no. 1 (1983): 107–122; Fol, *Thracian Orphism;* Fol, "Kouker without Mask," 81–85.

23. About the territory over which the rite spread, see Raychevski and Fol, *Kouker without Mask,* 41–46.

24. See the descriptions of the rites' personae, classified according to village, in Raychevski and Fol, *Kouker without Mask,* 136–184, which includes the authors' personal observations.

25. Arnaudov, *Studies in the Bulgarian Rituals;* Raychevski and Fol, *Kouker without Mask,* 7–40; Fol, "Kouker without Mask," 83–99.

26. Vizyinos, "The Kalogeroi"; Kakouri, *Dionysiaka;* Arnaudov, *Studies in the Bulgarian Rituals;* Puchner, "Die thrakische Karnevalsszene"; Raychevski and Fol, *Kouker without Mask;* Fol, *Der thrakische Dionysos;* Fol, "Kouker without Mask," 81–85; Valeria Fol, *The Rock, the Horse, and the Fire: Early Thracian Ritual Tradition* (in Bulgarian; Sofia: Arges, 1993).

27. I thank all the residents of these villages, who keep the tradition and welcome researchers with open hearts.

28. H. Reich, *Der Mimus* (Berlin: Weidmannsche Buchhandlung, 1903), 26.

29. Ibid., 82.

30. Ibid., 26.

31. For more information about the ancient roots of this ritual, see W. Burkert, "Euenios der Seher von Apollonia und Apollon Lykeios: Mythos jenseits der Text," *Kernos* 10 (1997): 73–81, and Valeria Fol, "Le Loup en Thrace Hyperboréenne," in *I Congreso de mitología mediterránea: La Razón del mito. Terrasa, Julio de 1998* (Madrid: Universidad Nacional de Educación a Distancia, 1998), 110–118.

32. About the Orphic cosmogony as an initiation, see D. Obbink, "Cosmology as Initiation vs. the Critique of Orphic Mysteries," in *Studies on the Derveni Papyrus,* eds. A. Lacks and W. Most Glenn (Oxford: Clarendon, 1997), 39–54. For information about the masquerade rites as initiation, see G. Kraev, *Bulgarian Masquerade Games* (in Bulgarian; Sofia: Publishing House "Alice-7," 1996).

3.22 Kouker masquerader in the village of Pavel Banja. *Photograph by Shirley and David Rowen, 1998.*

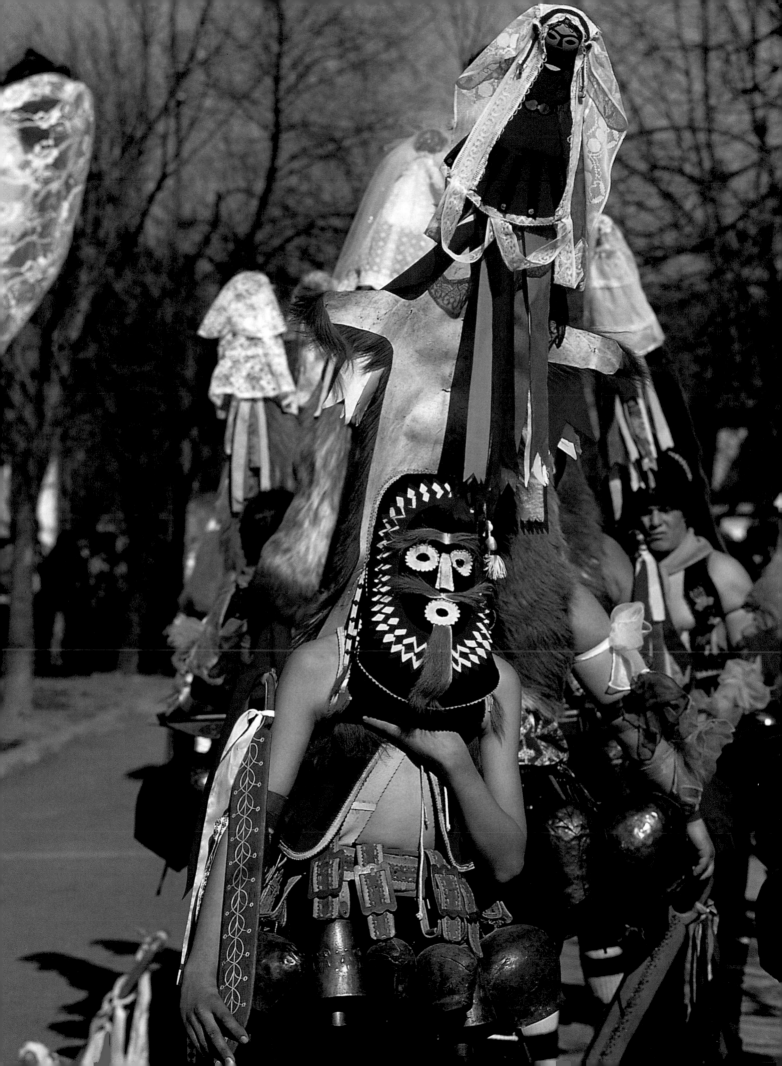

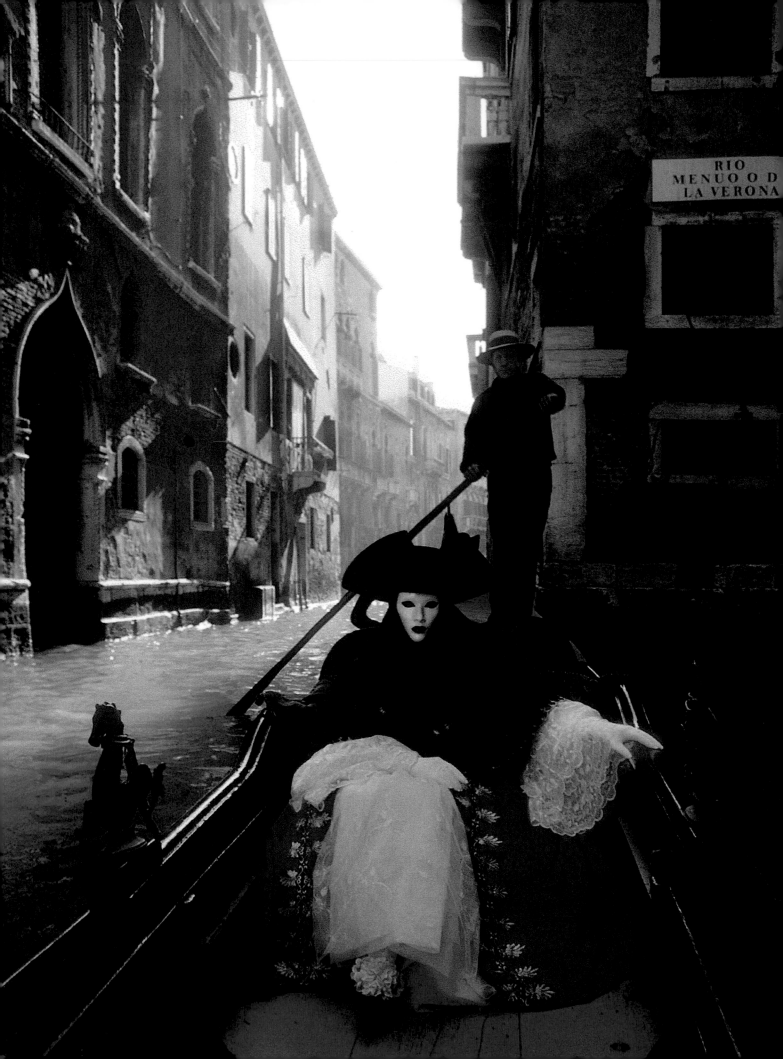

4 The Mask, the Mist, and the Mirror

CARNEVALE IN VENICE, ITALY

ALESSANDRO FALASSI

Go gentlemen, will you prepare you for this masque to-night? I am provided of a torch-bearer.
—*William Shakespeare, The Merchant of Venice*

She is the Shakespeare of cities—unchallenged, incomparable, and beyond envy.
—*John Addington Symonds*

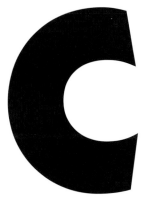

ASANOVA, FELLINI'S famous film, opens with a nocturnal image of long streaks of light reflecting upon a mirror of water. We are in Venice, La Serenissima, on the Grand Canal, at the opening ceremony of an eighteenth-century *carnevale* (fig 4.2). The doge cuts the ceremonial ribbon; an angel on a rope flies down and dives into the water. A large crowd of masks, among them Casanova, throngs to the shores of the canal as the imposing Rialto Bridge looms in the background. A web of ropes slowly brings up from the water an enormous, dark, woman's mask (fig. 4.4). Rising above the surface is the Sun and Moon headdress—the forehead and then the eyes, wide open and staring. But the ropes give way, and the mask sinks to be swallowed up forever by the dark waters of the lagoon, amid the clamor of the crowd.

Fellini stated explicitly that his gigantic mask was a symbol of Venice, arguing through images a sort of poetic syllogism: the mask is the symbol of Carnival; Carnival is the symbol of Venice; ergo the mask is the symbol of Venice.[1] Some have gone farther, to the point of asserting that the city itself is a mask. Lord Byron, who lived in a palace on the Grand Canal adorned with twelve lion masks, called Venice the "Mask of Italy!"[2] Georg Simmel, defining the city as "artifice now without substance," accorded it only "the deceptive beauty of the mask,"[3] a mask from which, according to Viktor Gomulicki, emanated a fatal attraction: "She has the face of the mythological Medusa: wondrously beautiful, but to look at her at length brings about a lethal shudder."[4]

The present-day Venetian essayist Alessandro Scarsella writes, "Venice is a mask without a face behind it, or a mask put on over another mask."[5] Or, it has been said, it is a mask placed on the earth or on water, on a mirror or on nothing. The Venetian painter Gianni d'Este says Venice is a mask that absorbs all that stands behind it: history, social structure, the fabric of the city.[6]

This has always been a city of masks, beginning with that of its patron saint. "Long live St. Mark, our lion!" goes the ancient popular chant, which invokes St. Mark in the form of a lion. The omnipresent lion is the holy mask of the Evangelist, or better yet, the masked Evangelist (fig. 4.5). For this reason, the lion is almost always portrayed without the saint, with disquietingly anthropomorphic features and a halo—as in the famous lion painted by Carpaccio or the one

4.1 Masquerader riding through the canals of Venice. *Photograph by Shirley and David Rowen, 1990.*

4.2 (overleaf) *Baùta* masquerader in Piazza San Marco. *Photograph by Shirley and David Rowen, 1986.*

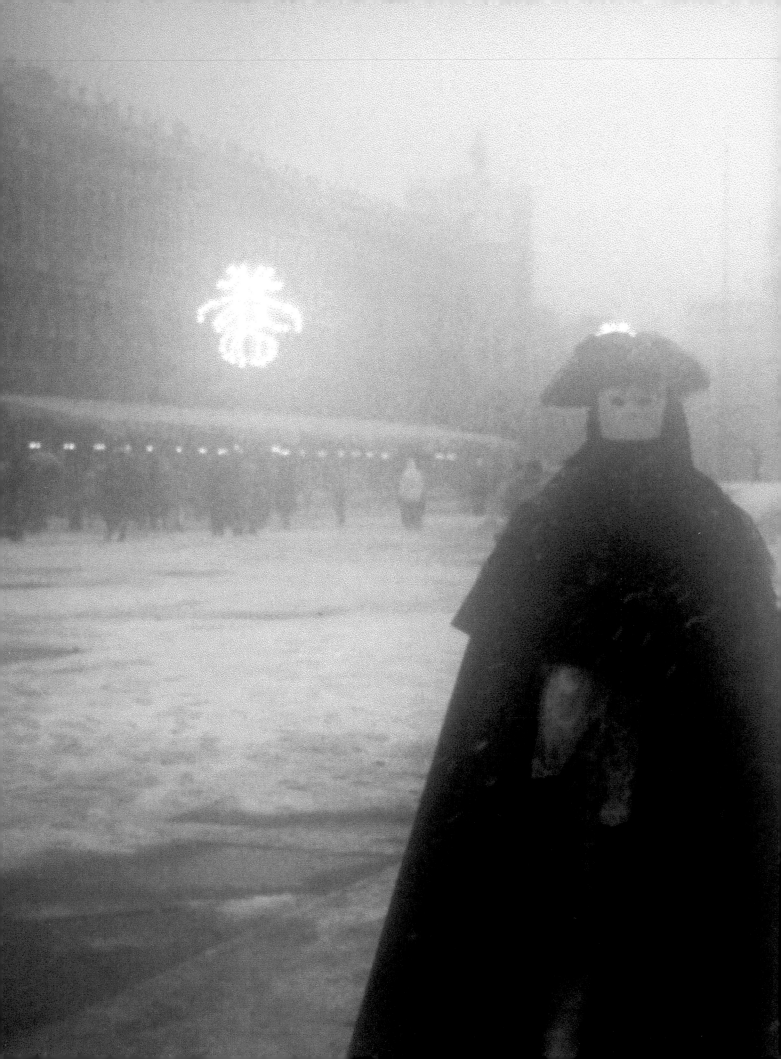

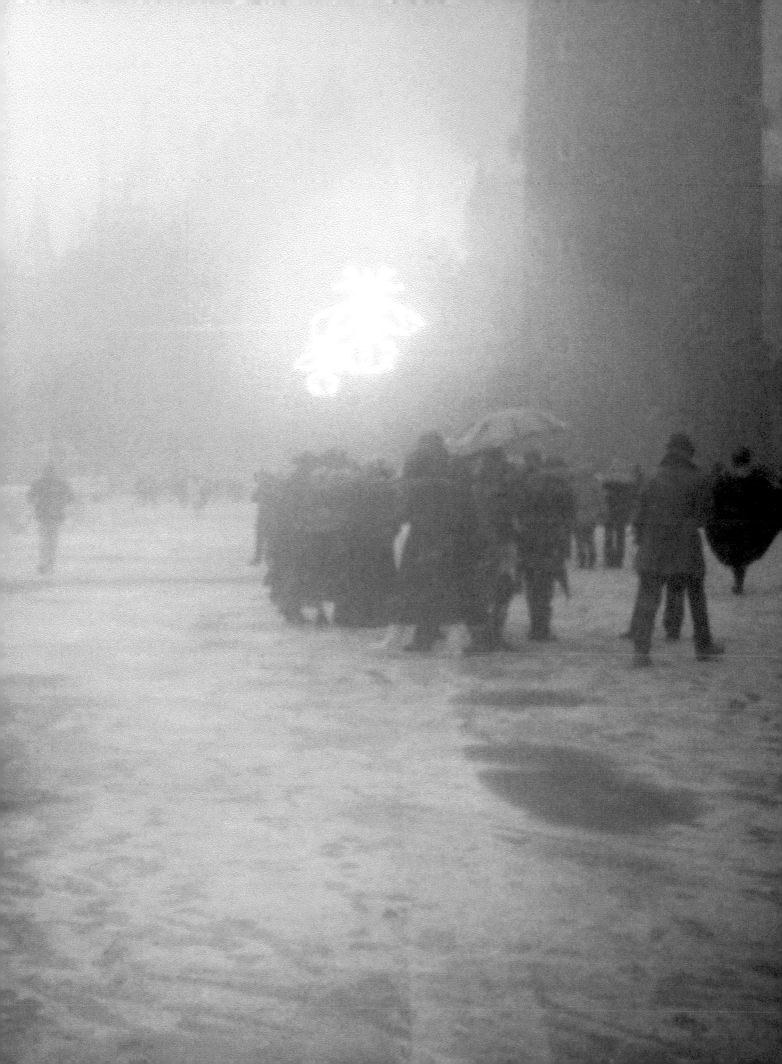

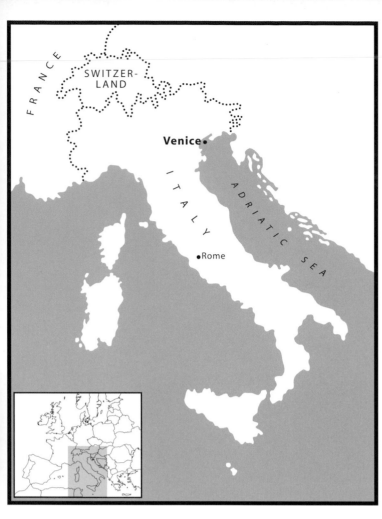

that, from the cupola in the Basilica of St. Mark, looks straight down into worshippers' faces (fig. 4.6).

On the other hand, Venice also reveres St. Pantalon, a fairly legendary saint, whom oral tradition presents ironically as the holy replica of the most Venetian mask of all, Pantalone, in turn a distant relative of Shakespeare's Shylock. The game of mirrors and reflections, of opposites and metamorphoses, in Venice must always pass through the mask.

Marchioness Luisa Casati, the femme fatale who animated Venetian social life between the world wars, adopted the mask as a personal trademark. She had large dark eyes and made them appear enormous by putting makeup around them, so as to appear masked. In 1922, Man Ray made a famous photographic portrait of her with three pairs of eyes and wrote, "One could take it for a surrealist version of Medusa." The marchioness indulged in metamorphoses. Once, she

4.3 Italy and Venice.

4.4 Mask from Fellini's film *Casanova,* now at Cinecitta Studios, Rome. *Photograph by Pietro Rosai, 2001.*

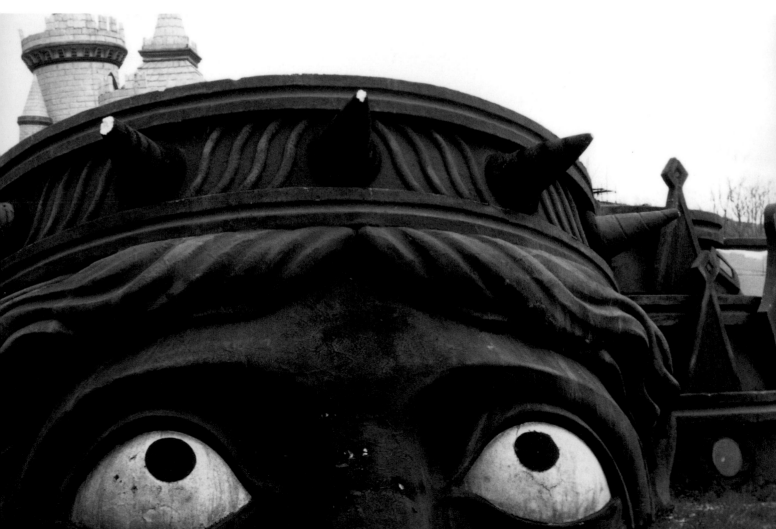

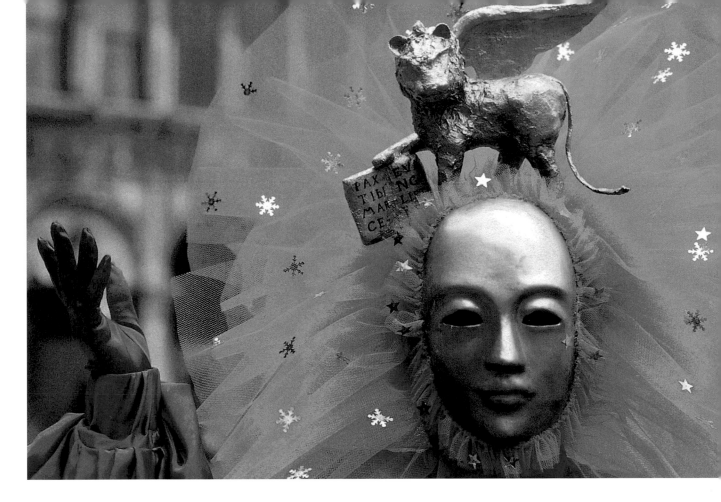

4.5 Masquerader with the lion symbol of St. Mark as a headdress. *Photograph by Shirley and David Rowen, 1991.*

4.6 Pulcinella masquerader from the commedia dell'arte with a lion statue of St. Mark in background. *Photograph by Shirley and David Rowen, 1992.*

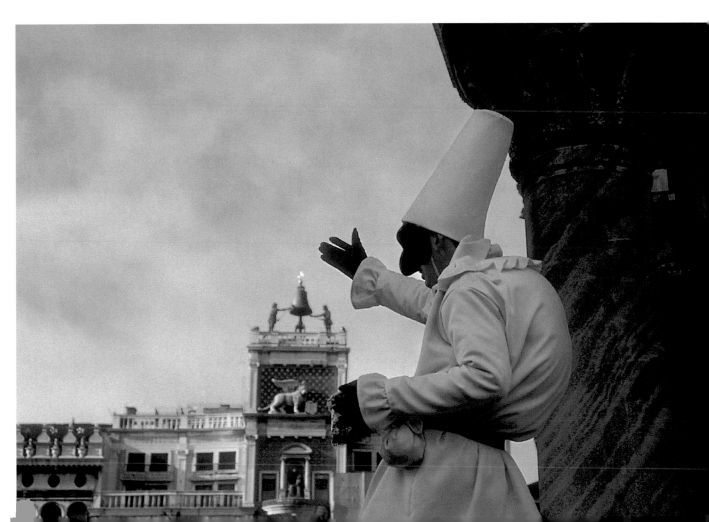

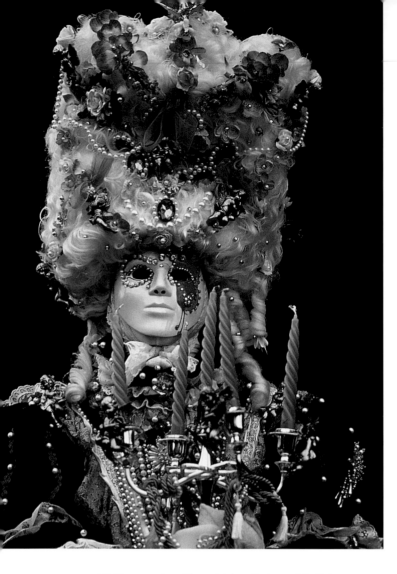

4.7 Masquerader with candelabra. *Photograph by Robert Jerome, 1995.*

looked at herself in the many mirrors in her hall and said excitedly to her portraitist, Alberto Martini, "Make my portrait with a lion head. . . . I see myself, I feel like a lion. Make me like a lion, not a lioness."[7] As the art critic Vittorio Sgarbi writes, she impersonated the magic of Venice, "city of enchantments and melancholies, of exhaltations and anguishes, of life and death".[8]

The myth of Venice is as ancient as the city. (Here I mean "myth" in the broad and current sense of the term, indicating a stereotypical, fantasy-like creation, an ideal and artificial portrait, a widespread and shared idea.)[9] Everyone agrees that this "mythological"— today we would say "virtual"—Venice exists, but some judge the construction of the myth a conscious act, whereas others call it unconscious. The poet Diego Valeri wrote that Venice had grown "unconsciously[,]

elaborating its own myth."[10] Gianfranco Bettin, on the other hand, pointed out "a conscious elaboration of the 'myth,' therefore functional to a political and historical plan, which gradually evolved through time." In order for Venice to achieve success, he believed, it chose to use, among its many resources, "the instrument of enchantment".[11]

It is certain in any case that, as Guido Piovene noted, "the life of Venice has always been accompanied by a fantasy of Venice. The real Venice has always been, even at its peak, simultaneously a Venice in disguise"— that is, carnivalesque (see fig. 4.1).[12] This of course obliged Venice to wear a mask.

Carnevale has always been an important part of Venice's myth, to which it often provides an evocative backdrop. Furthermore, as the historian Peter Burke observed, the Carnival of Venice is at times a "myth" in and of itself. Throughout history people have tended "to believe that *carnevale* belongs in some special way to Venice"[13]—and not only the mass public thinks this way. Another historian, Fernand Braudel, seeking something to which to compare the Venetian Carnival, first contrasted it with Rio de Janeiro's *carnaval* but then concluded that the only possible solution was to compare it to itself. Even for Braudel, the Carnival of Venice was one of a kind.[14]

Over the centuries, *carnevale*'s personality has allowed it to become character and theme in many artistic works. Comic operas in France and Germany, as well as in other countries, used the Carnival of Venice as their title or principal theme. The same is true for musical compositions, such as the *Carnevale di Venezia* ("Variations for Violin and Orchestra"), by Paganini, and for cinematography, the history of which begins with a group of short films by the Lumière brothers, one of them titled *Le Carnaval de Venise*.

The city itself has been portrayed in theatrical pieces as a female character who is either masked or in costume. In paintings, Venice is a regal, allegorical character depicted continually from the Renaissance to the Risorgimento.

Less grand are some more recent symbolisms. Mark Twain in 1867 portrayed Venice as "the humblest among the peoples of the earth—a peddler of glass beads . . . and trifling toys and trinkets."[15] In 1902 O. J. Bierbaum defined the city as "a queen, who for money, must show herself to curious people who possess money but no respect for the ancient majesties" (fig. 4.7).[16] More recently—and more degradingly—Mary McCarthy wrote that "Venice is a folding picture-post-card of itself."[17] And Truman Capote supposedly said, "Venice is like eating an entire box of chocolate liqueur in one go (fig 4.8)."[18]

The Carnival of Venice, throughout its long history, has remained the festival par excellence in La Serenissima's substantial festival calendar. Inaugurating the 2001 edition of the Carnival program, the head official from the city's Department of Culture and Tourism (significantly, what were formerly two departments have now been combined into one) went so far as to say that "Venice perpetuates the spectacle of *carnevale* because it belongs, so to speak, to her own genetic heritage."[19]

Even without involving genetics, historical memories of Carnival are as ancient as the city. Fat Thursday, celebrated during the week before Fat Tuesday, has its origin somewhere between history and legend. In 1162, Ulrico, patriarch of Aquileia, attacked Venice by surprise, but Doge Vitale Michiel II, acting swiftly, captured him and his court of clerics. The ransom agreement obliged Aquileia to provide Venice every year with one bull and twelve pigs—a crude and derisive, yet effective, metaphor for the prisoners. On Fat Thursday, after the doge and his entourage had personally destroyed several miniature wooden castles with iron clubs to commemorate the victory, the animals were brought before them and publicly slaughtered. The meat was then distributed among the city's most prominent citizens.[20] Games, hunts, and mimed battles took place in various locations throughout the city.

4.8 Store window with elegant *carnevale* costumes and masks. *Photograph by Doran Ross, 1997.*

4.9 Masquerader in the guise of the evil Medusa. *Photograph by Doran Ross, 1997.*

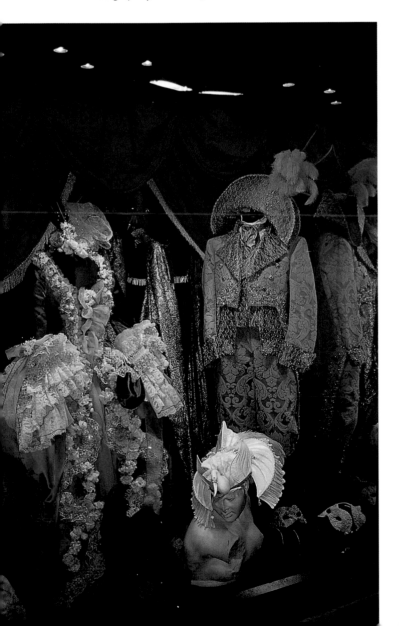

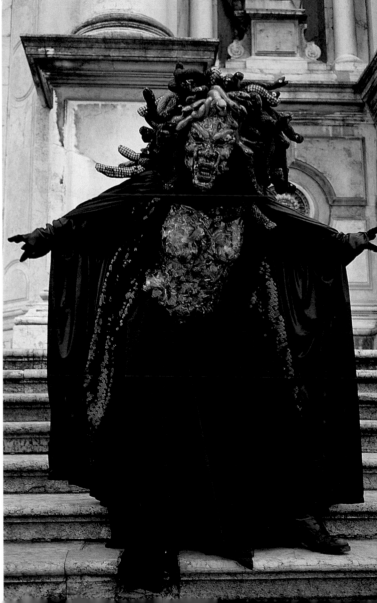

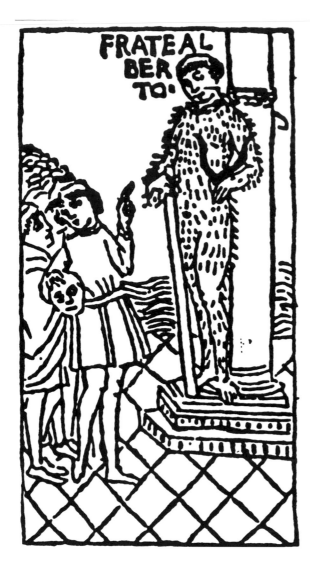

4.10 Venice Carnival revelers chastising a dishonest priest, who is dressed as a wild man and tied to a column near the Piazza San Marco. Print from Giovanni Boccaccio's *Decameron,* illustrated edition published in Venice in 1492. *Photograph by Luca Betti.*

Even the mask parade that takes place in the center of Venice has ancient origins. On December 26, the feast day of St. Stephen, the doge with his court of dignitaries would march solemnly to the church of San Giorgio Maggiore to pay homage to St. Mark's relics. This ceremony was perhaps the first paradigmatic model of *corteggi,* the formal and informal walks involving masked groups or single masks that continue even to the present.[21]

The medieval Carnival of Venice was a pandemonium of masks. First and foremost stood the mask of the devil, testimony to Christianity's obsession with the periodic eruption of evil and pantheism during

the *renovatio temporis,* the renewal of Time. In his *La Piazza universale,* printed in Venice in 1585, Tomaso Garzoni wrote that the first mask was that of the devil, who, "behind the face of the malicious serpent," convinced Eve of "horrid excess," of original sin (fig. 4.9).[22]

Variations on the demoniacal masks were the menacing Mattacini, throwers of perfumed or smelly eggs. The city council prohibited them from that game in 1268, though apparently with little success, for we find them still active in the middle of the seventeenth century.[23] Then there was the Wild Man, a character on the border between human and beast, which Boccac-

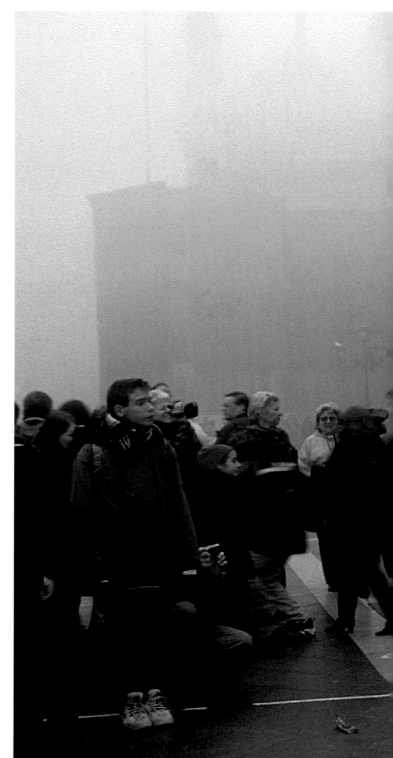

cio portrayed in a novella of the *Decameron* as typical of the Venetian Carnival (fig. 4.10).[24]

During the Renaissance, the bloody Fat Thursday ritual of pork butchery came to be considered distasteful and inelegant. Moreover, in Venice, as everywhere else in Italy, Renaissance festivals divided the participants into three clearly distinct categories: audience, actors, and patrons. Consequently, the doge had to watch, not act.[25]

The sacrifice of the bull—with the meat now distributed to prisoners and the sick—and bullfighting in the streets remained, along with games of strength and acrobatic feats (fig. 4.11). Such performances included the *pugni,* collective fistfighting by two teams, the Nicolotti and the Castellani, over the possession of a bridge; human pyramids; and tightrope walking by an angel or a Turk across a rope extended between St. Mark's bell tower and the ducal palace.[26]

The masks of the commedia dell'arte (fig. 4.12), each with its own history and past incarnations—several dating back to the ancient Roman theater—all found

4.11 Masqueraders performing on stilts in the Piazza San Marco. *Photograph by Shirley and David Rowen, 1997.*

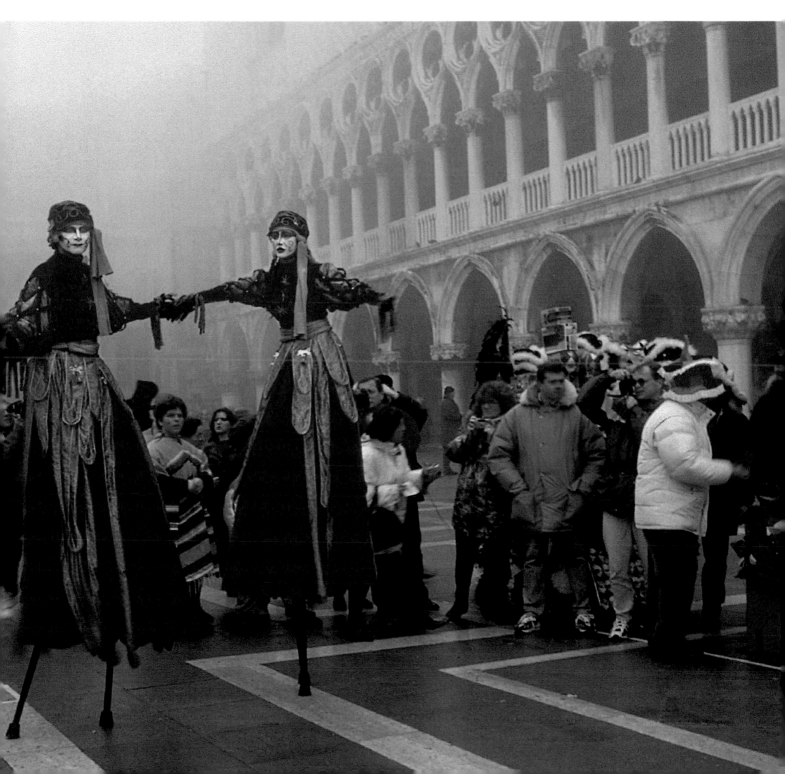

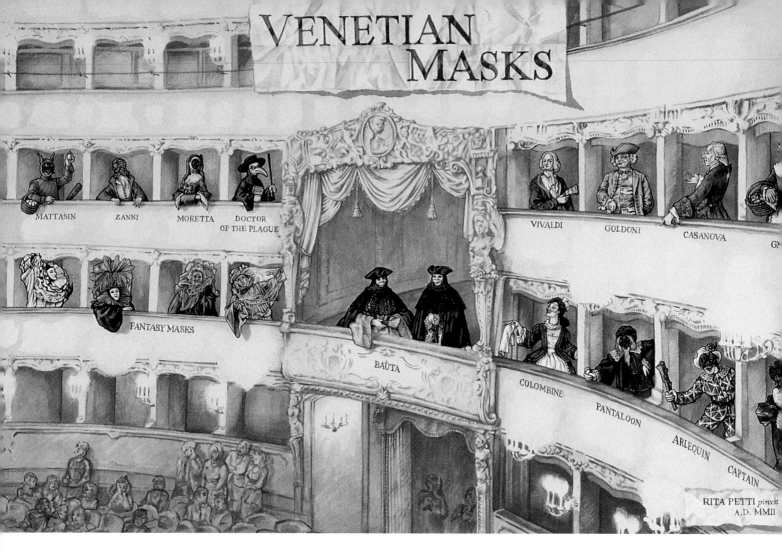

VENETIAN MASKS

MATTASIN   ZANNI   MORETTA   DOCTOR OF THE PLAGUE

FANTASY MASKS

BAÙTA

VIVALDI   GOLDONI   CASANOVA   G...

COLOMBINE   PANTALOON   ARLEQUIN   CAPTAIN

RITA PETTI *pinxit*
A.D. MMII

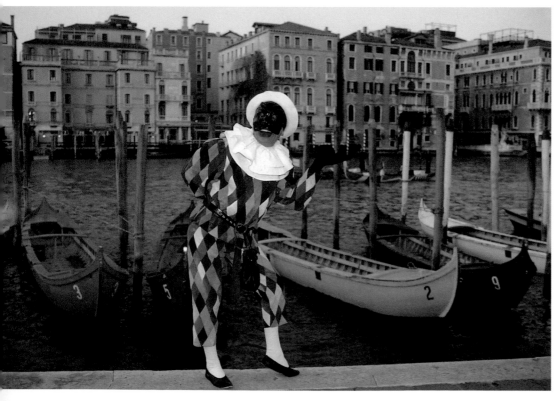

4.12 Masks of the commedia dell'arte and other masquerades that appear in Venice Carnival. Watercolor by Rita Petti. *Photograph by Blair Clark, 2002.*

4.13 Arlecchino (Harlequin) masquerader. *Photograph by Shirley and David Rowen, 1993.*

in the *carnevale* of Venice their ultimate forms and definitive personalities: Arlecchino (Harlequin; fig. 4.13), Brighella, Columbina, the consummate Venetian merchant Pantalone, the cosmopolitan Capitano (captain), Il Dottore (the doctor), the Venetian variation of the Neapolitan Pulcinella (see fig. 4.6), and all of their companions (fig. 4.14), including Domino, an elegant parody of the cassocks that Casanova liked so much, and the Plague Doctor (said to be the idea of the seventeenth-century French doctor Charles de Lorme; fig. 4.15). From the theaters of Venice, the masks of the commedia dell'arte would carry their messages and adventures throughout all of Europe.[27]

In the seventeenth century, the baroque taste for symbols, meanings, and plays on words brought to Carnival the "Masquerade of Proverbs." In the still famous spectacle of 1664, forty-eight proverbs were presented, each with its own text and corresponding "living portrait."[28]

As for the most famous of all Venetian masks, the white *baùta* (see fig 4.2), its origin is uncertain. Alvise Zorzi, the most illustrious among today's historians of Venice, suggests a fascinating hypothesis in his *Life of Marco Polo the Venetian:* "Perhaps in Marco's satchel there was something that would become the symbol of the great frantic festival of decadent Venice, 500

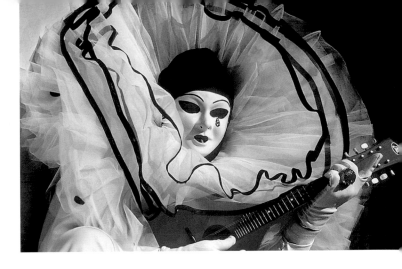

4.14 Pierrot masquerader. *Photograph by Shirley and David Rowen, 1992.*

years later, the festival among festivals, the Carnival, a mask with almond-shaped eyes, with a nose covering the mouth. Even today, instead of the traditional chador, . . . the women of Minab cover their faces with a leather mask, exactly identical to the baùta of the protagonists of the paintings by Giandomenico Tiepolo and Francesco Guardi."[29]

The Venetian Carnival of the eighteenth century had two principal protagonists. In the theater, there

4.15 Plague Doctor masqueraders visiting the produce market. *Photograph by Shirley and David Rowen, 1991.*

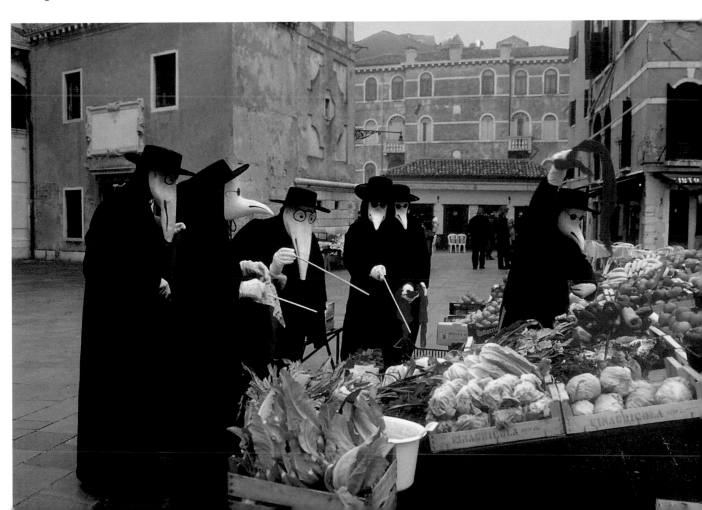

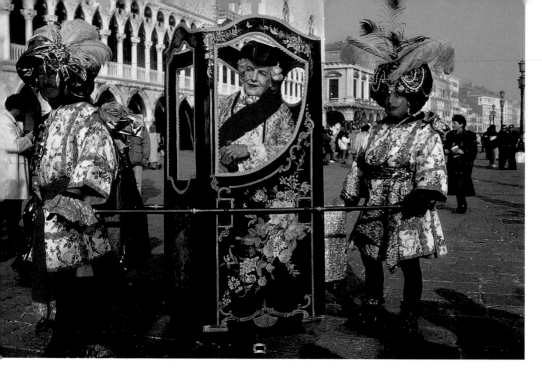

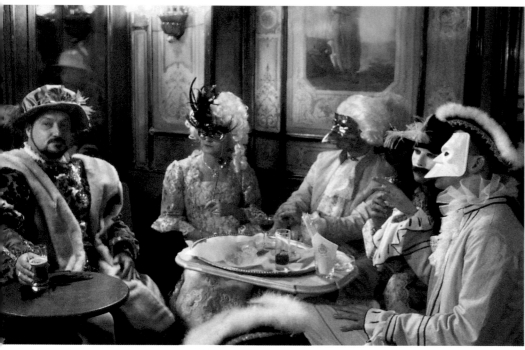

4.16 Count Emilio Targhetta masquerading as a seventeenth-century count. *Photograph by Shirley and David Rowen, 1990.*

4.17 Masqueraders stop for a drink in the famous Café Florian. *Photograph by Shirley and David Rowen, 1988.*

was Carlo Goldoni (his two hundred plays laid a new foundation for the commedia dell'arte),[30] and there was Casanova in the labyrinthine Venetian republic,[31] which was both hedonistic and dying yet still able to realize great public works and to dream grand utopias, as the poet Andrea Zanzotto contends. Writing on the subject of Doge Paolo Renier's death, which took place at the height of *carnevale* in 1789 and was concealed in order not to disrupt the events, Zanzotto interprets the episode not as a "tourist" maneuver but as the "auto-carnivalization" of power. That is, the doge,

representative of history, no longer mattered; the true power was that of Carnival. Therefore, it was logical that ceremonies for the former be subordinate to those of the latter.[32] Indeed, the cycle of La Serenissima's Carnival gradually expanded until eventually it took up half the calendar.

Venice surpassed every other European city in the splendor and variety of its festivals. Burke cited the impressive figure of 1,274 operas performed in one year.[33] Charles de Brosses, president of the Dijon parliament, after his visit to Venice in 1739 wrote, "This

Carnival begins on the 5th of October and there is another shorter one on the Day of the Ascension that lasts 15 days; so one can count about six months here in which no one walks around without wearing a mask; priests and lay people, even the apostolic delegate and the Father Guardian of the Capuchins."[34]

This view was reiterated in 1764 by a self-proclaimed Chinese spy who in reality was the French writer Ange Goudar; the topic of Venice could induce even essayists to masquerade themselves as exotic and ambiguous characters. Goudar affirmed that if "in the other European states the madness of the Carnival lasts only a few days, here one has the privilege of being an eccentric five or six months out of the year."[35] Carnival rendered the city "a perpetual masque and revelry,"[36] capable of "charming hither all the idlers of the world by its peculiar splendor and variety of pleasures" (figs. 4.16, 4.17, 4.18).[37]

The mask, especially the omnipresent *baùta* mask with its guarantee of anonymity, was accessory to the frenetic spread, in eighteenth-century Venice, of various games of chance. Before that, gambling had been a metaphor for the risk economy, with its enormous gains and losses, that over the centuries had made La Serenissima's fortune. Now gambling became an entrepreneurial activity in itself, taking place in the foyers of the theaters, the predecessors of the modern casinos.

Montesquieu, in his *Persian Letters* (1721), testified to the presence of thirty thousand to thirty-five thousand foreigners at Venice's Carnival.[38] Voltaire had his Candide (1759) meet with no fewer than nine sovereigns at a table in his Venetian hotel, all of them in the city for Carnival.[39] No longer in power, however, the sovereigns, like Venice, were reduced to wearing masks of their past regality.

The collapse of the exhausted Venetian Republic in 1797 at the hands of Napoleon, who took the city practically without bloodshed, signaled, in general opinion, the simultaneous death of its Carnival. "As for the carnival . . . it is dead," pronounced William Dean Howells, the American consul in Venice during the Lincoln administration.[40] Some forty years later, Henry James

4.18 Masqueraders in fantasy-style costumes. *Photograph by Shirley and David Rowen, 2001.*

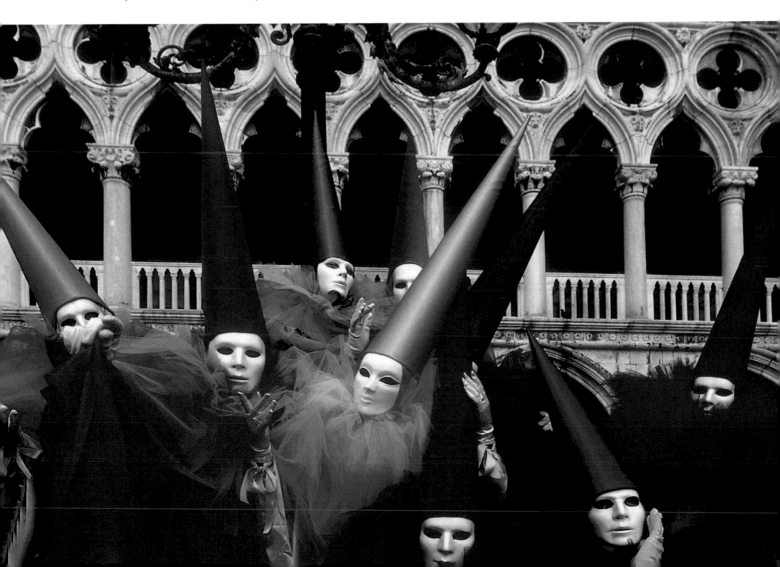

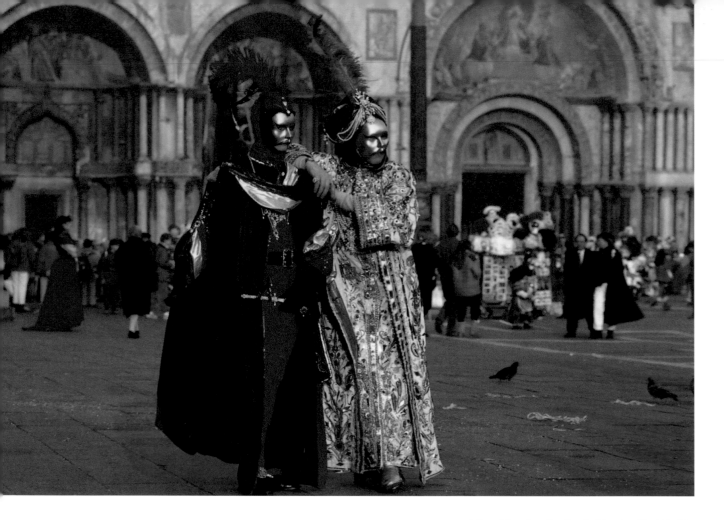

4.19 Masqueraders in historic-style costumes. *Photograph by Shirley and David Rowen, 1990.*

4.20 (overleaf) Masqueraders posing for a group photo. *Photograph by Shirley and David Rowen, 1997.*

would echo from his Venetian room at Palazzo Barbaro, "The carnival is dead."[41]

It was basically true. The festivities continued somehow—and not without some splendor. Alvise Zorzi points out that in 1846, thirty-seven hundred tickets were sold for the grand ball at La Fenice Theater, and in 1856, the impressive number of forty-five hundred. Sovereigns and important people continued to come to Venice; Emperor Francis Joseph and his wife, Sissi, Giuseppe Garibaldi, and the king of Italy all participated in the Venetian festivities.[42]

But suddenly, *carnevale*'s most intimate reason to exist had vanished. The Venetian Carnival had lost its character as a national festival simply because Venice was no longer the nation it had been for more than half a millennium. There was no longer that Venice of which Carnival was—to use both an anthropological

concept and the title of a play by Goldoni—*The World Upside-Down*.[43] The city of the eternal Carnival had become a city of eternal Lent.[44] It continued so—a shadow of its former self and a part of the new myth, *Death in Venice*[45]—under the French, the Austrians, and the mainland Italians until, almost two centuries later, the times were ripe for its return.

Prompted by Fellini's film, preceded by the growing revitalization of small Venetian Carnivals such as those on the island of Burano and in the neighborhoods of the Ghetto and Via Garibaldi, and finally propelled by the growing trend of grand events being organized by the new Departments of Culture in major Italian cities, the Carnival of Venice celebrated its revival in 1980.[46] The director Maurizio Scaparro, president of the Biennale Teatro, is credited with having been the principal author of this revival.[47] The Carnival of Venice was revitalized through interaction between the theaters, where spectacles were continually being performed, and open spaces throughout the city, where street artists, unlicensed musicians, and ordinary people wearing masks staged improvised shows of music, dance, and pantomime (figs. 4.19, 4.20).

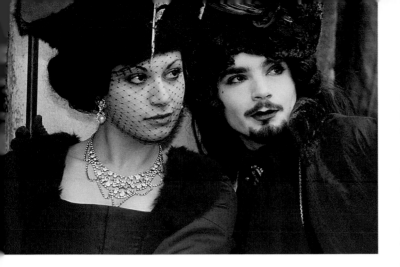

4.21 Costumes inspired by historic court attire. *Photograph by Robert Jerome, 1995.*

"Even the Rialto Bridge is a thoroughfare, a market, a theater," wrote Aldo Rossi, the architect who planned the "Theater of the World," a floating stage situated on the Grand Canal in front of St. Mark's.[48] More stages were built in different parts of the city, renewing the city's dedication to theatricality.

The event grew with the 1981 version of Carnival, but then Scaparro and his team stepped back. Organizations specializing in mass stage productions took over, and behind them came a new wave of tourism involving both the masses and the elites. Those "walls of suitcases, suitcases, suitcases," about which the writer Aldo Palazzeschi had complained arrived in Venice.[49] In 1993 the person responsible for the Società Grandi Eventi-Publitalia 80, of the Fininvest group, which had been entrusted with organizing the Carnival, wrote that now, "far from the implementation of chaos, the festival embodies the pinnacle of organized activity." During ten days of festivities, he claimed, more than seven hundred spectacles involving more than a thousand artists had been organized, attracting an influx estimated at nearly a million people.[50]

Since then, Venice's Carnival has completed its definitive passage from "rituality" to "sociality," as Simonetta Franci aptly put it.[51] In its first installment of the new millennium, *carnevale* found Volkswagen its official sponsor and the "Bellini," mass-produced by the Canella firm, its official cocktail.[52]

The formal Carnival organization coordinated its own events with those created by local committees and associations, trying to decentralize *carnevale* over all of Venice's urban space and on the mainland.

The official daily program listed events by geographical location: the Piazza San Marco, the city squares, the neighborhood "quarters" (in reality, Venice is divided into "sixths"), the mainland. It also listed them by type: theater performances and concerts, nightlife, parties and receptions, the residual category "other events," and finally "Buskers! Music in the City," with programs of ethnic music, Gypsy, African, Asian, rock, blues, and fusion. Altogether there were more than five hundred events, an average of more than forty per day.[53]

The ancient ritual paradigm disintegrated into a series of single, mixed, repeated events, as in a comic strip series or the episodes of a soap opera. The opening events took place from Friday through Sunday. After Saturday, there were fireworks, typically a signal of the closure of a celebration, in the Cannaregio neighborhood. The "bonfire of the puppet," no longer occurring in the city, took place only at a festival on the island of Burano.[54] At San Marco, groups of people wearing coordinated medieval and Renaissance costumes—ten Robin Hoods, fifteen Leonardo de Vincis—paraded by in waves, invited from various European cities by the European Consortium for

4.22 Young Carnival participant in a costume adapted from eighteenth-century court clothing. *Photograph by Robert Jerome, 1995.*

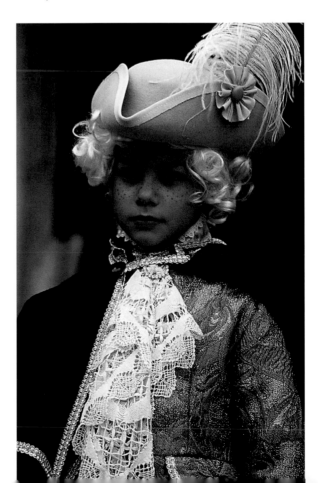

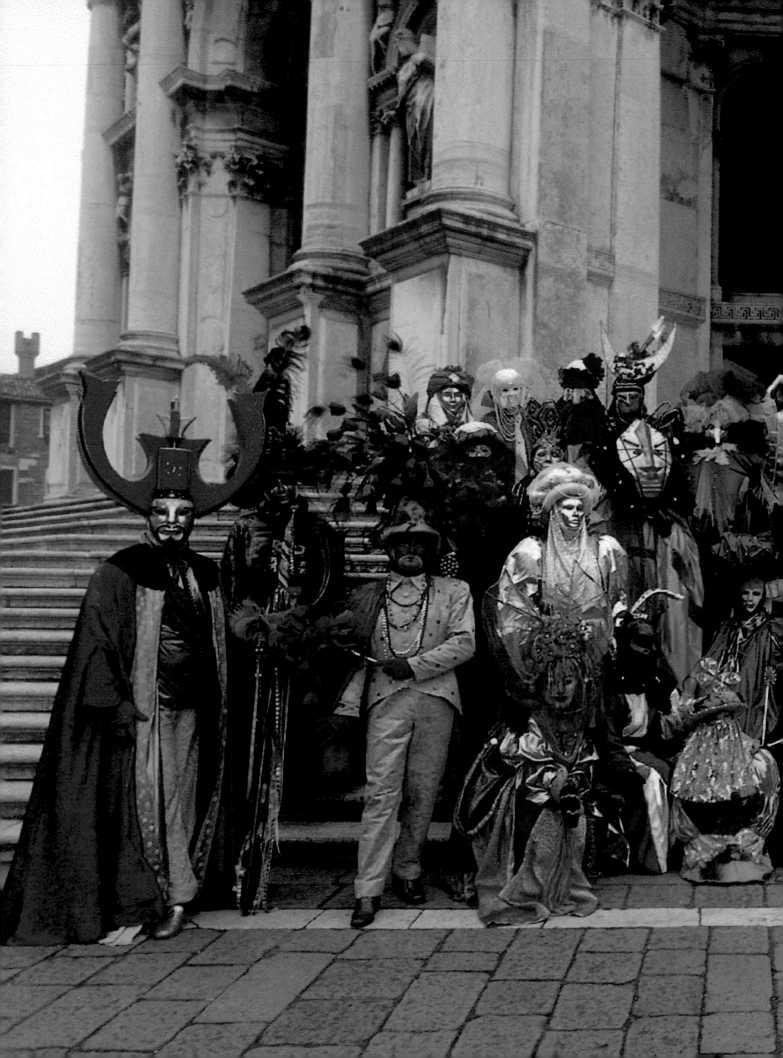

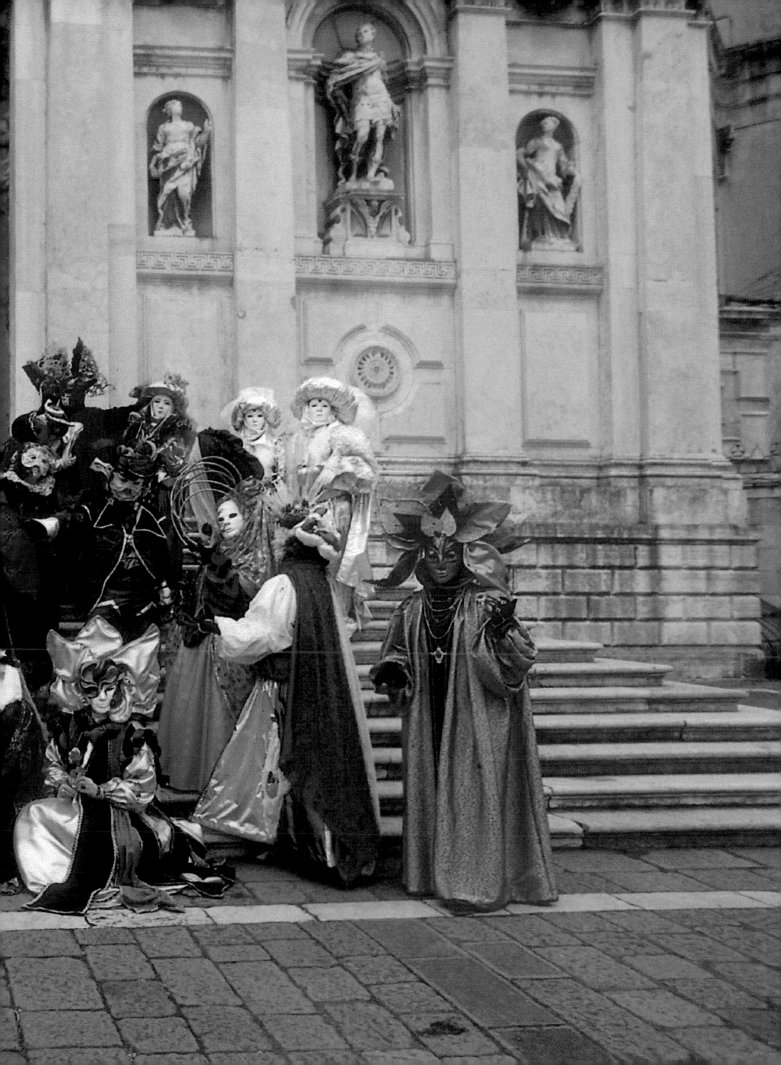

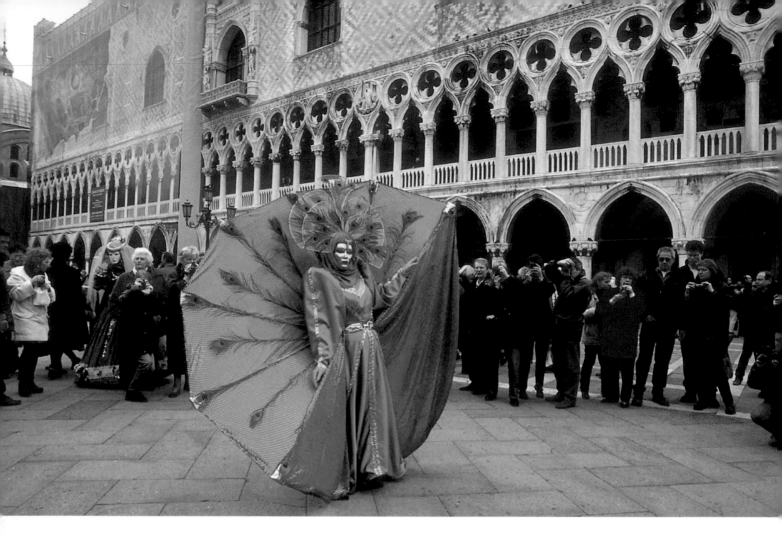

4.23 Masquerader in a fantasy-style costume posing for
the cameras. *Photograph by Shirley and David Rowen, 1998.*

4.24 Masquerades with a seashell theme. *Photograph
by Robert Jerome, 1995.*

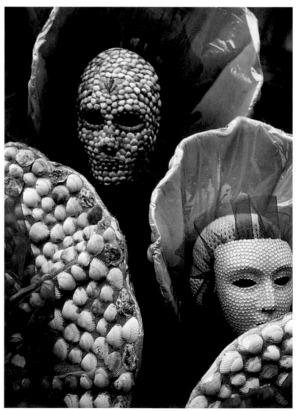

Historical Commemorations and lumped without
any apparent reason or cohesive plan.

Even the history of Venetian social life and customs
was freely plagiarized (figs. 4.21, 4.22). The Festival of
the Marys, a festival within a festival, commemorated
the medieval ritual of introducing into Venetian society a group of young "debutantes," who marched in
a perambulatory rite on the Day of the Purification
of the Virgin Mary. The ritual also commemorated
the legend of a failed "rape of the Sabine women"
attempted in 944 by pirates and thwarted by the
Venetians.[55] But the ancient event was now
transformed into a costumed beauty pageant, in
installments, which in the end crowned the "Mary
of the Year."

For spontaneous dancing, St. Mark's Square was transformed into a multipurpose space with a band stage facing the basilica and a giant screen at the foot of the bell tower, on which the crowd was projected "live," as in a giant mirror at a hi-tech disco (or a supermarket). It did not fail to display promotional messages.

With its medieval roots lost and those of the commedia dell'arte forgotten, the Carnival of Venice in the early twenty-first century appears to have adopted two reference models. On one hand, there is the Carnival devoted, through its elitist and costly events, to imitation of the eighteenth-century Carnival of Goldoni, Casanova, and Vivaldi. On the other hand, there is the depersonalized individualism of the "fantasy masks" or the "masks à la Roiter," given birth for photography and christened with the name of their most famous photographer.[56] Made of synthetic materials and as ephemeral as they are photogenic, these masks are the postmodern counterparts of the *baùta,* which concealed without representing any precise character (figs. 4.23, 4.25, 4.25).

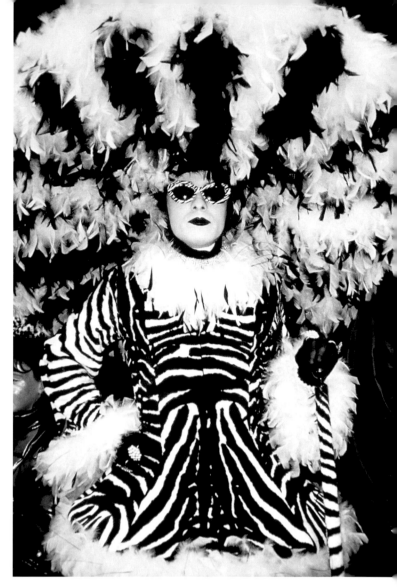

4.25 Masquerader in fantasy-style costume with sunglasses. *Photograph by Doran Ross, 1997.*

4.26 Pumpkin carriage in the Grand Canal. *Photograph by Shirley and David Rowen, 1994.*

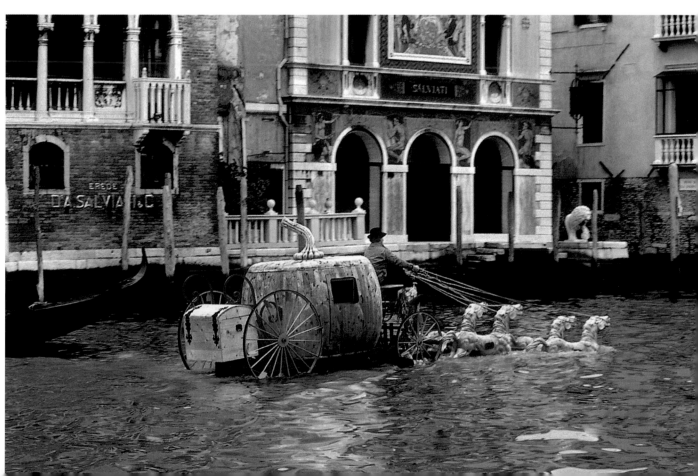

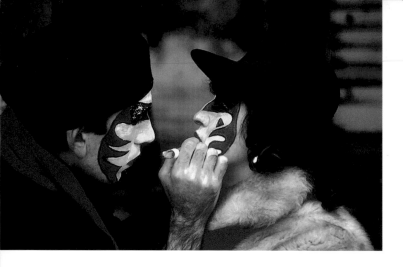

4.27 Face painting as a form of masquerade. *Photograph by Shirley and David Rowen, 1986.*

Visitors to Carnival have primarily these two possibilities open to them; a lesser alternative is that of going to the neighborhood Carnivals in the Ghetto or on Via Garibaldi or to the satellite Carnivals of Murano, Burano, Pellestrina, and Mestre, which, however, relatively few people ever visit.

What attracts the huge numbers of visitors—a million people to every Carnival in a city of forty thousand residents—is mostly the city itself, "the city of color

and rhythm," as Scaparro characterized it.[57] Venice has inevitably been viewed as a permanent stage, with incomparable scenery.[58] It offers an ideal location for theatricality, for celebration, and for the mask—and consequently, for Carnival, which encompasses all three of these elements (fig. 4.26).

Carnival takes place in Venice in a setting that it is unnecessary to "embellish" or to submit to a preliminary rite of valorization, because it is already fit for any celebration.[59] It is still the "high place of the religion of beauty" that Proust saw from his room at the fabulous Danieli Hotel, overlooking the Grand Canal and the golden angel atop St. Mark's campanile, "glittering in a sunshine that made it almost unbearable to the sight."[60]

Here, all that is needed is a minimal costume, some face paint (fig. 4.27), a luminescent bow tie, two dark circles drawn around the eyes, a cap with bells on it, in order to step into the illusion of the Carnival, to make believe that one is a participant in the festival or even

4.28 Group of Penguin masqueraders taking a break. *Photograph by Shirley and David Rowen, 1987.*

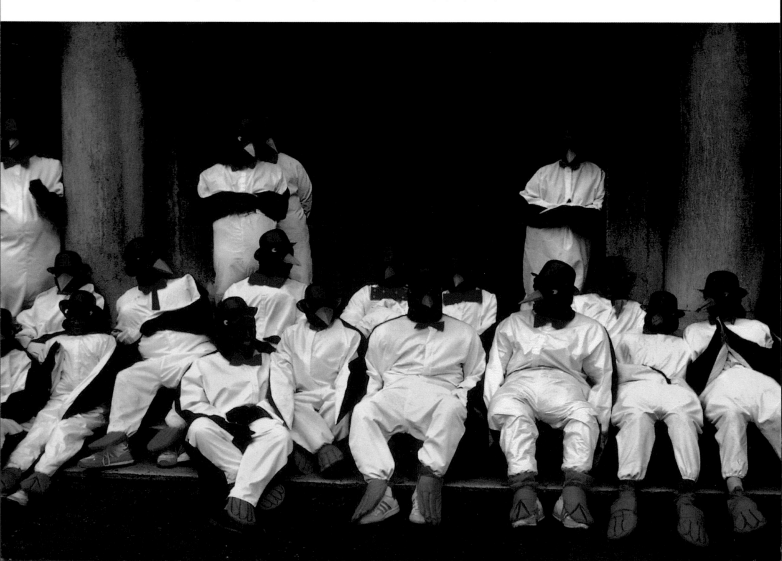

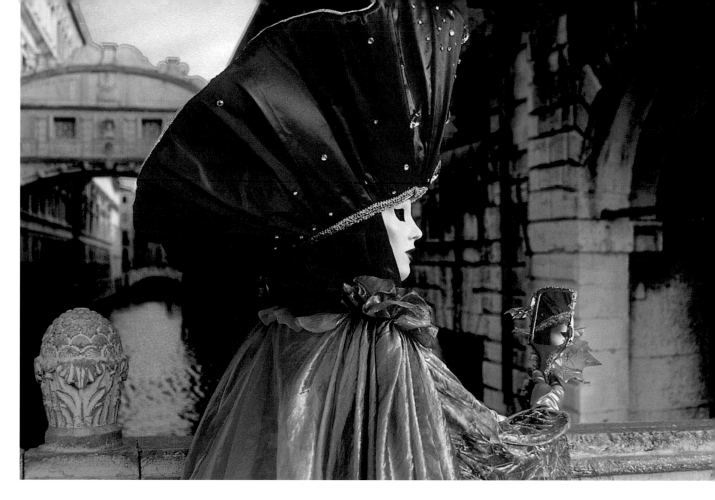

a principal character in one of its events. "The surrounding beauty is such that one instantly conceives of an incoherent animal desire to match it, to be on a par. . . . the city offers bipeds a notion of visual superiority absent in their natural lairs, in their habitual surroundings," wrote the Nobel laureate Joseph Brodsky.[61] The scenario goes from the picturesque to the sublime, making it impossible to "defend oneself from beauty."[62] After all, it was Venice that provoked the "Stendahl syndrome" in Stendahl. "The upright lace of Venetian facades is the best line time-alias-water has left on terra firma anywhere," wrote Brodsky, noting the dramatic contrast between the peerless form of Venetian architecture and the water, the fluid and ubiquitous negation of form.[63]

For the same reason, Venice is the ultimate liminal space, having been built rather backward, with all of her marble resting upon eleven million wood pilings turned over and driven into the mud, which protects and cements them.[64] It is a city where homes have two doors, one on land and the other on water. It is a city where, as Jean Cocteau noticed, pigeons walk and lions fly (fig. 4.28).[65]

"Neither land nor sea," say Venetians proudly. In

4.29 Mask reflected in the mirror. *Photograph by Shirley and David Rowen, 2000.*

spite of its two bridges to the mainland—a railroad bridge built by the Austrians and an autostrada bridge commissioned during Fascism—the city remains an island. The spatial scissure brings with it a temporal scissure. Social times move only half as quickly in Venice as they do on the mainland. The city, born from the waters like Aphrodite and frequently on the brink of plunging back in like Fellini's mask, is a space where two labyrinths cross each other—one of narrow streets and 400 bridges, the other of 177 rivers and canals.[66] It stands between the East and the West, between the land and the open sea, between water, mist, and sky, with its "white sun" of winter seeming, in its surreal light, like the daytime mask of the moon. "We chew the mist," wrote Gabriele D'Annunzio. "The city is full of ghosts. Men walk without making noise, swathed in the fog. The canals steam."[67] The artist Lucio Zorzi is famous for his effective mimic rendering of the mist.[68]

It is in this venue that the altogether Venetian games of misty mirrors, of double images, of metamorphoses that multiply, offer themselves to the

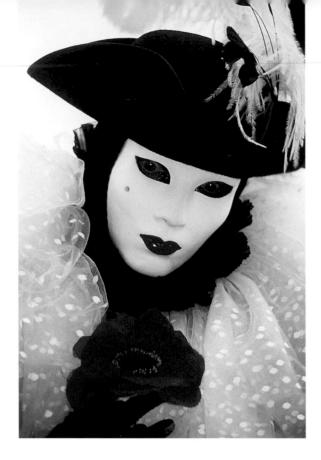

4.30 Eyes looking out from behind the mask. *Photograph by Robert Jerome, 1995.*

4.31 Painted masks reflecting on each other and in a mirror. *Photograph by Shirley and David Rowen, 1992.*

masks (fig.4.29).[69] In Venice, the semiotic status of the mask complicates itself. The mask is in any case a complex sign, because it hides, shows, and announces artifice all at the same time (fig. 4.30). But the sign, as Umberto Eco noted, is something that replaces something else in its absence. Here, instead, because of the ubiquitous mirrors, the sign duplicates something in its presence.[70]

The mask in the mirror is a case of reverse introspection. The ego looks not inward but outward, not at itself but at its own disguise. It confronts itself with the role it has chosen to assume in the Carnival. It sees it reflected in one of the countless mirrors of Venice, so fixed and ever-present in her history, which duplicate not only the images but also their context of space and luminescence. Or it watches it appear in the mirror of water in the lagoon, which is constantly moving. It sees the image becoming distorted until it is unreadable, becoming a caricature, a monstrosity—and then it becomes whole and recognizable again.[71] This is a kind of meta-narcissism, because it occurs not between the self and its own image but between the self and the image of the image. Narcissus fell in love with his own image, but here one risks falling in love with the image of the image. He who looks at his own mask in the mirror measures the limits of the extendibility, the readability, and the recognizability of his own meta-

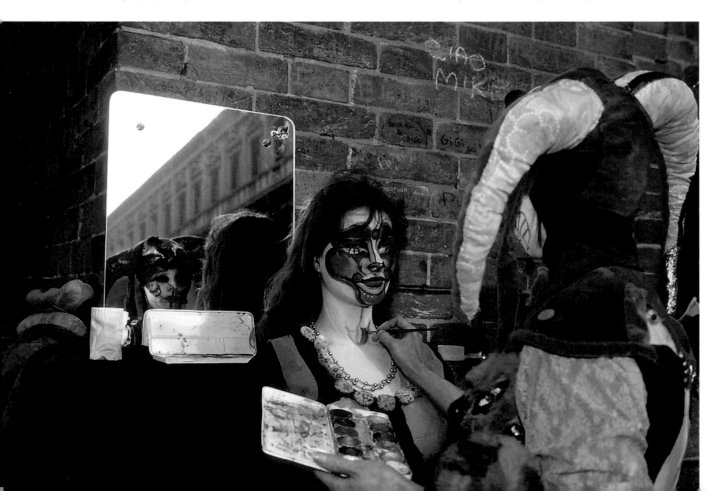

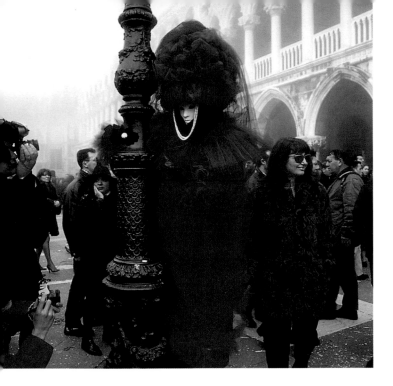

4.32 Masquerader posing for the cameras. *Photograph by Shirley and David Rowen, 1997.*

morphosis. He can control the metamorphosis or fall inside of it. The mirror, as Lacan asserted, is the door to symbolism and the symbol of it.[72] If the masks of today have no soul, it is because they have lost it in the Venetian mirrors (fig. 4.31).

In contrast, the meeting between one mask and another is a variation of the eternal I-Thou confrontation contemplated so much by philosophers. From inside my mask I look not at you but at your mask, while you from inside yours look not at me but at my mask. We are no longer individuals but impersonations interacting, as in the puppet theater that is so much a part of *carnevale*'s long history.[73]

Finally the mask meets a person without a mask. In the current Carnival, the old game of unmasking—"I know you, little Mask!"—has been replaced by its opposite, the encounter between the mask's exhibitionism and the camera's voyeurism, which authenticates the metamorphosis rather than unmasking it. As early as 1993, Fulvio Roiter was writing about the crowd of photographers swarming around the masks of Venice: "Never before has anyone seen so many cameras per square foot."[74] The current Carnival is, among other things, a photographic safari in which the models, as a rule, are unnaturally docile, like novice Hollywood actors, like the young Marilyn

Monroe.[75] The mask lets itself be watched and photographed without the ancestral taboos (fig. 4.32). It is not afraid of having its soul stolen with the image, because the camera steals, reproduces, and multiplies the "double" and not the ego that inhabits it and moves it—an ego that by itself, without the mask, might not attract attention, approval, deference, or desire. Here, one is "queen for the night," like Cinderella, but the metamorphosis is not irreversible, nor its end unforeseeable. Here it is reassuringly reversible at will.

The Carnival of Venice is a phenomenon now widely maligned by full-blooded Venetians. "Venice is Disneyland, and the carnival is its Mickey Mouse parade," snapped a Ca' Foscari University professor.[76] Arrigo Cipriani, owner of the legendary Harry's Bar, wrote to me in a letter that Venice Carnival is "a demential farce that has nothing to do with this city." He continued sarcastically: "Last Saturday in town there were 109,000 people. 89,000 were disguised as curious onlookers without a mask. 97,800 of those had a knapsack, 3 a suitcase, 19,700 the headgear of the stupid jester. The others were wearing D.O.C. [Denominazione di Origine Controllata] certified costumes"—that is, "officially" certified like a mass-produced wine bottle.[77]

Other Venetians, from all walks of life, criticize Carnival for its artificiality and superficiality, for its ever more televised "kitsch," for its exhibition of virtual images, for its rampant commercialism, and for its distressing refusal to offer some alterity with respect to the daily world. It is, as Paolo Puppa wrote, "without folkloric past, without present ritual, without future plan."[78] Nor is it possible to find real occasions for transgression, one of the city's ancient appeals. The acclaimed mask maker Guerrino Giano Lovato notes ironically that transgressive behavior is by now essentially expelled from Venice into the commercial red-light circuit on terra firma.[79]

In Venice, however, the Carnival mask, though currently lacking anthropological reasons and roots (which is not the mask's fault; it is the fault of those who do not know how to use it), offers a nowadays increasingly rare opportunity for metamorphosis, a game of chance with ever higher stakes and an uncertain outcome (fig. 4.33). On one hand, there is the ever greater risk of living a useless and illusory fantasy, of submit-

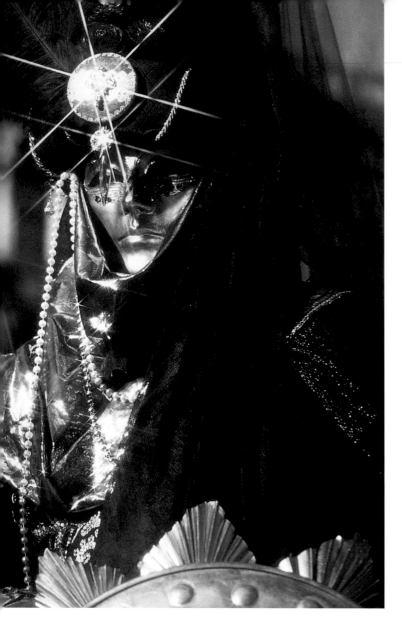

4.33 Elegant costume with gold mask. *Photograph by Robert Jerome, 1995.*

unreal realm of this Carnival, the real world seems to show more and more clearly its vast folly.[85]

In Venice, one can still seek an illuminating and liberating reflection, going beyond the appearance of things and self and toward their real essence, their "truth behind the mask." Or else one can dream of a knowledge that is a complete (that is, "specular") adequacy between the things to be known and the intellect, which "speculates" about them as if they were in a mirror.[86] The mirror, as Borges notes, is a mute surface where all is event and nothing is memory. That is why the mirror can give the hope of an instant knowledge, free from the burden of the past.

This perhaps is the unconfessed hope of many of those—possibly all those—who have chosen to take on Venice, this extraordinary city that is always in masquerade, that remains so "blissfully surreal" and capable of dreaming of a luminous happiness.[87] It was this same hope that caused Shakespeare's Richard II to exclaim, "Give me the glass, and therein will I read!"[88]

NOTES

Fieldwork at the Carnival of Venice took place in February–March 2001, after preliminary visits to the Carnivals of 1998, 1999, and 2000 and to the Marciana library of Venice. Photographing and filming, strictly connected with this essay, were done in 2001. I wish to thank Barbara Mauldin, the ¡CARNAVAL! project director, for her support and liberality in letting me make wider use of the materials produced for the project. Special thanks to my crew, who happily shared the excitement and challenge of taking on a city like Venice. They were Rodolfo Mascelloni, cameraman; Simone Madioni, second cameraman; Luca Betti, black-and-white photographer; Piero Rosai, color photographer; and Naki, gondoleer and marine. Silvana Goldmann (University of Venice) and Angelo and Francesco Goldmann offered a home base and served as local liaisons and family at large. Gianni d'Este Widmann served as a head unit and factotum.

I also wish to acknowledge the generous help and sympathy I recived from Alessandro Corsi, librarian; Gianna Bardotti, librarian; Francesca Bisutti, University of Venice; Serena Bruttini, librarian; Angelo Silva, hotelier, Leonardo Hotel; Alvise Zorzi, historian and president of the International Committees "Let's Save Venice"; Mary Serventi, research assistant; Mauro Costantini, street artist; Ciocio, gondoleer; Mirella Ambrosini, A. Barbarigo Institute, Venice; Claudio Ambrosini, composer; Anna Ponti, educator; Guerrino Giano Lovato, owner and mask maker, Mondo Novoatelier; Arrigo Cipriani, owner, Harry's Bar; Gianfranco Bettin, essayist and politician; Nicoletta Lucerna, owner, Lucerna Atelier; Claudio Staderini, general manager, Danieli Hotel; Lucio Marco Zorzi, mime and poet;

ting to yet another manipulation, to a "baby-sitting of the masses."[80] On the other hand, noted Massimo Cacciari, norms are masks. Our normal attire is a mask.[81] To dress, to undress, to dress up, to get into costume, on stage and in the mirror, is essentially to compel oneself to break away from the guise that we wear every day, to tell one's own "truth in masquerade," to take a deep, long "look at oneself in the mirror."[82] And, as we know, the mirror in its own way always tells the truth[83]—"Mirror, mirror, on the wall"—even the most painful truth, and especially those misty Venetian mirrors, which for centuries have been famous for "having reflected so much, before reflecting."[84] In the

Paola Semenzato, owner, Semenzato Atelier; Francesca and Cristina, Arlequin masks; Giovanni, Pokemon mask; Pino Zennaro, architect and painter; Marco Ceresa, University of Venice; Claudio Vergani and family, owners, Trattoria Vesuvio; Maria Antonietta Grignani, University for Foreigners, Siena; Francisco d'Andrea, natural sopranist; Silver Carpanese, manager, Hotel Danieli; Baroness Romana von Schilgen, owner, Ballo Tiepolo Shop; and Alberto Mioni, University of Padua.

1. Federico Fellini and Bernardino Zapponi, *Il Casanova di Fellini* (Turin: Einaudi, 1976), 6.

2. Lord Byron, *Childe Harold,* Canto 4 (abridged), stanza 3, verse 9.

3. Georg Simmel, quoted in "La verita delle maschere," by Alesssandro Fontana, in *Venezia e lo spazio scenico,* ed. Manlio Brusatin (Venice: Editions La Biennale, 1979), 21–22.

4. Viktor Gomulicki, quoted in "I viaggiatori dell'Est europeo," by Piero Cazzola, in *Venezia dei grandi viaggiatori,* ed. Franco Paloscia (Rome: Abete, 1989), 156.

5. Alessandro Scarsella, *Le maschere veneziane* (Rome: Newton Compton, 1998), 12.

6. Gianni d'Este Widmann, personal communication, February 2001.

7. Vittorio Sgarbi, "La Marchesa Casati, Dandy," in *Dell'Italia: Uomini e luoghi* (Milan: Rizzoli, 1991), 167–169.

8. Ibid., 172.

9. This wider meaning of the term "myth" in the social sciences owes much to the fortunate book by Roland Barthes, *Mythologies* (Paris: Seuil, 1957). On the myth of Venice, see, for instance, Alessandro Scarsella,"Proposte per una topica del mito di Venezia," *Ateneo Veneto* 25, nos. 1–2 (1987): 161–176. Bruce Redford (*Venice and the Grand Tour* [New Haven: Yale University Press, 1996], 51–80) discusses Venice's "mythical aura," as he calls it, in three aspects: Venice's governmental structure, its reputation for tolerance, and its culture of diversion and display.

10. Diego Valeri, "Il mito del settecento veneziano," in *Storia della civiltà veneziana,* vol. 3, ed. Vittore Branca (Florence: Sansoni, 1979), 119. For Diego Valeri's poetic portrait of Venice, see Valeri, *Guida sentimentale di Venezia* (Florence: Giunti-Martello, 1978 [1942]), and Valeri, *Fantasie veneziane* (Venice: Neri Pozza; Milan: Mondadori, 1994 [1934]).

11. Gianfranco Bettin, *Dove volano i leoni* (Milan: Garzanti, 1991), 16–17.

12. Quoted in Scarsella, "Proposte per una topica," 161.

13. Peter Burke, "Le Carnaval de Venise: Esquisse pour une histoire de longue durée," in *Les Jeux à la Renaissance,* eds. P. Aviès and J. C. Margolin (Paris: Vrin, 1982), 56.

14. Fernand Braudel and Folco Quilici, *Venise* (Paris: Arthaud, 1984), 115–119.

15. Mark Twain, *The Innocents Abroad* (New York: Oxford University Press, 1996 [1867]), 217: "a peddler of glass beads for women, and trifling toys and trinkets for school-girls and children."

16. Quoted in Doris Maurer and Arnold E. Maurer, eds., *Literarischer Führer durch Italien* (Frankfurt: Insel Verlag, 1988), 140.

17. Mary McCarthy, "Venice Observed," in *The Stones of Florence and Venice Observed* (London: Penguin, 1972 [1956]), 177.

18. Oral tradition in Venice credits Truman Capote with this statement.

19. Marino Cortese, quoted in *"Leo Bussola" Carnevale di Venezia 2001,"* special pamphlet of the Venice Tourist Board (Venice: Azienda di Promozione Turistica, 2001), 1.

20. Alvise Zorzi, "La Serenissima in festa," in *La Festa,* ed. Alessandro Falassi (Milan: Electa, 1988), 66. Zorzi ascribes the legendary episode to the year 1164. See also Burke, "Carnaval de Venice," 57–58, and Danilo Reato, *Storia del Carnevale di Venezia* (Venice: Filippi, 1988), 23–30; 33–34, illustration on p. 25.

21. Danilo Reato, *Venezia: Una Città in maschera* (Venice: Filippi, 1998), 17–22; Giuseppe Tassini, *Feste spettacoli divertimenti piaceri degli antichi Veneziani* (Venice: Filippi, 1961 [1890]), 173–176; Giustina Renier-Michiel, *Origine delle feste veneziane* (Venice: Filippi, 1994), 87–90.

22. Tomaso Garzoni, *La Piazza universale di tutte le professioni del mondo* (Venice: Gio. Battista Somascho, 1585), 548.

23. Reato, *Venezia,* 70–71. For demonic masks in Italian Carnival and archaic theater, see Paolo Toschi, *Le Origini del teatro italiano* (Turin: Edizioni Scientifiche Einaudi, 1955), 166–227.

24. Giovanni Boccaccio, *Decameron,* day 4, novella 2 (Venice, 1492). For the figure of the "savage man," see Toschi, *Le Origini del teatro italiano,* 134–139.

25. For this phenomenon in Italian festivities, see Falassi, *La Festa,* 9–12; Burke, "Carnaval de Venice," 59; Alvise Zorzi, *La Repubblica del Leone (Storia di Venezia)* (Milan: Rusconi, 1979), 304–305.

26. Alvise Zorzi, *Repubblica,* 66–67; Reato, *Storia,* 24, 27. The tightrope-walking tradition was revived, with uncertain results, in 2001. A young woman in a white dress, visibly terrified, descended, securely tied to a steel rope, from the top of the campanile to a stage in the piazzetta to meet an impersonator of the doge.

27. Reato, *Venezia,* 27–50. For general works on Italian ritual and theatrical masks, see, for instance, Loredana Stucchi and Mario Verdone, *Le Maschere italiane* (Rome: Newton Compton, 1984), and Nicola Fano, *Le Maschere italiane* (Bologna: Il Mulino, 2001). An extensive visual catalogue of Venetian masks and costumes drawn in color in the eighteenth century and recently reprinted is in Giovanni Grevembroch, *Gli Abiti de' Veneziani di quasi ogni età con diligenza raccolti, e dipinti nel secolo XVIII* (Venice: Filippi, 1981). Volume 3 contains many commedia dell'arte characters.

28. Reato, *Storia,* 81–83.

29. Alvise Zorzi, *Vita di Marco Polo veneziano* (Milan: Rusconi, 1982), 113.

30. The complete works of Carlo Goldoni (1707–1793) were published in a monumental edition of thirty-four volumes by the Municipality of Venice on the two-hundredth anniversary of his birth. See Carlo Goldoni, *Opere complete di Carlo Goldoni edite dal Municipio di Venezia nel II centenario della nascita* (Venice: Istituto Veneto di Arti Grafiche, 1907–1935).

31. Giacomo Casanova (1725–1798) wrote his memoirs in

French, as *Histoire de ma vie.* For a critical edition see Giacomo Casanova, *History of My Life* (New York: Harcourt, Brace and World, 1966–1971 [1826–1838]). For a recent assessment of his legendary appetites, including eros and *gastròs,* see the recipes in Comune di Venezia, *Il Carnevale veneziano del Casanova: Passioni enogastronomiche* (Venice: Municipality of Venice, 1998).

32. Andrea Zanzotto, "Carnevale di Venezia," in *Sull'altopiano e prose varie* (Vicenza: Neri Pozza, 1995), 183–192. The doge's death occurred on February 13 and was announced on March 2. See Zorzi, *Repubblica,* 483.

33. Burke, "Carnaval de Venice," 61. For Venetian theaters in general see Nicola Mangini, *I teatri di Venezia* (Milan: Mursia, 1974). The eighteenth century is discussed on pages 91–182.

34. Discussed in Zorzi, "Venezia, mito e antimito," in Paloscia, *Venezia dei grandi viaggiatori,* 15, 20. Charles de Brosses wrote his perceptive travel journals between 1739 and 1740. See Charles de Brosses, *Lettres familières écrites d'Italie en 1739 et 1740* (Paris: Librairie Academique, 1869).

35. Ange Goudar, *L'espion chinois* (1764), quoted in Jean-Claude Simoën, *Le Voyage à Venise* (Paris: Lattès, 1992), 20. On Goudar, see Paolo Preto, *I Servizi segreti di Venezia* (Milan: Il Saggiatore, 1994), 579.

36. James Morris, *Venice* (London: Faber and Faber, 1974), quoted in Toby Cole, *Venice: A Portable Reader* (New York: Frontier Press, 1995), 38.

37. William Dean Howells, 1866, quoted in Cole, *Venice,* 29.

38. Montesquieu, *Persian Letters,* 1721. Letter 31 discusses various aspects of Venetian life.

39. Voltaire, *Candide,* 1759. Chapter 26 is dedicated to this famous episode.

40. William Dean Howells, 1866, quoted in Cole, *Venice,* 29.

41. Henry James, *Italian Hours* (New York: Grove Press, 1959 [1909]), 41.

42. Alvise Zorzi, *Venezia Austriaca* (Gorizia: Libreria Editrice Goriziana, 2000), 327–352.

43. On symbolic inversion in Carnival, see Giuseppe Cocchiara, *Il Mondo alla rovescia* (Turin: Boringhieri, 1963).

44. Zorzi, *La Repubblica,* 566.

45. See Thomas Mann, *Der Tod in Venedig* (Berlin: Fischer, 1912). For a recent critical edition in English, see *Death in Venice* (New York: Norton, 1994). The book was decisive in earning Mann a Nobel Prize and in 1971 became a film, *Morte a Venezia,* by Luchino Visconti, with Dirk Bogarde and Silvana Mangano.

46. See the collected essays in Paolo Portoghesi and Maurizio Scaparro, eds., *Carnevale del Teatro* (Venice: Editions La Biennale, 1980), and Fabio Santagiuliana and Giuliano Scabia, *Venezia i giorni delle maschere* (Udine: Magnus Editions, 1980).

47. See Portoghesi and Scaparro, *Carnevale del Teatro,* 5.

48. Aldo Rossi, "Il Progetto per Il Teatro del mondo," in *Venezia e lo spazio scenico,* ed. Manlio Brusatin (Venice: Editions la Biennale, 1979), 7.

49. Aldo Palazzeschi, *Il Doge* (Milan: Mondadori, 1967), 16, 20, 22, 66.

50. Davide Rampello, "Progettare il Carnevale," in *Carnevale di Venezia: Che la festa cominci,* ed. Fulvio Roiter (Milan: Electa, 1994), 14.

51. Simonetta Franci, "Carnevale di Venezia (biennale e teatro): La Socialità come produzione e consumo" (Ph.D. dissertation, University of Bologna, 1983), 1–28, 58–62.

52. This cocktail of peach pulp and prosecco wine (inspired by the magical luminescence of Giovanni Bellini's Renaissance paintings) was invented in 1948 and made famous by Arrigo Cipriani and his Harry's Bar. An oral tradition collected in Burano in 2001 ascribes its invention to Ernest Hemingway himself, who anyway mentions it in his writings. For the recipe, see Arrigo Cipriani, *The Harry's Bar Cookbook* (New York: Bantam Books, 1991), 16–17. See also *"Leo Bussola,"* back cover.

53. See *"Leo Bussola,"* 2–16.

54. For this tradition in Venice, see Nantas Salvalaggio, *Attenzione caduta angeli* (Vicenza: Neri Pozza, 1995), 38–40; for Italy in general, see Paolo Toschi, *Le Origini del teatro italiano,* 323–324.

55. See, for instance, Tassini, *Feste spettacoli,* 9–13; Giuseppe Tassini, *Aneddoti storici veneziani* (Venice: Filippi, 1965 [1897]), 1–2; and Renier-Michiel, *Origine delle feste,* 50–54. Obviously, legends do not agree on the date, ranging from the sixth century to 939, 941, 942, 943, 944, and 959.

56. See, for instance, Fulvio Roiter, *Carnevale di Venezia tra maschera e ragione* (Padua: Dagor, 1981), and Roiter, *Carnevale di Venezia: Che la festa cominci.* Roiter has authored myriad photographic calendars, books, and individual postcards on the Venice Carnival.

57. Quoted in Manlio Brusatin, ed., *Venezia e lo spazio scenico* (Venice: Editions La Biennale, 1979), 5.

58. Brusatin, ibid., explores many aspects of the concept of Venice as a permanent stage in fields such as art and landscape.

59. Alessandro Falassi, ed., *Time Out of Time: Essays on the Festival* (Albuquerque: University of New Mexico Press, 1987), 4.

60. Marcel Proust, "La Fugitive," in *A' La Recherche du temps perdu* (Paris: Gallimard, 1954), 3: 623. Proust (1871–1922) was in Venice with his mother in 1900. The room they allegedly occupied at the Danieli Hotel is still in great demand.

61. Joseph Brodsky, *Watermark* (New York: Farrar, Straus and Giroux, 1992), 25–26.

62. Tiziano Scarpa, *Venezia è un pesce* (Milan: Feltrinelli, 2000); pages 114–120 offer ironic instructions on how to defend oneself from the beauty of Venice.

63. Brodsky, *Watermark,* 43–44.

64. On the Venetian pilings, see Paolo Barbaro, *Venezia la città ritrovata* (Venice: Marsilio, 1998), 89, and Scarpa, *Venezia è un pesce,* 9–10.

65. Quoted in Jan Morris, "Venice en hiver," *GEO* 33 (1981): 148.

66. Data from Venice City Administration, Ufficio Tecnico Comunale, 2001.

67. Gabriele d'Annunzio, *Notturno* (Milan: Garzanti, 1995 [1921]), 22–23. On fog and Venice, see, for instance, Valeri, *Fantasie veneziane,* 13–14; Diego Valeri, *Guida sentimentale di Venezia* (Florence: Giunti-Martello, 1978 [1942]), 113; and Bar-

baro, *Venezia la città,* 129–131, 147–150. As for fog in paintings, see Auguste Renoir's *Fog in Venice* and John Singer Sargent's *Venice par temps gris,* in Hugh Honour and John Fleming, *Venice and the Grand Tour* (Boston: Bulfinch Press, 1991), 57–59.

68. Lucio Marco Zorzi, *Fregole no xe fragole: Poesie* (Venice: Editoria Universitaria, 1996), 9, has his poem "Caligo" (mist), which he sometimes recites while performing the mimic routine.

69. On mirrors, see, for instance, Umberto Eco, *Sugli specchi e altri saggi* (Milan: Bompiani, 1985); Jurgis Baltrušaitis, *Le Miroir: Révélations, science fiction et fallacies* (Paris: Le Seuil, 1978); and Jean-Thierry Maertens, *Le Masque et le miroir* (Paris: Aubier Montaigne, 1978). On masks and metamorphosis, besides the seminal Claude Lévi-Strauss, *La Voie des masques* (Geneva: Skira, 1975), see, for instance, David Napier, *Mask: Transformation and Paradox* (Berkeley: University of California Press, 1985), and a recent assessment in John Nunley and Cara McCarthy, *Masks: Faces of Culture* (New York: Abrams, 2000).

70. Eco, *Sugli specchi,* 232.

71. Massimo Cacciari, "Memoria sul Carnevale," in *Psicologia storica del Carnevale di Venezia,* by Florens Christian Rang, edited by Franco Desideri (Venice: Arsenale, 1983), 84–85.

72. Eco, *Sugli specchi,* 321. Maertens, *Le masque,* 22, discusses the mirror stage of Lacan's theory.

73. Zorzi, *Venezia Austriaca,* 337–338; Grevembroch, *Gli abiti de' Veneziani,* vol. 3, no. 164 (Grevembroch numbers by images and not by pages); Tassini, *Feste spettacoli,* 132. For Italian puppetry and masks, see Dora Eusebietti, *Piccola storia dei burattini e delle maschere* (Turin: Sei, 1966).

74. Roiter, *Carnevale di Venezia,* 7.

75. Donald Spoto, *Marilyn Monroe: The Biography* (New York: HarperCollins, 1993), 112–113. Writing about Monroe's famous flirting with the camera as a way of connecting herself with anonymous admirers, Spoto notes: "With the lens aimed at her, she was learning how to fix its glance on herself."

76. Professor Marco Ceresa, personal communication, February 2001.

77. Arrigo Cipriani, personal letter, March 9, 2001.

78. Paolo Puppa, "Il Carnevale veneziano: La Forza e la forma l'energia della piazza," *STILB* 3, nos. 14–15 (1983): 7.

79. Guerrino Giano Lovato, personal communication, February 2001.

80. Ugo Volli, *Teatro o festa: Il Carnevale di Venezia* (Treviso: Arcari, 1980), 2.

81 Cacciari, "Memoria," 83.

82. For a general discussion of the various cultural patterns in dressing, undressing, and wearing costumes, see Ernesta Cerulli, *Vestirsi spogliarsi travestirsi* (Palermo: Sellerio, 1981).

83. Eco, *Sugli specchi,* 320–323, discusses truth and the specular image.

84. I am referring to Jean Cocteau's famous aphorism: "Les miroirs feraient bien de refléchir un peu, avant de renvoyer les images" (mirrors should reflect a little, before reflecting images).

85. A similar note, but about Venice in general, is in Mary McCarthy, "Venice Observed," 186. Maybe this quality of the city was one of the reasons for the revival of Venice's Carnival.

86. Eco, *Sugli specchi,* 320.

87. Gianfranco Bettin said that "Venice is built between water and light, and this fact alone already indicates in which sense it tends to project itself, and which happiness it dreams of" (personal communication, February 2001).

88. William Shakespeare, *Richard II,* act 4, scene 1 (and only).

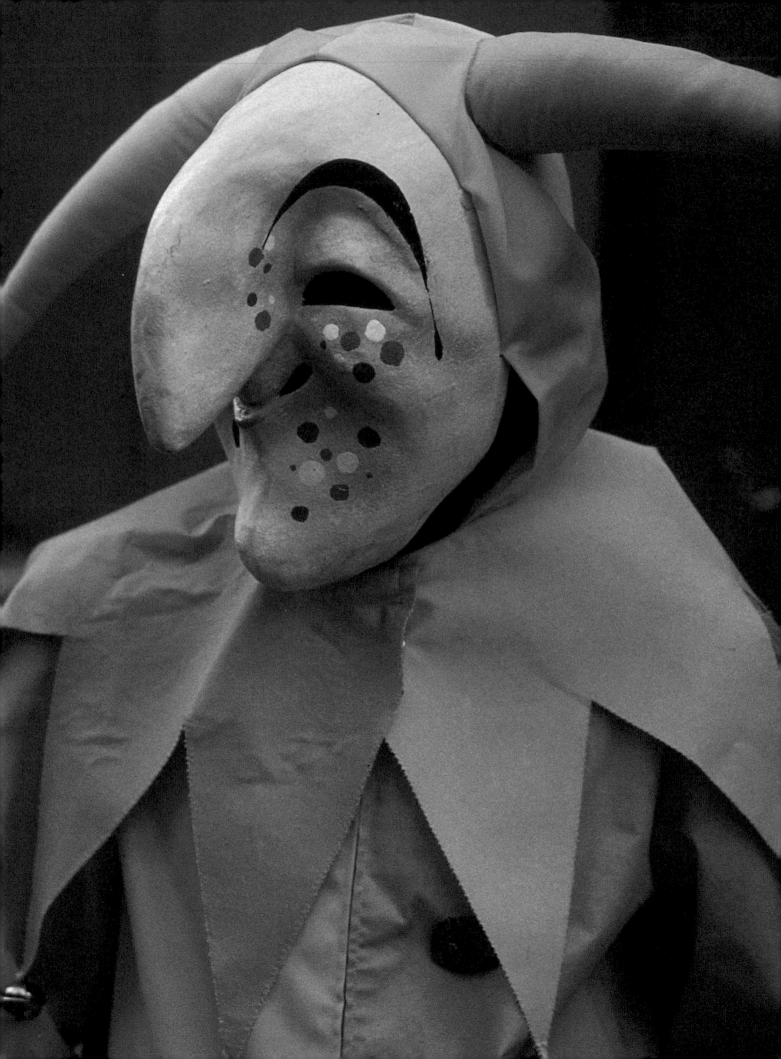

5 *Fasnacht* in Basel, Switzerland

A CARNIVAL OF CONTRADICTIONS

PETER TOKOFSKY

ASNACHT IN BASEL IS A Carnival of contradictions. This unique festival subverts the very premise of Carnival by taking place during the week after Ash Wednesday—specifically, from four o'clock in the morning on the first Monday after the onset of Lent until the same hour the following Thursday. Moreover, although surrounded by Catholic regions in Germany and France, Basel is a predominantly Protestant city, hardly the expected setting for a spectacular Carnival celebration. In further contrast to the typical Carnival, a sense of orderliness and near-militaristic precision prevails during much of *Fasnacht* in Basel, despite the presence of colorful masks and costumes. And although Carnival in Basel bears unmistakable similarities to its counterparts in other parts of Switzerland and throughout southern Germany across the border, it creates its own distinctive mood and traditions, which set it apart from related celebrations nearby and beyond. Perhaps these anomalies are fitting for Carnival in the city of Basel, which, from its important location on the Rhine River (fig. 5.2), at the intersection of three countries and two languages

5.1 An Ueli, or jester, masquerader wears the character's classic hat with two large horns protruding from the sides. *Photograph by Gianni Vecchiato, 1982.*

(dialects aside), has blazed its own path throughout centuries of history.

Basel sits on the "knee" of the Rhine, where this river rich in history and lore flows from its meandering mountain tributaries into a long, broad river plain and turns northward as a powerful shipping lane charging toward the North Sea (fig. 5.3). The Rhine divides the city into "Great Basel," the historical settlement on the left bank, and "Small Basel," the working-class neighborhoods on the opposite side. With a total population under three hundred thousand (including the administratively separate areas around the city), Basel is not the largest metropolitan area in Switzerland, yet for centuries it has consistently exceeded its size to stand out as an economic, political, and cultural center in western Europe. In previous centuries the manufacture of silk ribbon and other trades brought a steady flow of diverse new residents to Basel from other parts of Switzerland and internationally. Today Basel is home to major pharmaceutical and other industrial and service firms, which employ residents of the city as well as workers from neighboring Swiss cantons, Germany, and France, who simultaneously cross city and country frontiers in their commute to work. The substantial working class in Basel created the city's liberal social-democratic politics for much of the twentieth century and also played a significant role in determining the present form of *Fasnacht*.

Yet even before Basel emerged as an industrial center, it had a long history as a thriving economic hub.

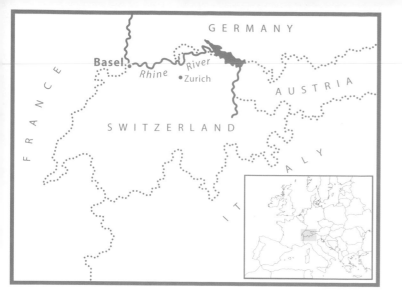

5.2 The location of Basel in Switzerland and Europe.

With its university, founded in 1460, and a liberal social and political atmosphere, Basel has always been the native or adopted home to prominent humanists, scientists, and artists, such as Erasmus of Rotterdam, the mathematician siblings Jacob and Johann Bernoulli, Friedrich Nietzsche, the influential historian Jacob Burckhardt, and the artists Jean Tinguely and Josef Beuys (who joined in *Fasnacht* parades himself).[1] In his substantial study *Basel in the Age of Burckhardt,* Lionel Gossman effectively captured the distinctive mood of Basel:

Not so long ago, old Baslers still spoke of "going to Switzerland" just as they might speak of going to France and Germany. Today, at the end of the twentieth century, as the influence of the old nation-states wanes in the context of European union, Basel has again turned outward beyond the frontiers of Switzerland and is engaged in an ambitious project to strengthen connections with communities in neighboring Alsace and Baden and to provide the *regio basiliens,* as the Basel agglomeration is called, with a powerful economic, cultural, and communications infrastructure.[2]

This legacy of cultural distinction and unique character lives on in the creative expressions of *Fasnacht* in Basel.

History of Basel Carnival

It is usually impossible to identify the precise origins of a complex, centuries-old festival such as Carnival. In Basel we must piece together the historical development like a jigsaw puzzle, slowly watching the current form of *Fasnacht* take shape as different components merge over the years. Before 1529, Basel was home to a typically excessive Catholic Carnival. This festival of abundance created a topsy-turvy world generally tolerated, if not condoned, by the Church authorities centered in the cathedral, which was built on the banks of the Rhine in the thirteenth century. During the infamous Carnival of 1376, rioting even broke out. In 1521, the sovereignty of the Catholic bishop over the city ended, marking the increasing influence of Protestantism. *Fasnacht* serves as a remarkable barometer of the changing religious and social tenor in Basel. In 1529 a Carnival band vandalized the cathedral, demonstrating the victory of the Reformation as well as the decline of the medieval Catholic Carnival.[3]

In most parts of northern Europe, the loss of ties to the Catholic Church and its observances meant the complete disappearance of Carnival and many other festive occasions; indeed, eliminating such excesses provided the very motive for many reformers. In Basel, historical records reveal explicit bans on masking throughout the first half of the sixteenth century and a complete proscription on Carnival in 1546, with the justification that the Reformation did away with the forty-day fast and hence with the need to indulge before its onset.[4] Protestantism does not tolerate indulgence.

Around the same time as these official attempts to eliminate Carnival, we find the earliest record of public festivities in Basel on the first Monday of Lent, the current starting point of *Fasnacht.*[5] A historical chronicle of the city notes that on this Monday in 1540 a general military muster was presented, followed by a parade of guilds, each with its banner and "symbol," that is, its representative masked figure.[6] With the Reformation and thus the cessation of Church authority over the city, elite neighborhood organizations such as those displaying their militias in 1540, as well as trade guilds having roots in medieval occupational systems, played an increasingly important role in struggles for power in Basel.[7] The parading tradition noted for 1540 continued through the following centuries and became increasingly associated with local districts in the city, which presented themselves annually with young men in military formation marching to beats provided by their drum corps. The ongoing tradition of neigh-

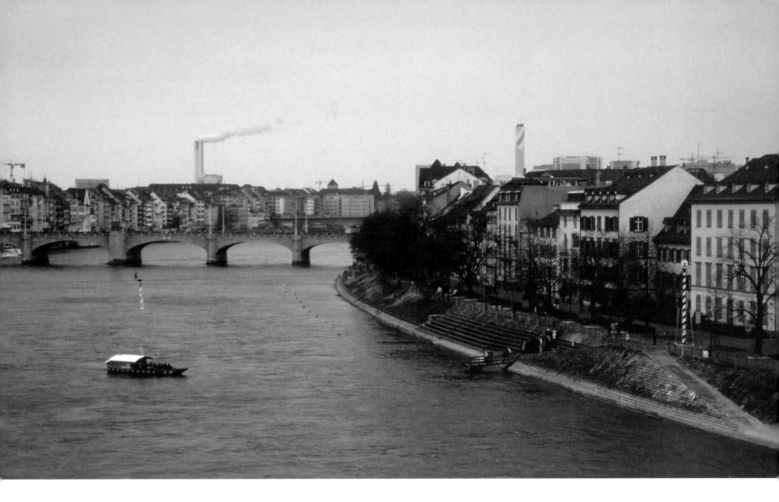

5.3 View of the Rhine River as it runs through Basel. *Photograph by Peter Tokofsky, 2001.*

borhood presentations experienced a significant change in 1798, when French troops entered Basel and a centralized Helvetic (Swiss) Republic was established. The new government abolished the local regiment system, thus draining the Monday morning presentations of their original purpose.[8]

Nonetheless, the district parades continued. Some observers have suggested that the Monday festivities in Basel remained popular because they provided an opportunity to mock and disturb the remaining Catholics during their holy days of prayer and penance. Yet rather than attribute this mean streak, albeit one not entirely alien to the spirit of Carnival,[9] to the marchers without evidence of motive, we would do better to presume that Carnival attached itself to this day out of convenience after the processions lost their more serious significance.[10] On *Fasnacht* Monday, as the day is known in Basel, marches now became more open, spontaneous, and less organized than they had been when they were tied to the political structure of the

city.[11] Like those who stormed the Cathedral in 1529, however, many masqueraders throughout the centuries have no doubt viewed this Lenten Carnival as an occasion to criticize the Catholic Church and torment its adherents.

At roughly the same time the processions were changing, a stream of immigrants brought new influences to the celebrations in Basel. At the onset of the nineteenth century, a majority of residents In the city had not been born in Basel, and by the end of the 1850s, almost 70 percent were non-natives.[12] Many of the new residents came up the Rhine from German cities to the north, such as Cologne, that were famous for their Carnival parades and balls. Through the immigrants' influence, traditional Carnival, nearly forgotten in Basel, began to reappear. The celebration that emerged bore greater similarity to the Carnival of Cologne, with its masked balls, Prince Carnival, and social satire, than to the *Fasnacht* of today. Indeed, nineteenth-century sources frequently employ the German terms *Fasching* and *Karneval* rather than *Fasnacht,* the only currently acceptable name in Basel.[13] However, since Ash Wednesday had long ceased to represent a significant end point for the celebrations in Protestant Basel, many of the new Carnival events bled over into the following week.

Celebrants in Basel could even draw on tradition to extend the festivities past Ash Wednesday. The date marking the beginning of Lent had changed over time, and different calculations were used in various parts of Europe. As a result, the period of fasting began either on Ash Wednesday or on the following Monday.[14] In southern Germany and parts of Switzerland, Catholics observed the later date, and even today Carnival celebrations and hillside bonfires take place on the Sunday after Ash Wednesday in those regions. This day is frequently known as Old *Fasnacht,* Farmer's *Fasnacht,* or *Funkensonntag* (the Sunday of sparks). For these communities, Lent began on the Monday after Ash Wednesday, the very day Carnival in Basel begins.

The immigrants invigorating Carnival in Basel did not always have easy lives in their new home. As in other times and places, wealthy and established citizens of nineteenth-century Basel marginalized the new settlers in public affairs. The new residents had little opportunity to enter the social hierarchy of Basel, and unless they managed to join a guild they could not vote in local elections. As an alternative to the elite organizations that excluded them, many "foreigners" (including those from other parts of Switzerland) formed social clubs. These groups wisely recognized *Fasnacht* and the Monday processions as an important point of entry into the life of Basel. They frequently joined in, mixing their own masking and parading with the more serious tone of the now purely symbolic military presentations, which gradually succumbed to the newer, more playful masking traditions.[15] Because the majority of the working class resided in Small Basel, many of the new Carnival clubs were based in that part of the city. By the middle of the nineteenth century, these groups had introduced the first painted *Fasnacht* lanterns carried in procession, as well as other innovations, in Basel (fig. 5.4).

By the early twentieth century, Carnival in Basel had taken a shape we recognize in the celebration today. The orderly, regimented processions and drum corps remained (minus military uniforms, and now accompanied by piccolos), but so, too, did the painted lanterns, costuming, and social critiques introduced by the *Fasnacht* clubs. A Fasnachts-Comité, still active today, was founded in 1910 to regulate the clubs and

help promote and finance the festival, ensuring that parade routes would be predictable and that the groups participating would adhere to a standard form. Carnival became important enough that clubs dedicated exclusively to enacting the festival were founded. Today they are known as "cliques," and the older ones date to the start of the 1900s. *Fasnacht* cliques are now active throughout the year in Basel, making preparations for the next Carnival but also playing a significant role in the social life of the city.[16] All of these changes and adaptations of Carnival during the period of immigration left in place the festival's Monday-morning focus, and today the *Fasnacht* of Basel plays out entirely during Lent.

Fasnacht Today

In a country renowned for its punctuality and efficiency, *Fasnacht* in Basel is no exception and annually follows a rigid schedule. At the moment churches throughout the city finish striking four o'clock on the morning of *Fasnacht* Monday, the lights in the central zone go dark. As soon as the reverberations of the fourth chime cease, more than ten thousand maskers, who have tightly arranged themselves throughout the streets in the heart of the city on either side of the Rhine, spring into action. The sounds of piccolos and drums suddenly resound through the darkened avenues and into the narrow alleyways. For the next several hours, groups ranging from a few individuals to massive cliques of several hundred march their way through the packed city, always in the special measured marching pace of Basel *Fasnacht,* releasing an energy accumulated over the past year in anticipation of this *Morgestraich,* the morning "tattoo" (fig. 5.5).[17]

The *Morgestraich* is undoubtedly and deservedly the most famous element of Carnival in Basel. It wows participants and spectators alike with its cacophony of sights and sounds. The early morning marchers bring out their most treasured costumes, creating a sea of diverse appearances ranging from traditional figures such as Harlequins, jesters, and old women to imaginative fantasy figures constructed in recent years (fig. 5.6). As spectators gaze upon this seemingly endless stream of images, they find their ears ringing with military marches emanating from dozens of piccolo and drum bands. In the midst of all this, most troupes of

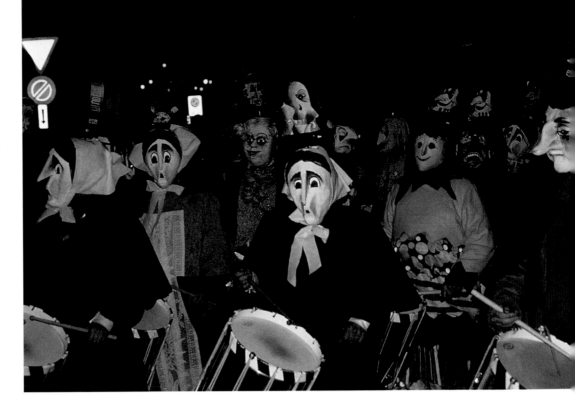

5.4 (overleaf) *Morgestraich,* the opening of Carnival in Basel, 1873. Engraving taken from a painting by the German artist Theoder Huth. *Courtesy of the New York Public Library, Picture Collection.*

5.5 A troupe, or clique, of drummers makes its way through town during the *Morgestraich,* the opening event of Carnival on early Monday morning. *Photograph by Peter Tokofsky, 1997.*

5.6 Members of a clique of piccolo players wear a variety of costumes and lanterns on their heads as they march through the streets of Basel during *Morgestraich. Photograph by Doran Ross, 1997.*

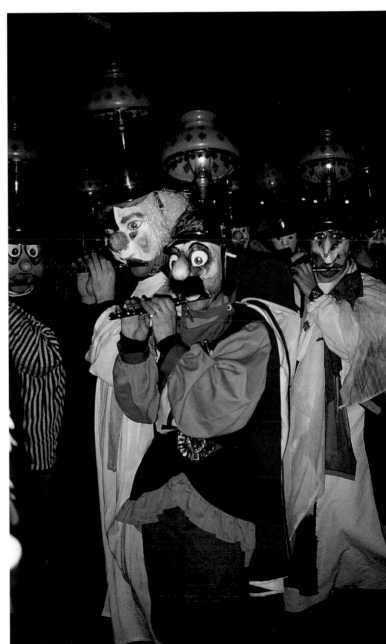

maskers are led by a front guard (*Vortrab*) who clear a path and carry the cliques' standards in the form of *Steckenlaternen,* painted lanterns glowing atop eight-foot poles. Much larger lanterns, carried on wagons or occasionally by four people, follow the *Vortrab* (fig. 5.7). These lanterns are actually more like floats. They consist of a wooden frame as high as eight feet or more placed on a cart or gurney. The constructed frame supports stretched canvases on which an artist has painted satirical depictions of selected current social or political themes. Within the framework, pipes provide propane-fed flames to illuminate the translucent canvases (fig. 5.8). Additional, smaller lanterns sit atop the masks of many musicians marching along the streets. Throughout Basel, dozens of lanterns of all sizes cast their distinctive glow during the *Morgestraich.*

The bitter-cold winter air typical for Basel during *Fasnacht,* the crowded spaces, and the cumbersome costumes take their toll on the hundreds of marchers during this predawn spectacle. At times they must hold their position for a quarter-hour or more while another group crosses in front of them. When the path

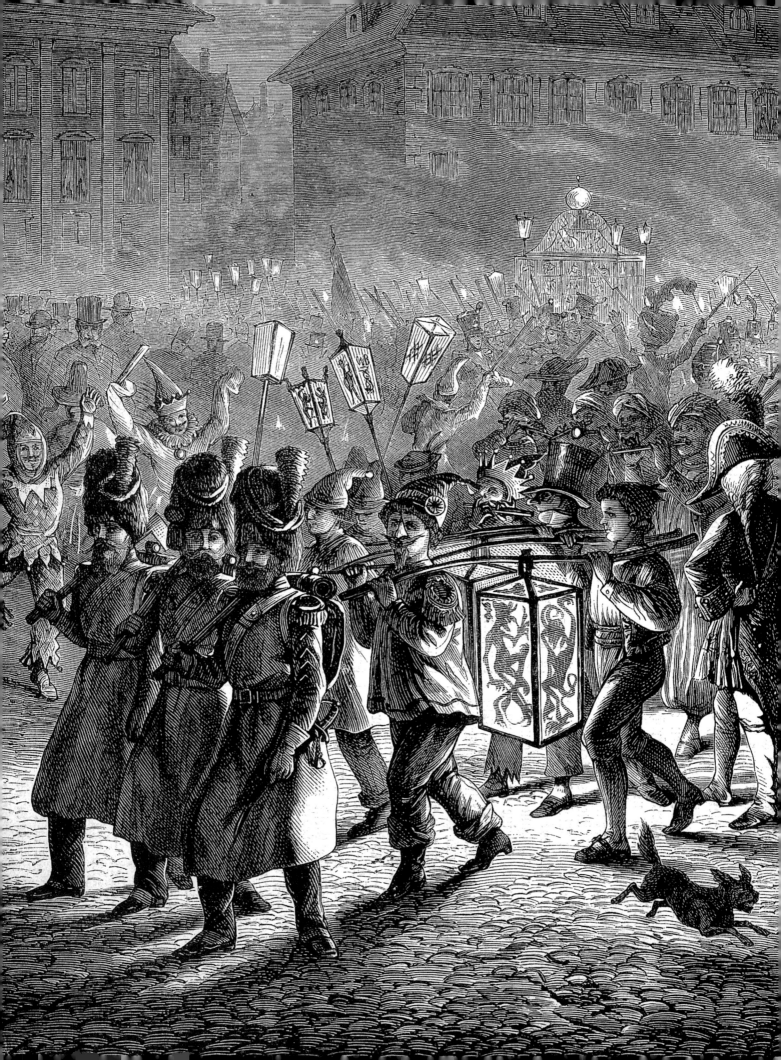

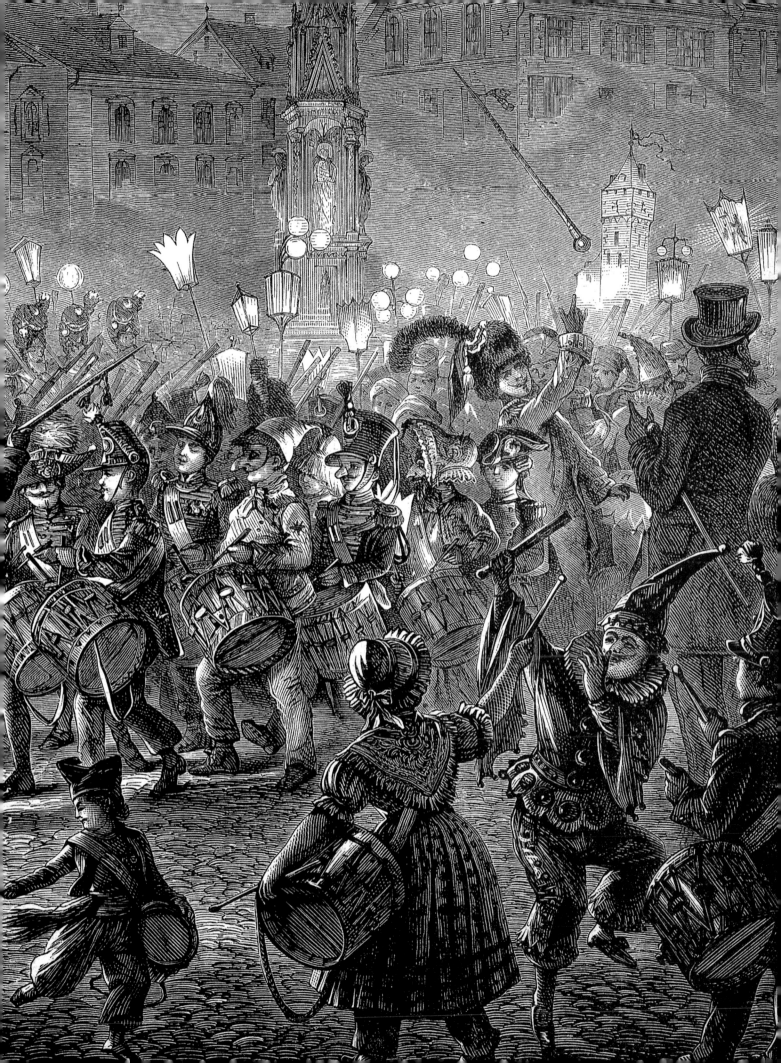

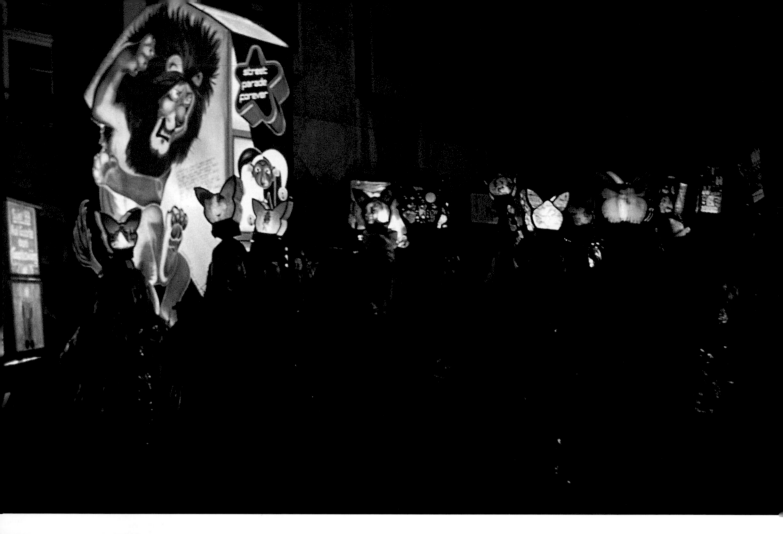

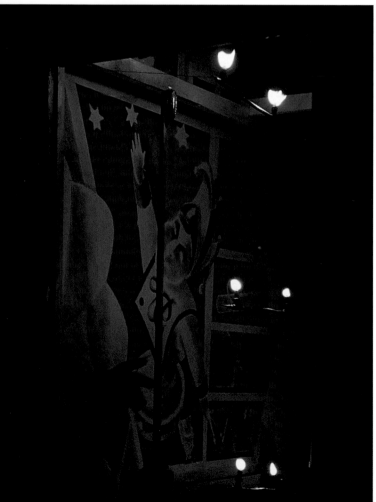

5.7 A clique of piccolo players with its standard, a painted lantern with the image of a lion on the front. *Photograph by Robert Jerome, 1999.*

5.8. Interior view of a painted lantern with pipes for propane to fuel the flames. *Photograph by Robert Jerome, 1999.*

clears, their drum major (*Tambormajor*), who wears a large mask and carries a staff so that he remains visible to those following, might cut a brisk pace for a considerable distance in order to reach a desired destination. The entire group always steps in the distinctive Basel manner, which is practiced well in advance to match the repertoire of instrumental marches. Despite widely publicized prohibitions, spectators frequently snap flash pictures, which, because of the constricted eyeholes of the masks, momentary blinds the marchers. All of these irritations give the groups good cause to take frequent rest stops at pubs and taverns throughout the city.

During the *Morgestraich,* and indeed throughout *Fasnacht,* rows of masks and lanterns line sidewalks outside these establishments as paraders gather inside

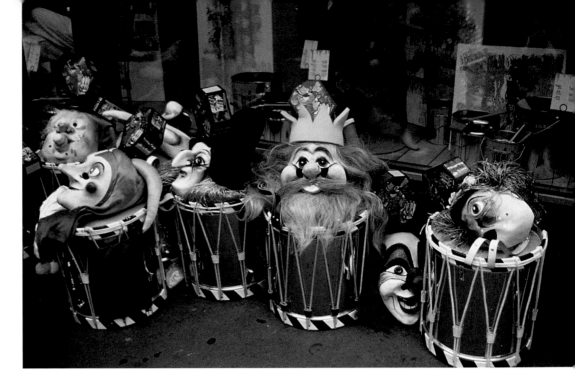

5.9 Drummers leave their instruments and masks outside a tavern where they replenish themselves when dawn breaks after *Morgestraich. Photograph by Peter Tokofsky, 1997.*

to warm themselves, socialize, and get some nourishment for the rest of the morning (fig. 5.9). *Fasnacht* would not be *Fasnacht* without two items in particular at these rest stops: *Määlsuppe* and *Ziibelwaije,* flour soup and onion tart (*Mehlsuppe* and *Zwiebelweihe* in standard German). Perhaps the former sounds a bit dull, but finding a seat to be served these Carnival delights is actually a challenge, for people savor the soothing warmth of the rich soup and the restorative, tasty proteins in the tart. By daybreak, more people might be found indoors warming themselves than continuing to march. Sometime after dawn, many of the maskers, especially those in a clique, head home for a few hours of rest and a change of costume.[18]

FASNACHT MASKS AND COSTUMES

For the *Morgestraich,* each participant chooses his or her own mask and costume. Baslers call this form of masking "charivari," borrowing the historical term for the chaotic, noisy processions once common in Europe to reprimand and ostracize unruly citizens.[19] In Basel's *Fasnacht,* charivari merely indicates a contrast with the more organized masking that takes place during the cortèges, or processions, on Monday and Wednesday afternoons. Masking is a central and vital aspect of Carnival in Basel. The local word *Maske* actually designates the entire outfit, not just the head covering; a more appropriate translation might be "masquerade." For "mask," Baslers use *larve,* cognate with "larva," thus emphasizing the transformative power of putting on

a new face. During charivari in Basel, thousands of different masqueraders appear, each somehow different from the next. Yet unlike the case in other Carnivals around the world, this diversity is not an invitation for visitors and spectators to put on some makeup or a rubber mask and join in. The current form of *Fasnacht* in Basel, despite being a relatively recent achievement, is closely protected and preserved by participants, leaving no room for random, uninitiated additions.[20]

Nonetheless, a great deal of innovation can occur within the established parameters. Any Basler who masquerades owns at least a few costumes. Clique members have their annual thematic costumes, which they wore in previous years, in addition to some more personal guises. Some costume types are better suited for warm weather, and others provide better protection in the rain. Some people prefer more traditional types of masks, many of which derive from the commedia dell'arte, whereas others try to be more inventive and introduce entirely novel constructions such as exotic animals, aliens from outer space, and fantasy figures (fig. 5.10). In any case, maskers always add their individual touches through choice of color scheme, accessories, and manner of animating the costume. The following are the more commonly encountered masquerades in Basel.[21] Each of these figures includes a traditional form of papier-mâché *larve* made with negative molds, usually in professional mask workshops (fig. 5.11). For piccolo players, the mouth area of the mask is cut away.

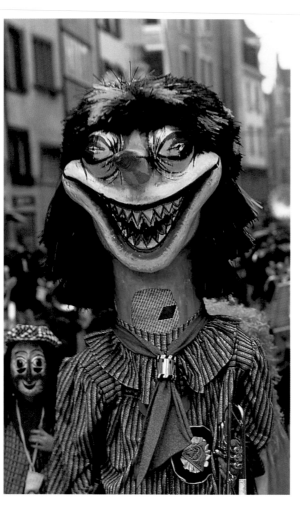

5.10 Innovative masquerade of an alien from outer space. *Photograph by Gianni Vecchiato, 1992.*

5.11 A display of generic papier-mâché *Fasnacht* masks at Larve Atelier Charivari. Maskers can choose one of these forms and then decorate it to suit their wishes, or they may ask for an original design. *Photograph by Peter Tokofsky, 2001.*

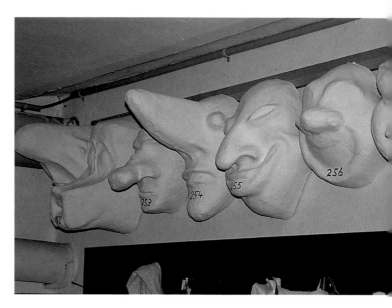

5.12 A group of Alti Dante masqueraders pulls its lantern in front of the red City Hall of Basel during the Monday afternoon procession. *Photograph by Robert Jerome, 1999.*

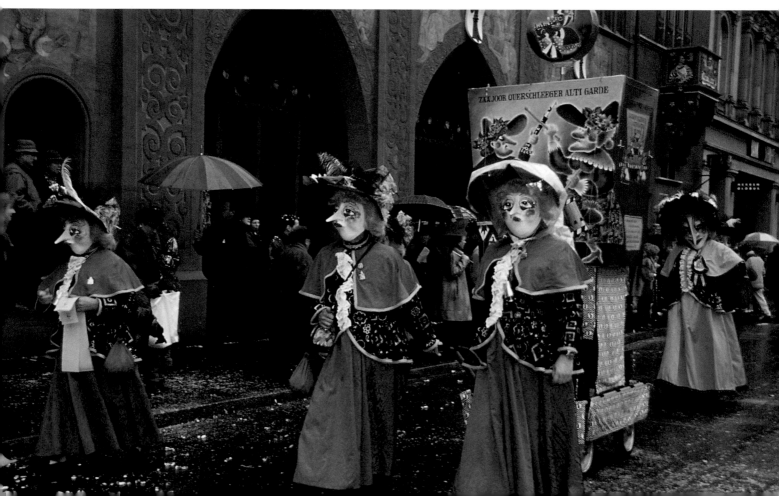

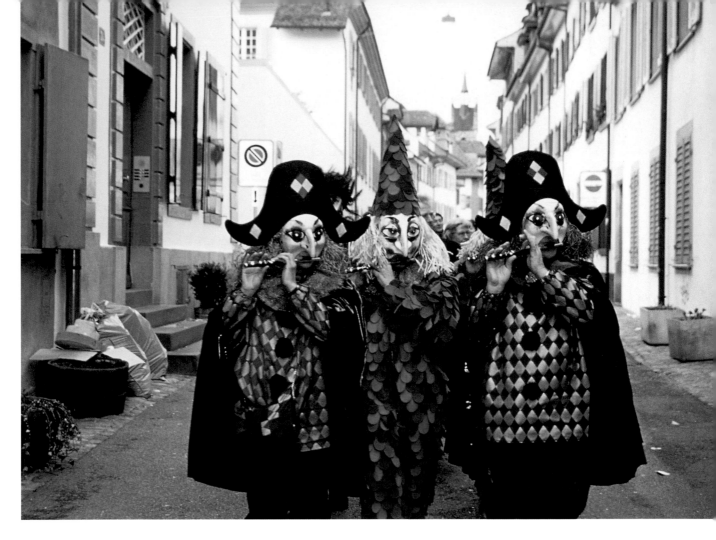

5.13 Two Harlequins and a Blätzlibajass play piccolos as they march through the streets of Basel. *Photograph by Peter Tokofsky, 2001.*

The Alti Dante ("old aunt") is an elegant old woman with a narrow, pointed nose and a gray wig. Her outfit is strictly high fashion from some time in the second half of the nineteenth century. It includes a large straw hat decked out with long feathers, plastic flowers, and perhaps even a little bird; an elegant long skirt of heavy material and a blouse with puffy arms and ruffled lace cuffs; and gloves, an umbrella, laced boots, and a neat purse called a reticule (fig. 5.12). The Alti Dante parodies an old maid. She moves very deliberately and during the cortège frequently sits atop a horse-drawn carriage, handing out roses to special recipients. From her reticule, she might also offer up a spritz of perfume, some hard candies, or a sip of spirits. But before you become too enamored of an Alti Dante handing you a gift, beware that a bearded man might be behind that elegant face. The costume elements place the Alti Dante in the Biedermeier period. However, it might

not be too far-fetched to relate the popularity of this figure to the much more general impulse that causes boys and girls to dress up in mother's fancy clothes.[22]

A character from the commedia dell'arte is Harlequin. Harlequin masqueraders in Basel wear broad Venetian hats and usually have colored hair of plastic straw that matches their outfits, which consist of tights and an overshirt. A frilly ruffled collar is essential. A Basel development on this figure is the wearing of a corresponding cape (fig. 5.13).[23]

Another traditional character, known as Blätzlibajass, dons a sacklike outfit completely covered with colorful fabric "tongues," or patches, layered on top of one another. This costume consists of a tall conical hat and either a jumpsuit or pants and a loose shirt (figs. 5.13, 5.14). The Blätzlibajass also frequently wears a broad white collar, and his mask often has a long nose. He resembles numerous figures found in German Carnival and elsewhere who also wear loose outfits decorated with layers of fabric patches.[24]

The rather silly character called Dummpeter might be my namesake ("Dumb Peter"), or his name might

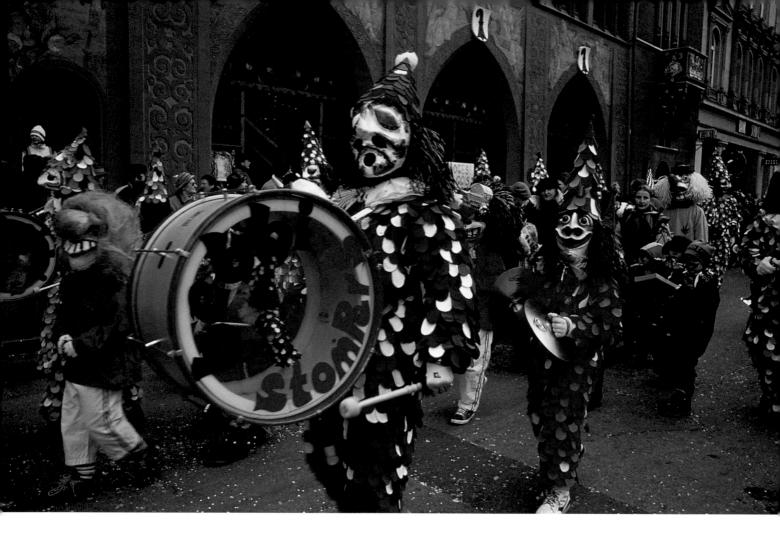

be a corruption of "trumpeter" said in a lisping voice unable to make out the *r* sound. He does have a small trumpet hung around his neck, but he never plays it. In any case, his mask features a broad, dumb smile, blushed puffy cheeks, and an innocently ignorant skyward gaze. He wears a fancy little cap atop a powdered wig with curls and a small pigtail. His matching two-piece outfit, cut from patterned material, has fine linen cuffs and a jabot. Beneath his knickerbockers, colorful mismatched socks provide further evidence of his obliviousness to the everyday world. Dummpeter's fancy black shoes are topped with white bows.[25]

The classic jester figure, Ueli, has medieval ancestry but is still very active in *Fasnacht* today. His mask features a large hooked nose and a mischievous grin, and two large horns protrude from the sides of his cap. Small bells are sewn onto the ends of these protuberances as well as at the tips of his collar, cuffs, and shoes, so that he jingles with every step. His two-toned outfit consists of a jester's tights and shirt (see fig. 5.1).[26]

Next is the character Pierrot, a classic commedia

5.14 A group of Blätzlibajass wears jumpsuits and conical hats covered with "tongues" of fabric. *Photograph by Robert Jerome, 1999.*

dell'arte theatrical figure that entered *Fasnacht* in Basel by way of France. He wears a simple costume consisting of a baggy top (which can easily cover layers in cold weather) and loose-fitting pants. Three large pom-poms cover the line of buttons on his shirt. A broad ruffled collar surrounds his neck below a pretty, rather serious, and perhaps somewhat melancholy mask. Like several other figures, he has colorful hair of plastic straw. His small, circular felt cap is topped by a single peacock feather.[27]

Altfrangg, the seldomly seen masquerade of a French soldier, is a reminder of the history of *Fasnacht* in Basel. His uniform—triangular hat, gold-buttoned coat and vest, formal pants tied off below the knees, and white socks—recalls the elite military corps that once made up the Monday morning marches. His powdered wig with ponytail and his proud face mark him as a member of the bourgeoisie (fig. 5.15).[28]

Last but certainly not least in this list of typical figures are the Waggis masquerades, who are truly in a class by themselves during *Fasnacht* in Basel. Mostly associated with the wagons entered in the afternoon processions, from which they shower crowds with confetti (*räppli* in Basel German; locals shudder when they hear someone use the Italian word *confetti*) and treats (oranges, small bottles of schnapps, yellow mimosa flowers, etc.), Waggis masqueraders love to rough-house throughout *Fasnacht*. Children and young women beware! A Waggis might jump down from his wagon or appear around a corner at any time and rub handfuls of *Räppli* deep into your hair and clothing. You will still be picking it out months later.

Waggis, the most common *Fasnacht* figure, is a caricature of the French Alsatian farmers who used to bring their produce to market in Basel. Hence his blue farmer's smock, his white pants (perhaps with red and blue stripes to complete the tri-color), and the red kerchief tied around his neck with a matchbox or other inappropriate item. A headful of usually yellow hair (again plastic straw) and large wooden clogs—frequently heard clopping along the cobblestones of the old town—complete the outfit (fig. 5.16). His mask

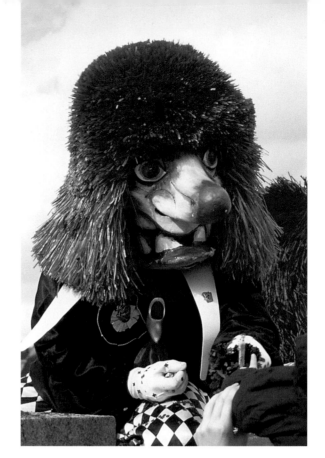

5.16 A red-headed Waggis with a fistful of *räppli* (confetti) searches for a victim at whom to throw it. *Photograph by Peter Tokofsky, 2001.*

5.15 The masquerade Altfrangg, or the French soldier, is a reminder of the elite military corps that once participated in the Monday morning marches in Basel. *Photograph by Peter Tokofsky, 2001.*

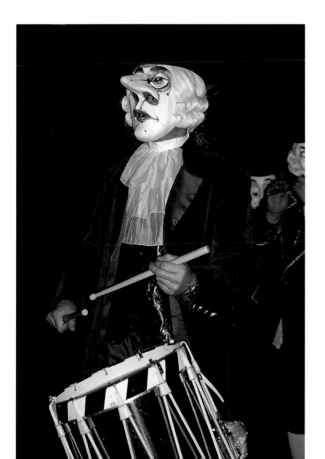

has an open mouth revealing a row of large teeth, and a long, fat, bulbous nose. A classic Waggis carries a bag of vegetables and makes a racket with a wooden ratchet. Modern Waggis masqueraders vary from the original color scheme, introducing hair and outfits of any imaginable color (fig. 5.17). They remain recognizable because of consistency in the basic form of the mask and costume. Although times have changed and Alsace is now a popular destination for travelers seeking spas or a taste of culinary tourism, Waggis provides a clear reminder of the role stereotypes and mockery of the "other" frequently play in Carnival.[29]

CLIQUES AND "WILD" FASNACHT

The twenty thousand-plus Carnival participants who appear during the three-day festival divide about equally between those who join cliques and those who prefer to remain "wild." The behavior of the latter is actually no more unruly than that of clique members. The differences lie, instead, in their form of organization. The cliques are registered clubs with officers,

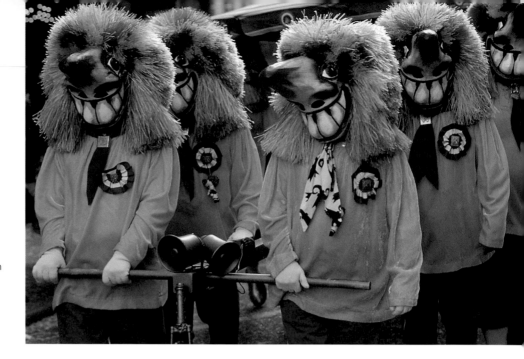

5.17 These Waggis masqueraders wear clothing and hair that vary from the traditional color scheme for this character, but the wide grin and bulbous nose leave no doubt about whom they are portraying. *Photograph by Gianni Vecchiato, 1990.*

statutes, dues, clubhouses, and all the other requisite features of an association. The structure of a clique does not differ from that of other voluntary clubs in Basel, such as those formed by ski enthusiasts or stamp collectors. Any club has its rules and procedures, regular meetings, fund-raising activities, and social events unrelated to its raison d'être. In Switzerland (and Germany) this type of formal organization for leisure activities is common and constitutes an important component of local life. In Basel, cliques are certainly the most prominent clubs, and in addition to organizing part of *Fasnacht,* they provide important personal and professional networks in the city. The Fasnachts-Comité coordinates among the cliques, prints a program listing the annual topics for all the *sujet,* or themes, and issues *Fasnacht* pins (*Blaggedde*) in bronze, silver, and gold, which are sold as a sort of admission ticket to visitors in order to raise funds. The committee also organizes drumming and piccolo concerts and competitions in the weeks prior to Carnival.

At last count, more than two hundred cliques participated in *Fasnacht,* but only about forty of them numbered among the largest, most established groups. If a clique grows large enough, it divides its membership into several units: the main group (*Stamm*), the young guard, and the old guard for the more elderly members who prefer a somewhat less strenuous pace during *Fasnacht.* The youngest members of the clique are *Binggis;* they receive special attention because they represent the future of the organization. The cliques arrange drum and piccolo lessons and thus serve a

vital function in perpetuating the central traditions of Carnival in Basel. Even with regular attendance at meetings of these instrumental schools, Basel musicians claim that it takes at least three years to become a proficient *Fasnacht* drummer, whereas a piccolo player can become skilled in enough tunes to march with a year or two of practice.[30] Over the years, a cohort of musicians becomes a well-coordinated band able to keep together during the *Morgestraich* and other *Fasnacht* processions despite acoustical interference from other groups.

Clique *Fasnacht* can become a highly ritualized affair, with activities such as the lantern *yypfyffe* ("piccolo-ing in" of the lantern). On Sunday evening before the *Morgestraich,* a contingent of piccolo players is dispatched to the lantern workshop, where it accompanies the transportation of this artistic creation back to the starting point for the clique's procession. This small ritual, repeated dozens of times throughout the city by various groups, caps months of preparations and truly sets off the anticipation for the *Morgestraich,* just hours away.

Wild *Fasnacht* groups have none of this organizational structure or ritual activity. Basically, anyone who participates in Carnival without a clique is "wild." Yet *Fasnacht* in Basel never exhibits the unrestrained street revelry of other Carnivals, so *wild* is a relative term here. Whether in a clique or wild, participation in Basel Carnival means to march with piccolo or drum, or at least in a group with these instruments. Even wild marchers spend time practicing their music during the year and put on costumes and masks before venturing out into the *Morgestraich.* A wild group might consist of only two or three members (one occasionally even sees a solo marcher on Monday or Wednesday evening) or might grow to a dozen or more. When several wild marchers form a small group, they become known as a *Schyssdräggziigli.* This peculiar Swiss term can be politely (but not precisely) translated as "dirty little parade."[31]

I befriended one such group during my latest visit to Basel. This *Schyssdräggziigli* has about ten members, men and women all around forty years of age, with a few newer members somewhat younger. Some of them know each other from childhood or university; others joined in later.[32] All of them play piccolo, the instrument that predominates among wild groups because learning a drum without the guidance and acoustical isolation of a clique's practice room is more difficult. The group meets weekly for a few months in advance of *Fasnacht,* and like many of their peers in cliques and other *Schyssdräggziigli,* its members hold final rehearsals on the move in a large park outside the city (fig. 5.18). During *Fasnacht,* rarely do all members of the *Schyssdräggziigli* manage to show

up at one time. Child care and other obligations can interfere. But the group has several scheduled meeting times and places during the hectic days, when latecomers can catch up and join in. The members of this particular group do not place great emphasis on their costumes. They have a nice set of traditional masquerades (Ueli, clowns, etc.), some of which are quite worn from years of use. One of their spouses provides technical support in the form of small battery-operated lanterns attached on top of their heads. In contrast, other wild groups make striking appearances in new, original costumes each year, belying the name *Schyssdräggziigli.*[33]

If you speak to *Fasnacht* participants, they will inevitably tell why they prefer one form of organization over the other. Wild marchers appreciate the lack of structure and the freedom for spontaneous decisions, such as turning up an unexpected alleyway, briefly joining forces with another small group, or extending an onion tart and wine break in a pub for an extra half hour. Wild masqueraders prefer to choose their march-

5.18 A "wild" *Fasnacht* group practices marching in the Lange Erlen park outside of Basel. *Photograph by Peter Tokofsky, 2001.*

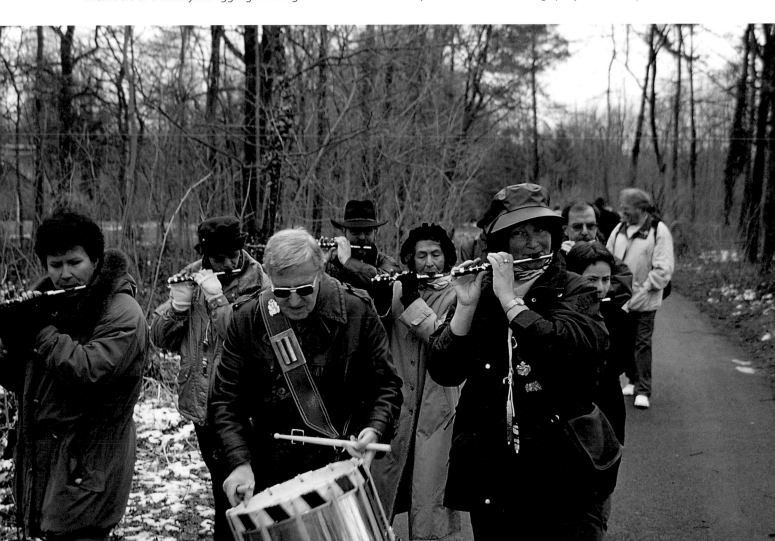

ing partners themselves and to make Carnival a time for connecting with old friends. Some of them disparage the rigidity of cliques or criticize their uncreative "*Fasnacht* in a sack" approach (implying that clique members just show up at a meeting and receive their costume in a bag before returning at the appointed time before the *Morgestraich*). Wild groups also enjoy the ability of their small troupes to wend their way through alleys so narrow that they could never accommodate a group larger than fifteen. Marching these alleyways in Great Basel is such an enchanting and characteristic part of *Fasnacht* that the Basel dialect even has a verb, *Gässle,* to describe it. *Gässle,* the diminutive of *Gasse,* means small alley or lane; used as a verb it means something like "do the little streets."

On the other hand, clique members will tell you that despite their obligations to the organization, they also find time to do all of the things celebrated by the wild groups while still having the year-round enjoyment of clique collegiality. They praise the music schools. Indeed, wild marchers will generally concede that a clique is the best place to learn to play; wild groups include many clique dropouts for this very reason. Cliques members enjoy their decorated clubhouses and their reciprocal relationships with other cliques, which allow them into these coveted spaces during Carnival. On several Sundays following *Fasnacht,* clique members take a *Bummel,* or casual walk, to nearby villages and have a chance to relive the recent festival in quiet conversation and fresh air.

Perhaps most importantly, clique members have the opportunity to participate in developing an annual theme, including original costumes in which they appear during the cortèges on Monday and Wednesday afternoons.[34]

CORTÈGE

By daybreak on *Fasnacht* Monday, the large *Morgestraich* crowds begin thinning as most participants and spectators make their way home. Some will catch a few hours of sleep before preparations begin for the next Carnival event, the cortège, or procession. The cortège commences at one-thirty on Monday afternoon and features all of the formally organized groups of *Fasnacht*—the cliques and *Guggemusik* bands, or brass bands that play cacophonous music. These groups station themselves at designated spots along two concentric loops passing through the center of town. When the procession begins, the groups in the two loops march in opposite directions. This unusual pattern was designed to enable thousands of maskers to complete the circuit in the few hours before nightfall. Unlike their custom for the *Morgestraich,* with its nearly limitless variety of costumes, cliques design original, coordinated outfits for the cortège, which repeats on Wednesday afternoon. The new guises correspond to the *sujet,* or theme, chosen by the clique for that year.[35]

A *sujet* is, as the French name suggests, a subject or theme selected for satirical treatment during *Fasnacht.*

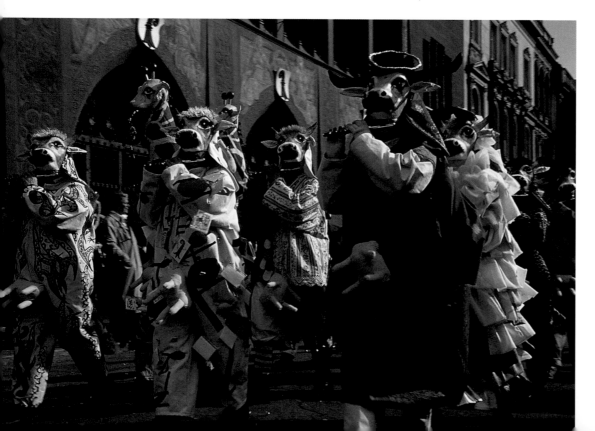

5.19 Members of a clique wear cow costumes as a comment on the threat of "mad cow" disease in central Europe. *Photograph by Robert Jerome, 1999.*

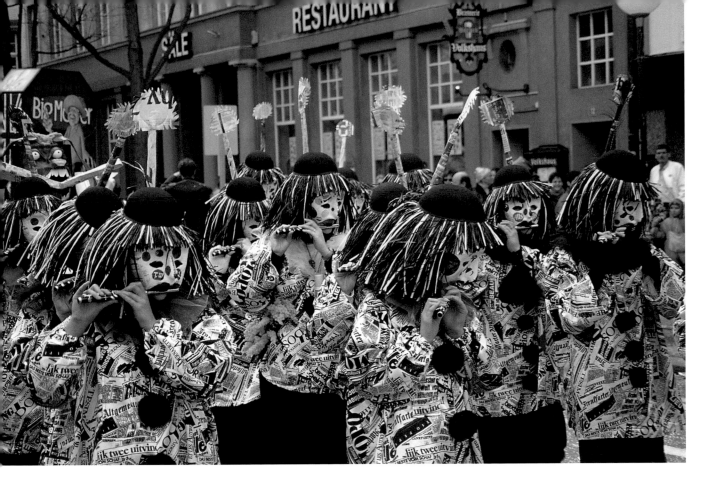

5.20 Newsprint outfits are worn by this clique to criticize the proliferation of free weekly newspapers in Basel. *Photograph by Peter Tokofsky, 2001.*

Each fall, special committees in the cliques convene to decide on an appropriate theme to play out in the coming Carnival. Clique members discuss any noteworthy political or social faux pas or scandals on the local, national, and even international scene that have transpired since the previous *Fasnacht.* Anything from the presidential balloting irregularities in Florida in 2000 to public transit policy in Basel, the threat of "mad cow" disease in Central Europe (fig. 5.19), and the financial problems experienced by Swissair in 2001 might provide material. Some cliques select weightier, even philosophical subjects, such as the global domination of English or greed in modern society. Other themes might seem relatively mundane, such as several popular subjects depicted during *Fasnacht* 2001: the proliferation of free weekly newspapers around Basel (fig. 5.20), a rubber ducky race on the Rhine used in a fund-raising drive, and the export of American Halloween customs to Switzerland. The balance between local and broader themes has varied over the decades.[36] However, the key to a successful

sujet is not so much the profundity of the topic as how the clique interprets and represents its point of view. These considerations enter into the initial discussion: What kinds of masks and lanterns might make for effective presentation of the subject? What does the clique want to say about the theme? Will the topic still merit attention in several months when unveiled during *Fasnacht?* By December, the clique will make its decision, and preparations for the masquerade and lantern begin.

The *sujet* chosen by the *Stamm* (main corps) and old guard divisions of the Rätz-Clique in 2001 make interesting examples of themes and their execution. The *Stamm* opted to depict the growing controversy over attack dogs in Switzerland with the *sujet* title "Don't be afraid—he just wants to play!" (*Kai Angscht— är wott numme spiile!*). Together with mask and costume designers, they decided to develop several different masquerade types representing various breeds of dogs. After the mask maker provided models of the forms these masks would take, the costume designer sketched out a variety of accessories to complete the figures (fig. 5.21). The result was a mix of dogs, from a stodgy, bespectacled English bulldog to St. Bernards headed for the Alps. Individual members of the clique added personal touches to the masks and costumes so that when the group appeared in the cortège, observers would find no two figures identical, even though the dozens of marchers had only five masks from which to choose (fig. 5.22).

Meanwhile, committee members met with lantern artist Christoph Knöll. During their discussions, Knöll recalled a childhood dachshund pull-toy consisting of several body segments that twisted and turned behind the dog's head. He sketched a model for a lantern based on this principle and soon found himself at work realizing his idea. Traditionally, Basel *Fasnacht* lanterns are vertical boxes with their largest painted surfaces facing front and back, which does not allow optimum viewing for streetside spectators. Knöll developed a horizontally oriented set of five segments, with large painted scenes facing the sides. On one side he depicted "good dogs gone bad": a guide dog for a blind man chasing a cat, a St. Bernard imbibing the whiskey from his own collar barrel, a guard dog snarling at an innocent girl, and a police dog snorting cocaine. The other side featured a large illustration of dogs viciously fighting (fig. 5.23). With the

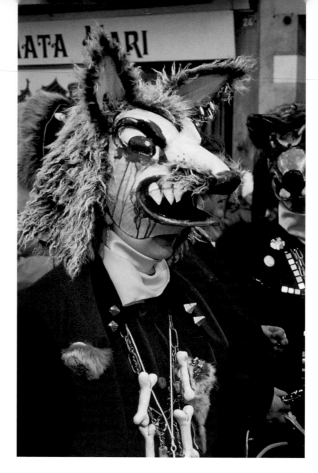

5.22 "Vicious dog" masqueraders from Rätz-Clique march in an afternoon procession. *Photograph by Peter Tokofsky, 2001.*

5.21 Costume sketch for a Chihuahua with material swatches. By Brigitta Bloch, costume designer and seamstress. *Photograph by Peter Tokofsky, 2001.*

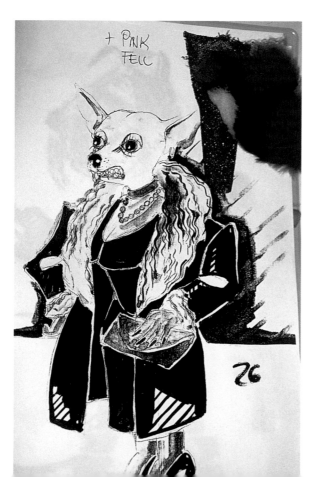

help of skilled clique members, Knöll successfully executed the pull-toy scheme to create an original form for the lantern.

For its *sujet*, "The fuss over the holes" (*s schyss um d Lecher*), the old guard of Rätz-Clique chose an international news item that resonated widely in Switzerland (indeed, several cliques independently selected this theme in 2001) while passing mostly unnoticed in the United States. It seems the U.S. Department of Agriculture had issued a regulation governing the size of the holes in imported Swiss cheese. As might have been expected, the Swiss did not react kindly to American bureaucrats meddling in their unofficial national symbol. (To give the USDA the benefit of the doubt, I assume the regulation was intended to prevent deceptive discrepancies between the size and the weight of a piece of cheese. Nonetheless, holes in Swiss cheese occur naturally, so to perpetrate fraud, someone would have to increase the size of the holes manually.)

On one side of the lantern made by the old guard to represent this theme, Uncle Sam, magnifying glass

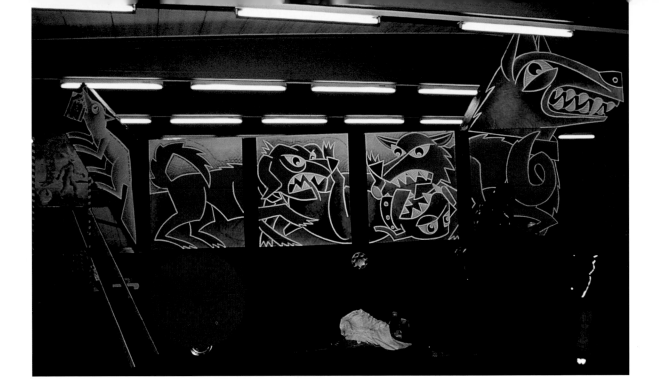

5.23 Side view of the Rätz-Clique's painted lantern depicting a dogfight, under construction in the workshop. *Photograph by Peter Tokofsky, 2001*

5.24 "The fuss over the holes" theme of the Rätz-Clique old guard's lantern addressed the US Department of Agriculture's regulation on the size of holes In imported Swiss cheese. *Photograph by Peter Tokofsky, 2001.*

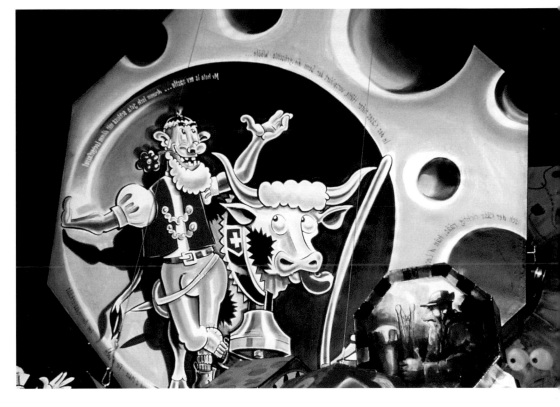

in hand, inspects a minute hole in a cheese; an agricultural stamp on the cheese reads, in mixed English and German, "Import not Bewilligt, Löchers too big," which translates, more or less, as "Import not approved. Holes too big." On the other side of the lantern, a large cheese hole comfortably accommodates a cow and farmer (fig. 5.24). The corresponding masks, produced in the old guard workshop (all those decades of mask-

ing add up to some expertise, which allows them to circumvent professional mask makers), depicted cheese-nibbling mice, many of them with manual drills destined to enlarge some holes (fig. 5.25).

These comical exaggerations of topics widely discussed and debated in local media and around tables in the pubs demonstrate the essential goal of depicting a *sujet* during *Fasnacht* with wit and humor. When

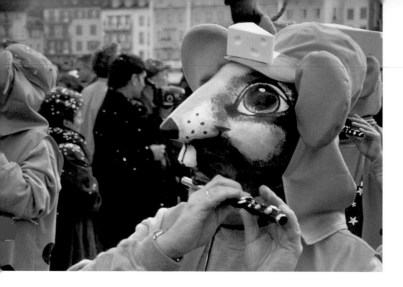

5.25 A mouse masquerader wears a slice of Swiss cheese (with small holes) on the brim of his hat. *Photograph by Peter Tokofsky, 2001.*

the clique makes its appearance in the cortège, two other elements contribute to its public commentary on the selected theme. First, members of the clique compose a satirical poem about the topic, which is then printed on long, colorful strips of paper (*Zeedel*) and distributed to curious spectators as the clique marches by (fig. 5.26). Second, a bit more commentary

on the *sujet* appears on the lantern itself in the form of so-called lantern verses, clever quips and puns written on the edges of the painting. These are best viewed and contemplated when the lanterns are put on stationary display in the cathedral square following the Monday cortège (fig. 5.27).[37]

The lantern verses and the poems distributed on paper are in local dialect, making comprehension of the lines a complicated process accessible to outsiders only through what I call "thick translation."[38] This means that it does not suffice merely to translate the words into a known language. A complete understanding of the nuances and wordplays in these texts requires an intimate knowledge of the subject and how it played out in local debate during the previous year. During one visit to *Fasnacht* in Basel, for instance, my Swiss friend Franziska joined me. She had lived in Basel for more than ten years, but during the months

5.26 Members of a clique hand out a satirical poem related to their theme, printed on long, colorful strips of paper. *Photograph by Gianni Vecchiato, 1992.*

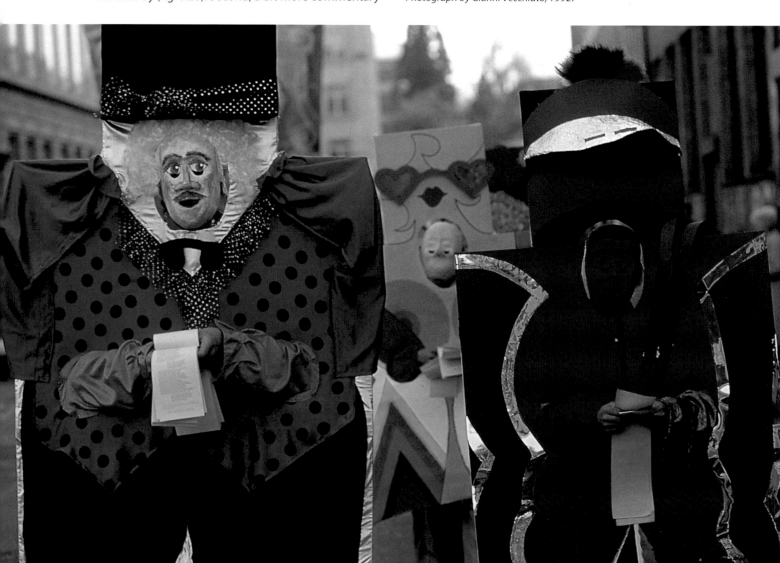

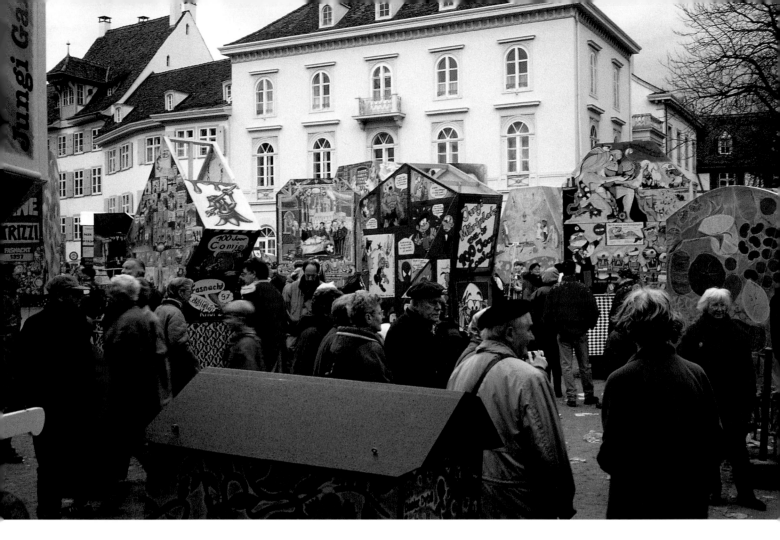

5.27 All of the cliques' lanterns are put on display in the cathedral square in Basel after the Monday afternoon procession. *Photograph by Doran Ross, 1997.*

leading up to Carnival she had resided abroad. Although she could easily discern the meaning of the words in Basel dialect, many of the themes and allusions did not resonate with her at all. In short, these *Fasnacht* texts serve as mechanisms for defining true Basel residents.[39]

TUESDAY

Spectators who manage to get a room in Basel and stay on for the second day of Carnival have an opportunity to enjoy a very different atmosphere in the city. Clique members put away their *sujet* costumes, for no formal parades are scheduled on this day. Instead, Tuesday is the day for children's *Fasnacht* and *Gugge-musik*. The maskers do not rise so early on Tuesday, for many of them celebrated the first day of Carnival well into the early morning hours. But by noon the streets of Basel slowly begin to fill again. An informal, almost

fairlike atmosphere envelops the city as families with children emerge from their homes dressed in the mixed costumes of charivari. From the smallest toddlers in strollers or riding in wagons (fig. 5.28) to preteens testing their *Fasnacht* legs while weighted down with costumes and masks, it seems as if every child in the city must be out, banging on miniature drums, joining family and friends in a mini-parade, or enthusiastically stuffing the shirts of friends and unsuspecting adults with colorful *räppli*. In fact, not all residents come out for *Fasnacht* (some parents prefer to imbue their children with other hobbies), but enough do to fill the streets and pass the tradition on to the next generation. Many of the children sport beautiful, small-sized versions of traditional masquerades (fig. 5.29). Their presence creates the special, joyous mood of sharing between young and old, familiar and new. Children run about enjoying their Carnival freedom while watchful but relaxed parents share a conversation over wine or coffee.[40]

The special atmosphere of informality on Carnival Tuesday gets an extra boost from the distinctive sounds

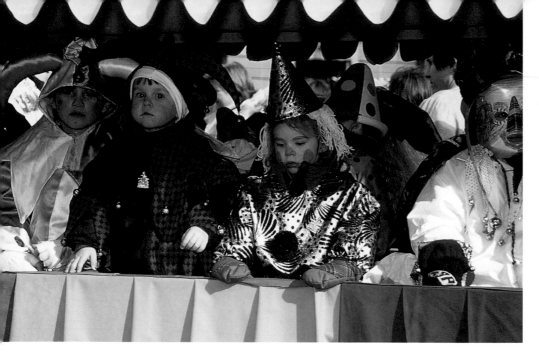

5.28 Young *Fasnacht* masqueraders ride in a trolley as part of the Tuesday children's parade. *Photograph by Robert Jerome, 1999.*

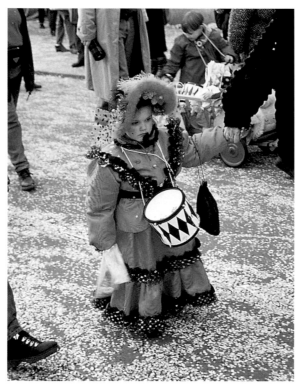

5.29 A small Alti Dante on *Fasnacht* Tuesday, with confetti covering the streets. *Photograph by Peter Tokofsky, 1998.*

of *Guggemusik* resounding throughout the city. *Guggemusik* is the true heir to charivari in Basel *Fasnacht*. In its original sense, charivari, also known as rough music or, in German, *Katzenmusik* (presumably because it sounds like the screeching of a cat), consists of clamorous "music" produced by any sort of noisemaker or instrument, from pots and pans to damaged brass

horns.[41] Bands of musicians playing brass and tin instruments joined *Fasnacht* festivities in Basel as early as the start of the nineteenth century, although they did not become known as *Gugge* bands until the 1900s.[42] Today, a *Gugge* is a brass band that plays familiar tunes in a cacophonous, even disharmonious fashion (fig. 5.30). As a result of this style of playing, listeners perceive the melody blown loudly by a portion of the band while contending with competing noise produced by other musicians blowing discordant notes. The overblowing and the apparently misplayed notes are all well planned to create the unique, almost indescribable *Gugge* music. Baslers value this peculiar, unusual sound so much that occasionally critics complain that the bands sound too good and thus are not truly *Gugge* musicians. "Good" *Gugge* musicians, according to this view, are those who "play demanding pieces 'capably wrong.'"[43]

Until the 1960s, *Gugge* bands participated in the *Morgestraich,* playing their versions of well-known jazz and popular tunes amid the drum and piccolo marches. By 1960, some people began complaining that these loud groups drowned out the marches and thus detracted from the *Fasnacht* experience. A compromise reached a couple of years later excluded *Guggemusik* from the *Morgestraich* and, in exchange, reserved the city center for the *Gugge* bands on Tuesday evening. This arrangement has allowed *Guggemusik* to thrive. The bands now have their own day, and members of cliques can also join *Gugge* bands without creating conflicts between their obligations.

Now the number of *Gugge* bands rivals the number of cliques. Each band has its own flair and repertoire, and audiences seek out their performances. As is usually the case, resistance to change slowly gave way, and now many people would consider *Fasnacht* incomplete without *Guggemusik*. The practical arrangement of confining *Gugge* to the cortèges and *Fasnacht* Tuesday allows both the old and the new to prosper without undue conflict. Similar controversies will surely continue to arise periodically as the creativity of Carnival continues to introduce new elements in Basel. For instance, over the past decade Samba bands have occasionally come out and joined the fun on Tuesday. Again, purists see no place for this Brazilian import, but if it appeals to enough people, *Fasnacht* in Basel will surely add yet another rhythm to its ongoing pastiche of sounds.[44]

As Carnival Tuesday wears on in Basel, strains of

5.30 A *Guggemusik* brass band in Waggis masquerades makes its way through the streets of Basel on Tuesday evening. *Photograph by Robert Jerome, 1999.*

Guggemusik begin to dominate the inner city. From all directions, the *Gugge* bands begin marching toward central squares. Band members wear costumes that, like the clique costumes, feature papier-mâché masks. Their leader wears an oversized "big head," peering out through the neck. As they march, the percussionists, playing drums and cowbells, keep a driving beat. When the band reaches a plaza or a wide intersection, it may pause to thrill the crowd with a set of loud tunes before taking a rest.

With dozens of *Gugge* bands streaming through the city and hundreds of families and other informal groups, including some "wild" troupes, spread around, Basel teems with *Fasnacht* energy well into the night on Tuesday. As darkness creeps in, the younger masqueraders head home while the *Gugge* musicians, known as some of the most enthusiastic celebrators among Carnival revelers in Basel, play on. Stages are set up in a couple of large squares so *Gugge* bands can offer open-air concerts to huge crowds. After its set, each one marches into the city, where together the bands provide an acoustically dominant contrast

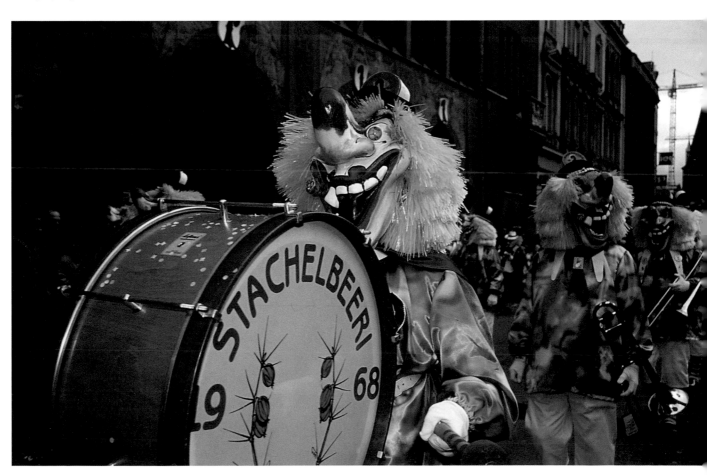

to the more solemn marches of the drums and piccolos. Still, in the narrow interstices of the *Gässle* (alleys), many small groups continue to play these instruments through the night on Tuesday. Because the cliques have no official activities on Tuesday, many of their members join in and find an opportunity to *Gässle*.[45]

SCHNITZELBANGG

On each night of *Fasnacht* in Basel, special performances take place inside selected restaurants and especially in the subterranean cellars run by some of the cliques. These *Schnitzelbangg* (in standard German, *Schnitzelbank*) performances are the modern versions of a centuries-old European carnival and fair tradition of "bench singing," in which traveling performers would come to a local festival and report important and titillating news from around the continent by singing and selling broadsheets telling of disasters and scandals. Poster-sized illustrations accompanied the orations, so all those in attendance could visualize the story as well. The bench singer frequently had an assistant who would point to and flip the illustrations as well as sell copies of the text to the curious audience.[46] Tabloid newspapers and television have replaced the function filled by these figures in today's world, but in Basel and neighboring southwestern Germany, Carnival performances retain the form of bench singing to create witty and humorous commentaries on current events.

There might be as many as a hundred *Schnitzelbangg* troupes in Basel, most consisting of fewer than five members. Although many of the troupes have become renowned for their wit and originality, the identity of most performers remains a strict secret concealed beneath their masks and costumes. The troupes enter establishments one after the other and quickly capture the attention of the crowd. Playing guitars, accordions, and other instruments, they sing brief verses (usually about four lines long) about a topical subject. Many of the same themes that appear as *sujet* in a given year will make repeated appearances in *Schnitzelbangg* texts as well. In 2001, mad cow disease, holes in Swiss cheese, the retirement of Swiss president Adolf Ogi, the nuisance of youths on scooters, and of course vicious dogs all received frequent treatment. As with *sujet,* it is not so much the selection of topics as the wit of the verse (in Basel dialect) that determines the success of a *Schnitzelbangg* performance. A skilled verse writer draws in the audience line by line before pouncing on it with a final line containing an unexpected play on words, association, or commentary. An easel with simple drawings helps key the audience into each topic (fig. 5.31). At the conclusion of the performance, the innkeeper usually offers the singers a drink, and the crowd grabs at the printed *Zeedel* distributed by the group in order to scrutinize the best verses more closely.

Generally speaking, there are two ways to experience *Schnitzelbangg:* by purchasing a ticket and reserving a seat in a designated restaurant on Monday or Wednesday evening or by hoping to find a spot where wild troupes will appear on Tuesday. An official

5.31 A *Schnitzelbangg* performer uses a drawing to help convey a verse he is singing. *Photograph by Robert Jerome, 1999.*

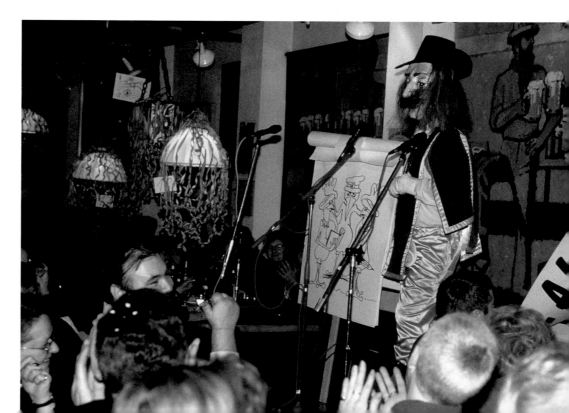

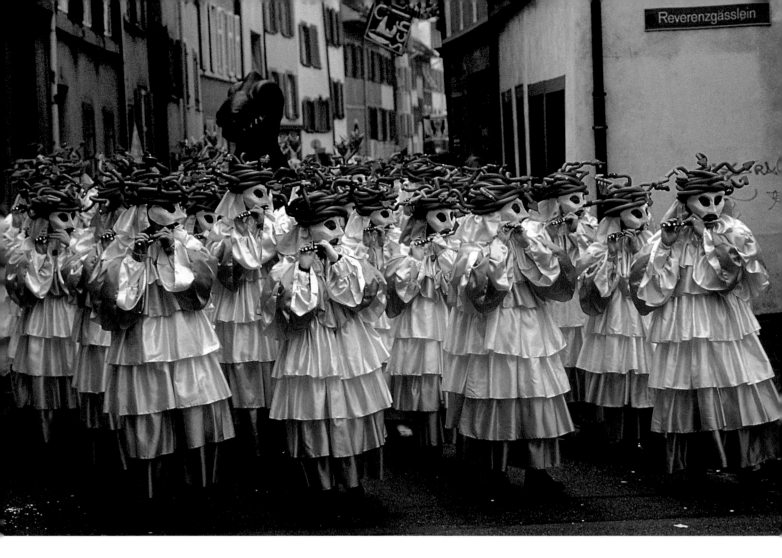

5.32 A clique makes its last circle along the *Fasnacht* route on Wednesday afternoon. *Photograph by Gianni Vecchiato, 1994.*

Schnitzelbangg organization sponsors the Monday and Wednesday "concerts" and designates in advance where performers will appear. Audiences for these shows can enjoy a comfortable dinner and the confidence that, over a few hours, they will see several dozen *Schnitzelbangg* troupes, but they give up the freedom of wandering the city for a more diverse experience. Spectators without tickets are not allowed to look on at these performances, which usually take place in a closed-off room.

For many, the ideal place to view *Schnitzelbangg* is in one of the intimate "*Fasnacht* cellars" usually open to the public only on these three special days. A small lantern outside the entrance marks their location. Anyone is welcome, but claustrophobics beware— these are indeed cellars, and space is limited. If a cellar is full, and too many people fill the waiting area, visitors will be sent away. But those fortunate enough

to get a seat at the right time might be surprised by a stream of unannounced *Schnitzelbangg* troupes. For me, very little can match the mood in one of these cellars when the audience enjoys the humor of the performance.[47]

PARTING VIEWS

By Wednesday morning, three nights of *Fasnacht* revelry (including the *Morgestraich*) have transpired. Fatigue is offset by the growing realization that only a few hours of Carnival remain. Crowds have thinned considerably, and the last surge of celebration engulfs the spaces opening up on the streets, which are now covered with a deep layer of *räppli*. Reminders of the unusual timing of this Carnival appear in bakery windows: plain pretzels with anise seeds, a good Lenten food. Easter tarts (*Osterfladen*) replace the onion tarts. Still, *Fasnacht* does not end with a whimper. In the afternoon another cortège circles the city route (fig. 5.32). In the evening wild groups and members of cliques continue to march, playing their drums and piccolos. *Schnitzelbangg* performances continue, and *Gugge* musicians stroll about. Completing the symmetry of the three days, Wednesday concludes with an *Ändstraich* (final romp or tattoo), which abruptly ceases exactly seventy-two hours after the festival began, at four o'clock Thursday morning. Quiet spreads over Basel, cleanup begins, and thoughts soon wander to next year.

NOTES

I would like to thank Stefan Ospel and all the members of the Rätz-Clique, who have been generous with their time and hospitality during my visits to Basel. Franziska Lauper, Brigitta Gerber, Peter Habicht, and Burckhard Frey also helped indoctrinate me into the subtleties of *Fasnacht*.

1. Lionel Gossman, *Basel in the Age of Burckhardt: A Study in Unseasonable Ideas* (Chicago: University of Chicago Press, 2000); Eugen A. Meier, ed., *Die Basler Fasnacht: Geschichte und Gegenwart einer lebendigen Tradition* (Basel: Fasnachts-Comité, 1985); Christina Burckhardt-Seebass et al., eds., *Zwischentöne: Fasnacht und städtische Gesellschaft in Basel 1923–1998* (Basel: Buchverlag der Basler Zeitung, 1998).

2. Gossman, *Basel in the Age of Burckhardt*, 6.

3. Peter Habicht, *Lifting the Mask: Your Guide to the Basel Fasnacht* (Basel: Bergli Books, 2001), 79.

4. Hans Trümpy, "Zur Geschichte der Basler Fasnacht," in *Unsere Fasnacht*, ed. Peter Heman (Basel: Verlag, 1971), 17–23.

5. The earliest record of *Fasnacht* in Basel in general dates from the fourteenth century, and the celebration may well have even older roots. See Trümpy, "Zur Geschichte der Basler Fasnacht," 18.

6. Trümpy, "Zur Geschichte der Basler Fasnacht," 19. Another Monday associated elsewhere with military musters followed by festive celebrations was Whitmonday, which occurs fifty-one days after Easter. See Henning Cohen and Tristram Potter Coffin, eds., *The Folklore of American Holidays* (Detroit: Gale, 1987), 198–200.

7. Habicht, *Lifting the Mask*, 79–80.

8. Thomas Bürgi, "Geburt der Fasnacht aus dem Geist der Immigration: Die Basler Fastnacht vom Ende des Zunftregiments bis zum Ersten Weltkrieg," in Burckhardt-Seebass et al., *Zwischentöne*, 17.

9. Emmanuel Le Roy Ladurie, *The Beggar and the Professor: A Sixteenth-Century Family Saga*, trans. Arthur Goldhammer (Chicago: University of Chicago Press, 1997), 105.

10. Even before the Reformation, *Fasnacht* activities bled into Ash Wednesday and beyond. Thus it is unlikely that the Lenten timing was originally motivated by anti-Catholic sentiments. Eugen A. Meier, "Die Fasnacht im Alten Basel," in Meier, *Basler Fasnacht*, 23. Of course certain individuals may have taken advantage of this opportunity.

11. Bürgi, "Geburt der Fasnacht," 17–18.

12. Ibid., 20.

13. Trümpy, "Zur Geschichte der Basler Fasnacht," 19.

14. Adolf Adam, "Aschermittwoch," in *Lexikon für Theologie und Kirche*, vol. 1, ed. Walter Kasper (Freiburg im Breisgau: Herder, 1993), 1058–1059. Also see William James O'Shea et al., "Lent," in *New Catholic Encyclopedia*, vol. 7 (Detroit: Gale, 2003), 468–469.

15. Bürgi, "Geburt der Fasnacht," 19–21.

16. Burckhardt-Seebass et al., *Zwischentöne*; Hans Dürst, "Das Cliquenwesen und die Basler Fasnacht," *Schweizerisches Archiv für Volkskunde* 69 (1969): 2–24.

17. *Morge* (standard German: *Morgen*) means morning. *Straich (Streich)* has many meanings, several of which might apply to the name of this event. *Straich* could indicate the beating of the drum, which provides the driving rhythm during the morning. It also means prank or escapade, which also surely describes the early morning event. The English translation that best captures the sense of *Morgestraich* is "tattoo," that is, a "display of military exercises offered as entertainment" (*American Heritage Dictionary*).

18. Personal observations by the author, who has visited and participated in Basel *Fasnacht* six times since 1989.

19. Peter Tokofsky, "Charivari," in *Folklore: An Encyclopedia of Beliefs, Customs, Tales, Music, and Art*, vol. 1, ed. Thomas A. Green (Santa Barbara: ABC-CLIO, 1997), 120–121.

20. Habicht, *Lifting the Mask*, 89. Since 1998, I have participated in Basel *Fasnacht* with the Rätz-Clique, and many observations in this essay are based on conversations with members of this club during Carnival.

21. For more detailed, illustrated descriptions of these and other Basel costumes, see -minu, *d'Goschdym-Kischte* (Basel: Gissler-Verlag, 1981), and Habicht, *Lifting the Mask*, 29–34.

22. -minu, *d'Goschdym-Kischte*, 46–47, and observations by author.

23. -minu, *d'Goschdym-Kischte*, 44–45, and observations by author.

24. -minu, *d'Goschdym-Kischte*, 30–31, and observations by author.

25. -minu, *d'Goschdym-Kischte*, 22–23, and observations by author.

26. -minu, *d'Goschdym-Kischte*, 48–49. For extended discussions of the costume of the fool and the symbolism of its various components, see Werner Mezger, *Narrenidee und Fastnachtsbrauch: Studien zum Fortleben des Mittelalters in der europäischen Festkultur* (Constance: Universitätsverlag Konstanz, 1991), and William Willeford, *The Fool and His Sceptre: A Study in Clowns and Jesters and Their Audience* (Evanston, IL: Northwestern University Press, 1969).

27. -minu, *d'Goschdym-Kischte*, 58–59, and observations by author.

28. -minu, *d'Goschdym-Kischte*, 18–19, and observations by author.

29. -minu, *d'Goschdym-Kischte*, 16–17, and observations by author.

30. Since their introduction in the second half of the nineteenth century, piccolos have become an extraordinarily popular component of Basel *Fasnacht*. Habicht, *Lifting the Mask*, 22, makes the startling observation that ten thousand people

play this instrument in Basel. As he remarks, "Can you imagine any other place in the world where more than 6% of the population play the same musical instrument?"

31. Personal observations by the author.

32. For an account of this group by one of its members, see Habicht, *Lifting the Mask,* 64–69.

33. Personal observations by the author.

34. Conversations held with members of the Rätz-Clique and others.

35. Habicht, *Lifting the Mask,* 35–39, and personal observations by the author.

36. Mercedes Matas, "'s goht um d'Wurscht!" Zeitgeschichte im Spiegel von Sujets der Basler *Fasnacht* 1923–1996, dargestellt am Beispiel der vier Jubiläumscliquen," in Burckhardt-Seebass et al., *Zwischentöne,* 101–112.

37. Personal observations and conversations with members of the Rätz-Clique during *Fasnacht* 2000–2001; Habicht, *Lifting the Mask,* 42–44, 55–57.

38. Peter Tokofsky, "A Tale of Two Carnivals: Esoteric and Exoteric Performance in the *Fasnet* of Elzach," *Journal of American Folklore* 113 (2000): 357–377.

39. Personal observations by the author.

40. Habicht, *Lifting the Mask,* 51–55, and personal observations by the author.

41. E. P. Thompson, "Rough Music," in *Customs in Common: Studies in Traditional Popular Culture,* ed. E. P. Thompson (New York: New Press, 1993), 466–538.

42. The origin of this designation for the bands is uncertain. In local German and Swiss dialects, *Gugge* means paper bag, especially the conical ones carried by children on their first day of school. Perhaps some of the bands produced their sounds by blowing through paper instruments. See Dominik Wunderlin, "Die Guggenmusiken in Basel: Die Entwicklung einer fastnächtlichen Bensonderheit," *Schweizer Volkskunde* 6 (1975): 91–92.

43. Ibid., 92–93.

44. Personal observations and conversations by the author during *Fasnacht* since 1989.

45. Personal observations by the author.

46. Tom Cheeseman, *The Shocking Ballad Picture Show: German Popular Literature and Cultural History* (Oxford: Berg, 1994).

47. Personal observations by the author.

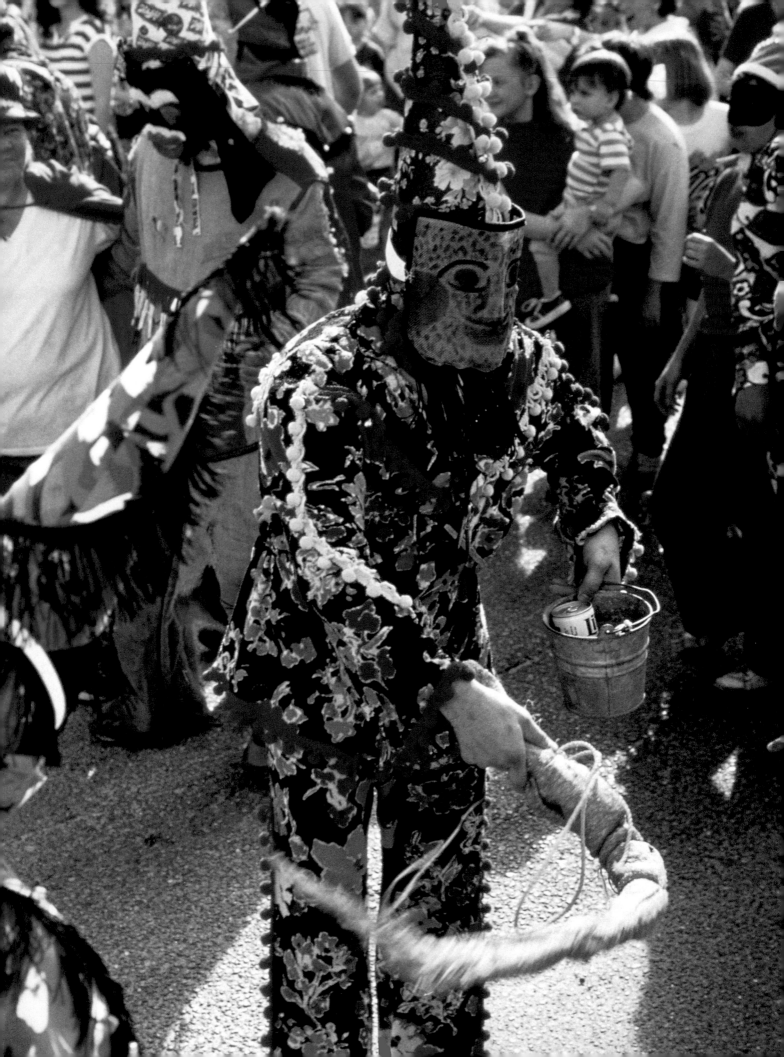

6 "That's My Day"

CAJUN COUNTRY MARDI GRAS IN BASILE, LOUISIANA, USA

CARL LINDAHL

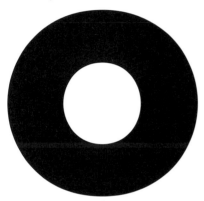

N THE PRAIRIES of southwestern Louisiana, late winter days are warm and still. Typically, the temperature hits seventy by noon. You seldom hear the thrum of tractor motors because farmers have flooded their rice fields and filled them with crawfish traps. In a good year the crawfish are fat by February, so you sometimes see men steering small, flat-bottomed boats through the fields to harvest their catch.

There are few other signs of human motion. Separated by sprawling fields, houses are set so far apart that you see only one or two others, if any, from the *gallerie,* or front porch, of your own.

At this time of year the land lacks color. The persistent brown of dead grass lines the highway. In the distance, the white feathers of low-flying egrets overlap the whiteness of the clouds. Most pervasively, all along the horizon, the blue of the flooded fields meets the often blinding blue of the sky.

To visitors, this hypnotically unvaried landscape is at best serene, at worst a portrait of monotony. It does not seem a likely stage for a wild, costumed, festive drama—which is perhaps one reason why, sitting on your *gallerie,* you easily sense the approach of the Mardi Gras revelers before you actually see them. In the fields, grazing horses raise their heads, flare their nostrils, start to dance. Seconds later, a rolling volley of whoops precedes any sight of the maskers. Simultaneously, you hear the Mardi Gras song blasting from the loudspeakers of an unseen truck.

Heads topped by tall conical hats (*capuchons*), the figures that now come into sight resemble invaders from another world (fig. 6.2). In many respects, they are exactly that. The Mardi Gras game and its past players were transported to these prairies over a period of centuries. The great majority of the ancestral revelers hailed ultimately from the Old World, though most arrived via numerous way stations in the Western Hemisphere.

Festive Roots

The base population of the culture now called Cajun was a cluster of families, predominately from west-central France, who left behind homes on two continents in the process of their long, slow journey to Louisiana. In 1632, some three hundred French peasants left their farms in Poitou and neighboring provinces on the eastern shores of the Atlantic to settle

6.1 His beggar's pail and beer in one hand and a whip in the other, Kim Moreau works the crowd during the street dance. *Photograph by Helena Putnam, 1992.*

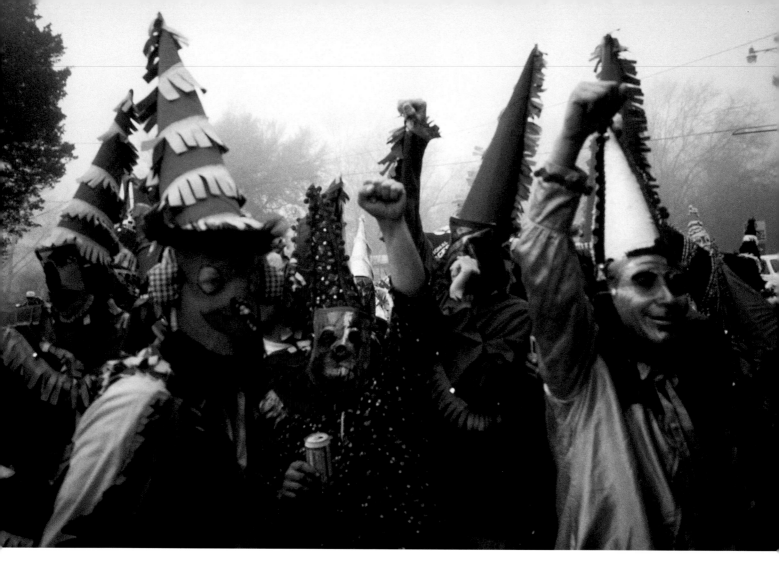

6.2 Mardi Gras *sauvages* suffuse the morning fog with unexpected color. *Photograph by Carl Lindahl, 1996.*

its chilly western shores in Acadie (or Acadia), the region known today as Nova Scotia. After more than a century in the New World, their descendants were forced into exile as the British undertook the conquest of French Canada. In a diasporic tragedy called the Grand Dérangement, or Great Displacement (1755–1770), British soldiers herded the Acadians onto ships, often dividing families in the process, and sent them off to separate destinations in England, France, Pennsylvania, Maryland, and other sites on both sides of the Atlantic. Many deportees lived migratory lives for decades before finding permanent homes; many others died without ever seeing their spouses, parents, or children again.[1]

Over time, the French culture of colonial Louisiana, still seemingly safe from the British, became a magnet for the exiles. Drawn to the isolation of the prairies,

Acadians began the process of transforming themselves into Cajuns. Having inhabited a region of extreme cold, they now had to find ways to survive the overbearing heat and humidity of the Gulf Coast. Difficult as the transition must have been, the Acadians had recently experienced far worse, and they were willing to do whatever was necessary to live reunited and unmolested.

The Cajuns were joined by other French speakers of greatly varied backgrounds who converged on the prairies from Europe and the Caribbean as well as elsewhere in North America. In 1763, as British troops drove French colonizers from the area known today as Alabama, francophone members of the Native American Koasati culture migrated into Louisiana, eventually settling a stretch of forest just west of present-day Basile. In the first decade of the nineteenth century, with the success of Haiti's slave rebellion, members of the island nation's French aristocracy fled to Louisiana; they brought with them numerous slaves who spoke Creole, a tongue born in the New World and based largely on standard European French but incorporating substantial elements from African and Caribbean Indian languages. A few years later, the collapse of Napoleon's power (1812–1814) sent numerous French soldiers to the New World, where they claimed farmland and settled alongside the Cajuns.

Thus French became the lingua franca of the prairies. The Spaniards who ruled the colony of Louisiana from 1762 to 1800 left traces of their surnames in Cajun country—Rodrique, Romero, Ortego—but their grandchildren spoke French. As slaves from Senegambia reached the colonial outpost of Pointe Coupe and joined brothers in bondage from Benin and the Bight of Biafra, all were forced to communicate with their French-speaking masters and thus began shedding their native Wolof, Bambara, Fon, and myriad other tongues. Later, substantial numbers of Germans and Irish poured into the region; after two generations they had left few traces of their old speech other than their surnames. The German Müller was Anglicized to Miller, but the inhabitants of Miller's Cove spoke French. The Irish surname McGee was retained but was considered a Cajun name by some because the great majority of the prairie farmers who bore it were French speakers.

Ultimately, it was the peasant dialect of the Cajuns that ruled. As the nineteenth century wore on, arrivals who did not speak Cajun French would have to learn it. By 1900, the great majority of the rural descendents of the Napoleonic officers and the Haitian slaves were speaking the rural French that the Acadians had brought with them from Poitou and Saintonge, with many modifications based on African and Native American speech.[2] South of the prairies it was the Africanized Creole dialect that dominated,[3] but on the prairies Cajun was the language everyone knew.

Cajun Mardi Gras

As the Mardi Gras wagons come into view, the world turns instantly bright and playfully menacing. Each of the two giant wagons carries some fifty masked *sauvages* ("Indians"). From the cuffs of their fringed pants to the tips of their *capuchons* (tall, conical, pointed hats), the *sauvages* sport colors so loud

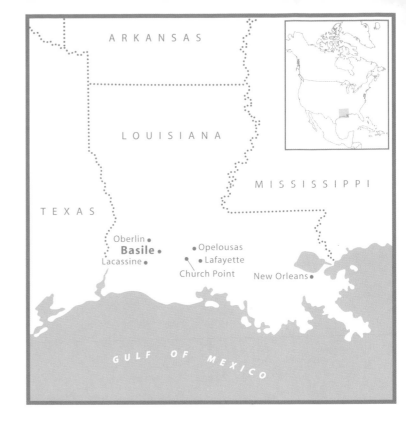

6.3 Location of Basile in the Cajun region of Louisiana.

as to do violence to the monochromatic landscape. Screaming players strain against the wooden walls of their wagons and stamp their feet on its wooden floor. As the truck draws to a halt, masked invaders race out of the wagons and into your yard. Many of them are running right at you—and it doesn't take them long to have you surrounded.

If the Cajun language seems a strange and archaic survivor in the midst of a stridently monolingual nation, then the festive language of Cajun Mardi Gras seems even stranger and more out of place. With relative accuracy and confidence, linguists can trace the various words and morphemes that constitute Cajun French back to their geographic and cultural roots, but the symbols and patterned behavior through which Cajun Mardi Gras speaks are delightfully and chaotically elusive. We know that many of the actions and trappings of Mardi Gras, as well as the name of the holiday itself, were imported from the Old World, but exactly who brought what, and when, is most often impossible to say. Poitevin France, identifiable as the ancestral home of most Cajuns and their language, cannot be established as the cradle of the Cajun Mardi Gras. Arnold van Gennep, in his magisterial survey of French calendar customs, was unable to find any written or oral memories of a festival closely parallel to

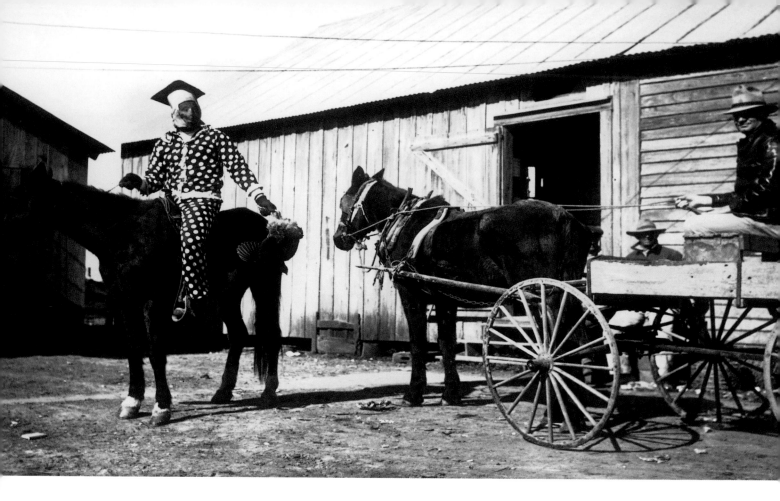

6.4 Mardi Gras reveler Ray Babineaux on his horse, holding a chicken he has taken from a neighbor's barn, 1935. *Photograph by Lauren Post.* Lauren Chester Post papers, Mss. 2854, Louisiana and Lower Mississippi Valley Collection, Louisiana State University Libraries, Baton Rouge, LA.

this one in Poitou or, for that matter, anywhere else in France.[4] Though many first-time spectators of Cajun Mardi Gras have felt themselves transported to medieval Europe, the prairie Carnival has as much to do with the cultural convergences and social environment of the New World as with memories of the Old.

Cajun country is a triangle-shaped section of southern Louisiana, occupying about one-third of the state's total territory, but the area in which the longest-documented rural Mardi Gras have taken place is even more circumscribed—a two-thousand-square-mile rectangle bounded by Lafayette, Lacassine, Oberlin, and Opelousas (fig. 6.3). This is a country of open prairies and occasional pine forests, much different from the coastal swamps that tourists typically associate with Cajuns. The region first attracted farmers. Subsistence farmers grew rice and sweet

potatoes; plantation owners grew cotton and (at the southern extremes of this region) sugar cane.

Most of the immigrants came to Louisiana bearing living festive traditions that could have contributed to the celebration of Mardi Gras. Many of the visual, kinesic, and verbal markers of Cajun Mardi Gras suggest ties to specific European, Caribbean, or African traditions, but connections cannot be definitively established. Consider, for example, the *capuchon*: it has been repeatedly claimed that this conical hat parodies the headgear worn by aristocratic women in late medieval France, but similar conical hats are also found in Spanish American and Mexican American *penitente* traditions, Irish mumming costuming, Cuban Carnival and Haitian Rara celebrations, and numerous African festive practices.[5] Similarly, Basile's Mardi Gras song, with its call-and-response pattern, has been presumed by some to derive from African tradition, and by others, from the military call-and-response chants of Napoleonic officers. Yet the closest analogues to the song's text come not from the Caribbean or France but from enclaves of French Americans in rural Missouri, near the Mississippi River, where costumed beggars yearly sing a New Year's song resembling the Mardi Gras song.[6] Was the text of this song brought to Louisiana by Frenchmen traveling from the north? Was the style in which the song was sung imported by Haitian-born slaves traveling from the south? And what is the source of the pervasive figure of the *sauvage,* or Indian? Was it derived from New Orleans Mardi Gras "Indians," from the proximity of the Koasati tribe, or from a pervasive tendency of Carnivals worldwide to identify their most unruly players as savages or wild men?

Guessing can go on forever, especially because what we can say about the history of Mardi Gras is so little. Surviving evidence from before 1900 is extremely scant. A register dating to about 1877 from an Opelousas general store records orders for New York-made wire-screen masks.[7] There is a late-nineteenth-century handwritten text of a song, similar to current Mardi Gras songs, that is described as having been sung by "a chorus of bearded men" (from *barbus,* a term still applied to masks that have yarn or horsehair "beards" dangling from their chins). A few newspaper items, more suggestive than informative, date from around 1900.[8] In the face of such meager evidence, almost any one of the dozen competing theories concerning the origin of Mardi Gras can be considered as valid as any other. All that can be said for certain is that by the early decades of the twentieth century, the rural celebration had taken on the traits and assumed the form by which it is known today, as evidenced by early photographs (fig. 6.4).

Where Cajun Mardi Gras ultimately came from may be an unanswerable question, but such historical confusion does nothing to shake revelers' convictions concerning ownership of the festival. In each of twenty small rural communities on the prairie today, Mardi Gras's most ardent players know that the game is theirs, that it belongs to them, and that it reflects who they are so fully that they take pride in saying that they live for Mardi Gras. To begin to figure out why they identify so passionately with the holiday, we must watch and listen to the festive actors.[9]

The Power of the Mask

Dozens of masked figures are moving toward you at various speeds and in unsettling postures. In some ways more disconcerting than those who charge are those who stalk. Although there is no place to hide in this naked landscape, maskers pretend they are sneaking up on you. One crouches as he lopes toward you with a simian gait. Another approaches crawling on his hands and knees (fig. 6.5) while uttering a wordless threat: "Ooo-ooo-ooo-ooo," a sound somewhere between the moan of a ghost and the hoot of an owl. The crawling *sauvage* doesn't stop until he's wrapped an arm around your leg. He starts to untie your shoe, while the loping *sauvage* drops to one knee and thrusts an empty palm in your face, a wordless demand for money (see fig. 6.20). As you empty a handful of coins into the masked man's palm, a third *sauvage,* charging up from behind, thrusts his hands into your pockets to make sure you've given enough (fig. 6.6).

You are suddenly surrounded by a dozen faces: six masks shaped from seemingly transparent window screens and six half-revealed human faces just behind

6.5 Mardi Gras *sauvages,* stealthy and conspicuous, stalk a chicken at one of the houses they visit during their day-long invasion of Basile. *Photograph Carl Lindahl, 1998.*

125

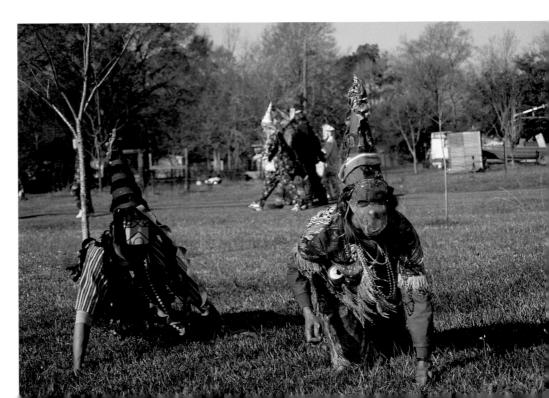

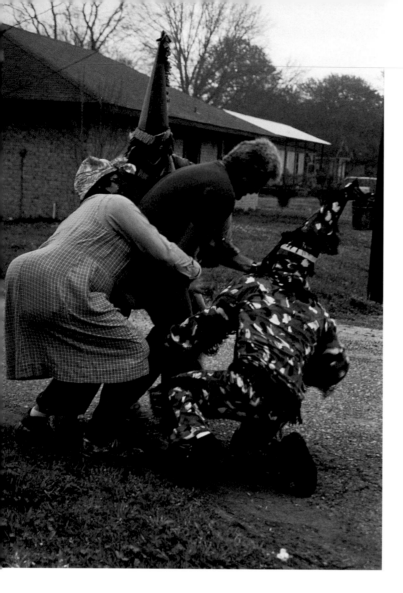

6.6 Three Mardi Gras surround their victim, intent on having either his money or his belt and shoes. *Photograph by Helena Putnam, 1991.*

the wire mesh. You half-know all of these *sauvages*. Each face is both reassuringly familiar and hauntingly strange.

In celebrations of Carnival worldwide, the mask most commonly transforms the wearer by obscuring the real face. But in Basile, Louisiana, the masks both hide and reveal the faces behind them—by offering just enough of the wearer's identity to tease you with the notion that you should be able to know the man on the other side of the screen.[10] Masks that transform their wearers and wearers who transform their masks together shape a festival that will reveal two faces from almost any angle from which it is viewed.

Outsiders are pleased and startled by the immediate sensory appeal of these disguises. But insiders tend to

center their love and understanding of the festival exactly at that point where the mesh of the screen mask meets the flesh of the wearer—and on the ways in which the wearer's features and personality can animate the homely tools of disguise to create something astonishingly new from the most timeworn and familiar. The Cajun neighbors tend to be less impressed by the disguise than by the art of the player lurking behind it.

What the entire traveling troupe does to transform the prairie landscape, each creative practitioner of Mardi Gras does to enliven her mask, his costume, so that the momentary strangeness and surface appeal of the suits, *capuchons,* and masks become merely the platforms upon which well-known neighbors parade their play selves. For its core participants, Mardi Gras in Basile, Louisiana, is both the most public and the most intimate moment of the year. The better you know the players, the more delight you draw from their play.

True to the nature of the festival, the best masks are themselves two-sided. One great Basile mask maker, J. B. LeBlue, most enjoys fashioning a mask "so ugly that it's beautiful and so beautiful that it's ugly."[11] Viewed empty, held in the hand or hanging on the wall, one of J. B.'s more spare and abstract masks takes on the appearance of a skull or the face of a monkey—marvelously suggestive, but much more beautiful than ugly, much more likely to attract than repel the viewer's eye (fig. 6.7). Once the mask is fitted to a face, however, the mutual transformation takes place, and a Carnival grotesqueness suffuses the mask as the pattern and the face run together (fig. 6.8). All of these artworks are tools, simple and adaptable. Each mask may approximate, but will never supplant, the wildly two-sided nature of the player who wears it.

The term Mardi Gras carries four distinct meanings for Cajuns.[12] Most literally, it is a slot on the calendar: "Fat Tuesday," the day preceding Ash Wednesday. Mardi Gras also names the celebration that falls on that date. But Mardi Gras is human, too: the term is used to label a person or, more characteristically, a group. In using "Mardi Gras" to name both the holiday and its celebrants, Cajuns set their celebration apart from the far better known festivities that take place in New Orleans and other Gulf Coast cities. The urban maskers who parade on floats through crowded streets identify themselves as "krewes," but there are no krewes

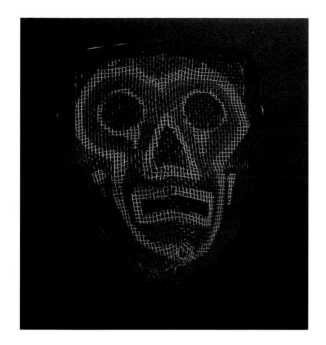

6.7 "So ugly that it's beautiful": Mardi Gras mask by J. B. LeBlue. Window screen, acrylic paint, hot glue, felt. *Photograph by Carl Lindahl, 1996.*

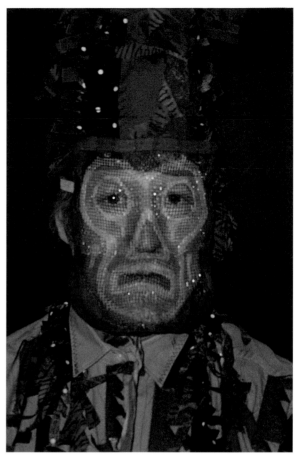

6.8 "So beautiful that it's ugly": the same mask, when worn, meshes with facial features to create an unsettling image. *Photograph by Heather Bohannan, 1996.*

in the Cajun countryside; the roving revelers simply call themselves "the Mardi Gras," and wherever they go, they transform everything they touch into more Mardi Gras. In the cities, tourists crowd the parade routes to watch the krewes, but the Cajun Mardi Gras carry their festival right to the front doors of their hosts. The name attaches itself to special players: an exceptional performer may receive the title "Best All Around Mardi Gras" from the leaders of the Basile celebration. And when the troupe overruns your front yard, clusters around your porch, and starts to sing, the whole group identities itself as "the Mardi Gras":

> C'est les Mardi Gras, ça devient de loin, ça devient
> de l'Angleterre.
> The Mardi Gras, they come from far away, they come
> from England.[13]

With these words, your closest neighbors present themselves as foreigners on their own home turf, temporarily turning your shared world upside down. Thus, linguistically, as in so many other ways, the holiday and its celebrants are so tightly intertwined as to become indistinguishable. Some community members watch the Mardi Gras; some host the Mardi Gras;

but a significant portion of the population of Basile—as much as 10 percent—*is* the Mardi Gras. The maskers are the festival.

Preparations

In many locales—most immediately, New Orleans—Mardi Gras encompasses not just one day but a whole festive season. Cajuns, however, tend to be more literal minded in their observance, confining their play to one day. Some communities spread out the festivities to accommodate two or more groups. In Basile, for example, the children hold their Mardi Gras on the Sunday before their parents run. In a few places to the west and south of Basile, at the western fringe of the Cajun prairies, the same Mardi Gras troupe travels through the neighboring countryside on two or three successive days. But these are the exceptions.

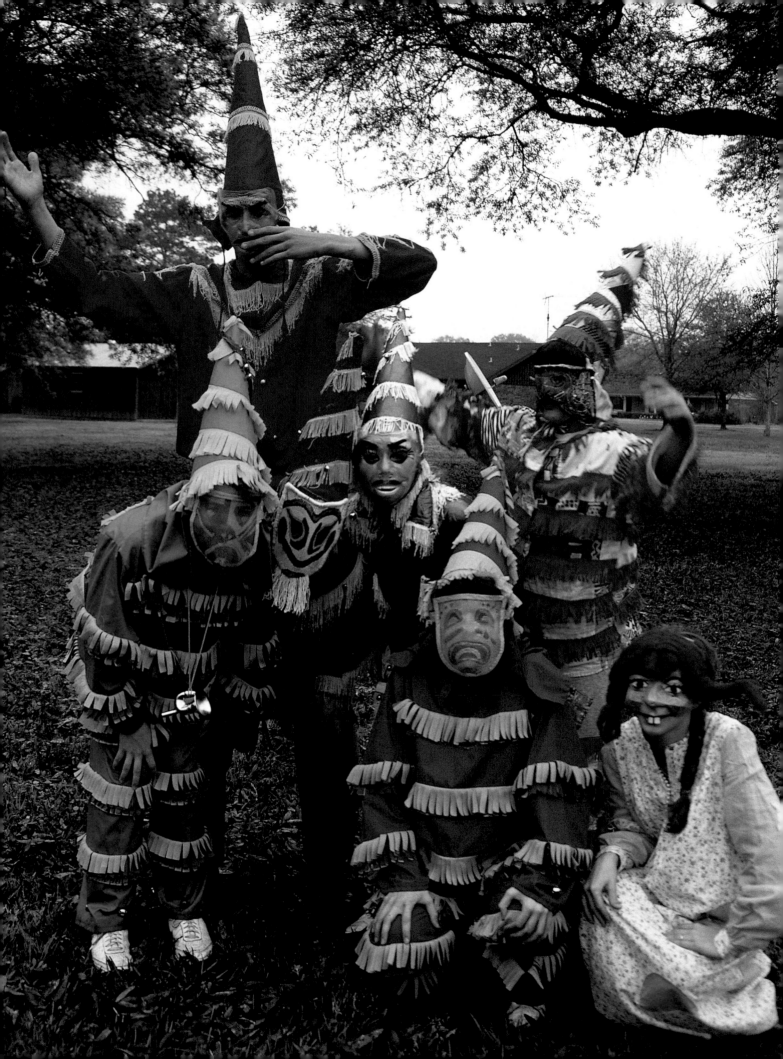

For the great majority of Cajuns, Mardi Gras is only one day.

There is no substitute for this one day, and no consolation for missing it. The brevity and small scale of the festival seem only to intensify the performance as the core revelers unload months of anticipation into fourteen hours of play. Cajun Mardi Gras may seem to end almost as soon as it has begun, but like American Christmas, it is preceded by a long period of anticipation and, once past, is recollected and retold by its participants and witnesses for years to come.

Although Cajun Mardi Gras has no season, it is nevertheless preceded by a "season of expectation" just as long as, and far more intense than, the period of planning. Basile—like a dozen neighboring prairie communities—possesses a Mardi Gras association. This official arm of the festival secures the logistic frame for the revelers' one-day ride through the countryside. In a series of meetings beginning after Epiphany, a small group of elected officers meets with other members to determine who will drive the trucks to pull the wagons and who will staff the support vehicles needed to carry the celebrants' beer and the chickens they capture. These meetings also refine strategies for institutional begging—determining which local organizations to solicit for funds, beer, or food to supplement the money raised through last year's festive begging.

In Basile, few participate in the official business of Mardi Gras, but the most dedicated players have their own unofficial, small-scale ways of counting down the days. They feed each other's festive appetites by singing and playing the traditional Mardi Gras song. Basile was the home of the great accordionist Nathan Abshire, and "Mr. Nathan's" recording of "La Chanson de Mardi Gras" plays repeatedly throughout January and early February, especially in public venues such as Da Office Bar, where the song is featured on the jukebox. Before jukeboxes came to Basile, "Bad-eye" Bellon, a great Mardi Gras of the World War II era, would phone his neighbors or stop them on the street to sing

a verse of the *chanson*—without so much as an introductory "hello." Indeed, for that one month, the Mardi Gras song served effectively as a greeting among celebrants, a way of sharing the otherwise private feelings of eagerness surging inside them.[14]

Crafting of costumes is typically a seasonal affair, both a utilitarian preparation and a psychic buildup for the holiday. Although some professionals sew and market costumes throughout the year, costume making remains largely a family matter. Females almost invariably fashion the Mardi Gras "suits" for themselves and their husbands, brothers, and children. The suit is generically amorphous: a pair of baggy pants topped by an equally loose-fitting shirt worn outside the pants and hanging down well below the belt line. Top and bottom are cut from the same material to convey a one-piece appearance, a look so standard that it could be called a Mardi Gras uniform. The suits so obscure the shape of the wearer that even the host-neighbors are sometimes unable to determine the sexes of the revelers who crowd their yards (fig. 6.9).

Women also typically make the Mardi Gras hats. By far the most common shape is the conical *capuchon*,

6.10 Kim Moreau wears a shell-shaker screen mask made by his father, Vories, in 1950, together with a costume and *capuchon* decorated in chili peppers. *Photograph by Carl Lindahl, 1996.*

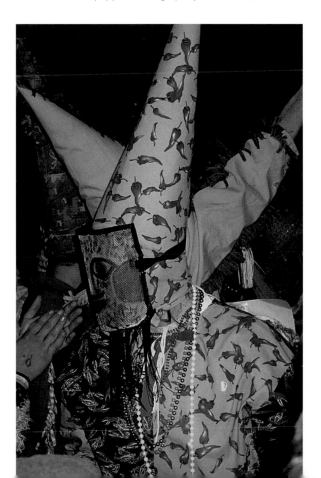

6.9 The Mardi Gras "uniform." Seven *sauvages* display the aesthetic norm and the range of costume styles. Here are six traditional fringed suits and one makeshift dress, six conical *capuchons,* four traditional wire screen masks, and three plastic masks. *Photograph by Helena Putnam, 1992.*

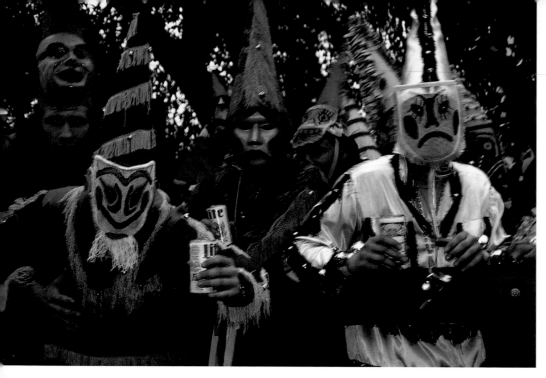

6.11 Inside the men's wagon, Basile *sauvages* begin to menace their audience even before departing on their daylong journey. *Photograph by Carl Lindahl, 1992.*

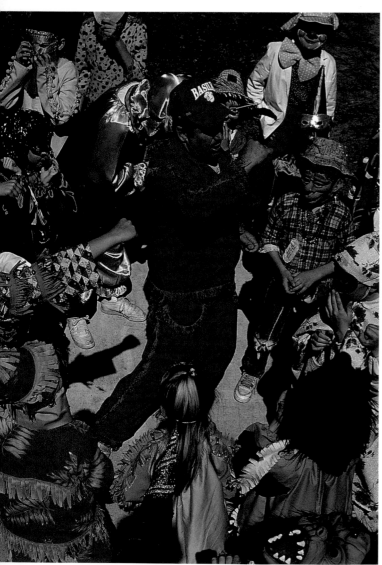

6.12 Potic Rider, president of the Basile Mardi Gras Riders Association, leads the children's Mardi Gras in the begging song. *Photograph by Helena Putnam, 1991.*

which typically displays the same pattern that adorns the wearer's suit. Suspended from the back and sides of the *capuchon* is a flap of cloth long enough to cover the ears and hair of the guiser. These three pieces are calculated to create mass anonymity, giving all members of the group a shared and nearly shapeless appearance.[15]

In Basile, masks are as likely to be made by males as by females. Only the mask offers a potential window into the identity of the wearer. Most often fashioned from wire mesh, the mask is in fact a sort of screen window. With her face up against the screen, the wearer clearly sees the features of those she encounters, but the mesh distorts her face to those who attempt to recognize her as they stand on the outside, looking in.[16]

This costume, like the entire celebration, combines the simplest and most homely ingredients with the richest imagination. The essential materials have always been relatively inexpensive and easy to find—by-products of everyday home life, broken down and now ready for recycling. In the first half of the twentieth century, burlap feed sacks constituted the major material for the suits and the coverings of the *capuchons*. Most of the suits shared the same dead-brown color of the grass lining the roads in late winter. This

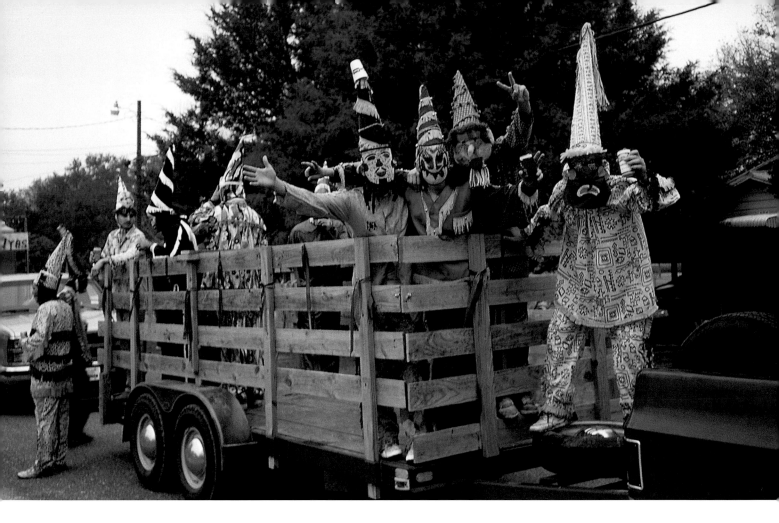

6.13 The men's Mardi Gras wagon begins its journey.
Photograph by Carl Lindahl, 1992.

pervasive brown was relieved by colorful fringes: rows of small cloth strips hanging from the arms, legs, and torso. Such fringes render the suit reminiscent of the buckskin clothing of Plains Indians. For many, this resemblance is more than coincidental. Mardi Gras guisers are called "Indians" (*sauvages*), and in their play they impersonate Indians in broadly stereotypical ways—with their high-pitched, birdlike whoops and the stealthy gestures they use in stalking their hosts.[17] Today's suits are no longer buckskin brown but vary brilliantly in color because they are made from patterned cloth.

Most mask makers favor discarded window screens, though some of the Basile men, notably those of the Moreau family, use a very heavy-gauge "shell-shaker" screen, a mesh used to filter gravel from the pipelines in the oilfields where many Cajuns work (fig. 6.10). In the nineteenth century, before screen windows were commonplace on the prairies, general stores sold metal mesh masks. Those who could afford them, bought

them, because they offered cooling facial ventilation on a hot February day. As late as the mid-twentieth century, players who could not afford a screen mask fashioned a close-fitting head covering from the denim of discarded blue jeans—a material that could make the mask oppressively hot.

Mask and costume makers intensify the mounting spirit of anticipation by doing most of their work in the days just before Mardi Gras. Many costumes remain unfinished even on the eve of the celebration; neighbors borrow and trade material and finished masks and *capuchons* almost up to the moment that Mardi Gras begins.[18]

Mardi Gras Day

Cajun Mardi Gras combines two simple acts: a daylight progress through town and country, followed by an evening *bal* (ball) in the center of the community.[19] The masked journey is advertised as a quest for chickens and other foodstuffs to create a gumbo for the people of the town. In the words of Basile's "Chanson de Mardi Gras":

C'est les Mardi Gras, ça demande à la maitresse, à la
maitresse,
Pour une petite poule grasse, et du riz ou de la graisse.
It's the Mardi Gras who ask the mistress of the house,
the mistress of the house,
For a little fat hen, and some rice or some grease (lard).

The group passes from home to home not merely to collect food but equally to prepare for a giant party. Most particularly, the maskers seek company for the dance that will end the festivities. In one of the song's stanzas, the Mardi Gras enjoin their *capitaine* to make haste to ensure that there will be time to invite everyone:

Capitaine, capitaine, voyage ton flag and hale ton camp;
La route est grande, la nuit est longue, et les belles sont
pas invitées.
Captain, captain, wave your flag and get moving;
The road is long, the night is long, and the pretty girls
haven't yet been invited.

Thus, the Mardi Gras's morning mission is to secure food for the town, and its goal for the evening is to bring the whole town together to feast, to dance, and to court.

On the Monday night preceding Mardi Gras, groups of young men and women stay up late to party, sometimes missing sleep altogether. The most fervent participants are too excited to sleep, even if they try. They often compare their sleepless anticipa-

tion to the insomnia experienced by American children awaiting Santa's arrival on Christmas Eve, the major difference being that for the key players, Mardi Gras has always been "bigger than Christmas."

Many revelers haggle with their employers to make sure that their jobs will be secure if they miss work on Mardi Gras. Even since Mardi Gras has become a Louisiana state holiday, some companies will fire those who miss work to join the guisers. Residents of Basile often describe the lengths to which they've gone to ensure their freedom to play. Vories Moreau had a set speech prepared for any boss who might threaten his holiday: "I'll work for you Christmas. I'll work for you Sunday. I'll work overtime every day. But I won't work on Mardi Gras. That's my day."[20] Vories always succeeded in counteracting his employers' threats, but many other Basile *sauvages* have lost their jobs, paying palpable tolls for favoring their play world over the "real" one.

The day's play begins in the predawn hours as maskers assemble at a central location—most recently, the metal-roofed pavilion in Basile's town park. Many arrive in full costume, guarding their identities even from their closest friends, and thus begin the festive activities with inwardly directed play calculated to trick their fellow Mardi Gras. A good deal of role testing and basic training takes place during this warm-up period (fig. 6.11).

Once the participants have paid their fees and submitted to a frisking, Potic Rider, president of Basile's Mardi Gras Riders Association, lays out the rules: no weapons, no fighting, no vandalizing the hosts' prop-

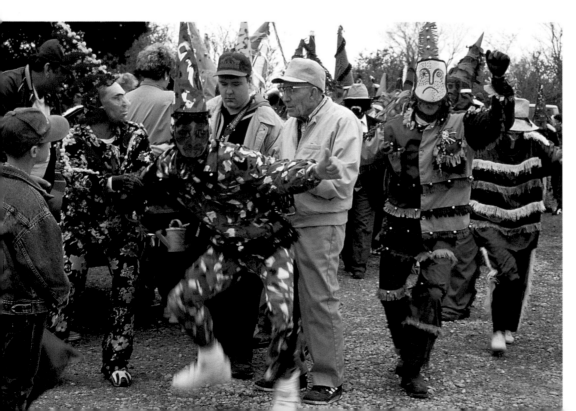

6.14 Mardi Gras maskers overrun their host's yard. *Photograph by Helena Putnam, 1992.*

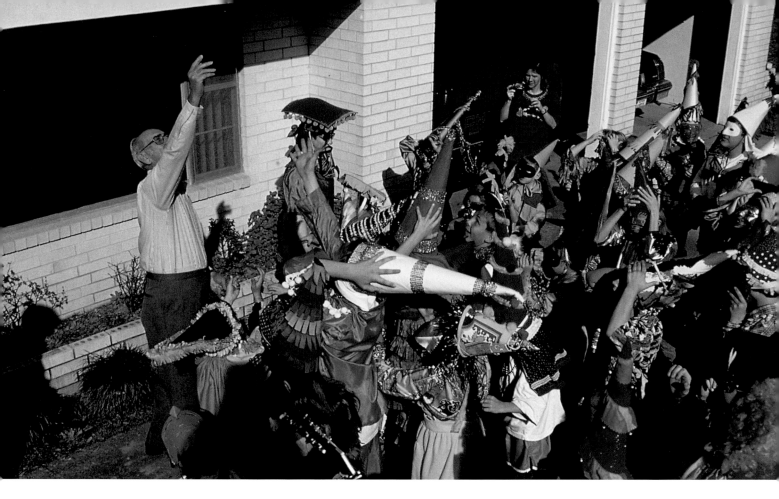

6.15. During a house visit, the host throws coins into the air to reward the masked troupe of children for their begging song. *Photograph by Helena Putnam, 1992.*

erty, and above all, no challenging the rule of the *capitaines*. Potic then leads the maskers in singing "La Chanson de Mardi Gras," a performance they will repeat dozens of times before the day has ended (fig. 6.12). Then, as the *capitaines* read their names aloud, the Mardi Gras file into two long, tall-sided trailers (fig. 6.13)—one for the men and one for the women—and the festival begins. It is seven AM.

About one hundred masked, costumed Mardi Gras, both male and female, and four or more unmasked *capitaines* with capes and whips have begun their motorcade through the town. The procession stops at many homes and small businesses in town, a few on the outskirts, and one or two in the outlying farmlands that, fifty years ago, formed the heart of Mardi Gras country. Before three PM the masked troupe will perform as many as forty visits to neighboring houses and businesses, during which celebrants perform potentially infinite and often inspired variations on a simple pattern.

When the procession draws to a halt, maskers wait in their wagons as their *capitaines* walk up to the host's house to ask permission for the Mardi Gras to enter the yard. Once invited, a *capitaine* waves a flag in the air, summoning the troupe onto the host's property (fig. 6.14).

The group clusters tightly around the gallerie to sing the Mardi Gras song for its benefactors. Potic Rider and a few other seasoned Mardi Gras sing most of the words, with the whole group joining in on the chorus:

Les Mardi Gras, ça vient une fois par an demander la charité.
Une fois par an, c'est pas trop souvent pour vous quand même.
C'est les Mardi Gras, c'est tout des bons jeunes gens,
Des bons jeunes gens, ça devient de toutes des bonnes familles.
(Chorus:) Tout le tour autour du moyeu.
C'est pas des malfaiteurs, c'est juste de quémandeurs.

The Mardi Gras come once a year to ask for charity.
Once a year is really not too often for you.

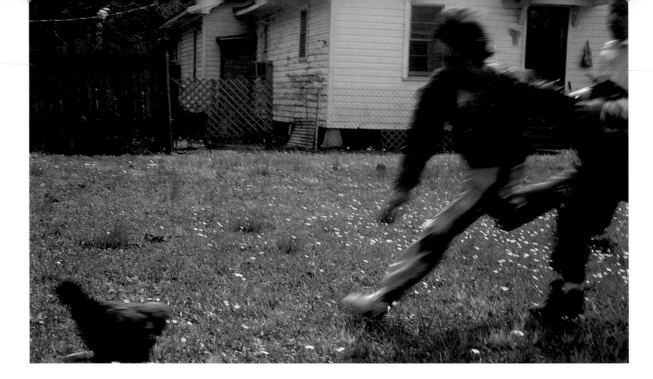

6.16 Running down a chicken at Basile's children's Mardi Gras. *Photograph by Carl Lindahl, 1991.*

> *It's the Mardi Gras who are all good people,*
> *Good people who all come from good families.*
> *(Chorus:) All around the hub.*
> *They are not evildoers, they are just beggars.*

The players pump their fists in the air as they sing the chorus. Then the unmasked musicians who are traveling with the Mardi Gras play a waltz and a Cajun two-step as masked Mardi Gras engage their unmasked watchers in dancing.

Once they have put on a "good show" at the house, the troupe receives a gift from the host: a chicken, rice, onions, or other ingredients for the evening's gumbo—or money (fig. 6.15). In the minds of most Mardi Gras, the chicken is the grand prize. This gift is not simply handed over to the Mardi Gras but presented to one of the *capitaines,* who throws the bird into the air. The Mardi Gras must run it down and capture it. Sometimes the chase ends instantaneously as the chicken flies directly into the masked crowd. Other times, pursuit continues for ten or twenty minutes while the chicken outruns the Mardi Gras, threading the lines of a barbed-wire fence as the pursuing runners get tangled in it. Or the chicken might run under a house or car, only to dash out the other side when maskers crawl after it. No matter how long the pursuit, the Mardi Gras procession will not resume without the

captured chicken. And no matter how easy the chase, catching a chicken is considered a triumph. The captor is regarded, at least momentarily, as a community hero. The value placed on catching a chicken is so high that few people forget when and how they caught their first (figs. 6.16, 6.17, 6.18).

Finally, once the chicken has been captured, *capitaine* Gilbert Leblanc breaks up the revelry by sound-

6.17 *Sauvage* Helena Putnam salutes the chicken she has just caught. *Photograph by Maida Owens, 1993.*

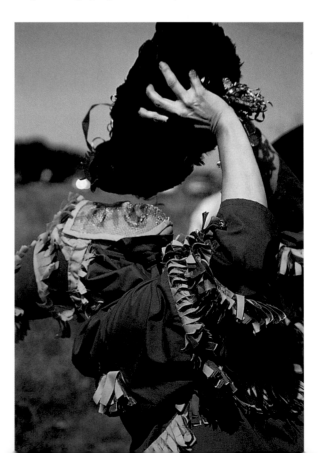

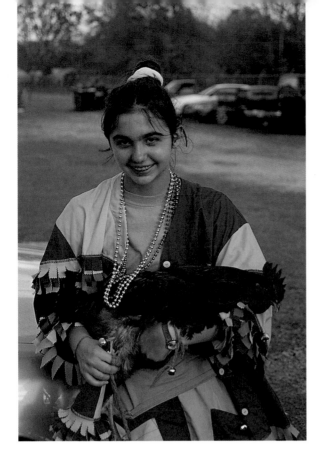

6.18 Even at the end of the day, one young *sauvage* still has trouble letting go of her captured chicken. *Photograph by Carl Lindahl, 2001.*

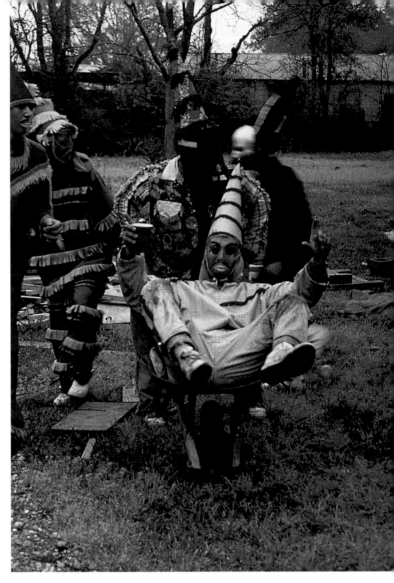

6.19 Having run off with their host's wheelbarrow, two *sauvages* take a third for a ride. *Photograph by Helena Putnam, 1992.*

ing his horn to summon the *sauvages* back to the road to resume their procession.

Such is the prescribed traditional form of Basile's Mardi Gras, a shape generally shared with other prairie communities. Equally traditional, though not confined to a structural slot, are a number of *niches* (practical jokes) and extempore games that various Mardi Gras perform whenever they can get away with it. For example, every time the troupe enters a host's yard, some Mardi Gras invariably run loose, climbing trees or telephone poles (see p. vi), commandeering a water hose and turning it on to soak other players, or riding off in any wheeled object that can be found in the yard (fig. 6.19). At such times, the whip-bearing *capitaines* lash them back into the fold.

Anything goes during these improvised moments, but in Basile the most common tricks are variations on begging. Anyone without a costume is fair game. The Mardi Gras sometimes present themselves as supplicants to their victims. Walking on her knees, mask level with her victim's belly, a *sauvage* will thrust her hands outward, pointing with the forefinger of one

hand into the empty palm of the other, and in a high-pitched, "Indian" voice demand *tits cinq sous,* "five little pennies" (fig. 6.20). If such tactics do not produce immediate results, beggars quickly grow aggressive (fig. 6.21). They surround civilians and unlace their shoes, remove their belts, run off with their hats. The players often refuse to return these possessions until the owner coughs up cash. The boldest extortionists surface when the procession crosses a highway. They lie down in the road to stop traffic, buying time for their companions to bang on the windows of stalled cars and wrangle money from the drivers (fig. 6.22).

The more outrageous the stunt, the more likely that the *sauvages* will be whipped by the *capitaines*. In Basile, there are four or more whip-bearing *capitaines,* at least two males and two females. Their weap-

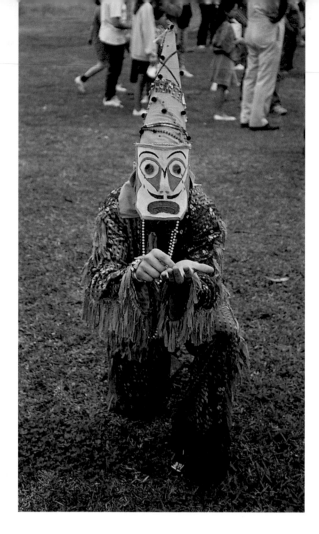

6.20 The classic Basile beggar's pose. *Photograph by Carl Lindahl, 1992.*

6.21 A pitch for charity with an undercurrent of extortion. Two Mardi Gras aggressively gesture for money. *Photograph by Mary Caroline Ancelet, 1992.*

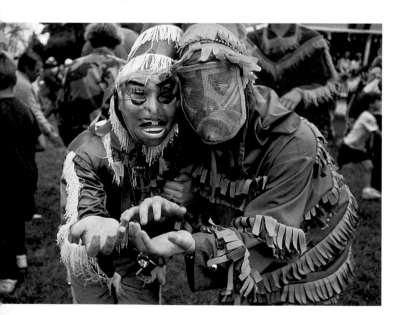

ons are not merely props. Made of leather, they range from buggy whips to bull whips. Sometimes a *capitaine* restores order just by waving or cracking the whip, but the most playful Mardi Gras invariably attract at least a few lashes. These strokes can be painful, but they neither put an end to the *niches* nor create animosity between the *capitaines* and the *sauvages*. As appallingly brutal as these whipping episodes seem to many outsiders, the Mardi Gras and their community regard them as an essential ingredient of the day's entertainment.

Climactic Processions

By about three PM the cycle of house visits has ended and the Mardi Gras—having, in the space of eight hours, performed forty songs and eighty dances, chased twenty chickens, pulled off innumerable athletic stunts, submitted to several whippings, and consumed prodigious quantities of beer—are understandably exhausted. The players rest for half an hour, gather their strength, straighten their costumes (by now torn and dirtied from the effects of chicken chasing and other acts of madness), and prepare for a series of more formal and less wild theatrics.

On Main Street, an open-air party is in progress. A band is playing, booths staffed by local charitable organizations are vending food and drink, and perhaps two hundred of Basile's citizens are milling, waiting for their Mardi Gras to return. The players assemble at the quiet end of the street, beyond the press of the crowd, to form a double-file line headed by the senior members of the troupe. As the band strikes up the Mardi Gras song, the players dance in procession to the bandstand (fig. 6.23), where they perform a waltz and a two-step and sing their Mardi Gras song, as they did earlier during the house visits. This time, they linger for an hour, some continuing to work the crowd for money (see fig. 6.1), others dancing with the unmasked spouses, girlfriends, or boyfriends who have come to welcome them back.

After the street dance, the *sauvages* return to the pavilion, where their day began, and eat the ceremonial gumbo. As a reward for securing food for the town, the Mardi Gras are served first; after them, all comers are invited to eat (fig. 6.24).[21]

Now follows another period of rest and regrouping

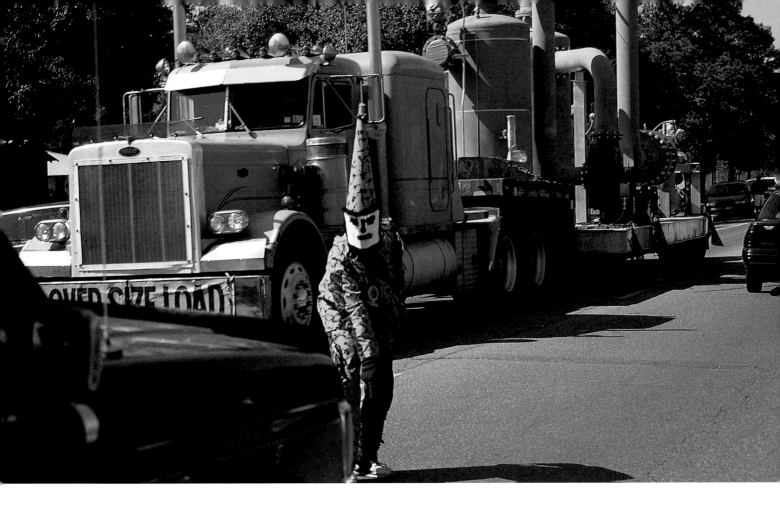

6.22 Stopping trucks on US 190. *Photograph by Carl Lindahl, 2000.*

6.23 Parading with a "Men Working" sign, a large plastic pail, and other props they have picked up on their journey, the Mardi Gras dance down Main Street. *Photograph by Carl Lindahl, 2001.*

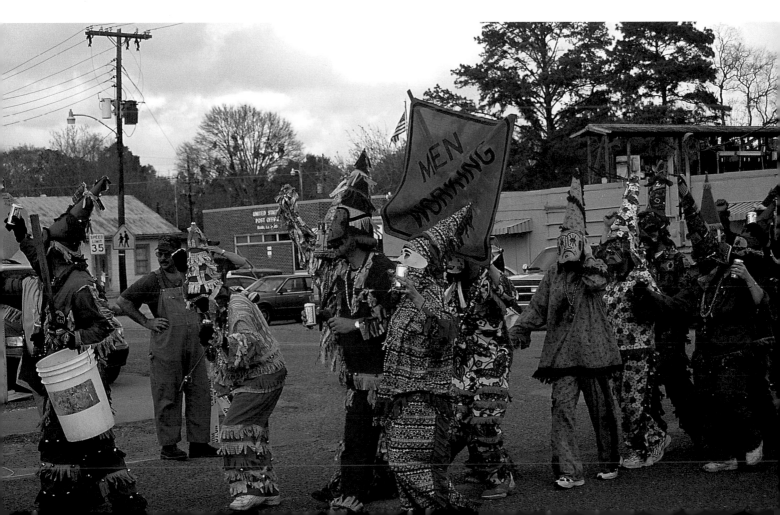

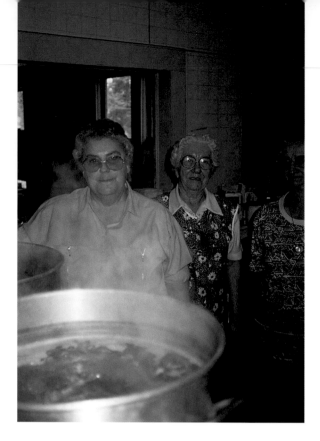

6.24 Euta Young, Agnes Miller, and Alice Young nurture Basile's Mardi Gras gumbo. *Photograph by Carl Lindahl, 1992.*

6.25 Flanked by their *capitaines,* the Basile Mardi Gras open the *bal* with a processional dance. *Photograph by Carl Lindahl, 1998.*

for the Mardi Gras's final and most formal festive act, the evening ball. Many Basile players wear two costumes on Mardi Gras day: a play suit and a *bal* suit. The play suit is the more rugged and the less expensive: it has to serve for a day of wild play and will almost certainly be damaged by day's end. But because the evening ball is more a visual spectacle than an occasion for insane play, and because prizes are awarded for costumes at the ball, the more lavish, delicate suits will be worn there.

The ball repeats, with elaboration, the structure of the street dance: a grand processional, the guisers dancing two by two to "La Chanson de Mardi Gras" (figs. 6.25, 6.26), followed by a series of waltzes and two-steps performed by the maskers and one last a cappella rendition of the Mardi Gras song. Now the judges bestow awards for most original (which is often construed, ironically, as most traditional), prettiest, and ugliest costume. The *capitaines* then decide the winner of the most coveted trophy: "Best All Around Mardi Gras." Then the rest of the town joins in the dance, which must end by midnight—because, hard as they might play on Mardi Gras day, most of the players are devout Catholics and will be on their knees tomorrow morning, begging forgiveness for their sins

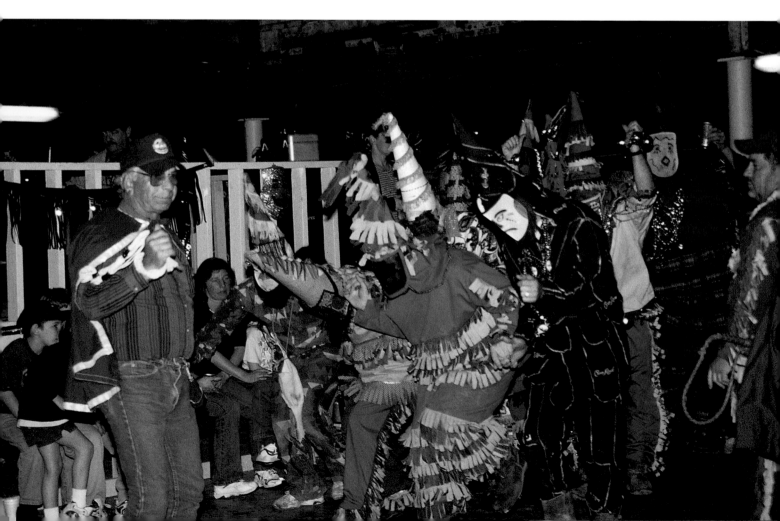

and receiving penitential ashes from their priest. As one Mardi Gras player told me, "If you do Mardi Gras right, you'll have plenty to pray about in church next morning." Indeed, those who have done Mardi Gras right are already feeling the effects as the dance continues. After a day of almost uninterrupted excess and madness, most of the revelers have left the dance by nine o'clock.

Remembered History, Rural Roots, and Their Importance for the Current Celebration

The yearly masked procession that unfolds on the Cajun prairies at the dawn of the twenty-first century seems at first glance so archaic and otherworldly that it naturally invites outsiders to speculate over how such an "ancient" game can persist with such vitality. Scholars quarrel endlessly over the origins of this vibrant play, seeking simple strands of descent in the unruly cultural weave of southern Louisiana. Yet when Cajun Mardi Gras is practiced today, few players find much need to invoke unknowable origins.

The current festival is in many respects consciously old-fashioned, but it is not archaic. Although many devotees think of their festival as an ancient legacy, connecting them to an otherwise unremembered time when all Cajuns were French or all Creoles were African, most of the players, born in an English-speaking world, most strongly identify Mardi Gras as an immediate hand-me-down from their grandparents, who were quite literally born in another world, a world of French speakers and subsistence farms. No matter which origin theory a Cajun may espouse, she most persistently experiences Mardi Gras as a time-defying bridge leading her back to the days when the oldest people she knows were children. Core revelers talk about how the older people "gave us" the Mardi Gras that is celebrated today. The general shape of the festival and many of its leading traits stretch back to the limits of, but seldom beyond, living memory, to enact the values and patterns of life, both as experienced by the oldest living Cajuns and as idealized by the youngest celebrants.

Many of the central props and actions point back to the agrarian lifestyle that predominated in the region before 1950. The chicken chase reflects a time when most Cajuns lived on farms and owned poultry.

The gumbo served on Mardi Gras was a traditional holiday meal for prairie farmers. The cycle of house visits and the climactic gumbo fill the day from sunup to sundown, reflecting the rural workday as older Cajuns experienced it.

Many Cajuns, feeling the loss of their traditional lifestyles in the face of a homogenizing American culture, work to preserve what they see as the "oldest" and "purest" aspects of the holiday. Accordingly, some Mardi Gras associations have taken steps to institute rules that work against change. All participants in the Tee Mamou celebration, for example, are required to wear *capuchons*. Such regimentation may conform to an ideal of the past, but it does not really reflect any given past era, for older Cajuns cannot recall a time when Mardi Gras costuming was uniform.

6.26 In twin Mardi Gras suits, sisters Heather and Brandi Putnam dance at the Mardi Gras *bal. Photograph by Helena Putnam, 1991.*

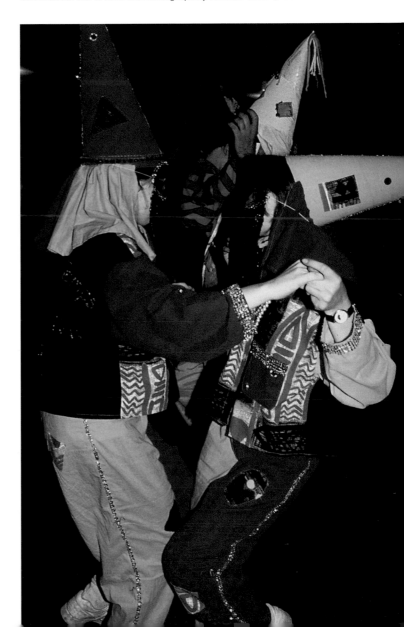

Cajun attitudes toward Mardi Gras are two-sided, combining a reverence for tradition with a willingness to accept, even embrace, change. Two of Basile's most radical departures from established tradition occurred two generations ago, and both departures are now themselves traditional for the town's players. First, the Mardi Gras processions of the first half of the twentieth century took place on horseback (although a few communities traversed their routes on foot or in horse-drawn buggies). By mid-century, Basile was losing most of its family farms; as former farmers moved to town, horseback Mardi Gras processions became increasingly impractical. Changing its mode of loco-motion to accommodate the changing shape of its community, Basile became one of the first Mardi Gras to convert to mechanized transportation. Second, at mid-century, nearly all Cajun Mardi Gras were all-male affairs. Basile was one of the first communities to wel-

come a separate women's Mardi Gras, which later merged with the male run, creating perhaps the first sexually integrated such celebration on the prairies. Currently, Basile is the only Mardi Gras with female *capitaines* (fig. 6.27), whose positions of power allow them to whip male *sauvages*.

If some players revere what they consider to be the "ancient" nature of their game, few are deterred from absorbing changing fashions into their play. In Basile, some of the "newer" aspects of the festival—traits that would not have been considered traditional, or perhaps acceptable, two decades ago but which are now embraced by most of the players—include increasingly elaborate costuming, competition for most original, prettiest, and ugliest costumes (a feature that some neighboring towns dismiss as "too much like New Orleans"), and wearing and throwing beads, New Orleans style.

Some of these changes are important, but they do not compromise the central ethos of the festival as perceived by it core participants. The shared conviction of Basile's most dedicated revelers might be summarized in this sentence: "Mardi Gras comes from our grandparents, and we are here to give it back to them."

6.27 Mardi Gras *capitaines* hoist Cassie LeBlue into the air. Cassie had suffered a heart attack shortly before Mardi Gras, as had a fellow *capitaine,* but both rode herd on Basile's *sauvages* throughout the daylong ordeal. *Photograph by Carl Lindahl, 2001.*

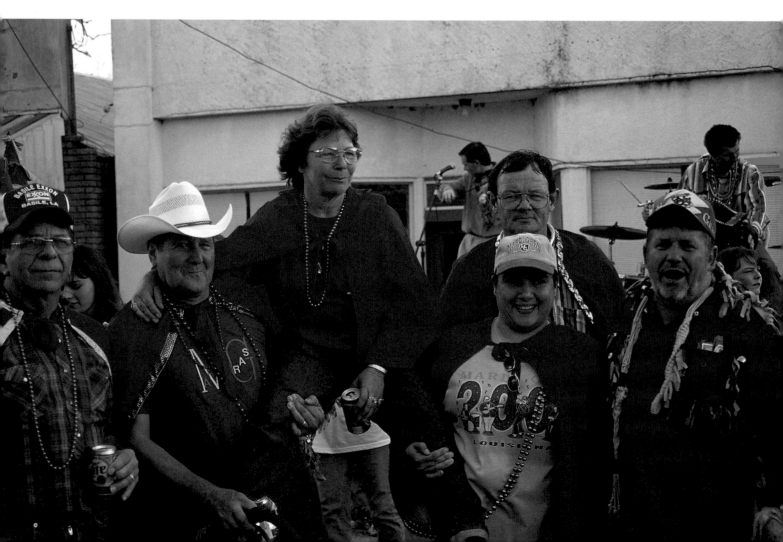

More specifically, "giving back" their ancestors' festival entails, first, a commitment to putting on a good show, a commitment greater than the commitment to fun. No matter how tired or injured the revelers may be, they persist in their game, and they will not stop reveling until onlookers are fully entertained.

Equally crucial is a commitment to the idea of redistribution and charity. This celebration mirrors a deeply embedded system of mutual social support in which the rules of the native community require dedication to a common good. Individual aspirations must be surrendered when they stand in conflict with a shared responsibility.

Every year the members of the Basile Mardi Gras association scrimp and beg, working exhaustively for weeks just to mount what an outsider might view as one day of chaotic, irresponsible fun. Every year the wealthier institutions in Basile, such as the bank, contribute less and less; some of the richest local powers have stopped giving altogether.

But their richer neighbors' lack of charity has only intensified the Mardi Gras's resolve to share. Every year, they offer a free gumbo to the people of Basile—including, perhaps most pointedly, those who did not contribute a cent. Every year, Potic Rider gives some variation of the same speech: "The Mardi Gras is not doing this for them now, not for the Mardi Gras. They're doing it to feed the people of Basile."

This spirit of charity goes far beyond the gumbo. Every year, the band visits the old folks' home in Basile, not to beg for chickens and rice, as elsewhere, but, in the words of Kim Moreau, "to take Mardi Gras back to where it came from." *Sauvages* sing for, hug, and kiss relatives, old friends, and total strangers, because, in the words of another Basile man, "We're giving the Mardi Gras back to the people who gave it to us" (fig. 28).

This defiant insistence on charity in the face of greed is perfectly aligned to the daily lives of the people who put on their Mardi Gras masks once a year. Knowing what the average Basile adult knows (that is, a great variety of anything-but-average skills), you could make a lot of money, but only if you left town or, like the bankers, turned your back on the reciprocal system by which the community lives. On Mardi Gras, the most committed players assemble to prove that they can give their town more than their richer neighbors can even hope to have.[22]

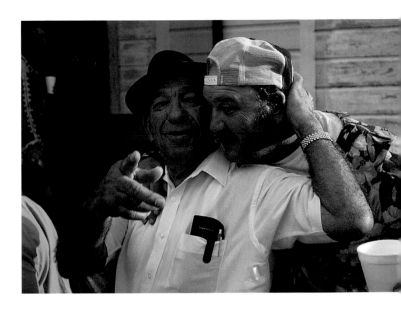

6.28 Bonding is not an abstraction on Mardi Gras day in Basile. Most obvious is the reciprocal hug around the neck, exchanged more often than hellos or handshakes. Here, Vories Moreau and Mike Broussard celebrate the return of the Mardi Gras to Basile. *Photograph by Carl Lindahl, 1992.*

Finally, the most engaged players display a generally religious, if often anticlerical and antiestablishment, cast of spirit. Most *sauvages* consider themselves good Catholics even if they are not regular churchgoers. And there is a sort of religiosity in their self-sacrificial fervor, so much so that it could be fairly said that, for them, Lent begins on Mardi Gras day. There are men who drink a case of beer that day and yet who will not touch another between Ash Wednesday and Easter, but their intoxication does not prevent them from reaching deep into themselves to perform repeated acts of play so exhausting as to challenge their survival. Nothing that they do to themselves, or that their health has done to them, can stop them from running that day-long self-sacrificial circuit of their town. At Basile's 2001 celebration, two of the *capitaines* had suffered heart attacks within the preceding two weeks. Nevertheless, both suited up and played their holiday games as fervently as ever, in the company of the oldest player, Gilbert Leblanc, seventy-nine, who had postponed an angioplasty in order to throw himself into the festival. All three were still standing at the end of the day. For these three *capitaines,* as for many younger runners, Mardi Gras celebrates a triumph of the spirit over the weakness of the flesh. This is the ultimate Day of Obligation, quite literally a matter of life and death.

On that same Mardi Gras day in 2001, Vories Moreau, one of Basile's greatest Mardi Gras, lay in a hospital in neighboring Mamou. Robbed by mortality of his hopes for running Mardi Gras in Basile that year, he planned instead to don his mask, suit, and *capuchon* inside the hospital and run the halls to entertain his fellow patients. Vories ultimately proved too sick to suit up on Mardi Gras day, and by the end of Lent he was dead. But he carried Mardi Gras with him past the threshold of death. At the funeral home, his mask and *capuchon* lay at his side, close to a floral arrangement sent by the Basile Mardi Gras association. At the end of the funeral, a group of musicians played the Mardi Gras song as they walked Vories to his grave.

NOTES

This essay is dedicated to the memories of Vories Moreau and Mrs. Agnes Miller and to Basile's living Mardi Gras community, with gratitude for their unfailing generosity.

1. Carl A. Brasseaux, *The Founding of New Acadia: The Beginnings of Acadian Life in Louisiana, 1765–1803* (Baton Rouge: Louisiana State University Press, 1987), 1–89.

2. Barry Jean Ancelet, Jay Edwards, and Glen Pitre, *Cajun Country* (Jackson: University Press of Mississippi, 1991), 12–28; Carl A. Brasseaux, *Acadian to Cajun: Transformation of a People, 1803–1877* (Jackson: University Press of Mississippi, 1991), 89–111.

3. Gwendolyn Midlo Hall, *Africans in Colonial Louisiana: The Development of Afro-Creole Culture in the Eighteenth Century* (Baton Rouge: Louisiana State University Press, 1992), 194–200.

4. Arnold van Gennep, *Manuel de folklore français contemporain,* vol. 1, *Les Ceremonies périodiques cycliques et saisonières,* Section 3, *Carnaval/Carême-Pâcques* (Paris: A. et J. Picaud, 1937–1938).

5. Henry Glassie, *All Silver and No Brass: An Irish Christmas Mumming* (Bloomington: Indiana University Press, 1975), 80–82; Samuel Kinser, *Carnival, American Style: Mardi Gras at New Orleans and Mobile* (Chicago: University of Chicago Press, 1990), 195–214; John W. Nunley and Judith Bettelheim, eds., *Caribbean Festival Arts: Each and Every Bit of Difference* (Seattle: University of Washington Press, 1988), 56–57, 71–73, 142–145; Alexander Orloff, *Carnival: Myth and Cult* (Wörgl, Austria: Perlinger Verlag, 1981), 75–78.

6. Rocky L. Sexton and Harry Oster, "Une 'Tite Poule Grass ou la Fille Ainée: A Comparative Analysis of Cajun and Creole Mardi Gras Songs," *Journal of American Folklore* 114 (2001): 204–224.

7. Carl Lindahl and Carolyn Ware, *Cajun Mardi Gras Masks* (Jackson: University Press of Mississippi, 1997), 31, 34.

8. Ibid., 30–34; Ronnie E. Roshto, "Georgie and Allen Manuel and Cajun Wire Screen Masks," *Louisiana Folklore Miscellany* 7 (1992): 33–49.

9. Carl Lindahl, "The Presence of the Past in the Cajun Country Mardi Gras," *Journal of Folklore Research* 33 (1996): 128–148; Carl Lindahl, "Finding the Field through the Discovery of the Self," in *Working the Field: Accounts from French Louisiana,* eds. Jacques Henry and Sara LeMenestral (Westport, CT: Praeger, 2003), 33–50.

10. The nearly transparent mask, requiring so much of the acting abilities of its wearer, is more common in Basile than in other Mardi Gras communities—one reason I use this mask as a metaphor for Basile's celebration. Nevertheless, as the photographs accompanying this chapter reveal, Basile's *sauvages* practice diverse forms of disguise, ranging from face paint to fully concealing rubber masks. On the range of facial disguise in Cajun communities, see Patricia E Sawin, "Transparent Masks: The Ideology and Practice of Disguise in Contemporary Cajun Mardi Gras," *Journal of American Folklore* 114 (2001): 175–203, and Carolyn Ware, "'Anything to Act Crazy': Cajun Women and Mardi Gras Disguise," *Journal of American Folklore* 114 (2001): 225–247.

11. Lindahl and Ware, *Cajun Mardi Gras Masks,* 40.

12. Cajun Mardi Gras shows extraordinary continuity and diversity across the two dozen prairie communities that observe the festival. In some ways, Basile is representative of most or all these communities; in other ways, Basile is unique. See Lindahl, "Presence of the Past"; Carl Lindahl, "One Family's Mardi Gras: The Moreaus of Basile," *Louisiana Cultural Vistas* 9, no. 3 (1998): 46–53; Lindahl, "Finding the Field"; Lindahl and Ware, *Cajun Mardi Gras Masks;* Carolyn Ware, "'I Read the Rules Backward': Women, Symbolic Inversion, and the Cajun Mardi Gras Run," *Southern Folklore* 52 (1995): 137–160; and Ware, "'Anything to Act Crazy,'" for specific treatments of Basile. Studies of other Cajun Mardi Gras include Barry Jean Ancelet, *"Capitaine, voyage ton flag": The Traditional Cajun Country Mardi Gras* (Lafayette: Center for Louisiana Studies, *1989*); Barry Jean Ancelet, "Mardi Gras and the Media: Who's Fooling Whom?" *Southern Folklore* 46, no. 3 (1989): 211–219; Ancelet, Edwards, and Pitre, *Cajun Country;* Carl Lindahl, "Ways Inside the Circle of Mardi Gras," *Journal of American Folklore* 114 (2001): 132–139; and Pat Mire, director, *Dance for a Chicken: The Cajun Mardi Gras,* 57–minute, 1/2-inch video format, color (Eunice, LA: Attakapas Productions, 1993).

13. Basile's "Chanson de Mardi Gras" has changed over time and is currently sung with varied words and interpretations. In this essay I quote from a performance by Potic Rider with two variations noted as alternatives by the transcribers. See Helena Putnam and Barry Jean Ancelet, "Chanson de Mardi Gras (Basile)," in *Cajun Country Mardi Gras: Variety within a Culture,* program for a performance at the Liberty Theater, Eunice, LA, February 18 (Eunice: Liberty Cultural Association, 1995), 5–6. Like several other Mardi Gras communities, Basile recognizes two Mardi Gras songs: first, the a cappella song quoted here, unique to Basile and sung only by members of the Mardi Gras, and second, a more generic, instrumental and vocal version (bearing some textual similarities to the Basile song but

based on the version of Mamou) that has been recorded by many Cajun artists and that plays on the radio and in live performances throughout Cajun country on Mardi Gras day. The instrumental version is far easier to dance to, hence its popularity at *bals* and street dances. On Cajun Mardi Gras songs, see Sexton and Oster, "Une 'Tite Poule Gras."

14. Interviews with Vories Moreau conducted by Carl Lindahl, December 1991 and February 1992.

15. Lindahl and Ware, *Cajun Mardi Gras Masks,* 14–15.

16. Ibid., 14–15.

17. Many Mardi Gras, however, do not think of themselves as play Indians. According to Vories Moreau, even by the 1940s, the "Indian" nature of the Mardi Gras was largely a thing of the past. "We called each other 'Indians.' But we didn't really think we were acting like Indians. . . . The fringes on our suits . . . were more a decoration than a symbol" (interview with Moreau, February 2000; also see Lindahl, "Presence of the Past," 35). Although Basile's *capitaines* refer to all the maskers as *sauvages,* the troupe sometimes includes two figures who play more differentiated roles: the *nègre* and the *négresse,* a male and female in blackface whose comedy plays upon stereotypes about African Americans. Blackface figures are not considered essential to Basile's Mardi Gras; I have seen a *nègre* in only five of the thirteen celebrations I have attended and a *négresse* in only one.

18. Carl Lindahl, interviews with and observations of Basile Mardi Gras participants, 1991–2003.

19. The description of Mardi Gras day and the festivities of Mardi Gras evening are based on my field observations of thirteen Mardi Gras celebrations in Basile, 1991–2003; see also Lindahl, "Presence of the Past," 127–131, and Lindahl, "Finding the Field."

20. Lindahl, "Presence of the Past," 134.

21. In Basile, as in other prairie communities, a group of women (or men, in L'Anse Maigre) takes on the daylong job of preparing the communal gumbo. Two generations ago, the gumbo was made from the same chickens caught by the *sauvages* that day: periodically, a member of the Mardi Gras's support staff would collect the chickens caught up to that time and drive them back to the cooks. Today, however (the sole exception being at L'Anse Maigre), chickens are purchased before Mardi Gras, to ensure that all the chickens will cook long enough to be tender by the time the troupe returns. Chickens captured that day are either donated to charity or consumed by the Mardi Gras themselves after Lent ends.

22. This and the preceding two paragraphs are adapted from Carl Lindahl, "The Power of Being Outnumbered," *Louisiana Folklore Miscellany* 12 (1997): 58–59.

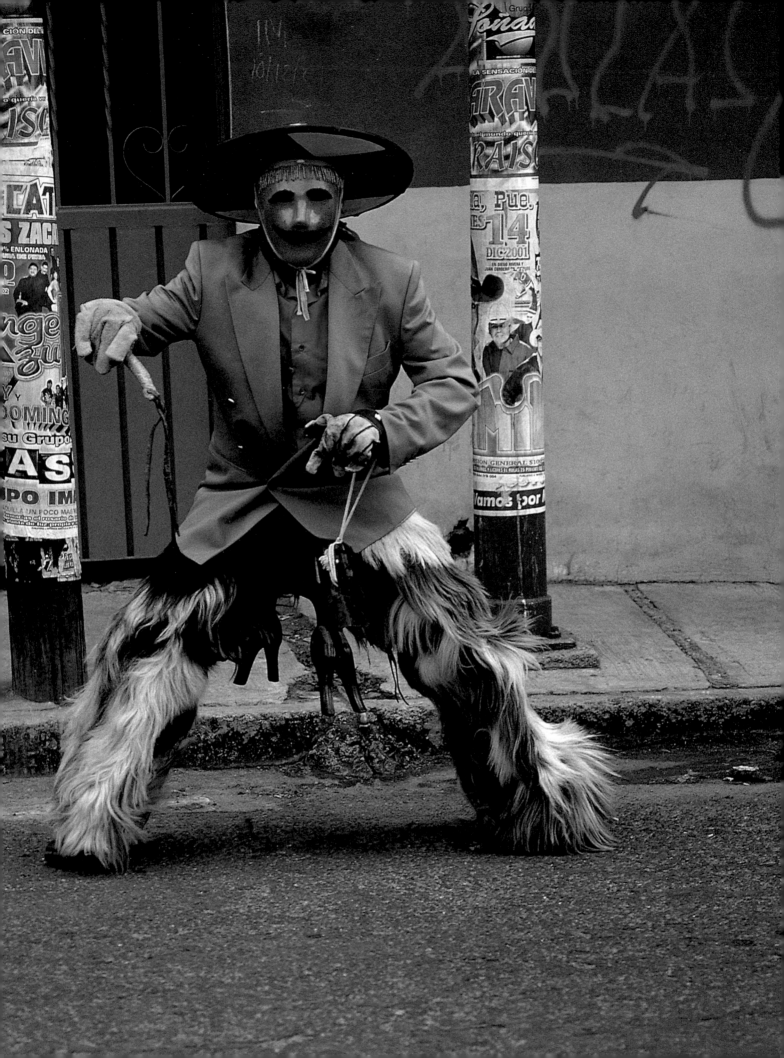

7 Ritual and Play

CARNAVAL IN NAHUA INDIAN COMMUNITIES
OF TLAXCALA, MEXICO

BARBARA MAULDIN

NTENSE SUNLIGHT BEATS DOWN ON concrete buildings and paved streets in the rural Nahua Indian community of Papalotla, located in south-central Mexico in the small state known as Tlaxcala (fig. 7.2). Somewhere in the distance we hear trumpets and drums playing a lively tune, and after turning a corner we see a group of masked dancers in front of one of the houses, performing a European-style *cuadrilla,* or square dance (fig. 7.3). These Carnival masqueraders are called *charros,*[1] a name that refers to the upper-class Mexicans or Spaniards who oversaw cattle ranches in this region during the mid- to late nineteenth century (fig. 7.4).[2] In keeping with this role, the Indian dancers wear realistic pink-skinned masks that portray young Caucasian men. They also wear a version of ranchero clothing consisting of tailored white shirts, neckties, black vests, pants, leather chaps, boots, and capes. Each carries a coiled rope in one hand. In an exaggeration of the nineteenth-century *charro* hats, these dancers wear large headdresses ornamented with draped fabric and an enormous framework of colored ostrich feathers.

At one point in the performance, the *charros* form two lines, uncoil their ropes, and begin trying to hit each other's legs and feet with the narrow tips (fig. 7.5).

7.1 A *chivarrudo* masquerader gallops on his "horse" in Papalotla, Tlaxcala. *Photograph by Barbara Mauldin, 2002.*

145

This action is in keeping with the character of the rowdy ranchers, who enjoyed showing off their abilities in handling ropes.[3] Local legend, however, says that the performance dates to pre-Hispanic times, when a beautiful but cruel young woman lived in this area and seductively mesmerized all of the young men. This led to both apathy and competition among the youths, who had no other aspiration than to obtain a smile from the girl. Finally, one of their deities, known as Tlacotecalotl, came to their rescue and transformed the young woman into a snake. She retained her evil spirit and continued to torment the people of the area. Eventually the young men developed a dance, known as the Danza de la Culebra (Dance of the Snake), in which they whipped the head of the snake against

7.2 The state of Tlaxcala and some of the major cities and towns in that region of Mexico.

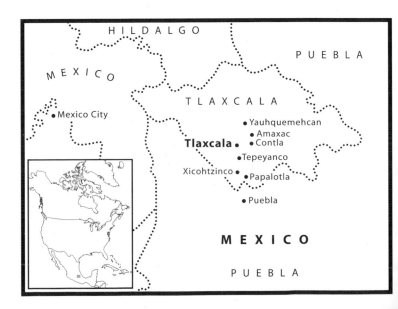

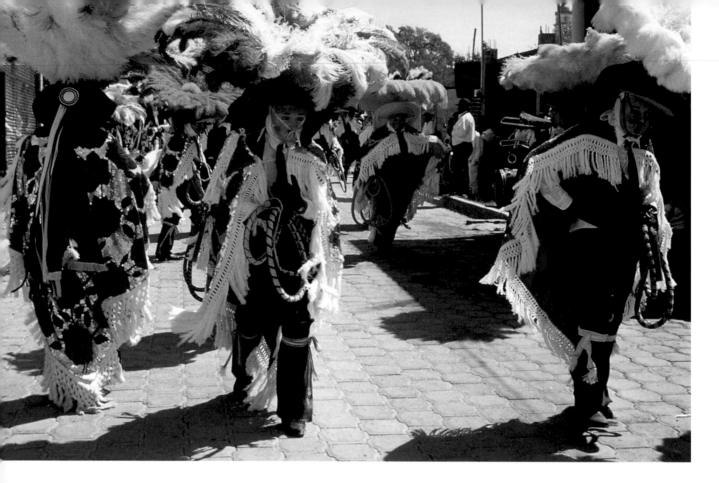

7.3 *Charros* perform a *cuadrilla,* or square dance, during Carnival celebrations in Papalotla, Tlaxcala. *Photograph by Barbara Mauldin, 1999.*

7.4 *El Ranchero.* Drawing by H. Iriarte, transformed into a lithograph by M. Murguía y Cia. Reproduced from *Los Mexicanos: Pintados por si mismos*, 1855. *Photograph by Blair Clark.*

7.5 *Charros* try to hit each other's legs with their ropes during the Dance of the Snake in Papalotla, Tlaxcala. *Photograph by Ruth Lechuga, 1971.*

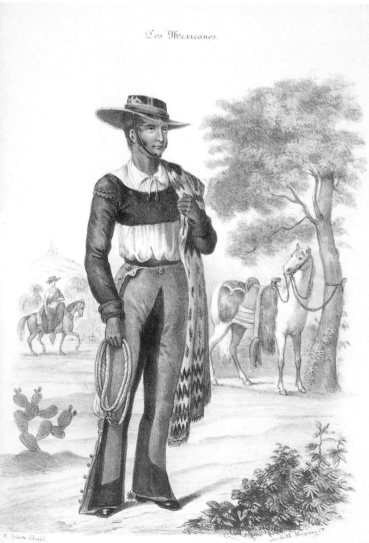

Los Mexicanos

EL RANCHERO

the legs of another man until it was subdued. At the end of the sequence, the injured snake, or spirit of the woman, was laid on the ground and the young men triumphantly danced around it (fig. 7.6).[4]

Another explanation for the Dance of the Snake also derives from pre-Hispanic times, but in this case it is said to have come from the rituals that the Nahua peoples of central Mexico carried out for their god of water, known as Tláloc. The cracking sound of the ropes is said to imitate thunder, and the aggressive acts of the men serve as a petition for storms and rain in the coming growing season. At the end, when the rope is laid on the ground, it looks like a snake. This reptile has traditionally served as a symbol for water,

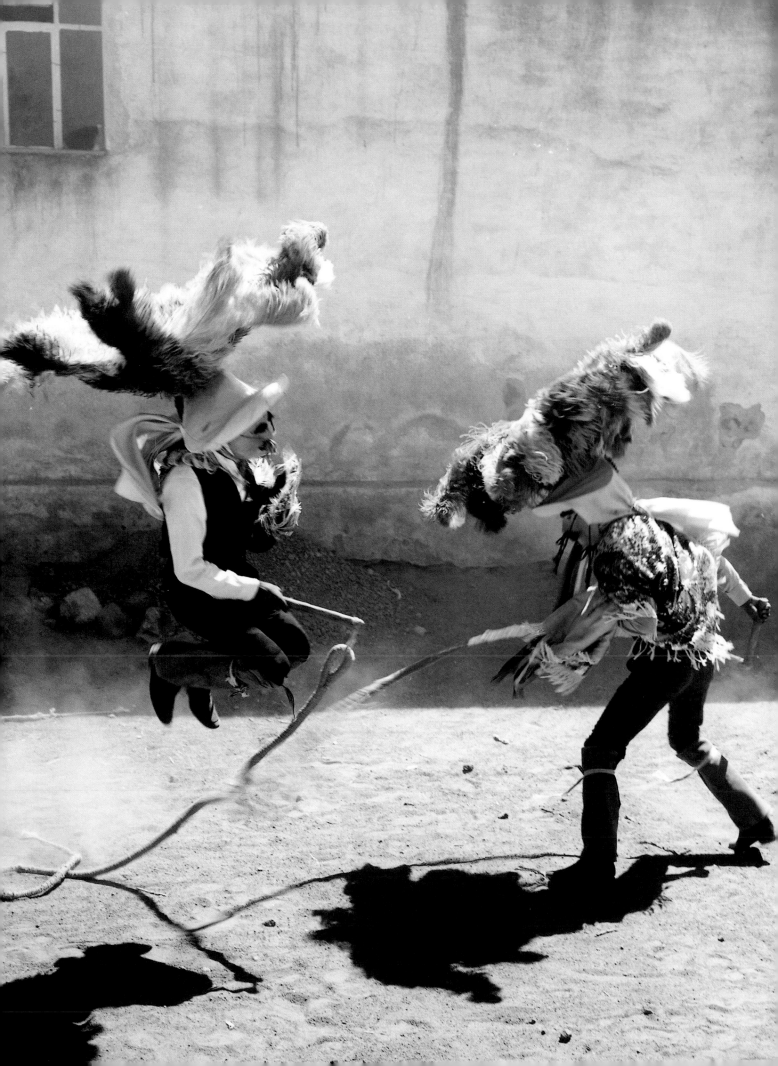

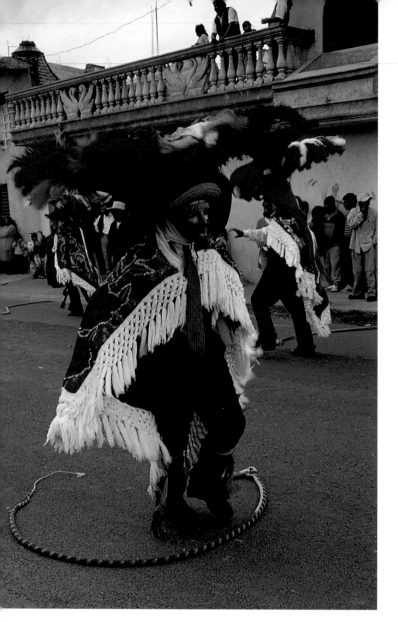

7.6 *Charros* perform the Dance of the Snake in Papalotla, Tlaxcala. *Photograph by Barbara Mauldin, 2002.*

A Brief History of Festivals, Dancing, and Masquerade in Mexico

Masked pageantry and dancing were important aspects of ceremonial practices in Mexico long before Spaniards invaded the area in the early sixteenth century. Chronicles written by Catholic priests during the first decades of European colonization describe a variety of ethnic groups with highly developed forms of political, social, and religious life, including a range of festivals that took place at specific times during the indigenous calendar year. Religion permeated every aspect of life, and it was important to carry out the festivities correctly in order to honor and entertain the pre-Hispanic deities and ancestor spirits, who in turn would bless the people with abundant rain, fertile crops, successful harvests, and good health. The celebrations also brought the people of the communities together for socializing and enjoyment.[7]

The larger festivals were generally sponsored by the elite rulers of a broad geographical region, but smaller celebrations were also carried out on the local level. Extended family groups bound by a common divine ancestor lived near one another in a cluster of houses either in the countryside or forming neighborhoods of larger towns. The land of the community was defined by the place where the spirit provided his or her special protection, and the religious festivals honored the ancestor as well as reinforcing the group's identity. Financial sponsorship for these local celebrations rotated from one member of the extended family to another.[8]

Although specifics of the festivals varied, the main part of the ceremonies involved processions and dancing as well as choreographed theatrical performances. These were usually followed by public feasts and social entertainment in the form of games, dancing, and comical or satirical dramas. The chronicles describe a variety of costumes and masks worn by men who participated in the events. Some masqueraded as old men and women who performed comic acts for the crowds. Other masqueraders participated in plays that made fun of members of the community or impersonated and ridiculed neighboring ethnic groups.

Great emphasis was placed on developing the performers' skills, and the religious priests maintained

and the performance of dancing around the "serpent" is another plea for rain.[5]

With either interpretation, it can be said that the masquerade and stories portrayed in the performance reflect the history of the region and the Indians' ability to observe, imitate, burlesque, and subvert. They carry out festivals and performances in appropriate ways to bring about the well-being of the whole community. Although their costumes, masks, music, and dances are taken primarily from European models, the underlying structure of the rituals and the performers' commitment to executing them have roots in pre-Hispanic cultural traditions.[6]

special schools in which to train and prepare composers, musicians, singers, and dancers. Prizes were given to those who did best, including performers who danced in groups, initiated dance steps, and made up farcical songs.[9]

After the Spanish conquest of Mexico in 1521, the Europeans dismantled most of the elite political-religious empires and banned the practice of pre-Hispanic religion. With the collapse of the imperial states, the local kinship communities of the various ethnic groups became autonomous entities; in many instances they were viewed by the Europeans as small villages. When they existed as neighborhoods in larger towns, the Spaniards referred to them as barrios.[10] European Catholic priests established churches in these communities and, as part of conversion to Christianity, instructed the Indians to adopt the Catholic festival calendar, including Holy Week, Corpus Christi, All Saints and All Souls Days, and Christmas. In between were a number of important feast days for Christ, the Virgin Mary, and other popular saints. The pre-Hispanic structure used by the kinship groups to carry out religious rituals and celebrations was gradually reconfigured to conform to the Spanish tradition of social-religious brotherhoods known as cofradías or mayordormías.[11]

By the late seventeenth and early eighteenth centuries, the native peoples of central Mexico had come to adopt Jesus, the Virgin Mary, and other Catholic saints into their pantheon of deities. They prayed to them and performed rituals that combined aspects of pre-Hispanic and Christian traditions, in the hope that they would help prevent illness, bring rain and fertility for the crops, and ensure well-being for the community.[12] The cofradías, or religious organizations of the barrios, remained highly structured and focused on carrying out complex rituals that went far beyond what the Catholic authorities condoned. Feast day celebrations were particularly important, and Spanish priests often complained about the amount of time, money, and other resources the Indian groups put into these events.[13]

The central region of Mexico was a fertile growing area, and the Nahuatl-speaking peoples who lived there at the time of the Spanish conquest had developed a ritual calendar oriented toward the agricultural seasons. The first day of their new year coincided with the European Gregorian calendar date of February 2.

This was the time when indigenous farmers began to cultivate their fields for the spring growing season. Rituals carried out during the first twenty days of their year were dedicated to their rain gods. It was hoped that this would bring the storms and rain that generally began in March. Thus the period that began with the feast day of Nuestra Señora de Candelaria (February 2) and continued through Ash Wednesday, Lent, and Easter was an important time in which to carry out rituals.[14]

Although some form of carnaval celebration may have been introduced into Mexico during the early phase of Spanish colonization, the first documented references date from the eighteenth century. These are found in complaints filed by Catholic priests and government officials about the rowdiness of the festivities and the scandalousness of some masquerades.[15] The Indians living in larger colonial cities and on haciendas and ranches no doubt saw these Carnival revels but would not have been allowed to participate in them.

With Mexico's independence from Spain in 1821 and the political and religious struggle for power that followed, the Indians were largely ignored and gradually became freer to carry on their lives as they saw fit. Yet even though Catholic priests no longer oversaw Indian religious activities, Mexican indigenous groups continued to embrace the Christian god and saints and carry out the rituals and festivals that had become part of their traditions under European rule.[16]

As the economic and social life of Mexico changed, mestizo people—those of mixed Indian and Spanish blood—were gradually allowed to wear the European-style clothing that was fashionable among the upper-class Mexicans, Spaniards, and Frenchmen living in the cities and on rural haciendas and ranches. Mestizos also admired the social life and parties of the upper-class citizens and often got together in town plazas or in the countryside to perform dances that imitated those being done in elite homes and salons (fig. 7.7).[17]

By the late nineteenth century, mestizo and Indian communities throughout Mexico were also carrying

7.7 (overleaf) Los Mestizos paseo de la vigas (The Mestizos dancing in the countryside). Drawing by M. Rugerdas, transformed into a lithograph by G. M. Kurz. Reproduced from México y los mexicanos, 1859. Photograph by Blair Clark.

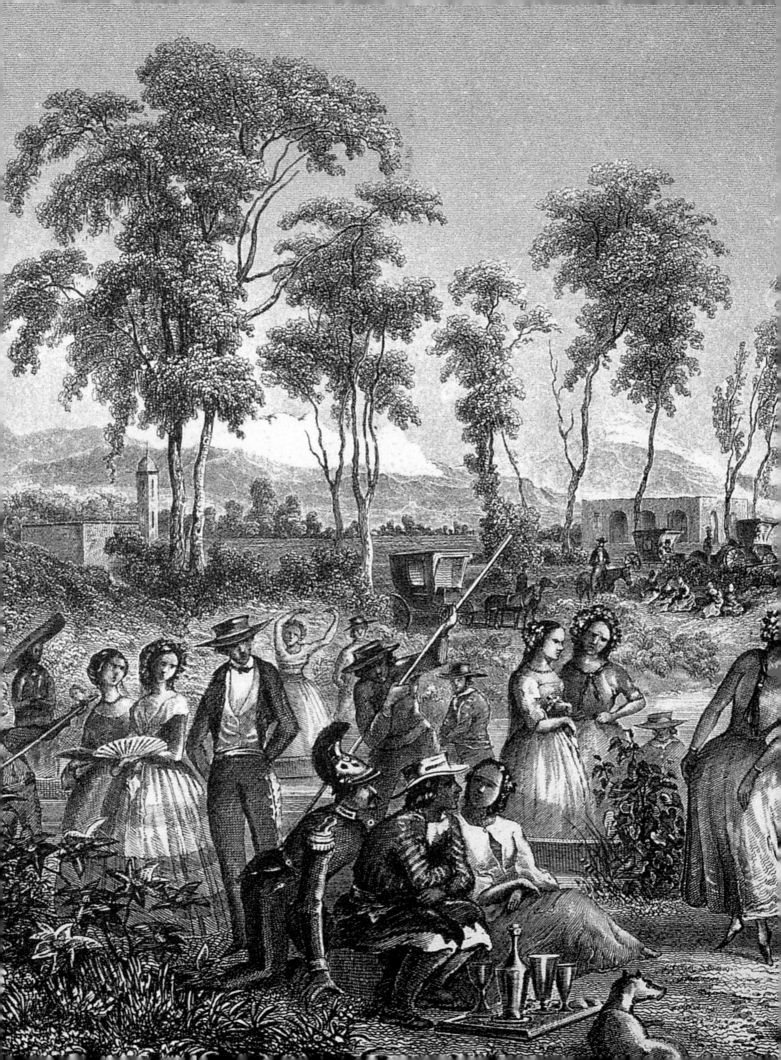

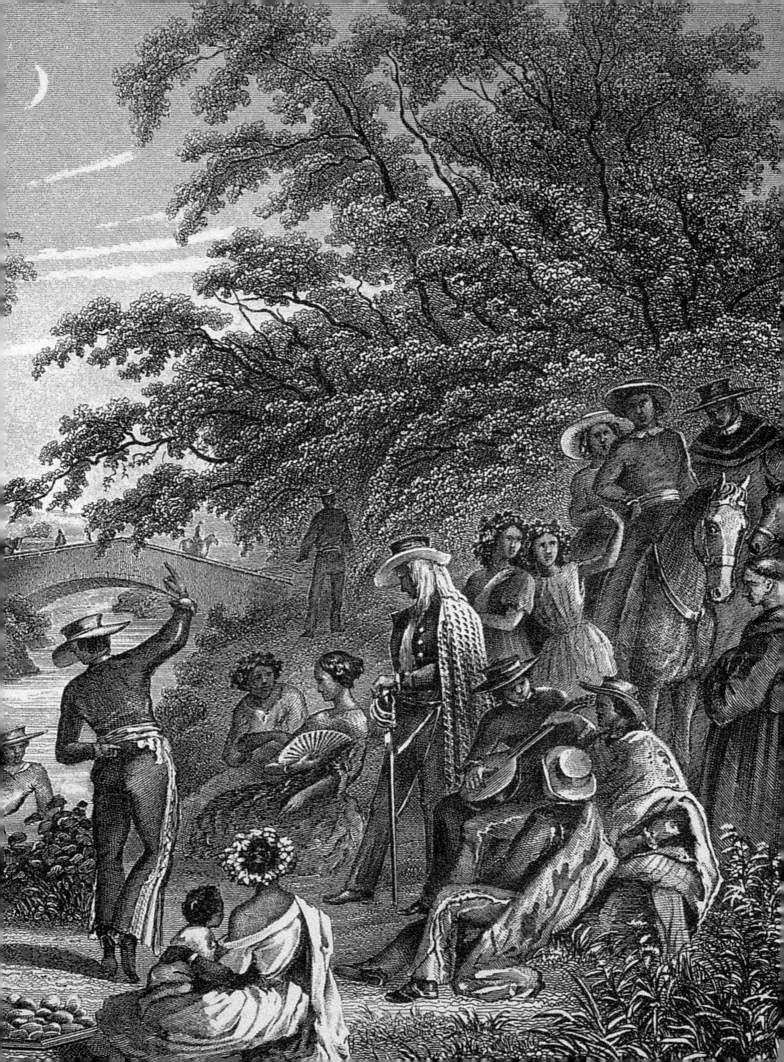

out Carnival, and it continued to evolve in the twentieth century as one of the most popular celebrations of the year. This was a time when communities came together to feast, sing, dance, and perform lively and often humorous masked dramas, some of which satirized the upper-class Europeans.[18] Underlying this celebration were religious concerns for the beginning of the spring agricultural season, and aspects of Carnival activities in Indian communities sometimes openly addressed this topic. An example was found in the Nahua town of Capuluhac in the state of Mexico, where masqueraders guided two oxen in circles around the dirt in front of the Catholic church to ritually plow the sacred earth. In some Indian villages in the Valley of Mexico and in the highlands of the state of Chiapas, Carnival participants carried cornstalks as a petition for abundant crops. In other towns in Chiapas, Tabasco, and Oaxaca, Indian masqueraders carried out dramas during the Carnival festivities that related to hunting and maintaining the natural environment.[19] For the most part these festivals have continued in the same form and with the same popularity into the twenty-first century.

History of Tlaxcala and the Introduction of Carnaval

The Tlaxcalan Indians and their relatives, the Aztecs, were seminomadic tribes that evolved in Mexico's northern wilderness. In the late thirteenth and early fourteenth centuries these Nahuatl-speaking groups began moving south, and the Aztecs settled in the Valley of Mexico. The Tlaxcalans established themselves in the highland basin to the east and became a dominant power in what is now known as the Puebla-Tlaxcala Valley (see fig. 7.2). By the middle of the fifteenth century, the Tlaxcalans had developed an antagonistic relationship with the Aztecs, which led to aggressive warfare that was still going on when the Spaniards arrived in Mexico in 1519. Because of their fighting abilities, the Tlaxcalans ended up playing a decisive role in helping Hernán Cortés and his Spanish troops defeat the Aztec ruler, Moctezuma II, and take control of his empire in the summer of 1520. Following the conquest, Cortés made a number of special concessions to the Tlaxcalans to show his gratitude. These privileges were to be held in perpetuity.[20]

Thirty years later the Indians drew up the *Lienzo de Tlaxcala* to remind the Spaniards of their important role as auxiliary troops in defeating the Aztecs. One of the many scenes depicted on the painted fabric portrayed Tlaxcalan lords and ladies presenting gifts to Cortés and his translator, Malinche, in 1519, when they first received the Spaniards into their territory (fig. 7.8). This image showed the Tlaxcalan men wearing long capes, known as *tilmatlis*. Worn knotted in front across the neck, each was beautifully embroidered and painted with patterns and colors that reflected the wearer's status. Each of the lords also wore a headdress from which tall, multicolored feathers projected up and over his head.[21] Other Spanish chronicles refer to the wonderful dances carried out by Tlaxcalan men and the beautiful clothing worn by the performers.[22]

The status of the Tlaxcalan Indian empire within the Spanish viceroyalty of Mexico faded quickly, however, and by the mid-sixteenth century the Spanish crown was giving large land grants to wealthy Europeans in various parts of Tlaxcala, where they set up ranches and haciendas. Much of this region was ill suited for commercial agriculture, so the Spanish colonists concentrated their efforts on cattle ranching.[23] By the mid-seventeenth century some hacienda owners had begun producing and marketing a pre-Hispanic alcoholic drink known as *pulque,* made from the local maguey plant.[24]

The first mention of *carnaval* celebrations being carried out in Tlaxcala dates from 1768, when the governor of the state published a pronouncement in the Tlaxcala city newspaper that ridiculed and banned certain types of behavior. Apparently, groups of men were running through the streets of the city late at night, banging on doors and windows, shouting insults, singing vulgar songs, and throwing seeds and confetti that dirtied the streets. The governor forbade them to carry on these activities or to wear costumes and masks that made fun of other people.[25] It is unclear who these men were, but lower-class Indians probably would not have been among them.

After Mexico gained its independence from Spain in 1821, the Catholic Church gradually lost much of its authority in the Tlaxcala-Puebla area, and by the late nineteenth century the priests overseeing the Indian communities had all but disappeared. As elsewhere in Mexico, the majority of Indians still called themselves

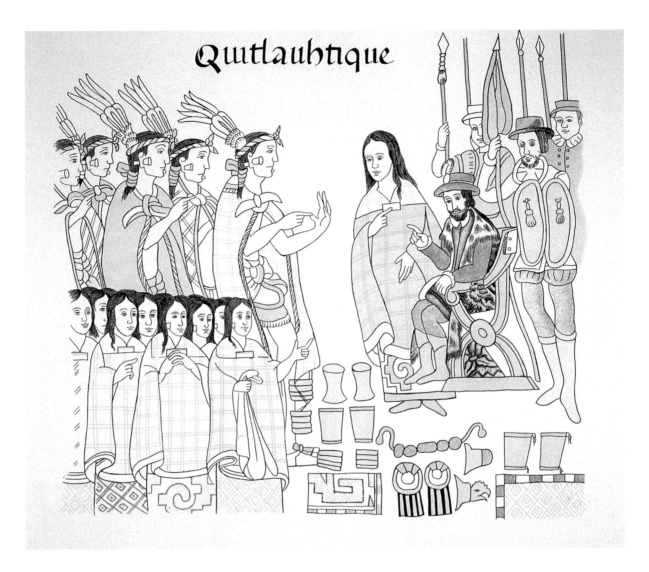

Quitlauhtique

7.8 The Spaniard Cortés and his Indian translator Malinche meet with Tlaxcalan lords and ladies in the early sixteenth century. *Lienzo de Tlaxcala, lámina 7. Photograph by Blair Clark.*

Catholics and prayed to the saints that had become an important part of their ritual lives and their struggle to survive. However, the Tlaxcalan people felt freer to organize and carry out festivals in ways that were appropriate to them.[26]

From the mid-nineteenth into the early twentieth century, the numbers of upper-class Mexicans and Europeans living in the Tlaxcala-Puebla region grew. With this growth came an increase in the number of cattle ranches and in *pulque* production on the haciendas. Other entrepreneurs took advantage of new railroad lines through the region and established textile factories and other businesses. More Tlaxcalan people began working for these employers and became famil-

iar with their lifestyles, mannerisms, clothing, and forms of entertainment.[27] The wealthy ranchers and businessmen organized elaborate parties and masked balls for themselves and their aristocratic friends that took place in their elegant salons. Household servants and field laborers were not invited to participate but watched eagerly from the sidelines. French quadrilles, or square dances, were particularly popular in upper-class society at this time, and the Indians learned to imitate the dances and music that accompanied them.[28]

Carnival in Tlaxcalan Indian Communities Today

By the late nineteenth and early twentieth centuries, most Tlaxcalan Indian communities were organizing Carnival festivities that included performances by men wearing masquerades and carrying out the dances

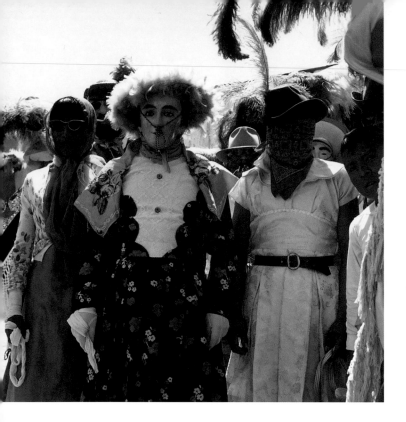

7.9 Men used to masquerade as women during Carnival celebrations in Papalotla, Tlaxcala. *Photograph by Ruth Lechuga, 1965.*

they had learned from the upper-class Mexicans and Europeans.[29] This celebration continued to gain popularity until it became the most important festival of the year among Nahua people. Most were still dependent on farming for a portion of their food and continued to observe the spring ritual calendar, with the period from Carnival to Easter being particularly important for carrying out festival activities. This was also a time to strengthen social relationships and bring communities together to share in a happy occasion.[30]

Today, approximately thirty-eight towns in the state of Tlaxcala celebrate Carnival, their festivities extending over a few days or several weeks. In most of the towns, activities begin on the Sunday before Ash Wednesday, when everyone can participate.[31] Nowadays many people work during the week and travel to jobs away from their homes, so only a handful of communities celebrate Carnival on the Monday and Tuesday before Ash Wednesday. Ignoring the Catholic ban on celebrations during Lent, groups in at least sixteen towns repeat the Carnival performances on the following Sunday, and eight of these communities repeat them again on the next Sunday. A few continue to repeat the celebration over the following three Sundays leading up to Easter.[32]

Until the late 1960s and 1970s the dancers were all young men, because the Indians' conservatism did not allow women to participate in this kind of activity. The all-male performance lent itself to rowdy behavior, particularly among the cross-dressers, who often played out the feminine role with great satire (fig. 7.9). Gradually attitudes changed, and girls between the ages of eight and twenty began learning the dances and joining in as partners. Villagers explain that one of the reasons this was allowed to happen was that there were a limited number of young men to act out both parts. With the influx of girls, the number of available participants greatly increased, but the style of the performances also changed, becoming less rowdy and more formalized. Because of the change in atmosphere, a growing number of younger children, particularly boys, have been participating in the performances as well. Families take pride in dressing them in the same outfits as the older dancers and teaching them the beat of the music and how to carry out the dance steps (fig. 7.10).[33]

From the late nineteenth century until the middle of the twentieth, the costumes of the Tlaxcalan Indian dancers featured a variety of satirical and comical masquerades. These ranged from representations of upper-class Europeans and Mexicans to exotic Arabs, Catholic priests, political officials, movie stars, and other famous people from contemporary times.[34] Young men played the roles of women, which often led to humorous or dramatic masquerades.[35] A few folk artists living in small towns throughout the region produced masks for the performers. Some of these were made of leather that was shaped in ceramic molds. Others were carved from a soft wood known as *tzompantle* or *colorín* (coral tree). Both types of masks were painted to create a realistic appearance of the character or person being portrayed.[36]

In 1966, the conservative governor of the state of Tlaxcala, Conde de San Román, promoted a law prohibiting satires of certain known people.[37] Moreover, by this time increasing numbers of communities were

7.10 A young boy performs with his father as a *charro* in Papalotla, Tlaxcala. *Photograph by Barbara Mauldin, 2002.*

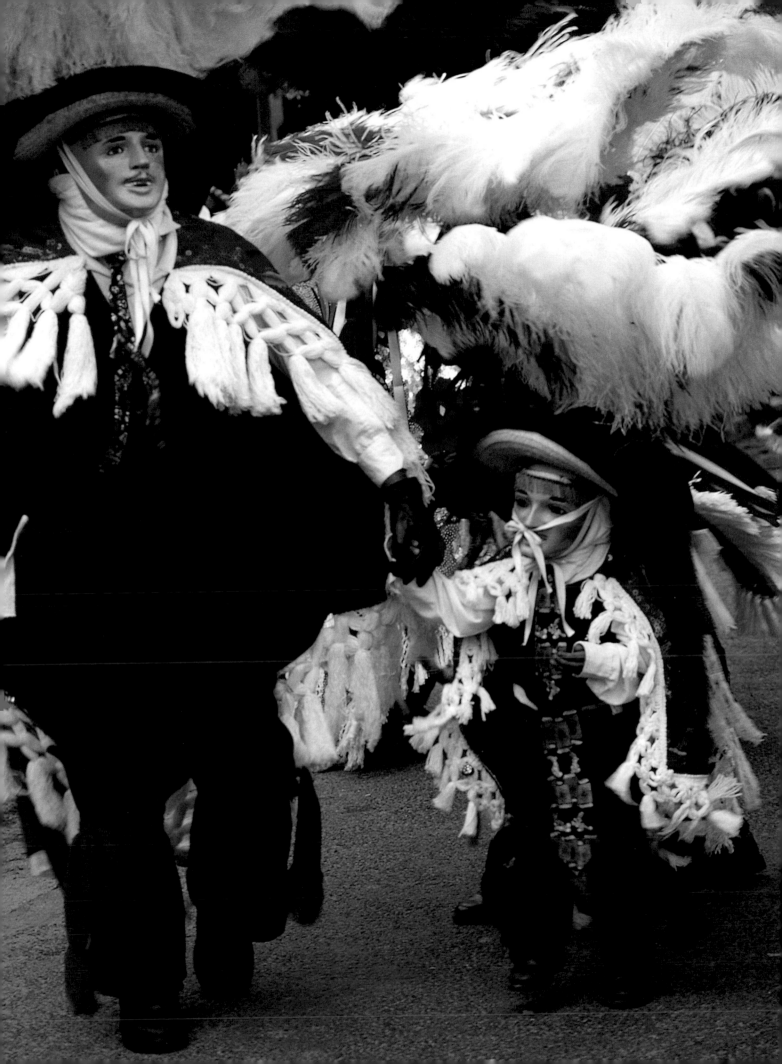

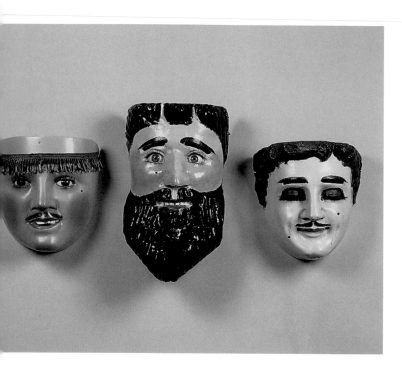

7.11 Carnival masks. Left: mask by the Méndez Hernandez family, Puebla, circa 1985. Center and right: masks by Carlos Reyes, San Pablo Apetatitlán, Tlaxcala, circa 1953 and circa 1935, respectively. International Folk Art Foundation collection in the Museum of International Folk Art. *Photograph by Blair Clark.*

allowing girls to participate, reducing the variety and number of humorous and satirical female characters that had been portrayed by men. Since the early 1970s, the masquerades have been narrowed down to a few types, and most masks worn by Tlaxcalan Carnival performers represent generic Caucasian men with pink skin, beauty marks, blue or light brown eyes with long eyelashes, and white teeth with gold fillings. Some also have beards and mustaches. The majority of these masks are now produced in two workshops, one in the town of San Pablo Apetatitlan in central Tlaxcala and the other in the city of Puebla. These mask makers use hardwoods to carve the face coverings and sophisticated painting techniques to create extremely smooth, realistic skin surfaces. Many of these masks have been fitted with glass eyes, and in some, the eyelids were designed to open and close when the dancers pulled thin strings extending down to their chins (fig. 7.11).[38]

Following are brief descriptions of the various characters or types of masquerades one sees nowadays during Carnival in the state of Taxclala.

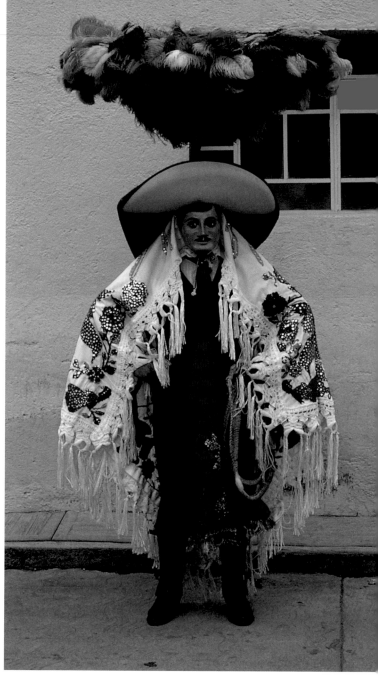

7.12 *Charro* masquerader in Tepeyanco, Tlaxcala. *Photograph by Barbara Mauldin, 2002.*

CHARROS

The *charro* Carnival masquerade (fig. 7.12) is worn by dance groups in a few of the Nahua Indian communities in the southern half of the state, in the valley below the sacred volcano La Malinche. The townspeople of San Francisco Papalotla, Tenancingo, San Cosme Mazatecochco, and San Francisco Tepeyanco, once heavily involved in rituals to the gods associated with the volcano, were also exposed to wealthy Mexicans and Europeans who established ranches in the region. As I mentioned earlier, *charros* represent the dashing, upper-class cowboys who oversaw ranches in this area during the mid- to late nineteenth century.

An important part of the dancer's outfit is the cape, decorated with colorful embroidery and sequins that reflect the sunlight as they twirl. In the more prosperous towns, such as Papalotla, families take great pride in providing new capes for their sons each year or at least every three years.[39] These garments are often said to derive from the embroidered Chinese shawls or intricately woven serapes worn by upper-class Mexicans in the nineteenth century.[40] Some scholars, however, have also pointed out the similarity of these capes to the *tilmatli* worn by Tlaxcalan lords at the time of the Spanish conquest (see fig. 7.8).[41] The use of feathers in the dancers' hats can also be compared to the feathered headdresses worn by Tlaxcalan lords in the sixteenth century. In the modern version, the tall, colored feathers cascade down over the dancer's head like an umbrella, a feature that has led some people to refer to these masqueraders as *paragüeros,* or umbrella carriers.[42]

VASARIOS AND VASARIAS

Accompanying the *charros* as they make their way through the streets of their neighborhood is a group of male and female dancers known as *vasarios* and *vasarias* (vassals). In Papalotla, Mazatecochco, and Tenancingo, the men wear the same type of mask and tailored white shirts, black vests, and pants as the *charros*. But in keeping with their subservient role, they do not wear the elaborate cape and feathered headdress or carry the coiled rope. Their young female partners wear newly made, matching dresses.[43]

NANA

Dancing with the *vasarios* is a man wearing a female Caucasian mask and dressed as a matronly woman (fig. 7.13) This character represents the mythical Mexican character Maringuilla, the young Indian or mestizo girl who fell in love with the dashing Mexican or Spanish *charro*. At one point in the dance she presents a baby doll to the crowd as a symbol of that relationship (fig. 7.14).[44] In her role as a mother she is referred to as *nana*. As the musicians play a special tune, she dances

with the doll carried over her head and then holds its face to her breast as if she were feeding it. All the while *nana* loudly recites a poem meant to lull the baby to sleep. Traditionally this poem was sung in Nahuatl, but today Spanish is more common.

The *muñecas,* or toy figures, used in this performance are usually female dolls with long, curly hair. The lullabies *nana* sings, however, are the same as those recited to images of the Christ child during the Christmas season, with references to the Son of God, the Virgin Mary, and the adoration of the three kings. At the end of the poem, two of the *vasarias* unfold a blanket and hold it taut, placing the doll on top. They gently rock the blanket back and forth as a means of helping the baby to sleep, another practice carried out

7.13 *Nana* dances with *vasarios* in Papalotla, Tlaxcala. *Photograph by Barbara Mauldin, 1999.*

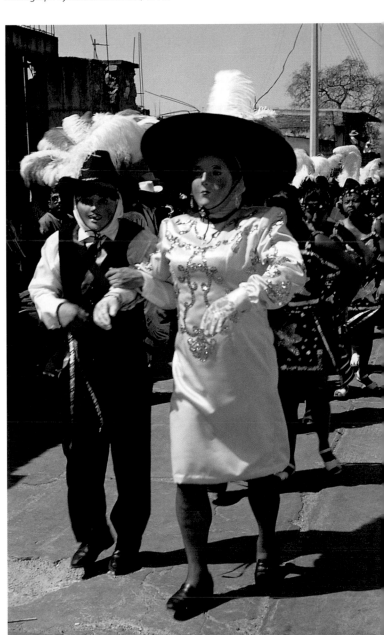

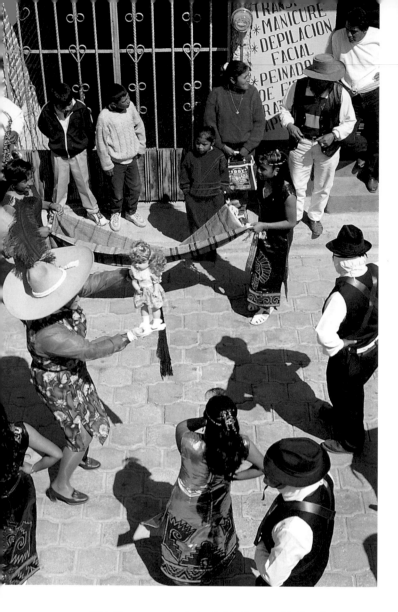

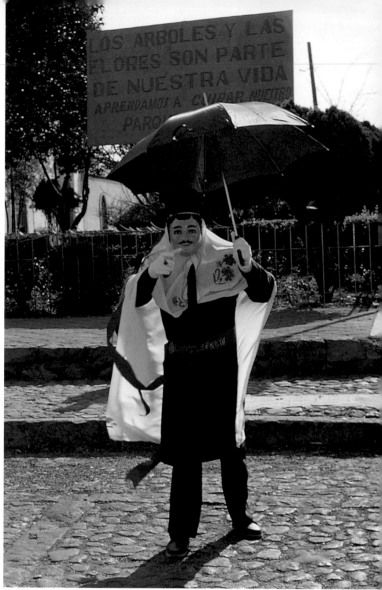

7.14 *Nana* presents a baby doll to the crowd in Papalotla, Tlaxcala. *Photograph by Barbara Mauldin, 1999.*

7.15 *Catrine* masquerader in Amaxac de Guerrero, Tlaxcala. *Photograph by Barbara Mauldin, 1999.*

with images of the Christ child on Christmas Eve. After a while *nana* takes the baby doll back into her arms and continues to dance to the music. At the end of the sequence she presents the doll to the woman of the house in front of which the group is performing.[45] This is said to be a blessing of fertility and prosperity for that household as well as the rest of the neighborhood and town.[46]

EL CATRINE

El catrine is the dominant type of masquerade worn by groups of men from barrios in the Nahua towns in the central part of Tlaxcala state, such as San Bernardino de Contla, Amaxac de Guerrero, and Panotla. It is an impersonation of the French dandies who were seen

on the streets of large cities such as Puebla and Tlaxcala in the latter part of the nineteenth century (fig. 7.15). Along with beautiful Caucasian masks, the dancers wear tuxedos, top hats, and gloves and carry umbrellas, all of which are generally purchased in Mexico City at the Lagunilla clothing market. Among most groups the *catrine* costume also includes a wide sash around the waist and an embroidered white scarf billowing over the back, adding to the character's elegance. The *catrines* carry castanets in their hands which they play while dancing or click as they walk through the streets. The young women who serve as their dance partners wear matching dresses, ranging from short skirts to full-length evening gowns (fig. 7.16). Between dances the *catrines* often clown around and strike poses that

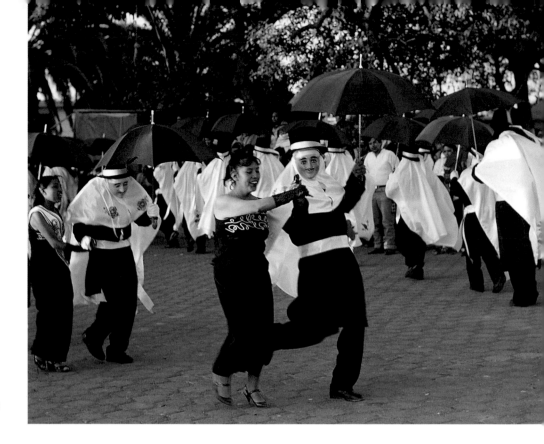

7.16 *Catrines* dance in Amaxac de Guerrero, Tlaxcala. *Photograph by Barbara Mauldin, 1999.*

emphasize the effeminacy of their costumes and beautiful masks. They hold the open umbrellas over their heads to protect their "delicate white skin" from the sun.[47]

One of the *catrine* groups in the town of San Bernardino Contla has retained the tradition of using young men to play the role of the female dance partners (fig. 7.17). None of them wears a mask, but some use dark sunglasses to cover their eyes. All of these "females" wear some type of dress, ranging from matronly outfits to sexy miniskirts. This creates a humorous effect that is played out as the group makes its way through the streets of town. Its dance performance is taken seriously, however, and it is clear that all of the participants have practiced the choreographed steps and movements necessary to please the watching crowds.[48]

EL ESPAÑOL

In many towns in central Tlaxcala, such as San Dionisio Yauhquemecan, Santa María Atlihuetzía, and San Esteban Tizatlán, male dancers wear a different type of outfit, one known as *el español*. In contrast to the black tuxedo of the *catrine*, this outfit consists of a jacket and three-quarter-length pants said to derive from a Spanish bullfighter's outfit that was adapted for wealthy gentlemen's clothing in the nineteenth century. Today

most of these costumes are made of brightly colored satin decorated with shiny sequins and beads, and the dancers wear colorful hats or headdresses ornamented with mirrors, feathers, paper flowers, and other decorative items (figs. 7.18, 7.23). Their female partners often wear satin dresses decorated similarly to the men's outfits.

Español-style costumes are also worn by some of the male groups in San Francisco Tepeyanco, located in the southern part of the state, but there they are made of black velvet embroidered with colorful floral patterns, and the dancers wear black cowboy hats with feathers (see page iv). Their "female" partners today, as in the past, wear white knee-length dresses fashioned in a style that was popular among upper-class Mexican women in the mid-twentieth century (fig. 7.19).[49]

TRAJE TRADICIONAL DE SAN JUAN TOTOLAC

Male dance groups from the town of San Juan Totolac, west of the capital, used to wear *catrine* costumes, but they complained about the weight of the clothing and the way their bodies got overheated when they danced. Finally, in the mid-1940s they decided to wear a style of Mexican Indian clothing that would eliminate these problems. The costume consisted of loose-fitting shirts and knee-length pants made of white cotton, along with leather sandals, or *huaraches*.

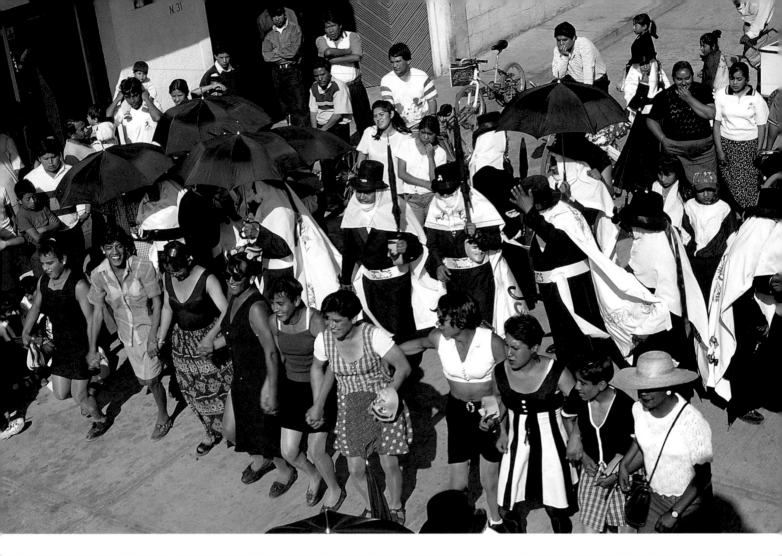

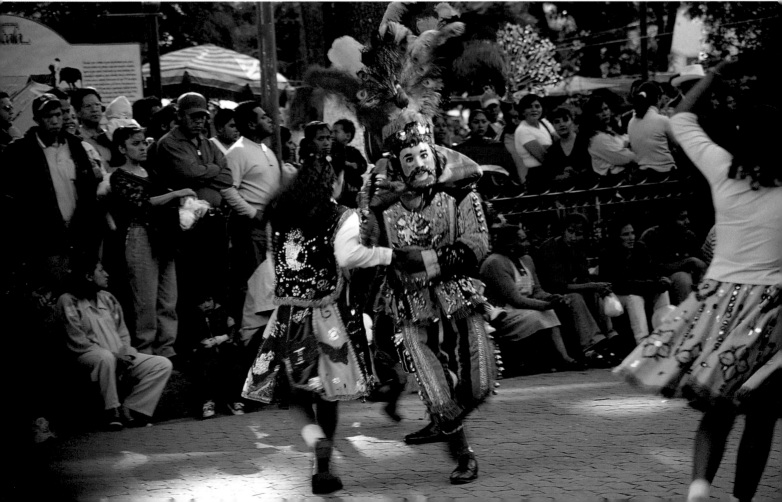

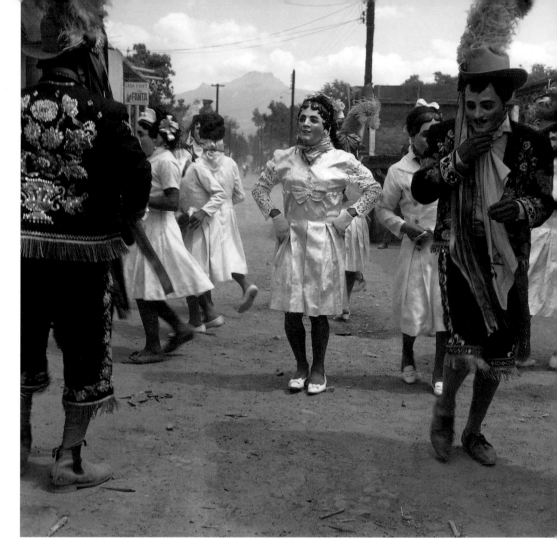

7.17 *Catrines* dance with "female" partners played by men in Contla, Tlaxcala. *Photograph by Barbara Mauldin, 1999.*

7.18 *Español* masqueraders from San Esteban Tizatlán dance during Carnival celebrations in the city of Tlaxcala. *Photograph by Barbara Mauldin, 2002.*

7.19 *Españoles* once danced with "female" partners played by men in Tepeyanco, Tlaxcala. *Photograph by Ruth Lechuga, 1969.*

Eventually they changed to full-length pants and began wearing a short cotton cape over their shoulders. They call this style *traje tradicional,* or traditional dress.

By the 1970s, the white cotton fabric was being decorated with brightly colored ribbons and the men were wearing cowboy hats with tall feather plumes. Throughout all of these changes the men's faces continued to be covered with Caucasian-style masks, many of which sported dark beards and mustaches. Since the late 1950s, when Totolacan girls began participating in the dance performances, their outfits have complemented the men's, being made of the same white cotton fabric and ornamented similarly. Today, dance groups in neighboring towns such as San Francisco Ocotelulco, San Miguel Tlamahuco, and San Lucas Cuauhtelupan have adopted similar outfits. Besides *cuadrillas,* dancers in San Juan Totolac are known for carrying out another type of performance derived from the European maypole tradition. In Tlaxcala it is called the Danza de Las Cintas, or Ribbon Dance (fig. 7.20).[50]

CHIVARRUDOS

Another category of Carnival masquerade is found in a few Tlaxcalan villages in the southern part of the state, such as Zacatelco and San Toribio Xichotzingo. There, groups of young men are dressed as *chivarrudos,* or comical cowboys, wearing large painted hats, wool jackets, full-length pants, and chaps made from the hides of goats (*chivos*). A small wooden horse is attached to the crotch of each masquerader's pants, as if he were riding it, and he carries a short whip that he uses to coax the tiny "steed" into action (fig. 7.21). The *chivarrudos'* faces are covered with different types of masks, but most are made of painted leather and portray Caucasian men with furry mustaches.[51] These masqueraders represent the lower-class mestizo cowboys who ran cattle through Tlaxcala in the late nineteenth and early twentieth centuries. The cattle drive often followed the main road that passed from north to south, and the cowboys stopped in towns along the way to get food and other supplies. Residents in some of the southern towns on this route, such as Zacatelco

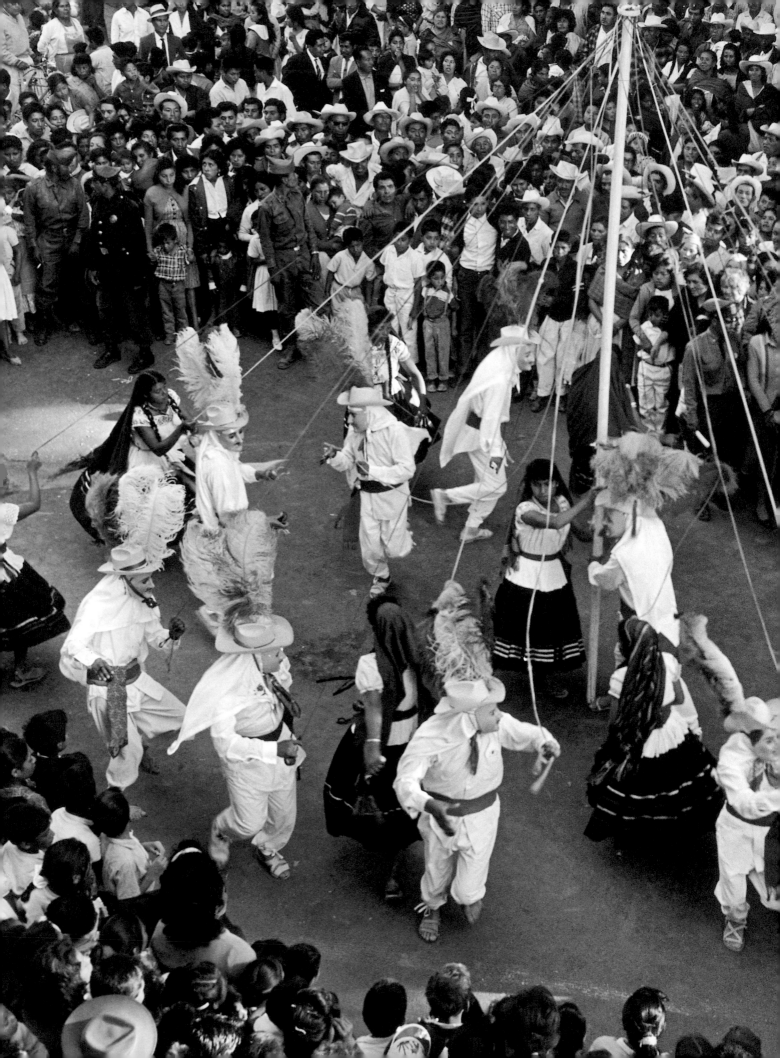

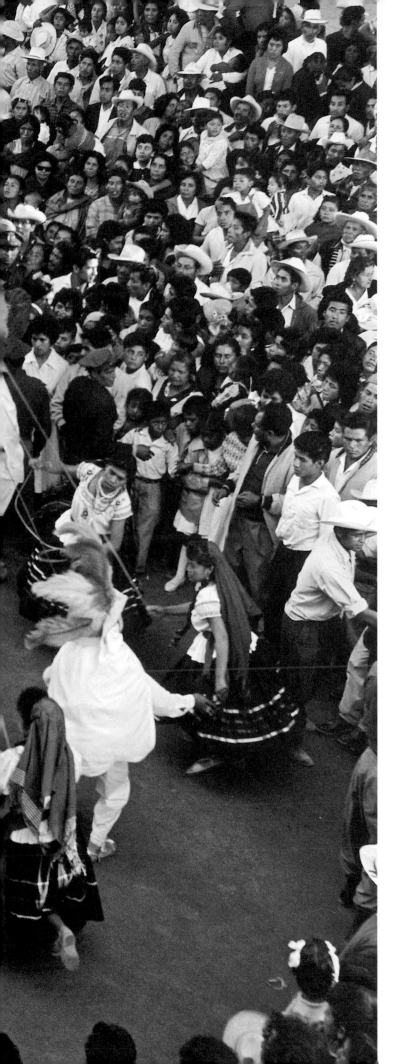

and Xichotzingo, viewed these cowboys with great humor and developed the *chivarrudo* Carnival masquerade to imitate and make fun of them.[52]

Unlike other Tlaxcalan Carnival groups, the *chivarrudos* do not have female participants. Indeed, they perform a different type of line dance from those found elsewhere, and their music is solely percussive, using a pre-Hispanic style of drum known as a *teponaxtle*. Some of the dancers also sing songs that tell about the beautiful women of their town. In keeping with the cowboy theme, the group usually includes a man carrying a cane and a papier-mâché sculpture of a bull, called a *torito*. He holds the bull over his head and dances with the cowboys as part of the performance.[53]

Since the 1970s, men in neighboring communities, such as Papalotla, have also been wearing the humorous *chivarrudo* Carnival masquerade, but they usually come out by themselves or with only one or two other men (see fig. 7.1). Instead of performing their own dance, they simply gallop around the streets "riding" the little wooden horses attached to their pants or join in with the *vasario* dance groups. During breaks they sit down on the pavement and rest on the backs of their tiny "animals." All of these antics bring great amusement to the crowds.[54]

CUCHILLOS

Another type of dance performed in a few villages in the northeastern part of the state, such as Toluca de Guadalupe, is said to have originated on a Spanish colonial ranch known as La Concepción. The dancers are referred to as *cuchillos,* or knives, because they perform with knives tied to their ankles, pointing toward the insides of their legs. They take turns showing off their ability to carry out the precarious dance steps, which require grace and exactness in movement. Their outfits consist of short jackets and knee-length skirts made of brightly colored fabrics decorated with contrasting ribbonwork. Short shawls of a different fabric are worn over their shoulders, and they wear hats decorated with paper flowers and long ribbons. Like *chivarrudos,* they use painted leather masks that portray Caucasian men.[55]

7.20 Masqueraders from Totolac perform the Ribbon Dance in the city of Tlaxcala. *Photograph by Ruth Lechuga, 1963.*

In contrast to the Carnival music found in most of the other Tlaxcalan villages, the musicians who accompany the *cuchillos* play a violin and a guitar. The masqueraders perform dances that are unique to this part of the state, with names such as La Entrada, El Tlaxcalteco, El Peine, El Porrazo, and El Jarabe. The men form two lines or a circle and take turns executing fast dance steps that allow the knives to click against each other in time with the music. Sometimes the men skip rope as part of the performance.[56]

OSOS AND PAYASITOS

In many villages in central and southern Tlaxcala, groups of young men and boys wander through the streets wearing costumes and masks that are inexpensive and easy to purchase at a commercial costume shop. The two most common types are the *oso,* or furry bear, and the *payasito,* or clown (see fig. 7.27), both of which bring back memories of the circuses

7.21 *Chivarrudo* masqueraders pose for a photograph during Carnival celebrations in San Toribio Xichotzingo, Tlaxcala. *Photograph by Barbara Mauldin, 2002.*

that used to come through Tlaxcala. Sometimes the bear and clown masqueraders join in the performances of the other groups.[57]

INDIVIDUALES

Despite the mid-twentieth century ban on satirical masquerades of known people, individuals or small independent groups sometimes appear on the streets wearing masks that make fun of local politicians and other famous people, such as Fidel Castro (fig. 7.22). These rubber masks are sold in costume shops in Puebla and the larger towns in Tlaxcala; the Carnival revelers put together the rest of the costume.[58]

Organization of Carnival Activities

Although the organizational systems used to carry out the Carnival festivities vary somewhat from town to town, some general structures and sequences of events can be found in most of them. The mayor and city council members oversee the broad aspects of the celebration and coordinate the events that take place in the main plaza.[59] Most of the dance performances,

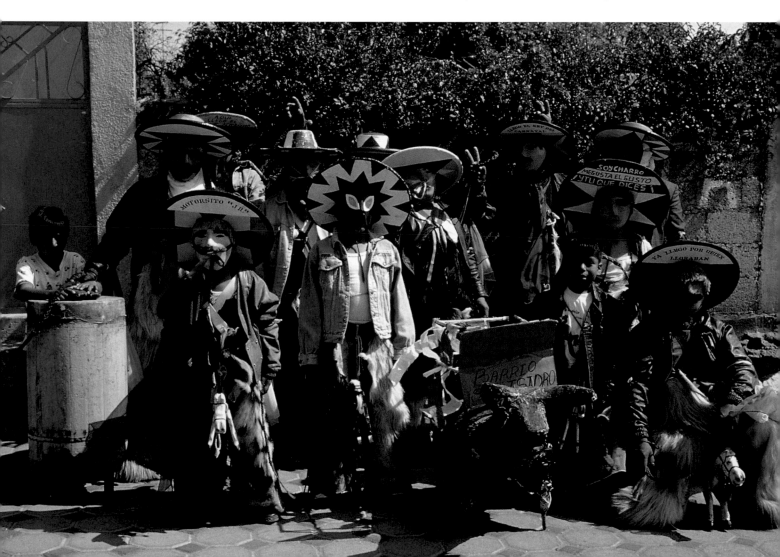

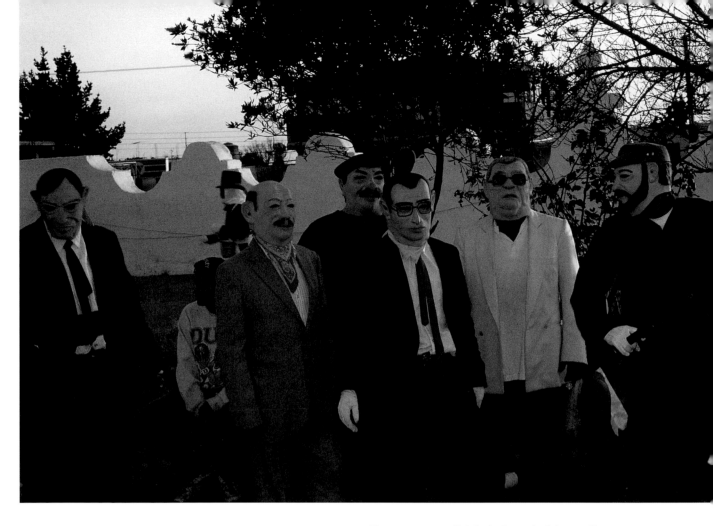

7.22 Masqueraders impersonate Fidel Castro and Mexican politicians in Contla, Tlaxcala. *Photograph by Barbara Mauldin, 1999.*

however, are organized by the neighborhood, or barrio, associations, which continue to function somewhat like the pre-Hispanic kinship groups. In some towns there are as many as ten barrios, each with its own association.[60] Many participants view their role as a religious commitment to Christ, the Virgin, and other Catholic saints, and they carry out the festival rituals as a spiritual promise and sacrifice. They also take a great deal of pride and pleasure in helping to bring about a successful celebration.[61]

One or more people from the barrio volunteer to sponsor a group of dancers, known as a *camada* or *comparsa*. The sponsors, generally called *encargados* or *encabezados,* are responsible for selecting the dancers from the barrio, teaching them several types of *cuadrillas,* or square dances, and then making sure they attend the rehearsals that begin a few months before Carnival. They must also pay the musicians who will accompany the dancers and provide meals for the performers, families of the barrio, and other invited

guests. The sponsors solicit help from their immediate families, other relatives, and neighborhood friends to collect money to pay the musicians and to cook food for the community meals, the menus for which include dishes such as *mole* (turkey stew), beans, corn, tortillas, and sweet breads. The dancers also volunteer their time and are responsible for acquiring their own costumes, which are made by women in their families or commissioned from someone else in the town. This involvement of most residents in the neighborhood helps to bring the community together so that everyone feels part of the activity.[62]

On the days of the Carnival festivities, the musicians and fully costumed dancers sometimes go to church to pray and ask for support from the Christian saints.[63] Then they assemble at the house of the main sponsor at around ten o'clock in the morning and eat a meal with his family, other sponsors, and invited guests. After completing a performance of all of the dances in front of this house, the group moves through the streets of the neighborhood, repeating the dances in the front of the homes of other sponsors. Along the way the dancers stop and perform in front of

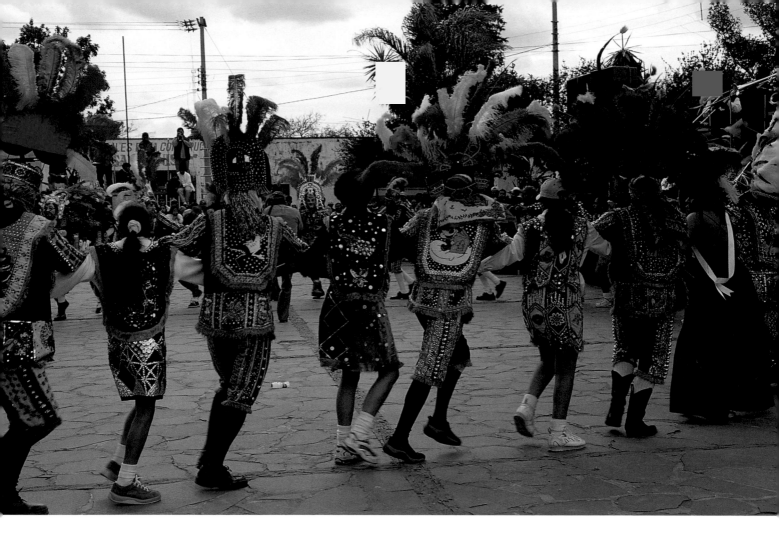

7.23 *Españoles* and their female partners perform a square dance in Yauhquemecan, Tlaxcala. *Photograph by Barbara Mauldin, 2002.*

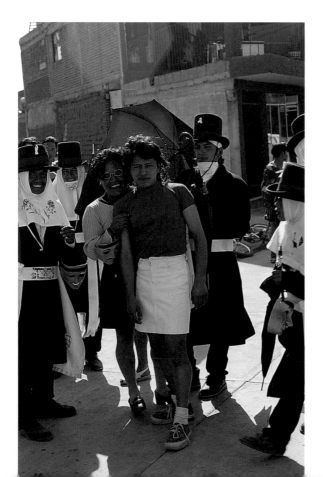

other houses where families have paid for the honor of watching the dances. Food and drink are also offered to the performers as they pass through the neighborhood streets.[64]

Cuadrilla is a generic term referring to the square or rectangle that the dancers form to carry out their performance, with six to eighteen or more couples participating (fig. 7.23). Variations on this formation are used for different dances, each with its own choreography and music. Some of the most popular dances are known as the Lancers, Franceses, Taragotes, Cuatro Rosas, Españoles, Cuatro Estaciones, Virginias, and Pañuelos, and the music that accompanies each of them is usually referred to by the same name. Some of these dances have several parts and can go on for two to four hours. However, the performances in the streets of the barrio are generally cut short so the groups can do a number of different dances and then

7.24 Unmasked *catrines* and their "female" dance partners take a break between performances in Contla, Tlaxcala. *Photograph by Barbara Mauldin, 1999.*

move on to visit other houses. Between performances the young men often remove their masks to get fresh air on their faces and socialize with the other dancers (fig. 7.24).[65]

The *bandas,* or groups of amateur musicians, that accompany the dancers usually consist of six to eight men and teenage boys who play wind and percussion instruments with varying degrees of proficiency (fig. 7.25). This type of musical group developed in most Indian communities throughout Mexico in the second half of the nineteenth century through the influence of Mexican military marching bands. Gradually the Indian musicians learned to play a wider selection of tunes for their local fiestas, such as the polkas, mazurkas, and schottische-style music used in the Tlaxcalan Carnival dances.[66] The *banda* generally follows the dancers on foot as they move from house to house, setting up on the sidewalk at each new location. In some of the larger towns the musical groups have been enlarged to include electric guitars and pianos, and they travel in the back of a truck with speakers blasting into the neighborhood.[67]

As I mentioned earlier, the festivities may be repeated over two or more Sundays, culminating in

a last day that is called the *remate* (conclusion). On that day the performances in the barrios are carried out again, and then in the late afternoon each neighborhood's group of dancers and musicians makes its way to the main plaza of the town. There it joins the other dance groups, and they all form a long procession. In the meantime, residents from the various neighborhoods have assembled downtown to watch the groups as they pass by (fig. 7.26). Often this procession leads the performers to the central church, where they enter and offer a prayer to the patron saint (fig. 7.27). Then the dancers and their musicians go to a space assigned to them in the central plaza, and all the groups begin performing at once. In some of the larger towns, officials present prizes and even name a queen of Carnival for the overall event.

Hundreds of strands of cordage decorated with small streamers and pendants have been stretched across the plaza. The loud music produced by the different bands and the swirling motion of the dance groups creates an atmosphere of chaos and energy that everyone, performers and spectators alike, can feel. Around the periphery, vendors sell food, games, and other items that add to the festive atmosphere (fig. 7.28). As the late afternoon sun fades away and darkness takes over, city officials set off a fantastic array of fireworks and rockets that illuminate the night sky. The music, dancing, and other festivities continue

7.25 *La banda* provides dance music during Carnival celebrations in Tepayanco, Tlaxcala. *Photograph by Barbara Mauldin, 2002.*

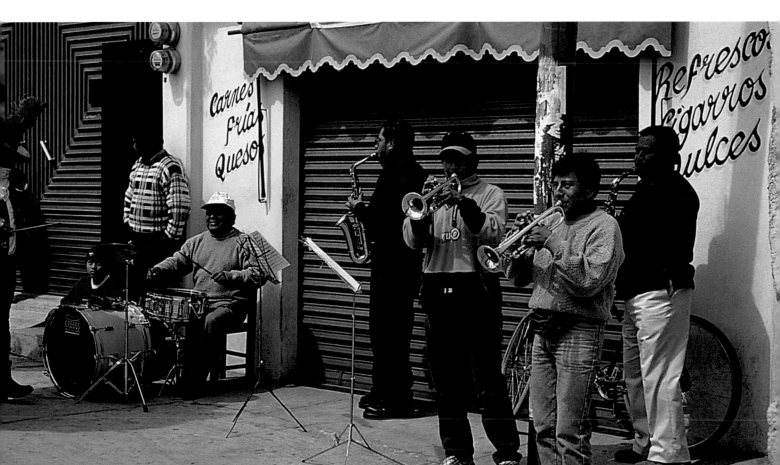

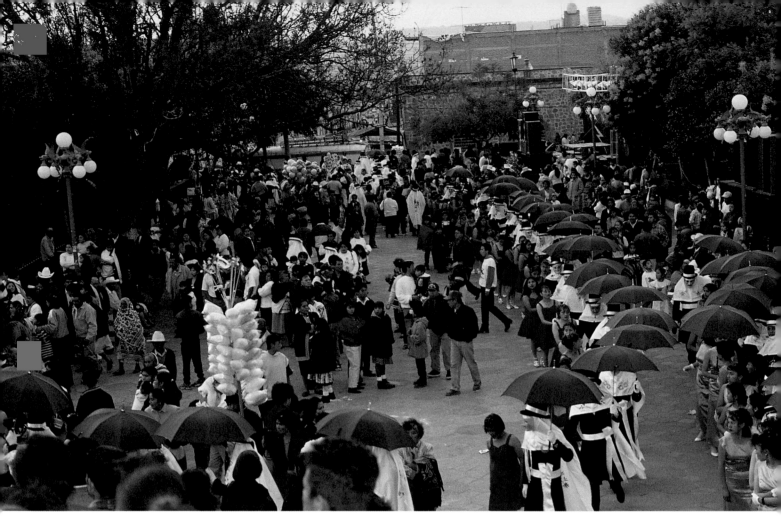

7.26 Groups of *catrines* and their female partners come into the main plaza of Contla, Tlaxcala, amid a crowd of onlookers during the *remate,* or final day of Carnival celebrations. *Photograph by Gabriel Alatriste Montoto, 1999.*

7.27 Groups of *catrines* and their female partners visit the church in Contal, Tlaxcala, late in the afternoon of the *remate*. On the left are two young masqueraders in clown masks. *Photograph by Barbara Mauldin, 1999.*

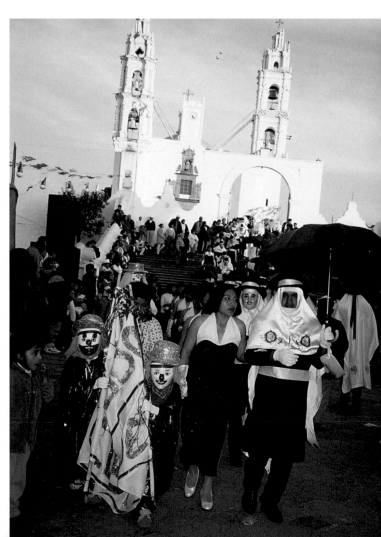

for a few more hours, until everyone is tired and at last ready to go home.[68]

Traditionally, the Carnival groups from some of the neighborhoods around the city of Tlaxcala came together to perform in the *atrio,* or courtyard, in front of the sanctuary dedicated to Nuestra Señora de Ocotlán, an image of the Virgin Mary that is said to have miraculously appeared to Tlaxcalan Indians in the mid-sixteenth century on the Sunday before the beginning of Lent. In the mid-twentieth century, however, city officials moved the *remate* performances to the bull-ring in the central part of the city.[69] The organizers also started inviting Carnival dance groups from towns

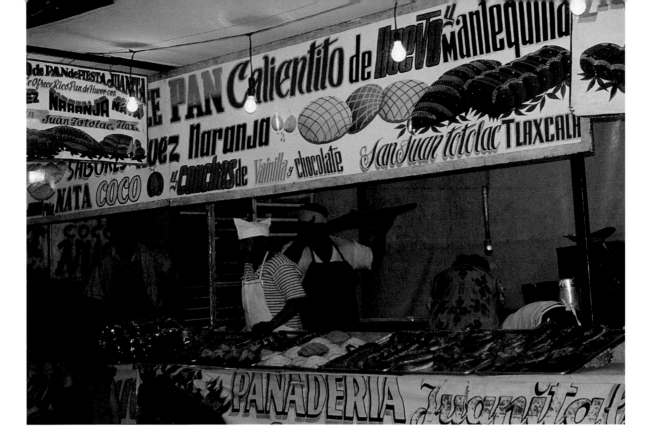

7.28 Booths sell varieties of sweet *pan,* or bread, during the festivities in Contla, Tlaxcala. *Photograph by Barbara Mauldin, 1999.*

around the state to come to the capital city, and they set up several areas for them to perform in. Now, a published schedule shows when each group will dance, beginning on the Friday before Ash Wednesday and continuing until the Tuesday night before Lent begins. Besides providing a means for Tlaxcalans from the different towns to see each other's costumes and performances, this was done to encourage tourists to come from other states and countries and to recognize the quality and significance of Tlaxcala's Carnival celebration.[70] To date, however, very few outsiders attend the festivities.[71]

Conclusion

Despite the efforts of city and state officials to turn Tlaxcala's Carnival celebrations into larger civic events, the primary impetus and significance for the festivities remain within the barrios. Following pre-Hispanic ritual traditions, extended family members and other residents of the neighborhoods work together each year to see that the dance performances and related activities are carried out in appropriate ways to bring about the well-being of the whole community. Under-

lying the festivities are religious concerns of pleasing the Catholic saints and adhering to a spring ritual cycle. There is also pride in wearing beautiful or interesting costumes and performing the dances with skill and endurance. Overall it is a time for everyone to come together to socialize and enjoy the celebrations.

Following pre-Hispanic and Spanish colonial practices, the masquerades worn by the performers are impersonations of someone other than themselves—in this case, interesting foreigners who were seen in the Tlaxcala-Puebla region in the late nineteenth and early twentieth centuries. This was the time when Indian communities were freer to begin carrying out festivals and masked pageants in their own ways, and it was natural for them to imitate and burlesque the exotic costumes and dances of upper-class Europeans and Mexicans or mestizo cowboys. Although the range of masks, costumes, and dances seen in Tlaxcalan Carnival celebrations today has narrowed since the early twentieth century, the masquerades' endurance shows the importance of adhering to "tradition" once norms were established. At the same time, new generations of sponsors and performers have allowed some changes, such as the participation of young women dance partners, to keep the festivities alive and relevant within the evolving world around them.

NOTES

I want to thank Ruth Lechuga, the well-known scholar of Mexican folk culture, for providing valuable information in the early stage of my research on Carnival in Tlaxcala and for allowing me to go through her archive of photographs and select a few to accompany this essay. I am also indebted to Yolanda Ramos Galicia, former director of the Museo de Artes y Tradiciones Populares de la Casa de las Artesanías de Tlaxcala and current director of the Museos del Centro INAH-Puebla, for her hospitality and guidance while I conducted field research in Tlaxcala. The anthropologist Hugo Nutini and the scholar and artist Desiderio H. Xochitiotzin were both generous with their time and comments in answering many questions about their own research in Tlaxcala. Andrew Mauldin provided valuable editing of the essay, and special acknowledgment must also go to some friends and colleagues who accompanied me to Carnival festivities in various towns in Tlaxcala: Gabriel Alatriste Montoto, Antonio Alvarez, Consuelo Rodríguez de Ramos, Nicolás Ahuactzin, and Lee Carter.

1. Amparo Sevilla, Hilda Rodriguez, and Elizabeth Camara, *Danzas y bailes tradicionales del estado de Tlaxcala* (Tlahuapan, Puebla: Premiá Editora de Libros, 1983), 80, 118, 148.

2. José Ramon Ballesteros, *Origen y evolución del charro mexicano* (México, DF: Librería de Manuel Porrúa, 1972).

3. José Alvarez del Villar, *Hombres y caballos de México: Historia y práctica de la charrería* (México, DF: Panorama Editorial, 1980), 61–65. During the late nineteenth century the *charros* often performed rope tricks during the fiestas on the ranches. Some of these performances were combined with music.

4. José Guadalupe H. Xochitiotzin Ortega, "Los Carnavales de Tlaxcala," *México Desconocido* 180 (1992): 20.

5. Isaura Ramos de Temoltzin, *Danzas de carnaval en Tlaxcala* (Tlaxcala: H. Ayuntamiento de Tlaxcala, 1997), 21–22; Ruth Lechuga, "Carnival in Tlaxcala," in *Behind the Mask in Mexico,* ed. Janet Brody Esser (Santa Fe: Museum of New Mexico Press, 1988), 165.

6. Andrés Santana Sandoval, "Carnaval, la fiesta colectiva," in *Tlaxcala es una fiesta: Mesa redonda sobre el Carnaval Tlaxcala 90* (Tlaxcala: H. Ayuntamiento de Tlaxcala, 1990), 29–34.

7. Marilyn Ekdahl Ravicz, *Early Colonial Religious Drama in Mexico: From Tzompantli to Golgotha* (Washington, DC: Catholic University of America Press, 1970), 1–25.

8. Francis Joseph Brooks, "Parish and Cofradía in Eighteenth-Century Mexico" (Ph.D. dissertation, Princeton University, 1976), 45–51.

9. Ravicz, *Early Colonial Religious Drama,* 16–25.

10. Charles Gibson, *The Aztecs under Spanish Rule: A History of the Indians in the Valley of Mexico* (Stanford, CA: Stanford University Press, 1964), 152–153, 182.

11. Brooks, "Parish and Cofradía," 61–75.

12. One of the most insightful studies and analyses of the Mexican Indians' adoption of Catholicism into their religious beliefs and practices is found in Serge Gruzinski, *The Conquest of Mexico: The Incorporation of Indian Societies into the Western World, Sixteenth-Eighteenth Centuries,* trans. Eileen Corrigan (Cambridge: Polity Press, 1993).

13. Brooks, "Parish and Cofradía," 75–296.

14. Fray Bernardino de Sahagún, *Florentine Codex: General History of the Things of New Spain,* Book 2, *The Ceremonies,* trans. and eds. Arthur J. O. Anderson and Charles Dibble (Salt Lake City: University of Utah Press, 1981), 1–10.

15. Higinio Vázquez Santana and J. Ignacio Dávila Garibi, *El Carnaval* (México, DF: Talleres Gráficos de la Nación México, 1931), 19–20.

16. This continued into the twentieth century, as documented by John M. Ingham, *Mary, Michael, and Lucifer: Folk Catholicism in Central Mexico* (Austin: University of Texas Press, 1986), 47–54.

17. Carl Christian Sartorius, *Mexico and the Mexicans* (London: Trubner, 1859; reprint, México, DF: San Angel Ediciones, 1973), 41–44.

18. Vázquez Santana and Dávila Garibi, *El Carnaval,* 73–130.

19. Ruth Lechuga, *Máscaras traditionales de México* (México, DF: Banco Nacional de Obras y Servicios Publicos, 1991), 81–96. Lechuga examines the Carnival celebrations and underlying significance for the Indian communities within a broad cycle of time that continues into Holy Week.

20. Charles Gibson, *Tlaxcala in the Sixteenth Century* (Stanford, CA: Stanford University Press, 1967), 1–27.

21. Alfredo Chavero, ed., "Lienzo de Tlaxcala," in *Antigüedades mexicanas publicadas por la junta colombina de México en el cuarto centenario de descubrimiento de América* (México, DF: Secretaría de Fomento, 1892), *lámina 7.*

22. Diego Muñoz Camargo, *Historia de Tlaxcala,* facsimile edition (México, DF: Secretaría de Fomento, 1966 [1892]), 135.

23. Gibson, *Tlaxcala in the Sixteenth Century,* 79–88.

24. Ricardo Rendón Garcini, "Las Haciendas pulqueras," in *Tlaxcala: Textos de su historia,* eds. Lía García Verástegui and Ma. Esther Pérez Salas C. (México, DF: Instituto de Investigaciones Dr. José María Luis Mora, 1990), 1: 74–75.

25. Alberto Xelhuantzi Ramírez, "El Carnaval o carnestolenda en Tlaxcala en el siglo XVIII," *Caceta Cultural del Tlaxcala de Xichténcatl* (February 10, 2002): 2A.

26. This situation continued into the twentieth century and was well documented by Hugo G. Nutini in *San Bernardino Contla: Marriage and Family Structure in a Tlaxcalan Municipio* (Pittsburgh: University of Pittsburgh Press, 1968), 63–82.

27. Hugo G. Nutini, "An Outline of Tlaxcaltecan Culture, History, Ethnology, and Demography," in *The Tlaxcaltecan Prehistory, Demography, Morphology, and Genetics,* ed. Michael H. Crawford (Lawrence: University of Kansas Press, 1976), 27–29.

28. Sevilla, Rodriguez, and Camara, *Danzas y bailes,* 178–181; J. Arturo Chamorro, *La Música popular en Tlaxcala* (Tlahuapan, Puebla: Premiá Editora de Libros, 1983), 14–15.

29. Isaura Ramos de Temoltzin, "Aspectos históricos de la danza en México," in *Tlaxcala es una fiesta,* 25–28; Sevilla, Rodriguez, and Camará, *Danzas y bailes,* 28–33, 76.

30. Santana Sandoval, "Carnaval, la fiesta colectiva," 29–34.

31. Yolanda Ramos Galicia, *Calendario de ferias y fiestas tradicionales del estado Tlaxcala* (México, DF: Instituto Nacional de

Antropología e Historia, 1992); *Programa de Carnaval Tlaxcala, 2002* (Tlaxcala: Secretaría de Turismo, 2002), 3–5.

32. Lechuga, "Carnival in Tlaxcala," 145; *Programa de Carnaval Tlaxcala, 2002,* 3–5; personal observation in Tlaxcala during Carnival celebrations in February 2002.

33. Sevilla, Rodriguez, and Camara, *Danzas y bailes,* 107–115.

34. Vázquez Santana and Dávila Garibi, *El Carnaval,* 41–53, 111–123; Ramos de Temoltzin, *Danzas de carnaval,* 16–18.

35. Interview with Desiderio H. Xochitiotzin, artist and scholar of Tlaxcalan Carnival, at his home in Tlaxcala, February 2002.

36. For more information about the older mask makers and the types of masks they made, see Lechuga, "Carnival in Tlaxcala," 153, 157, 161.

37. *Programa de Carnaval Tlaxcala, 1999* (Tlaxcala: Secretaría de Turismo, 1999), 1.

38. Lechuga, "Carnival in Tlaxcala," 153, 157; personal observation of Carnival performances in Contla, Tlaxcala, in February 1999.

39. Sevilla, Rodriguez, and Camara, *Danzas y bailes,* 200.

40. Ibid., 148–150.

41. Lechuga, "Carnival in Tlaxcala," 163.

42. Ibid., 163, 165.

43. Sevilla, Rodriguez, and Camara, *Danzas y bailes,* 150.

44. Interview with Desiderio H. Xochitiotzin, February 2002.

45. Sevilla, Rodriguez, and Camara, *Danzas y bailes,* 131–138. One explanation the authors give for including rituals to the Christ child in the dance of the *nana* is that many residents in Tlaxcala associate the Carnival festival cycle with Holy Week and the persecution of Jesus. I think it is also related to the strong devotion that Indian and mestizo people in Tlaxcala (and most other regions of Mexico) have for the Christ child and the elaborate ritual patterns that have been developed to carry out this devotion in a community setting. See Hugo G. Nutini and Betty Bell, *Ritual Kinship: The Structure and Historical Development of the Compadrazgo System in Rural Tlaxcala* (Princeton: Princeton University Press, 1980), 1: 101–172. Even though the doll used by the *nana* does not actually represent the Christ child, the implied involvement of the baby Jesus brings a deeper religious significance and sense of well-being to the festivities.

46. Interview with Desiderio H. Xochitiotzin, February 2002.

47. Sevilla, Rodriguez, and Camara, *Danzas y bailes,* 146–148, 158; Ramos de Temoltzin, *Danzas de carnaval,* 28–29.

48. Personal observation of Carnival performances in Contla, Tlaxcala, in February 1999.

49. Sevilla, Rodriguez, and Camara, *Danzas y bailes,* 150–152.

50. Ibid., 117–118, 152–154.

51. Sevilla, Rodriguez, and Camara, *Danzas y bailes,* 140.

52. H. Xochitiotzin Ortega, "Los Carnavales de Tlaxcala," 21.

53. Sevilla, Rodriguez, and Camara, *Danzas y bailes,* 139–142.

54. Ibid., 140; personal observation in Papalotla, Tlaxcala, during Carnival festivities in February 2002.

55. Ramos de Temoltzin, *Danzas de carnaval,* 25–27.

56. Sevilla, Rodriguez, and Camara, *Danzas y bailes,* 115–117.

57. Ibid., 148; Desiderio Hernández Xochitiotzin, "Conclusions," in *Tlaxcala es una fiesta,* 39.

58. Personal observations in Contla and the city of Tlaxcala during Carnival festivities in February 1999 and February 2002.

59. Lechuga, "Carnival in Tlaxcala," 145, 153.

60. Hugo G. Nutini, "Clan Organization in a Nahuatl-Speaking Village of the State of Tlaxcala, Mexico," *American Anthropologist* 63 (1961): 67–76.

61. Hernández Xochitiotzin, "Conclusions," 36–37.

62. Lechuga, "Carnival in Tlaxcala," 145, 153.

63. Hernández Xochitiotzin, "Conclusions," 37.

64. Lechuga, "Carnival in Tlaxcala," 145; personal observation in Tlaxcala during Carnival celebrations in February 1999 and February 2002.

65. Sevilla, Rodriguez, and Camara, *Danzas y bailes,* 93–106.

66. Chamorro, *Música popular,* 14–17.

67. Personal observation in various towns in Tlaxcala during Carnival celebrations in February 1999 and February 2002.

68. Sevilla, Rodriguez, and Camara, *Danzas y bailes,* 82–84; personal observation in San Bernardino Contla during the Carnival *remate* in February 1999.

69. Desiderio Hernández Xochitiotzin, "Orígenes del carnaval en Europa, México y Tlaxcala," in *Tlaxcala es una fiesta,* 18–19.

70. *Programa de Carnaval Tlaxcala, 2002,* 6–7.

71. Personal observation in Tlaxcala during Carnival celebrations in February 1999 and February 2002.

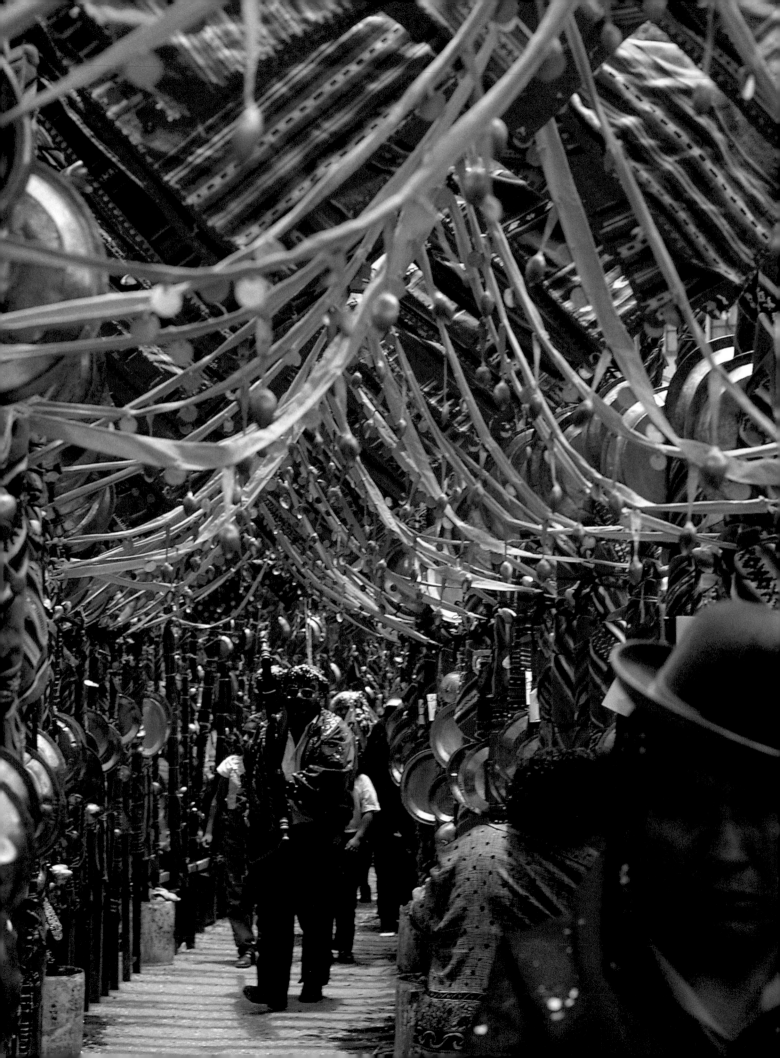

8 Dancing for the Virgin and the Devil

CARNAVAL IN ORURO, BOLIVIA

CYNTHIA LECOUNT SAMAKÉ

Historical sections by Barbara Mauldin

THE FLAMBOYANT *CARNAVAL* of Oruro, Bolivia, has become the country's most important religious, social, and artistic event. In May 2001, UNESCO declared the celebration a "Masterpiece of Oral and Intangible Heritage of Humanity" (Patrimonio Oral e Intangible de la Humanidad), with prestige and importance similar to those of a UNESCO World Heritage site.[1] Bolivians are extremely proud of this international distinction, because world news outlets typically ignore their peaceful country. Bolivian tourist brochures call Oruro the "Folklore Capital of Bolivia," and indeed, the remarkable masks, costumes, and performances of Oruro's Carnival constitute the most vital and exciting expression of modern Bolivian creativity (figs. 8.1, 8.2).

The Evolution of Bolivian Festivals and Carnival

At the time of the Spanish arrival in the Andes in the early sixteenth century, Indian groups throughout the highlands were carrying out festival celebrations with songs and dances that told stories about their past. These performances relayed the history of their ancestors, places and events, and myths and legends important to the group's identity. The performances enforced community memory and ensured that history would be passed down to future generations. The celebrations were part of a ritual cycle that observed the summer and winter solstices, the agricultural seasons, and the annual initiation of young people. Heavy consumption of *chicha,* a potent alcoholic beverage fermented from corn, generally accompanied the festivities. Ritual offerings of the alcohol, called *ch'allas,* were given to the sun god, Inti, to the mother goddess, Pachamama, and to other important spirits and ancestors.[2]

At first the Catholic priests encouraged the Indians to perform their traditional dances and songs for Catholic feast day observances. Some of the largest festivals took place in the new Spanish centers, such as Cuzco in Peru and Potosí in Bolivia.[3] The latter was the site of silver deposits that turned out to be one of the richest finds in all of the Americas. European entrepreneurs quickly set up mining operations and forced Indians from the region to work as their laborers. Soon the entrepreneurs became extremely wealthy and began to sponsor lavish feast day celebrations as symbols of their success. The Indians were instructed to perform their traditional songs and dances as part of the festivities.[4] By the latter part of the sixteenth century, however, Church and civic authorities in Potosí and elsewhere were condemning the practice because

8.1 A tunnel of fabric-draped wooden arches is set up in the plaza in front of the church on the Monday of Carnival, and people walk through it to honor the Virgin and receive her blessings. *Photograph by Barbara Mauldin, 1997.*

of excessive drunkenness and promulgation of the traditional religious beliefs. Many Spaniards took note of the subtle ways in which the Andeans were able to keep the memory of their idols and other aspects of their past alive.[5]

In 1569 the Spanish Crown sent Francisco Toledo to the Andes to serve as the new viceroy for Peru and the surrounding region. He immediately implemented a series of ordinances aimed at resolving certain problems Spain was experiencing with the indigenous population. As part of this effort he instituted a systematic reorganization of traditional practices and relationships to the land by forcing many groups to move and resettle in Spanish-style towns, where the Indians served as laborers. The Villa Imperial de Potosí became a model for colonial mining towns,[6] and in 1606 a new settlement, known as the Villa de San Felipe de Austria, was established in an adjacent mining region known as Oruro.[7]

During Catholic feast days, Indians living in the resettlement towns were required to participate in

Spanish-derived processional dramas in which performers acted out epics such as that of the Incas being defeated by Pizarro and biblical stories about good conquering evil. In many cases the Indians were allowed to wear traditional clothing and speak their own language, but the choreography, music, and text of the dancing and dramas were new and intended to do away with ancient Andean identities and establish a new colonial self-image.[8] One of the traditional performances the Indians in the Potosí region were allowed to continue was the *tinku,* a ritual battle between two groups. A dramatic effect was given to the conquest plays when the Indians performed a short fight sequence.[9]

By the late sixteenth century the Spaniards were also importing enslaved West Africans to work in the mining operations. The high altitude, cold climate, and harsh labor, however, were difficult for them, and many did not survive. Eventually the slaveholders realized that they would get a better return on their investment if they sent the Africans to work on agricultural plantations that had been established in the temperate lowlands of western Bolivia, known as the *yungas.*[10] Some of the plantation owners and over-

8.2 Devil masqueraders perform in the Oruro Carnival parade. *Photograph by Barbara Mauldin, 1997.*

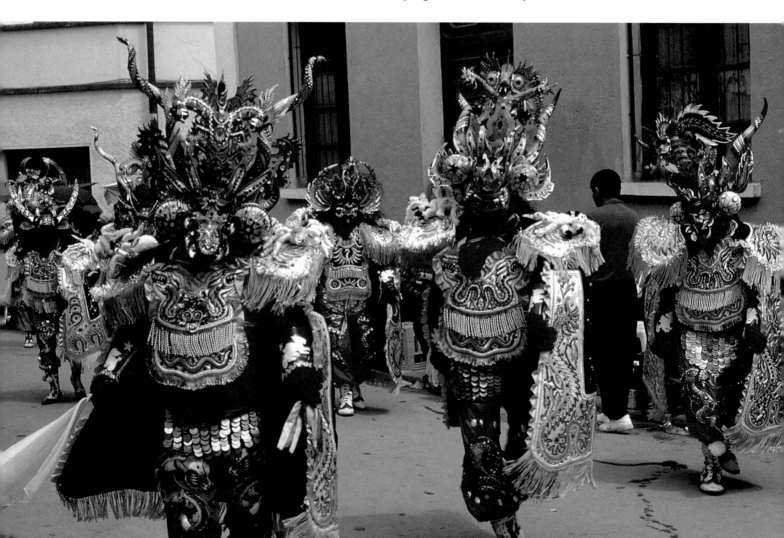

seers there allowed the Africans to play drums and carry out singing performances that came to be known as *saya.* Among the participants was the captain, who led the singing, and the corporals, or *caporales,* who wore strings of bells around their knees and guided the music.[11]

As the seventeenth century progressed, the Spanish authorities became increasingly convinced that the Andeans had converted to Christianity, and the priests became less concerned with monitoring their festival performances. Meanwhile, the Indians appropriated aspects of Christianity into their own religious beliefs and practices and figured out ways to carry on their lives under the guise of orthodox Catholicism. By the early eighteenth century, ritual systems honoring the Catholic saints had become a principal means by which town- and rural-based Indian groups defined themselves. The cycle of Catholic feast days was overlaid on the Andean calendar of important celebrations, and the festival activities included dancing, singing, and drinking as well as animal sacrifices and *ch'allas,* or offerings, to both Christian saints and Andean gods.[12]

This situation continued throughout the first half of the eighteenth century, until groups of laborers in some of the Spanish towns began staging rebellions during festivals to try to get rid of the Spaniards. One of these occurred in Potosí in February 1751, on the Wednesday and Thursday nights before the annual Carnival celebration, when a group of drunk miners descended on the city waving white flags, banging on drums, and shooting off firearms.[13]

The resistance escalated over the next three decades and peaked in the 1780s. A series of events took place around Oruro in 1781, beginning in late January and continuing into April, when local miners attacked Spaniards in protest over taxes they were being forced to pay. During one of these events, Indians cut off the head of a sculpture representing the Virgin of the Rosary, because she was thought to be a witch and was owned by a religious brotherhood of the elite class.[14] The Carnival celebration in Oruro that year was marked by drunken revelry, and it was noted that the city's market was full of Indians selling looted gold and silver back to its owners.[15] Fears of another possible uprising were reported in the Villa de San Felipe de Austria on March 3, 1783, the Monday night

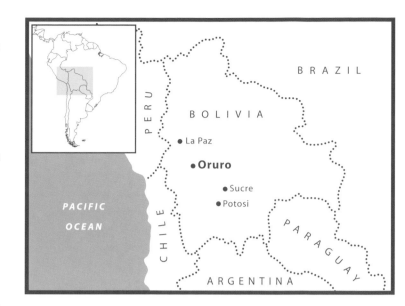

8.3 The location of Oruro in Bolivia and South America.

of Carnival, when nearly three hundred Indians and mestizos danced and sang through the streets of the city.[16] These fears were not unfounded, because festivals were being used in other Andean towns to carry out attacks. When the Indians came out to perform their ritual *tinku* battle as part of the conquest drama, instead of fighting each other they turned on the Spanish and Creole observers and tried to kill as many as they could.[17]

Spain eventually suppressed these rebellions, only to come under attack from Creoles living in Peru and Bolivia who wanted to rid themselves of the European authorities. After gaining independence from Spain in 1825, the new government of the Republic of Bolivia tried to "civilize" the rural Indians by doing away with communal landownership and privatizing their holdings. In general, however, they were allowed to carry on their ceremonial lives as best they could. The Indians continued to practice the forms of worship, rituals, and festivals that had evolved during the colonial period, utilizing aspects of both pre-Hispanic Andean traditions and Christianity.[18]

The class system that had evolved during the colonial period remained in place, with Indians who lived in small rural communities and who were known as *campesinos* on the bottom. Most of the Indians who had been resettled or had migrated to the larger Spanish towns were given a higher status, for they had adopted aspects of European clothing and lifestyle. They came to be known as *cholos* (male) and *cholas* (female) or as mestizos, indicating their adoption of a Spanish lifestyle or their actual mixed blood. On top were the *criollos* or *blancos,* born of European-Spanish heritage.[19] A small percentage of the lower-class Bolivian population was called *zambos,* descendants of West African slaves, Indians, and Spaniards.[20]

During the nineteenth century, few elite Bolivians took notice of the urban *cholo* or rural Indian festivals. An exception was Melchor María Mercado, who was born of Creole parents in 1816 and grew up in Sucre in the southern part of the country. After graduating from the university in Sucre, Mercado pursued a variety of interests, including drawing and painting, in which he documented the flora and fauna of his beloved country as well as the native people. He eventually published a collection of his work that included a number of illustrations showing both urban and rural men and women in festival costumes and masquerades, with inscriptions providing the names of the dances and the characters being portrayed. Some of these, dating from 1859, are labeled "Carnabal" in La Paz. One image shows Indians wearing feathered condor outfits and playing Andean panpipes (fig. 8.4). Next to them are *cholos* and *cholas* wearing European-inspired clothing: knee-length pants, tailored jackets, pleated full skirts, tailored blouses, shoulder scarves, and brimmed hats. In other paintings Mercado portrayed some elite Bolivian *señoras* wearing fancier costumes inspired by upper-class European fashions of the time.[21]

The Bolivian economy prospered in the late nineteenth and early twentieth centuries, when Oruro became a major tin-producing region. In the 1920s the "tin barons" of Bolivia were among the richest men in the world. Then the worldwide depression of the 1930s hit, and the Bolivian economy collapsed. This led to a succession of military coups and a series of ineffective presidents. In the 1940s a leftist movement began to evolve, and the National Revolutionary Party took control of Bolivia in 1952.[22]

As part of the socialist ideology, leaders and intellectuals of Bolivia began to look at the Indian lifestyle and hold it up as an ideal model for a communist society. Correspondingly, indigenous festivals, with their lively costumes, music, and performances, came to be viewed as national folkloric pageants that celebrated the true heritage of Bolivia. Suddenly the rural Indian and urban *cholo* and mestizo people's status was elevated, and elite citizens of Bolivia flocked to their communities and neighborhoods to witness the pageants

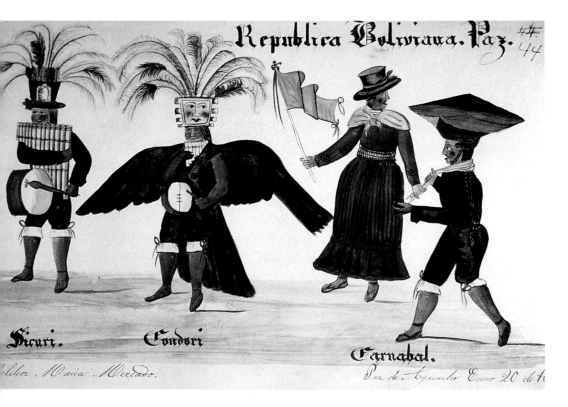

8.4 Illustration showing costumes worn by Bolivian Indians and *cholos* during Carnival celebrations in La Paz, 1859. Watercolor by Melchor María Mercado. *Photograph courtesy of the Fundación del Banco Central and Servicio Gráfico Quipus.*

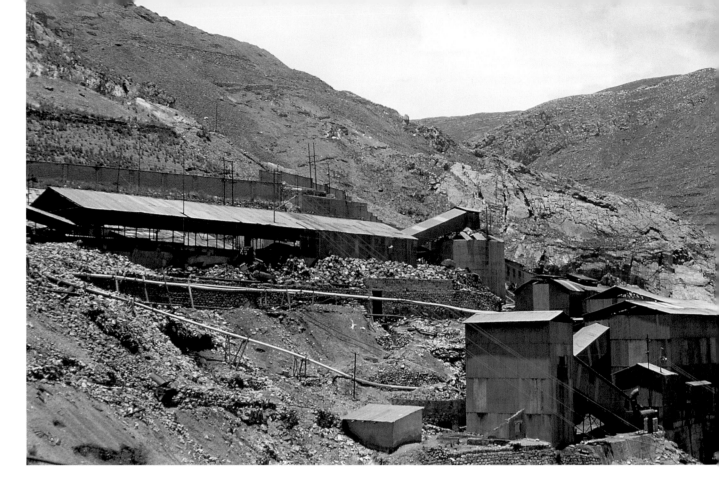

8.5 Tin mines still operate today in the stark, high-altitude landscape of the Oruro area. *Photograph by Barbara Mauldin, 1997.*

firsthand. Eventually they even appropriated some of the Indian costume and performance themes to wear for their own celebrations and, in some cases, as in Oruro, joined in the processions they had once looked down on.[23]

The History of Oruro and Evolution of Its Carnival Traditions

Oruro, formally known as the Villa de San Felipe de Asturia, is located in the altiplano, or high plateau, region of Bolivia, at 12,144 feet above sea level. The name for the city and the region surrounding it derives from the Uru-Uru people, who were the first to inhabit the area. Over time they were joined by Aymara-speaking groups, who eventually came to dominate the region. In the mid-fifteenth century, Quechua-speaking peoples from Peru began moving into Bolivia to establish colonies and spread the Inca empire southward. By the end of the century they had discovered silver in the mountains around Oruro and were

extracting the precious metal for use in jewelry, adornment of clothing, and ceremonial objects (fig. 8.5).[24]

The indigenous miners believed in an underground spirit called Supay, who was viewed as the patron or owner of the minerals in the mountains. He could either help the miners locate the riches or prevent their extraction, even to the point of causing disastrous cave-ins. The miners created images of Supay that they placed in the mines and made offerings to, since it was believed that the spirit's attitude depended on correct offerings and proper respect from his *sobrinos* (nephews).

As part of the Spanish conquest of Bolivia and exploitation of the mines, the Indians living around Oruro became laborers for the Europeans. As soon as the Spanish clergy became aware of the Indians' devotion to Supay, they tried to dissuade the miners from continuing this worship. The priests told them that this spirit was actually the devil and would only be an evil force in their lives. The Catholic priests added horns to the Supay images to further emphasize the spirit's frightening character. The miners, however, secretly continued their devotion to Supay and came to adopt the horns as an aspect of his appearance (fig. 8.6).[25]

The earliest account of Indians participating in an Oruro Carnival dates to 1781, and by 1783 local Spanish citizens were complaining of seeing nearly three hundred laborers dancing and singing through the streets on Monday night of Carnival week. They feared this performance might escalate into a rebellion.[26] Indians and mestizos continued to participate in Oruro's Carnival in subsequent years, but the ruling class was determined to remain in control of the festivities. In 1789 an image of the Virgin of Candlemass was named the patron for Oruro Carnival, a designation that grew out of a miracle she was reported to have performed in a cave near one of the mine shafts.[27] It is likely that the Spanish citizens and Catholic clergy of Oruro promoted the story of the miracle and the Virgin's patronage of Carnival as a way to insert a religious element into the celebration and create a less rebellious environment. They obviously wanted the Indians to worship the Virgin Mary for her benevo-

lence rather than view her as a witch and cut off her head, as they had done in one of the 1781 attacks.[28]

The miracle legend recounts that a thief called Chiru-Chiru was hiding out in a den near one of Oruro's silver mines, and every evening he lit candles before an image of the Virgin of Candlemass. One night Chiru-Chiru went out and tried to rob a poor mine worker. The Virgin appealed to the thief's conscience, but he ignored her, so she withdrew her protection and the worker wounded him. Then the Virgin took him to his den and cared for him. The grateful thief repented before he died of his wounds. Not long afterward, miners discovered the den and found Chiru-Chiru dead in his bed. On the wall above the corpse's head, a picture of the Virgin of Candlemass and her child had appeared.[29]

Allegedly, the miners were so awed by the miraculous appearance of the Virgin's image that they decided she would be known as the Virgen del Socavon, or "Virgin of the Mineshaft," protector of workers and patron saint of Oruro (fig. 8.7). Because her feast day, February 2, often coincided with the timing of Carnival, they would honor her on the Saturday of Car-

8.6 Miners continue to make offerings to images of Supay, the Andean god of the underworld. *Photograph by Peter McFarren, 1989.*

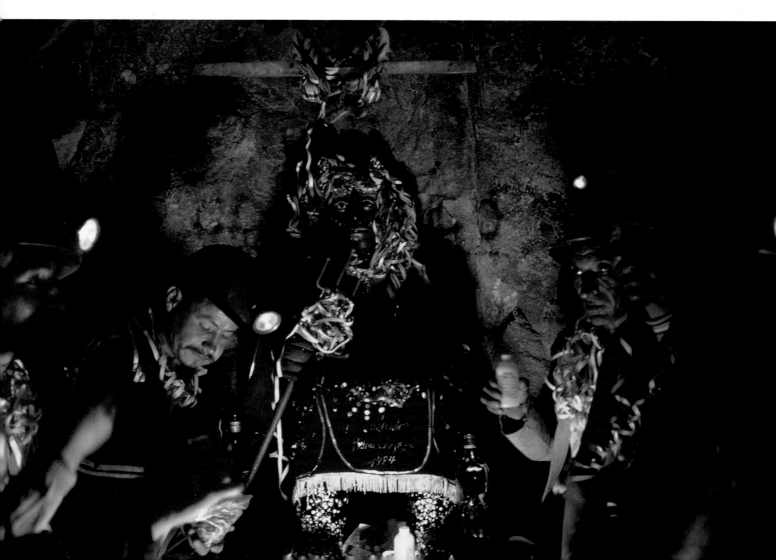

nival. However, fearing that Supay would be jealous of the attention paid to the Virgin, the miners decided to honor him during Carnival as well. They impersonated him in masquerades, and adopting the descriptions of Supay promoted by the Catholic priests, they designed their costumes and masks in the form of devils.[30] Following the colonial pageant format, the miners performed a processional drama in which different devil characters took part. In 1818 the French Catholic priest Montalegre reportedly introduced the biblical drama of the seven capital sins as part of the devil's performance. The miner's group then stopped performing the *diablada* drama in Oruro's Carnival.[31]

From the late nineteenth into the early twentieth century, two Carnival celebrations were carried out in Oruro, one for the elite citizens and one for the Indians and *cholos*. It has been reported that the upper-class participants had a small procession on Saturday, when they dressed in exotic costumes representing figures such as sheiks with harems of women. The Indians and *cholos* had their procession on Sunday, performing the same types of processional dance dramas as in the colonial period, such as the Conquest of the Incas, and wearing masquerades corresponding to those themes. The music consisted of men playing Andean panpipes or drum-and-brass bands playing European marching tunes.[32]

Decades passed with no organized Indian or *cholo* devil groups. Then, in 1904, a new group of miners got together under the name "Gran Tradicional Diablada Oruro." They danced together for several years, disbanded, and started again in 1914 when friends from nearby mining communities decided to join the festival. By 1917, a group of butchers had joined the miners. Since then, the Gran Tradicional group has danced continuously except when Carnival was canceled during the Chaco War in the early 1930s. After the war, many *cholo* veterans decided to dance, and for the first time the professional class participated. Other *diablada* groups were formed in Oruro in the following years. The original group renamed itself the "Definitiva Gran Tradicional Auténtica Diablada de Oruro," or Great Traditional Authentic Diablada of Oruro.[33]

The processional dance drama of the Black Man, called the *morenada,* was also begun in the early twentieth century as part of the Indian-*cholo* Carnival

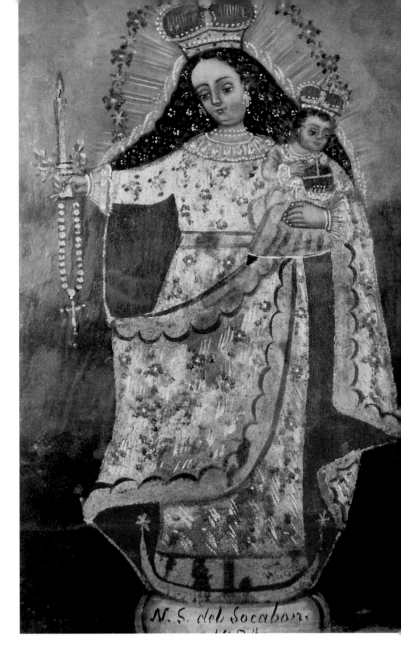

8.7 Nuestra Señora del Socavon (Our Lady of the Mineshaft), 1884. Painting by anonymous artist, reproduced as a lithograph. Private collection. *Photograph by Blair Clark.*

procession. The first group, Morenada Oruro, was started in 1913 by ten of the wealthiest *cholos* in Oruro, coca leaf sellers and candle vendors. In 1924, another group of coca leaf sellers started the Morenada Central, to commemorate the sacrifice of the slaves.[34] The dancers' performance, masks, costumes, and accessories symbolized elements in the history of slavery in Bolivia, and the masquerades included slaves, slave drivers, and blue-eyed Spaniards, called *achachi*. The earliest *achachi* outfits consisted of ostentatiously embroidered jackets and pants. The wearer's head and face were covered with a wig and false whis-

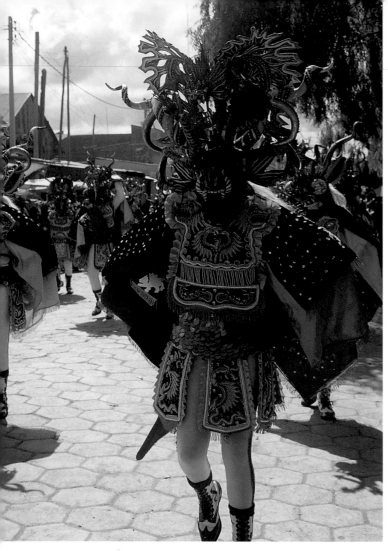

kers, intended to ridicule the Spaniards. Men representing slaves wore small, embroidered, barrel-like costumes with tin or plaster masks painted black.[35]

Oruro Carnival from the Mid-Twentieth Century to Today

As mentioned earlier, the Bolivian socialist political movement that began in the 1940s led to a new appreciation of indigenous culture by certain members of the elite class, who came to view the Indian lifestyle as a model for an idealized communist society. Indian-*cholo* religious practices and festivals were celebrated as the true heritage of Bolivian culture, and the masquerades and processional dance dramas were seen as national folkloric pageants. Soon the elite participants in Oruro Carnival began forming their own dance groups, modeled after those of the Indians and *cholos,* and the two separate days of processions were combined into one big event.[36]

8.8 Devil, or *diablo,* masqueraders in their elaborate costumes and masks. *Photograph by Barbara Mauldin, 2000.*

8.9 *Chinas diablas* (female devils) enjoy carrying out their role as sexy seductresses. *Photograph by Barbara Mauldin, 2000.*

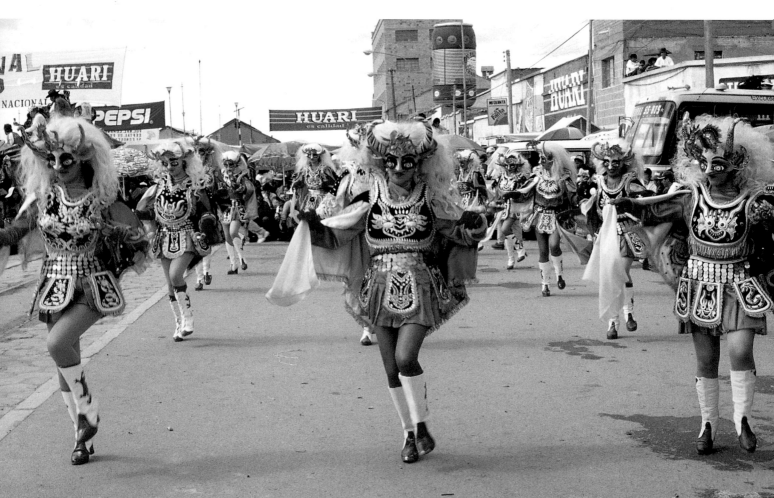

DIABLADAS (DEVIL GROUPS)

The elite participants created two new devil groups, known respectively as the Conjunto Tradicional Folklórico Diablada Oruro (1943) and the Fraternidad Artística y Cultural "La Diablada" (1944). Up until this point, the Indian-*cholo* devil groups had been somewhat disorganized, with dancers wearing regular clothes for practice sessions and improvising spontaneous dance steps. In 1945, dancers from the elite group Fraternidad began wearing matching outfits for practice sessions and more elaborate devil costumes for actual performances. They also began to develop choreographed dance steps with complex patterns. Other groups soon followed suit.[37]

The Fraternidad group reintroduced a biblical component into its drama and brought in the masked characters Lucifer and Saint Michael. It also added a seductress, a female devil character known as China Supay, who was played by men wearing feminine devil masks with large eyelashes and beauty marks. They wore *chola*-style outfits with full skirts and fitted jackets.[38] By the late 1940s, both regular devils and Lucifers were wearing a long, coin-studded chest plate like a coat of armor, with embroidered "skirt" panels similar to those worn today, along with a metal drum-major-style hat and a devilish mask (fig. 8.8).[39]

In 1956, railroad workers from the Oruro national railroad union started the group Diablada Ferroviaria.[40] The Diablada Artística Urus made its debut in 1960.[41] Eventually, some groups added men dressed in furry bear costumes who walked alongside the devil and grabbed at spectators watching from the sidelines.[42] Some of the troupes also had at least one condor masquerader (similar to that seen in the 1859 Mercado painting), who wore a feathered mask and a costume with enormous wings that he opened and closed as he danced down the street.[43]

Since the late 1970s, elite and *chola* women have joined the devil groups, wearing female devil masks and calling themselves *chinas diablas*. They enjoy performing the role of lusty *diabladas* wearing sexy outfits that consist of extremely short *cholita*-style skirts and high boots, which they kick in the air with energetic dance steps (fig. 8.9). Other unmasked women and teenage girls, called *diablesas*, dress in similar short skirts and boots and often perform as lead dancers for a troupe of devils. A few young boys and girls, known

as *diabillos* and *diabillas*, are dressed in miniature male and female devil outfits and also perform as lead dancers for the adult groups.[44]

The existence of so many devil groups resulted in increased competition among dancers for ever more glorious costumes. At some point they began decorating their outfits and masks with images of ants, frogs, lizards, and snakes, symbols taken from an ancient Uru-Uru myth as well as being sacred in altiplano faith healing and witchcraft.[45] Costume and mask makers continue to develop this imagery with marvelous depictions of monster ants, neon-green frogs, and whimsical lizard-snake-dragon creatures (fig. 8.10).

8.10 Mask maker Benito Cruz holds one of his elaborate devil masks with snakelike dragon creatures rising out of the top. *Photograph by Cynthia LeCount Samaké, 1993.*

8.11 (overleaf) A large *diablo* group, led by a figure of St. Michael, dances up the steps to the Sanctuary of Our Lady of the Mineshaft. *Photograph by Barbara Mauldin, 2000.*

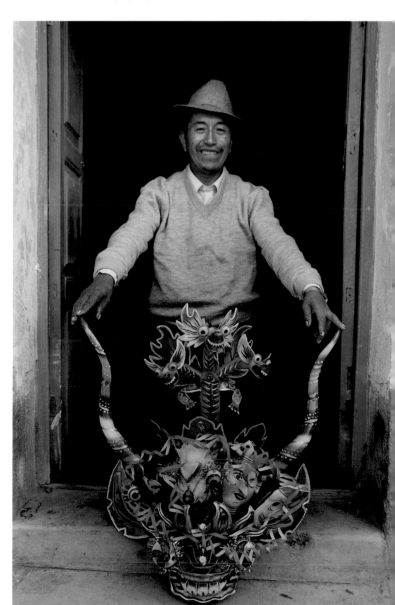

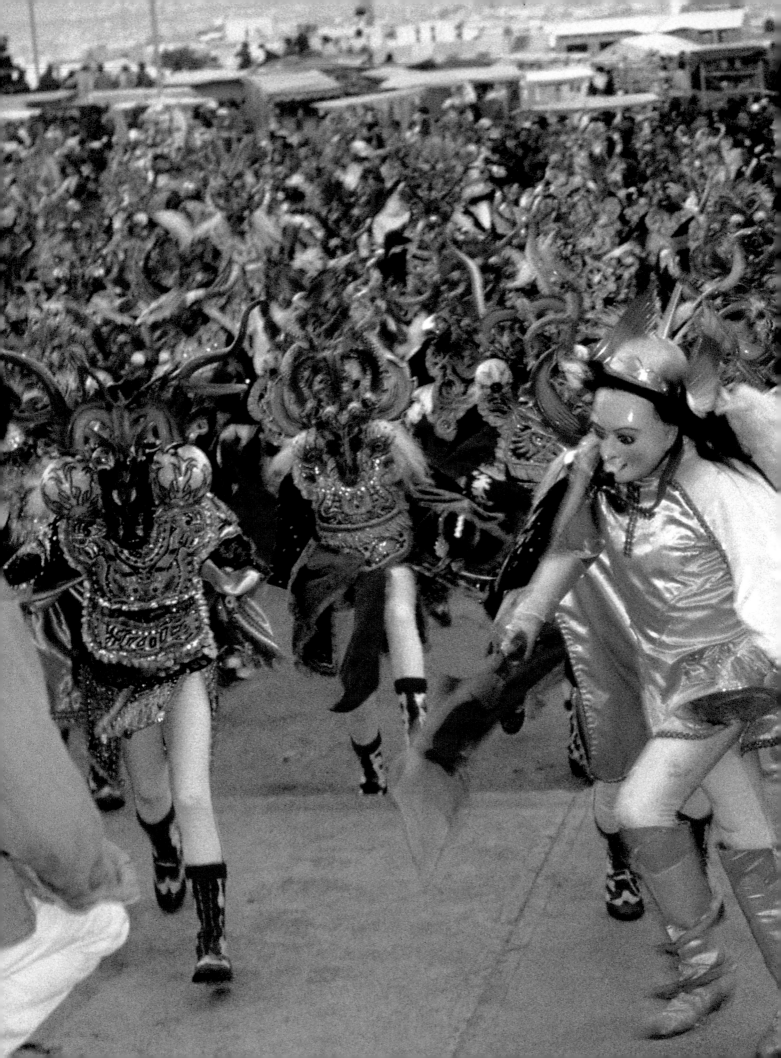

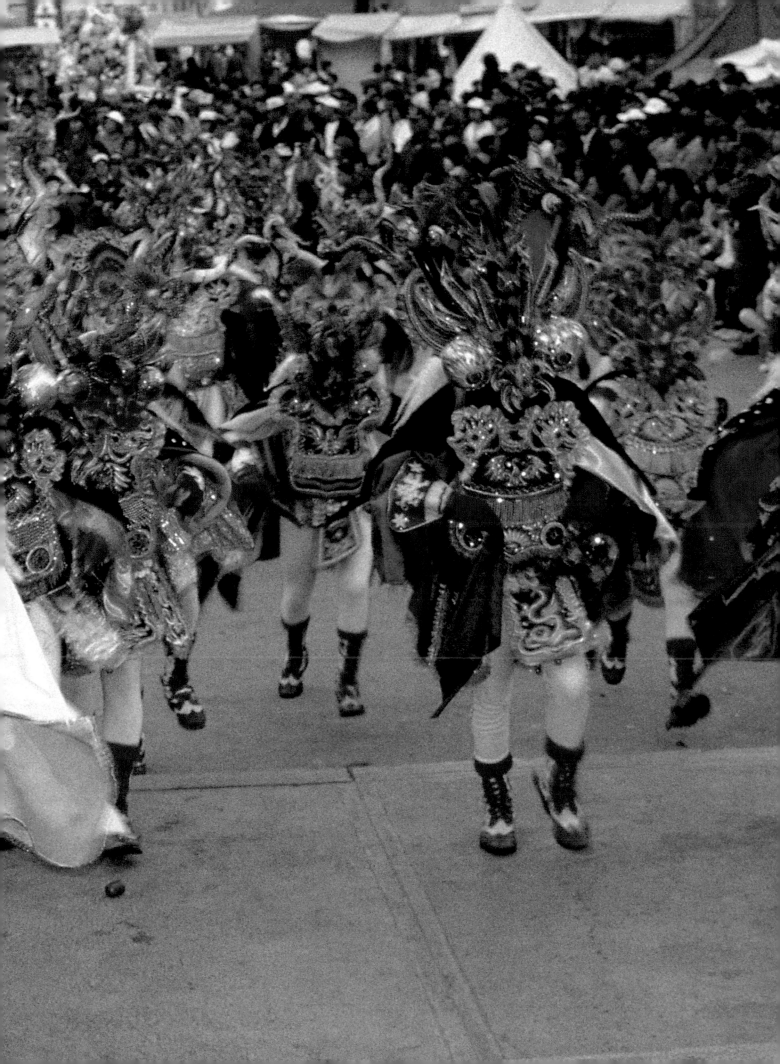

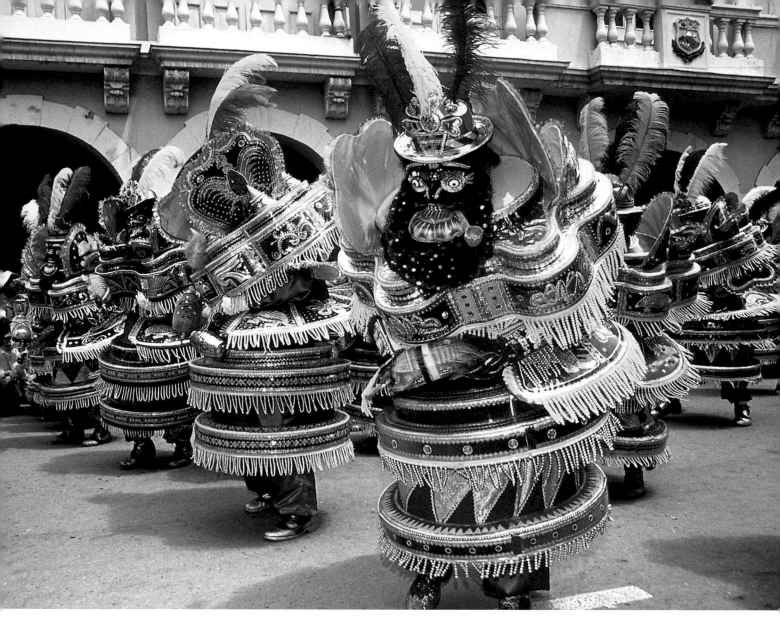

8.12 *Moreno* (African slave) masqueraders wear tiered, barrel-like costumes and twist the handles of their *matracas* (noisemakers), that are made from the carcasses of armadillos. *Photograph by Robert Jerome, 2003.*

Some dancers add working light bulbs to their masks for spectacular evening performances. Today the exciting and popular devil performances are practically synonymous with Oruro's Carnival, and the entire event is often referred to as the *diablada* (fig. 8.11).[46]

MORENADAS (BLACK MAN GROUPS)

The popular Morenada Central group grew in size after the 1940s, with new participants coming from the upper and middle classes. Today it has 450 to 500 members and four sections, and the dancers wear some of the most opulent and innovative of all the *morenada* costumes seen in Oruro. Over the years, workers' guilds have started several other *morenada* troupes. Truck drivers created the Morenada Mejillones in 1977, with the octopus as their symbol. Miners from COMIBOL, the Corporación Minera de Bolivia, began the Fraternidad Reyes Morenos in 1978. Later, mine technicians and professionals joined, and more recently, workers from the national telecommunications company have filled out the ranks. Employees of the Empresa Nacional de Fundiciones metal refinery began dancing as La Morenada ENAF in 1980.[47]

The *morenada* dance drama has gradually expanded to include more characters: *morenos* (black slaves), *caporales* (whip-wielding slave drivers), *reyes morenos* (traditional African kings or tribal leaders), *achachis* (Spaniards), *doñas* (native Aymara wives of the slaves), and *cholitas* (single young women). *Morenada* costumes have also grown in size and now weigh up to sixty pounds, making movement difficult and slow. The dancers do a lugubrious sideways step, said to be reminiscent of the slaves struggling along, dragging their chains. The costumes retain their barrel-like form, which some people say was inspired by wine barrels used in the wineries in the tropical lowlands of Bolivia, where the blacks labored. Their *matracas* (noisemakers) make a creaking noise when whirled that is said to imitate the sound of the winepresses (figs. 8.12, 8.32).[48]

The *doñas,* or women dancers who impersonate the wives of the slaves, generally wear calf-length, *chola*-style skirts, shawls, and derby hats (fig. 8.13). In recent years they have also begun wearing *moreno* female masks. The *cholitas,* younger single women who dance in front of the *morenos,* often choose

8.13 Female masqueraders impersonate the wives of the *morenos* (African slaves) and dance in one section of a *morenada* group. *Photograph by Robert Jerome, 2003.*

short skirts and high boots, similar to those worn by the female devil dancers described earlier. Children also participate in the *morenada* troupes, with young boys wearing smaller versions of the *moreno* costume and performing the same types of dance steps. Small girls wearing short skirts and high boots dance alongside the *cholitas* (fig. 8.14).[49]

SAYAS AND NEGRITOS

By the late 1950s, other groups began masquerading as blacks from the *yungas,* or the Bolivian tropical lowlands, who were now often referred to as *sayas,* and as *negritos* from the mining region around Oruro. The drummers who accompany such groups today play lively, African-derived music while the dancers chant, leap, and twirl. Although inspired by the *saya* performances of Afro-Bolivians in the *yungas,* the music and dance of these Carnival groups is not the same and has come to be know by its own name, *tundiqui.* The men wear satin pants, high boots, satin shirts with big, ruffled tulle sleeves, and huge hats. The women wear long, colorful, ruffled dresses. In keeping with their

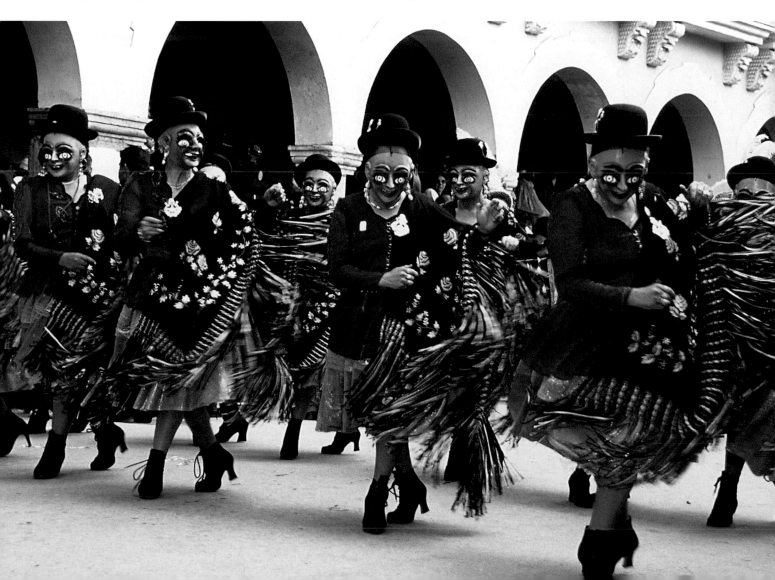

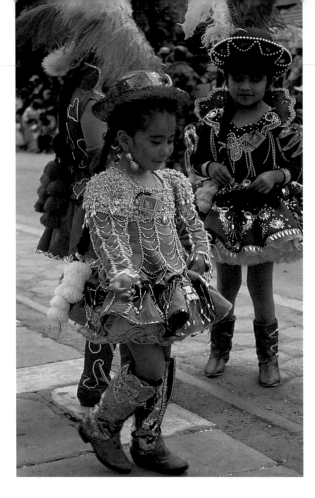

8.14 Young girls dressed in *cholita* costumes dance in front of the *morenada* groups. *Photograph by Cynthia LeCount Samaké, 1999.*

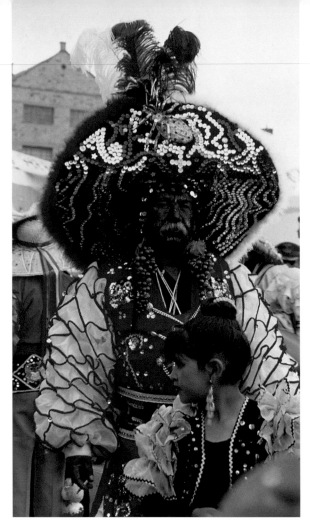

8.15 *Negrito* performers wear costumes inspired by those seen in the tropics of Cuba and Brazil. *Photograph by Cornelia Palmer, 1998.*

tropical character, they hang plastic tropical fruits such as bananas and grapes from their earlobes (fig. 8.15).[50]

CAPORALES

Another type of Afro-Bolivian-derived dance group is known as the *caporales*. The male dancers wear bells tied around their legs, similar to the *caporales* in the traditional *saya* performances. However, the Carnival *caporales* groups take their name from the colonial slave drivers, as was seen in the *morenada* masquerade. The troupe Negritos Centralistas, founded in 1961, performed *tundiqui*-style music and dance. In 1975, members transformed the group into the Caporales Centralistas, who began performing a highly choreographed version of this dance with energetic music provided by brass bands accentuated by the ringing of the bells on the dancers' legs. Other people eager to dance the lively steps to the infectious, high-spirited beat soon got together to form other *caporales* groups.[51]

The six large *caporales* troupes that perform today are composed mostly of upper-class young adults. They do not wear masks. The men generally wear sumptuously decorated satin pants and shirts with high boots decorated with a dozen tin bells (fig. 8.16). The women wear matching satin *chola*-style miniskirts and blouses and high heels. Specially hired designers and seamstresses produce new outfits every year, adding elaborate shoulder projections and complex sequined motifs to elevate their group's costumes to the most spectacular. The male *caporales* each carry a symbolic whip, but the slave-driver concept seems to have been forgotten in favor of electric performances of energetic choreography.[52]

Large groups of musicians wearing uniforms of slacks and sport coats accompany these dance troupes (fig. 8.17). In 2002, the band for the Caporales Centralistas included 126 musicians. They played brass sousa-

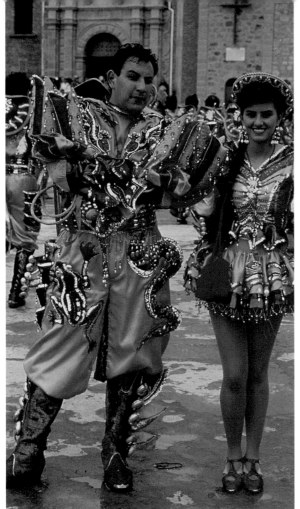

phones, cymbals, trumpets, and drums, swinging their instruments in time to the music or performing energetic dance movements, hopping along the ground.[53]

INCAS

The conquest drama about the Spanish defeat of the Incas is still performed by some groups, although it has diminished in importance as other types of groups have gained in popularity. The Incas wear wide capes with sun motifs and act out the battle of Atahualpa against the Spanish conquistadores while the Inca Virgins of the Sun look on (fig. 8.18). One man plays the Inca emperor, and another is the Spanish conquistador, Pizarro, dressed in black robes.[54]

8.16 Male and female *caporales* dancers typically wear elaborate costumes such as those seen here. *Photograph by Cynthia Le-Count Samaké, 1998.*

8.17 Large groups of musicians play brass horns, cymbals, and drums to provide the lively music for the dance troupes. *Photograph by Barbara Mauldin, 2000.*

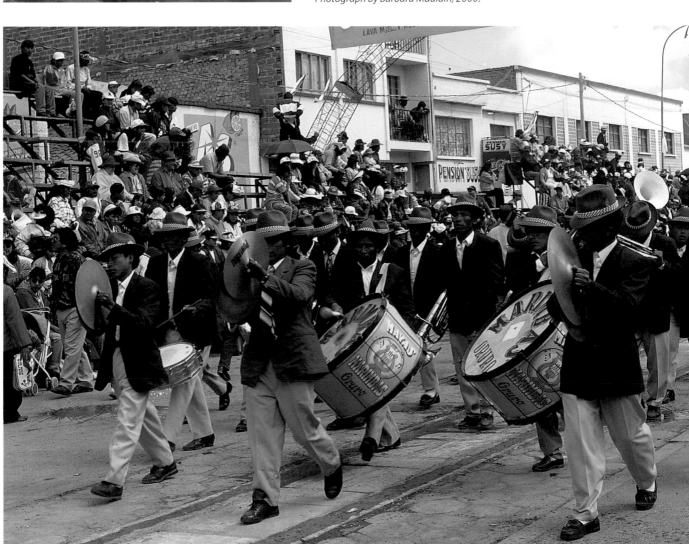

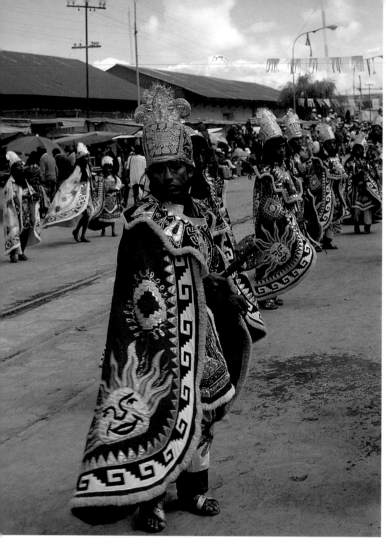

GROUPS WITH ANDEAN INDIAN THEMES

Dance groups with Andean Indian themes also gained in popularity in the mid-twentieth century among the middle and upper classes, and they continue to perform in Oruro Carnival today. These include the *llameros,* or llama herders, who twirl their *hondas,* or slings, as they dance (fig. 8.19). The *kullawada* groups represent rural village spinners. As part of their costumes, the women carry small spindles of spun yarn.[55]

The *tinkus* represent Aymara people of central Bolivia, who carried out the ritual battles as part of the colonial performances. The *tinku* men's costumes include a cowhide helmet, traditionally worn to protect their heads during the fighting. The *tinku* women wear beautiful embroidered dresses, handwoven mantas, and hats decorated with colorful feathers and ribbons hanging down over their faces (fig. 8.20).[56] Other groups wear the *pujllay* costume of the Tarabuqueños,

8.18 Inca troupes perform a dance drama about the Spanish conquest of Peru and Bolivia. *Photograph by Barbara Mauldin, 2000.*

8.19 *Llamero,* or llama herder, troupes twirl their herding slings as they dance. *Photograph by Barbara Mauldin, 1997.*

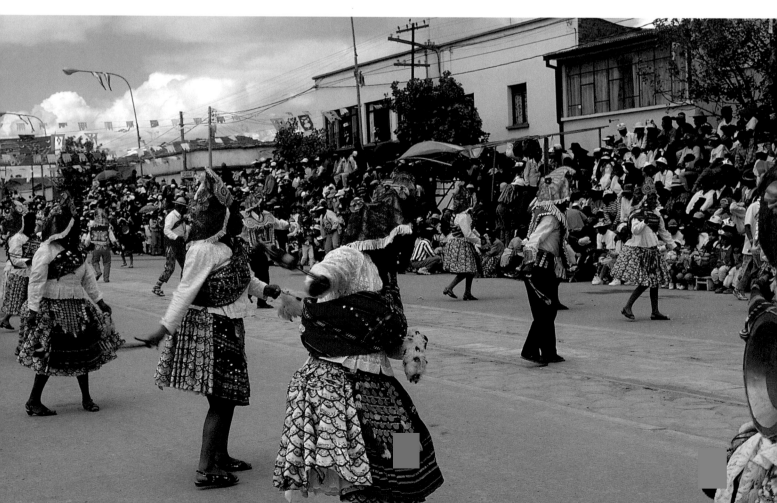

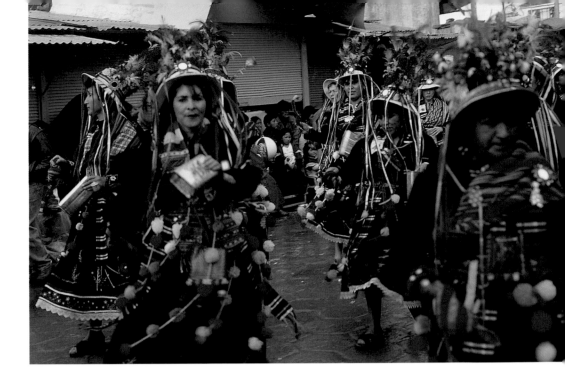

8.20 Women perform as part of a *tinku* group wearing the costume and hat of Aymara women from the Norte Potosí region of Bolivia. *Photograph by Barbara Mauldin, 1997.*

who live in the region around Sucre in southern Bolivia. Their outfits consist of beautiful handwoven striped ponchos, embroidered back panels, conquistador-style helmets, and four-inch-high wooden sandals with metal spurs, adopted from the footgear of the Spanish soldiers. Some of the performers also play four-foot-long wooden flutes (fig. 8.21).[57]

Tobas groups impersonate tropical Indians who once lived in the interior lowlands of Bolivia. They carry staffs, wear feathers and animal skins, and execute high-jumping dance steps as they move along the parade route (fig. 8.22).[58] Costumes worn by *siku-sikuris* groups derive from ceremonial dances in the Bolivian altiplano, where dancers wear large circular headdresses of rhea (*avestruz*) feathers and pantomime the graceful bounding movements of the Andean ostrich.[59]

COSTUME AND MASK MAKERS

Almost without exception, the mask makers (*masca-reros*) who create the *diablada* and *morenada* masks and the *bordadores* who make the sumptuous embroidered costumes are *cholos* who live in La Paz or Oruro. Specific neighborhoods of each city house the artists, and because they function in the same close-knit social and business environment, most of the artists and their families have close ties with the others. Many represent the third or fourth generation of artists from the same family.

To fill all the costume orders for the many festivals

held year-round throughout the highlands, the most famous artists, their assistants, and their family members work full-time making items that may be either sold or rented at festival time. Both men and women work in the family *talleres* (workshops), but men do most of the hard labor such as stitching the heavy outfits and the harsh production work such as soldering. Women often have active roles in management—organization, accounting, or designing new products—skillfully "multi-tasking" as they juggle babies, do the cooking, and handle customer relations. Teenagers of both sexes help out during school breaks, and some of them eventually join the family business.

Dancers either commission their outfits to be made for them or rent the items they want to wear. Many costume pieces, such as the devil's cape, chest plate, and waist panels, are quite expensive to buy, so dancers may rent these. Fabrication of a *diablada* or *morenada* costume takes months of tedious work. Some traditional artists, such as Gregorio Flores of Oruro, persist in making ever more detailed, intricate, and skillfully designed compositions each year (fig. 8.23). Numerous cobblers in La Paz and Oruro work full-time to fabricate the fancy custom boots and shoes for the various dance groups.[60]

Dancers who can afford it like to change their masks annually. They usually want novel and ever-larger masks, knowing that wearing an innovative, eye-catching, and costly mask made by a famous artist gives them status. Mask makers work constantly to

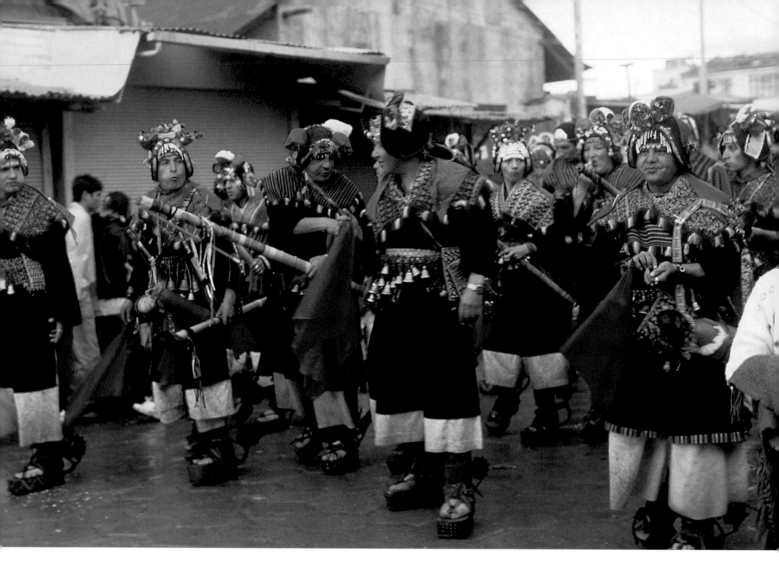

8.21 Some Oruro Carnival groups dress in costumes traditionally worn by indigenous people of the Tarabuco region of southern Bolivia for their *pujllay* festival. *Photograph by Barbara Mauldin, 1997.*

provide dancers with new creations. Typically, *morenada* masks are made of tin, and *diablada* masks, of plaster compounds. Mask makers generally specialize in one or the other. Artists also develop distinctive styles, so aficionados can identify the work of well-known mask makers such as Benito Cruz and German Flores by its unique characteristics (figs. 8.10, 8.24).

Mask makers also make *matracas,* the handmade metal ratchet-type noisemakers carried by certain masqueraders in all *morenada* groups. Each group has its signature *matraca,* often related to the occupation of the members or to a symbolic animal or object. For example, *morenos* dancing for the Ferrari-Ghezzi cookie factory carry a metal cookie box *matraca* with the company logo character perched on top. The bus

drivers' group carries foot-long minibus noisemakers. The animal mascot for Morenada Central is the armadillo (*quirquincho*), so each *moreno* dances with a *matraca* made from a dried armadillo carapace stretched over a wooden box housing the ratchet mechanism (see fig. 8.32). In recent years the animal body has been replicated in tin.[61]

CONTINUED DEVOTION TO THE VIRGEN DEL SOCAVON AND SUPAY

Over time, the thief's den, site of the 1789 miracle, became a pilgrimage destination. A sanctuary in honor of the Virgin of the Mineshaft was eventually built squarely on top of it and the adjoining mineshaft. Today in Oruro, important religious activities and masses take place in and around the Iglesia de la Virgen del Socavon. This is also the termination point for the Carnival processions, and most dancers make a vow to dance for three years in a row to receive the Virgin's blessing for good fortune in the coming year.

For most Carnival dancers, completing this vow and thus paying homage to the Virgin is their primary motivation.[62] Despite its decline, mining remains paramount in the character and history of Oruro. Some miners persist in digging new tunnels in the region or reworking the ore-bearing rocks from older mines for base minerals. Foot-high earthen Supay images are still present in most mines today, and on Friday night at the end of each work week, the miners perform a *ch'alla* to the figure, asking him for luck and protection (see fig. 8.6). This consists of sprinkling him with alcohol, sticking a lighted cigarette in his mouth, arranging coca leaves at his feet, scattering *mistura* (confetti) over him, and draping him with streamers. This is a particularly important ceremony on the Friday before Carnival, when the miners petition Supay for prosperity in the coming year with a special *ch'alla* that includes the sacrifice of a llama.[63]

8.22 *Tobas* troupes masquerade as tropical Indians who once lived in the interior lowlands of Bolivia. *Photograph by Cynthia LeCount Samaké, 1995.*

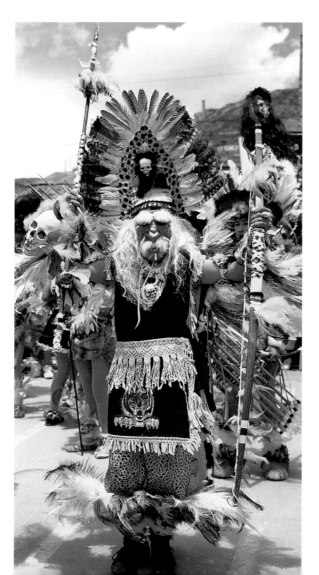

Oruro Carnival Unfolds

Approximately 175,000 people, known as "Orureños," now live in the city of Oruro.[64] It hunkers against arid, treeless hills on the altiplano and looks uninviting—dusty, windy, and monochromatic—for much of the year. But during the week of Carnival, Oruro bursts into brilliant color, resounds with the cacophony of brass bands, and overflows with hundreds of thousands of revelers wielding water balloons. The devotion of Carnival participants serves to affirm personal and communal spiritual values. Whether serving as a city official to organize the events, dancing in the parade, stitching sequins on a daughter's costume, selling beer or water balloons, playing the trumpet in a band, or doing any of the hundreds of other related activities, most Orureños participate in Carnival.[65]

For Carnival dancers and musicians, preparations and practice sessions begin on the first Sunday of November, four months before the event. During this time, each group must get a commitment from sponsors, called *pasantes,* usually a married couple, who pay for banquets and musicians' fees. Sponsors such as the national beer company, banks, and corpora-

8.23 The Oruro costume maker Gregorio Flores produces skillfully designed and intricately detailed costumes, such as this devil outfit, which he will rent to this performer. *Photograph by Sally Campbell, 1997.*

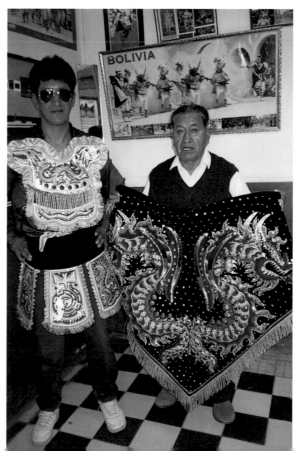

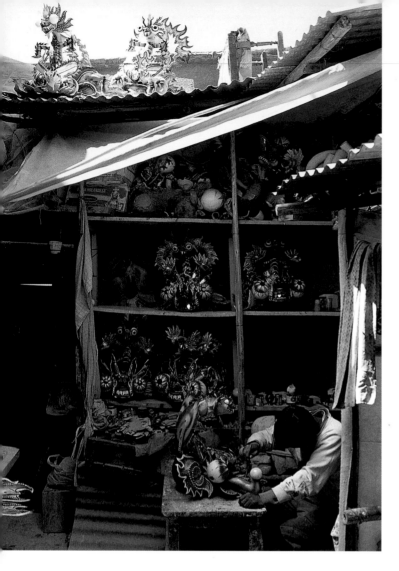

8.24 Workshop of the Oruro mask maker German Flores, with an assortment of elaborate devil masks. *Photograph by Cynthia LeCount Samaké, 1993.*

tions such as Pepsi and Fuji also contribute to various groups' expenditures, in exchange for advertisements in the groups' Carnival brochures.[66]

People who have moved away from Oruro, even as far as the United States, often return to dance and to reunite with family members and friends. Moreover, thousands of spectators, dancers, and musicians from La Paz, Cochabamba, and other Bolivian cities join the Orureños for Carnival. This universal involvement strengthens social ties and helps to unify the country. Although there are relatively few tourists from Europe and North America, thousands of spectators arrive from neighboring South American countries. This huge annual influx of people also greatly benefits the local economy. In 2002, it was estimated that four hundred thousand spectators would attend Carnival.[67]

Thirty-five blocks of Oruro's streets, or about three square kilometers, are officially reserved for the Carnival parade. In the days leading up to the events, workers bolt together temporary wooden bleachers along the route, and people buy tickets for numbered seats. The most desirable bleacher seats around the main plaza and along certain central streets cost more than those on narrow side streets.[68]

THURSDAY

In past years, a half-dozen groups of indigenous villagers from remote hamlets (as opposed to the larger groups described earlier) were always invited to participate in Oruro Carnival. Typically they danced in the Saturday *entrada* (opening day) parade, but so late at night that they were by then completely exhausted, cold, and inebriated. The implications of their rank in the Carnival order were glaring. The situation was greatly improved several years ago with the inauguration of an event called the *Anata Andina*. It is a separate version of Carnival, held on the Thursday before the Saturday *entrada,* and it provides essential recognition for the dozen or so groups of proud middle-aged folk and oldsters who participate.

They dress in traditional, handmade clothing—new or fancy versions of their everyday dress. The villagers play handmade wooden flutes, *charangos* (guitars), and drums instead of the brass instruments of the larger dance groups. They often bring a young llama, alpaca, or sheep to walk in the parade. Dancers sometimes carry potato plants or other greenery in their shawls, wear necklaces of corn and other vegetables, or wear wreaths of bread atop their heads to represent fertility and the harvest season and to honor Pachamama, the earth mother (fig. 8.25). *Anata Andina* ends with a dance contest for which judges hand out useful prizes such as wheelbarrows, shovels, and hoes.[69]

THURSDAY AND FRIDAY

Meanwhile, on the Thursday and Friday before the Saturday *entrada,* most local people hold important ancestral *ch'allas,* or offerings of food, drink, coca

8.25 Indian groups from neighboring villages come into Oruro on Thursday to participate in an indigenous event known as *Anata Andina. Photograph by Barbara Mauldin, 2000.*

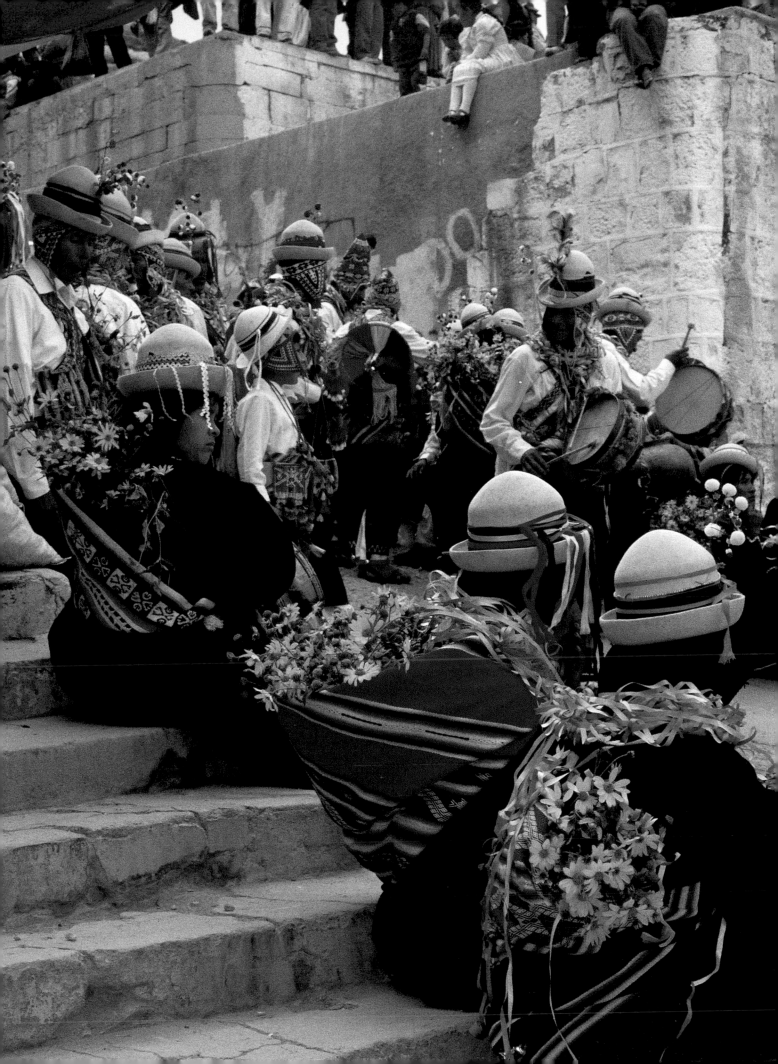

leaves, or blood to the spirits. The *ch'allas* done on the eve of Carnival protect mines, factories, workplaces, markets, offices, and schools. Devotees ask Pacha-mama for better work and working conditions, greater production, and general welfare. Every *ch'alla* is accompanied by music, alcohol, and food, and symbolic objects are festooned with multicolored paper streamers and confetti.

Revelers celebrate the eve of Carnival with street dancing, eating, and drinking. They congregate on the Avenida de Folklórico (where the Carnival parade will begin) or crowd into the plaza in front of the church of the Virgin of the Mineshaft until far beyond midnight, listening to the bands play, drinking beer, and snacking from the many food stalls. Special dishes include crisp fried dough strips (*churros*), a hot purple corn

8.26 Automobiles decorated with silver objects and statues of Our Lady of the Mineshaft honor the Virgin as the patron of Oruro's Carnival. *Photograph by Barbara Mauldin, 1997.*

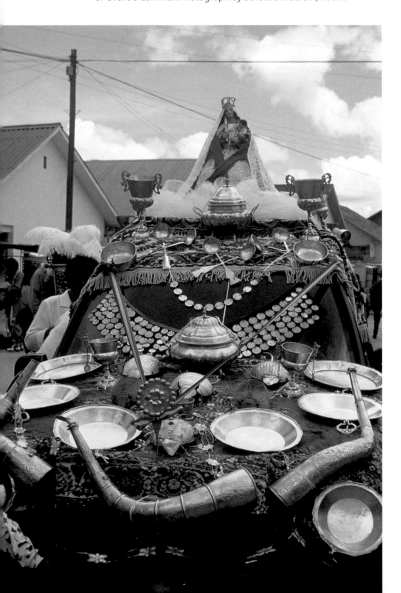

drink (*api*), skewers of beef hearts (*anticuchos*), and tripe soup. Many dancers dash off at the last minute on this night to pick up a mask or costume to wear the next morning.[70]

SATURDAY

Unlike many Carnival celebrations in Europe and elsewhere in the Americas, the primary festivities in Oruro take place on Saturday and Sunday, rather than on Monday and Tuesday. Saturday is known as the Gran Entrada de Peregrinación (grand opening-day parade). The dancing procession begins on the northern edge of town around nine in the morning and continues for about sixteen hours. Policemen on motorcycles clear the route, riding down Avenida Folklórico with sirens blaring. Several Catholic priests walk at the head of the parade, followed by altar boys swinging incense burners. Next comes a row of miners in mining gear, followed by dignitaries carrying banners and then dance sponsors cradling a glass case with a statue of the Virgin of the Mineshaft. Spectators fill the wooden bleachers; vendors walk in front offering their wares. Teens armed with plastic bags full of water balloons pelt pretty girls as they pass, and children drench each other with *bombas de agua,* water guns made from tin cans soldered to metal plungers. Children from more prosperous families squirt new plastic water guns.

Carnival officials stand in the street with walkie-talkies at the starting point of the parade and at intervals along the route, keeping the dance groups moving so the parade doesn't get jammed up. Police and soldiers are also present, having been recruited for traffic rerouting and crowd control, but usually the Carnival crowd in Oruro is relatively well behaved. Officials merely look on with amusement at the wild water balloon and soap foam fights.

As always, the oldest *diablada* group, Gran Tradicional Auténtica Diablada Oruro, begins the parade, and each group in turn then sets off along the route. Automobiles decorated with silver plates, woven cloths, and statues of the Virgin precede the larger groups and serve as offerings to the Virgin of the Mineshaft (fig. 8.26). The sponsors, or *pasantes,* come next, walking sedately and carrying large satin standards embroidered with the name of each group, its founding dates, and the current year. Forty-odd dance groups, each accompanied by several bands, prance

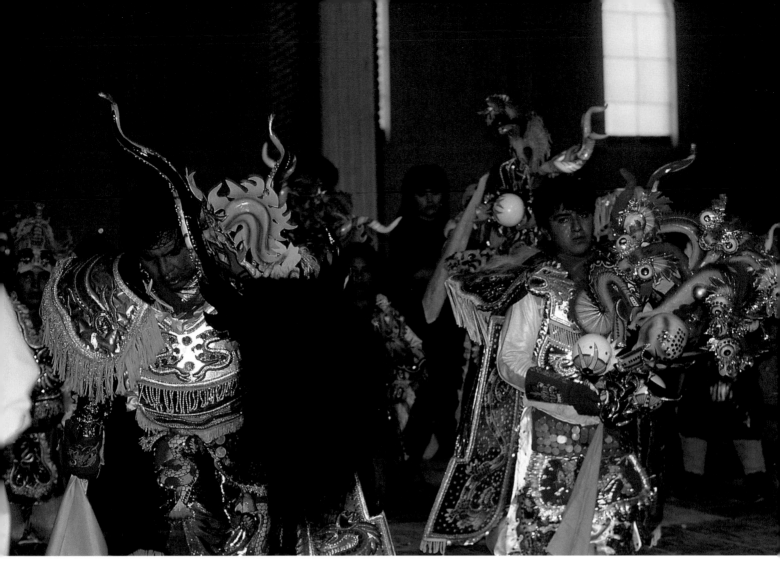

8.27 Devil masqueraders remove their masks and crawl up the aisle of the church of Our Lady of the Mineshaft to honor the Virgin. *Photograph by Barbara Mauldin, 1997.*

and twirl the entire three-kilometer parade route uphill through town. Each group arrives exhausted at the uppermost plaza in front of the church of the Virgin of the Mineshaft. Many musicians show off, hopping along the ground as they play their cymbals. Joyful dancers whoop as they arrive at the church, proud to continue dancing, even high-kicking, right up the steps to the church entrance.

As the dancers enter the light-filled church and gaze at the Virgin's holy image, emotions run high. Most of them kneel when they get to the main aisle and proceed to the first altar on their knees (fig. 8.27). Others walk slowly; many cry openly. Once the first dancers reach the altar, the whole group stops and the priest gives a speech, calling the *conjunto,* or group, by name, welcoming its members, and thanking them for their sacrifice to the Virgin. He then throws three

scoops of water over them and, still on their knees, they shuffle over to the main altar in front of the painting of the Virgin. After a moment or two, each dancer stands and proceeds to the left of the altar, where another priest greets and blesses each one with holy water before he or she exits (fig. 8.28). This process continues with each group as it arrives at the church.

SUNDAY

The last group of weary, footsore dancers enter the church around two o'clock on Sunday morning. Meanwhile, many bands of musicians converge outside the main entrance, assembling on the church steps to play ear-splitting music, each group performing a different tune. Band members wave their instruments and sway in time with the music as they play, and the masses of people below in the plaza dance, drink, and talk. Despite its rowdiness, this musical performance is in honor of the Virgen del Socavon.

At 4:30 in the morning, the Catholic priests preside

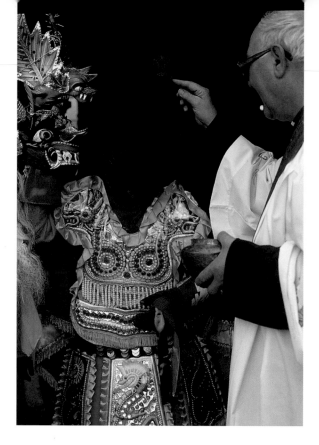

8.28 A Catholic priest anoints the dancers with holy water as they leave the sanctuary. *Photograph by Barbara Mauldin, 1997.*

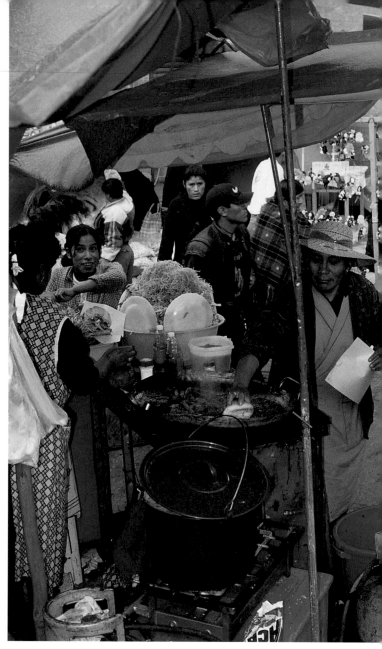

8.29 One of the many food booths set up in the plaza in front of the sanctuary to the Virgin on the Sunday of Carnival. *Photograph by Barbara Mauldin, 2000.*

at the *alba,* or dawn mass, in the church. Afterward, as the sun rises, the whole parade starts over again, with dance groups beginning in a different order from that of Saturday. Sunday is considered the non-serious day. Devil masks are usually decorated with balloons and streamers but are still worn, whereas *morenada* and *reyes morenos* dancers leave their masks at home. The parade continues, but more casually and less energetically than on Saturday. Everyone is tired from dancing the day before and partying most of the night. The foam and water fights escalate.

People crowd into the plaza below the church for games, food, and shopping in the outdoor market called *calvario* that is set up for Carnival Sunday. From dozens of booths, vendors sell snacks of sweet, fried *churros,* grilled, skewered meat and potatoes, and *api,* the hot drink made from blue corn (fig. 8.29. Other booths offer candies, sodas, doll clothes, and miniatures to add to the household "god" statue, Ekhekho. Boys try their luck at table soccer and games of chance, winning painted plaster dogs or pigs. Their parents relax and enjoy the last hours of the first Carnival weekend.[71]

MONDAY

On Monday, a tunnel of wooden arches is constructed on the plaza in front of the church steps. It is draped with brightly striped woven cloth and hung with silver urns, plates, and cutlery. Each section of an arch carries the name of the people who erected and decorated it in order to honor and receive blessings from the Virgen del Socavon. Some of the costumed dancers who perform on Monday pass through the arches, led by the *pasantes* of their group, who carry an image of the Virgin (see fig. 8.1).[72]

Later in the day, a drama takes place in a wide street below the church, the Avenida Cívica, which has permanent bleachers built on both sides. The original devil group, the Gran Tradicional Auténtica Diablada Oruro, acts out the *relato,* or mock fight, between the Archangel Michael and seven devils who represent the seven capital sins.[73]

TUESDAY

On Tuesday, *martes de ch'alla,* the town closes down as people relax and make ceremonial offerings to their places of business, market stalls, and homes. The *ch'allas* include tossing confetti into each other's hair and decorating whole buildings with streamers. People also burn offerings, known as *mesas,* which consist of sheets of paper covered with special herbs, sugar plaques, and small lead pieces in the form of objects or emotional desires one hopes to gain through the ritual. Families get together for bountiful meals and offer beer to Pachamama, even sloshing the foam over the floor of the house or restaurant (fig. 8.30). Up

8.30 A family carries out a *ch'alla,* or ceremonial offering to the Andean mother goddess, Pachamama, on the Tuesday of Carnival. *Photograph by Cynthia LeCount Samaké, 1996.*

on the plaza in front of the church to the Virgin of the Mineshaft, new car or minibus owners douse their vehicles with beer and scatter confetti over them. A Catholic priest comes out to bless them, praying for accident-free driving.[74]

FOLLOWING SUNDAY

Adhering to the old Catholic calendar, in which Lent begins on the Monday after Ash Wednesday, most communities throughout Bolivia culminate their Carnival celebrations on Sunday. This is also true in Oruro, where residents flock to various sites around town to dance, picnic, and perform rituals. One of the most popular gathering places is on the hillside overlooking Oruro, where two large rock formations, one in the shape of a snake and the other resembling a lizard, are found. According to ancient Uru-Uru mythology, these giant reptiles had been sent to destroy the people, but one of their gods intervened and turned the monsters into stone. They are considered to have supernatural powers connected to Pachamama, and offerings made to them are thought to bring good luck and prosperity. As part of the ritual observances, people drape colorful paper streamers on the rock formations and pour alcohol over them. Some people

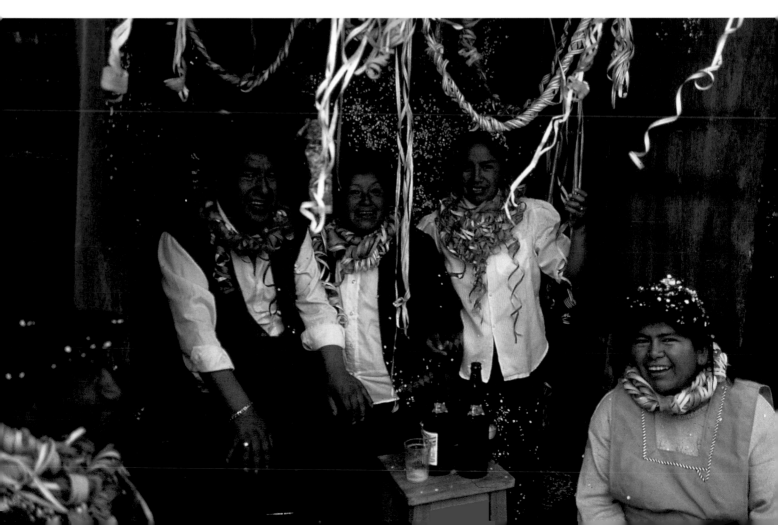

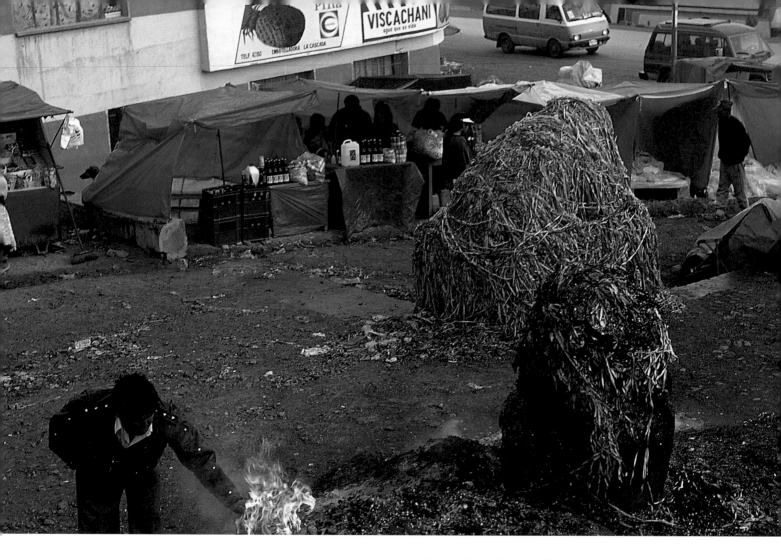

8.31 A concrete effigy in the form of a toad receives offerings during Carnival week from villagers who hope it will bring them good luck and prosperity in the coming year. *Photograph by Barbara Mauldin, 1997.*

buy *mesas* that they burn at the base of one of the outcroppings. They also shake up bottles of beer and shoot the foamy offering onto the rocks above the fire. Others construct little stone houses that represent either the homes they own and want to bless or their dream houses. A stone toad that once stood at the north entrance to Oruro has been replaced by one of cement, and similar offerings are made to this figure (fig. 8.31).[75]

Conclusion

Bolivian festivals have undergone considerable changes since the arrival of the Spaniards in the early sixteenth century. Remnants of pre-Hispanic religious beliefs and practices, however, are still enacted, such as the *ch'allas* and other offerings made to Andean gods and spirits during Oruro Carnival to help ensure well-being for individuals and their families. As the Catholic feast day calendar was overlaid on the Andean seasonal cycle, the pre-Lenten Carnival celebration coincided with the beginning of harvest season. Some rural Indian groups continue to observe the older ritual cycle today; they adorn their Carnival costumes with cuttings from early-sprouting potato plants and carry wreaths of bread to represent fertility and honor their mother goddess, Pachamama. A popular form of Christianity adopted by indigenous people during the seventeenth and eighteenth centuries also plays an important role in their religious and festival life. An example of this is seen in the strong devotion given to the Virgen del Socavon during the Carnival season in Oruro, despite the fact that Carnival is generally celebrated as a non-Catholic event in most communities in Europe and the Americas.

Dance, song, and music are still significant aspects of Bolivian festivals, as is seen in the Oruro Carnival, but their forms reflect changes that took place under Spanish Church and civil authorities. Rather than telling stories that enforce community memory of a group's history and identity, the dance dramas now focus on themes relating to a more general cultural history of Bolivia as portrayed through costumes and masks. It is interesting to note, however, that the same types of themes have persevered for fifty to a hundred years, perhaps reflecting the Andeans' desire to stay with tradition once it has been established. The major recent change in Oruro's Carnival performance has been the participation of young women in the unconventional role of *chinas diablas,* wearing masks and extremely short skirts and playing up their seductiveness. It is also interesting that a few women now wear *caporales* costumes with trousers instead of miniskirts, though they let their long hair flow and do not attempt to look masculine. Both cases reflect a relaxing of conservative attitudes in the broader Bolivian society.

Class is another important issue in Oruro's Carnival. As a result of the socialist thinking of the mid-twentieth century, Indians, *cholos,* mestizos, and middle- and upper-class *criollos* and *blancos* all come together to participate. Some class divisions are seen in the quality of costumes, the degree of complexity of choreographed dance steps, and the size and quality of the musical groups that accompany the dancers. All the groups, however, contribute to UNESCO's declaration that Oruro's Carnival is a "Masterpiece of Oral and Intangible Heritage of Humanity."

NOTES

Many years ago, the late Daniel J. Crowley, intrepid traveler and Carnival scholar, inspired me to specialize in Bolivian festivals; I still hear him cheering me on. Hundreds of other wonderfully generous people have helped over the years, both in Bolivia and in the United States—most recently, Barbara Mauldin, who researched and added the historical section of this chapter. Helping with interviews and photography during Carnival were a group of stalwart field research assistants with the University of California Research Expeditions Program (UREP): Akemi Ichiho, George Rich, Miep (Cornelia) Palmer, Alexis LeCount, Patricia Dodson, Lloyd Stephens, Rosalie Dolmatch, Jim Piojda, Josie Riley, Dace and John Sheffield, Dee Cole, Kathryn Laeser, Catherine Edwards, Shelby Sampson, Sarah Campbell, Robert Schilling, Leanna Erickson, Kristi Wessenberg, Lisa Duffek, Gretchen Bronke, and Ginger Moehring. Roger La Jeunesse, R. Wagner, and Philip Palmer offered sound advice on numerous occasions.

In Bolivia, the following people deserve sincere thanks: Johnny Molina and Ruth Mier de Molina; Eusebio; the late Pablo Sanchez, dancer extraordinaire of the Caporales Centralistas; Jimmy Andrade; Benito and Bernadino Cruz and their family, Mary, Veronica, Gonzalo, and Martin; German and Sra. Flores; Alfredo Flores; the late Mario Paz Salinas and his family, Alejandro and Bertha; Basilia and her son Roberto Gironas; Mario Llave Fuentes; Elena Magne and Jose Luis; Simon and Dominica Quisbert; Ricardo Mamani; Bertha Lunario de Gutieirez; Milton Eyzaguirre; Hugo Ruiz; Julio Mendez; Gregorio Flores; Claudio and Elizabeth Vera Llosa; Freddy Leaño; Juan Carlos Parilla; Mauricio Suaznabor Solari; Pacifico Gamboa; Teodocio Choquehuanca; and Jimmy Andrade Siles.

1. Josermo Murillo Vacarreza, "Un Hipotesis sobre el origen del baile de los diablos," *La Patria* (special Carnival edition), February 9, 2002: 4.

2. Thomas A. Abercrombie, *Pathways of Memory and Power: Ethnography and History among an Andean People* (Madison: University of Wisconsin Press, 1998), 179–185, 189, 218–219.

3. Juan Carlos Estenssoro Fuchs, "Los Bailes de los indios y el proyecto colonial," *Revista Andina* 10, no. 2 (1992): 360–361.

4. Bartolomé Arzáns de Orzua y Vela, *Historia de la villa imperial de Potosí,* eds. Lewis Hanke and Gunner Mendoza (Providence, RI: Brown University Press, 1965 [1735]), 1: 33–46, 63–66, 95–97.

5. Abercrombie, *Pathways,* 216–221; Estenssoro Fuchs, "Los Bailes," 362–367.

6. Abercrombie, *Pathways,* 214, 223–225, 235; Arzáns de Orzua y Vela, *Historia,* 1: 64.

7. June Nash, *We Eat the Mines and the Mines Eat Us: Dependency and Exploitation in Bolivian Tin Mines* (New York: Columbia University Press, 1993), 23.

8. Abercrombie, *Pathways,* 235–236, 256, 262.

9. Ibid., 301

10. Arturo Pizarro Cuenca, *La Cultura negra en Bolivia* (La Paz: Ediciones ISLA, 1977), 51–57.

11. Juan Angola Maconde, *Raíces de un pueblo: Cultura afroboliviana* (La Paz: Producciones Cima, 2000), 100–105. For a discussion of *saya* performance today, see Robert Whitney Templeman, "We Are People of the *Yungas:* We Are the *Saya* Race," in *Blackness in Latin America and the Caribbean: Social Dynamics and Cultural Transformations,* eds. Norman E. Whitten, Jr., and Arlene Torres (Bloomington: Indiana University Press, 1998), 435–440.

12. Abercrombie, *Pathways,* 271, 278, 281–284; see 346–351 for a description of *ch'allas* still being made today.

13. Thomas A. Abercrombie, "Q'aqchas and la Plebe in Rebellion: Carnival vs. Lent in Eighteenth-Century Potosí," *Journal of Latin American Anthropology* 2, no. 1 (1996): 62–111.

14. Fernando Cajías, "Los Objectivos de la revolución de 1781: El Caso de Oruro," *Revista Andina* 1, no. 2 (1983): 407–428.

15. Marcos Beltrán Avila, *Capítulos de la historia colonial de Oruro* (La Paz: La República, 1925), 308–309. Also see Max Harris, *Carnival and Other Christian Festivals, Folk Theology, and Folk Performance* (Austin: University of Texas Press, 2003), 206–

207, for a discussion of the 1781 rebellion and its relationship to Oruro Carnival.

16. Fernando Cajías, "Carnaval de 1783," *Presencia* (special edition, *Oruro carnaval, historia y tradición*), February 8, 1997: 5–7.

17. Abercrombie, *Pathways,* 300–301.

18. Ibid., 304–305, 317–407.

19. Thomas Abercrombie, "La Fiesta del carnaval postcolonial en Oruro: Clase, etnicidad y nacionalismo en la danza folklórica," *Revista Andina* 10, no. 2 (1992): 286, 292–295.

20. Robert Whitney Templeman, "AfroBolivians," in *Encyclopedia of World Cultures,* vol. 7, *South America,* ed. Johannes Wilbert (New York: G. K. Hall/Macmillan, 1994), 7.

21. Melchor María Mercado, *Album de paisajes, tipos humanos y costumbres de Bolivia (1841–1869)* (Sucre: Archivo y Biblioteca Nacional de Bolivia, 1991); the festival clothing is shown in figures 37–45.

22. Herbert S. Klein, *Bolivia: The Evolution of a Multi-Ethnic Society* (New York: Oxford University Press, 1982), 161–245.

23. Abercrombie, "Fiesta del carnaval," 298–300.

24. Klein, *Bolivia,* 15–24; Nash, *We Eat the Mines,* 18–20, 22–23; Heather Lechtman, "Andean Value System and the Development of Prehispanic Metallurgy," *Technology and Culture* 25, no. 1 (1984): 9–15.

25. Nash, *We Eat the Mines,* 7, 19–20; Manuel Vargas, "El Carnaval de Oruro," in *Máscaras de los Andes bolivianos,* ed. Peter McFarren (La Paz: Editorial Quipus, 1993), 99–107.

26. Beltrán Avila, *Capítulos,* 308–309; Cajías, "Carnaval de 1783," 5–7.

27. Vargas, "Carnaval de Oruro," 107–108.

28. Although most scholars writing about Oruro Carnival traditions state that the local miners were responsible for developing the devotion to the Virgen del Socavan, it is more likely to have been a concerted effort on the part of a Catholic priest.—Barbara Mauldin

29. Antonio Paredes-Candia, *Tradiciones orueñas* (La Paz: Ediciones Ilsa, 1980), 70–77.

30. Ibid.

31. Agusto Beltrán Heredia, "Carnaval de Oruro," in *Carnaval de Oruro, Tarabuco y Fiesta del Gran Poder* (La Paz: Editorial los Amigos del Libro, 1977), 69–70.

32. Abercrombie, "Fiesta del carnaval," 298.

33. Fabrizio y Mauricio Cazorla Murillo, *Gran Tradicional Auténtica Diablada de Oruro* (Oruro: Gran Tradicional Auténtica Diablada de Oruro, 2000), 4–6.

34. "Coca y tradición se combinaron en la Morenda Central Cocanis," *La Patria* (special Carnival edition), February 9, 2002: 11.

35. Alicia O. Overbeck, "Bolivia, Land of Fiestas," *National Geographic* 66, no. 5 (1934): 645–660.

36. Abercrombie, "Fiesta del carnaval," 300–301.

37. Cazorla Murillo, *Gran Tradicional,* 4–6.

38. Jorge Enrique Vargas Luza, *La Diablada de Oruro: Sus máscaras y caretas* (La Paz: Plural Editores, 1998), 15–21.

39. This is seen in a 1946 photograph of a devil group shown in McFarren, *Mascaras de los Andes bolivianos,* end plates.

40. Augusto Beltrán Heredia and Josermo Murillo Vacarreza, "Diablada Ferroviaria," *La Patria* (special Carnival edition), February 9, 2002: 4.

41. Alberto Guerra Guiterrez, *Diablada Artística Urus* (Oruro: Diablada Artistica Urus, 2000), 1–4.

42. Vargas Luza, *Diablada de Oruro,* 26–27.

43. Ibid., 27.

44. Ibid., 22–25; personal observations during Oruro Carnival, 1994–2002.

45. For information about the significance of these symbols in the Myth of Wari, see Nash, *We Eat the Mines,* 18–19.

46. Personal observations during Oruro Carnival, 1994–2002.

47. Humberto Apaza Orozco, "La Morenada ENAF reivindica el trabajo de los metalurgistas," *La Patria* (special Carnival edition), February 9, 2002: 10.

48. Overbeck, "Bolivia, Land of Fiestas."

49. Personal observations during Oruro Carnival, 1994–2002.

50. "Negritos," *Presencia* (special edition, *Oruro carnaval, historia y tradición*), February 8, 1997: 19; David Mendoza Salazar, "Caporales," *Presencia* (special edition, *Oruro carnaval, historia y tradición*), February 8, 1997: 4.

51. Mendoza Salazar, "Caporales," 4; Templeman, "We Are People of the *Yungas,*" 440; Ramiro Orozco, ed., *Caporales centrales* (La Paz: Producciones Gráficas Tauro, 1998), 6.

52. Personal observations and interviews during Oruro Carnival, 1994–2002.

53. Personal observations during Oruro Carnival, 1994–2002.

54. Beltrán Heredia, "Carnaval de Oruro," 41–42.

55. Ibid., 47–53.

56. Antonio Revollo Fernández, "Tinku," *Presencia* (special edition: *Oruro carnaval historia y tradición*), 8 February 1997, 18.

57. Rafael Cejas Pabón, "Pujllay," *Presencia* (special edition, *Oruro carnaval, historia y tradición*), February 8, 1997: 18–19.

58. Beltrán Heredia, "Carnaval de Oruro," 42–47.

59. Hugo Boero Rojo, *Fiesta boliviana* (La Paz: Editorial los Amigos del Libro, 1991), 61. This costume is similar to one of those illustrated by Melchor María Mercado in the mid-nineteenth century (see fig. 8.3).

60. Personal observations and interviews in La Paz and Oruro, 1994–2002.

61. Personal observations and interviews in La Paz and Oruro with mask and *matraca* makers, 1994–2002.

62. Personal observations and interviews with dancers during Oruro Carnival, 1994–2002.

63. Nash, *We Eat the Mines,* 134–138; personal observations during Oruro Carnival, 1994–2002.

64. Mario Montaño Aragon, *Raices semíticas en la religiosidad Aymara y Kichua* (La Paz: Biblioteca Popular Boliviana de UH, 1979), 80–88.

65. Personal observations and interviews during Oruro Carnival, 1994–2002.

66. For example, the Caporales Centralistas San Miguel

1998 brochure has ads for Pepsi, Nissan, Dove soap, Bolivian Cascade soft drinks, and Banco de Crédito. The dancers' costumes, however, never carry such ads or logos.

67. "El Carnaval de Oruro apasiona y atrae a millones de personas," *La Patria* (special Carnival edition), February 9, 2002: 1A.

68. Personal observations during Oruro Carnival, 1994–2002.

69. Personal observations and interviews during Oruro Carnival, 1994–2002.

70. Ibid.

71. Ibid.

72. Personal observations during Oruro Carnival, 1994–2002. For more information on this tradition and its symbolism, see Nash, *We Eat the Mines,* 145.

73. Personal observations during Oruro Carnival, 1994–2002.

74. Ibid.; Nash, *We Eat the Mines,* 135–136.

75. Personal observations during Oruro Carnival, 1994–2002.

8.32 A *moreno* (African slave) masquerader from the group Morenada Central. *Photograph by Cynthia LeCount Samaké, 1999.*

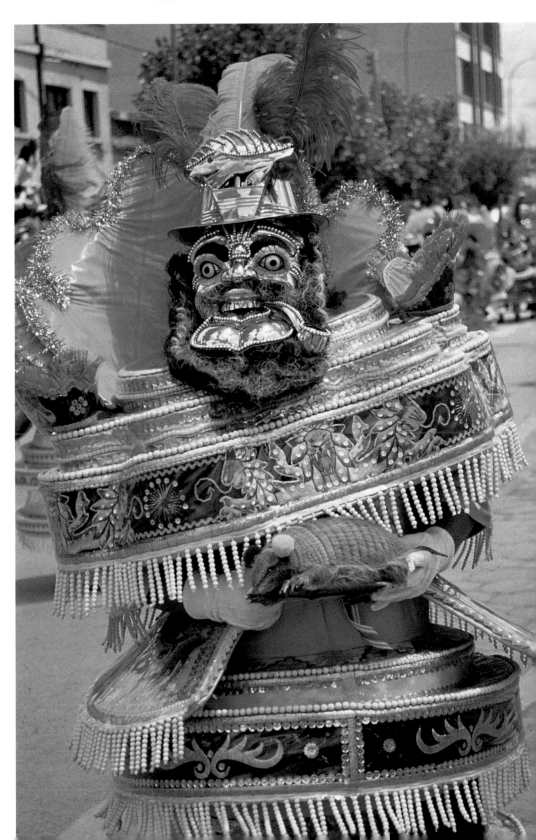

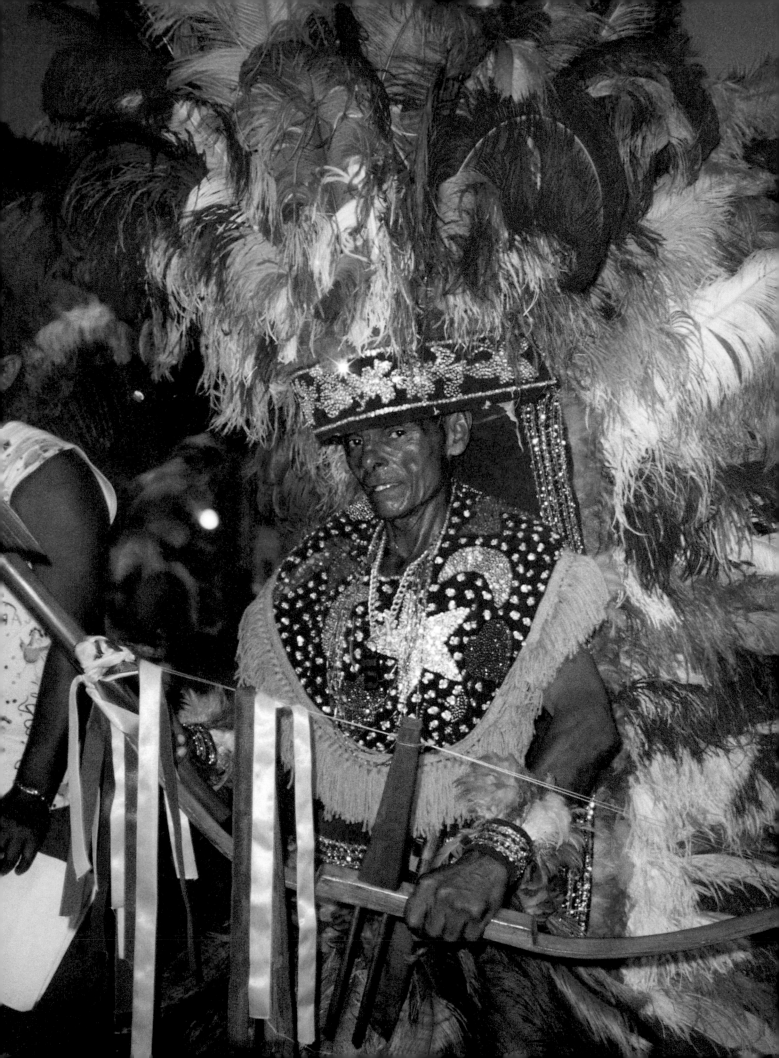

9 Evoé!

THE *CARNAVAL* OF RECIFE AND OLINDA IN PERNAMBUCO, BRAZIL

KATARINA REAL

"FOUR DAYS THAT SHAKE THE nation" is the way the Brazilian journalist Hernane Tavares de Sá described his country's *carnaval* celebrations.[1] Brazil's renowned writer Jorge Amado entitled his first novel *O País do Carnaval* (Carnival country).[2] And the anthropologist Roberto da Matta characterized his country's pre-Lenten festival as a major "national ritual."[3] I am tempted to describe Brazilian Carnival as something of a national obsession. Its importance is such that, to imagine anything remotely comparable in the United States, one would have to combine all the festivities of Christmas and New Year with the fervor and excitement of the Superbowl, the parades and fireworks of the Fourth of July, and some of the pagan mystery of Halloween.

Fans of New Orleans Mardi Gras will insist that their festival is comparable, but it is not held nationwide. Moreover, what is unique about Carnival in Brazil is that it constitutes one of the key determinants of the national ethos and influences virtually every facet of the country's life. Politics, economics, sports (*futebol*—soccer in the United States), literature, the arts, music,

dance, costume, sexual values, and even family relationships cannot resist the overwhelming power of this great national festival.

Although my focus here is on the colorful celebrations in the cities of Recife and Olinda in the northeastern state of Pernambuco (fig. 9.2), one cannot ignore the world-famous festivities in Brazil's former capital, Rio de Janeiro, birthplace of the *escola de samba* (samba school) parades immortalized in the film *Black Orpheus*. In downtown Rio, the colossal Sambódromo (Sambadrome), similar to a giant football stadium, has been constructed for these groups to present their lavish theatrical pageants, often numbering more than seventy thousand costumed dancers and musicians.[4] Nor can one ignore the less-well-known *carnaval* of Salvador, Bahia, often referred to as "the Rome of the Africans," where massive sound trucks called *tríos elétricos* attract thousands of revelers. There, at least nine different types of costumed groups, almost all influenced by Brazil's African cultural heritage, sing and dance in the streets for more than a week prior to Ash Wednesday.[5]

Recife, considered the economic capital of northeastern Brazil, with a population approaching two million, and neighboring Olinda, with around four hundred thousand inhabitants, are two quite different cities. Recife is sometimes described as an "amphibious city" because it sprawls over a vast floodplain bisected by two rivers that divide the area into an island, a peninsula, and a mainland, all connected by

9.1 The "king" in the Caboclinhos folk drama dances with a wooden bow called a *preaca* that is also a percussion instrument. *Photograph by Katarina Real, 1996.*

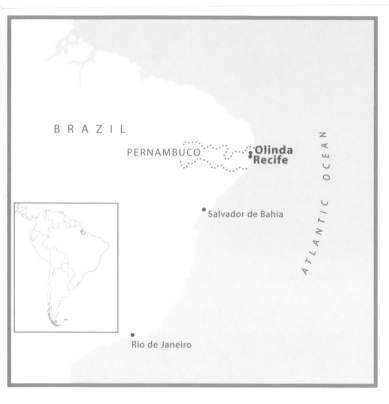

9.2 Location of Recife and Olinda in Brazil and South America.

numerous bridges (fig. 9.3). Olinda, located about five miles distant, is a charming colonial hilltown overlooking the Atlantic Ocean, with cobblestone streets, exquisite baroque churches, and quaint, brightly colored houses (fig. 9.4). It was recently designated a World Heritage Site by UNESCO.

Both of these coastal cities were founded by Portuguese in the 1500s. At that time, the coast of what was to become Brazil was inhabited by diverse groups of tropical forest Indians who had not developed advanced civilizations comparable to those on the other side of the South American continent. Sugarcane, originally from the Canary Islands, was soon introduced into this tropical region, later to be known as the Province of Pernambuco. Cane production required a vast labor force, and the Portuguese began capturing and enslaving Indians to do the work. Members of these seminomadic tribes were poorly adapted to the arduous labor in the cane fields. Many died of diseases, and others escaped into the jungle interior. So the Portuguese turned to their extensive African colonies for black slaves. It is estimated that

9.3 View of Recife with one of the rivers that bisect the city. *Photograph by Katarina Real, 2000.*

9.4 Looking down one of the cobblestone streets of Olinda during the Carnival celebration. *Photograph by Helga Ancona, 2000.*

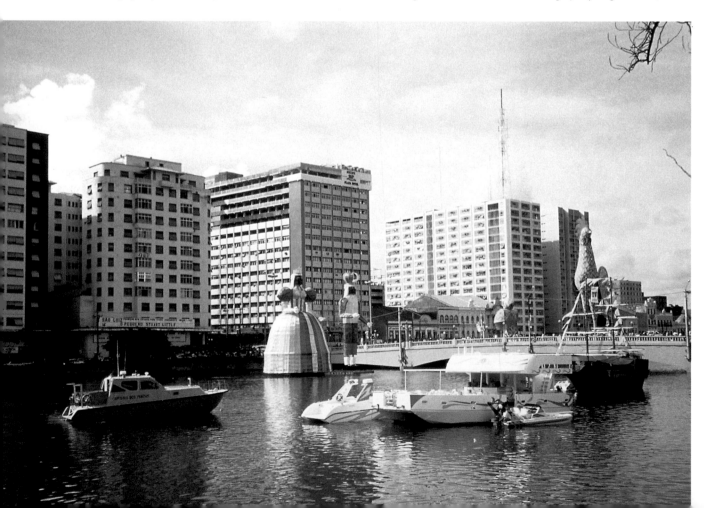

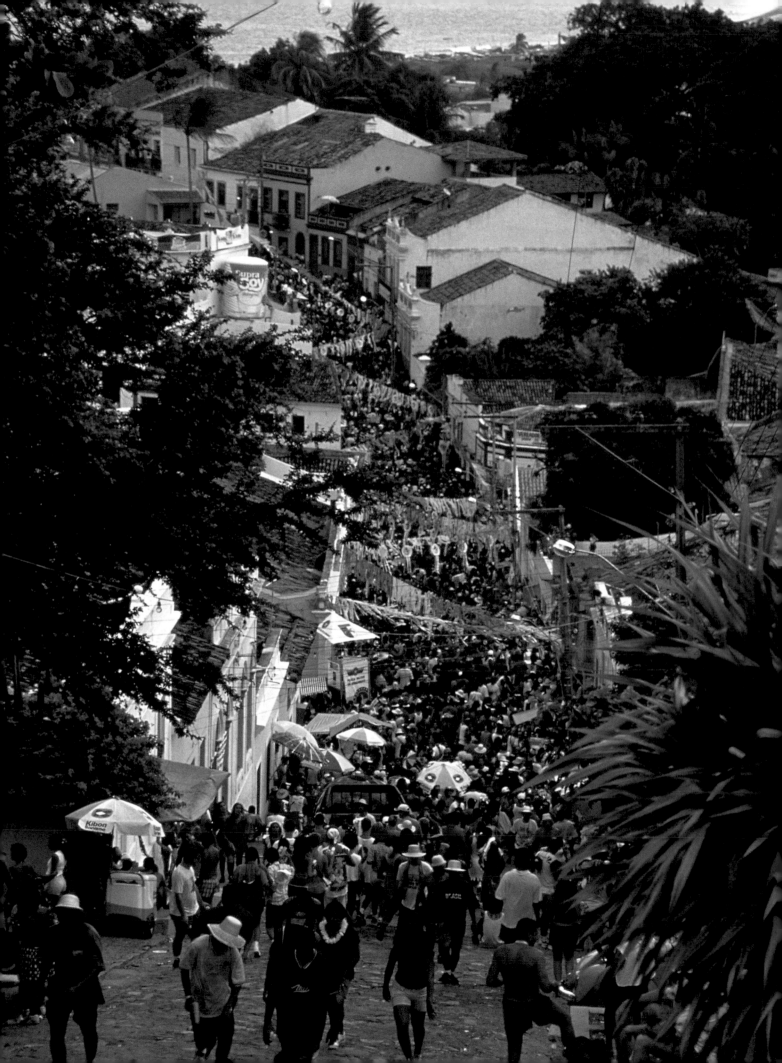

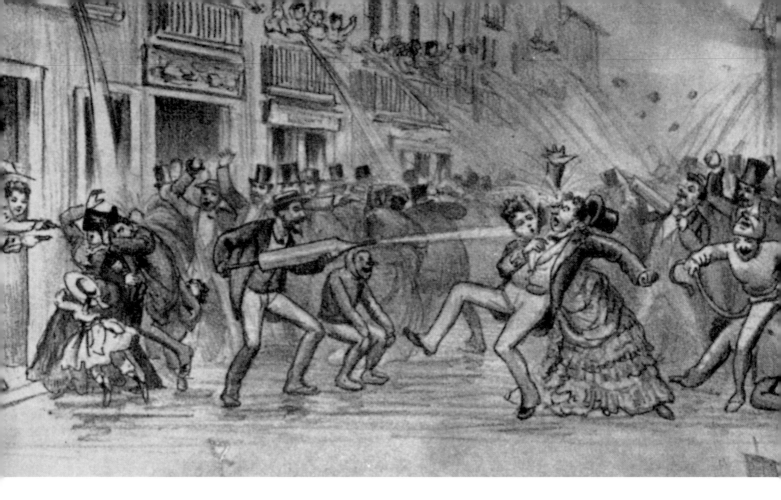

9.5 *Entrudo* celebrations in Rio de Janeiro, early 1800s. Sketch by Angelo Agustinho, reproduced as a lithograph. Private collection. *Photograph by Blair Clark.*

over some three hundred years, until the abolition of slavery in 1888, approximately three million to four million slaves were imported into Brazil from Sudan, Congo, Portuguese Angola, and Mozambique.[6]

Over the years, a prosperous plantation society developed in Pernambuco, as was admirably described by the anthropologist-historian Gilberto Freyre in his classic work *The Masters and the Slaves.*[7] It was a rigidly patriarchal system in which the plantation owner held supreme authority over every activity and person on his estate, including his wife and family, his employees, and, of course, his slaves. In this semifeudal society, the master's authority exceeded even that of the local Catholic priest. A salient aspect of life on the sugar estate was the high degree of miscegenation—the master, his sons, and male relatives cohabiting with African and Indian slave girls, thereby producing a large number of *mestiço* (mixed-blood) offspring.

From a sociocultural perspective, perhaps the most distinctive characteristic of plantation life was the type of Catholicism the Portuguese brought to Brazil. Often described as folk Catholicism, this religious tradition included the cult of the saints, fervent belief in miracles, and community-wide festivals with folk dramas, comic figures, music, dancing, singing, and drinking. Most of these festivities took place during the Christmas season, extending to Epiphany on January 6, and in them even the slaves were often enthusiastic participants. The colonists also introduced special saints, such as Saint John and Saint Gonçalo, who were considered *santos foliões* (jovial or playful saints) and who could be joked with and manipulated for the pleasure of the believers. Freyre described all this as Brazil's "lyric, festive Christianity,"[8] and it was to have a major influence on the development of *carnaval*.

By the turn of the eighteenth century, the old rural aristocracy was in decline and a prospering urban society was growing in the coastal cities, aptly described once again by Freyre in *The Mansions and the Shanties.*[9] This society was rigidly structured in a hierarchical configuration reminiscent of ancient Rome's. At the top of the social pyramid, all political and economic power was held by the civil, military, and religious authorities. The civil leaders, appointed by the Portuguese Crown, were responsible for political control of the colony by maintaining order and preventing uprisings and social upheaval. They accomplished this in part by promoting elaborate civic parades and celebrations of national events in which the total community was obliged to participate. The working classes, composed largely of enslaved and free blacks, were organized into a hierarchy of trade guilds (*corporações de ofício*), which were expected to parade in costume and present dances symbolizing their particular skills, a medieval tradition inherited from Portugal.[10] Survivals of these Negro trade sodalities are still to be found in Pernambuco's Carnival today.

Sociopolitical control was also exercised by Church authorities. Along with their role of inculcating Christian values into the ethnically diverse populace and catechizing the newly arrived slaves from Africa,[11] they were instrumental in developing a hierarchy of Catholic brotherhoods based on social class and ethnicity. There were confraternities designed specifically for the white populace, others for *mestiços* (known as *homens pardos*) and Indians, and special ones for slave and free Negroes. On saints' days and other religious holidays, all the brotherhoods, as well as civil and military groups, joined in opulent street processions with marching bands, lavish costumes, and imposing, heraldic finery. An unusual aspect of these religious processions was the inclusion of profane or even comic elements such as Adam and Eve with the serpent, the seven deadly sins, clowns, devils, bats, satyrs, nymphs, and ancient Greek figures such as Bacchus, Mercury, and Apollo.[12]

The Negro brotherhoods, honoring Our Lady of the Rosary (Nossa Senhora do Rosário) or the black Saint Benedict, were to become of particular importance in the development of Recife's modern Carnival. During the colonial period, such groups were organized into "nations" according to their tribal origins and were allowed to honor their patron saints with dance pageants called *congadas,* consisting of a mock Portuguese royal court accompanied by African drums and other percussion instruments. Associated with these groups was the crowning of the Rei do Congo (Congo King), a tradition involving the selection by civil officials of a prominent black leader to "rule" over the slave and free Negroes. These black brotherhoods were multifunctional, providing social benefits such as bur-

ial services and the raising of funds for freeing their slave brethren. They also provided the opportunity for blending African deities with certain Catholic saints in a process known as religious syncretism, as well as providing a façade for the surreptitious retention of original native religions, known as *candomblé* in Bahia and *xangô* in Pernambuco.[13]

The Entrudo

In addition to the religious festivals and civic celebrations just described, the Portuguese brought to Brazil the bizarre and somewhat primitive pre-Lenten custom of the *entrudo*.[14] Described by various writers as "barbaric," "savage," "innocent madness," and "the stupid water festival,"[15] the tradition consisted of raucous water fights in which buckets or giant syringes filled with various liquids were used to douse friends, family, and unsuspecting strangers during the three days prior to Ash Wednesday (fig. 9.5). Revelers plastered their rivals with flour, soot, whitewash, mud, and other substances, and euphoric attackers threw rotten eggs, fruits, and vegetables with abandon. More genteel weapons were homemade wax oranges and lemons filled with perfumed water (*limões de cheiro*) with which people splattered selected opponents; these were especially popular among courting teenagers. Even Brazil's emperors Dom Pedro I and II were known to be enthusiastic "players" in this crude game.[16] Among the upper classes, the *entrudo* was played inside the home by family members, including even the house slaves. It gave the women, cloistered in an almost Moorish manner, a rare opportunity for a merry free-for-all.[17]

In the streets and public squares, this bedlam was carried on by the rest of the populace, with merchants, tradesmen, laborers, and even members of the clergy joining in. Many of the leading authorities were scandalized by this "barbaric" practice, and several attempts were made to abolish it. Laws (*alvarás*) were promulgated imposing fines and jail sentences for those caught playing the *jôgo do entrudo,* the most stringent dating from 1822.[18] But the tradition was highly resistant to withering away, and today a much tamer version of it can still occasionally be observed in suburban slums and middle-class residential neighborhoods.

Noteworthy is that most of the Negro populace

seems to have had little interest in "the stupid water festival," preferring instead to use the pre-Lenten holidays for performing their *congadas* and other Christianized African dances in ornate costumes with dancing, singing, and drumming.[19]

The mid-nineteenth century was a time of radical socioeconomic and cultural change in Pernambuco as well as the rest of Brazil. With independence from Portugal (1822) and the opening of the ports to foreign commerce, European influences and bourgeois values from more industrialized nations flowed into the country. Foreign visitors, often Protestant, described with astonishment and sometimes scorn the pagan nature of the regional festivals. The Pernambucan intelligentsia, along with civil and clerical leaders, became deeply concerned about their image

9.6 Harlequin costumes from the Italian commedia dell'arte are still popular today in Recife Carnival. *Photograph by Katarina Real, 1998.*

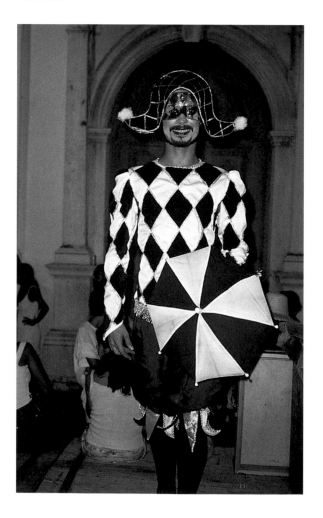

abroad and renewed their efforts not only to abolish the *entrudo* but also to prohibit the profane and comic elements in the religious processions. A more rigidly orthodox Catholicism was instituted, and even the festivities of the Negro brotherhoods were treated as threats to the country's moral and political stability.[20]

Along with this "Europeanization" process, the exuberant Carnival traditions of Venice, Rome, Paris, Nice, and other great cities of the Continent were imported and gradually came to fill the void left by the old *entrudo*. This marked the beginning of the Pernambuco Carnival as we know it today.

At first the festival was almost entirely an upper-class affair, with lavish costume balls and elaborate street parades featuring floats, mounted cavalry, and pedestrian orchestras playing classical and popular music. Themes from the Italian opera were popular, as were those from Roman and Greek mythology. At elegant masked balls held at theaters and private clubs, costumes from the Italian commedia dell'arte were also favored, including Harlequin, Colombina, Pulcinella, and the tragicomic figure of Pierrot. Many of these masquerades are still seen in Recife Carnival today (fig. 9.6).

By the 1860s, the newly founded Carnival societies (*sociedades carnavalescas*) of the elites had taken control of the street festivities, leaving the seclusion of their private clubs to parade before the enthralled populace. Imitating a European model, these groups were made up of students, doctors, lawyers, and other professionals and often had republican, abolitionist, or other political aims. A recent wave of modernization in Recife, such as the paving of the avenues, had allowed the *sociedades* to develop their outdoor street pageants and attempt to win the approval of the crowds in competitions with their archrivals for the most extravagant allegorical floats.[21]

The lower classes were not permitted to participate in these elite parades. Severe police restrictions against their *entrudo* games continued, and laws were enacted prohibiting the use of masks by the Negro populace in its festival practices—a result of constant fear of slave rebellions. Many of these restrictions came to an abrupt end when Princess Isabel, acting as regent for her father, Dom Pedro II, signed the historic edict proclaiming the total abolition of slavery in 1888. This brought about a dramatic change in Pernambuco Carnival the following year, when the euphoric urban

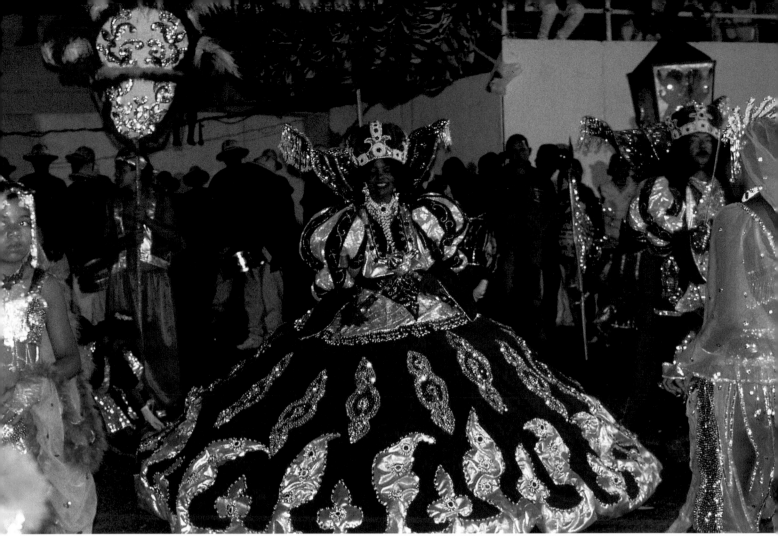

9.7 The *maracatu* group known as Porto Rico, with its queen, doña Elda Viana. *Photograph by Barbara Mauldin, 1998.*

masses surged into the open avenues to celebrate their newly achieved freedom. The Negro trade guilds, which had metamorphosed into Catholic brotherhoods (and often secret *xangô* cults), now were able to make their final transformation into the popular Carnival parading organizations we know today as *agremiações carnavalescas*.[22] Groups with names such as Pás de Carvão (Coal Shovelers), Vassourinhas (Street Sweepers), Lenhadores (Wood Choppers), Ferreiros (Ironmongers), and Caiadores (Whitewashers), some of which still exist today, began competing with each other and soon developed intense rivalries that sometimes led to bloody encounters. It is noteworthy that these organizations retained the names of their guild professions rather than taking titles to celebrate their African roots as was the case with similar groups in Salvador, Bahia, during the same period.[23]

By the turn of the last century, these *agremiações* had secularized and incorporated many features of their original religious confraternities into their parades, such as ornate heraldic standards, brass band accompaniment, and opposing cordons of dancers carrying symbols of their trade on long poles. A similar secularization process occurred with the *congada* pageants of the black Rosário brotherhoods. Sometime in the nineteenth century they had transferred their courtly parades (which had drawn increasing disapproval from the Church) into Carnival and had come to be known as *maracatus*. These groups, which continue to consider themselves "African nations," still survive and flourish in Pernambuco and are among the most exciting features of the festival today (fig. 9.7).[24]

The Frevo and the Passo

It was from the music of the brass orchestras in the military parades that two of the most original aspects

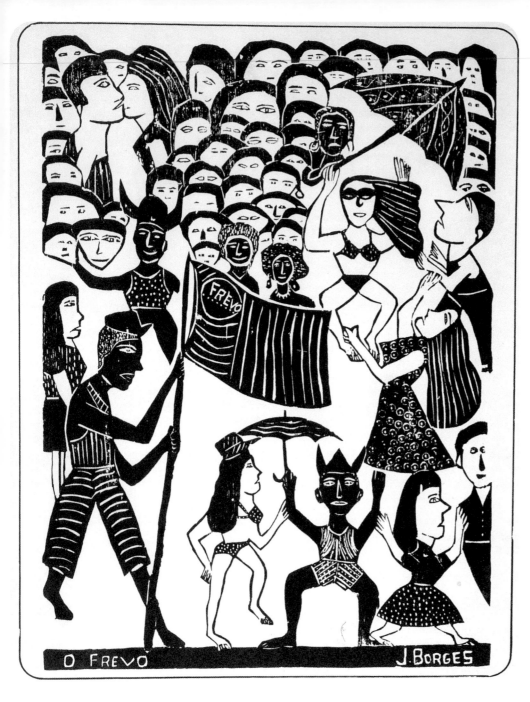

O FREVO   J. BORGES

9.8 *O Frevo*. Woodcut print, 1982, by José Borges, Bezerros, Pernambuco. Private collection. *Photograph by Blair Clark.*

of Pernambuco Carnival developed: the rhythm of the *frevo* and its accompanying dance, the *passo*. The *frevo* (a corruption of the verb *ferver*, meaning "to boil") evolved as Afro-Brazilian musicians from the parades of former times began syncopating the march rhythms and adding improvised fanfares and solos in a manner similar to that developed by the jazz bands of New Orleans in the United States. Over time, polka, quadrille, and other elements were infused into the *frevo*, producing what has come to be known as "the great hallucination of Recife Carnival" (fig. 9.8).[25]

The *passo* also has intriguing Afro-Brazilian roots. During the nineteenth century, bands of dark-skinned ruffians known as *partidos de capoeiras* became partisans of specific military bands. Brandishing long knives or clubs, they performed acrobatic dance steps to the march rhythms ahead of their favorite orchestras as they paraded along the avenue. The word *capoeira* also describes the well-known dance-game-martial art that was brought to Brazil by African slaves from Portuguese Angola.[26] The *partidos de capoeiras* were often involved in lethal street fights with rival bands, terrorizing the populace and causing great concern to the authorities. Local politicians sometimes hired them as henchmen during elections, enabling them to avoid arrest for many years, but the *capoeira* "gangs" were finally abolished by law in 1890.[27] Then the *passo* began to crystallize into the much tamer Carnival dance of today, with multicolored umbrellas or parasols replacing the slashing knives of old (fig. 9.9).

This dance, often called the *frevo* rather than the *passo* today, requires a variety of complex steps, leaps, and bodily contortions in which the parasol is sometimes necessary for balance. Valdemar de Oliveira points out that although the choreography of the *passo* grew out of the *capoeira* game, it retained more of *capoeira*'s virile spirit than the offensive aggressiveness characteristic of the martial art itself.[28] In contrast to the sensuality associated with the Brazilian samba, the uniquely Pernambucan *passo* is completely asexual, with individualistic solo steps more closely resembling those of Russian Cossack dances.[29] For many years, the *frevo/passo* was considered a lower-class activity to be performed in the streets only by the masses, but by the 1950s it had begun to gain accept-

ance at Carnival balls in private clubs. In recent years, dozens of dance schools have started giving classes to children and teenagers, hoping to keep the intricate choreography of the *passo* alive and competitive with the increasing popularity of dances done to the Bahian samba-reggae rhythm, as well as to save it from being engulfed by the invasion of rock music imported from the United States.[30]

Pernambuco Carnival Today

In cities throughout Brazil, Carnival actually starts on New Year's Eve. On that occasion, elegant balls called *reveillons* are held at private clubs in Recife, during which the affluent celebrate both the New Year and the coming Carnival. Soon after the first of the year,

9.9 Children in the typical *frevo* costume performing the *passo* with their colorful parasols. *Photograph by Katarina Real, 1999.*

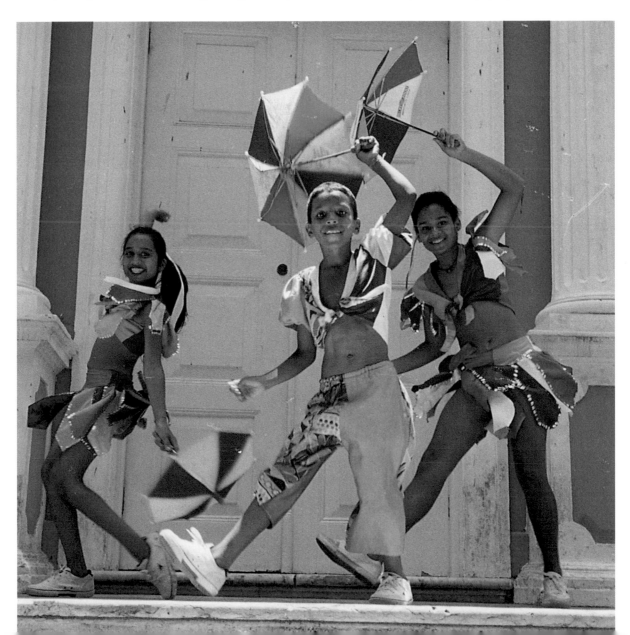

the pace of pre-Lenten activities accelerates. Colorful street decorations begin to appear, bleachers are constructed in many parts of both Recife and Olinda, and gaily decorated stalls soon line the downtown avenues, selling a panoply of Carnival "toys" (*brinquedos*; fig. 9.10). These include noisemakers, papier-mâché masks, bags of multicolored confetti, plastic water squirters (*bisnagas*), coils of paper streamers (*serpentina*), small hobby horses (*burrinhas*), exotic wigs, false noses and mustaches, inexpensive children's' costumes and accessories such as Hawaiian leis and "grass" skirts of gold and silver tinsel, and dozens of other items.[31]

Because Carnival falls in late summer in the Southern Hemisphere, usually during the dry season in Pernambuco, there are limitless opportunities for outdoor celebrations. In order to make room for both the tourists and much of the regional populace, the municipal governments (*prefeituras*) have developed a number

of *polos* (poles or sites) in which to spread out the Carnival activities. A few of the most important in Recife are the broad avenues in the heart of the city, where massive sound stages are set up for local musicians and singers to entertain the crowds and where the Carnival parading organizations are to perform; the Bairro do Recife Antigo, the attractively restored port district of the city, where the upper classes gather at swank sidewalk cafés and often dance along with specially contracted Carnival groups as they pass; and the Boa Viagem Beach area, where a wall of luxurious apartment houses and expensive hotels lines the wide avenue adjacent to one of the most beautiful beaches in Brazil.

At the last site, traffic is rerouted, and block-long grandstands requiring paid admission are constructed. This is where foreign tourists, visitors from other Brazilian cities, and the younger generation congregate to dance to the music from dozens of the large, noisy *tríos elétricos* (electric sound trucks). The revelers who make up these groups, called *blocos,* must pay a fee for participation; a T-shirt and baseball cap (*boné*) with the group logo guarantee a spot in an area cordoned off

9.10 One of the street stalls in Recife where residents can buy Carnival toys and costume accessories. *Photograph by Katarina Real, 2000.*

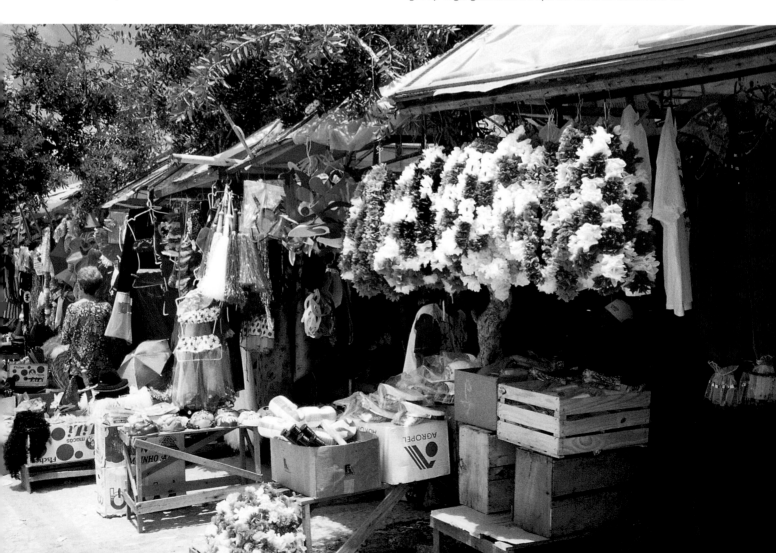

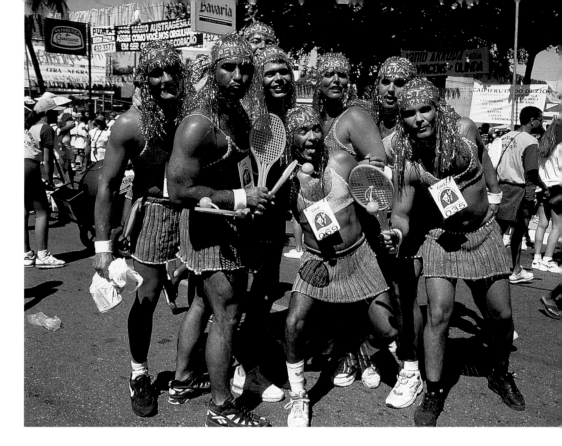

9.12 A group of men dressed as female tennis players participates in the Parade of "Virgins" in Olinda. *Photograph by George Ancona, 1998.*

behind the *trio,* isolating the participants from the non-paying crowds. Dozens of *blocos,* mostly from the middle classes, jam the avenue from morning until the following dawn during pre-Carnival week (*semana precarnavalesca*) and up to Ash Wednesday. They have the advantage of a refreshing swim in the ocean when the tropical heat starts to overwhelm them.[32]

Olinda's *polos* are concentrated in two major areas: the lower city, which borders the Atlantic Ocean, and the historic upper city (*sítio histórico*). Whereas the *tríos* attract thousands of revelers in the former, they are unable to maneuver the steep hills and narrow winding streets of the latter—something of a blessing, for their thunderous sound would surely endanger the foundations of the old colonial churches, which are protected today by the National Historic Patrimony. This leaves the upper city free for the most extraordinary agglomeration of masqueraders to be seen in all of Brazil, along with *frevo* bands, folkloric groups, giant puppets, and families, teenagers, and children dancing in the streets (fig. 9.11).[33]

During the weeks prior to Shrove Tuesday (Mardi Gras), there is a steady buildup of Carnival events far too numerous to describe here. Mention should be made, however, of the annual Bal Masqué at the palatial Clube Internacional. Following a European model, this is a lavish, black-tie affair for the elites in which

the women, in bejeweled gowns, compete for prizes for the most elaborate mask creations.[34] Another major event is the annual parade of the Turma da Jaqueira (Crew of the Jackfruit) of the Joaquim Nabuco Research Foundation in the historic suburb of Casa Forte. Five or six gargantuan *tríos elétricos,* blaring forth *frevos,* samba-reggae, and other popular rhythms from amplified instruments, attract more than fifty thousand revelers who dance and sing around the streets of the suburb under a searing tropical sun from noon until sunset.[35]

Undoubtedly, one of the most bizarre events is the Desfile dos Vírgens do Bairro Novo (Parade of the "Virgins" of the Bairro Novo suburb), which takes place in Olinda on Saturday of pre-Carnival week. This is an all-male group of several hundred from the upper and middle classes, who revel in a major ritual of cross-dressing for an enormous all-day parade in the lower city. The men are all considered heterosexual—no gays are allowed—and are dressed by their wives, girlfriends, or male colleagues in hilarious satires of the female body and comportment (fig. 9.12). The

9.11 (overleaf) Street in Olinda crowded with *carnaval* revelers dressed in a variety of masquerades. *Photograph by Helga Ancona, 2000.*

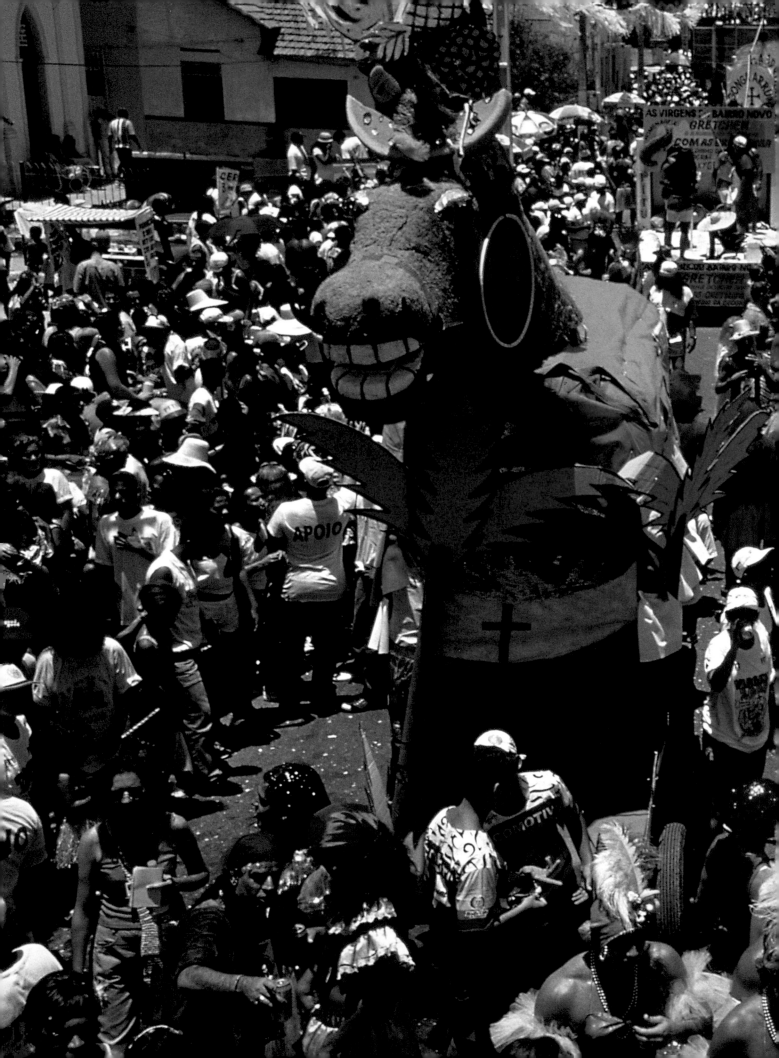

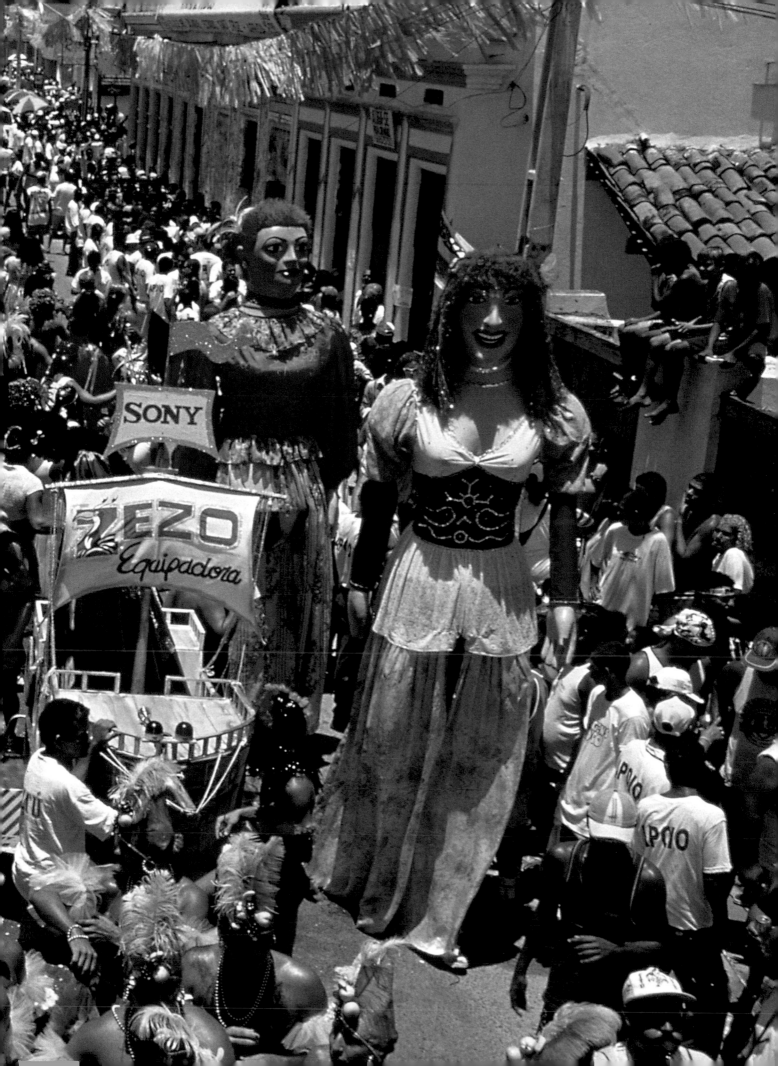

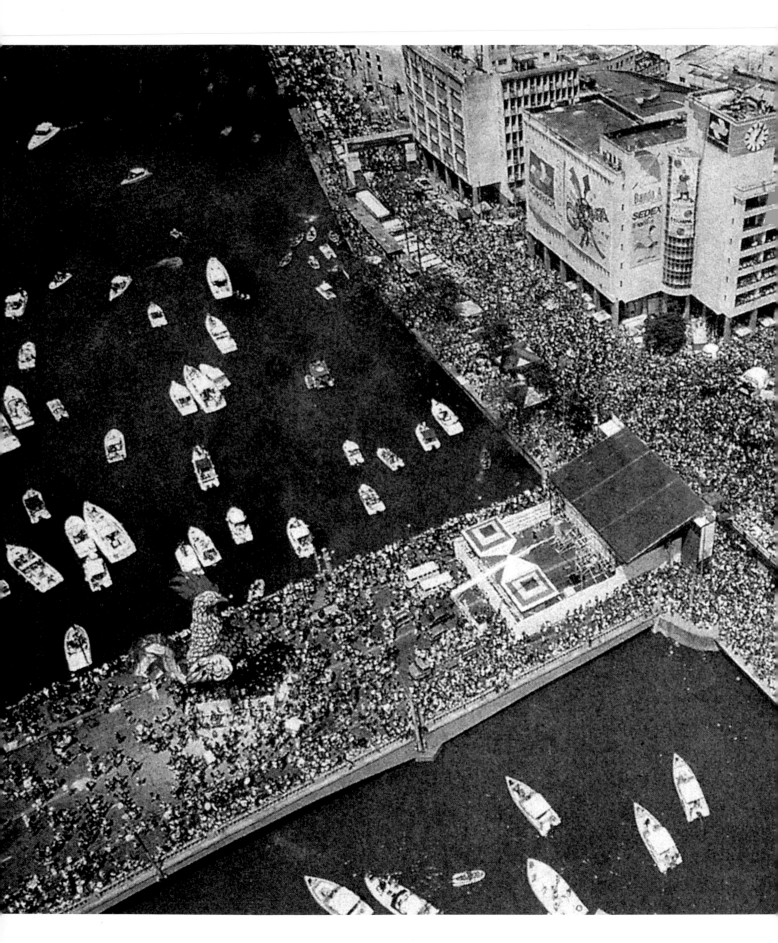

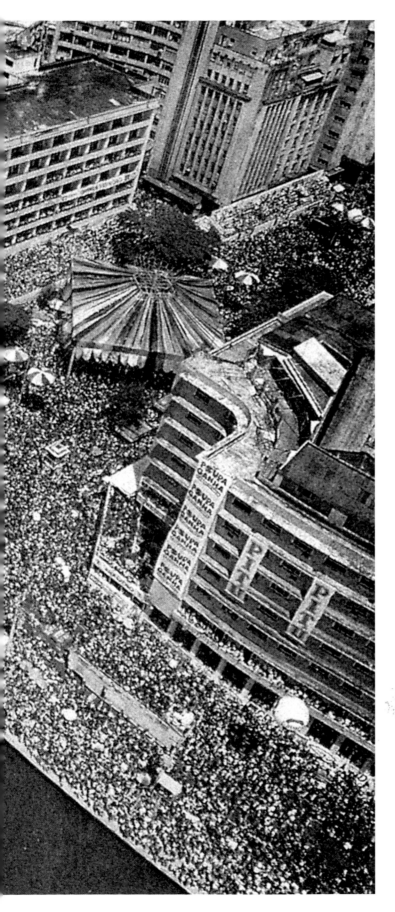

"virgins" don absurd wigs, voluptuous plastic or coconut "breasts" (sold in the shops), exaggerated makeup, and sexy female costumes in order to sashay and wiggle to the music of a dozen *tríos elétricos.* Some of the men even feint sexual advances toward male spectators along the way. Tens of thousands, along with the press and television crews, line the avenue to admire or ridicule or be amazed by the comic creativity of these muscular transvestites. This parade might seem appallingly vulgar to some Americans, but Brazil is gifted with a non-Puritanical culture, and everyone in the crowd, including the women who are being so grossly caricatured, seems to be enthralled by this outlandish rite of gender reversal.[36]

Saturday of Carnival! Recife is in a frenzy of anticipation for the stupendous parade of the Clube de Máscaras Galo da Madrugada (Cock of the Dawn Mummers' Club). In 1995, the Galo parade filled the streets, avenues, and bridges of downtown Recife with over one million revelers (fig. 9.13). In the middle of it, an enormous float carried a replica of the *Guinness Book of Records* open to a page that referred to the famous Carnival group as the largest of its kind in the world.[37] The makeup of the Galo parade, which lasts all day (and leaves the city littered with tons of trash), is almost too complex to describe. It includes masqueraders of all types, nubile young women in bikinis, dozens of floats and *tríos elétricos,* pedestrian *frevo* orchestras, giant puppets, antique cars, trucks selling beer and other refreshments, fire hoses spraying water on the packed crowds, hundreds of uniformed and plainclothes policemen, and several first aid wagons. Television cameras and journalists from various countries are there in force. Owners and guests on sail and motor boats fill the nearby River Capibaribe to admire the spectacle. And all this takes place under another burning tropical sun.[38]

It is among the lower classes and the urban poor that the greatest cultural riches of Pernambuco festival are to be found. From this segment of the populace come the hundreds of diverse *agremiações carnavalescas* (popular Carnival parading clubs), many of which

9.13 Aerial view of the gigantic parade of the Galo da Madrugada (Cock of the Dawn) *carnaval* association, with over one million revelers, 1995. *Photograph reproduced from the "Viagem" section (February 22, 2000), courtesy of the* Jornal de Commércio.

are unique to this region of Brazil and most clearly reflect its striking European, African, and Amerindian ethnic mix and resulting blend of cultural traditions. Most of these groups start preparing their costumes, designing their *alegorias* (plots or dramas), and rehearsing their choreographies in early September prior to Carnival of the following year.

Well over four hundred of these *agremiações* are legally registered in Recife and Olinda. Most of them are year-round voluntary and recreative associations that provide a variety of annual activities for their memberships, although their principal focus is to appear in the Carnival parades. Many are mutual aid societies, providing benefits such as funeral aid and even primary schooling for neighborhood children. The better-off groups have clubhouses with large dance floors used for fund-raising parties and rehearsals of choreographic pageants. For the smaller groups, the house of the elected club president usually serves as headquarters.[39]

In Recife, most of the *agremiações* are affiliated with the Federação Carnavalesca Pernambucana (FCP), an entity founded in 1936 with the aim of organizing the parades, collecting funds, and controlling the intense rivalries between competing groups. The FCP establishes the requirements (*regulamentos*) for the presentations of the diverse categories of festival associations, chooses the judging committees, and offers first-, second-, and third-place trophies. Some of the requirements are quite rigid, specifying acceptable numbers of musicians to be included and types of costumes to be presented, but there is still room for innovation and creativity on the part of individual clubs. The FCP is also in charge of distributing stipends from the city and state governments to the associated groups, stipends that are calculated on the basis of a group's size, its importance, and the expenditures necessary for its performances. Although these stipends cover only a minimal portion of any group's expenses, they provide a strong incentive for new clubs to try to join the FCP, thereby acquiring legitimacy as officially recognized organizations.[40]

Olinda's Carnival is far more loosely structured. Small amounts of financial aid from the municipality are sometimes available to local groups. Although a few of them have chosen to affiliate with the FCP in Recife, most prefer to remain independent and thus freer to perform when, how, and where they choose. Because of the proximity of the two cities, a good deal of interchange takes place between them, so that most of the *agremiações,* as well as groups from the interior of the state, can make the rounds of the different *polos* in both Recife and Olinda.

Among the notable restrictions on these organizations are, first, that although monetary contributions from local politicians and business firms are acceptable, political propaganda is not allowed and commercial advertising is severely limited and, second, that the *agremiações* are prohibited from ridiculing the Catholic Church or the Brazilian armed forces.

Even more extraordinary than the large number of Carnival associations is the variety of such groups in the parades. There are at least fifteen categories of *agremiações* with special repertoires of festival pageantry that portray some of the multiplicity of urban and rural subcultures in Pernambuco today.[41] The Brazilian musicologist Tiago Pinto has noted that in addition to the sambas of Rio and the *bloco afro* music of Bahia, the Pernambuco Carnival includes "almost the whole of the music and dance spectrum of the northeast region of Brazil."[42] I have suggested that the Carnival of Recife and Olinda presents the richest variety of folk traditions in the Western Hemisphere and quite possibly in the world. A brief typology of the fifteen categories of *agremiações* includes the following.[43]

CLUBES DE FREVO

These are the famous brass band clubs that are Pernambuco's greatest pride and joy. The *clubes de frevo* are among the oldest and most traditional Carnival associations, tracing their ancestry to the trade guilds of the colonial era described earlier. They are groups that parade at night in elaborate heraldic finery, led by a standard bearer in Louis XV costume with powdered wig, ornately embroidered jacket and breeches, lace jabot, and high-heeled shoes with gold or silver buckles. He dances while twirling a large quilted velvet standard, embroidered in gold or silver heraldic design and fringed with gold, which is hung from a tall metal frame—a total weight of up to a hundred pounds. There may be three or four standard bearers in a single *clube,* giving each one a chance to rest after performing with such a heavy artifact (fig. 9.14).

The standard bearer is followed by the brass orchestra of twenty to thirty musicians blaring forth the intoxicating *frevo* rhythms on trumpets, trombones, saxophones, and tubas, with snare and bass drum accompaniment. Then come the tuxedo-attired directorate; rows of teenage girls and boys and a few small children dancing the *passo* while waving multicolored parasols; *alas* (wings or sections) of men and women in lavish, bejeweled costumes with enormous feather headdresses; and finally two cordons of dancers carrying the symbol of the *clube* on a long pole while performing intricate choreographic figures. There may be several more *alas,* including one of homosexuals in costumes such as bats or butterflies. The pageantry of each group is based on an *alegoria,* or theme, different each year, on a fantasy or historical subject such as "The Court of the Caliphs," "The Reign of the Pharaohs," "Othello and Desdemona," and "The Dutch Occupation of Pernambuco." More than twenty *clubes de frevo* paraded in the year 2000, with up to five hundred dancers and musicians in each.

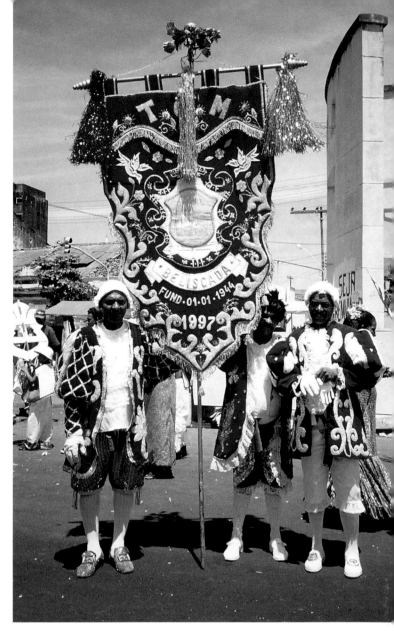

9.14 The heraldic quality of Recife *carnaval* is evident in the elaborately embroidered standards of the *carnaval* clubs. The *porta-estandarte* (standard bearer) is required to dress in powdered wig and costume of the Louis XV period. *Photograph by Katarina Real, 2000.*

9.15 A brass band from one of the *troça carnaval* clubs plays *frevo* music for an enthusiastic crowd. *Photograph by Katarina Real, 1996.*

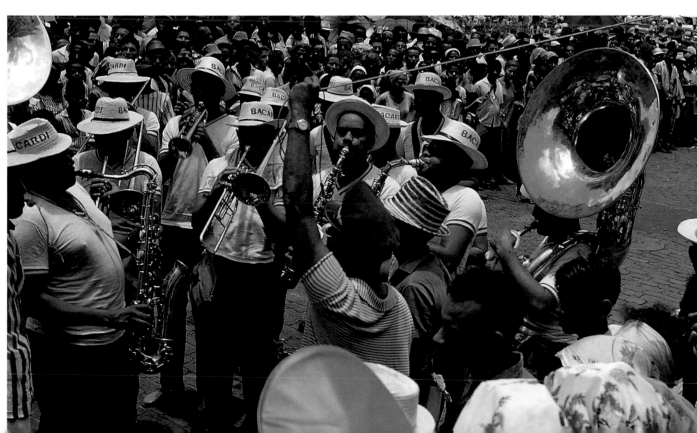

THE TROÇAS

Troças are daytime groups, similar in structure to the *clubes* but generally smaller. Few of them parade with more than two hundred costumed dancers, and their orchestras comprise no more than twenty musicians (fig. 9.15). While some of the *clubes* have retained the names of their ancestral guilds, such as Lenhadores (Woodchoppers) and Vassourinhas (Street Sweepers), the *troças* reveal a more lighthearted and frivolous spirit by names such as Pão Duro (Stale Bread), Camisa Velha (Old Shirt), and Cachorro do Homem do Miúdo (Dog of the Chitlins Vendor). In the Carnival of 2000, more than thirty of these groups appeared in the parades. If they grow in size and luxury and have sufficient financial resources, they can move up to the *clube de frevo* category in the FCP. Most of the *troça* participants are of mixed race and come from the urban working classes. Interestingly, the choreographic structures of both these categories in many ways resemble that of a Catholic religious procession, albeit in a totally secularized form, showing the influence of the ancestral brotherhoods on these organizations.

CLUBES DE BONECOS

Clubes de bonecos are relatively small groups that parade with a *frevo* orchestra of ten or twelve brass musicians and have as their central figure a fifteen-foot-tall puppet (*boneco gigante*), which dances and spins along the avenue to the delight of the crowds. The *clubes de bonecos,* like the two previous categories, must develop a theme, and they present fancy costumes and an *ala de passistas* (wing of *frevo* dancers). A few of the members appear in T-shirts bearing the logo of the *clube* and act as reliefs for the person dancing under the giant puppet, which weighs up to sixty pounds. These groups are a recent addition to Pernambuco Carnival, first appearing during the 1980s. There were ten of them in the 2000 parades, several from Olinda, and their popularity is attributed to their being less costly to produce, in comparison

9.16 A string band *carnaval* club, known as a *bloco lírico,* performs in one of the nighttime parades in Recife. *Photograph by Barbara Mauldin, 1998.*

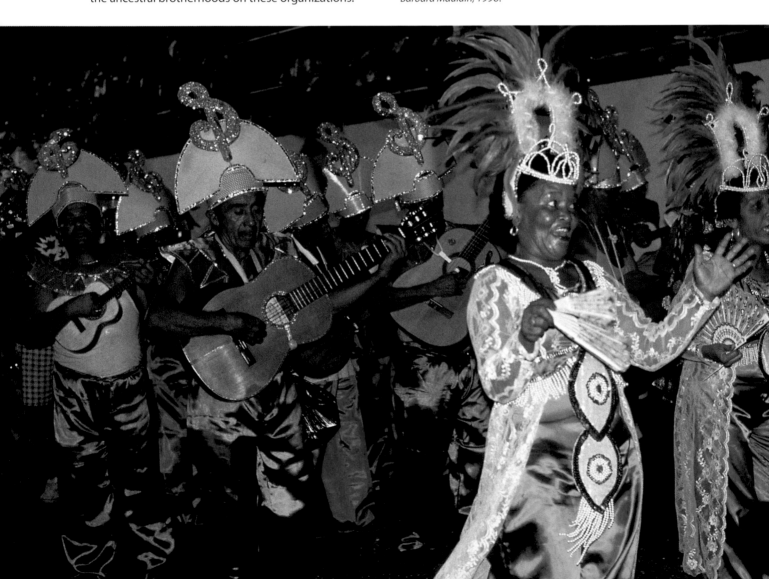

with the enormous expense necessary to put a *clube de frevo* or a *troça* into the parades.

BLOCOS (LÍRICOS)

Undoubtedly, the most melodious and elegant *agremiações* to appear in Pernambuco Carnival are the string band clubs known as *blocos*. Because *bloco* is a generic term applied to several other types of groups, the adjective "lyric" is sometimes added to identify them more specifically. These are nighttime organizations that parade with at least fifteen musicians playing stringed instruments (guitars, banjos, mandolins, etc.) and woodwinds; these musicians are called an *orquestra de pau e corda* ("wood and string"). Sometimes a few brass instruments are included to reinforce the sound on the open avenues. The *blocos líricos* are one of the few categories not to appear with a heraldic standard; instead, they are introduced by a figure bearing a large cutout placard, ornately decorated, in the shape of a fan or a lyre and called a *flabelo*. Then comes the directorate, often in top hats and tails, followed by dozens of dancers, swaying and spinning in lavish costumes to the typical lilting music, called *marcha-de-bloco*. The high point of their presentation is the well-rehearsed female chorus, which sings nostalgic songs about the beauty of Recife or Olinda Carnival, famous *blocos,* composers, and musicians of the past, or the deep sadness felt when the festival comes to an end. Each *bloco* presents a plot (*alegoria*) on such themes as "Discovery of Brazil," "Homage to France," and "Splendor in the Land of the Dragon." At least fifteen of these associations usually parade each year, with from two hundred to three hundred participants apiece, mostly from the lower middle class but also including popular recording artists and television personalities (fig. 9.16).

Historically, the *blocos líricos* originated from bands of young men who sang serenades to their neighborhood sweethearts and friends during the nineteenth century. When women were later allowed to join these groups, they introduced traditions from the Pastorinhas, a Christmas pastoral play in which two cordons of girls representing shepherdesses on their way to Bethlehem sing and dance in honor of the Christ child. In the 1980s, groups from the upper and middle classes began to found their own *blocos líricos* and to parade on the avenues in a nostalgic attempt to relive and preserve the pedestrian serenading traditions of earlier decades. Each year, individual groups from the bourgeoisie present special themes, the members appearing in identical costumes representing figures such as Spanish bullfighters and señoritas, Gypsies, folkloric rag dolls, or, as in 1977, Harlequin, Pierrot, and Colombina from the Italian commedia dell'arte. The upper-class *blocos* are not affiliated with the FCP and do not compete for prizes or trophies but often utilize string band musicians from the more proletarian groups.

ESCOLAS DE SAMBA

The world-famous "samba schools" are a nationwide phenomenon, and Recife and Olinda present the largest groups in Brazil after Rio, São Paulo, and Manáus.[44] Each group carries before its title the initials GRES (Grêmio Recreativo Escola de Samba) and can number as many as two thousand costumed singers, dancers, and musicians in the parades. Samba schools were initially brought to Recife by dark-skinned Brazilian sailors from Rio prior to World War II and since then have grown enormously in size, prestige, and political power. Originally, all the *escolas* belonged to the FCP, but in later years, some of them opted to form a separate organization called FESAPE (Federação das Escolas de Samba de Pernambuco) in order to obtain their own commercial and political support and not have to depend on the small stipends distributed to the FCP *agremiações*. In the years 1996–2000, seventeen samba schools belonged to FESAPE while fifteen remained with the FCP.

The structure of these groups as they parade is incredibly complex, consisting of dozens of *alas,* several gigantic floats, and a sound truck to amplify the voices of the lead singers. The heart of the *escola* is the *batucada,* a drum corps made up of separate rows of percussionists playing hand drums (*tamborins*), snare drums (*taróis*), friction drums (*cuícas*), cowbells, tambourines (*pandeiros*), bead-strung calabashes, and various other rhythmic instruments. The *batucada* can number as many as two hundred musicians, and each group has its own distinctive set of polyrhythmic samba beats. The hypnotic roar of so much percussion can drive the crowds into a delirium.

Other traditional elements include the *baianas,* female singers in voluminous Afro-Bahian costumes, these groups. The dark-skinned *batucada* players are mostly from the lower class; the whiter middle-class participants can finance their own extravagant costumes and sometimes even pay the *escola* leaders to appear in the parades.[45]

MARACATUS-NAÇÃO

The *maracatu* "nations" are also known as *maracatus de baque virado,* referring to the "spun-beat" rhythms played by the drummers. These groups are the direct descendants of the previously described Rosário brotherhoods and the tradition of crowning the Rei do Congo in the colonial era. Several of the oldest *maracatu* nations trace their founding to the early nineteenth century, when they were composed of enslaved and free blacks and were allowed to dance on their patron saint's day and during the Christmas season. Exactly when they joined the Carnival parades is unknown, but amazingly, they have survived into the twenty-first century and are growing in popularity.[46] In the 1960s, when I first studied them, only three still existed, parading with no more than fifty figures. Today, at least thirteen *maracatus-nação* are performing in dazzling choreographic parades with up to six hundred figures.

These groups represent a regal court (see fig. 9.7) and are led by a standard bearer in Louis XV costume. He is followed by the "court," made up of dukes and duchesses, princes and princesses, ambassadors—all in lavish European court attire—and ladies-in-waiting (*damas de paço*) who dance and spin in immense hoopskirts while holding luxuriously dressed black wooden dolls, called *calungas,* which represent the African ancestors and protectors of the "nation" (fig. 9.17). There follows an *ala* of *baianas* (Bahian-style women) in colorful head ties and sparkling bead necklaces, whose dance is similar to those seen in *xangô* rituals, and two cordons of men and women dressed as Roman soldiers. Finally come the king and queen, also in Louis XV finery, with long trains held by juvenile pages. They proceed majestically under a massive velvet canopy fringed with gold and held by a "slave" (fig. 9.18). Large animal figures such as lions and elephants, riding on wheeled platforms, represent the symbols of the group, and a charming children's court wears costumes similar to those of the adult participants (fig. 9.19).

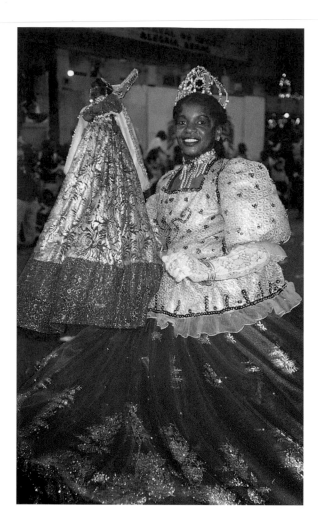

9.17 A lady-in-waiting of the *maracatu* nation Porto Rico holds a wooden doll called a *calunga* that represents the African ancestors and protectors of the "nation." *Photograph by Katarina Real, 1996.*

the *malabaristas,* dark-skinned male dancers performing acrobatic steps similar to those of *capoeira,* and most important of all, the *mestre-sala* (a type of majordomo) and the *porta-bandeira* (female banner carrier). Dressed in Louis XV court costumes, this couple performs an elegant minuet to the samba beat, the girl spinning in a hoopskirt as she waves the *escola*'s multicolored flag on a pole while the male dancer prances around her, gently holding the tips of her fingers.

Each *escola* develops a *samba de enrêdo,* a storytelling choreographic pageant that may take up to an hour to pass by, and most of them rely on themes from the Afro-Brazilian *orixás* (deities from the *xangô* religion) or themes based on prominent black figures from Brazilian history. There is some class division among

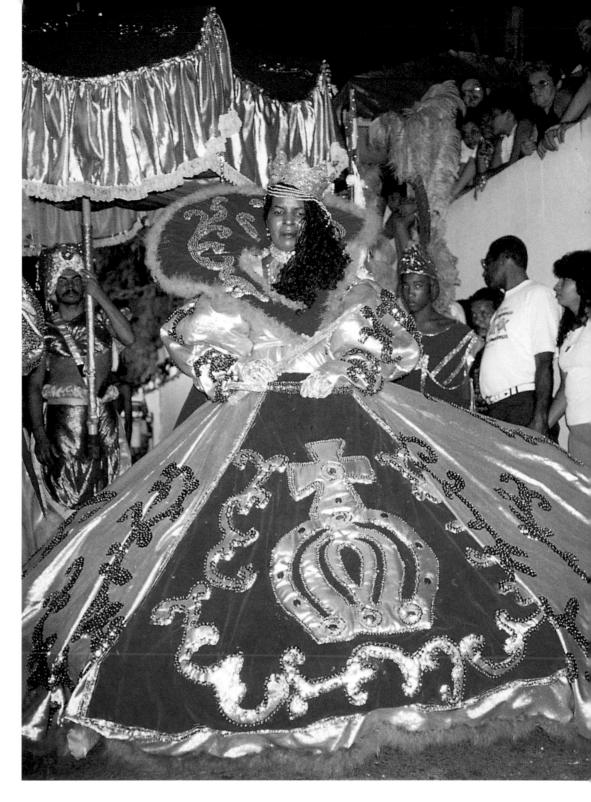

9.18 The queen of the *maracatu* nation Estrela Brilhante parades under a large canopy held by a costumed "slave." *Photograph by Katarina Real, 1997*.

A unique feature of the *maracatu* nation is the *batuqueiro* drum corps, made up of percussionists who beat complex polyrhythms on large, barrel-shaped wooden drums with thick sticks (fig. 9.20). These drums, called *bombos,* are required to have goat-skin heads tightened by heavy cords—no plastic drumheads or metal frames like those in the *batucadas* of the *escolas de samba* are allowed. Double cowbells (*gonguês*) and snare drums add to the complexity of the rhythms and make the sound of the orchestra, created by as many as forty musicians, audible from a great distance. At intervals in the drumming, the *mestre* (lead singer) introduces verses (*toadas*) in Portuguese, praising the valor of the "nation" or expressing a longing for its African homeland, which are repeated by the *baiana* chorus.

Most of the dark-skinned *maracatu* participants come from the urban poor, and the majority have close ties with the Afro-Brazilian *xangô* religion. Usually, the queen is a *mãe-de-santo* (mother of the saint), a high priestess of one of the *xangô* temples, which also serves as headquarters for the group. One of the most dramatic events in Recife is the annual Noite dos Tambores Silenciosos (Night of the Silent Drums) ceremony, which is held in a historic square on Monday night of Carnival. All the "nations," with their regal courts and batteries of drummers, gather to await the stroke of midnight, when the drums are silenced for a few moments to pay homage to the many Brazilian slaves who died in the struggle for freedom.

MARACATUS RURAIS

Among the most extraordinary groups to be seen during Pernambuco Carnival are the *maracatus rurais*, or

9.19 The king and queen and their attendants in a children's *maracatu* group in Olinda. *Photograph by George Ancona, 1998.*

rural *maracatus*, also known as *maracatus de orquestra* or *maracatus de baque solto* ("loose-style" rhythm). These *agremiações* originated on the sugar plantations in the interior region northwest of Recife (the *zona da mata*) in past centuries and are still largely composed of former cane cutters and rural farmworkers, most of whom are poor, often unemployed, and semiliterate. They have few ties with the *xangô* religion, considering themselves *índios-africanos* ("African Indians"), an identity that closely corresponds to their ethnic makeup. They have their own folk religion, called *catimbó*, which involves hallucinogenic trances in order to become possessed (*atuado*) by Amerindian or African spirits. Originally the *maracatus rurais* were seen only during the Christmas and New Year festivities celebrating the end of the cane harvest on the plantations. Over the years they have incorporated elements from several different Christmas folk plays, traveling circuses, folk troubadours, and the *maracatus-nação* to produce a highly original "polyglot" type of *agremiação*.

The most spectacular figures in the *maracatus rurais*

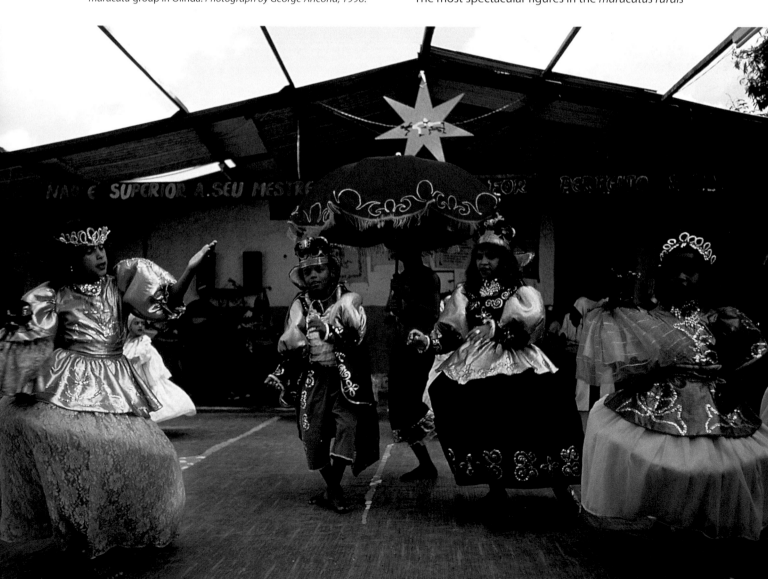

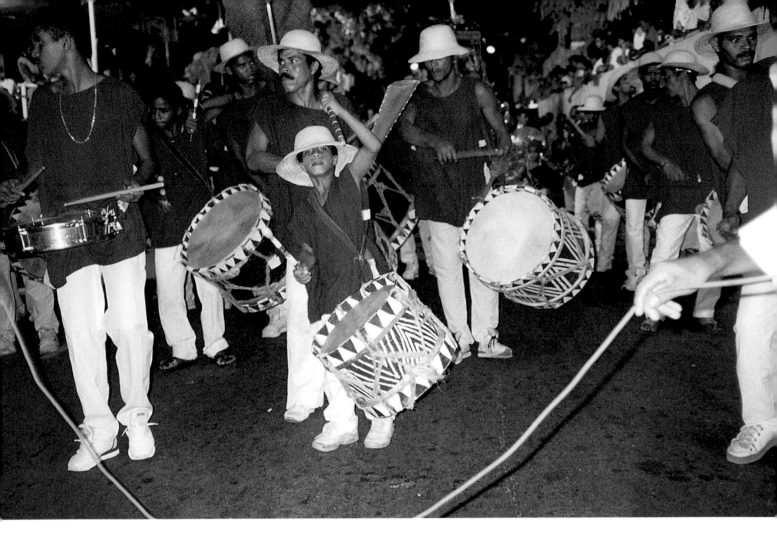

9.20 A *batuqueiro* drum corps from the *maracatu-nação* Elefante. *Photograph by Katarina Real, 1996.*

are the *caboclos de lança* ("lancer warriors"), who dance, leap, drop to the ground, and sometimes duel while slashing six-foot-long spears (*guiadas*) covered with multicolored ribbons. They wear tall headdresses made of thousands of strips of shiny, colored cellophane, which are tossed back and forth like a lion's mane when they dance (fig. 9.21).[47] The rest of the costume consists of an enormous pectoral cloak (*gola*), completely embroidered with sequins or bugle beads, which extends almost to the ankles, along with breeches and scarves of bright flower-print cotton, tennis shoes, and a strange artifact called a *surrão*. The last is worn over the buttocks and has several large cowbells attached, which clank noisily as the *caboclo de lança* runs and dances. The lancers also wear dark glasses, often paint their faces with red dye (*urucum*), and sometimes hold a flower in their teeth, indicating possession by an Amerindian spirit.

Other figures in the rural *maracatus* include the standard bearer, again in Louis XV attire, a women's chorus in *baiana* costumes, a hobby-horse figure who asks for donations, two or three *tuxáus* (Indian shamans), who wear gigantic headdresses of peacock and dyed rhea feathers (fig. 9.22), and occasionally a somewhat incongruous king and queen (see p. 19). The group is led by a *tirador de loas* (verse caller), who improvises folk poetry into song, utilizing complex rhyme schemes inherited from medieval Portugal. The female *baiana* chorus picks up the verse in a call-and-response pattern, accompanied by a small orchestra of cowbell, snare drum, *cuíca* (friction drum), metal cylindrical rattle (*mineiro*), and trombone that plays samba, *marcha,* and the regional *galope* rhythms.

The phenomenal growth of the rural *maracatus* in recent decades has led to the founding of over one hundred of these groups in Pernambuco, some sixty of which perform in both Recife and Olinda during Carnival. Some of them parade with as many as two hundred figures, including more than eighty *caboclos de lança.* They have recently organized their own fed-

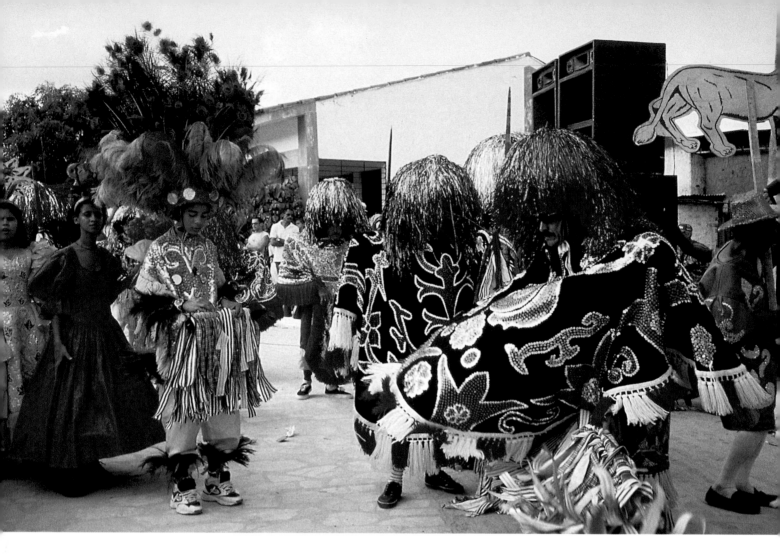

9.21 The *caboclo de lança* (lancer warrior) costumes of the rural *maracatus,* with their enormous capes, are the most spectacular in Pernambuco Carnival. *Photograph by Katarina Real, 2000.*

eration, with headquarters both in the interior and in the town of Paulista, near Olinda, where, on Sunday of Carnival, all the groups must gather to present a brilliant display of choreographic pageantry before scattering to the various urban *polos* or out to towns in the interior.

CABOCLINHOS AND TRIBOS GROUPS

The Indian cultural heritage of northeastern Brazil is celebrated in the Caboclinhos and Tribos folk dramas, although in a highly romanticized form. Both types of choreographic pageants are probably descended from folk dramas called *autos hieráticos* that were introduced by Jesuit missionaries in the seventeenth century as a means of Christianizing the Amerindian tribes. Their choreographic structure—two opposing cordons of warriors—resembles the structure of medi-

eval sword dances known as *moriscas* but is atypical of any dance pattern found among unacculturated tropical forest Indians. Once again, we find that both the Caboclinhos and the Tribos dramas were originally part of the Christmas festivities on sugar plantations and were incorporated into Carnival in the last century. They are still sometimes performed at Christmastime, when their lengthy spoken verses are heard, but at Carnival, because of the brief time allotted to the performers during the parades, the verses are usually curtailed.

The Caboclinhos drama is essentially a battle mime about a planned attack on an enemy, a rival group, or the Portuguese invaders, during which disloyalty is discovered within the tribe. The *cacique* (tribal chief) resolves the conflict and punishes the traitor, who begs for forgiveness. The dance presentation is led by a standard bearer with a tall headdress and a skirt and anklets of dyed rhea feathers, who leaps and shouts as he spins the standard around him. He dances barefoot, as do all the other dancers in the group—

quite a challenge on the rough concrete or cobblestone pavement. He is followed by *alas* of costumed "Indian" children (*perós*), teenage girls in discreet rhinestone bikinis with enormous fan-shaped headdresses of multicolored ostrich feathers (*cocares*), cordons of boys and men, naked to the waist and wearing similar headdresses, and finally the male and female tribal chiefs, or the king and queen, with gold crowns and long velvet trains.

Most of the dancers carry an artifact called a *preaca*, which looks like a bow and arrow but is actually a percussion instrument (see fig. 9.1). It makes a sharp clicking sound when the flange on the arrow strikes the wooden bow and provides the accelerating rhythm for the dancers, who leap up and down from a squatting position. Accompaniment is provided by three musicians in feather costumes playing a snare drum, a vertical flute (*gaita*), and one or two metal rattles (*caracaxás*).

More than twenty-five Caboclinhos groups perform in the parades each year, some affiliated with the FCP and others coming in from the interior. Most are relatively small, numbering fewer than one hundred dancers, but a few of the more prosperous groups appear with as many as three hundred.

The Tribos dancers, originally from the neighboring state of Paraíba, are similar in structure to the Caboclinhos groups but present a different folk drama in which there is a "death and resurrection" scene. Their feather costumes are also different, and the dancers are often painted red from head to toe. Instead of *preacas,* the women carry small hatchets, and the men, short spears. Four Tribos groups belong to the FCP and parade with fifty to sixty figures apiece.

The participants in both of these "Indian" categories are mostly dark-skinned or mixed-race members of the urban or rural underclass. Although few of them are truly Indian, all the groups have adopted names of the Tupi-Guarani tribes that formerly inhabited northeastern Brazil, many of which are now extinct. These folk dramas, however, continue to memorialize their bravery and valor during present-day Carnival celebrations.

URSOS DE CARNAVAL

The *ursos,* or Carnival bear clubs, have been described by the folklorist Roberto Benjamin as "a European influ-

ence in an Afro-Indian Carnival."[48] It is indeed startling to see a man dressed in a grizzly or polar bear costume dancing in the streets of tropical Recife. This figure wears a large bear mask over a body suit covered with shredded burlap or fabric remnants or velvet (depending on the type of animal being represented) and shuffles along in a grotesque fashion (fig. 9.23).

How did "bears" make their way into Carnival? In the nineteenth century, Italian Gypsies arrived in Pernambuco to work as coopers in the sugar mills. Some

9.22 The *tuxáu,* with his tall headdress of peacock and dyed rhea feathers, acts as a shaman and protector of the rural *maracatu.* Photograph by Katarina Real, 1997.

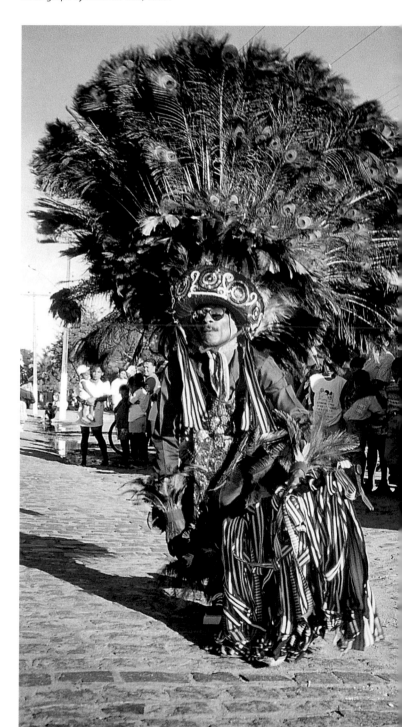

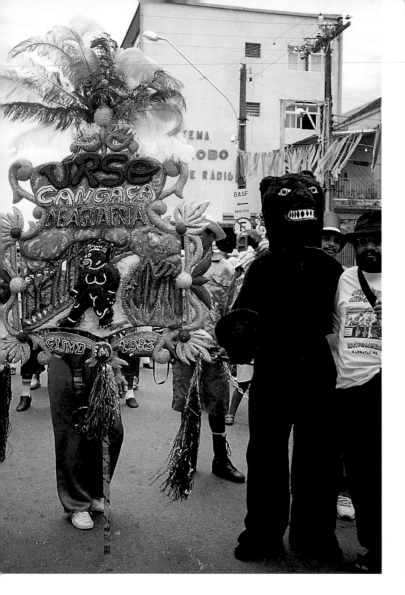

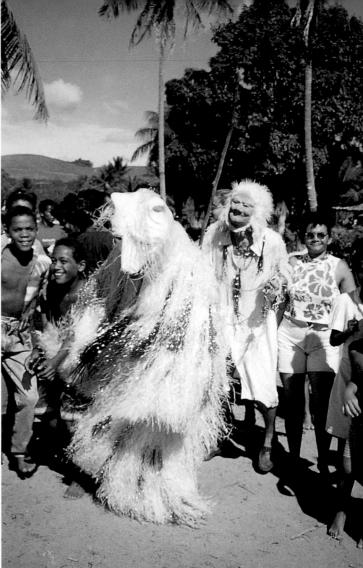

9.23 An *urso de carnaval* (Carnival bear) group dances along the parade route with an ornate standard called a *cartaz*. *Photograph by Katarina Real, 2000.*

9.24 A Carnival "bear" with his "Italian trainer" dances in a village in the interior of Pernambuco. *Photograph by Katarina Real, 1996.*

of them brought specially trained bears, a survival of medieval bear-baiting, which ended up performing in small traveling circuses, where they captivated the local populace. The northern European animals did not long survive in the tropical climate, but people kept the tradition alive by inventing the folkloric *urso de carnaval agremiações,* in which the central figures include a dancing "bear" tied to a chain, his elegantly dressed Italian trainer (*Italiano*) with whip, who pulls and yanks the animal to make it dance, and a *caçador* (hunter) buffoon, who prances around keeping an old musket trained on the beast (fig. 9.24). While this hilarious act is being performed, two cordons of small children, teenage boys and girls, and a few adults, dressed in Gypsy, Italian, or *passo/frevo* costumes,

encircle the group, dancing and singing praises of the ferocious "bear." The European origins of these *agremiações* are apparent in their original songs, which are composed each year and accompanied by an orchestra playing march, polka, and schottische (*xote*) rhythms on accordions, guitars, tambourines, triangles, drums, and clarinets.

In the 1960s, there were around fifteen *urso* groups, mostly to be seen only in the remote suburbs.[49] By *carnaval* 2000, there were over thirty-five such groups in the FCP competing for first, second, and third place. The bear clubs parade in the daytime with no more than forty figures each, made up mostly of extended families. Children, parents, grandparents, and other relatives all work together on costume preparation, choreography, and the verses to be sung. Each *urso* group is preceded in the parade by a large *cartaz* (cut-out placard) with a picture of its special bear and its date of founding.

Originally, the *ursos de carnaval* appeared to demonstrate a covert criticism of slavery, but according to Benjamin, in recent years they have taken on an overtly sexual connotation of cuckoldry, because the "bear" is believed to be able to seduce the wife while the husband is absent.[50]

BOI DE CARNAVAL

Among the most important survivals from medieval Europe to be found in Pernambuco Carnival are the heraldic standards, the *urso* clubs, and the "Bumba-meu-boi" ("Whup my ox!") folk dramas.[51] These "bull dramas," known as *autos populares,* are found, with certain regional variations, from southern Brazil to the Amazon and are considered by Renato Almeida to be the major expression of Brazilian folklore theater.[52] In most regions, including Pernambuco, they are performed during the Christmas season by a "company of players" of ten or twelve actors who, in true Shakespearean tradition, are able to play as many as fifty different roles among them. The hilarious slapstick comedy revolves around the misfortunes of a much prized bull while satirizing the society of the colonial sugar plantation or cattle ranch, from the master down to the field hands and cowboys, with broad criticism of corruption, hypocrisy, stupidity, and other human foibles. It also includes a variety of animal and monster figures, mythical or imagined, that are designed to amuse or terrify the spectators.

At Carnival in Recife, most of the actor roles and spoken lines are dropped, and it is principally the clowns and the animal and monster figures that parade as *boi de carnaval* players (fig. 9.25). These groups are introduced by a dancing "nobleman" carrying a somewhat rustic standard with an embroidered bull figure. Then comes a motley assemblage of comic figures swirling around each other, including hobby-horse dancers (*cavalo-marinho* and *burrinha*); three clowns clobbering the other figures—one of whom (the *catirina*) is a man-woman in blackface and rags—with inflated pig bladders (*bexigas*); a quack doctor; a corrupt soldier (*sordado-da-gurita*); and even a mock priest. The *boi*'s head is made from a cow's skull, and the monster figure, called a *babau,* uses a horse's skull. Each is attached to a large painted canvas carapace under which a hidden dancer performs. The *boi*

9.25 A *boi de carnaval* (Carnival bull) group performs with clowns and monster figures from the Bumba-meu-boi ("Whup my bull!") folk drama. This is one of the most hilarious types of groups to appear in Pernambuco Carnival. *Photograph by Katarina Real, 2000.*

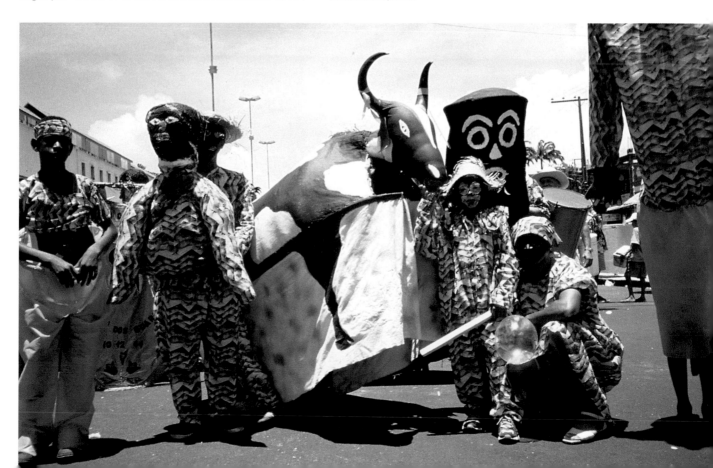

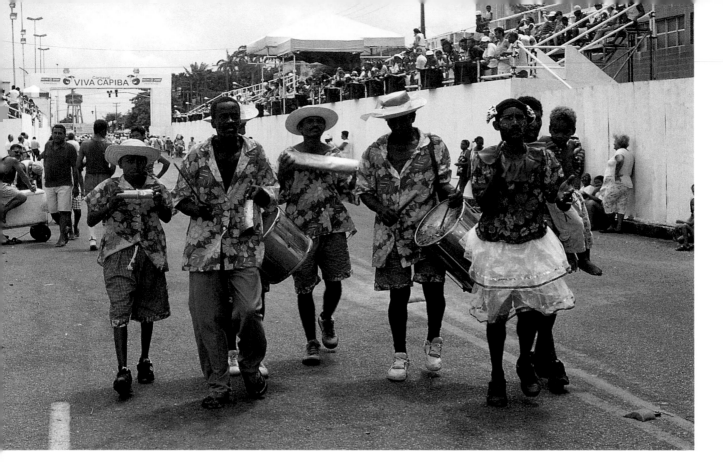

9.26 A small group of musicians plays lively percussion music for a *boi de carnaval* troupe. *Photograph by Barbara Mauldin, 1998.*

9.27 A young "African" dancer from the *afoxé* Ilê de Egbá. *Photograph by Katarina Real, 1999.*

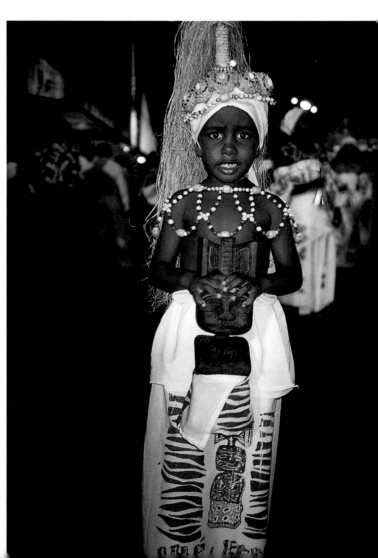

charges around, wildly butting back the excited crowds, while the *babau* snaps its teeth at spectators, particularly at unruly children. The *jaraguá* is a tall "bird," articulated by a man underneath pulling a cord attached to its beak, which pecks at the audience, and there is the horrific *morto-carregando-o-vivo* ("dead man carrying the live one") and far too many more ludicrous figures to be described here. Adding to this bedlam is the raucous music played by a small band of percussionists beating drums, cowbells, and other noisemakers (fig. 9.26).

Usually presenting no more than thirty figures, the *boi de carnaval* companies are the smallest groups to appear in the downtown parades. Nine belong to the FCP, but there are many more unaffiliated groups in the suburbs and the interior, some with only a few of the figures mentioned above. Although their membership is drawn mostly from the poorest of the poor, it is apparent that these often semiliterate revelers (*folgazões*) have an extraordinary sense of the absurd and the art of comedy.

The *afoxé* associations are the most African, or rather Africanized, groups to be seen in Recife-Olinda Carnival. In Salvador, Bahia, they date from the late 1940s. There, according to Crowley, their number had grown to some twenty-five parading groups by the 1980s, with as many as three thousand figures in each.[53] In Pernambuco, they are among the most recent additions to the festival, first appearing in the parades in the late 1980s, spurred by the burgeoning "black consciousness" movement in Brazil and the celebrations marking the centenary of the abolition of slavery in 1888. It is difficult to estimate how many *afoxés* there are, because they are not affiliated with the FCP and do not always welcome visits from curious anthropologists. Probably no more than six exist in Pernambuco today, four in Olinda and two in Recife. All the *afoxés* are closely associated with the *xangô* and *candomblé* religions, adopting names honoring some of the Afro-Brazilian *orixás* (deities). They parade with no more than a few hundred figures dressed in white Afro-Muslim robes and turbans (fig. 9.27) or various types of pseudo-African costumes. They sing verses praising

their African heritage in a mixture of Yoruba and Portuguese, accompanied by an orchestra of conga drums, calabashes, and other percussion instruments plus a giant papier-mâché figure of the group's special *orixá*.

TURMAS

The *turmas* make up a catch-all category for the hundreds, perhaps thousands, of small groups of masqueraders to be seen dancing and playing in Recife, in the suburbs, and especially up and down the steep streets of Olinda. The extraordinary variety of traditional and original costumes that appear during the four days of Carnival include bats, bears, bulls, cocks, "ghosts" in white sheets (*almas*), bandits, cowboys, Gypsies, odalisques, "babies" in diapers and nursing bottles (worn by grown men), American Indians, Pierrot, Colombina, and Harlequin, various types of masks (fig. 9.28), and many other creations. Three distinctive Recife-Olinda costumed groups include the *burrinhas,* dancers wearing small "hobby-horse" donkeys around their waists (fig. 9.29); the *papangús,* revelers in headmasks with pretty white female faces and plastic curls in garish colors (fig. 9.30); and the *palhaços de coração,* "heart clowns," wearing gold or silver headmasks, ruffled collars, and embroidered velvet boleros (fig. 9.31).

Many groups of mummers are made up of families, friends, students, or business colleagues who come out

9.28 The Julião mask shop in Olinda sells a variety of masks to individuals or small groups who join in the *carnaval* festivities. *Photograph by George Ancona, 1998.*

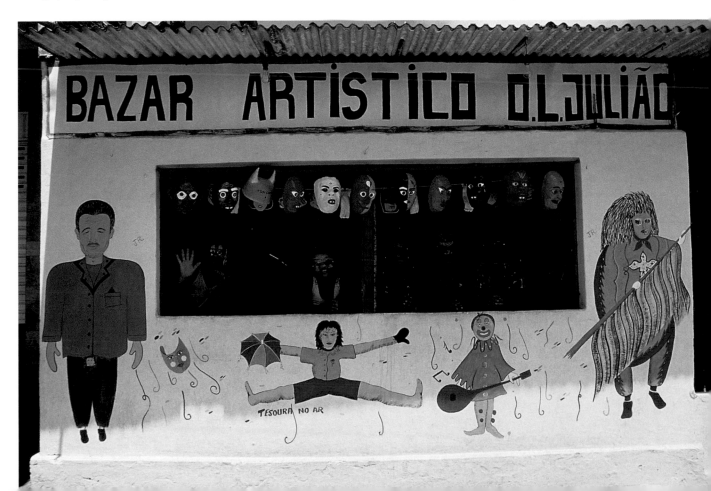

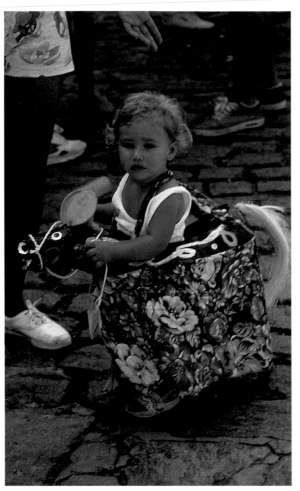

to play at Carnival one year and may not decide to masquerade again. However, some of the more traditional groups, such as the heart clowns, are permanent year-round organizations with their own directorates, and they appear each year to add colorful fantasy to the festivities. While actually not "costumed," the *turmas de ensaboados,* covering themselves with soapsuds, and the *enlameados,* pouring yellow mud over each other, contribute to the ambiance of generalized hilarity. A new *turma* of evangelical Protestants, called Jesús é Bom Abessa (loosely, "Jesus is really cool"), has recently been parading on the avenues. Wearing T-shirts and accompanied by a *batucada de samba,* they pass out leaflets calling for repentance, salvation, and the acceptance of Christ.

BLOCOS EMPRESARIAIS

The associations known as *blocos empresariais,* which began to parade in the 1980s, are composed mostly

9.29 Many small children wear *burrinhas,* or hobby-horse donkeys, for their Carnival costume. *Photograph by George Ancona, 1998.*

9.30 The narrow cobblestone streets of Olinda are filled with *papangús* masqueraders. *Photograph by Katrina Real, 1997.*

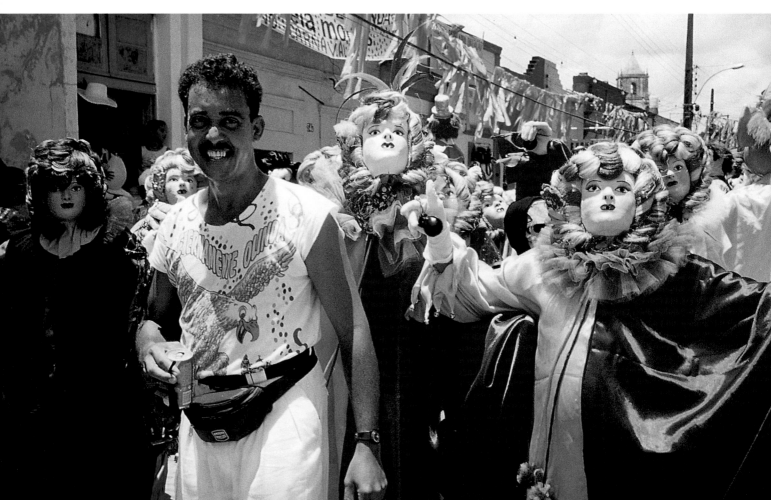

of middle-class employees of the public utility companies, private business firms, and the labor unions. In 1996, forty-six of these groups filled the avenues of downtown Recife and Boa Viagem Beach during pre-Carnival week.[54] Bank workers, journalists, security police, teachers, hospital employees, and dozens of other professionals each have special parading organizations, many with funny names, such as the Bloco da Lingua Ferina ("savage tongue") of the journalists' union. Some of these groups are immense and include the families of the employees as well as clients of the enterprise, all dressed in identical T-shirts and baseball caps (*bonés*). In 2001, the parade of the Bloco da Parceria, composed of employees, colleagues, and fans of the giant Bompreço supermarket chain, drew almost a million revelers to the broad avenue of Boa Viagem, accompanied by eleven *trios elétricos*. It even included a hundred *caboclos de lança* from Pernambuco's most famous rural *maracatu*, the Piaba de Ouro.[55]

PARADE OF THE GIANT PUPPETS

As dawn approaches on Fat Tuesday (Mardi Gras), the Carnival of Olinda is ready to explode. Many of the smaller *agremiações* I have described—the *ursos, bois, troças, tribos de índios*, and so forth—are ready to join the throngs of *turmas* and other masqueraders for a final day of revelry. Larger groups such as the *escolas de samba* and many of the *blocos* are absent, being unable to maneuver on the steep, narrow streets and in the midst of the densely packed crowds. The whole populace awaits what is considered the apogee of Olinda Carnival: the parade of the giant puppets (*bonecos gigantes*), organized by a master puppet artisan named Sílvio Botelho (fig. 9.32). As many as eighty of his famous *bonecos gigantes* gather on a square high above the city and, with several *frevo* orchestras interspersed among them, begin a descent down the winding cobblestone streets. Dancing, spinning, and bowing to applauding crowds of thousands, the giant puppets make their way past the colonial churches and other historic buildings to the lower city in a parade that lasts far into the night (fig. 9.33). Botelho's giants, measuring up to fifteen feet tall, are each borne by a man underneath the figure, balancing it on his head, who is called the *alma* ("soul"), since he "gives life" to his charge. Some of the *bonecos* honor important individuals in Recife-Olinda Carnival—musicians,

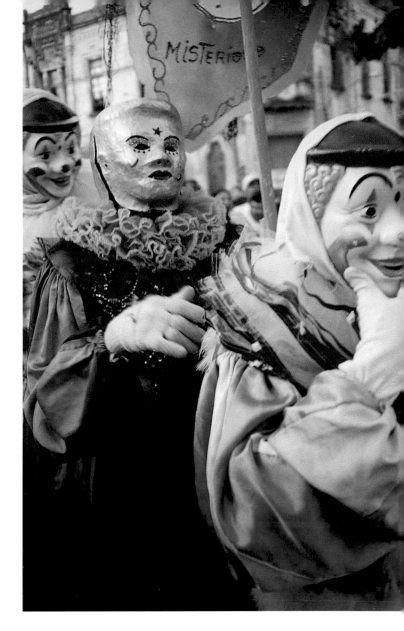

9.31 *Palhaços de coração* (heart clowns) are a popular masquerade for individuals in Recife *carnaval* parades. *Photograph by Katarina Real, 1996.*

composers, club leaders, and so forth; others portray local types such as the newspaper boy, the tourist, the mailman, and the waitress. Pierrot is also included, as well as a devil, John Travolta, and a host of others.[56]

Carnival Is Reluctant to Die

During Carnival, the Catholic priesthood has been on a retreat (*retiro*), cloistered in the monasteries or seminaries along with a few devout parishioners (mostly older women) wishing to escape the noise and confusion. On Ash Wednesday, the priests reopen the churches for the ritual of placing ashes on the brows

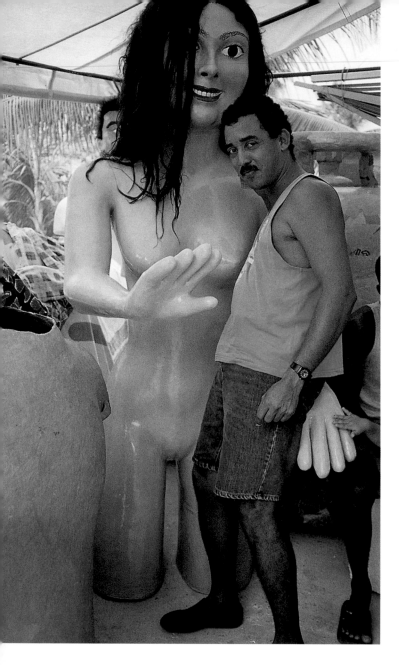

9.32 The giant puppet artisan Silvio Botelho with one of his recent creations in his Olinda workshop. *Photograph by Katarina Real, 1997.*

Lenten dish of codfish, potatoes, and spices (*baca-lhoada*), washed down with copious amounts of beer. And Carnival still does not end, for there are the all-important victory parades, the awarding of trophies the following Saturday, and the celebrations on ensu-ing weekends of all the winning *agremiações* that have made the Pernambuco festival such a glorious event. Many believe that Recife and Olinda, and for that mat-ter much of Brazil, do not really return to a normal rou-tine of everyday life until the Monday after Ash Wednesday.[57]

Brazilian Carnival may be considered a rite of inten-sification, a joyous national *rite de passage,* almost a religion itself, and should be judged less for its empha-sis on sexuality, irrationality, and chaos than for its role in unifying a diverse people by undermining racial, class, religious, and political barriers for a few momen-tous days of unbridled merriment each year.

NOTES

Among the many people who made invaluable suggestions on the essay, I should include Roberto Benjamin, current presi-dent of the Pernambuco State Folklore Commission, and my friends Cléa Brasileiro and Olímpio Bonald Neto in Brazil. Spe-cial thanks also go to Professor Robert Bender of Annapolis, Maryland, and to Barbara Mauldin of the Museum of Interna-tional Folk Art in Santa Fe, New Mexico.

The *Evoé* in the title of this chapter is also the title of the hymn of the Federação Carnavalesca Pernambucana (Pernam-buco Federation of Carnival Clubs). The interjection *evoé!* comes from the ancient Greek and is defined by *Webster's New International Dictionary of the English Language* (2d edition, vol. 1, 1943), 886, as "an exclamation expressing exhilaration; —the cry of bacchanals."

1. The Brazilian author and journalist Hernane Tavares de Sá wrote the classic work *The Brazilians: People of Tomorrow* (New York: John Day Company, 1947). In chapter 8, "A Play-ground for a Capital," he described the unbridled merriment of Rio de Janeiro's Carnival as "spontaneous, unaided by any stimulant. The sale of liquor anywhere in the city is strictly prohibited during the four days" (78). This is no longer true in most Brazilian cities, and certainly not in Recife and Olinda, where hours of dancing under the hot tropical sun would be intolerable without cold beer or rum-flavored fruit juices.

2. Jorge Amado, *O País do Carnaval* (São Paulo: Martins Editôra, 1931).

of the penitent. But for many revelers, the festival still has not ended. Groups with names such as "Parou, por quê?" ("Why did it stop?") and "Eu quero mais!" ("I want more!") continue to frolic in the streets on Ash Wednesday, along with the enormous parade of Bacalhau do Batata, formed by the hundreds of wait-ers and bartenders (and their supporters) who have had to work all during Carnival and not yet had a chance to "play." After their parade, the Batata revel-ers gather for a sumptuous banquet of the traditional

9.33 *Mestre* Silvio Botelho's annual parade of the giant puppets fills the streets of historic Olinda all day on the Tuesday of Carnival. *Photograph by Katarina Real, 1996.*

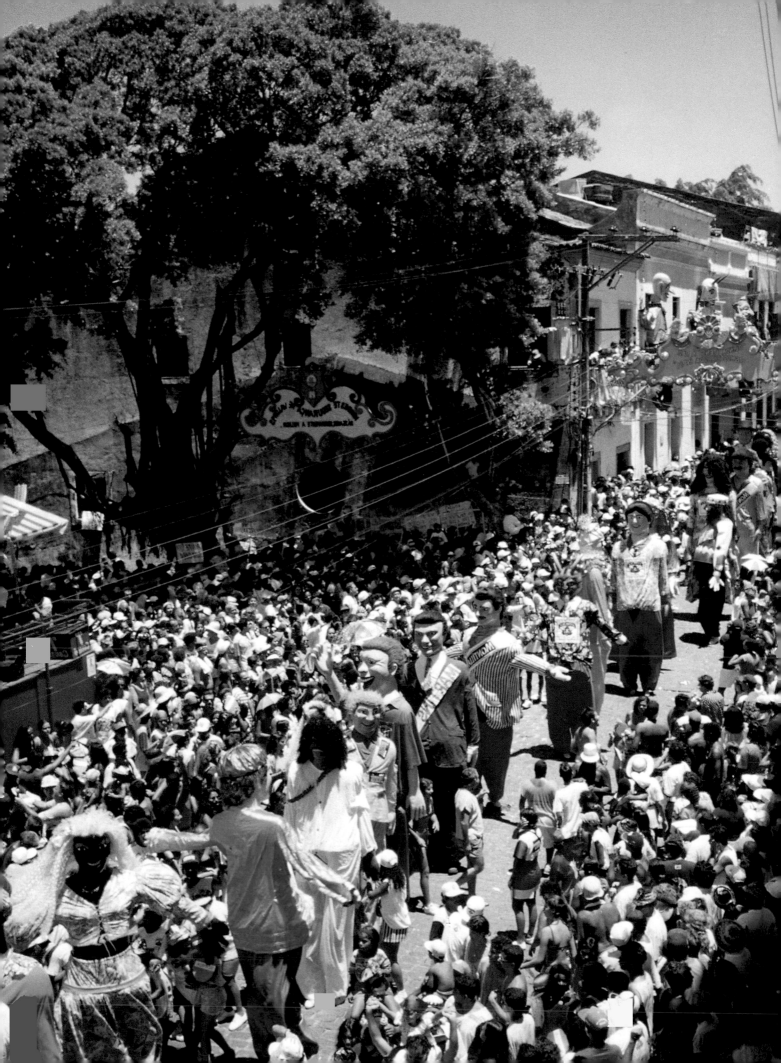

3. Roberto da Matta, *Carnavais, malandros e heróis: Para uma sociologia do dilema brasileiro* (Rio de Janeiro: Jorge Zahar Editores, 1978), 36, 53. He also described Carnival as "marked by a universalist orientation, cosmic, emphasizing such all-embracing categories as life as opposed to death, joy as opposed to sadness, the rich as opposed to the poor, etc." (my translation).

4. Designed by Brazil's premier architect, Oscar Neimeyer, and inaugurated in 1984, the Sambadrome consists of a mile-long stretch of paved roadway flanked by concrete bleachers, luxury boxes, and ground-level seating with the capacity for ninety thousand spectators. Joseph A. Page, *The Brazilians* (New York: Addison-Wesley, 1995), 446–485. Page gives an accurate and colorful description of Rio's spectacular Carnival.

5. Daniel J. Crowley's monograph *African Myth and Black Reality in Bahian Carnaval* (Los Angeles: UCLA Museum of Cultural History, 1984) presents a comprehensive analysis of the festival in Salvador, Bahia, particularly of its Afro-Brazilian component.

6. Phillip Curtin, *The Atlantic Slave Trade: A Census* (Madison: University of Wisconsin Press, 1969), 47–49.

7. Gilberto Freyre, *The Masters and the Slaves: A Study in the Development of Brazilian Civilization* (translated by Samuel Putnam from the Portuguese *Casa grande e senzala,* first published in 1933; New York: Alfred A. Knopf, 1964).

8. Ibid., 239. Freyre commented: "An ascetic, orthodox Catholicism, by hampering the freedom of the senses and the instincts of generation, would have prevented Portugal from straddling half a world."

9. Gilberto Freyre, *The Mansions and the Shanties: The Making of Modern Brazil* (translated by Harriet de Onís from the Portuguese *Sobrados e mucambos,* first published in 1936; New York: Alfred A. Knopf, 1963).

10. Rita de Cássia Barbosa Araújo, "Festas públicas e carnavais: O Negro e a cultura popular de Pernambuco," in *O Negro e a construção do carnaval no nordeste,* organizers Luis Sávio de Almeida et al. (Maceió: Universidade Federal de Alagôas, 1996), 41.

11. Donald Pierson writes in his classic work *Negroes in Brazil: A Study of Race Contact at Bahia* (Chicago: University of Chicago Press, 1942), 91, that the imported slaves "were required by law to be baptized into the Christian religion on penalty of forfeiture to the state. Those from Portuguese Angola were baptized in lots before they left their native shores. . . . With slaves from other parts of Africa, the master was allowed a year for the instruction requisite for baptism."

12. Freyre, *Masters and Slaves,* 239.

13. René Ribeiro, *Religião e relações raciais* (Rio de Janeiro: Ministério de Educação e Cultura, 1956), 76.

14. The word *entrudo* comes from the Latin *introito,* meaning "introduction," referring to the period that introduces Lent. This is the same term used to refer to the rowdy Carnival celebration in Laza, Spain (chapter 2).

15. Rita de Cássia Barbosa Araújo, *Festas: Máscaras do tempo-entrudo, máscara e frevo no carnaval do Recife* (Recife: Fundação de Cultura Cidade do Recife, 1996), 118–167.

16. Eneida Moraes, *História do carnaval carioca* (Rio de Janeiro: Editôra Record, 1987), 21.

17. Henry Koster, *Travels in Brazil,* 2d ed. (London: Longman, Hurst, Rees, Orme and Brown, 1817), 1: 322.

18. Katarina Real (Katharine Royal Cate), "The Brazilian Urban Carnaval: A Discussion of Its Origins, Nature, and Ethnological Significance" (master's thesis, University of North Carolina, Chapel Hill, 1960), 88. Portuguese has two verbs for the English "to play," with different connotations. *Jogar* means to play with the aim of winning and is used for activities such as sports, gambling, and the *jôgo do entrudo.* The verb *brincar* means to play innocently like a child, with no specific goal in mind, and is used for Carnival participation. Hence, *brincar carnaval* is to play simply for the sheer joy of it all.

19. Araújo, "Festas públicas," 31–62.

20. Ribeiro, *Religião e relações,* 90–93.

21. Araújo, *Festas: Máscaras,* 197–198.

22. Katarina Real, *O Folclore no Carnaval do Recife,* 2d ed. (Recife: Editôra Massangana, Fundação Joaquim Nabuco, 1990), 10.

23. Araújo, "Festas públicas," 50.

24. Real, *Folclore,* 55–59.

25. Valdemar de Oliveira, *Frevo, capoeira e passo* (Recife: Companhia Editôra de Pernambuco, 1971), 27–34.

26. *Capoeira* is often described inadequately as "foot boxing." This does little justice to the exciting Afro-Brazilian dance-game-martial art, because the athletic combatants use not only their feet but also their arms, legs, and entire body. *Capoeira* has recently become popular in the United States.

27. Araújo, *Festas: Máscaras,* 332–334.

28. Oliveira, *Frevo, capoeira e passo,* 100.

29. Real, "Brazilian Urban Carnaval," 98.

30. Personal observation in Recife, 1960–2000.

31. Ibid.

32. Ibid.

33. Ibid.

34. Ibid. During pre-Carnival week, the annual Municipal Ball (*Baile Municipal*) is also held. Prizes are awarded for the most luxurious and/or original costumes, many of which are incredibly ornate, weighing up to seventy pounds, and must be displayed without any additional supporting apparatus. The newly elected Rei Momo (King Momus), who must be fat and jolly, and the Rainha de Carnaval (Carnival Queen), chosen for her beauty as well as her expertise in dancing the *passo,* also appear at the ball. The whole event is televised and covered in detail by the local press.

35. Personal observation in Recife, 1960–2000.

36. Ibid.

37. Personal observation in Recife, 1995.

38. Personal observation in Recife, 1960–2000.

39. Real, *Folclore,* 20–128.

40. Ibid., 48.

41. Ibid., 158–160.

42. Tiago de Oliveira Pinto, "The Pernambuco Carnival and Its Formal Organizations: Music as an Expression of Hierarchies and Power in Brazil," *Yearbook for Traditional Music* 26 (1994): 20–38.

43. This information is based primarily on my own research, published in Real, *Folclore.*

44. Pinto, "Pernambuco Carnival," 26.

45. For a colorful description of the emotions involved in dancing with an *escola de samba,* see Alma Guillermoprieto, *Samba* (New York: Vintage Books, Random House, 1991), 219–242.

46. Leonardo Dantas Silva, "A instituição do Rei do Congo e sua presença nos maracatus," in *Estudos sobre a escravidão negra,* ed. L. D. Silva (Recife: Editôra Massangana, Fundação Joaquim Nabuco, 1988), 2: 1–7.

47. Pedro Ribeiro and Maria Lúcia Montes, *Maracatu de baque virado* (São Paulo: Serviços de Imprensa Quatro Imagens, 1998), 28.

48. Roberto Benjamin, "Os Ursos: Uma influência européia num carnaval afro-indigena," in *Suplemento cultural: O Carnaval de Pernambuco* (Recife: Diário Oficial, 2001), 3.

49. In 1965, as a member of the organizing committee of Recife Carnival, I was instrumental in originating the first *urso de carnaval* competitions in an attempt to draw them from the suburbs into the downtown parades. In that year only six came to town.

50. Roberto Benjamin, "Os Ursos," 3–6.

51. Katarina Real, "Sobrevivências medievais no carnaval de Pernambuco," in *Anais da I Jornada de Estudos Medievais-1996* (Aracaju, Sergipe: Secretaria de Estado da Cultura de Sergipe, 1997), 105–122.

52. Renato Almeida, *Inteligência do Folclore* (Rio de Janeiro: Livros de Portugal, 1957), 82.

53. Crowley, *African Myth,* 23.

54. Severino Alves Lucena Filho, *Azulão do BANDEPE: Uma Estratégia de comunicação organizacional* (Recife: Author's edition with support from the Banco de Pernambuco, 1998), 73.

55. Personal observation in Recife, 1960–2000.

56. Olímpio Bonald Neto, *Os Gigantes foliões em Pernambuco* (Olinda: Fundação Centro de Preservação dos Sítios Históricos, 1992). Although dancing processional giants had long been part of Catholic saints' festivals in Brazil, Olímpio Bonald points out that the first *gigantes* in Olinda Carnival date from the early 1930s. He considers the massive figures of the festival in Nice, France, to have given a significant impetus to the growth of the tradition in Pernambuco today (61).

57. Personal observation in Recife, 1960–2000. Recife actually holds a second Carnival, the Recifolia, in September or October each year. That month marks the start of the summer beach season in the region, so Recife, along with several other cities in the northeast, instituted the second festival in order to attract tourist dollars and fill the beachfront hotels. It is criticized by many as detracting from the more genuine, traditional pre-Lenten festivities.

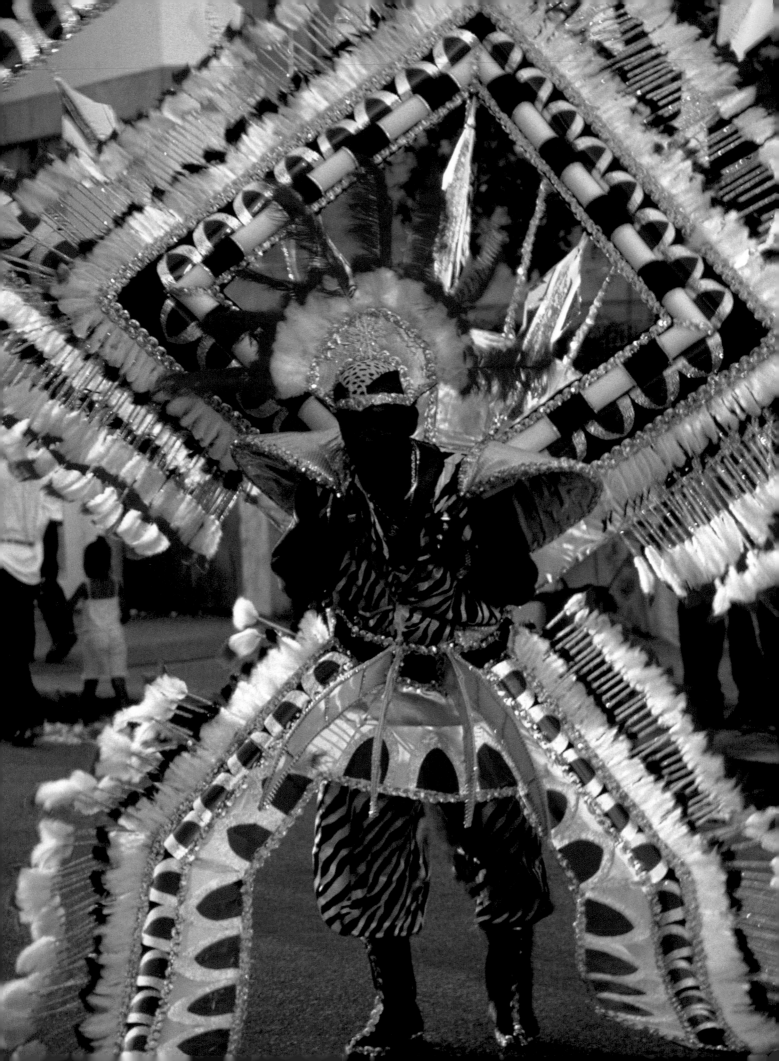

10 Playing *Mas*

CARNIVAL IN PORT OF SPAIN, TRINIDAD AND TOBAGO

JOHN NUNLEY

HEAR IT COMING. IT ROLLS INTO town from the Levantille Hills, from Belmont, Woodbrook, Saint Anne, Maraval, Cascade, St. James, and Diego Martin. Commercial jets bring them in from London, New York, Brooklyn, Boston, Toronto, Miami, and Los Angeles. Port of Spain is seething with creativity. It is Carnival, or *mas,* hungry for presentation, hungry to be heard and seen and just plain hungry. The term *mas,* an abbreviation of the word *masquerade,* recalls a time when most Carnival participants actually wore masks. Over the last several decades it has been used to refer to Carnival in general, even though most people no longer wear masks. African *bata* music played on steel drums emerges from the ancient sound of the plantation slave crews beating iron in praise of the African *orisha* spirits: Ogun, god of iron, and Shango, god of thunder. These *orisha* raised their heads proudly along the Middle Passage, giving hope to millions of victims of colonial abuse. *Tassa* drums from India excite the crowd; the Hindu god of luck, Ganesh, blesses the Carnival; and followers of the Bible and the Koran turn to the big ritual, the one that dances through the streets to the cool and easy beat of *soca.* This music sings in the shuffle steps of the Carnival dancers as their feet beat the pavement. What an eyeful: glitter, beads, sequins, copper, cardboard crowns, bodies glistening in mud, chocolate, and oil, and just simply bodies (figs. 10.1, 10.2). Yes, this is Trinidad, a destination of the world, a crossroads of global culture before the term *global* was used in that fashion.

The belly of the Carnival fills with coconut curries, oysters in hot sauce, burgers, ice cream, roasted corn, coconut milk fresh from the source, rotis (an East Indian Creole food consisting of curried vegetables, meats, seafood, or fowl wrapped in a large wheat- and chickpea-flour pancake), fried chicken, and chips. The calories burn, the "souls" of feet blister, the sun beats down, it is Hot! Hot! Hot! Wet me down! (as the songs go). Cool me with Carib beer, ice cold; pep me up with rum and Coca-Cola. It is going on midnight on Carnival Tuesday. The last lap, the last gasp, dust from the Savannah park blesses all (fig. 10.3). From dust to ashes, that's where it's going. Costume fragments lift in the thermoclines; Carnival is dying. Crowds thin, the cacophony unravels, leaving loose musical threads that struggle like worms on hot pavement. It comes to a dead stop; it is quiet. The three-month buildup has reached another end. It is Ash Wednesday. Hallelujah![1]

10.1 Some designers create elaborate costumes that evoke the rich African heritage of black Trinidadians. *Photograph by Barbara Mauldin, 2003.*

10.2 (overleaf) A huge, glittering Carnival group moves across the Savannah stage in Port of Spain. *Photograph by Gianni Vecchiato, 1994.*

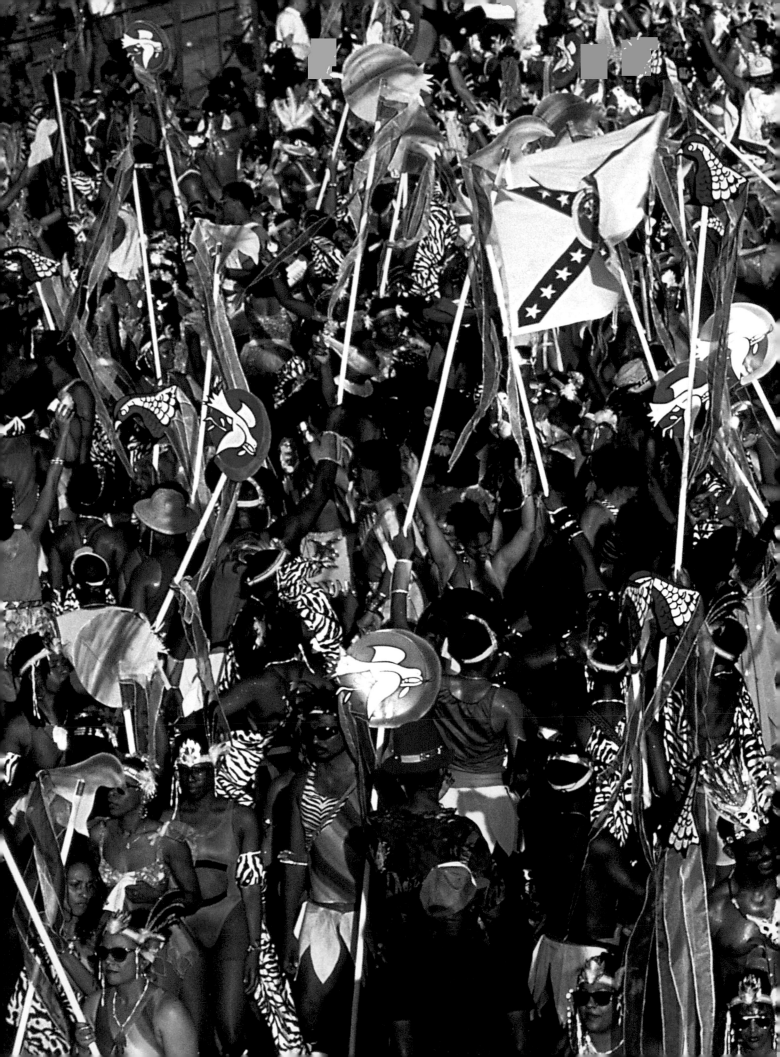

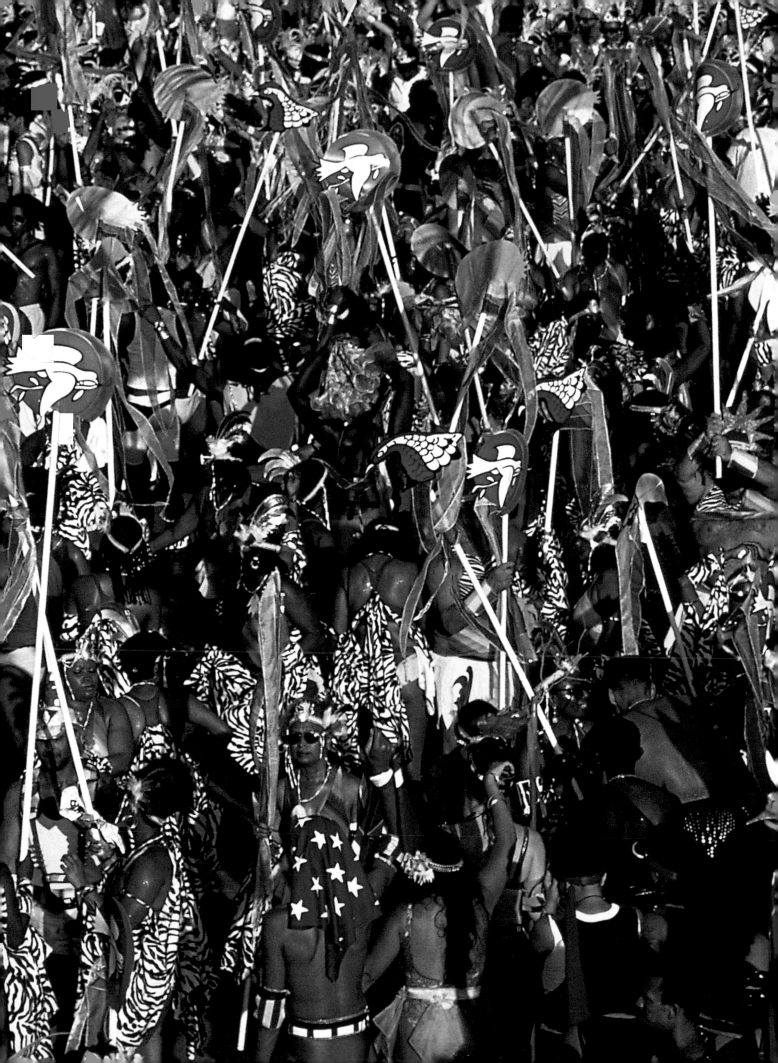

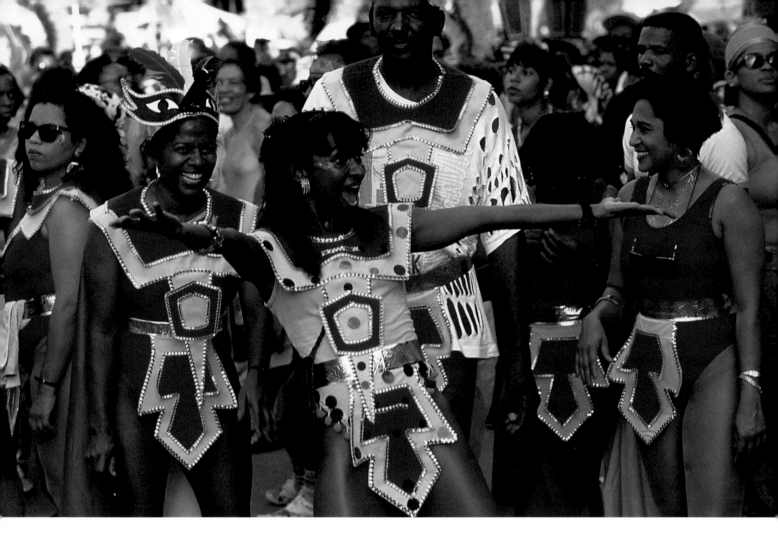

10.3 Carnival revelers in one of the large groups wait to make their appearance on the Savannah stage. *Photograph by Gianni Vecchiato, 1994.*

History of Carnival in Trinidad

Why did Carnival emerge on this small Caribbean island, and what were the forces of historical destiny that made this cultural flower larger than life? Why does it have such an impact on so much of the world? The answer: Trinidad, and later its national sister island Tobago, was always a socially complicated place; diversity there has always carried the day. Geographically, Trinidad is an extension of the Andean Cordillera Mérida just four or five miles away, where the great mountain chain bends on the northern coast of South America and breaks northeast, forming the island (fig. 10.4). In contrast to the Andean altiplano are the tropical lowlands and watershed of the Orinoco River in what is now called Venezuela, from which the river pours its contents into the dragon-shaped mouth of the Gulf of Paria on the west coast of Trinidad. Thus

the island is blessed with a tropical zone as well. Given the juxtaposition of these two environments, the flora and fauna of the islands are extremely diverse. This complexity was bound to attract inhabitants of the South American mainland, and with the building of ocean-going canoes starting around seven thousand years ago, the first immigrants arrived from the tropical regions of the Orinoco.

At the end of the fifteenth century, an estimated forty thousand Amerindians lived in Trinidad. They grew cotton, practiced hunting and fishing, and processed cassava flour as their staple crop. The cultivation of maize, peppers, squashes, and beans was supplemented by the gathering of crabs and turtle eggs. Tobacco was the primary stimulant. Many tribes were represented on the island; just as it is today, it was ethnically diverse. The dominant language of the first settlers was Cariban-Arawakan, and the social organization was based on chieftaincy and shifting alliances of village settlements.[2]

These indigenous peoples held festivals around harvests, warfare, and the deaths of important people.

We can only imagine on these occasions the music and ritual dress, which included pearls and gold ornaments, feathered headdresses, cotton wrappers, and body paint. Thus, from the beginning of European occupation, colorful presentation at festivals was the aesthetic norm. European settlement of the island, in the long run, spelled the death of Amerindian culture, although some indigenous terms, such as *hammock* and *tobacco,* still reflect its early presence.[3]

In July 1498, Columbus turned his fleet westward from Sierra Leone, West Africa, and headed for the southern Caribbean seas. On the seventeenth day of the journey he wrote that "as the sun's strength increased and our supply of water was falling, I resolved to make for the Caribee islands and set sail in that direction; when by the mercy of God which he has always extended to me, one of the sailors went up to the main-top and saw to the westward a range of three mountains. Upon this we repeated the 'Salve Regina' and other prayers and all of us gave thanks to Our Lord."[4] Columbus named the island Trinidad, after the Trinity symbolized by the three mountains in its southern range. During the following three hundred years, under Spanish rule, the island was used as a staging ground for men of fortune looking for the city of gold, El Dorado, in South America. Under the Spaniards, the Indians suffered and the population quickly diminished.

Throughout the Spanish occupation, the Crown showed little interest in developing Trinidad, in part because Spain chose to invest men and money in its continental interests instead. There was no gold in the islands. It was the Royal Cédula of Population issued by King Charles III of Spain in 1783 that brought Trinidad into the global picture. Urged by French planters from other Caribbean islands, the king issued this *cédula,* which invited all members of the Catholic faith to settle the country—including free people of color. The size of the free property that each planter received was directly related to the size of his family and the number of slaves under his control. Thus, overnight, a French and Creole plantation life developed, and with it came French and Creole cultural practices.[5] Carnival appeared as the event of the year, with fancy dress balls and house-to-house visitations. The primary costumes of the estate elites during the festival were those of the *negre jardin* (field slave) for the men and

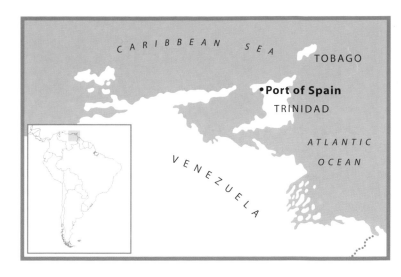

10.4 The location of Trinidad and Tobago off the northern coast of South America.

the *mulattras* for the women. *Fêtes* (parties), balls, and hunts were staged, all culminating in Carnival.

The island prospered with the new immigrants, and by 1797 the population had grown to 2,250 French, 4,700 "colored," and 9,700 slaves. The Indian population had been reduced to 1,127.[6] During this period French culture was dominant, yet a warring Europe with Napoleon at its center was to add another element to the growing mix of peoples. The British were coming, and their presence would challenge the French genteel culture and its Carnival.

Recognizing that the defeat of the French under Napoleon would depend upon who controlled the seas, Britain commenced a campaign to destroy the French navy and its ports. This was particularly true in the Caribbean, where the production of sugar products was a powerful generator of the industrial revolution. To that end, in 1797, General Sir Ralph Abercromby was ordered to attack French fleets and the islands of the West Indies. Because of Trinidad's size, great port, fertility, and proximity to South America, he was ordered to take the colony. Rear Admiral don José María Chacon, governor of the island, saw the British fleet off the coast and wisely surrendered.[7]

Whereas the French had maintained their plantation lifestyle, with Carnival as the climax of the social season, the newly arrived British, who were anti-Catholic, looked upon the pre-Lenten festival with misgivings. They much preferred Christmas. As in other parts of the British Empire, they declared martial law during the Christmas holidays to demonstrate to the colonized that even at a time of high spirits the British were still firmly in control. Young males of the business community were drafted into the militia during this time, and as a result the city closed down, allowing leisure time to celebrate. Military reviews were held in the public parks. Each regiment was divided into sections and demonstrated maneuvers while parading to marching bands of the black Caribbean regiments. Many of these soldiers had served in West African regiments or fought for the British in the American Revolution. Members of both groups had retired to Trinidad, in many cases with their North American Indian wives. These new immigrants may have contributed to the Indian-style Carnival costumes that would appear later in the century.

10.5 *The End of the Day.* Drawing by Richard Bridgens, 1820, copied and printed by Peter Shim. *Photograph courtesy of Paria Archives.* When the day's labor was done on a Trinidadian plantation, the slave gang that had cut the most sugarcane would play instruments and sing to announce its success.

During militia days, tents were pitched to protect the crowds from exposure to the hot sun. Food and drink added to the merriment of the day, and the many fancy balls spilled out into midnight.[8]

Because of the perceived need for tight security, slave celebrations (fig. 10.5) were highly restricted. British fears of insurrection during the holidays were confirmed when the government uncovered a conspiracy on Christmas Day in 1805. The "conspirators" had grouped themselves, like the British, into regiments with queens and kings and members of the court, all dressed in elaborate costumes. That slaves were not permitted to celebrate as the whites did would become a point of contention in later Carnivals.[9]

The hard work and deadening routine of plantation life were occasionally interrupted by the outbreak of fires. On these occasions, slaves from nearby plantations would gather at the burning estate to put out the fire and grind the damaged cane before it rotted. These events must have been highly charged and dramatic, with the wailing of conch-shell horns and the crackling of torch fires that cast strange shadows and created dramatic images as the workers charged

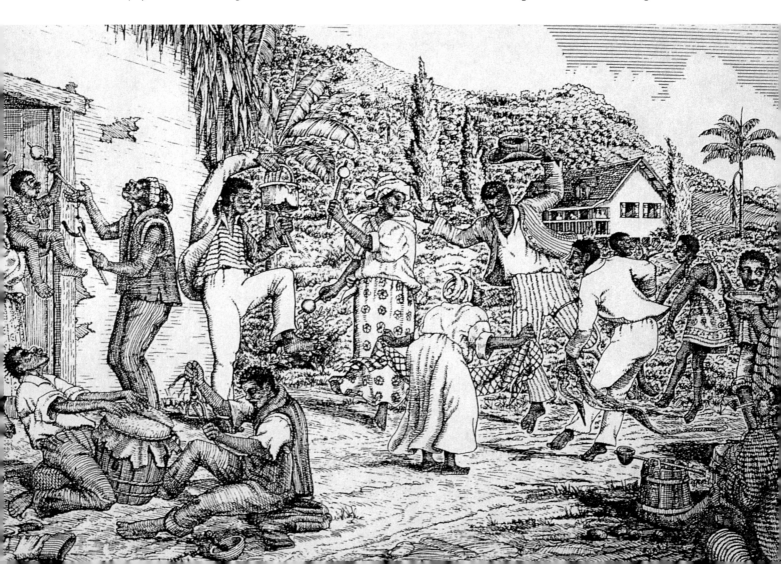

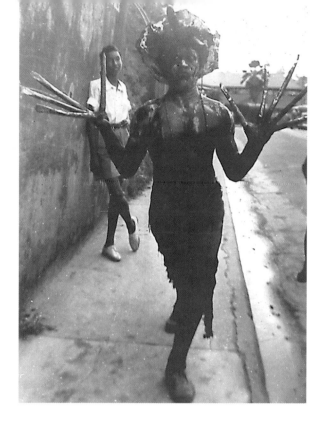

10.6 A *jab-jab* devil masquerader roams the streets of Port of Spain during Carnival in the 1950s. *Photograph from the Carrington Collection in the Paria Archives.*

through the night. It was an opportunity for slaves to mix, share news, and, most importantly, experience their collective power. Such events, called *cannes brûlées,* were ritualized and reenacted on August 1, 1838, the date emancipation was effected and the anniversary of Columbus's landing on the island. The years after emancipation saw freed slaves take Carnival to the streets of Port of Spain, the capital of Trinidad. By mid-century, Carnival opened at midnight on the Sunday before Lent with a ritualized *canne brûlée* similar to that which had been celebrated on Emancipation Day.[10]

After emancipation, Port of Spain grew rapidly, becoming a major center of commerce in the West Indies. Freed blacks from the West African country of Sierra Leone were imported to the city; many were of Yoruba origin, which helped refresh the cultural memory of their brothers and sisters who were already in Trinidad.[11] The population of Port of Spain continued to grow as large numbers of freed slaves left the hated rural estates to seek their fortunes in the city. An urban black culture emerged behind the shops in the interior of every block. In these spaces, small dwellings with a common water source and latrines housed the newly

freed. These "barracks," as they were called, formed little neighborhoods that competed with one another through their music, singing, and playing at Carnival. Competitions held during Carnival now included stick fighting, singing, drumming, and the extemporaneous delivery of news and gossip known as *picon,* all of which the white community despised. This new Carnival included groups of black women dressed in costumes of uniform colors, similar to groups of Yoruba women in Africa, where they are known as *ashoebi.*[12]

Throughout the remainder of the nineteenth century, Carnival masquerading included different types of devils such as the *jab-jab* (fig. 10.6), imps, beasts, Lucifer, and Beelzebub (the Bookman). Other characters also appeared: Pierrot and Pulcinella from the commedia dell'arte, pirates, sailors, royalty, Indians of South America, Death, Turks, Highlanders, transvestites, stickmen, and stilt walkers. Stilt walkers, known as *moco jumbies,* appear in many island festivals in the West Indies and were most likely introduced by Africans. *Jumbies* on both sides of the Atlantic represent spirits that bring peace wherever they appear. Stickmen evolved from the *negre jardin* (garden Negro) costume worn by white planters in imitation of slaves during Carnival. When blacks played this character, they transformed it into a fancy costume with satin or velvet breeches and colorful shirts. They also used staffs to fight each other in opposing groups. The fighting was more like a dance accompanied by stick-fighting music, known as *calinda,* which was produced by drums and rattles (*shack-shacks*). Later, when stick fighting was outlawed, these masqueraders turned their costume into the clown character from the commedia dell'arte, Pulcinella. This character later evolved into Pierrot, who carried a whip, danced in fancy dress, and competed with other Pierrots by demonstrating his agility with his whip and his highly stylized verbal ability.[13]

The parading, costumed revelers danced to African-based drumming and to musical arrangements sung by the "chantwells," groups of exslaves who once sang songs of praise and satire for their master and his friends during late evening entertainments on the plantations. This tradition was passed on to the calypsonians, whose lyrics championed their own barracks while ridiculing others. During this time the white establishment withdrew from public participation in

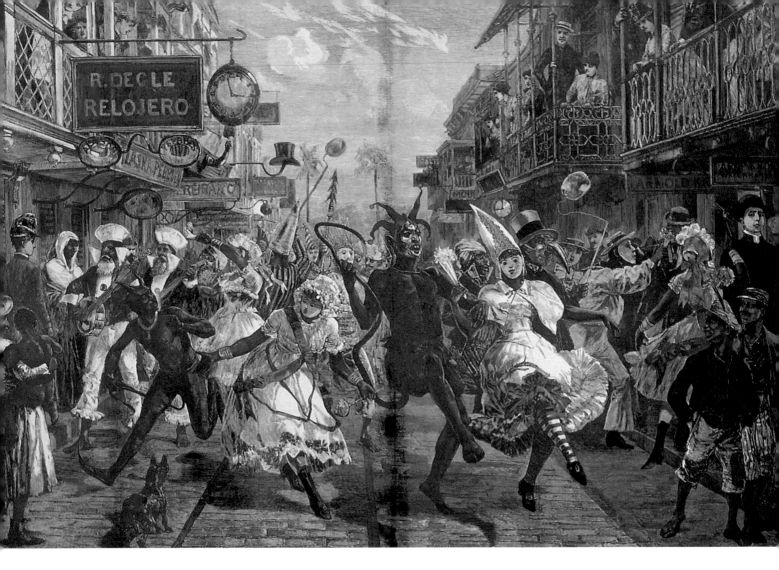

10.7 *Carnival in Port of Spain*. Print by Milton Prior, 1888, for the *Illustrated London News*, reproduced as a color lithograph by Paria Publishing Company. Private collection. *Photograph by Blair Clark*. By the late nineteenth century, the upper-class citizens of Port of Spain had begun to come back onto the streets and balconies to watch or take part in the rowdy Carnival parades.

Carnival but continued to celebrate in private homes. Eventually the festival become a major dividing point between the white citizens and the black population, and by 1880 the upper class was attempting to abolish the rowdy street celebration altogether.[14]

Thanks to one enlightened governor, public hearings and meetings were held between Carnival troupe leaders and government officials. In a conciliatory mood, the Carnival groups, known as bands, agreed to "clean up" their presentations and discourage violence among themselves. As Carnival took on a more respectable appearance, businesses began to sponsor bands in order to advertise their goods and services and support the will of the people. By 1880, the population of Port of Spain had reached thirty thousand and become increasingly international, with a growing East Indian component, which from 1845 had replaced the slaves as indentured servants on the plantations. Slowly the upper class returned to Carnival, and by the end of the century it was quickly becoming an integrative institution that would one day be the national festival (fig. 10.7).[15]

The African slaves of the late eighteenth century made a soup called *callaloo*. The recipe included many diverse ingredients: crab, sausage, the green leaf of the *dashin* (taro) plant, okra, coconut milk, hot peppers, and more. *Callaloo* has become a metaphor for the diversity of Trinidad's cultural life: the more diverse the ingredients, the sweeter the soup, and likewise for the population and its culture.[16]

By the end of the nineteenth century, the torches of the *cannes brûlées* that opened Carnival were forbidden, and a law was passed prohibiting street parades before six o'clock Monday morning. Thus, the midnight revelry was replaced by *jour ouvert* (opening day), beginning on Monday at six. This component of Carnival consisted of people wearing last year's costumes and old-time masquerades, featuring characters such as *jab-jab* devils, transvestites, dragons, bats, and imps, as well as Pierrots and Pierrot Grenades (lower-class Pierrots from the island of Grenada).

Improvisational skits consisting of biting political and social satire were also performed. Drums were outlawed, but in their place appeared *tamboo-bamboo*, groups of musicians who struck pieces of bamboo of various sizes, the ancestors of the steel drum. Men who dressed as women in long nightgowns that had been stained with urine were prohibited from parading. Their antics, which included carrying cloths with imitation menstrual blood and other lewd acts, proved too offensive to the general public.

By this time, most of the roads of Port of Spain were paved. With a "cleaner" environment, devoid of

mud and extreme debauchery, more people began to participate in Carnival, and the middle class took it to the streets. Many of them masqueraded in groups on small trucks and trailer beds. Some even danced in the streets with the lower stratum of society. Musicians accompanied all the masking groups. The French Creole elites still held their fancy dress balls at Government House and in the mansions, all paid for by the growing cocoa economy.[17] Meanwhile, in the lower-class neighborhoods, the masked Pierrots, who competed with each other with whips and lively debates (fig. 10.8), and the stickmen had to obtain licenses in order to perform.[18]

Most importantly, the Boer War, which commenced in 1899, galvanized Trinidadian society. That the British fought this war against the Dutch and German settlers of South Africa in the name of British imperialism caught the attention and support of Trinidadians from all walks of life. Trinidad was now intensely loyal to the Crown, and many of its men volunteered for the British regiments. "We Are Marching to Pretoria" became the most popular song that year, drawing the classes closer together. At the same time, the chantwells sang patriotic songs and shifted from patois to English.[19]

The developing sense of unity in Trinidad and the

10.8 Whip-masters perform during Carnival in Port of Spain. *Photograph by Robert Jerome, 2001.*

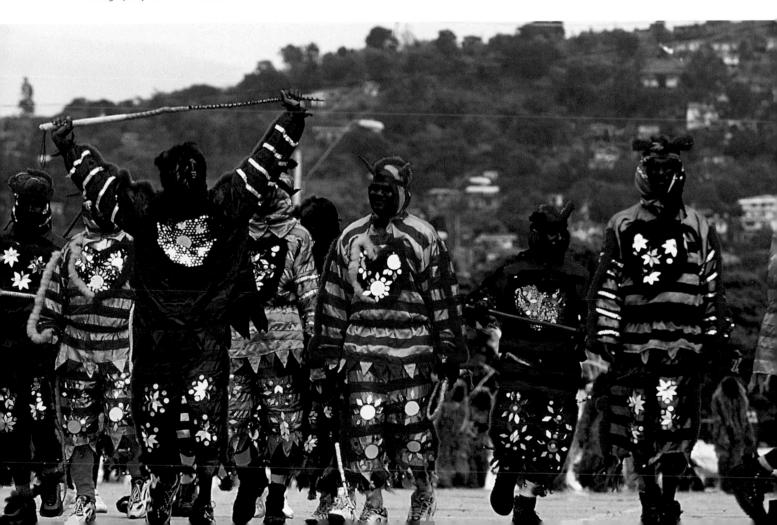

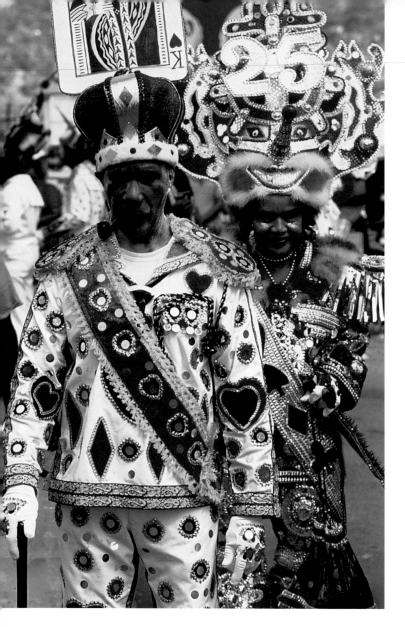

10.9 Fancy sailor masquerades such as those worn here by Sylvia and Stanley Beguesse maintain their popularity. *Photograph by Gianni Vecchiato, 1994.*

gradual acceptance of Carnival over the next thirty years led to the relaxation of most prohibitions. The festival was now relatively free to create its own destiny.

Carnival in the Twentieth Century

The neighborhoods of the part of Port of Spain known as Belmont were, in the 1930s, creating sailor troupes, known as bands. Young groups of athletes with leaders such as "Diamond" Jim Harding were playing sailors with masks. Members of Harding's group would look for trouble by stealing from a grocer or grog shop, lowering their papier-mâché or wire-screen masks to

conceal their identities. Many mask groups were now dancing to percussion music played on used bicycle frames, biscuit tins, brake drums, and other metal containers—music that became more melodious while remaining rhythmic. Harding and his circle marked the beginning of the great sailor tradition, which is a mainstay of Carnival today (fig. 10.9).[20] This genre was further stimulated by the hundreds of thousands of American sailors and servicemen seen in uniform on the streets of Port of Spain during and after World War II, from 1941 to 1954. The impact of sailors ashore produced entire flotillas of commandos in Trinidad Carnival.

The character called the Midnight Robber has played a prominent role in Carnival throughout the twentieth century. Although such masqueraders are few these days, their black clothing, their large ter-raced hats decorated with toy skulls, and the coffins that many pull on a rope strike powerful and intimi-dating images. Robbers carry plastic weapons to fur-ther enhance their fierce appearance. As crowds gather around, each one presents a monologue describing his great and terrible feats, fights with Satan, and destruction of entire armies and civiliza-tions. The origins of this character are unclear, but its cowboy-like appearance may have been inspired by illustrations of cowboys in comic books that were sold in Trinidad from the early part of the twentieth cen-tury. In the 1920s this character may have acquired his speech from the Pierrots, who by that time were fading from the scene (fig. 10.10).[21]

The Indian masqueraders, who celebrated North American indigenous culture, also evolved during the 1920s, especially in the Woodbrook neighborhood, with such notables as Bomparte and Mack Copeland. In an explosion of feathers and beadwork, these groups danced with tomahawks, bows, or spears to celebrate and honor American Indians (fig. 10.11).[22]

During World War II, the American military pro-tected the oil reserves of Trinidad from the Germans, whose submarines often patrolled outside the harbor of Port of Spain. The Americans brought to the colony many jobs and a big payroll, and thus a middle class of all colors grew. Port of Spain now had a population of over two hundred thousand. During these years, Harold Saldina and the young Bailey brothers, who had inherited Carnival from their father, Sunny Bailey,

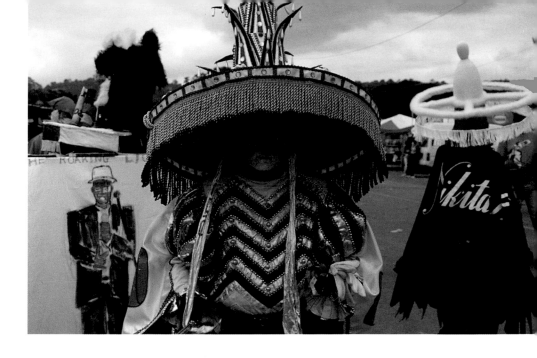

10.10 Midnight Robber masquer-
aders still perform in Port of Spain
Carnival. *Photograph by John
Nunley, 2000.*

pioneered Carnival for Woodbrook. The brothers Albert and Alvin Bailey would push the Carnival Mas in new dimensions under the leadership of their famous brother George Bailey. Although Carnival was banned during the war for security reasons, the Baileys, who were taught basketball by the young Americans, were also watching American cinema, like other would-be band leaders. Basketball demonstrated to them that blacks and whites could work together, and the public library gave them ideas about band productions and spectacles.[23]

Other young Trinidadians, such as Ellie Manette, were experimenting with the fifty-five-gallon steel drums in which oil had been stored, developing the

10.11 Some Carnival groups wear elaborate masquerades portraying North American Indians. *Photograph by Robert Jerome, 2001.*

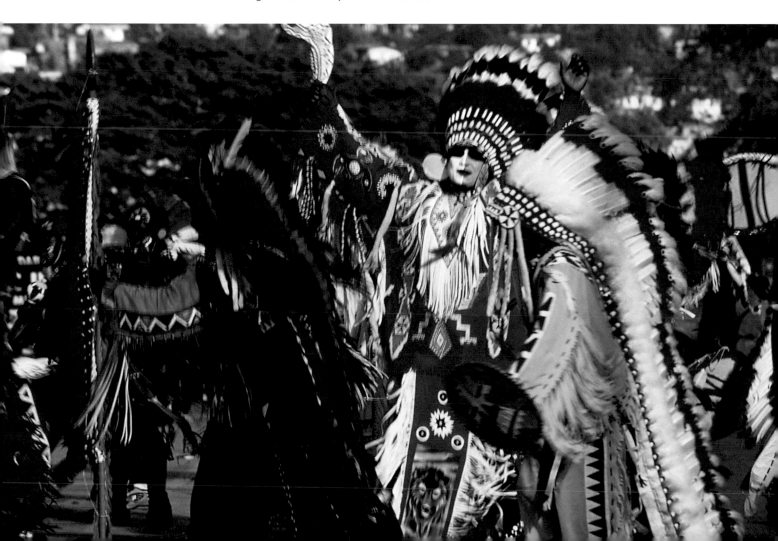

steel band from its biscuit-tin days. Cutting the drums to various lengths, just as the bamboo of *tamboo-bamboo* had been cut, and creating beveled pods on the lids of the pans that could be struck to achieve different notes, Manette and his peers established a new sound that covered the entire musical scale. Band musicians now had full control of melody, while the driving beat of the slave crews heard in Trinidad 150 years earlier was now carried out in the "engine room," the rhythmic section of the steel band, which played snare and conga drums (fig. 10.12).[24]

The war years without Carnival created a longing and recognition that this festival had become part of an emerging national consciousness. Trinidadians dreamed of Carnival. With new ideas about costumes, production, and music, artists, musicians, and the people were ready to express their evolving sense of identity through Carnival. Nationalism and Carnival had arrived, and the festival exploded in the 1950s.

A Rhodes scholar named Eric Williams returned from Oxford University in England and entered Trinidad politics. As chief minister, in 1956 he instituted the Carnival Development Committee (CDC), and

10.12 Musicians from the band Phase II play drums made from fifty-five-gallon steel containers that have circular pods beveled into the surfaces to create a range of notes. The conventional snare and conga drums in background-the "engine room"-provide the rhythm. *Photograph by Barbara Mauldin, 1994.*

through this organization the various components of today's Carnival were created. Incidentally, Williams would in 1962 become the first prime minister of the independent country of Trinidad and Tobago. He championed Trinidadian culture, especially as it was expressed at Carnival.[25]

The *mas* bands of Carnival ranged from a few hundred to several thousand members. Old houses in the neighborhoods served as centers for the organizations, where people could congregate to socialize and view current designs for costumes (fig. 10.13). In the last months leading up to Carnival, the buildings were filled with workers making the outfits. Each year the bands would choose themes, which often reflected the changing social identity of the country. Until 1957, band themes such as "The Ten Commandments," "The Fall of Babylon," and "The Glory That Was Greece" resulted from a British sense of history that was taught in public school textbooks and portrayed by feature films lavishly produced in Hollywood.[26] In that year, however, George Bailey's "Back to Africa" portrayed elegantly dressed African royalty based on careful art-historical research. The dignified characters simply stunned the crowds, who were accustomed to seeing stereotyped witchdoctors, fierce Zulu warriors, and crocodile-loving Zambezis. Black people felt empowered by such spectacle (see fig. 10.1). It signaled the emergence of a large black middle class that would

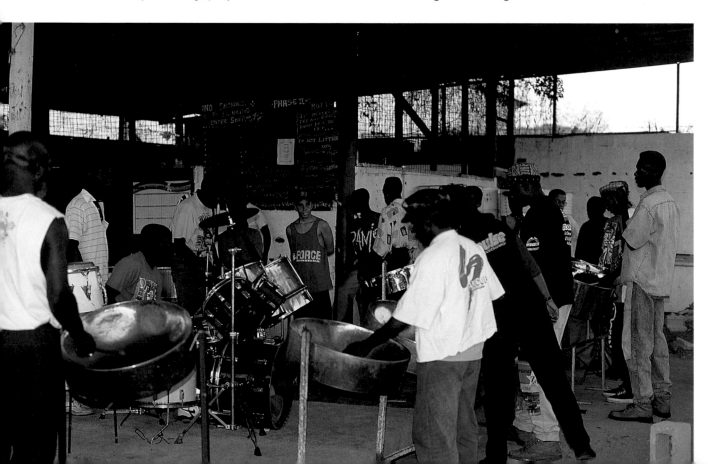

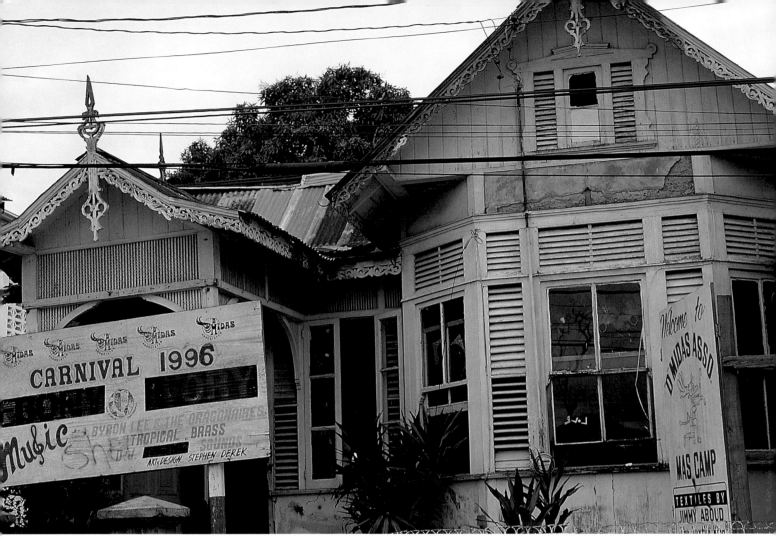

10.13 This old Victorian-style house once served as the *mas* camp, or center, for the D'Midas Carnival troupe. *Photograph by John Nunley, 2000.*

run the government of Trinidad and Tobago for over three decades while the East Indian minority waited in the opposition benches of the nation's parliament.

In 1968 Bailey came out with "Fantasia," a theme that broke entirely from Western history and opened the minds of Trinidadians to building a national sense of identity based on their own history and environment.[27] As a result, band leaders and designers turned to local Trinidad and Tobago themes for Carnival. After exploring the beautiful reefs of Tobago, for example, Irving McWilliams was inspired to bring out a band entitled "The Wonders of Bucco Reef." Band members were dressed as fish, shell life, living rocks, corals and anemones, and lobsters.[28] The country had finally found respect for its own beauty, not that of jolly old England or the "make-believe" of Hollywood. Likewise, the band "A la Carte," produced by Stephen and Elsie

Lee Hueng and designed by Wayne Berkeley, featured members dressed as locally prepared foods such roasted corn and gin and coconut milk, along with dancing salt and pepper shakers symbolizing the racial mix of the island.[29] Through the end of the twentieth century, Carnival would reflect citizens' complex heritage and compel them to recognize it.

Peter Minshall's theme "River" introduced East Indian culture into Trinidad Carnival in a dramatic presentation in 1983. Participants were dressed as mosques and pandits, and the king of the band was a multi-armed crab symbolizing the greediness of many-armed Hindu deities (fig. 10.14). The three thousand costumed members danced to the East Indian drums known as *tassa*. Appearing onstage for competitions at the Queen's Park Savannah, the entire band was sprayed with various colors of paint (fig. 10.15), an element Minshall borrowed from the East Indian festival called Pagwa, which the first indentured East Indians had brought to Trinidad early in the nineteenth century.[30]

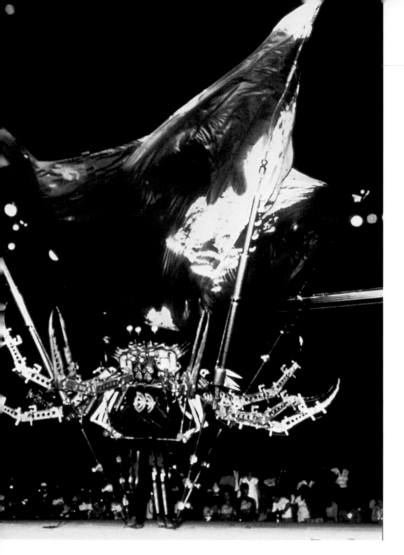

Carnival at Present

The term *mas* comes from the word *masquerade,* and indeed the majority of Carnival participants from 1910 through the 1930s wore masks. With the ban on the festival during World War II, Trinidadians appeared to lose the habit of masking, and when Carnival was again celebrated in 1946, few participants wore masks. Nevertheless, the term *mas* was retained and still refers to Carnival. When a person participates in a band, he or she is said to "play *mas.*" Similarly, the studios where Carnival costumes are produced are called "*mas* camps."[31]

Carnival begins with the Christmas season and ends on Ash Wednesday. Thus the British preference for Christmas and that of the French for Carnival, expressed in the early nineteenth century, are combined in one grand festival season. Artists and designers establish a theme for each band. Artists themselves are sometimes band leaders, and as such they must oversee the management, productions, and finances of the band. Often, a committee carries out

10.14 The Crab King costume designed by Peter Minshall in 1983 symbolized the greediness of many-armed Hindu deities. *Photograph by Noel Norton.*

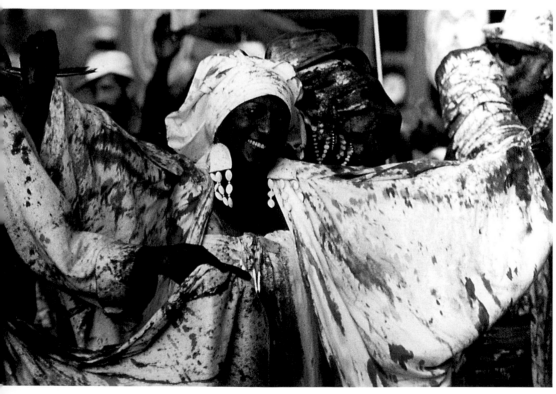

10.15 A member of Peter Minshall's Carnival band "River" wears a costume sprayed with various colors of paint, inspired by the Pagwa festival of East Indian residents of Trinidad. *Photograph by John Nunley, 1983.*

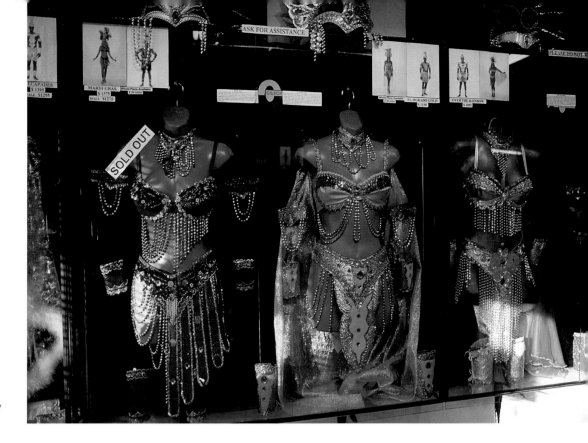

10.16 Drawings and costume samples for the "Bedazzled" theme of the Carnival group Legends. *Photograph by Barbara Mauldin, 2003.*

these responsibilities. Bands must be licensed by the National Carnival Bands' Association (NCBA), as it is known today, and must abide by rules and regulations ordained by that governmental body.

Mas launchings are held mostly in November and December, when each band may sponsor a barbecue, hire a music group for a dance, or have a formal, gallery-type opening. On the eve of the launching, people eat, dance, and discuss the Carnival season. They pay careful attention to band themes and look at the illustrations and samples of the costumes for each section of the band to see how it helps develop the main theme (fig. 10.16). Illustrations of the king's, the queen's, and "individual" costumes are also considered. Usually the persons playing kings and queens have close relationships to band leaders and artists, as do those playing "individuals." The latter costumes are generally much more elaborate than the section costumes but less so than those of the queens and kings. The cost of king and queen costumes can easily exceed US$15,000, whereas section attire may sell for $200 to $300. Large bands such as Legends or Poison may have as many as four thousand members, while medium-size bands such as D'Midas and Jason Griffith's Old-Fashioned Sailors have over three hundred, and small bands such as Breakaway Productions, around one hundred.

During the Christmas season the talk is all Carnival—who is playing in which band, which bands are hot, and which seem dull or boring, their membership growing old. Eventually participants select their band and band section and pay the *mas* manager in advance for their costume. Major local businesses and international corporations such as Angostura Distillers and BP Amoco also sponsor bands.

As Carnival heats up, musicians are turning out the new *soca* and calypso songs. Steel bands begin rehearsing in the pan yards, which are large open spaces in the various neighborhoods. The sounds of a one-hundred-member steel band such as Phase II Pan Groove attract people to the pan yard, where drinks and food may be purchased while one enjoys the music (see fig. 10.12). The spirit of Carnival carried in steel band music can be heard as one moves through the neighborhoods (fig. 10.17). There are the Renegades from Belmont, the Desperados from Levantille, the Invaders from Woodbrook, Starlift from St. James, and Exodus from St. Augustine. Much excitement is generated in these modern-day, barracks-like environments; alliances are formed, and fans make it clear whom they are backing. Not every steel band player will make the cut to play in the Panorama competition, and when the official list of a hundred appears, many are disappointed.

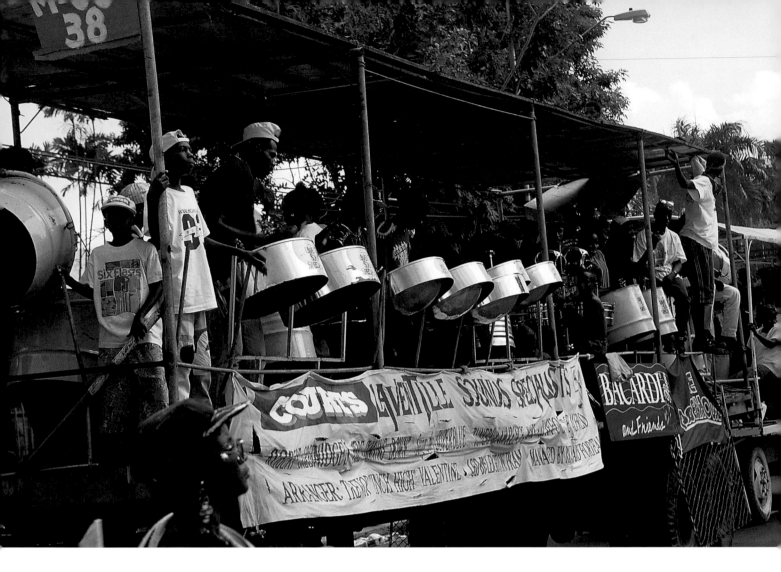

10.17 Many of the steel drum bands set up their instruments on trucks and play music for the large groups as they dance along the Carnival parade route in Port of Spain. *Photograph by John Nunley, 2000.*

Carnival gets big and fat with the approach of Lent. You can hear it on the radio, see it on television, read about it in the papers. You can consume its foods in portable take-out kitchens placed around the Savannah. Other Trinidadian cities, such as San Fernando, have their Carnivals as well, but the big one is in Port of Spain. The major site for all the competitions is the Queen's Park Savannah, which was once a huge sugar plantation. Ironically, the liberation of Carnival today is experienced on a property where slavery formerly existed. Where there once were *cannes brûlées,* there is now *mas.*

The competitions are held on a temporary stage built about five feet off the ground. The 150–by-70–foot stage, with its long entry and exit ramps,

stands at the former finish line of the horse-race track that once occupied the area. Portable bleachers are added on the north side of the stage, across from the permanent seating on the south side. Three Saturdays before Carnival, the steel bands enter the competition. It starts with as many as fifty bands, but by the time of Panorama on the last Saturday before Lent, it is down to fourteen.

Meanwhile, the *mas* camps are turning out costumes around the clock. Men are bending wire for costume frames (fig. 10.18), women are sewing, and volunteers are gluing glitter and sequins onto pants, shorts, shirts, skirts, and skimpy bikinis and bathing suits in the current styles. A constant hum of gossip is interrupted by a frustrated designer who yells harsh words at an artisan who can't balance a 30–foot-high, 130–pound king costume on a particular metal and fiberglass frame. "Christ maan, this design, it's fucked!" exclaims the worker. People stop talking and stare at the red-faced designer, his mouth tense and snarled.

Nerves are edgy. Finally the designer calms down and says, "Today we take care of the impossible, tomorrow the miracles." Everyone is relieved. Someone checks to see who wants pizza or Chinese food to go. *Mas* costume makers grab a soft drink or a beer from the fridge, and work resumes. The place is humming.

On the Tuesday before Carnival Monday, the kings and queens of each band compete. Crowds pack the north and south stands of the Savannah stage, and the judges gather just in front of the stage on the south side. These critics carefully watch each contestant as he or she dances across the stage (fig. 10.19). On a score sheet, each judge enters a number of points out of a maximum of thirty each for creativity-authenticity and craftsmanship and a maximum of twenty points each for visual impact and presentation, for a total perfect score of one hundred.[32]

Band leaders gather on the east runway with their kings and queens as attendants dress them and apply makeup. Last-minute instructions are given, and with a deep breath and an occasional shot of rum, contestants arrive onstage in performance. If the rhythmic motion of the dancer's arms, legs, and pelvis are in sync with the musical beat of the orchestra, and if the parts of the costume reflect that motion, then the crowds roar. It is the motion and the color of the *mas* that makes it work. The Savannah heats up. In the year 2000, kings with names such as D'Rough Rider, the Balance of Life, D Spirit of D Tribe, M' Ganga, Witch Doctor, and Quetzal Coatl-Feathered Serpent all performed across the stage. The queens that year included Miss Tourist, D African Queen Bulolo, Tears of Africa, National Heraldry, A Vision Deep from Bucco Reef, and Jewel of D Jungle. By the Friday before Carnival, the queens and kings are down to sixteen finalists.

All day Saturday, children celebrate Kiddie Mas, officially called Junior Carnival. The children's groups are organized through public and private schools or by the adult Carnival bands, and like the adult groups, junior bands have themes with costumes varying from section to section. In 1994, one group with an ecological theme had children elaborately dressed as plants covered with bumblebees (fig. 10.20). Other groups wear simpler costumes that reflect Caribbean life (fig. 10.21). One man has organized a large group of underprivileged children to perform as stilt walkers

(fig. 10.22). Kids from ages three to fourteen play this *mas* for about six hours in the hot sun. The groups convene at camps, public squares, and parks, where they find their sections and wait for the music trucks to appear. When they move out into the parade route, the children wave their banners and dance to the *soca* music blasting from the trucks and speakers set up on the sidewalks. Adults keep a close eye on each section of the band, looking for signs of fatigue and heat exhaustion and also out of fear of an accident, especially around the moving music trucks. After performing on the Savannah stage, the participants retire to the park for a rest and something to eat. East Indian rotis, pilau, and a filled pocket-bread sandwich called "doubles" help, and a cold drink or snowcone is quickly consumed.

10.18 An artist prepares a large Carnival costume. *Photograph by John Nunley, 2000.*

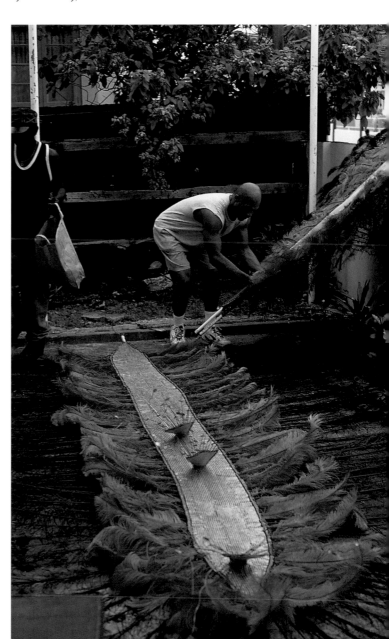

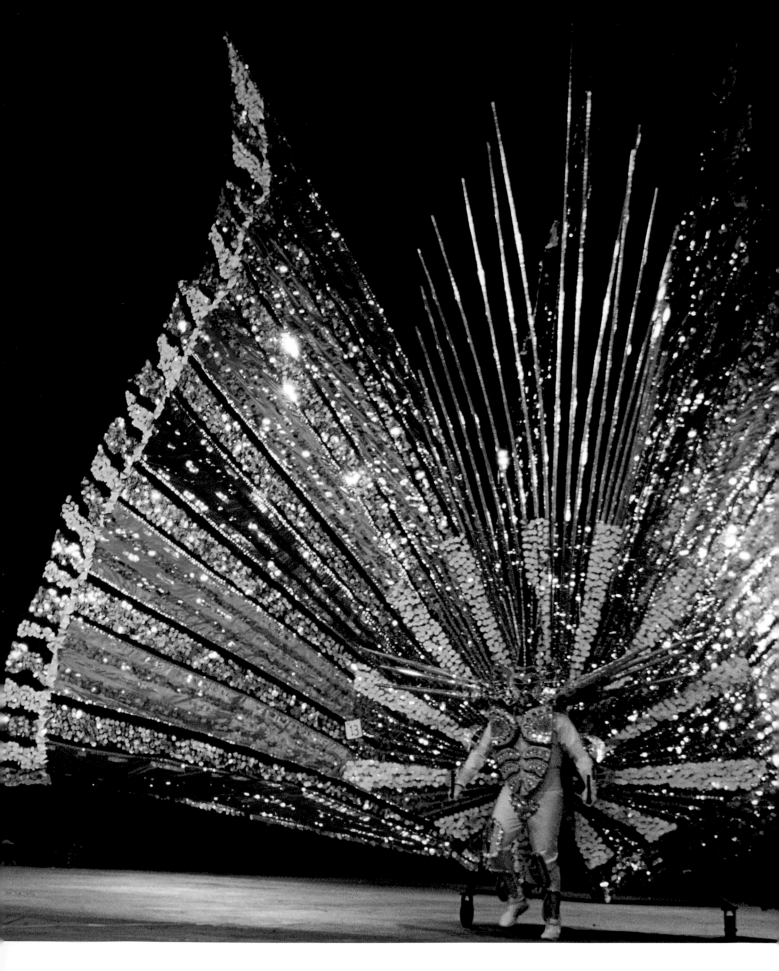

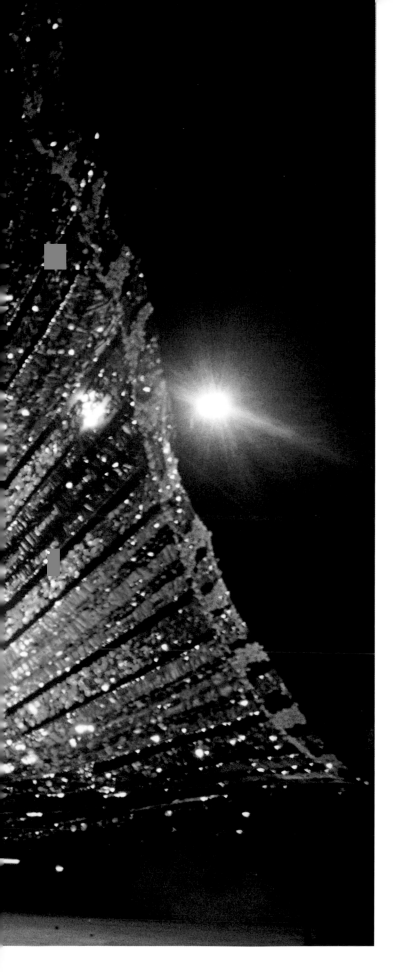

Kiddie Mas is a serious event, judged by panels of adults who select the king and queen and band of the year. The event offers some of a child's most important experiences. In these groups, lifetime relationships are formed and future musicians, designers, and artists are developed. A sense of both individual identity and community is established by participating in Carnival. Children are also made aware of social problems in their country and the rest of the world by playing *mas* in bands with themes concerning war, the environment, and diseases such as AIDS. After this celebration, people rest for a few hours and then shower and change clothes.

Saturday night—it is time for the Panorama steel band competition. The fourteen steel band finalists assemble at the Savannah for the clash of steel. Before each band sets up, the stage lights are turned off, leaving a black void before the spectators. By this time, everyone is transformed by the bacchanal (a term commonly used to denote the high spirit of Carnival), which includes the consumption of prodigious amounts of food and drink stored in ice chests at the center of each partying group. *Liming* is what Trinidadians call these group sessions. The term comes from the eighteenth-century British navy tradition in which every sailor received a half-pint of thick rum diluted in a quart of water and fresh-squeezed lime juice. Thus, drinking was referred to as "liming."[33] Dramatically, the stage is relit, and suddenly before the crowd appears a band, standing resolute, prepared for battle. For months the young men and women of these bands have given their energies to long nights of practice. Now, success hinges on a single ten-minute performance.

In one opening sentinel blast, in an instant, the band beats out the song. The complexity of the Caribbean polyrhythms, its nanosecond yet laid-back precision, the blending of the hundreds of percussionists, and the melody, which has its own life, begin to thrill the listeners and dancers who lime in the stands. With the name of their band printed on flags, flag bearers twist, jump, and turn from side to side onstage, cheering their orchestra on to victory. The

10.19 The 2003 King of Carnival, Curtis Eustace, performs on the Savannah Stage in his glittering costume entitled "D Sky is D Limit." *Photograph by Noel Norton, 2003.*

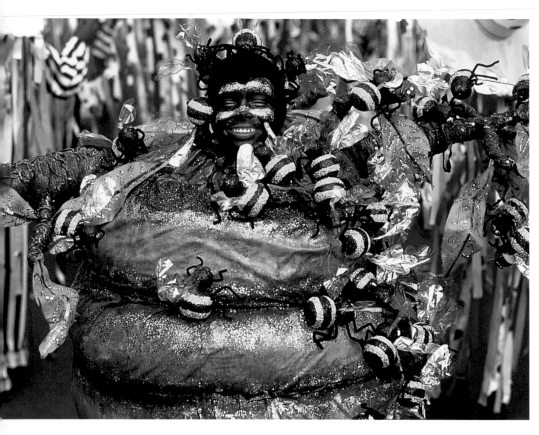

10.20 A young boy partici-
pates in Port of Spain's Junior
Carnival dressed as a plant
covered in bumblebees.
*Photograph by Gianni
Vecchiato, 1994.*

10.21 A group of girls in
the Junior Carnival is dressed
in matching beachwear.
*Photograph by Gianni
Vecchiato, 1994.*

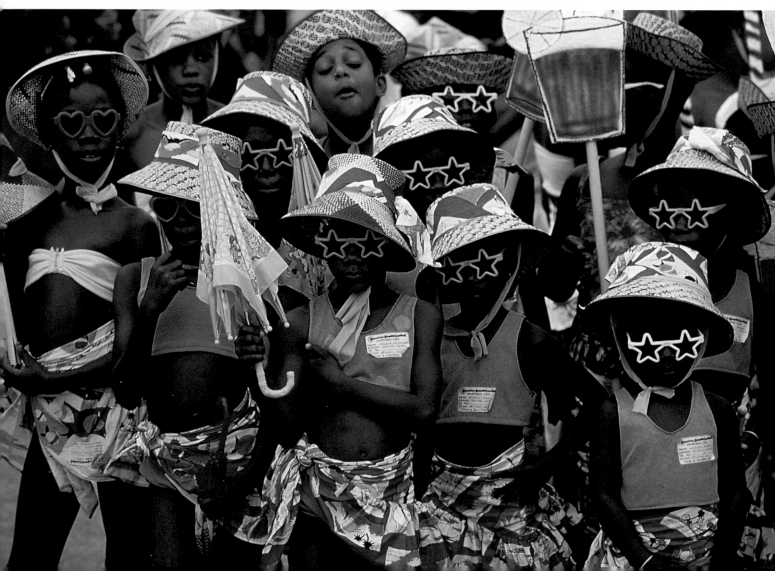

mutable shapes these flags take in the wind and the twisting movements of the dancers remind everyone that change is irrefutable. The abstract patterns take on spirit shapes that shift with the raging beat of the music as it nears its climax. This is bacchanal: feel it in the head, the body, the bones. It rolls through the gut as one stands on the swaying bleachers. The event casts a transcendent spell; it is a big surge heading one step closer to Carnival. The sounds die down. It is three AM before the winners are announced.

The big show, *Dimanche gras* (Fat Sunday), takes on an air of French refinery, with the aristocratic countenance of the fancy masquerade balls once celebrated on the sugar estates. The African-based drumbeat of the steel band and its engine room gives way to the lighter beat of calypso and *soca* music. Pretty colors, shapes, and movements offer a more watchable experience. The sensational movement of a particular king or queen draws the shouts and applause of the crowd, but this is an intermittent response, not the continual roar of the previous night. During this event, the sixteen finalists in the king and queen competition make their appearance before the crowds and the judges; the latter select the winners and runners-up (fig. 10.23).

This is also the night for the calypsonian competition. These performers sing lyrics that make fun of human sexuality or offer bitter political analysis of the government, much to the scorn and horror of the politicians being so scrutinized. The slow pace of the events on Sunday night is punctuated by surprise guest appearances, skits, and presentations of awards. This splendid show gently concludes shortly after midnight. *Jouvay* is waiting.

The term *jouvay* may derive from the French *jour ouvert*, opening day, for the event known as *jouvay* does open the gate to the *mas* parade of the bands. It may also derive from the French word *jeu*, which means play. In any event, both explanations apply to this great "ludic enactment" on opening day. *Jouvay* used to begin a few hours after midnight, but new laws have moved it to five AM. Members of organized bands meet at the specified location dressed in old clothes, bathing suits, or underwear. Everyone is smeared with oil, paint, mud, or even chocolate (fig. 10.24). People lime while they wait for the music trucks that carry live *soca* bands, steel drum orches-

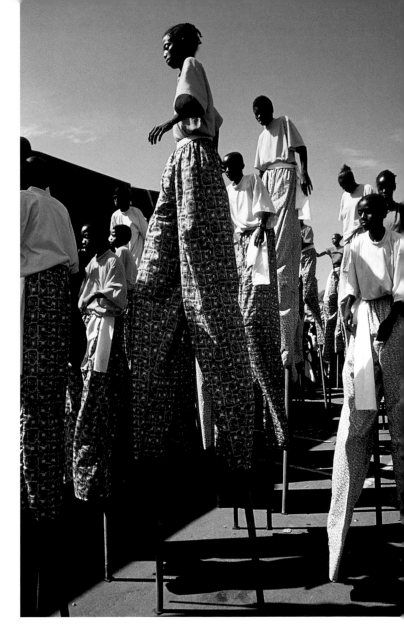

10.22 Children from Port of Spain are trained to perform as stilt walkers in Junior Carnival. *Photograph by Robert Jerome, 2001.*

tras, or disk jockeys who play taped music. Soon they begin the dancing journey, jumping and using a shuffle step called "chipping" down the streets of the city to Independence Square. They also run into improvisational music groups beating rhythms on automobile brake drums, large glass or plastic containers, sticks, anything that makes listeners want to jam jam jam (fig. 10.25). The closer one moves toward the city center, the denser the sound and the more crowded the streets as the many *jouvay* groups converge (fig. 10.26).

By eight o'clock, the mud-, paint-, and oil-covered people have melted into one smeared vision of humanity. The slippery, erotic fluid acts as a lubricant for hips

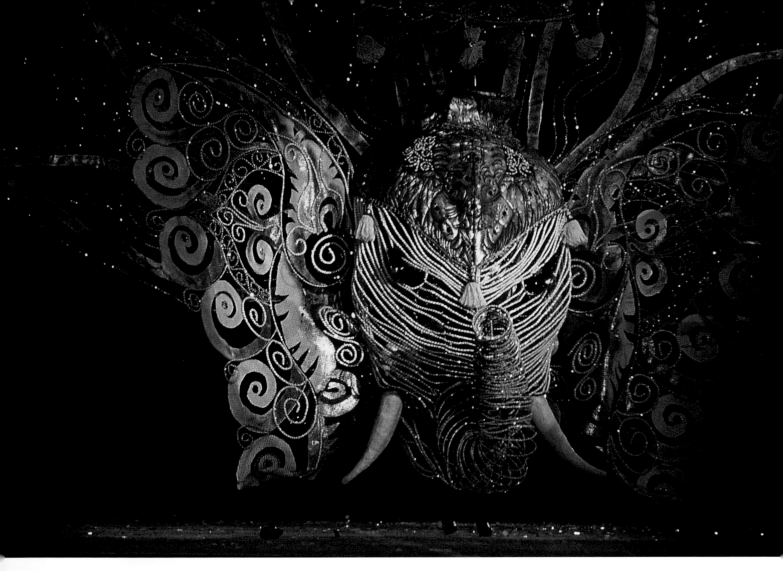

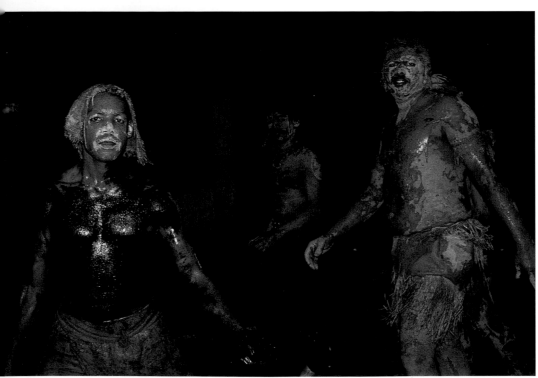

10.23 A king masquerader makes a dramatic presentation on the Savannah stage during the final king and queen competition on Sunday night. *Photograph by Robert Jerome, 2001.*

10.24 Carnival revelers participate in *jouvay*, when band members cover their bodies with oil, paint, or mud. *Photograph by John Nunley, 1988.*

10.25 Improvisational music groups perform on the streets of Port of Spain during *jouvay,* beating rhythms on automobile brake drums, glass or plastic containers, or whatever is at hand. *Photograph by John Nunley, 1988.*

10.26 *Jouvay* groups join in downtown Port of Spain as the sun rises on Monday morning of Carnival. *Photograph by John Nunley, 1987.*

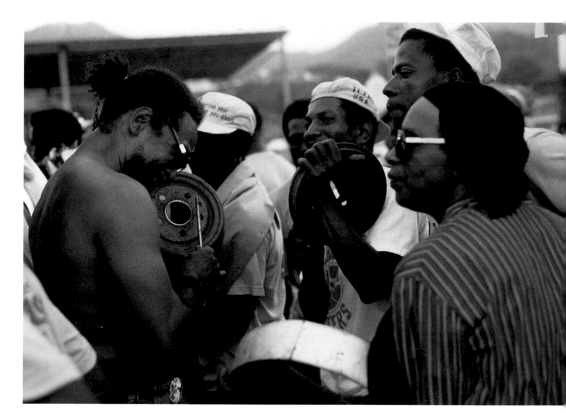

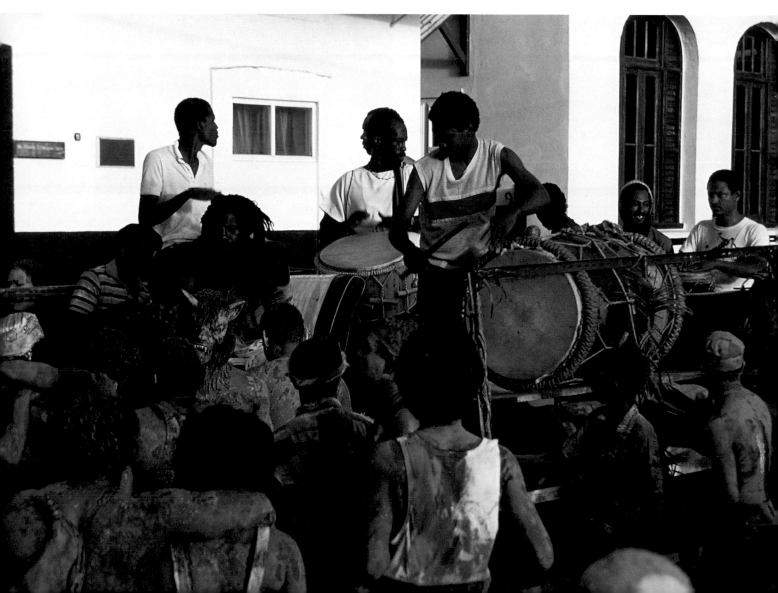

and stomachs, which move back to belly, back to belly in the jamboree. The old streets of the city, like blood-carrying arteries, have conveyed sixty thousand wet, slippery *jouvay* players to the square, the heart of this city of one-half million people. The sun lifts itself over the Levantille Hills, delivering its bristling heat. *Jouvay* has reached full potential, jamming, jamming, jamming! Everyone is moving to all of the music. Hands are raised toward the sky, the sun, toward freedom and the new year, toward loved ones and past experience. People are poised between the old and the new in a crossing of times. A sense of wonder and expectation fills the air. The genie's lantern has been opened, and everyone inhales the air of magic. As the wise and understated *mas* man Albert Bailey says, "*Jouvay* morning is a real refresher course."[34]

Jouvay has set the tone for Carnival Monday. In general, bands are required to proceed along an official route through the city, performing on two smaller stages in town and at the Savannah. However, not all bands comply with this ordinance. Jason Griffith, an elder statesman of Carnival who has brought out sailor bands for over fifty years, greets members of his Old Fashioned Sailor Band outside his house on Pelham Street in Belmont. From Brooklyn, London, and Toronto they arrive in sailor dress. Greetings, hugs and kisses, and handshakes anoint the reunions. Band members put on their headdresses and gather in their respective sections. Sylvia and Stanley Beguesse, members of the band, dress in their unique, fancy, and outlandish uniforms (see fig. 10.9). Other sailors, dressed in standard white uniforms, assemble behind the music truck and begin to "wine": their shoulders rotate, their hips roll, sway, and dip with knees slightly bent (fig. 10.27). The truck moves and feet slide-step along the way to the Savannah. The sounds of chipping feet on the pavement recall similar sounds produced by the old British marching regiments, which, like *mas* bands, were grouped by section. The acoustic

10.27 Sailor masqueraders dressed in traditional white navy uniforms begin to dance behind a music truck. *Photograph by John Nunley, 2000.*

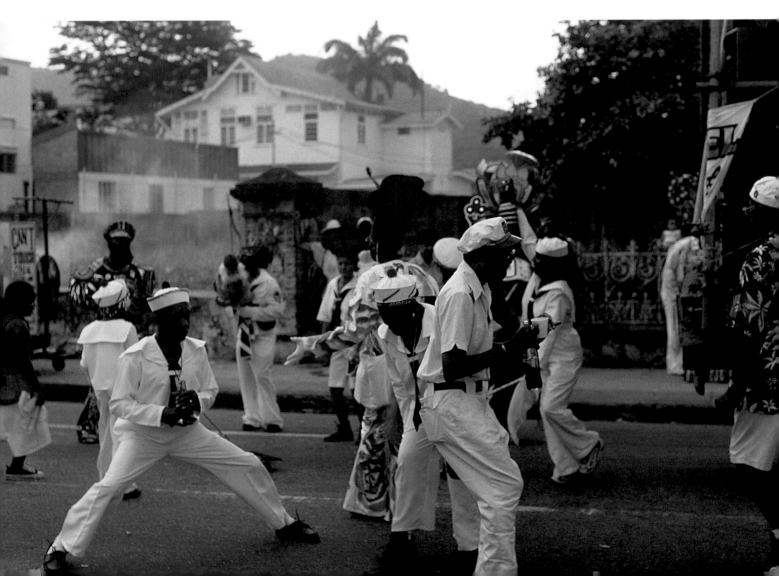

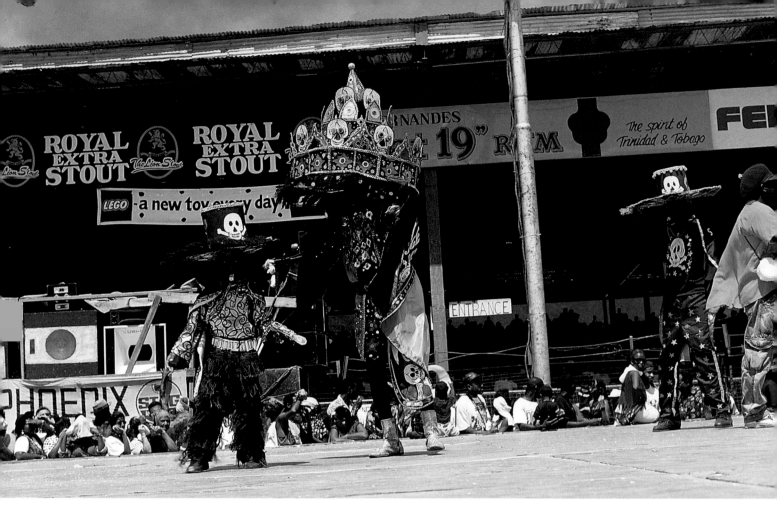

10.28 Midnight Robber masqueraders perform as a group on the Savannah stage during Port of Spain Carnival. *Photograph by Barbara Mauldin, 1994.*

history of the militia days revives to energize and give memory to Carnival.

The sailors move west on Jerningham Street to the southeast corner of the Savannah at ten o'clock Monday morning; then they head north to the east runway leading to the Savannah stage. Sailors with canes and pipes and stokers who pretend to stoke fires with coal dance onstage as the crowd looks on. Sailors carrying boxes of baby powder christen their mates with the white dust, which can whip itself into a halo of fog, depending on the wind. After sailors, many other bands pass this way. For some, it is the only time they will cross over the Savannah stage; for others, it is a practice run for the more important parade on Tuesday or the first of a two-part performance.

On Tuesday morning, the bands follow the same route, but now everyone is dressed in full costume. Wayne Berkeley's well-disciplined band New Moon makes its appearance at the Savannah promptly at

nine o'clock. Its theme this year portrays the timeless cycle of death and renewal as reflected by the lunar cycle. Between bands, traditional *mas* characters such as Midnight Robbers, performing their robber talk, make their way across the stage (fig. 10.28). Some of the devil masqueraders, too—such as the Bookman—make an appearance and compete with one another through their calculated steps and posturing (fig. 10.29). Next comes a group of "Indians" wearing elaborate feather and bead costumes (see fig. 10.11, 10.30). Other traditional masqueraders are the *moco jumbies*, or stilt walkers, who perform acrobatics and other tricks for the crowd (fig. 10.31).

Several of the big bands now pass by, including Funtasia, with its theme "Take One," and Hart, depicting "Life . . . A Helluva Time.'" At noon, Legends is ready to burst onto the stage, four thousand strong in sixteen sections, to portray the theme "Streets of Fire." One section, entitled "Saturday Night," honors the late calypsonian Lord Kitchener, who died the previous year. The snaps and pops of firecrackers and the layers of colored smoke add to the excitement while *soca* singer Super Blue's "Pump It Up" and Iwer George's

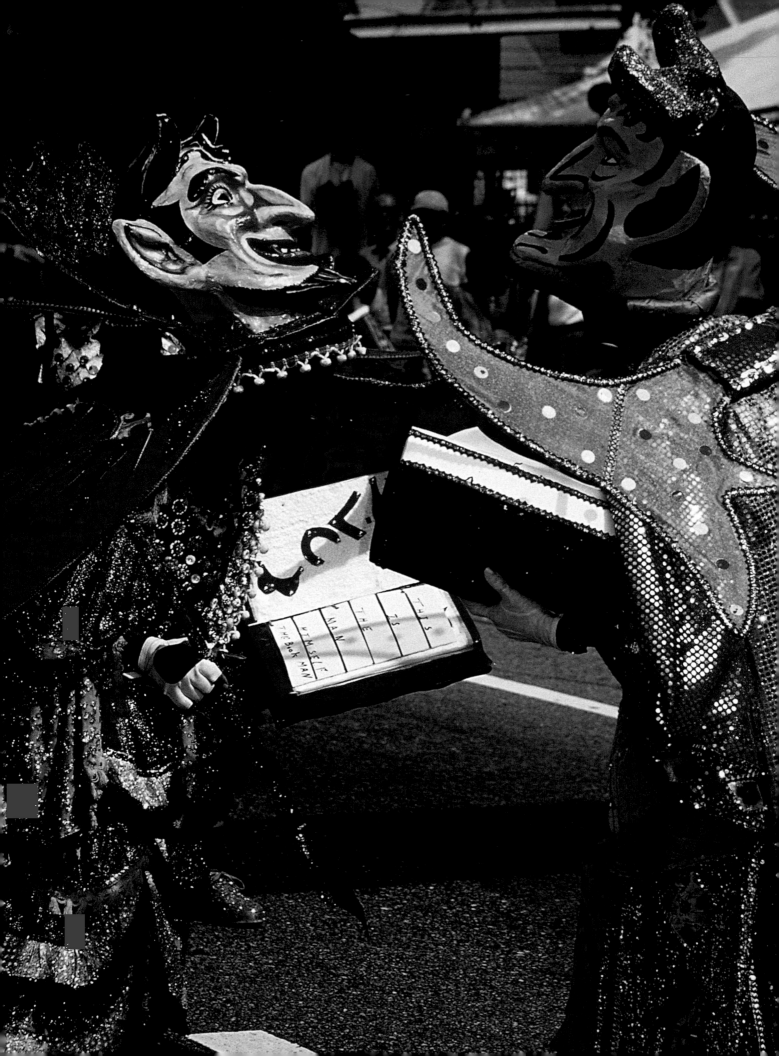

"Carnival Come Back Again" keep the *mas* men and women "winin'" across the stage.

Peter Minshall's presentation of "M2K" avoids the Savannah; band members assemble on the west side of the park at the Queens Royal College. Like his great theme "River" of 1983, his band's theme in 2000 celebrates racial diversity as Trinidad and Tobago's greatest resource. Members of the band section called "White Planet" process behind a giant white ball while those of the "Black Planet" move toward them on a planetary collision course. When the two spheres meet, balloons inside them are released, and clouds of silver and gold float in the air. Armed with squeeze bottles of white and black paint, members of the White and Black Planets spray one another, symbolically integrating white and black to create racial harmony.

It is now late afternoon, and all the main streets of Port of Spain are alive with color and sound. It is diffi-

cult to distinguish participant from onlooker. This is the last lap. Whole costumes and pieces of them lie discarded in the streets and city squares, the corpses of Carnival foreshadowing the coming of Lent. Gradually the streets begin to empty, the colors fade, and music soft and disparate replaces the solid blast. By midnight the revelry has come to an end. It is Ash Wednesday.

At Piarco, Trinidad's international airport, expatriates from Miami, Toronto, London, New York, and Los Angeles line up for the return trip. They carry their costumes proudly as they discuss the experiences of Carnival. The music, the spectacle, and memories of friends and relatives are carried with them to their homes in North America and Europe. Emigrants who left their West Indian island homes after World War II have transplanted this powerful festival of renewal to their new homes. Thanks mostly to Trinidadians, new festivals such as Caribana in Toronto, the West Indian

10.29 Devil Bookman masqueraders compete with one another by gesturing with their bodies. *Photograph by Robert Jerome, 2001.*

10.30 Fancy Indian masqueraders wait to perform on the Savannah stage. *Photograph by John Nunley, 2000.*

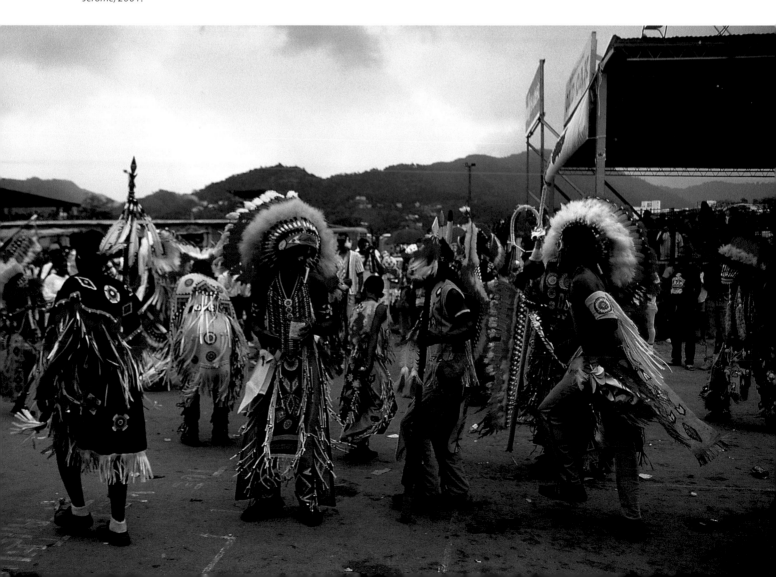

Labor Day celebration in Brooklyn, the Columbus Day celebration in Miami, and Carnival at Nottinghill Gate, London, have become large and vital events in these urban centers. Yes, Trinidadians have invaded these metropolises and begun a process of "Caribbeaniza- tion." Yet each year they return to the source to make it happen all over again.

NOTES

I would like to thank Gerard Besson for his critical review of this work and, in general, his great contribution to the preser- vation of Trinidadian culture through the numerous publica- tions of his company, Paria Publishing Company Limited.

1. My experience of Carnival derives from repeated visits to Trinidad and Tobago since 1983. Some of the research sup- porting this chapter resulted from a Fulbright-Hays Post Doc- toral Research Grant dispatched from 1990 to 1991.

2. Gerard Besson and Bridget Brereton, *The Book of Trinidad* (Port of Spain: Paria Publishing, 1992), 3–4.

3. Ibid.

4. Ibid., 17.

5. Ibid., 45–46.

6. Andrew Pearse, "Carnival in Nineteenth-Century Trinidad," in *Trinidad Carnival* (Port of Spain: Paria Publishing, 1988; a re-publication of *Caribbean Quarterly* 4, nos. 3–4, 1956), 5.

7. Besson and Brereton, *Book of Trinidad,* 72–74.

8. Pearse, "Carnival in Nineteenth-Century Trinidad," 13–14.

9. Kim Johnson, "Introduction," in Paria Publishing, *Trinidad Carnival,* xi–xxii.

10. Errol Hill, *The Trinidad Carnival* (London: New Beacon Books, 1997), 11, 23, 30.

11. John Nunley, "Masquerade Mix-up in Trinidad Carnival: Live Once, Die Forever," in *Caribbean Festival Arts: Each and Every Bit of Difference,* eds. John Nunley and Judith Bettelheim (Seattle: University of Washington Press, 1988), 111.

12. Pearse, "Carnival in Nineteenth-Century Trinidad," 24, 37–38.

13. Hill, *Trinidad Carnival,* 25–27, 87–90.

14. Pearse, "Carnival in Nineteenth-Century Trinidad," 34.

15. Ibid., 34–35, 40.

16. Nunley and Bettelheim, *Caribbean Festival Arts,* 31.

17. Pearse, "Carnival in Nineteenth-Century Trinidad," 26.

18. Daniel J. Crowley, "The Traditional Masks of Carnival," in Paria Publishing, *Trinidad Carnival,* 198.

19. Michael Anthony, *Parade of the Carnivals of Trinidad 1839–1989* (Port of Spain: Circle Press, 1989), 13–14.

20. Jim Harding, personal communication, October 25, 1990.

21. Daniel J. Crowley, "Midnight Robbers," in Paria Publish- ing, *Trinidad Carnival,* 90–91.

22. Mack Copeland, personal communication, February 1984.

23. Albert Bailey, personal communication, 1990.

24. John Nunley, "The Beat Goes On: Recycling and Impro- visation in the Music of Trinidad and Tobago," in *Recycling, Reseen: Folk Art from the Global Scrap Heap* (New York: Abrams, 1996), 135.

25. Ibid., 137.

26. Anthony, *Parade of the Carnivals,* 263.

27. Albert Bailey, personal communication, 1990.

28. Anthony, *Parade of the Carnivals,* 352.

29. Wayne Berkeley, personal communication, March 1983.

30. Personal observation in February and March 1983.

31. This and the following information is based on my field research and personal observation during the Carnival season in Port of Spain in 1983, 1990, 1991, 1994, and 2000. A col- lection of essays about Carnival activities in Trinidad and Tobago can be found in Milla C. Riggio, ed., "Trinidad and Tobago Carnival," *Drama Review* 42, no. 3 (1998).

32. Judge's scoring sheet from the National Carnival Commission.

33. Anthony Dias Blue, "Feeling Groggy," *American Way* (January 2003): 44.

34. Albert Bailey, personal communication, 1990.

10.31 *Moco jumbies,* or stilt walkers, perform acrobatics and other tricks for Carnival crowds. *Photograph by Gianni Vecchiato, 1994.*

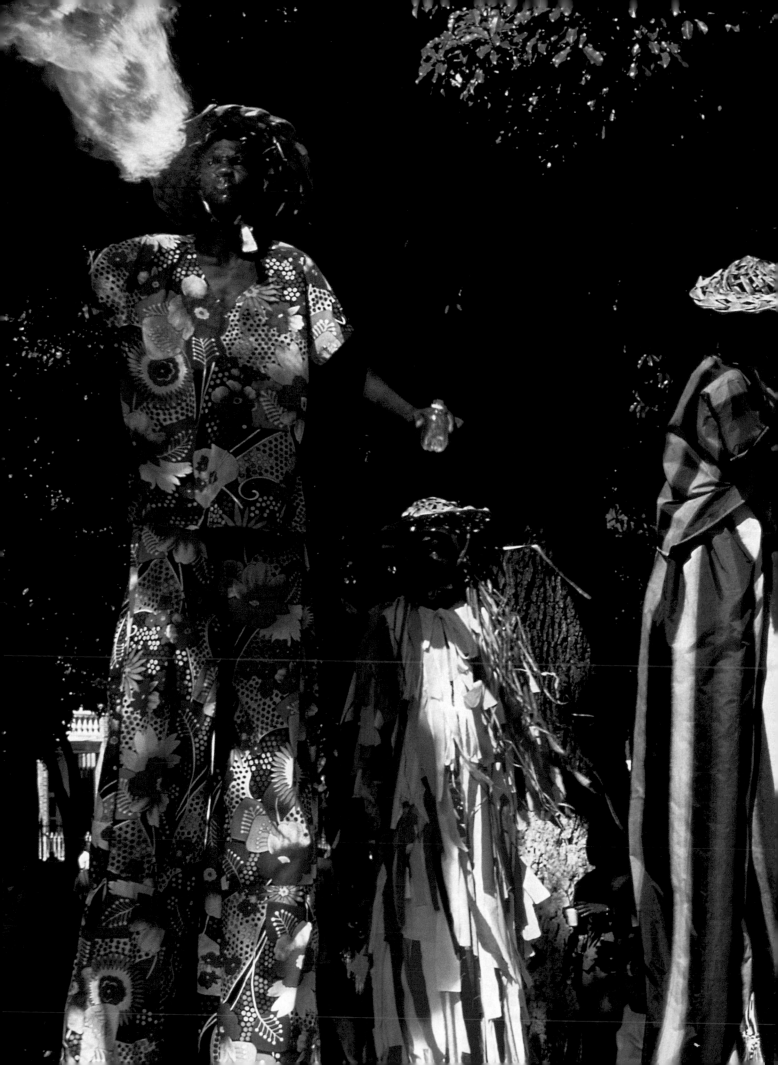

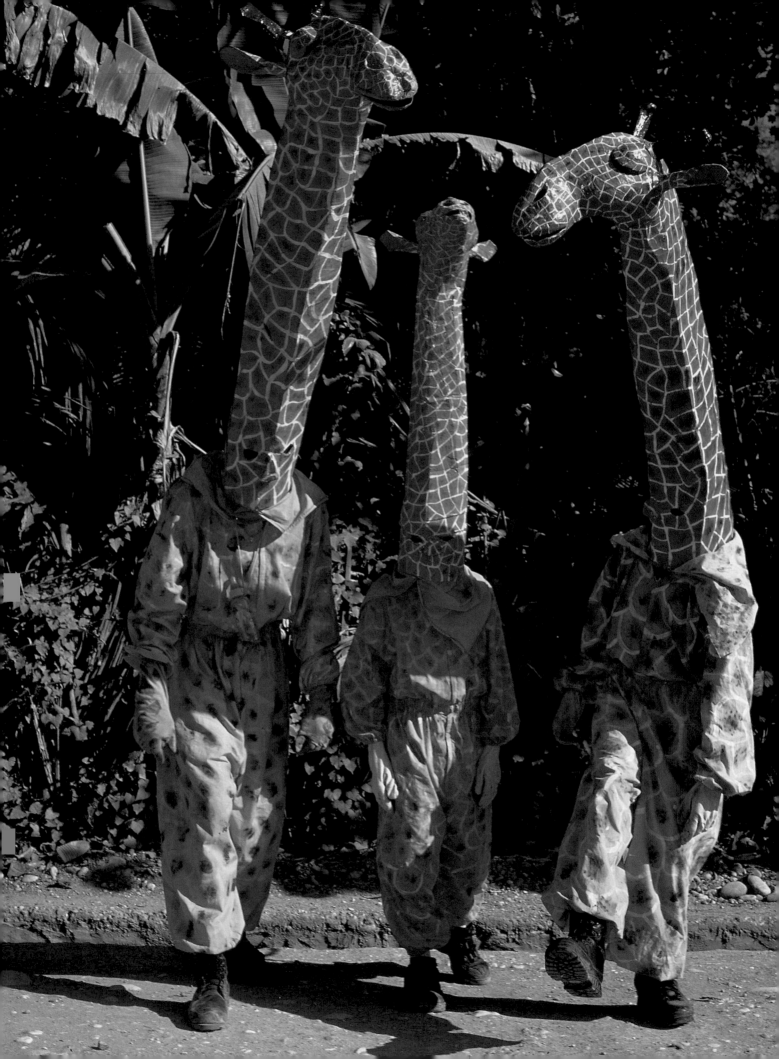

11 "My Heart Don't Stop"

HAITI, THE CARNIVAL STATE

DONALD COSENTINO

ARNIVAL IN HAITI IS AS unique as the history of the people who celebrate it. In other places, Carnival is a three-day disruption of daily life, a brief letting-up on the social REPRESS BUTTON. In Haiti, Carnival is a continuation of daily life *by other means.* It intensifies rather than disrupts. In other and more Christian lands, Carnival collapses at midnight on Fat Tuesday: violent exaltations of the body give way to the spiritual mortifications of Lent. In Haiti, things are just getting started on Ash Wednesday. Carnival morphs into Rara. Rowdy marching bands emerge from the *ounfo* (Vodou temples) to dance their way through the season of penitence all the way to their final blowouts on Easter Sunday. There is no doubt an element of institutional mockery in this refusal to let Carnival die. But in Haiti, Carnival celebrations stand not so much in opposition to the state religion of Catholicism as in complement to the national religion of Vodou. Carnival's reigning spirit is not comely Bacchus but ghastly Gede—Captain Zonbi, the Hard-On Mas-

ter. Finally, there is nothing merely compensatory or simply symbolic in the outrages of this Carnival. In Haiti, Carnival really can and does change things (fig. 11.2).

"My Heart Don't Stop"

At the heart of Carnival celebrations is music, and no one writes better about contemporary Haitian music than the gonzo ethnomusicologist Gage Averill. Consider what he has to say about these lyrics to "My Heart Don't Stop," a *chan pwen* (point song) composed by the renowned Haitian "roots" band Boukman Eksperyans for the 1990 Carnival in Port-au-Prince:[1]

> *My heart don't stop, my heart don't stop,*
> *My heart don't stop this year.*
> *Boukman's in Carnival, my heart don't stop.*
> *Go forward, don't fight among yourselves [in the band].*[2]

As Averill explains, such songs are meant to send a *pwen* (point), or serious message of censure, against someone whose identity can only be inferred, since he or she is never directly named.[3] The lyrics go on to denounce *magouye* (frauds), *sendenden* (idiots), and *paranoye* (paranoids), without naming names, though activists were using just those terms to describe the military thugs who ruled Haiti in the dark days following the 1986 overthrow of "Baby Doc" Duvalier's regime.

11.1 Giraffe Carnival masqueraders. Jacmel. *Photograph by Phyllis Galembo, 1998.*

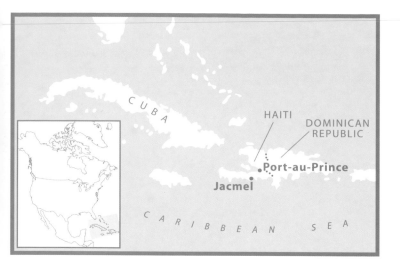

11.2 The location of Port-au-Prince in Haiti and the Caribbean.

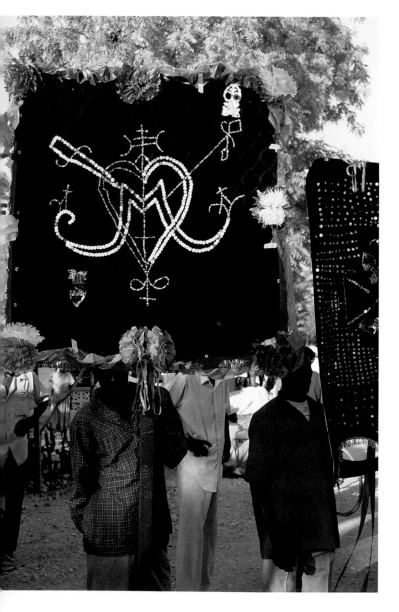

The song proceeds to an invocation of Ogou Bal-endjo ("Poison can't harm those possessed by Bal-endjo"), the Vodou *lwa* (deity) most closely identified with the insurgent slaves and freemen of color who rose against another alien military force during the mythic beginnings of the 1791 Revolution. It calls for unity "in the band," a metonym for the *pep ayisan* (common people) who are the foot soldiers of Carnival. The song ends with this Jacobinic warning: "I didn't know you at all before—but now I know you all too well!"

Boukman Eksperyans' 1990 Carnival song put the dictator du jour, General Prosper Avril, in a quandary. It had already been picked up during rehearsal by other Carnival bands and diffused throughout the countryside by Rara, that peculiar Haitian tradition of dueling Carnival bands that wend their obstreperous way through town and countryside between Ash Wednesday and Holy Saturday (fig. 11.3). Avril could have banned "My Heart Don't Stop" from being performed during Carnival, thereby affirming that he indeed was the target of the *pwen,* or he could pretend that the lyrics were pointed at someone else.

It was a classic case of damned if you do, damned if you don't. In the end, Avril allowed the song to be played, but its refrains were not silenced on Ash Wednesday. Inspired by the angry lyrics, the marching, shouting, swearing, laughing bands of Rara sang their own songs, insisting that the *dechoukaj* (uprooting) that began with the overthrow of Baby Doc was not yet finished.[4] By April 1990, General Avril was himself gone—another in a line of corrupt and venal politicians undone by the one-two punch of Carnival and Rara.

In order to appreciate Carnival's power to change Haitian society, one must first understand its symbiotic relationship with Rara. Carnival, as we shall see, is a quasi-official event, a state compromise with popular expression forced by custom and tradition. Aspects of Carnival can be legislated (though seldom successfully). Carnival can and sometimes has been co-opted by the state. The same cannot be said for Rara. Its only organic links are to the *ounfo,* from which it derives its magical powers (fig. 11.4). If Carnival is understood as

11.3 Rara wends it way through the Haitian countryside on Good Friday. Cabaret. *Photograph by Marilyn Houlberg. 1992.*

an annual parliament of fools, then Rara is
its armed extension—its reification into a provisional
regime of guerilla bands who hold their ground for
several months before retreating into the *ounfo,* where
they will regroup to sally forth next year.

Liza McAlister describes this consolidation of Carnivalesque power into what might legitimately be called
an alternative Haitian state:

Rara bands are organized local groups with formal ranks,
costumes, and rituals, and they conceive of themselves as
armies connected to imaginary states that move through
territory, carry out armed maneuvers, and conduct diplo-
matic relations with other groups in the process of their
musical celebrations. As local groups under the leadership
of "big men," Rara bands mirror the politics of patronage
that characterized Haiti's national government. In their performances of maneuvers, diplomacy, and tribute to local
notables, Rara bands distribute and redistribute prestige,
reputation, and local resources.[5]

There really are no parallels to the decisive role that
Carnival has played in the national life of Haiti. Indeed,
Mikhail Bakhtin, Carnival's most persuasive and influential modern theorist, assigned an ahistorical role
to its "ritual of social liberation." As Richard Burton
argues, "at the heart of [Bakhtin's] widely held view is
the belief that what happens during Carnival is essentially *different* from what happens during the rest of
the year, that the three or four days it lasts are a negation in every respect of the laws and behaviors that
hold good for the remaining 360 odd."[6] Although he
allows for some exception in Trinidad and Haiti, Burton assigns a similar ineffectiveness to Caribbean
Carnival:

The dominant order first represses the cultural challenge by
force, and then neutralizes it by absorbing it into the structures of power (as happened with Haitian Vodou and Jamai-
can Afro-Christianity) . . . by [transforming] it into exotic
spectacle and commodity. . . . All this defusing does not,
of course, render future disruption of public order impossible, but it suggests that such disruption, when it occurs,
will be dealt with relatively easily by the structures of
power: there is nothing, it seems, that cannot first be
repressed and then recuperated and neutralized by the
"shitstem."[7]

What Burton seems to be asking rhetorically is,
"What does Carnival really change?" For Haiti, the

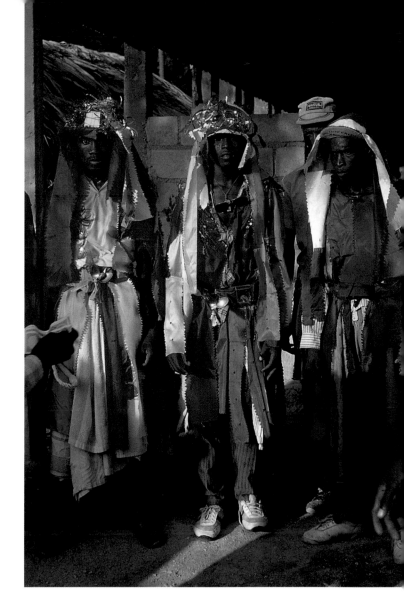

11.4 Rara derives its awesome magical powers from the *ounfo,*
or Haitian Vodou temples. Artibonite countryside. *Photograph
by Donald Cosentino, 1992.*

short answer might be, "Not everything, but a lot."
A longer answer would force some fancy footwork
between metaphysics and history, a *kontredans* that
Gage Averill executes with great elan:

Carnival is the most important crossroads of music and
power in Haiti. The *koudyay* ambience of Carnival, the tradition of *chan pwen* in Carnival songs, the powerful impres-
sion made by tens of thousands of lower-class Haitians in
control of the streets, and Carnivalesque (Gede-esque)
exuberance (obscenity, exaggeration, verbal play, parody,
excessive consumption, the grotesque, debasement, sexuality, license, transgression, masking, conflict, and signi-
fying on hierarchies) all contribute to an event that is
potentially threatening to the state and to the elite.[8]

I would ratchet up Averill's argument several notches by describing Haiti as a "functioning" rather than "potential" Carnival state. By that I mean two things: first, that Carnival has played a determinant role in shaping the country's history, and second, that the Black Republic itself has played a Carnivalesque role on the world stage ever since its Revolution of 1791–1804. For two hundred years, Haiti's history has been a continual affront to prevailing hegemonies of race and power. It was born in bloody ceremonies of reversal in which the reigning colonial-racial-social orders—at the apogee of their powers—were all overturned. Its armies were led by self-liberated slaves whom Napoleon Bonaparte dismissed as "gilded Negroes" before he, or at least his brother-in-law, was trounced by golden Toussaint in one of the most amazing turnarounds in military history.[9]

One of the hero-generals of this revolution, Henri Christophe, appropriated the prerogatives of both *le roi soleil* and Frederick the Great, constructing his own Versailles near Milot and naming it Sans Souci after the royal residence in Potsdam.[10] Christophe, the slave turned general turned emperor, was eventually followed by Soloque, another foot soldier, who crowned himself Emperor Faustin I, and then by ranks of *generalissimi,* by various bagmen-stooges for American military occupiers, by the family of a country doctor who channeled Bawon Samdi, the divinity of death, and finally by the current president, an ex-Catholic priest whose devoted supporters identify him alternatively with Ogou, divinity of war, and with the Gedes, sons of the Bawon Samdi and trickster divinities of the Vodou pantheon whose avatars are in fact the patrons of Carnival.[11] Obviously, Haitian revelers have never lacked rich material for festive inversions.

In his seminal essay on Vodou art, Robert Farris Thompson ascribed just such an international festive role to Haiti when he wrote that "it is permissible to greet black Haiti as the *coumbite* of the western hemisphere, the *rara* of the universe, a school of being for us all."[12] To extend Thompson's similes, we might position Haiti below the *kalunga* line, that mystical divide between visible and invisible worlds everywhere discernable in Kongo art and philosophy. From its inverted position at the bottom of the Atlantic socioeconomic triangle, Haiti mirrors the power arrangements that created the colonial inequalities of Saint Domingue and sustains them till today in the Black Republic. The unfinished agenda of the Haitian Revolution continues to throw up all sorts of interregnum political monsters (to borrow Antonio Gramsci's elegant phrase), whose annual court summonses are delivered during the three days of Carnival.

By employing these analogies, I certainly do not mean to discount the real historical importance of the Revolution of 1791–1804. In assessing the impact of that cataclysmic event, we would do well to consider the rejoinder that Henry Kissinger received from Chou En-Lai. In the course of their conversation (to prepare for the operatic state visit of Richard and Pat Nixon in 1972), the Chinese foreign minister mentioned the French Revolution to the American secretary of state. Intrigued by the reference, Kissinger asked Chou whether he thought the Revolution had been a success, to which Chou replied, "It's too early to tell." I think we all need to take that Chinese long view in assessing the import of the Haitian Revolution, which will not be complete until the inequities against which it rose are resolved on some wider pan-African scale.

What is grotesque in this history are the political and social arrangements forced upon the Haitian people by the corrupt trustees of their incomplete revolution. What is Carnivalesque is the popular resistance to these trustees, or, as they are now called, MREs (morally repugnant elites), through enraged song and laughter and occasionally through the swift and terrible justice of the street. Edouard Duval-Carrié's painting *Les Mardigras au Fort Dimanche* exquisitely captures such Jacobinic table-turning (fig. 11.5).

In the painting, all the Duvaliers are dressed in Carnival costumes, as if posing for a photograph, in the gangrenous cell of Fort Dimanche, the family's torture chamber. The daughters are tarted up in black, a *pwen* on their bourgeois tastes and their familial alliance with Bawon Samdi. Everyone is wearing sunglasses, another dual reference to the family of the Bawon and to the Duvalier goon squads, the Tontons Macoutes, who favored Ray-Ban sunglasses. Behind the daughters are the in-laws, an army general and the archbishop of Port-au-Prince, both church and army having been co-opted, as indeed even Carnival had been co-opted, during those dark days of the *dictatur.*

At the center of the painting is the (Un)Holy Family. Mama Simone is dressed in widow's weeds, like Gran

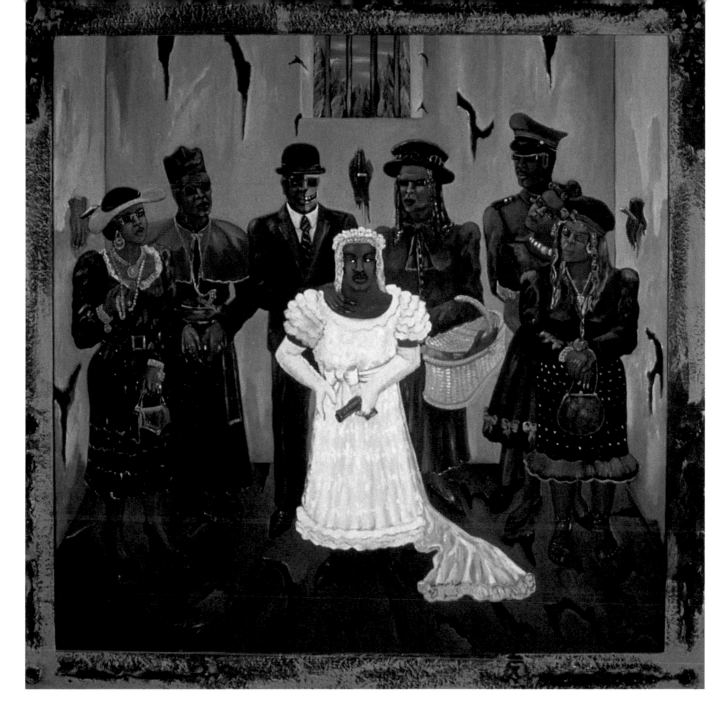

11.5 *Les Mardigras au Fort Dimanch*. Oil painting by Edouard Duval-Carrié, Port-au-Prince, 1992–1993. Collection of Sanford A. Rubenstein. *Photograph by Ive Breton. Courtesy of the UCLA Fowler Museum of Cultural History.*

Brijit, the Bawon's wife. A severed hand pokes out of her wicker basket, companion to three other hands nailed to the walls. Papa Doc wears his familiar dark Masonic suit. Dead since 1971, his skull is half-eaten into the leering rictus of Bawon Cimitiere, brother of Samdi and spiritual keeper of the cemetery to which Papa had dispatched so many enemies during his time on earth. Between them is Baby Doc, wearing a wed-

ding dress and holding a pistol. That dress bristles with *pwen*, mocking references to Mama Simone's status as a *manbo* (Vodou priestess), to rumors of Baby's own gender confusion and his devotion to the campy love goddess Ezili, and to his disastrous marriage to Michelle Bennett, the Marie Antoinette of the regime. Her nouveau riche pretensions were the target of *chan pwen* years before his regime collapsed on the eve of Carnival 1986.

After the family's flight, this painting inspired the most popular poster of the *dechoukaj*, a reproduction of another painting by Duval-Carrié. In it, Baby Doc, dressed again in his wedding dress, now has the pistol

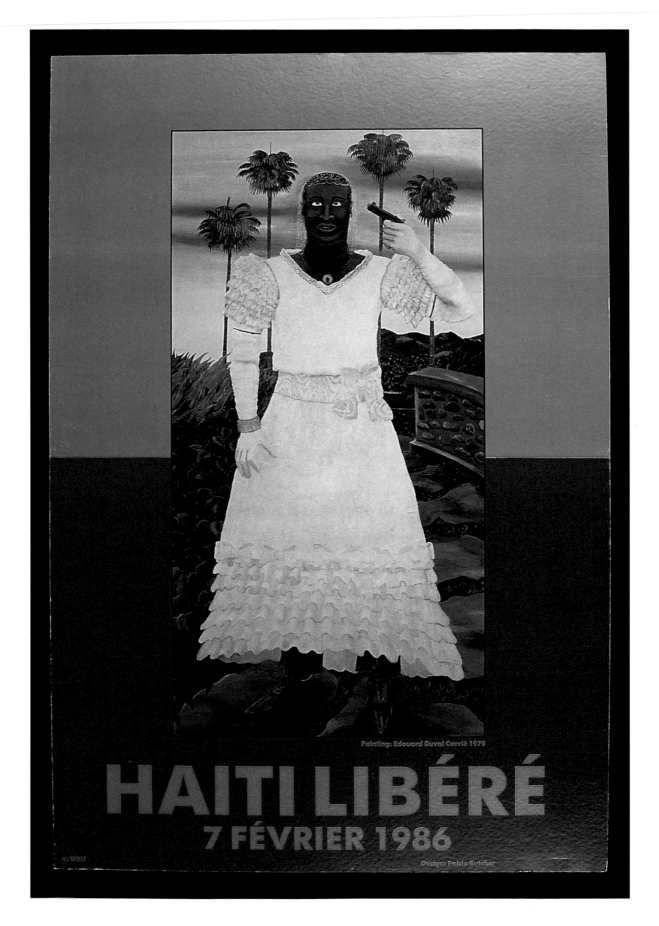

11.6 *Haiti Libéré, 7 Février 1986.* Oil painting by Edouard Duval-Carrié, Port-au-Prince, 1986. Reproduced in poster form by Pablo Butcher. Collection of Donald Cosentino. *Photograph courtesy of the UCLA Fowler Museum of Cultural History.*

raised to his head. At the bottom of the poster is written (in ungrammatical French), "Haiti Libéré, 7 Février 1986" (fig. 11.6).

As an artist, Duval-Carrié shares in the work of musicians, dancers, mimics, mimes, and street clowns who transform the three fat days preceding Ash Wednesday, and the forty that follow, into a kind of annual parliament. Each year they conjure alternative realities, and they sometimes manage to bring their mocking images to life. I was lucky enough to participate in and observe the Carnivals of 1991 and 1995, which bookended the inauguration and restoration of President Jean-Bertrand Aristide, or, as he is sometimes called, M'se Mirak ("Mr. Miracle"). Aristide's near-miraculous career illuminates the transformational powers of Carnival and leads to a deeper appreciation of the pivotal role Carnival has played in Haiti's surreal history.

"Squat and Piss"

Carnival in Haiti is as old as the French colony of Saint Domingue, established in 1697. During those early colonial days, street celebrations began on the second Sunday of January, following the Feast of the Three Kings (an important holiday throughout the Black Caribbean), and continued through *Dimanch gra, Lindi gra,* and *Madi gra,* the three official days of Carnival preceding Lent.

Revelers brought with them their Breton and Norman traditions, which were among the most raucous in the so-called Christian world, including *tresser ruban* ("moving maypole"), *danse des batonnets* (baton fencing dance, with flutes, whistles, and tambourines), and the squalidly amusing *baisser-pisser* ("squat and piss").[13] From the beginning, Carnival was deeply politicized, establishing tropes that have persisted from the colony to the republic. According to Ady Jeangardy, Carnival "thrives on political stories. It goes on throughout the eighteenth century . . . adding more and more buffoonery, including male transvestites, mercilessly mocking the effete lords of French

nobility, particularly the regent of state Phillipe d'Orleans, the homosexual, provoking his subjects [into wearing] his skirts and lacy frills everywhere. To this day, this character is part of the Carnival."[14]

These early revels were so lawless, even by the depraved standards of Saint Domingue, that by 1729 the Church succeeded in having Carnival banned. But the "squat and piss" crews would have none of that. Donning mock cassocks and play mitres, they hurled *pwen* at Church authorities, including the pope. They chanted a funeral dirge for the governor, who had been the bishop's stooge. The following year Carnival was restored, thus establishing its role as a transgressive political force to be reckoned with by most of the bizarre regimes that followed. Throughout Haiti's history, the political state and Carnival revelers have been engaged in a kind of pas de deux: co-option wrestling with transgression, authoritarianism with anarchy, for control of the Black Republic.

During the years of the Revolution (1791–1804), the Franco-Rabelaisian traditions of Carnival passed entirely to the blacks and mulattos, who celebrated their world turned upside-down through *ochan* (songs of praise) to their Jacobinic leaders. "Groups come out of everywhere banging their drums and loudly singing hymns of praise to Dessalines or in honor of the joyous celebration of freedom (*bamboche de liberte*) while soiling the memory of *les blancs*" (fig. 11.7).[15] Thus, by the end of the eighteenth century, Haitian Carnival had established precedents for both supporting and provoking political change. The *ochan* of praise and the *pwen* of mockery were locked in a dialectic that has remained the "X" factor in Haiti's culture and history.

Carnival dialectic is not the worst way to read the history of Haiti's nineteenth century. Presidents made broad and sometimes successful attempts to structure Carnival and then were run out of office by the very crowds they had tried to restrain. Bands marched through the streets wearing grotesque masks affixed with naughty epithets mocking the mulatto generals who inherited government from the original generation of revolutionary heroes. In 1843 their *pwen* ignited a political movement that ended with the flight of President Jean-Pierre Boyer, who had been dictator since 1818. This Carnival coup would be mirrored more than a century later in the hasty exile of

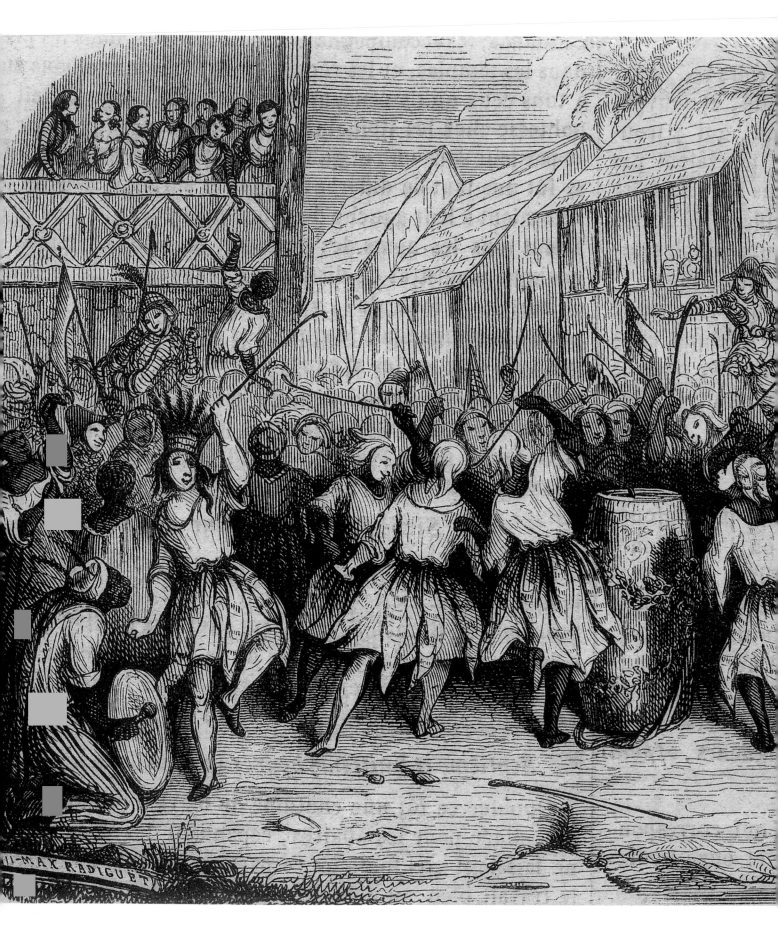

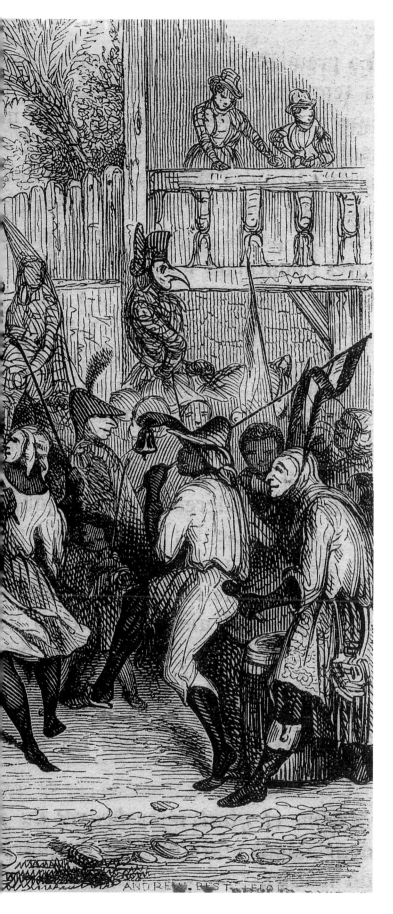

Baby Doc, Jean-Claude Duvalier, who fled the country rather than face the Carnival bands of 1986.

Throughout the nineteenth century, Carnival bands constituted a popular mock parliament, a kind of rough-and-ready "Estates General." Mock nobles with play titles collected for three days of annual (dis)order. Reflecting the nuances of national life, their songs shook political systems and inspired counterefforts at control. At century's end, President Antoine Simon attempted to fabricate national Carnival standards. Originally from Cayes, Simon decreed that the *tresser-ruban,* which had been known only in his hometown, would become national, as would the Danse des Balayeurs (Dance of the Sweepers) from Cap Haitien. The latter reform proved his undoing. Wearing T-shirts and boxers, mock *balayeurs* rose against the reforming president. On Mardi Gras day they pushed their brooms amid great clouds of dust, crying "a bas la dictatur."[16]

Following the first American invasion and occupation (1915–1933), Carnival groups once more marched under the red flag of Ogou, whose divine wrath would also precede the second invasion at century's end (1994). During the years of occupation, puppet presidents fulminated against Carnival revelers in rebel costumes, some of whom further undermined their American collaborators by carrying around *lamayots* (wooden boxes with "little surprises" inside). For a few pennies, *lamayot* lids would be opened to reveal a puppet labeled "Ti Lulu" (a nickname for President Louis Borno) being fucked by another puppet dressed as Uncle Sam. In 1928 a rowdy crowd roamed the streets of Port-au-Prince dancing to anti-Lulu *chan pwen* while a *prete savan* (mock Catholic priest) solemnly intoned his requiem. In 1929, Lulu struck back. Reacting to these outrages, he forbade Carnival rehearsals in January, officially limiting its celebration to the three days preceding Lent.

Inspired by Lulu's draconian counterattack, the Port-au-Prince mayor forbade unofficial participation in Carnival. Marchers would henceforth need to wear official Carnival uniforms, and musicians would perform from *chars* (floats). All other participants were

11.7 *A Scene of Carnival in Haiti in 1838.* Pen and ink drawing by Max Radiguet, printed by Andrew Best Liloir. *Photograph courtesy of the New York Public Library, Picture Collection.*

restricted to constructed stands. These decrees instituted the first *cortège carnavalesque* (Carnival parade)
and inspired what would become a lasting tension
between *chars* and street mobs. By employing police
to confine its various constituencies to predetermined
spaces, the president and the mayor thought they
could refashion Carnival into a bourgeois street party
(*bamboche*). But their drastic measures only ensured
the government's growing unpopularity and partly
explained its collapse the following year.

Lulu's successor, Stenio Vincent, retained the *cortège*

11.8 Masquerade of General Charles Oscar, or "Chaloska."
Jacmel. *Photograph by Donald Cosentino, 1995.*

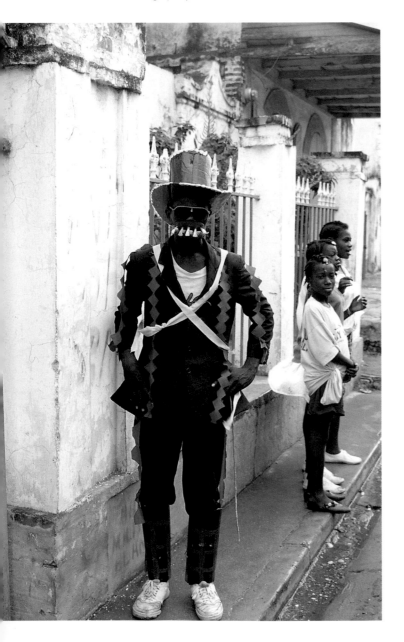

but liberated it from prior restraint. During Vincent's
regime a whole new platoon of military characters
marched into Carnival: the eternally popular and ridiculous General Charles Oscar, aka "Chaloska" (fig. 11.8),
assisted by Generals Kaka, PiTa-PiTris ("Later and Sad-
der"), Plim pa Gouye ("Nothing Stirs"), Ti-Zozo ("Little
Dick"), Pet Santi ("Stinky Fart"), and Gran Van ("Big
Wind").

Elie Lescot followed Stenio Vincent and fared even
worse than his predecessors. *Lamayots* were pried
open to reveal the president in a state of undress,
being fucked by the even more hated Dominican dictator (and *genocidaire*) President Trujillo, or as a huge
and savage cat wearing a face mask of the president.
In 1940, Lescot prohibited masks and costumes and
also forbade musicians to mention his name and those
of other political figures in the lyrics to their *merengues*
(forgetting that *chan pwen* had no need of anyone's
actual name). Perhaps with even less effect, Lescot
tried to chase the *lamoyots* off the streets.

Following the Second World War, President Dumar-
sais Estimé transformed Carnival into a tourist attraction. These were the golden years, when tourists,
mainly American, actually came to Haiti. Carnival was
just the sort of exotica they sought, and so Estimé set
aside an important part of the state budget to finance
merengue contests and encourage similar forms of
Carnival folly. "Leaf vendors" (*marchan fey*) peddled
pornography. Play wedding parties, stilt walkers, "big
butts" (*gwo derrieres*) showing huge female rear ends,
groups of werewolves, king devils, cowheads, Arabs,
Indians, Africans, slaves, kings and queens on magnificent floats—all of these groups and displays were
promoted and sanctioned as part of a government
effort to create a "fun Haiti" for newly flush visitors
from the north (fig 11.9).[17]

Such were the Carnival scenes shot by the ethnog-
rapher and filmmaker Maya Deren that were later
incorporated into *Divine Horsemen,* the oddly edited
montage of her fieldwork from the late 1940s and
early 1950s.[18] In this film, Harlequins in satin jumpsuits stand at crossroads whipping the ground. Floats
pass by carrying mulatto beauty queens. A bogus
diplomat in top hat and morning coat is tracked by
a cardboard movie camera. Marchers appear with
gigantic papier-mâché heads: hydrocephalic mock-
eries of the bourgeoisie. A large contingent suddenly

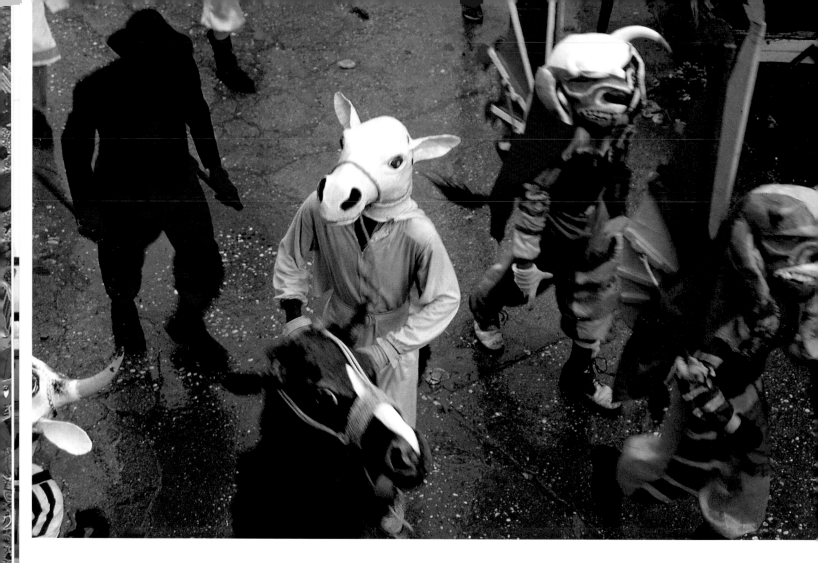

11.9 Groups masquerade as werewolves, devils, cowheads, and other creatures during Haitian Carnival festivities. Jacmel. *Photograph by Donald Cosentino, 1995.*

appears carrying signs advertising Ex-Lax. But always, amid these diverse groups, a figure with white powdered face and sunglasses keeps popping up. It is Gede: Mr. Bones in black top hat and smoking jacket, the divine undertaker bumping and grinding with the revelers.

Mr. Laughing-Death is the last frame in Deren's film, a chilling harbinger of what would happen to Carnival after Estimé. For sitting in the cabinet of this populist president was an obscure country doctor named François Duvalier. In 1957 "Papa Doc" wrested political power from his enemies and, after a fourteen-year reign of unparalleled brutality, passed that power on to his flaccid son, "Baby Doc." Together *père et fils* transformed the Haitian state into a grade B horror film. Papa Doc assumed the funereal attire and even the nasalized speech of the Bawon Samdi. Baby

became *président a vie* (for life) at nineteen. After a few more feckless years, he married the rapacious Michelle Bennett, and the two settled into a life of routinized terror. During the reign of the Duvaliers, what remained of Carnival's masquerading traditions were seized by the Tontons Macoutes, who became real-life monsters in Ray-Bans. Deren's final image of leering Gede foreshadowed that descending night.

Koudyay

Transformed by Estimé into a tourist commodity, Carnival was rescripted into a circus by Duvalier. The style of the state-sponsored Carnival-circus was *koudyay*, defined by Averill as "popular, festive songs that animate torchlight parades before national and church holidays, Carnival and political demonstrations." Through money and terror, Carnival troupes were coerced into performing *ochan* for the president with such inspiring lyrics as "Look at the jet airport Duvalier gave us." On the level of popular music, *koudyay*

Kanaval Lespwa (Carnival of Hope), following Aristide's return by a few months, was widely regarded as the best barometer for gauging the mounting political pressures. Indeed, this may have been the most closely scrutinized of all Haitian Carnivals, as is apparent from this *Miami Herald* news service report, datelined Port-au-Prince, February 28, 1995:

More than a quarter million hip-swiveling, foot-stomping revelers poured into the streets of Sunday for [the] "Carnival of Hope." A cacophony of tubas and trombones, maracas and drums, kazoos and whistles filled the air. The streets of the capital were alive with people and colorful kiosks and hawkers selling straw hats, kites and fried treats.

[Government sources claimed that] "anti-democratic forces are plotting to attack the parades to disrupt the Carnival," while President Aristide said, "The Mardi Gras should take place in peace. The Mardi Gras should take place in order. . . . These are days for you to rejoice, to enjoy yourselves."

Among the 80 floats planned for the opening parade were ones [touting] peace, justice and the environment, representing the priorities of the Aristide government. In front of the palace, a reviewing stand for Aristide to watch the parade was decorated with multicolored balloons and ribbons—and shielded with bulletproof glass.

The U.S. led multinational military mission was out in force to make sure all went smoothly. A helicopter gun ship and a plane circled Port-au-Prince, trying to spot trouble, and humvees with mounted submachine guns nudged their way slowly through the throngs on the streets.

Observers acknowledge that foreign governments and investors will be looking to the Carnival to gauge Haiti's progress under Aristide. This year's Carnival has been beset by a cash shortage because of a boycott by businessmen who supported past military dictatorships. . . . [One businessman who wished to remain anonymous commented that Aristide] "agreed to impose a three year embargo on us, all the promises of investment and aid have produced nothing so far, so now we are going to impose an embargo on the Carnival."

The Carnival's budget, initially set at $3 million by [the culture minister], was slashed to $850,000. [The suburbs of] Petionville and Delmas said they were too broke to contribute. All Haiti is broke. "We are going to try to do the best we can with the little we have," said [Port-au-Prince mayor Evans Paul].

On Sunday, a group of musicians got a whole streetful of people singing "Deposez, Deposez, Deposez!" When asked what they wanted deposed, a bystander answered, "The military of course—the soldiers." Even though the army is abolished, "we still fear the soldiers. They are still a threat."[39]

11.15 Pig Carnival masquerader. Jacmel. *Photograph by Phyllis Galembo, 1997.*

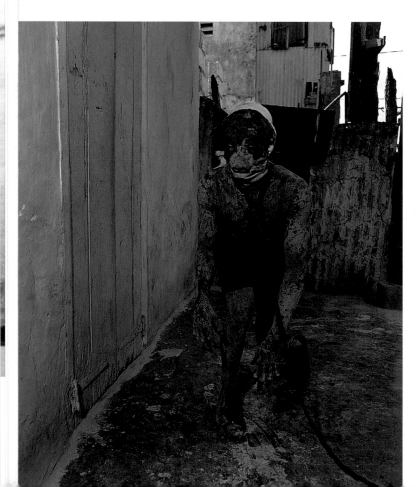

The *Miami Herald* got the look of this Carnival right. The Champs Mars, where the reviewing stands were set up, was all spruced up. A battery of rooster heads was perched on a pyramid across from the presidential palace. At the roundabout stood a billboard plastered with Titid's smiling face next to the legend "Li Tounen"—he's back! (fig. 11.17). Enormous papier-mâché statues of an Indian *cacique,* a Vodou daughter of Ogou, and Papa Gede, eternal king of Carnival, loomed over everyone (fig. 11.18). The look was good, but where was the energy? Movement around the Champs Mars felt more like a mall crawl than a samba. Everyone seemed tentative, not knowing what would happen next. Satire had died. No "Yo sezi," no "Pale, Pale." No looney Lafontants or marauding Macoutes. No raging *zozos,* just the nicely sheathed ones on the Pante condom poster boys. There was live TV coverage, but video splices of bands such as Ram were more

11.16 Alligator Carnival masqueraders. Jacmel. *Photograph by Phyllis Galembo, 1997.*

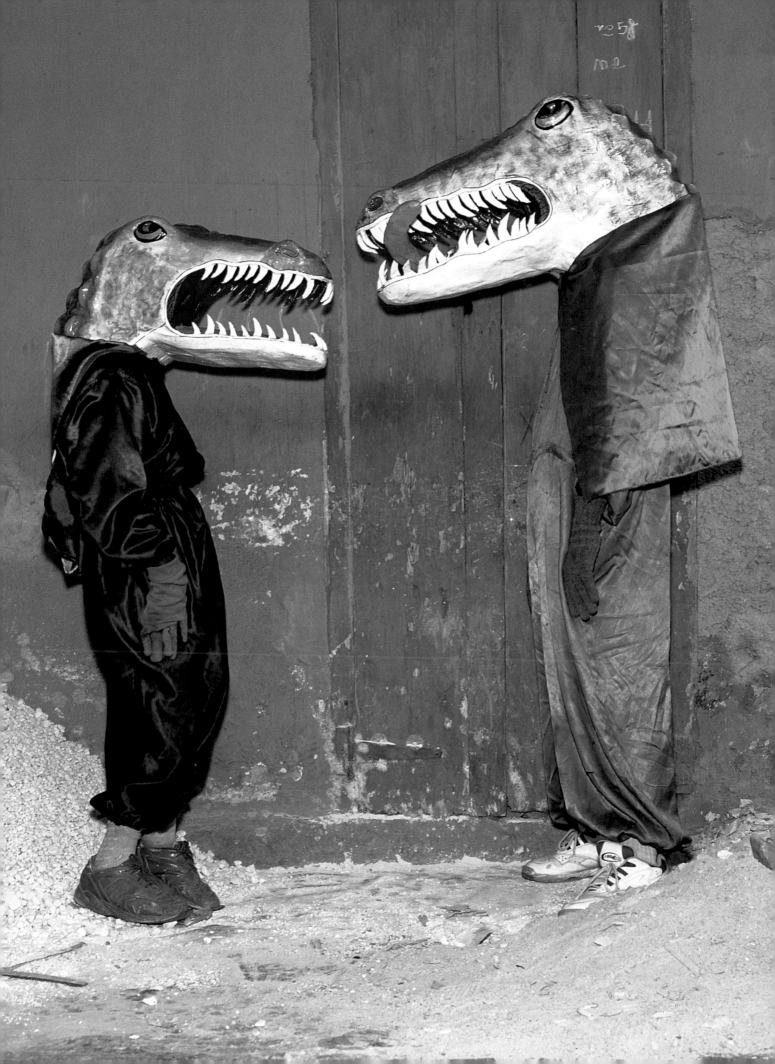

interesting than the live crowd shots. Watching TV, however, was still better than standing on the roof of the Holiday Inn looking down at the listless crowds where four years earlier all those triumphant roosters had strutted.

Why was this Port-au-Prince Carnival a dud? Was the tedium on the streets proof of Prince Hal's priggish warning:

> If all the year were playing holidays
> To sport would be as tedious as to work;
> But when they seldom come, they wish'd for come,
> And nothing pleaseth but rare accidents.
> (Shakespeare, *Henry IV,* Part 1)

The whiff of insurrection that gave such frisson to 1991 had been replaced by a kind of weary triumphal-

11.17 Billboard welcoming back President "Miracle." Port-au-Prince. *Photograph by Donald Cosentino, 1995.*

ism. Perhaps it is the genius of Carnival to overturn, not to rule. Or perhaps the requisite manic energy had been hijacked by another and more authentic Carnival that paraded down the Rue John Brown every day. I am speaking of the American soldiers, so much larger than any Haitians in their Star Wars uniforms, larded with weaponry and see-in-the-dark magic glasses. Crowds came out to watch the American tanks rumble down the potholed main drag, their tonnage rattling the old wooden Kreyol cottages. They looked for all the world like an invading army from the planet Neptune. I know not what security the United States' annual $300 billion or $400 billion defense budget buys, but it certainly produces one of the most enthralling shows on earth. It was the "immaculate invasion" that street urchins now pantomimed in discarded uniforms (fig. 11.19) or re-created in military toys made from GI trash.[40] In 1995, it was the American military display that produced the true festival of reversals.

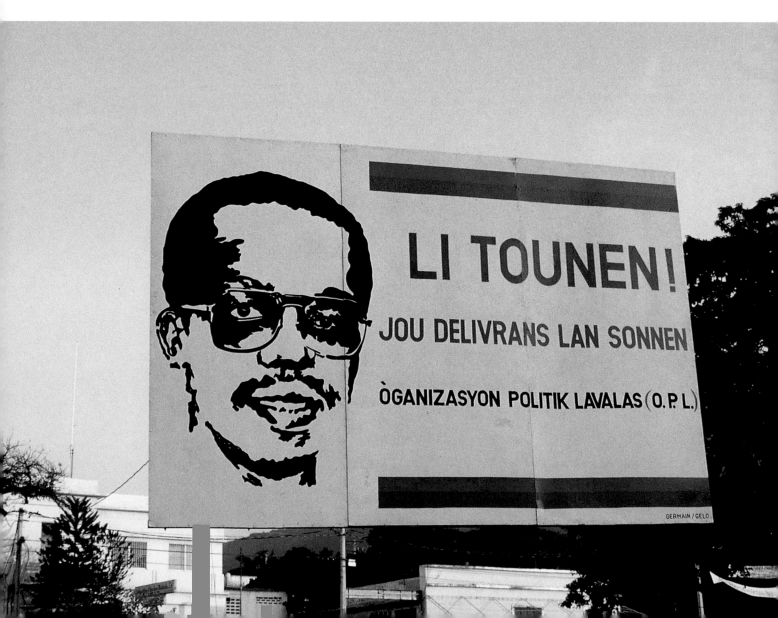

LI TOUNEN !

JOU DELIVRANS LAN SONNEN

ÒGANIZASYON POLITIK LAVALAS (O.P.L.)

GERMAIN/GELO.

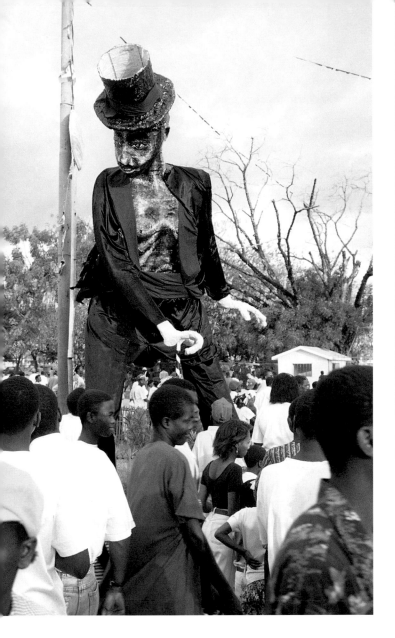

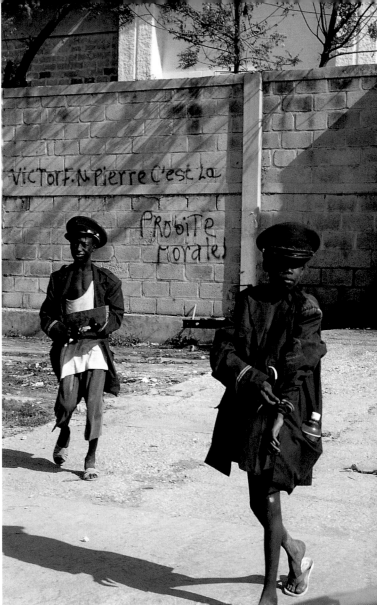

11.18 A giant papier-mâché figure of Gede at the Carnival of Hope. Port-au-Prince. *Photograph by Donald Cosentino, 1995.*

11.19 Street urchins pantomime U.S. soldiers during Carnival. Port-au-Prince. *Photograph by Donald Cosentino, 1995.*

Heading South

To catch the manic invention that has marked Haitian Carnival since colonial times, it was necessary to get out of the capital and head south to Jacmel. That harrowing trip up and over the Haitian Alps, fording three rivers whose bridges had been washed away, was also a journey backward in time to the ancient days of "piss and squat": Rabelais's Carnival captured and reinvented by Africa. Little troupes in costume wandered up and down the steep cobbled streets. Black-hooded contortionists in greasepaint twisted and wiggled around parallel bars as if their bodies had no bones (fig. 11.20). *Bakas,* those were-creatures from the Hait-

ian imaginary, swarmed everywhere, looking as if they had emerged right out of Zépherin's painting (see figs. 11.1, 11.15, 11.16).

Devils with flapping wings also swarmed, some with wings painted red, white, and blue in honor of the GIs stationed in town (fig. 11.21). Saints, kings, and patriarchs made the show, too: the archangel Michael (fig. 11.22), the Zulu king, dotted with Kongo *pwen* (fig. 11.23), Taino *caciques* (fig. 11.24), and Papa Jwif, the wandering Jew, sometimes called Patriarch Jerusalem, Ezekial, or Hezekiah (fig. 11.25). There was little in this last masquerader's costume—the black bishop's mitre with Masonic insignia, the golden cloak, the *egungun* stockings—to identify him with the eponymous character from European legend. But when I asked why he was charging crazily at the crowd, I was told, "He's acting demented because he's a Christ killer." How easily these ideas were transferred from Europe to the circumference of the Black Atlantic, where Jews are known only in Carnival transformation.[41]

From the balcony of the Dome Café, one looked down upon a Carnival world. Everyone swayed to the sounds of the trumpet and the drum and to the low moans of the *vaccine,* a wind instrument often played during Carnival and Rara. There was no division between the holiday crowds in finery—or fine bodies—and the beasts and heroes of the Carnival imaginary. A terrified old hag is dragged from the Iron Market by masquerade *bakas,* a fool forced to parade before the laughing people. You wince. You laugh. Very Victor Hugo. Very *egungun.*[42] And then the *chaloskas* and their bagman show up: monsters with huge red lips and great buck teeth, chasing each other and the laughing crowds with big waving sticks (fig. 11.26).

I first saw *chaloskas* in Jonathan Demme's film *Haiti Dreams of Democracy.* He caught them performing at the 1987 Jacmel Carnival. The *chaloskas* all wore

the usual mad military gear, said to be a mockery of the nineteenth-century general Charles Oscar, though their satire was clearly contemporary. Marching in a half-assed goose-step, they sang, "There are no Macoutes here," indicating precisely the opposite. The honcho *chaloska* then pulled out a notebook and barked at his idiot troops:

"You are accused of telling the truth!"
And they brayed back through their big buck teeth,
   like a stand of donkeys:
"Wawawawawawawawa . . ."
And the general shouted,
"You are accused of not kissing our ass!"
To which they replied, "Wawawawawawawawa . . ."[43]

It was easy to see that these new *chaloska* recruits were send-ups of the recently deposed junta. But if considered a little deeper, who else was it donning

11.20 Black-hooded contortionists twist and wiggle as if their bodies had no bones. Jacmel. *Photograph by Donald Cosentino, 1995.*

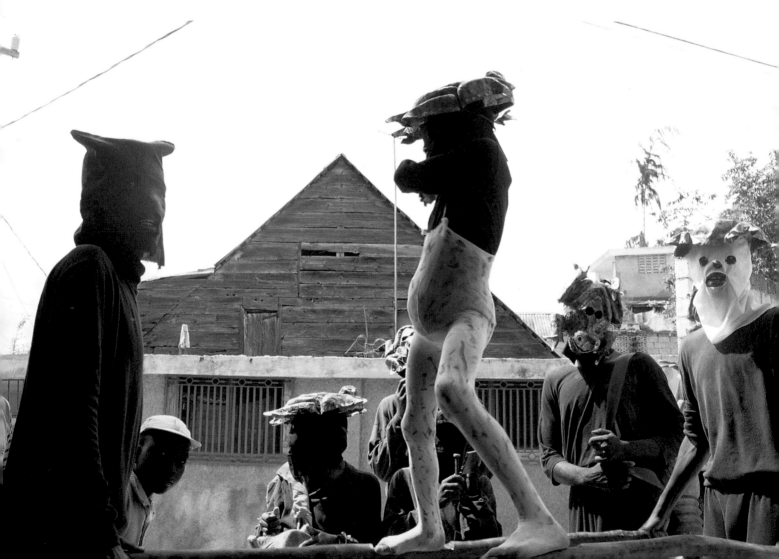

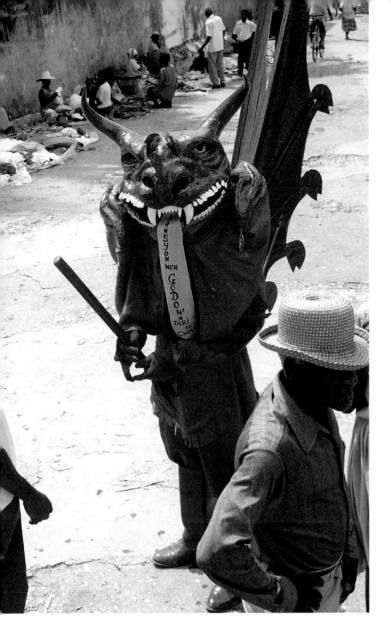

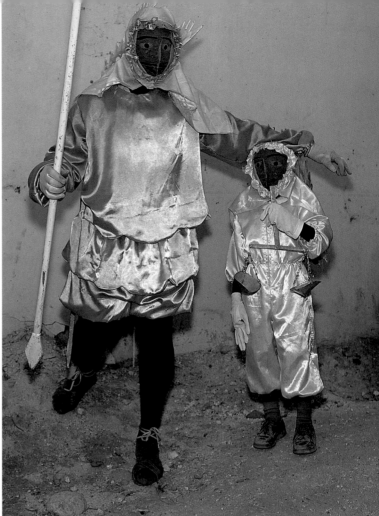

11.22 Carnival masqueraders dressed as the archangel Michael and his sidekick Justice, holding her scales. Jacmel. *Photograph by Phyllis Galembo, 1998.*

11.21 Young men masquerading as devils with flapping wings parade about town. Jacmel. *Photograph by Donald Cosentino, 1995.*

those crazy Sergeant Pepper military outfits but the Gede boys? I had seen a similar lineup of idiot Gedes in November 1987 at one of Baby Doc's favorite Vodou temples, where the great American dancer Katherine Dunham had been initiated as a Vodou priestess. Holding his phallic cane like a baton, the Bawon Samdi was leading his Gedes through a martial display, pausing every few steps to execute a bump and grind. The brass band hired for the ceremony was playing *Jingle Bells*. The audience upstairs was shouting "Zozo, zozo, zozo."[44]

But in this hard year of a hard Carnival, poor old Papa Gede had grown pretty limp. Indeed, his Jacmel supporters were carting him down the street in a wheelbarrow. An intravenous bag was attached to his arm, and he was attended by a battery of transvestite nurses. "Papa HIV," they called him with mock sorrow. The metaphor was almost too perfect. Gede on his last legs—like Haiti? The country (though not its people) shabby and diseased, but still rolling along. And singing, like Porgy, "O Lord, I'm on my way, I'm on my way to a heavenly land." Of course there was nothing so melancholy about Papa HIV. He was hilarious. Everyone knew his dying body sported an erect penis. That's why the god of death is patron of this steamy eruption of life. After every disaster he's still there. Each Carnival is his whistling in the dark. Laughing at the bogeymen. If you laugh, they will run away.

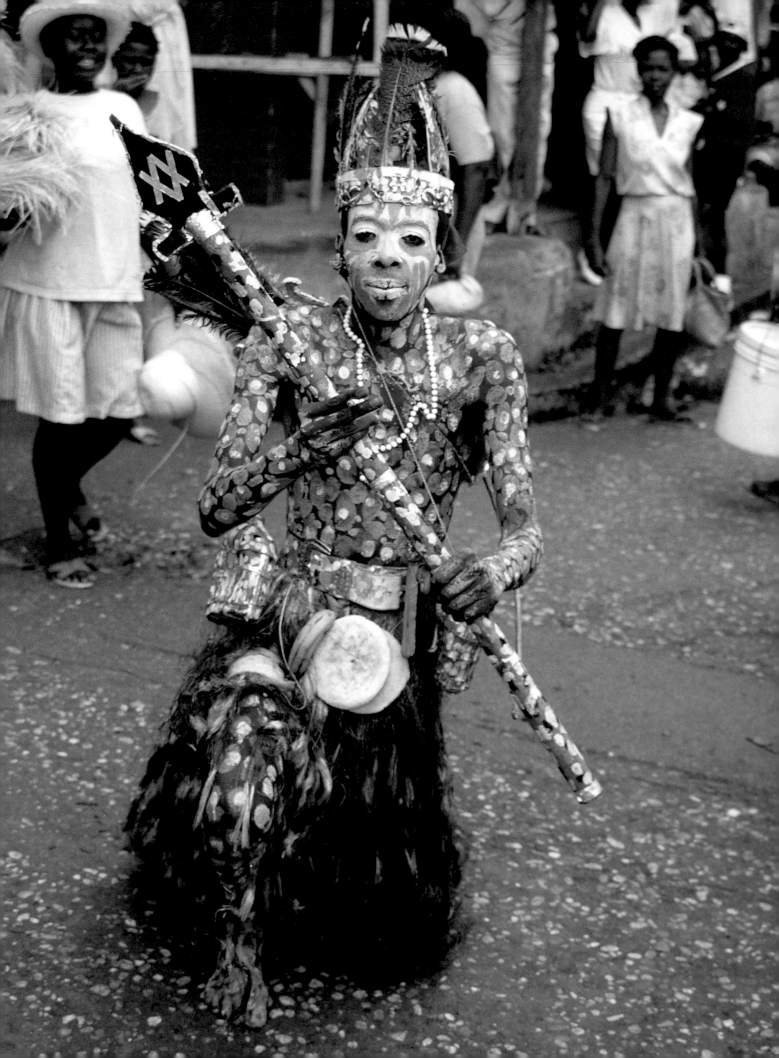

Postscript: Aristide's Last Carnival?

LOS ANGELES TIMES, SUNDAY,
MARCH 3, 2002, PORT-AU-PRINCE

Haitians were still dancing in the streets at the end of this year's Mardi Gras. But the moves were not lascivious, as they had been a week earlier. By Fat Tuesday, the dancing in this capital city was aggressive, furiously spirited, near riotous. . . . Port-au-Prince has become a tinderbox, with growing tensions between Aristide supporters and detractors. . . . A European diplomat warned, "Once the good cheer of Carnival wears off, we're expecting trouble." As a Haitian intellectual [warned], "The future holds more isolation for the country. And we are again part of a *mad dream*."[45]

NOTES

I thank the Academic Senate of the University of California, Los Angeles, for research funds that enabled me to travel to Haiti to participate in the Carnivals of 1991 and 1995. I also thank Phyllis Galembo, Marilyn Houlberg, and the UCLA Fowler Museum of Cultural History for permission to use their photographs, and Gage Averill, Liza McAlister, and Ady Jeangardy for their inspiring research on Carnival in Haiti. Most especially, I thank Papa Gede, my mentor and patron, for dancing me through Kalfou Danjere. Mesi mét tét.

1. The band Boukman Eksperyans identifies its inspiration and aspirations by naming itself after the Vodou priest Boukman Dutty, who exorted his fellow slaves to arise and destroy their oppressors ("Burn their houses! Cut off their heads!") at the legendary Bois Caiman ceremony that began the Haitian Revolution in 1791. See Sidney Mintz and Michel-Rolph Trouillot, "The Social History of Haitian Vodou," in *The Sacred Arts of Haitian Vodou,* ed. Donald Cosentino (Los Angeles: UCLA Fowler Museum, 1995), 138.

2. Averill transcribes the lyrics first in Kreyol: *Ke'm pa sote wo, ke'm pa sote wo / Ke'm pa sote ane sa / Boukman nan kanaval, ke'm pa sote wo / Avanse pa frape nan bann lan.* This

11.23 Zulu king masquerader dotted with Kongo *pwen.* Jacmel. *Photograph by Donald Cosentino, 1995.*

11.24 Taino chiefs, or *caciques,* live again in Carnival masquerades. Jacmel. *Photograph by Donald Cosentino, 1995.*

11.25 The "wandering Jew" Carnival masquerade. Jacmel. *Photograph by Donald Cosentino, 1995.*

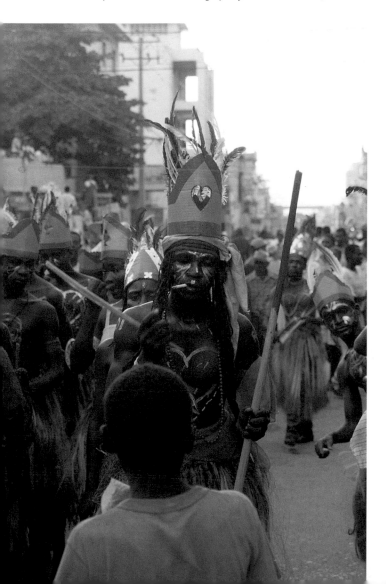

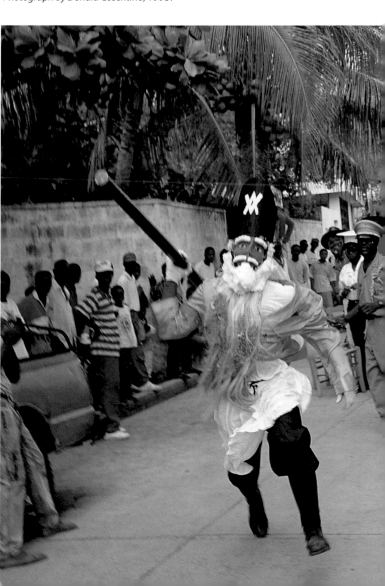

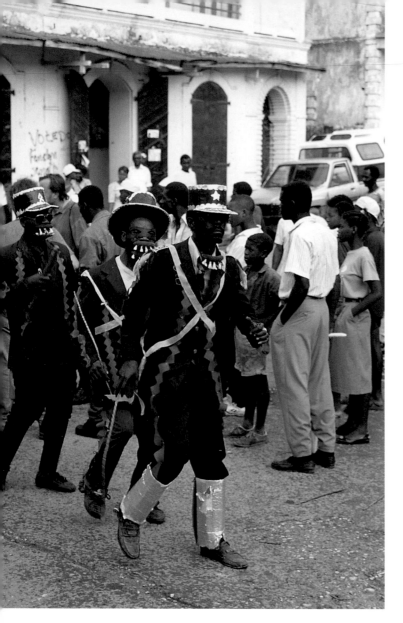

11.26 *Chaloska* Carnival masqueraders on the move. Jacmel. *Photograph by Donald Cosentino, 1995.*

transcription and much of the argument about this song's significance are borrowed from a masterful work on popular music and power in Haiti, Gage Averill's *A Day for the Hunter, a Day for the Prey* (Chicago: University of Chicago Press, 1997), 181–182.

3. Ibid., 238. The term is analogous to the Vodou term *voye pwen* (sending a point), meaning to cast a magic spell or place a charm against someone.

4. The irony is that while "K'em pa Sote" was inspiring revolution in Haiti, it was the main track on Boukman Ekspeyans' world beat hit album *Vodou Ajaye,* entertaining audiences who could appreciate its intoxicating rhythms but not its incendiary lyrics. It seems to be the fate of Haitian culture to produce tropes for other people's worlds.

5. Elizabeth McAlister, *Rara: Vodou, Power, and Performance*

in Haiti and Its Diaspora (Berkeley: University of California Press, 2002), 147–148.

6. Richard E. Burton, *Afro-Creole: Power, Opposition, and Play in the Caribbean* (Ithaca, NY: Cornell University Press, 1997), 156–157.

7. Ibid., 263–264.

8. Averill, *A Day for the Hunter,* 154.

9. "Gilded Negro" was a term Napolean used to describe Toussaint-Louverture, whom he subsequently tricked into imprisonment and caused to die of exposure in a Jura prison cell. For a description of Napoleon's treatment of Toussaint, see Wenda Parkinson, *"This Gilded African": Toussaint L'Ouverture* (London: Quartet Books, 1980), 179–207.

10. Christophe went on to create his own parodic nobility, including the Dukes of Marmalade and Limonade. See Hubert Cole, *Christophe, King of Haiti* (New York: Viking, 1967), 225.

11. See Donald Cosentino, "Titid Mon Amour: *Lwas* and Saints in the Haitian Heart," *The World and I* (October 1991): 616–625; Donald Cosentino, "Returning the Dead," *The World and I* (October 1994): 223–243.

12. Robert Farris Thompson, *Flash of the Spirit: African and Afro-American Art and Philosophy* (New York: Random House, 1983), 191. *Coumbites* are cooperative workforces and therefore an appropriate symbol of peasant fraternity.

13. The outline and details of this history are appropriated from Ady Jeangardy, "Carnaval Historie," *Sourire* 1, no. 3 (February 1995): 18–39. This Port-au-Prince magazine served as an unofficial program for Kanaval Lespwa, where I picked it up, and may no longer be available in archives.

14. Ibid., 18.

15. Ibid., 39.

16. Ibid., 32.

17. Ibid., 37–38.

18. *Divine Horsemen, The Living Gods of Haiti,* edited by Seiji and Cheryl Ito.

19. Averill, *A Day for the Hunter,* 154–160.

20. Ibid., 157.

21. *Tout Fanm se lougawou / Men pa devan Ti Maryann o / Li gen dwet long / E renmen kob.* "Although many of the Carnival songs of the period were never recorded, they were collected by Yves Robert Louis and printed by journalist Jean Fragat in an article in Haiti-Observateur" (Averill, *A Day for the Hunter,* 155).

22. *Yereswa, mwen rev yon bourik kap souse yon piwouli.* See Averill, *A Day for the Hunter,* 157.

23. I picked up these photocopies on the streets of Port-au-Prince in the spring of 1986. It is tempting to see these broadsheets as derivative from the earlier tradition of Lamayot, which so salaciously (and effectively) undermined "Lulu" Borno (among others).

24. Personal observation by the author.

25. Much of this description of the 1991 Carnival was published in Donald Cosentino, "Vodou Carnival," *Aperture* 126 (Winter 1992): 22–29.

26. Personal observation by the author.

27. McAlister, *Rara,* 59.

28. Ibid., 60–61.

29. Haitians are amused by Americans' fascination with

zombies, who play a small role in Haitian folklore but a major role in Hollywood's "voodoo" imaginary. The movie version of Wade Davis's best-selling zombie biography, *The Serpent and the Rainbow,* was playing to good houses at the Rex Theatre in Port-au-Prince the first time I visited in 1986. Herard Simon, the Vodou strongman who allegedly sold Davis the secret "zombie medicine," laughed as he told me, "We sold [Davis] the plans for the B-25, but we've kept the F1–11 secret."

30. McAlister, *Rara,* 95; Laennec Hurbon, "American Fantasy and Haitian Vodou," in Cosentino, *Sacred Arts of Haitian Vodou,* 194–197.

31. See especially Melville J. Herskovits and Frances S. Herskovits, *Dahomean Narrative: A Cross-Cultural Analysis* (Evanston, IL: Northwestern University Press, 1958), 125–126. "Legba manifested in the body of a young girl dressed in purple. When she reached the drummer, she put her hand under the fringe of raffia about her waist and brought out a wooden phallus, attached [so as to] remain horizontal [like] the erect male organ, and as she danced toward a large tree where many women were sitting, they ran away from her, shrieking with laughter."

32. McAlister recorded a sacrilegious variant of this song and offered an explication of its blasphemous humor: "All the sexual songs . . . implicitly satirize Catholicism, but the connection can be made explicity when a crowd sings a Catholic prayer song and follows it with a song about sex. The following song is particularly blasphemous [because it suggests] that the Virgin Mother has AIDS.

> Our Lady of Perpetual Help
> Watch over your children
> Our Lady of Perpetual Help
> Pray for us always
> If I fuck her I'll get AIDS
> Your Mama's clit.

This is a 'straight' French hymn until it delivers its ridiculous punch line in Kreyol. Just as 'straight' Catholics depend on Vodou as an oppositional evil, so too does the [betiz] depend on Catholic [and more recently, Protestant] decorum for its humor" (McAlister, *Rara,* 63).

33. Henry Drewal and Margaret Thompson Drewal, *Gelede* (Bloomington: Indiana University Press, 1983), 1–16.

34. Lyrics were collected, transcribed, and translated by the author.

35. Cosentino, "Returning the Dead," 229–230.

36. McAlister, *Rara,* 93.

37. Ibid., 73.

38. The painting was commissioned by the UCLA Fowler Museum for the traveling exhibition *The Sacred Arts of Haitian Vodou* (1995–1999). It appeared in the Fowler exhibition catalogue and as the cover art for the book by Bob Shacochis, *The Immaculate Invasion* (New York: Viking, 1999), which describes the problematic 1994 invasion.

39. Herald Wire Services, "Haitians Celebrate in 'Carnival of Hope,'" *Miami Herald* (February 28, 1995): 3A.

40. For an excellent description of the wall art inspired by the American invasion, see Karen McCarthy Brown, "Art and Resistance: Haiti's Political Murals, October 1994," *African Arts* 29, no. 2 (1996): 46–59.

41. For instance, Nigerian secondary school students have told me they thought Jews had tails. McAlister, *Rara,* 130, traces parallel developments of this figure in Haitian folklore: "'The Jews' are a stock figure in Haitian popular culture, inherited in the process of Catholic European missionizing that was part and parcel of the Latin American plantation enterprise. A figure used at once as a scapegoat and mystical forebear, 'the Jew' can also be a comedian who speaks the unspeakable. He shows up in Carnival as Papa Jwif, a wandering Jew who delivers satirical political commentary or enacts problematic issues in the community. In Port-au-Prince during the coup that ousted President Aristide, Papa Jwif was both a signal of the AIDS pandemic and a symbol of the corrupt military rulers, diseased beyond redemption. Here the 'Jew' was a Carnival character dying of AIDS. He was surrounded by an entourage of doctors perpetually treating him with useless remedies, coded as U.S. political forces propping up a violent and corrupt regime."

42. *Egungun* is the Yoruba word for both ancestor and ancestral masquerade. Kreyol uses the word *Nago* to refer to the Yoruba and indeed to a whole style of ritual performance signified by Nago costumes in Rara and Carnival.

43. Jonathan Demme, director, *Haiti Dreams of Democracy* (Clinica Estetico, 1987).

44. A couple of weeks later and a few blocks away from Gesner's temple, the Macoutes would massacre twenty Haitians waiting to vote in what would be an aborted election. It seems that Baron and the Gedes were being premonitory in the mockery.

45. J. Slavin, "As Aristide's Support Ebbs, Tensions Grow," *Los Angeles Times* (March 3, 2002): M3.

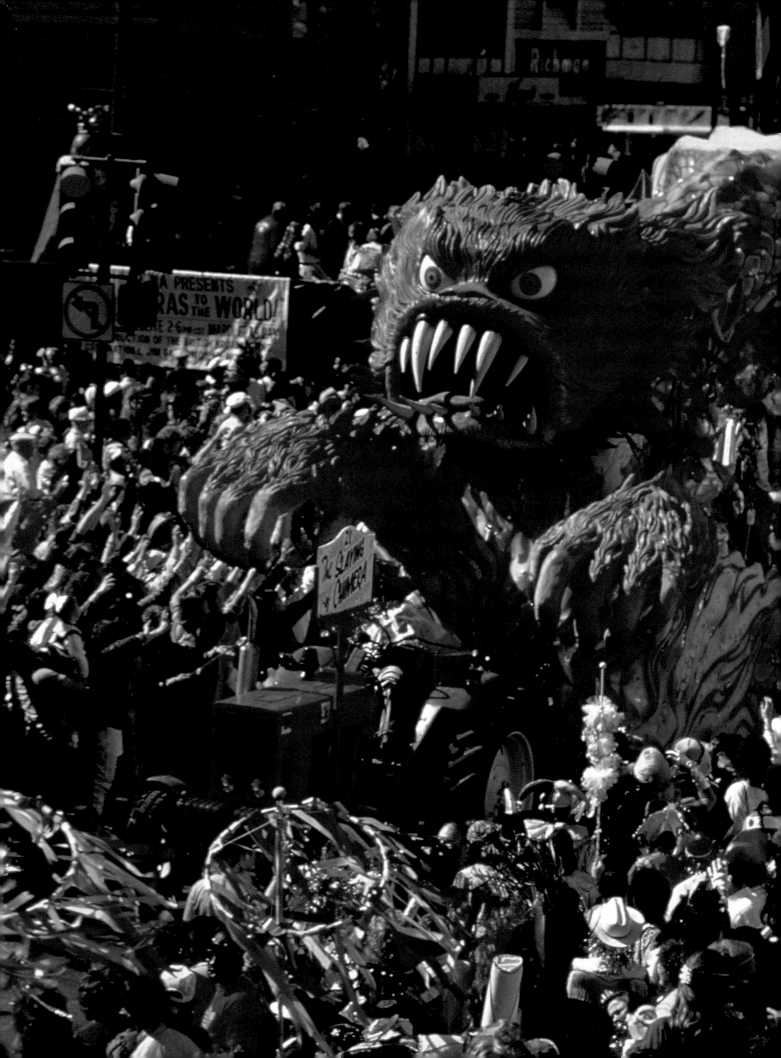

12 Mardi Gras in New Orleans, USA

ANNALS OF A QUEEN

JASON BERRY

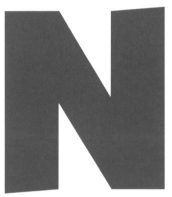

NEW ORLEANS IS A haughty dowager, laughing at the ravages of time. With beauty and decay rubbing cheek to jowl, she reigns as Queen City of the South, all the region's dreams and maddened sins fused into a single urban place. Shabby and seductive, she orders another round of drinks, commanding the band to play on while all around her disasters swell—hurricanes, floods, crime, viral mosquitoes, sinking soil, cracked streets, politicians stalking the money meat.

Who could possibly keep up with her? That's what those dead men think. And they should know: so many spouses and lovers, farmed out in scattered cemeteries, all those reformers who would make of her some display of progress.

The population is 62 percent African American, of whom nearly half live in poverty. Nightly TV news is a show about urban homicide. The collapse of public education is so severe that certain members of the civic aristocracy are trying to rescue the city from the depredations of race and class bequeathed by indolent patricians of yesteryear. Here is a city, teeming with cultural wealth, saddled by Third World sorrows sufficient to drive off businesses that might relocate there. And so we slog along, citizens all, dodging the bullets and street lakes left by monsoon rains that in the worst of summer make the town seem like a steaming halfway house caught between the inferno and purgatory. But then October comes, cool and sweet . . .

Above all the Queen City is a mythic place, her memory a spectacle in perpetuity, a baroque drama of Latin mores grafted onto this postage stamp at the bottom of America. People lean on balconies of floral iron grillwork to cheer the street dancers as they course along, swept by tides of African memory. Mardi Gras is a ritual theater at this crossroads of humanity. The late Marcus Christian, a poet and Creole of color, captured the urban character in a 1968 poem, "I Am New Orleans," celebrating the 250th anniversary of the city's founding:

> I am America epitomized
> A blending of everything—
> Latin, Nordic and Negro
> Indian, European and American . . .
>
> Out of the swamps of Louisiana,
> Out of the blue mud and sand of the Delta,
> Out of hurricanes, storms and crevasses,

12.1 A Krewe of Rex "monster" float brings cheers from spectators on the street. *Photograph by Syndey Byrd, 1988.*

Out of Indian massacres and slave insurrections;
Phoenix-like have I risen;
Out of French, Spanish and American dominations
I have preserved my soul . . .[1]

Spirit Tides

Mardi Gras draws deeply from the city's quaking spirituality. Names like Annunciation Street, Conception Street, Religious Street, Mystery Street, Saint Roch Street, and Saint Charles Avenue hint at the spiritual imagination. Sundays hum with a sinuous line of gospel choirs in churches stretched like an accordion across the urban grid, pews shaking, voices soaring to the skies. The prayers in Catholic churches begun each August echo into October: "Our Lady of Prompt Succor, spare us from the hurricanes." In the pews that fill all seasons at the St. Jude Shrine in Our Lady of Guadalupe Church on Rampart Street, novenas are offered to the saint for those in desperate need, the saint to whom the great Grammy-award-winning singer Aaron Neville made solemn prayers during the

12.2 The location of New Orleans and Louisiana in the United States.

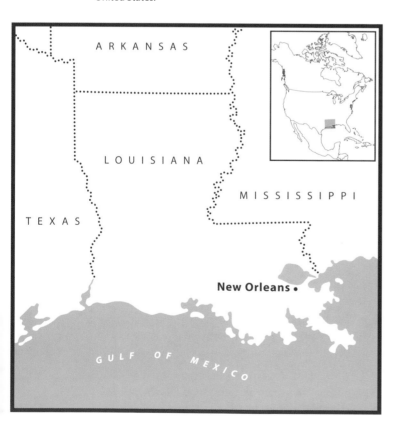

ravages of his smack addiction years ago, "'cuz believe me, Jack, I *was* a hopeless case."[2]

Essences of the sacred and the profane charge Carnival like an electrical current. Hundreds of thousands of people flock to "the annual audition just to be yourself," in the lyrics of A. J. Loria, a peerless lounge lizard.[3]

Carnival season begins at Twelfth Night, January 6, and ends on Shrove Tuesday, the day before Ash Wednesday. The dates are wedded to the Catholic seasonal calendar, in which ancient planting seasons and social rhythms culminated in a great feast to usher in the forty days of Lenten fasting.

How far the winter blowout has come from its earliest days.

Origins

Founded in 1718 by Jean Baptiste Lemoyne, Sieur de Bienville, a Canadian explorer for the French Crown, La Nouvelle-Orleans was laid out on soggy soil in a sub-sea-level bowl bounded by Lake Pontchartrain on the north, the Mississippi River curling around the southern rim like a lock of muddy hair (fig. 12.2). The plantation economy soon faltered, and landowners could not generate enough food to feed the enslaved Africans who worked their holdings. The rulers allowed slaves to trade food they grew, hides or meat they hunted, and vegetables and fruit they cultivated at a makeshift Sunday marketplace on the grassy public commons behind the ramparts of the town. The place became known as Place du Congo, or the Congo plains. Today, a portion of the area is contained in Louis Armstrong Park along Rampart Street, just outside the French Quarter.

Poor as it was, the port town was pervaded by a French idea of life's finer things. The second provincial governor, the Marquis de Vaudreil, "may have seen himself as a surrogate king, perhaps a king in his own right," wrote Errol Laborde. Vaudreil tried to "duplicate the grandeur" of Versailles under Louis XIV, with elegant balls and "dinners served on plates of gold."[4]

Carnival began more as a closed operation than as a public festival. Balls in the houses and halls of the wealthy were attended by enslaved servants, but on Sunday afternoons at the Place du Congo market, a tradition of public dancing mushroomed. As many as five hundred dancers at a time formed concentric rings, moving in counterclockwise circles, their hand-clapping and feet-shuffling forming cross rhythms to music made on conga drums, tom-toms, panpipes, and calabashes. Here was the African instrumental family replanted; nowhere else on North American soil did the force of African music sustain such a long history as in New Orleans.[5]

Remnants of the Choctaw Indians who lived in the cypress woods girding the area watched the dancers as the tradition surged into the nineteenth century. Costuming was fundamental to African ritual. Mask making as a specific tribal custom was lost in the Middle Passage, but the idea of mask-and-dance in a spiritual continuum lived on in a city where gentry flocked to see the exotic spectacles. Nowhere else in the South were slaves given such freedom of expression in music and dance. The Africans sometimes dressed as Indians, "ornamented with a number of tails of the smaller wild beasts," wearing "fringes, ribbons, little bells, and shells and balls, jingling and flirting about the performers' legs and arms."[6]

Here was the process of creolization, a melding of cultural identities as strands of cultural material fused into a synthesis of something new, much as the famous Creole cuisine formed in a melting pot of ethnic traditions.

The Spaniards found Louisiana a bad bargain and returned it to the French. In 1803, Napoleon sold the territory to the Americans in the best real estate deal of US history, the Louisiana Purchase. As the colony became a state, the *bal masques* of the aristocracy continued; so did the slave dances in the park, which became known as Congo Square, until the curtain lowered on the antebellum era.

The patrician love of masked balls and the high place of costumery in the danced religions of the African ritual psyche spilled into the streets as Carnival traditions unfolded. "Men and boys, women and girls, bond and free, black and white, exert themselves to invent and appear in grotesque, quizzical, diabolical, horrible, strange masks and disguises," reflected a visitor at the 1835 celebration. "Human bodies are seen with heads of beasts and birds, beasts and birds with human heads; demi-beasts, demi-fishes, snakes' heads and bodies with arms of apes; man-bats from the moon; mermaids; satyrs, beggars, monks and robbers parade and march on foot, on horseback, in wagons,

carts, coaches ... in rich profusion up and down the streets, wildly shouting, singing, laughing, drumming, fiddling, fifeing ... as they wend their reckless way."[7]

Beginning of the Krewes

The Mistick Krewe of Comus, formed in 1857, gave Mardi Gras its formal patina. People wearing costumes and parading in streets had been around for years when along came Comus, a group of elite young white men, only one of whom had a French surname. They were products not of the clannish white Creole aristocracy but rather of the arriviste Anglo-Americans. This was the first group to form an elite and secretive men's society, which came to be known as a krewe. "Their lavish balls could be attended only by those fortunate enough to have received invitations, but their processions of floats, lights, and music could be viewed by anyone who cared to, and vast crowds lined the city's streets," observes the artist and Mardi Gras chronicler Henri Schindler. "What they saw during this Golden Age was ebullient public art of the highest rank."[8]

As police protection accompanied the evolution of a parade aristocracy, late-nineteenth-century Mardi Gras drew a more benign inspiration from Parisian artists who produced beautiful invitations; the few artifacts of the masked tableaux suggest costumed performances on a large scale. Float designs were steeped in themes of antiquity and Renaissance drama. With the artistry of early Carnival rose the aspirations of a former slaveholding class that wedded its economic recovery to an idea of neoclassical glory. Mardi Gras became a time when "deities of forgotten pantheons and the splendors of long-vanished courts are restored for a season, summoned into being from the gilded vaults of the old city's memory."[9]

Within those gilded memory vaults lay an idealization of the slaveholding South that sent many krewe members into the White League and participation in violent attacks on a Reconstruction government supportive of blacks. Comus paraded at night, its way lit by black men carrying flambeaux, heavy poles studded with candles "set off in a blaze of light, flanked by elaborate costumed maskers on foot and bands playing martial music" (fig. 12.3).[10] Black men carrying torches, white men in costume—a cameo of race and class divisions. But is the split all that transparent?

stepped off with the famous General Custer: royalty and a celebrity to boot!

Lewis Salomon, a founder of Rex, borrowed his royal outfit from an actor performing in *Richard III*. Wardrobe for his dukes came from the Varieties Theatre. With flags and lamps and floral displays lining the route, Rex members sashayed along in outfits designed to make them look like Chinamen, clowns, monkey, devils, Indians, blacks, women, birds, and beasts. "Nobody thought, in the early days, to turn up his or her nose at the commercialization of Mardi Gras," writes James Gill. He adds:

The first Rex parade included advertising vans touting the Gem Saloon, Warner's Bitters, Singer Sewing Machines, Mme. Tigau's Elixir for Ladies, Carter's Mucilage, Leighton's Premium Shirts, the Old Reliable Furniture Company and Dr. Tichenor's Antiseptic, among others. Rex subsequently appeared in newspaper advertisements announcing that he dined at Mme. Begue's restaurant, drank at the St. Charles Hotel, and bought his comestibles at Chick Lalande's in the French Market and his hats from the Robert E. Lee store.[11]

As the parade came together with horse-drawn wagons and streams of masked marchers, gossip percolated that the Grand Duke was enamored of a young woman singer in a burlesque musical, *Bluebird*. The stories were not true, though in a long foreshadowing of another century's celebrity culture, the belief in a nobleman smitten by a woman of the stage made him all the more popular, thanks to the press buildup. A local music teacher organizing music for the parade set a ditty from the show, "If Ever I Cease to Love," in march time, with new lines as a tweak to the Grand Duke. The song became the theme of the Rex ball.[12]

Another parade krewe began in 1872, the Knights of Momus, whose members came from well-heeled backgrounds. The aristocracy continued its merriment with the founding of the Phunny Phorty Phellows in 1878 and the Krewe of Proteus in 1882.[13]

Of the old-line aristocracy, the four major krewes are Comus, Rex, Momus, and Proteus, many of whose members today trace family lines through the organizations back a century or more.

Comus's parade of 1873, entitled "The Missing Links to Darwin's Origins of the Species," was a satirical attack on the North. Louisiana's Reconstruction governor, Henry Clay Warmoth, was depicted by a masker

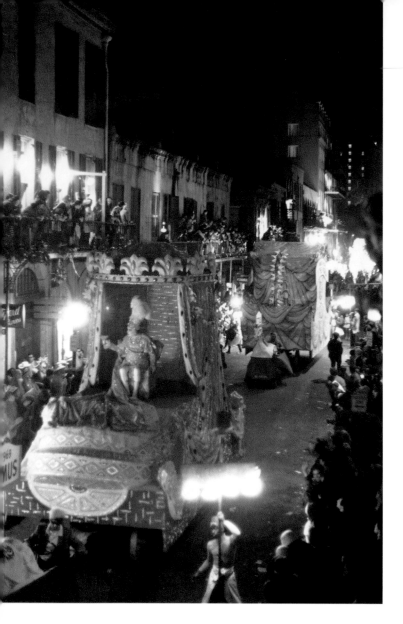

12.3 In 1969, the Krewe of Comus was still parading in the French Quarter as black men carried flaming torches to light the way. *Photograph by Michael P. Smith.*

Mardi Gras 1872 saw the first parade of another secret men's society, the Krewe of Rex. This coincided with a visit from a Russian nobleman, the Grand Duke Alexis of Romanoff, who was traveling in the United States. His arrival thrilled the city fathers, who, seven years after the Civil War, wanted to put on a new face for the northern press, sending signals of progress and, though the word was not in use then, tourism. The Grand Duke had been on holiday out west, shooting buffalo with a celebrity called Buffalo Bill and the Indian fighter General George Custer. Indeed, when the riverboat pulled into the port, the Romanoff duke

dressed as a snake. Another masker, dressed as a bloodhound, represented a despised police superintendent. Then, in the costume of a hyena with a silver spoon, paraded a parody of General Benjamin "Beast" Butler, the hated Union occupier.

Harper's Weekly's spectacular illustration of the 1873 Comus ball shows people dressed as insects, frogs, mushrooms, and turtles, a pair of dancing children center-stage with butterfly wings and gray wigs, and, atop the throne with a crown, an apelike figure with Negroid features. The picture is a construction of the ball, a re-creation of mythical figures more than a rendition of people in costumes. The vibrancy and range of characterizations are striking, like those in a painting by Bosch; the ape is a menacing sign of how whites saw the power shift (fig. 12.4).[14]

12.4 *Final Tableaux of the Mystic Krewe of Comus Ball,* 1873. Color print, *Harper's Weekly. Photograph courtesy of Henri Schindler.* The theme for the Comus parade that year was "The Missing Links to Darwin's Origins of the Species"; the costumes featured a variety of animals and insects.

Words of a Flambeau Man

A celebration built on the exaggeration of class differences was bound to spawn satires and parodies among the less advantaged. As the sprawling street crowd found masks and music of its own, Carnival turned into a vast arena of spontaneous theater. The line of krewes continued forming through the *fin de siècle* and parading into the early twentieth century.

Each krewe, then and now, strives to reflect a persona, a style, a tone in the quality of its float design, in the kinds of bands and marching groups that course along between the floats, and in the vitality with which the maskers toss plastic beads, toys, and trinkets to the people in the streets yelling, "Throw me somethin', Mister!" (fig. 12.5).

The throws consist mainly of plastic beads, necklaces, doubloons, and trinkets. Most have little value, save among collectors of doubloons. The thrill lies in catching something free, as if leaves were money. The tradition of maskers on floats tossing gifts to specta-

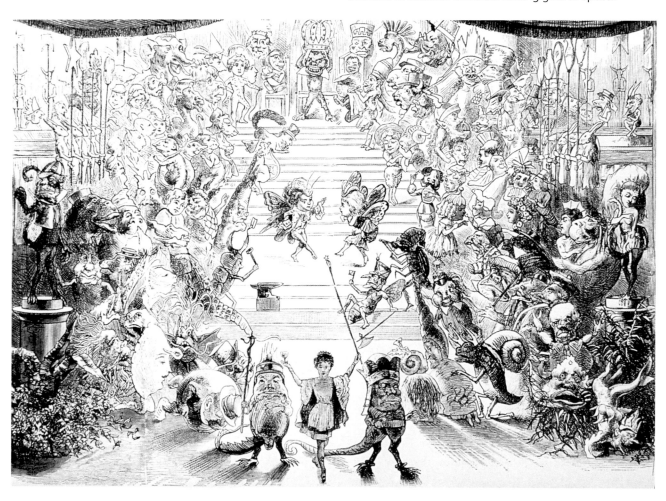

tors can be found in European Carnival as far back as the fifteenth century. Whether or not New Orleans Mardi Gras is a linear extension of such traditions is anybody's guess. In the 1840s, maskers often tossed sugar-coated almonds and candies to people in the streets. The Twelfth Night Revelers held their first parade in New Orleans in 1871. One of the maskers was Santa Claus, who distributed small favors to the crowds.[15]

In 1921, the Rex organization ushered in a new Carnival practice when krewe members began tossing custom necklaces to spectators from their floats. Doubloons came into existence in 1960, the invention of an engraver named H. Alvin Sharpe, who convinced the captain of Rex that his coins were sufficiently lightweight not to hurt anyone and could be customized with the krewe's insignia and motto. In a few short years, all of the parades were tossing doubloons.[16]

12.5 Crowds in the French Quarter beg krewe members riding on floats to throw beads into their eager hands. *Photograph by Syndey Byrd, 1999.*

The night parades roll down tree-shrouded St. Charles Avenue to the beat of the marching bands, suffused in the glow of candle torches hoisted along by black men called flambeau carriers (fig. 12.6). The sight of black men lighting the parade for white men in masks at first blush seems an image borne of Southern racial stereotyping. But in a public drama, each actor plays a role with his own inner logic.

"I've been doing it since I was twelve years old," said flambeau carrier Clarence Holmes, a burly custodian at Charity Hospital, who was forty-seven during the Mardi Gras of 2002. "I got into it from my daddy and my daddy's daddy and my great-grandfather. I'm the fourth generation. Carrying a flambeau is a tradition that somebody enjoys for years. The torches used to have two-burners and four-burners. Now we don't have the old four-burners. They have people making new ones; they're much lighter and use butane. And the smaller ones are kerosene. I toted both kinds, me. I started off toting the small one."

Clarence Holmes continued: "We used to line up on Jackson and Rousseau, and used to go to Municipal

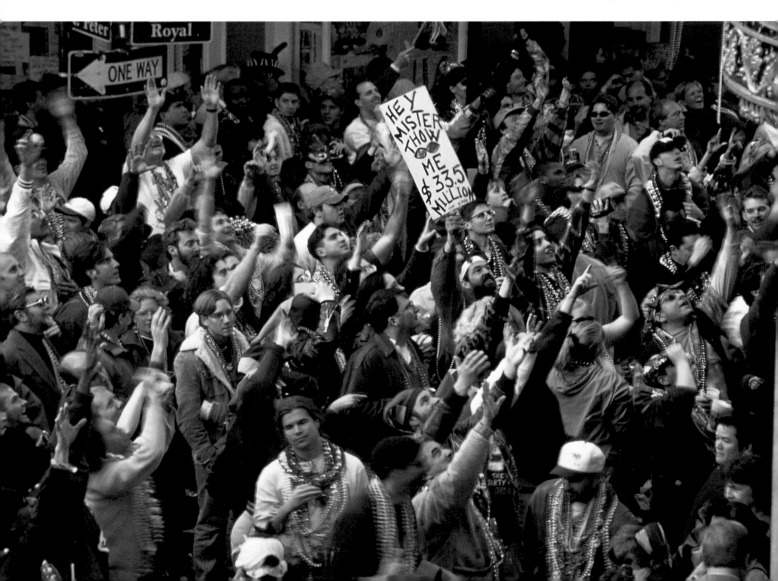

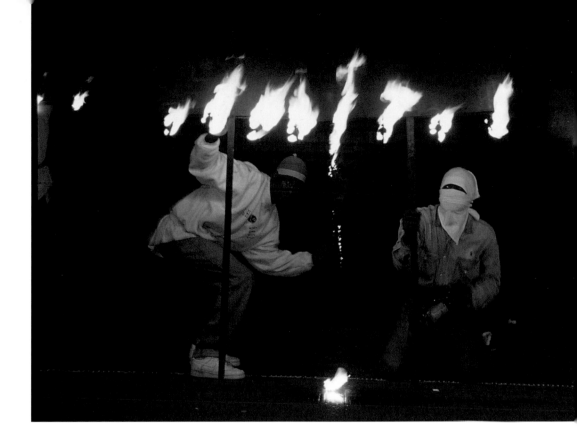

12.6 Flambeau carriers light the way for the krewes' floats in the night-time Mardi Gras parades. *Photograph by Syndey Byrd, 2001.*

Auditorium. When I first started I used to get like five dollars [for each parade march.] They went up to seven, then up to nine. Now they give you between ten and fifteen to tote the small torches. The big ones pay twenty-five and thirty dollars right now. . . . You get extra money from people in the street, throwing money."

What does being a flambeau carrier mean to Clarence Holmes?

"I have people admire me. The *Times-Picayune* has pictures when I used to tote. I'm still doing it cause it's a tradition and I love it. I was a little boy when I started. My wife does it, too, and I can't get her to stop doing it. People done took our picture together, husband and wife. I can't tote if she don't tote. She's been doing it about twelve years now."[17]

Fancy Balls and Newer Krewes

Some Carnival organizations did not parade, but only held balls. In 1930, when the Municipal Auditorium was completed, the winter ball season had a spacious arena, big enough for the colorful tableaux (fig. 12.7). The Elves of Oberon (who do not parade) held the first ball in that new venue. After World War I, the masquerade and fancy dress balls long popular with the middle class began a sharp decline. Costumes are still

worn at music clubs, concerts, and for some balls, but the shift after World War II, especially at the auditorium, looked back toward patterns of the past (figs. 12.8, 12.9, 12.10). As the Carnival savant Henri Schindler writes:

The new balls followed the method and manner of nineteenth-century Carnival. They were strictly private affairs, and admission was by invitation only. Those fortunate enough to receive invitations to any Carnival ball were expected to attend them, and every night brought new crowds dressed in ballgowns, tuxedoes, and tails. Ballgowns were de rigueur, and while men in black tie were admitted into the Auditorium, only those in white tie were allowed on the ballroom floor. These codes were strenuously enforced by all, and the length of a lady's gown became as important to the committeemen of Carnival as to the couturiers of Paris.[18]

As Mardi Gras evolved, the interest in krewes radiated through the middle class and petit bourgeoisie. Storeowners and merchants banded together in neighborhood-based groups such as the Krewes of Carrollton and Freret, whose float riders had businesses along the uptown streets for which the krewes were named, in the vicinity of Tulane and Loyola Universities.

Iris, the krewe that parades along Napoleon

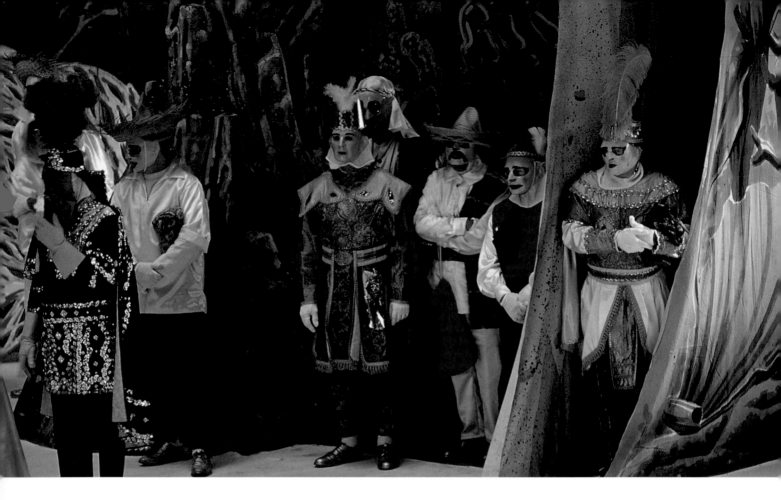

12.7 Masqueraders watch from the side of the stage as a tableaux is enacted at the beginning of the Krewe of Proteus Mardi Gras ball. *Photograph by Syndey Byrd, 1989.*

12.8 The king and queen of the Krewe of Comus make their entrance into the ballroom and welcome the other guests attending the exclusive event. *Photograph by Syndey Byrd, 1991.*

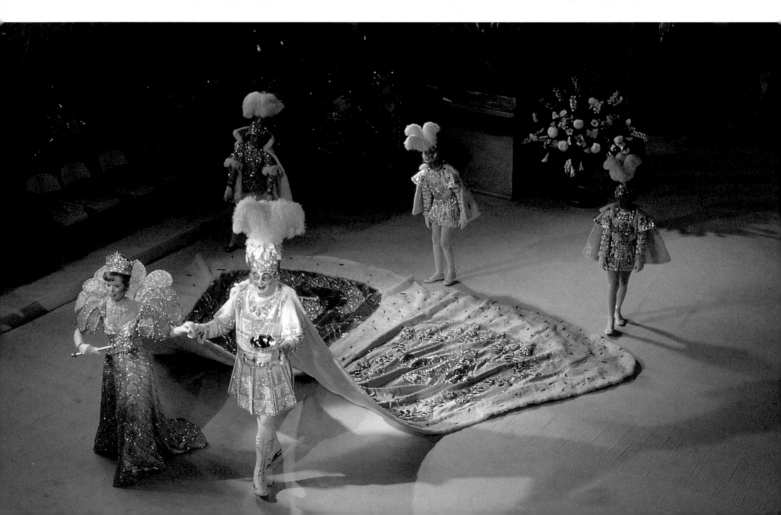

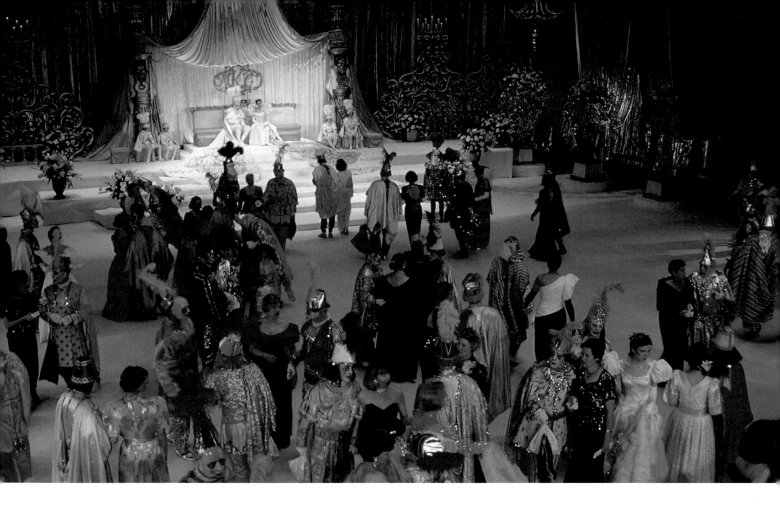

12.9 For the Mardi Gras ball of the Krewe of Comus, everyone is required to wear formal attire, and men cover their faces with masks. *Photograph by Syndey Byrd, 1991.*

12.10 Debutantes of the Krewe of Twelfth Night Revelers are introduced to guests at the Mardi Gras ball. *Photograph by Syndey Byrd, 1990.*

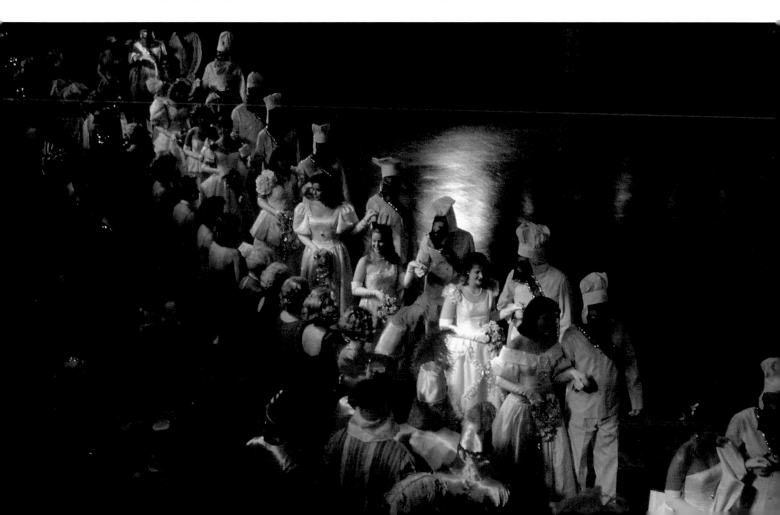

Avenue and down St. Charles on the last Saturday before Mardi Gras, is the first (and still one of the few) krewes made up entirely of women. Costumed and masked moms, some riding alongside *their* moms, mingle with aunts, daughters, sisters, homemakers, and career professionals, sashaying in place on the floats to the boom-box echo of rock songs—which also advance the high-stepping choreography of majorette groups—or to the pumping melodies of high-school bands as the caravan swims along beneath the canopy of oak limbs draping the big thoroughfares.

Today there are more than seventy krewes, including those that parade in the different parishes or suburbs around New Orleans. The names convey something of the region's multicultural whimsy: Choctaw, Saturn, Babylon, Zulu, Neptune, Shangri-La, Oshun, Chaos, Cleopatra, Jefferson, King Arthur, Lil Rascals, Morpheus, Pegasus, Pontchartrain, Ulysses, Pygmalion, Zeus, and Krewe D'Etat . . . among many others (figs. 12.11, 12.12).

Those krewes whose members come from pedigreed families are still quite exclusive and hold private balls. Public balls, which flourished before the advent of Comus, made a big comeback in the 1970s as large, upstart krewes lured celebrities to ride on their floats. While the handful of old-line krewes each numbers fewer than one hundred in its membership, super-krewes such as Bacchus, Endymion, and Orpheus have as many as two thousand members apiece, some of whom fly in from foreign countries such as San Francisco and New York to ride a huge float and throw swatches of beads to jubilant people in the street. The experience is quite a rush. Although elaborate costumes were part of the golden age of Carnival for the riders of floats and for the tableaux in the balls, today most of the riders (though certainly not all of them) wear one-piece costumes, color coordinated for each float, with the universal blank face masks. The floats tend to depict the krewe's annual theme more than the costumes do (see figs. 12.1, 12.13).

Mardi Gras today builds on the proposition that the rest of the world is irrelevant—save as a source of money-wielding tourists and TV cameras to capture the neon-tropical pageantry. Programs such as *Entertainment Tonight* thrive on Mardi Gras, although the national news media give scant reference to an urban spectacle of staggering proportions. That's another way of saying that nothing important happens in New Orleans except culture. With parades mushrooming around the suburbs, the krewes with fat budgets lure TV and movie personalities to fly in and ride their floats as faux royalty. Charlton Heston, Ernest Borgnine, Bob Hope, Raymond Burr, Henry Winkler, and talk-show host Larry King have each sat on the king's float of Bacchus, parading down St. Charles Avenue to Canal Street on a winter's night. The Krewe of Orpheus has made a point of inviting black celebrities to ride on its floats, including Whoopi Goldberg and Stevie Wonder.[19]

12.11 Masqueraders with the Society of St. Anne participate in a walking parade through New Orleans that begins at dawn on Tuesday and continues into the evening. *Photograph by Syndey Byrd, 1994.*

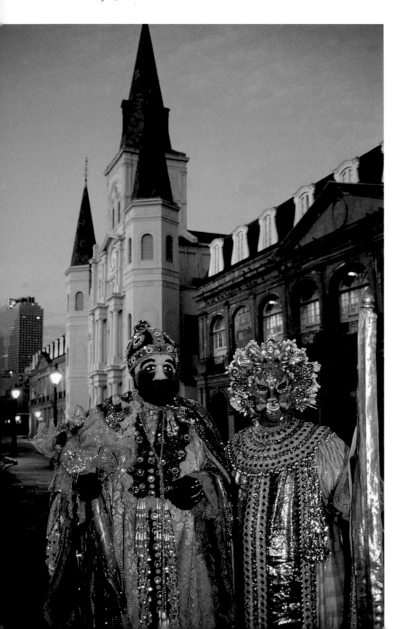

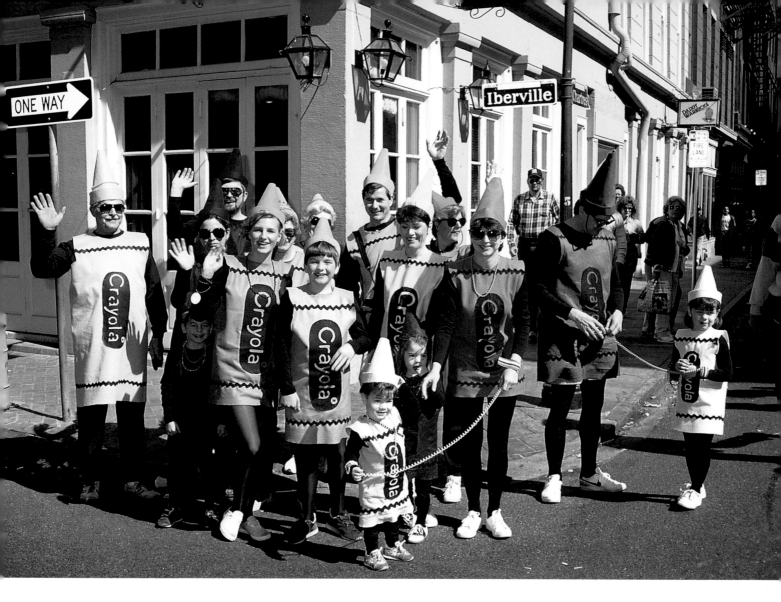

12.12 Families also join to take part in the Mardi Gras festivities. *Photograph by Susan Leavines, 1987.*

French Quarter Activities

The French Quarter is the Babylonian essence of New Orleans (figs 12.14, 12.15), a riot of erotica during the big day, with many people walking around semi-nude, nearly nude, or nude-but-painted (fig. 12.16). In recent years, rip-roaring men in the streets have been bellowing to women on balconies: "Show us your tits!" Those who do receive streams of beads in return.

The high point of Mardi Gras in the Quarter is the midday drag-queen beauty contest on a stage at the corner of Bourbon and St. Ann Streets (fig. 12.17). The dazzling costumes, many with rainbow feathers, dripping light, bespeak a tradition of the day-without-closets stretching back well before the rise of gay liberation in the 1970s. Gay Mardi Gras grew more for-

mal in the 1950s with the Krewe of Yuga, which satirized the traditional Mardi Gras balls. The police raided Yuga's first ball in 1958, and ninety-six members had their names printed in the newspaper in an arrest sweep (fig. 12.18). Undeterred, the Krewe of Petronius formed in 1961, marking a move by gay men into the Carnival mainstream (fig. 12.19). By the early 1980s some fifteen gay krewes were holding balls with elaborate floor shows. The AIDS epidemic, however, cut deeply into the community, and by 1999 only five krewes were active, including the Lords of Leather and the first black gay krewe, Mwindo.[20]

"The costumes are ornate, often topped with head pieces, shoulder pieces and collars," wrote David Lee

12.13 (overleaf) A Krewe of Orpheus float entitled "Mahalia Jackson," in honor of the famous gospel singer, makes its way down the parade route. *Photograph by Syndey Byrd, 1994.*

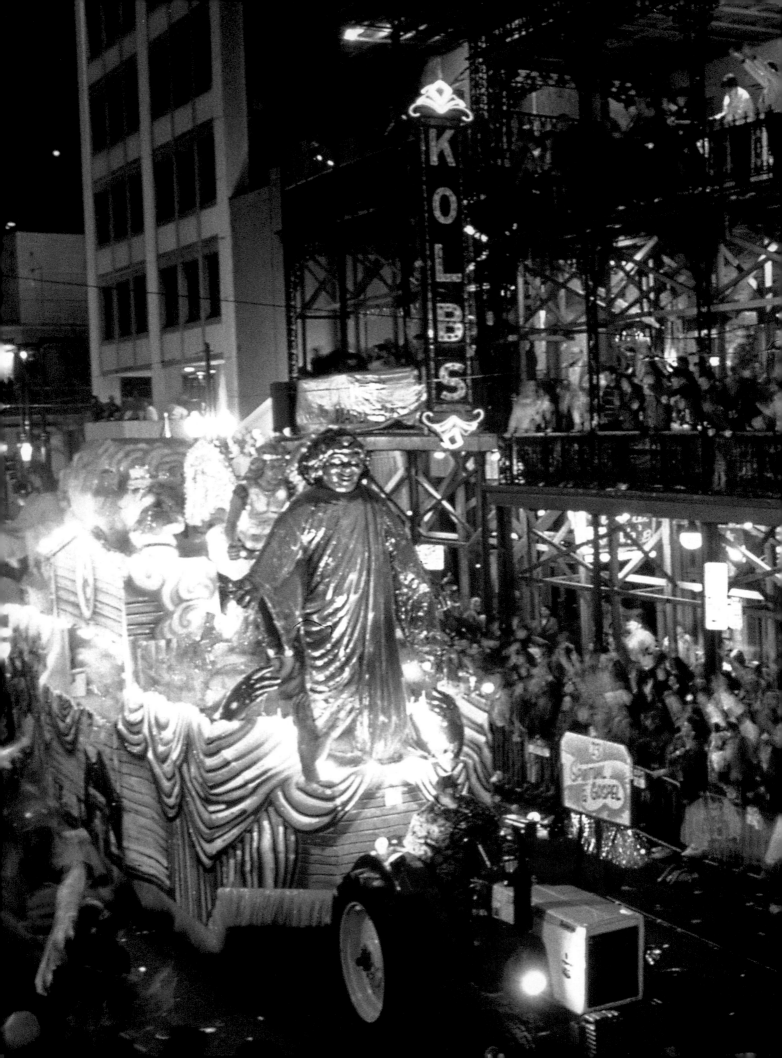

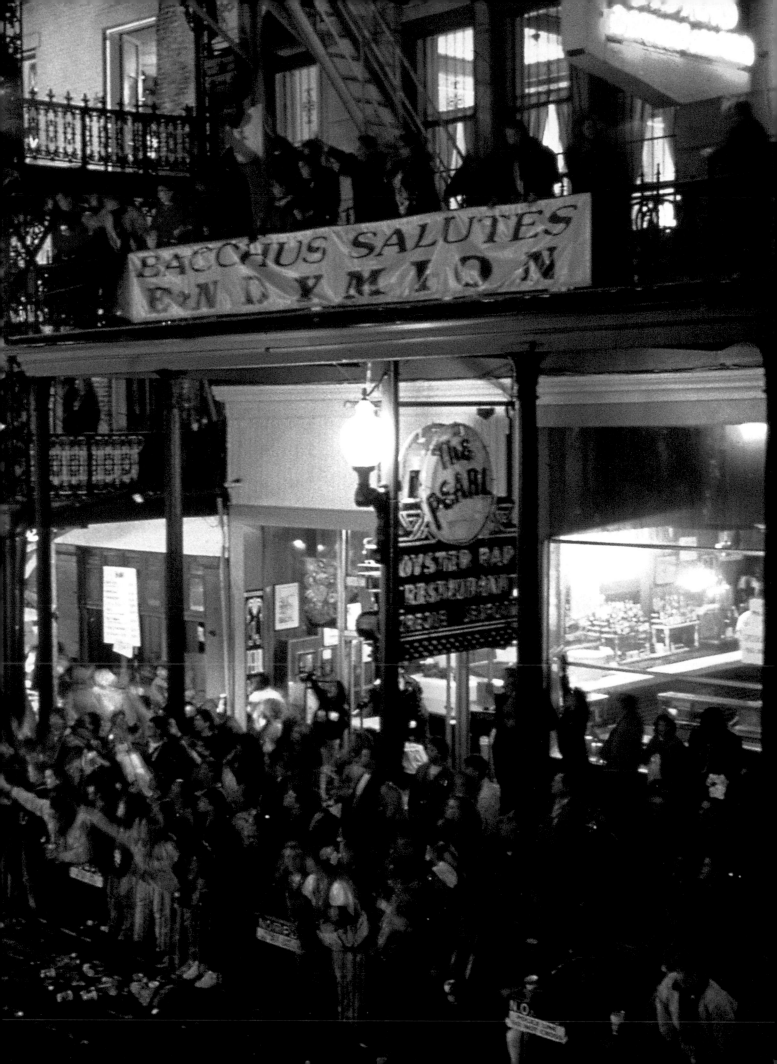

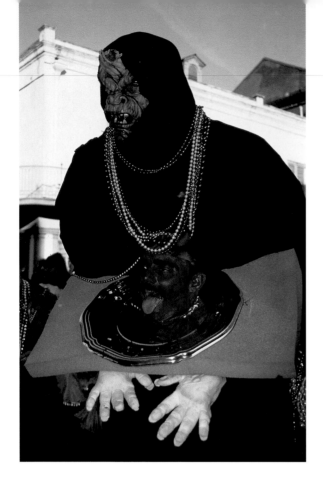

12.14 "Hell on a Platter" masquerade in French Quarter. *Photograph by Syndey Byrd, 1997.*

12.15 A trio in the French Quarter masquerades as the Three Blind Mice. *Photograph by Syndey Byrd, 1991.*

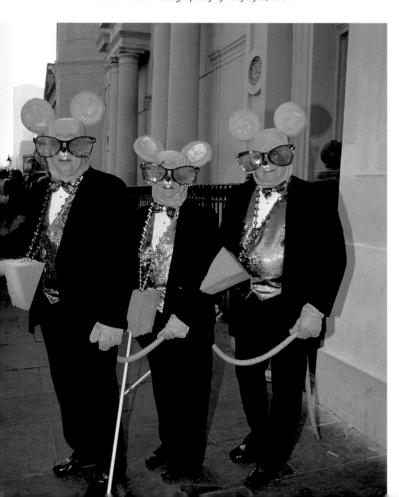

Simmons of a recent Krewe of Amon-Ra ball in the suburban St. Bernard Civic Center:

It's here that the feathers and sequins make their fashion stand. The ball, which to the uninitiated seems little more than a series of elevated drag shows, honors an oft-discussed tradition of gay culture that recalls the 1990 documentary *Paris Is Burning*. In that exploration of Harlem's gay ballroom scene, director Jennie Livingston conveyed the whole notion of a subculture of society reaching for the pinnacle of style and glamour in the face of years of oppression. The draft show and ball are equal parts self-parody, defiance and celebration.

After 13 musical performances, the year's king and queen are announced and presented in much the same style as kings and queens of mainline Mardi Gras krewes. They are received warmly by both the crowd and the returning royalty.[21]

Black Carnival: A Counterhistory

At one level, Mardi Gras can be seen as a vast set of hierarchies with Rex, Comus, and the white patrician society at the top, like figurines on a wedding cake, followed by a pyramid of descending faux royalty in the krewes of lesser pedigree. In this prism, an elaborate web of black organizations with their own kings,

12.16 Semi-nude "cats" enjoy Mardi Gras in the French Quarter. *Photograph by Michael P. Smith, 1998.*

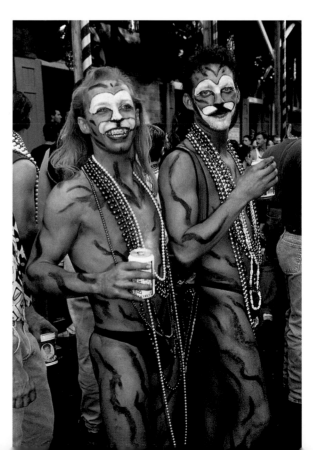

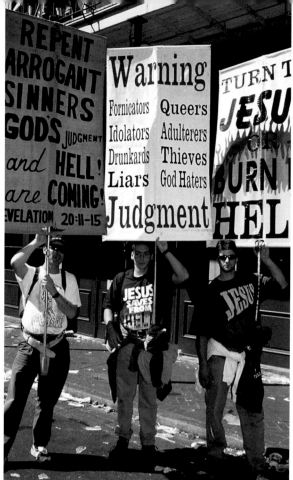

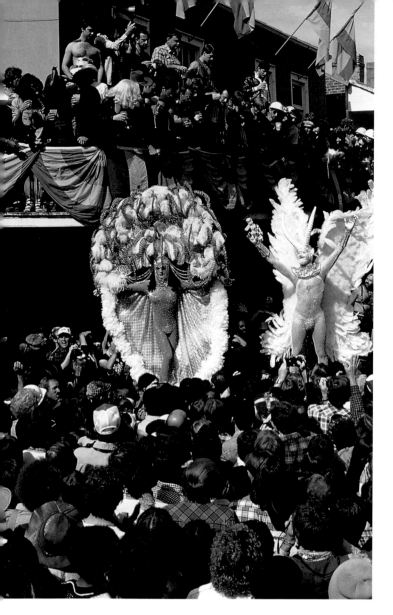

12.18 Young men from the Fundamentalist Christian Church carry signs to protest the wild behavior of gays and other Mardi Gras revelers in the French Quarter. *Photograph by Michael P. Smith, 1998.*

12.17 The drag-queen beauty contest in the French Quarter is a particularly popular Mardi Gras event. *Photograph by Syndey Byrd, 1979.*

queens, and debutantes takes the stage as a counter-royalty.

The Original Illinois Club, founded in 1895, is Creole-of-color upper crust, with a ball presenting young women as debutantes (fig. 12.20). "There are the obligatory courtesies, the outgoing court and queen, the new queen, maids and debutantes, and a grande marche ('If Ever I Cease to Love' is also played at the Original Illinois Club ball) and a *tableau vivante,*" writes Carolyn Kolb.

The [tableau] themes have included the classic "The Glory of Rome," the romantic "Romeo and Juliet," the adventur-ous "Pancho Villa: The Magnificent Bandito" and the senti-mental "The Robins Came Back to Nest." The same families' names recur. The king in 1971, Herman Antoine Sr., was a descendant of C. C. Antoine, who served as Lieutenant Gov-ernor of Louisiana during the Reconstruction era. The Mis-shore family has several representatives, as do the Barancos of Baton Rouge.[22]

A spin-off group, the Young Men Illinois, formed a debutante cotillion presenting young women from other parts of Louisiana, Atlanta, St. Louis, and cities beyond the Gulf South; some have family ties to mem-bers, others seek admission based on their academic or professional achievements. The Original Illinois has also broadened its geographic base of debutantes.[23]

The Zulu Social Aid and Pleasure Club, the leading black krewe, was formed in 1909 (its parade began seven years later). Zulu today is the longest and most imaginatively designed black parade, a rudder

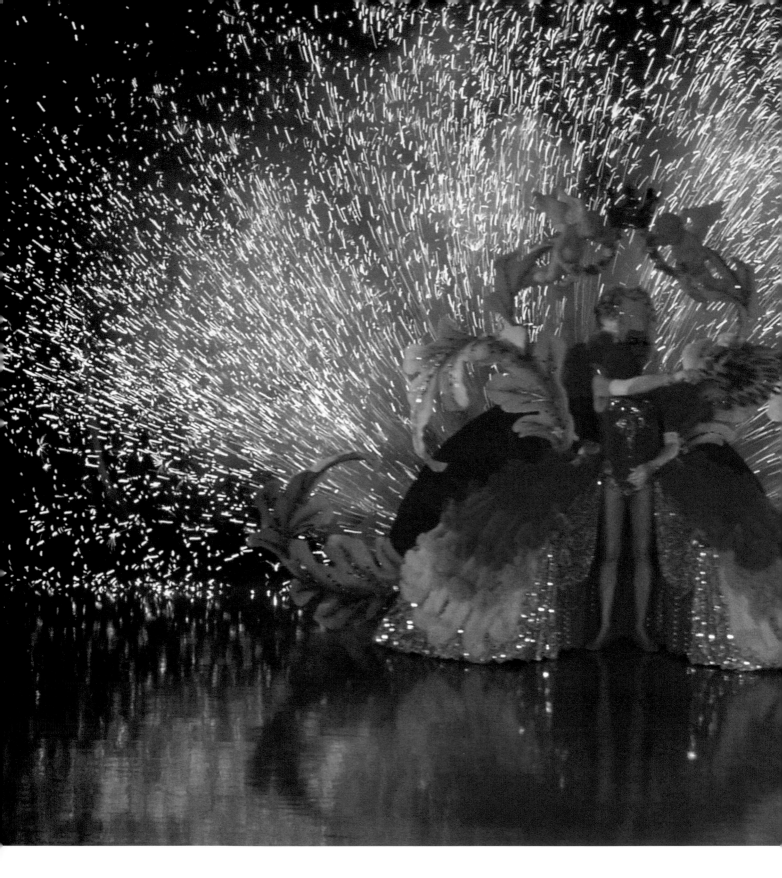

of Carnival. Black men in blackface, wearing grass skirts, hand out gilded coconuts from floats that roll down St. Charles Avenue on Mardi Gras morning, preceding the Krewe of Rex (fig. 12.21). But where the Rex ball is a pinnacle in the calendar of the white elite, with invitations difficult to come by even for those with personal ties to members, the Zulu ball is a sprawling affair with upwards of ten thousand people,

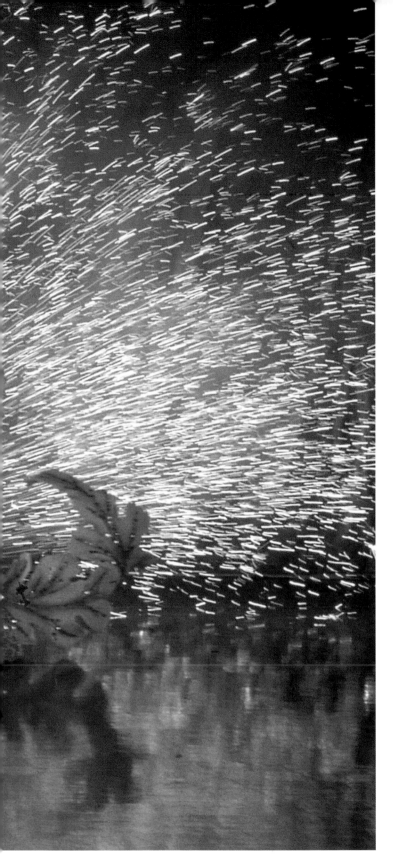

Zulu began as a double satire. A group of black longshoremen engaged in a parody of the Zulu tribe in South Africa and used their African costumes in a further burlesque of Rex and the would-be royalty of white folk. If Rex had a royal robe and scepter, King Zulu wore a grass skirt and waved a hambone. Out of this smirking parody evolved an organization rooted in the working and middle classes. Louis Armstrong rode as an exultant king of Zulu in 1949. Today the city's leading politicians, including several dozen whites, are members of Zulu. The krewe has a clubhouse on North Broad Avenue and performs various charity services during the year.

The Zulu parade has been and still is one of Mardi Gras's most loved traditions. The Zulu krewe consists of a nontraditional hierarchy of characters (fig. 12.22). It has a king but no nobles per se, and one character, the "Big Shot of Africa," outshines the king (the term *outshine* was used in earlier days and meant to look better than someone else in competition). A Zulu member created the Big Shot character in the 1930s. He is the man behind the throne; no one can see the king without seeing the Big Shot first.

Among the other Zulu characters, the Witch Doctor was one of the first. He prayed to the gods for good health for the members and the king, as well as for good weather and safety. The Ambassador, Governor, and Mayor were characters created in the 1970s, representing heads of government. Milton Bienamee, a long-time deputy sheriff, created the "Province Prince" in the early 1970s. This character represented the oldest former king. Also in the 1970s, James L. Russell and Sonny Jim Poole created the "Mr. Big Stuff" character, who tries to outshine the Big Shot. The idea came from the 1970 recording "Mr. Big Stuff," by Jean Knight.[24]

Africans and Indians

Another side to black Carnival is a symbolic revolt against the overlords of history. In 1883 or thereabouts, a group of black day laborers began masking as Indians. This tradition harked back to the slave

many of them bringing food to be laid out on a vast array of tables. Zulu is where privilege melds with the masses: just about anyone can go to the ball for the price of a ticket.

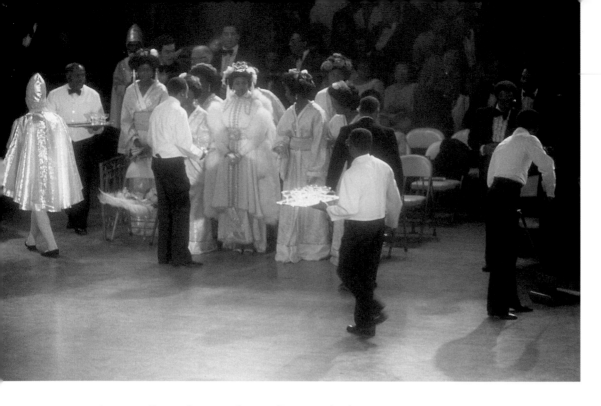

12.20 The Original Illinois Club ball is an elite affair for upper-crust Creoles of color in New Orleans. *Photograph by Syndey Byrd, 1987.*

dances at Congo Square, where Indians watched Africans who sometimes dressed as Indians.

Indians had harbored runaway slaves in Louisiana territory. Unlike Natives in many other parts of the South, where Indians were driven out by force, the Choctaws in New Orleans melted into the local population, many of them marrying blacks.

Traveling Wild West shows of the 1880s had a hold on the black population. But with sinuous street dances and improvisational rhythms pounded out on hand percussion instruments, the Mardi Gras Indians cast a spiritual searchlight onto the African past. Embracing the persona of the Indian, the black tribes paid the supreme compliment to another race by adapting their trappings as spirit figures. The black Indians used the

ritual stage of Carnival to parade as rebellious warriors for a day, stopping in bars, sometimes fighting, releasing passions otherwise bottled up by the daily grind of poverty and race (fig. 12.23).[25]

The trancelike possessions of African Americans in the vernacular churches found an analogue in the dancing of the black Indians, according to the late Big Chief Donald Harrison Sr., founder of Guardians of the Flame. "Trance," remarked the chief, a folk philosopher who worked for many years as a waiter and enjoyed the works of Albert Camus, "I can see winos, anybody, you can get to a certain point and go into a trance. To the casual observer they look like they're just jumping up and down, but in reality they're in a world by themselves, rhythmically."[26]

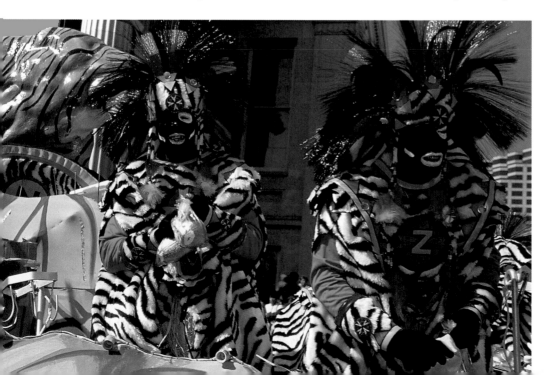

12.21 Zulu members dressed as blackfaced Soulful Warriors ride on one of the many Zulu floats, handing out coconuts to spectators on the street. *Photograph by Susan Leavines, 1999.*

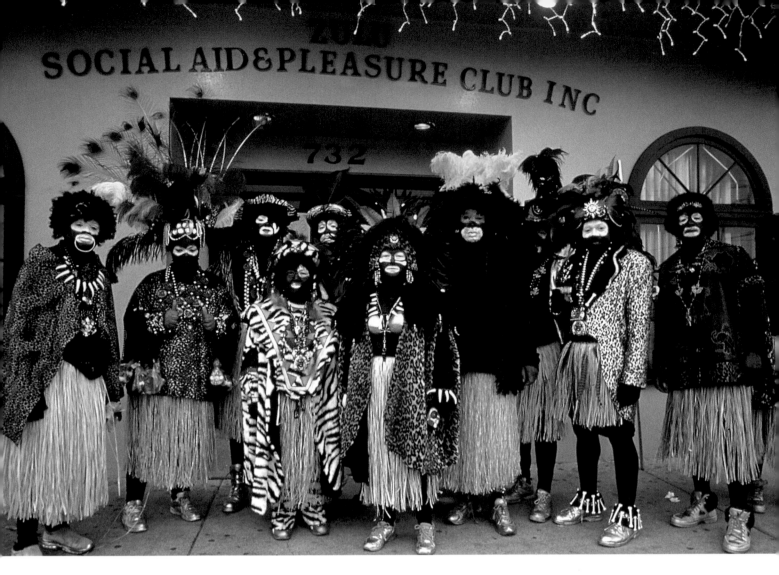

12.22 Characters in the Zulu Mardi Gras parade wear blackface and stylized African tribal outfits. A group of them stands in front of the Zulu Social Aid and Pleasure Clubhouse. *Photograph by Syndey Byrd, 2001.*

Some call it a trance; others say "with the spirit." The term "possessed" is another way of saying "fugue state." The sudden force of energy rushes into the body, throwing it out of control, into gyrations, while the mind—or spirit—spins into another zone. It happens often in spiritual churches.

"People go to churches of organized religion," the chief continued. "Every time they go to church it's a religious experience for them. When I'm into the Indian thing, that's a religious experience for me. I live it year-round. It's something for your inner self, expressed through your outer self."

Much of what we know of the early Mardi Gras Indians has come down the generations of an oral tradition, rich in folklore and coded lyrics that lie in the Afro-Creole patois. The tribe is led by the Big Chief, with a Spy Boy who scouts the streets to make sure the way is clear for the Big Chief to parade without bother. The gangs or tribes have names like the Ninth Ward Hunters, Creole Wild West, Wild Squa-toolas, Spirit of the Fi-Yi-Yi, Golden Eagles, and Wild Magnolias. Each tribe has Flag Boys and Trail Chiefs and the Wild Man, whose job is to be, well, wild.

"Wild Man Rock," recalls Allison "Tootie" Montana, Big Chief of the Yellow Pocahontas, "was a cat who lived out by a junk heap, way down Elysian Fields where people dumped their garbage. He fished old cigarettes out the trash and strung them over the roof where he lived, let 'em dry in the sun, and rolled himself cigarettes. You never saw him much till Carnival came. Then he'd come bargin' out with a ring in his nose and carryin' on, used to throw that spear and scare all hell out of people."[27]

Tootie Montana paraded for fifty years as Big Chief of the Yellow Pocahontas, the oldest tribe, which

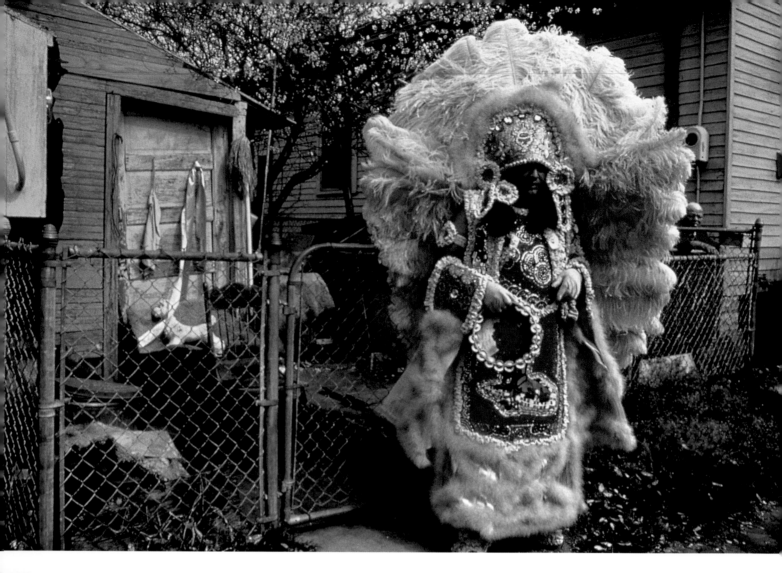

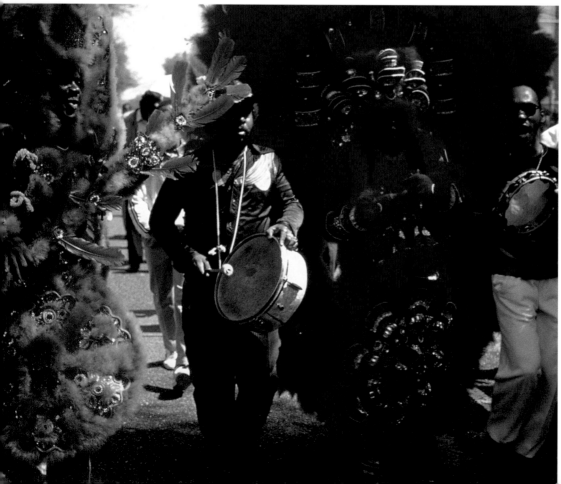

12.23 Big Chief Norman Bell of the Wild Tchoupi-toulas Mardi Gras Indian Tribe. *Photograph by Syndey Byrd, 1989.*

12.24 Big Chief Allison "Tootie" Montana and other members of the Yellow Pocahontas Mardi Gras Indian Tribe sing and dance through the streets of their neighbor-hood. *Photograph by Syndey Byrd, 1987.*

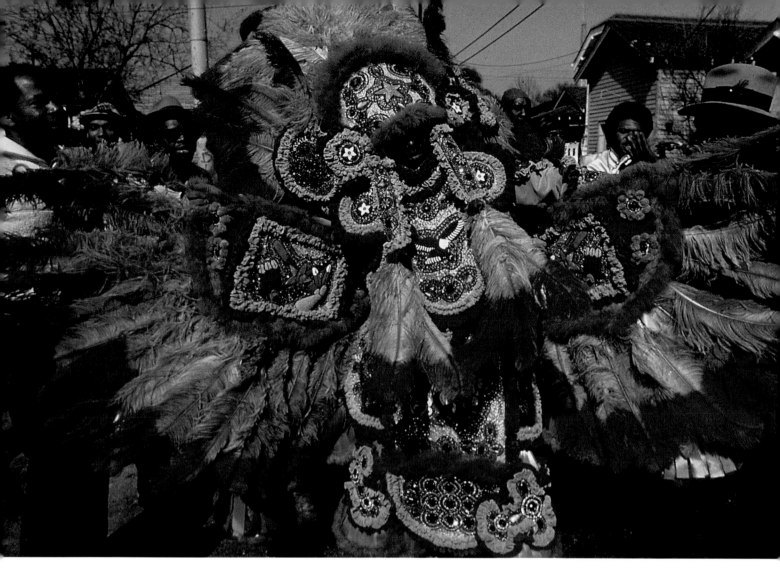

12.25 Big Chief Larry Bannock of the Goldenstar Hunters Mardi Gras Indian Tribe. *Photograph by Michael P. Smith, 1983.*

was founded by his ancestors (fig. 12.24). Montana received a National Endowment for the Arts National Heritage fellowship. The Indian costumes are dazzling sights—billowing ostrich plumes, red, yellow, turquoise, green; bead- and rhinestone-studded patches on chests and arms bearing images of everything from Indians on horses to casino dice. One could make a short film on the imagery of Indian costumes alone. The street dances have a fierce beauty, with their rhythms of tambourines and hand-held instruments.

Fights between Indian gangs of the early twentieth century are fact and lore. The tradition is peaceful now. "We used to fight with knives and guns," one Indian remarked. "Now we compete by the beauty of our costumes."[28] Since the 1970s, when record producers and film makers discovered the Indians, the folk tradition has generated a line of recordings by tribes, including eponymous CDs—*The Wild Tchoupitoulas, Wild Magnolias,* and *Guardians of the Flame,* among others.

When a Mardi Gras Indian chief endorsed a brand of cell phone in a newspaper advertisement, the tradition had come a far piece from Reconstruction.

For some Mardi Gras Indians, the commitment to tradition is more than just a commitment from the heart. It is a huge financial commitment as well. The chiefs design and make their own costumes every year. In an effort to be the "prettiest" Indian, chiefs can spend $5,000 or more on these lavish, colorful costumes (fig. 12.25). Like members of the more affluent white krewes, the Indians pay for their own costumes; this can be a real hardship for many. There are between twenty and twenty-five black Indian tribes who continue to parade on Mardi Gras as well as St. Joseph's Day (March 19) and Super Sunday, a day when a combined procession makes its flamboyant

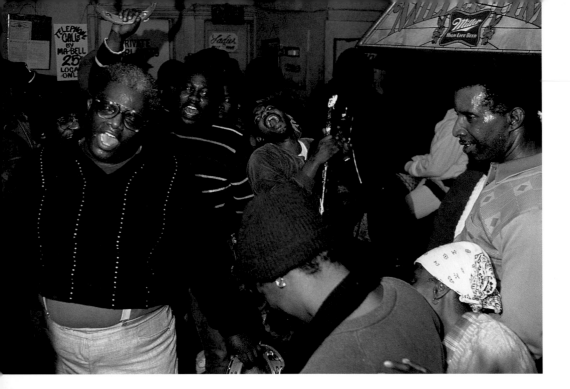

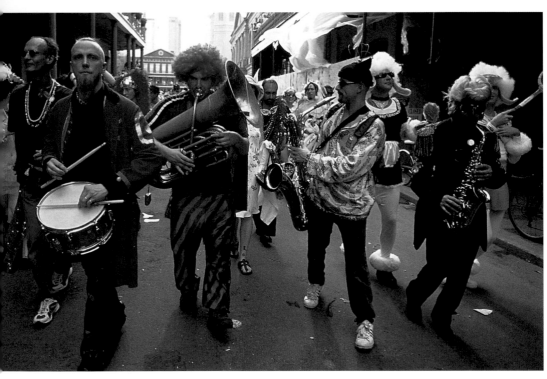

12.26 Big Chief Larry Bannock and Goldenstar Hunters practice their Mardi Gras Indian marching songs in a neighborhood tavern. *Photograph by Syndey Byrd, 1987.*

12.27 A small Mardi Gras marching band of well-known musicians makes its way through the French Quarter. *Photograph by Syndey Byrd, 2001.*

way down a main city street. A few of the well-known tribes travel around the world giving performances.[29]

Music: A Mosaic within a Mosaic

"I'm not sure, but I'm almost positive, that all music came from New Orleans," quipped the late Ernie K-Doe, rhythm-and-blues singer. If Mardi Gras is a mosaic of New Orleans society, then the music of Carnival is a mosaic within a mosaic. The unending thematic flow in early jazz, mid-century rhythm-and-blues, and the late-twentieth-century pop idioms of Mardi Gras Indians' music is the city itself, the folkways, neighborhoods, and rituals of public spectacle (fig. 12.26). In a very real sense, music is the memory of the culture.

Out of the city's vast musical product runs a long legacy associated with Mardi Gras, a line of lyrics and rhythms, parade and ball traditions entwined with var-

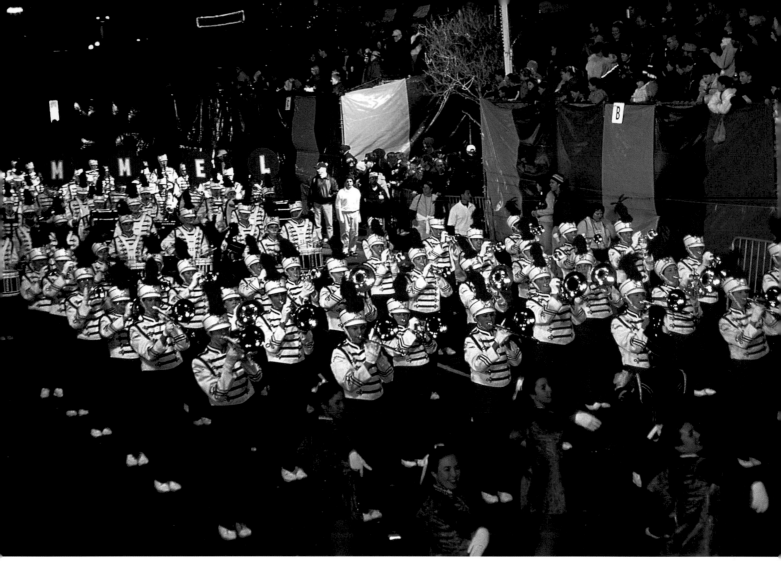

12.28 A school marching band provides music for one of the large krewe parades. *Photograph by Syndey Byrd, 2001.*

ied tiers of the society. "If Ever I Cease to Love" is still played when Rex and his queen begin the grand march at the ball on the night of Shrove Tuesday. Patrician balls have other sentimental favorites, such as "While We Danced at the Mardi Gras," played by orchestras whose members wear tuxedos. In recent years the orchestral repertoire has loosened a bit as band-leaders season the spread with tunes like Paul Simon's "You Can Call Me Al" and the Neville Brothers' "Hey Pocky-Way," a 1976 recording spun from street chants of the Wild Tchoupitoulas Mardi Gras Indians.[30]

Dancing is everywhere during Carnival—in private clubs, street fests, block parties, nightclubs, and fancier venues. Music permeates every layer of society (fig. 12.27). The parades rely on marching bands (fig. 12.28). High-school units from across the city, throughout the southern parishes, and far-off places like Florida and Texas march in the parades, proud youngsters in uni-forms pushing along between the tractor-drawn floats that carry maskers throwing beads and trinkets. The hundred-member band of the premier high school for black boys in New Orleans, the St. Augustine Purple Knights, high-stepping in their uniforms, plays with a bravura sound in eight to ten parades each season.

Bandleaders sift the pop charts for new songs each year, discarding others from the repertoire, maintain-ing a core of standards that draw cheers from people on the sidewalks. The bands rehearse in school yards for weeks before Mardi Gras; local TV stations pay vis-its to practice sessions before the final days. As the parades move along, the power of the horn sections and the booming drummers exert a magnetic effect on black kids who move down the neutral ground in a "second line"—a sinuous, snakelike parade of spon-taneous street dancing. Organized march-and-dance clubs from city and suburbs, high-school girls and

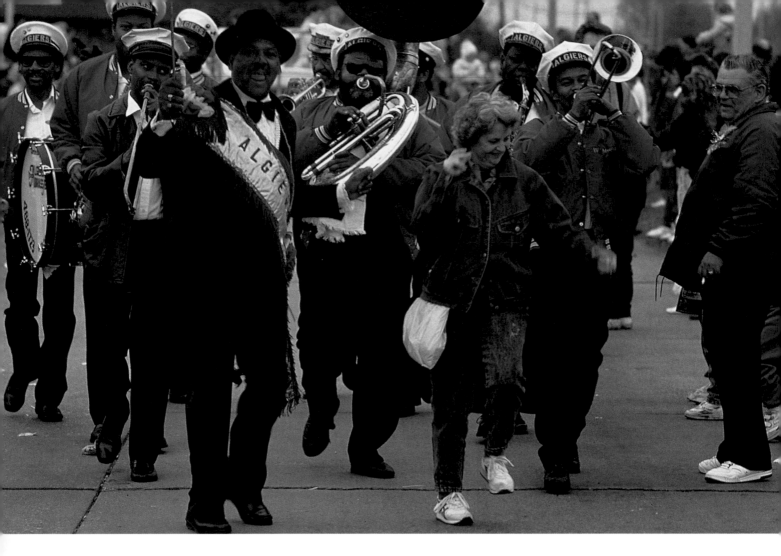

12.29 The Algiers Brass Band performs in a Mardi Gras parade. *Photograph by Syndey Byrd, 1989.*

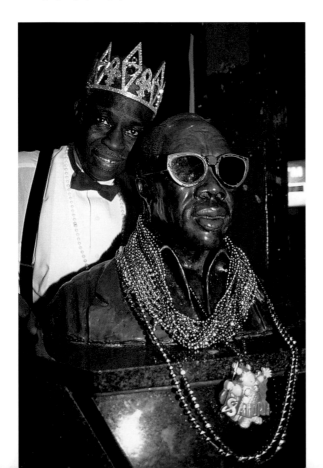

women into their thirties, prance in brightly colored outfits, waves of high-steppers with batons and pom-poms grooving to the latest rock hits blasting on industrial strength boom-boxes carried in vans.[31]

Most of the jazz brass bands march in several parades during the season (fig. 12.29). The Olympia Brass Band, which dates to the 1880s, is a fixture in the Krewe of Zulu parade, playing favorites like "When the Saints Go Marching In," "Bourbon Street Parade," and "The Second Line." Pete Fountain, the clarinetist and Dixieland jazz star, marched for many years with his own group, the Half-Fast Walking Club (with a Jesuit retreat master on second clarinet), winding along St. Charles Avenue and Canal Street in advance of Zulu and Rex.[32]

Mardi Gras has seasonal songs that become a

12.30 Al "Carnival Time" Johnson stands behind a bust of Professor Longhair. The music of these two musicians is widely played during Mardi Gras in New Orleans. *Photograph by Syndey Byrd, 2001.*

virtual soundtrack on radio and in clubs, each tune a slice-of-life cameo of the city that care forgot. From "Carnival Time," by Al Johnson:

The Green Room is burning
and the Plaza's burning down
Throw your baby out the window
and let the joints burn down
All because it's Carnival Time . . . everybody's
 drinking wine.

The late Professor Longhair (Henry R. Byrd; fig. 12.30), a legendary figure in the annals of black popular music, lives on in the rumba-studded keyboard licks that simulate the rushing sound of a train heading down the tracks, heading for "Mardi Gras in New Orleans":

Got you ticket in my hand
You're gonna go to New Orleans
Going to St. Claude and Dumaine
To see the Zulu Queen.

In 1954, the year of the *Brown v. Board of Education* school desegregation decision, a seventeen-year-old named Art Neville did the vocals on a song that became an overnight sensation among adolescents, white and black, "Mardi Gras Mambo."

Down in New Orleans
where the blues was born
takes a cool cat to blow a horn
On LaSalle and Rampart Street

The combos play with a mambo beat
Mardi Gras mambo, mambo, mambo,
Down in New-Awleens.

Food of Mardi Gras: King of the Bean

The only food designated as absolutely necessary during Mardi Gras is "king cake," a food so integrated into the festival that today's Carnival queens owe their reign to it. The story begins with the observance of Twelfth Night, or Epiphany, a religious holiday that can be traced back to the middle of the fourth century. There was also a separate feast of the kings in the early ninth century, in which Roman children drew lots with beans to see who would be king. Much later, in England, a large cake containing a bean was called a Twelfth-Cake. The cake was divided up and a bean was hidden in one of the pieces; whoever found the bean was proclaimed King of the Bean. Even Mary, Queen of Scots, celebrated this tradition, but with a queen, of course.

Now the story veers off to the title "Lord of Misrule," which comes from the English tradition of having a leader of revelry who saw to it that during the merry season all had a good time.[33] In New Orleans, the fourth organization to proclaim itself as an official Carnival krewe was called the Twelfth Night Revelers, and who should be their king but the Lord of Misrule? Krewe members instituted the tradition of hiding a golden bean in a giant cake (fig. 12.31), which was presented at their first Tableau Ball in 1870, though not so gracefully. Pieces of the cake were practically tossed at the ladies, and so the bean was lost. The next year,

12.31 A giant tiered king cake is served to guests at the Krewe of Shangri-La Mardi Gras party. *Photograph by Syndey Byrd, 2000.*

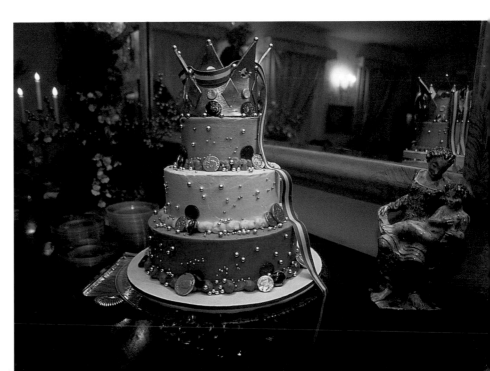

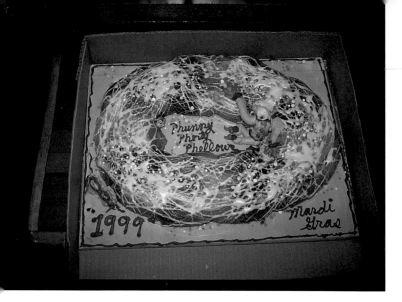

12.32 The more traditional Mardi Gras king cake is made in the form of a circular wreath, decorated in New Orleans Carnival colors of purple, green, and gold. *Photograph by Syndey Byrd, 2000.*

the art perfected, the Lord of Misrule carved slices for the ladies. Emma Butler chose the slice with the bean and thus became the first Queen of Carnival.[34]

The cake today is made from yeast dough, braided with cinnamon and sugar, baked, and topped with colored sugar in the royal Carnival colors, purple, green, and gold (fig. 12.32). Bakeries in New Orleans make between 750,000 and 850,000 cakes every year. Since we cannot all be kings or queens, the tradition now states that he who gets the bean must throw the next party. On Mardi Gras, besides the obligatory king cake, people celebrate with the usual New Orleans staples such as gumbo and boiled crawfish and the traditional Monday staple, red beans and rice. Many families with places staked out along the parade routes turn Mardi Gras into a picnic.[35]

Coda

In December 1991, barely a month after closet Nazi David Duke drew an army of reporters to Louisiana in his losing quest for the governorship, an African American city councilwoman proposed an ordinance to desegregate the Mardi Gras krewes, which utilized city streets for their parades. In the ensuing political battle, Comus and several other old-line krewes folded their parades rather than agree to admit blacks or Jews. The ordinance effort failed, but the society's exposed cleavages were painfully real just the same.[36]

History is clear that Mardi Gras helped perpetuate the serrated chasm of race and class, yet the momentum and life force spawned from the festival has created endless improvisations of a rough cultural democracy that loves to parody nobility. The evolution of the people's feast has been more than a safety valve for society. Mardi Gras is a family affair, as the many gathered with children and ladders on grassy neutral grounds, waiting for the parades, will ever attest. The tradition of Mardi Gras Indian Big Chiefs siring future chiefs has its mirror in the sons of Rex becoming Rex.

Behind the celebrities and commercialization lies a history of artists, many of them little known, who have produced the goods of culture—floats, gowns, throws, costumes, invitations, the tableaux of the balls, the performance art and dazzling costumes at the campy drag-queen beauty contest on Bourbon Street—the list goes on. Mardi Gras vistas, as many-sided as a kaleidoscope, do not happen by accident. People from across the society design, make, and deliver what they cherish.

Thus it goes, despite the worsening of objective data on crime, education, insects, pollution, and politicians. Come what may, the Queen City stands ever firm on the primacy of her spectacle. You must live among people who wear masks and dance in the streets to experience such embedded optimism for the human experiment.

NOTES

The author thanks the filmmaker Phoebe Ferguson for research assistance with this essay.

1. Marcus Christian, *I Am New Orleans: A Poem* (New Orleans: privately printed, 1968), 1.

2. Author's interview with Aaron Neville, 1978.

3. A. J. Loria, "Ain't Nothin' Like It," on the CD *King Nino: It's a Mardi Gras World* (KIMIK, 2003).

4. Errol Laborde, *Mardi Gras! A Celebration,* conception and photography by Mitchell Osborne (New Orleans: Picayune Press, 1981), 56.

5. Jason Berry, "African Cultural Memory in New Orleans Music," *Black Music Research Journal* 8, no. 1 (1988): 1; Henry A. Kmen, *Music in New Orleans: The Formative Years, 1791–1841* (Baton Rouge: Louisiana State University Press, 1966), 228. See also Dena J. Epstein, *Sinful Tunes and Spirituals: Black Folk Music to the Civil War* (Urbana: University of Illinois Press, 1977), 133.

6. Jerah Johnson, "New Orleans's Congo Square: An Urban Setting for Early Afro-American Culture Formation," *Louisiana History* 32, no. 2 (1991): 142–143.

7. James Gill, *Lords of Misrule: Mardi Gras and the Politics of Race in New Orleans* (Jackson: University Press of Mississippi, 1997), 36.

8. Henri Schindler, *Mardi Gras Treasures: Float Designs of the Golden Age* (Gretna, LA: Pelican Publishing, 2001), 10.

9. Henri Schindler, *Mardi Gras Treasures: Invitations of the Golden Age* (Gretna, LA: Pelican Publishing, 2000), 7.

10. Samuel Kinser, *Carnival American Style: Mardi Gras at New Orleans and Mobile* (Chicago: University of Chicago, 1990), 35.

11. Gill, *Lords of Misrule,* 99.

12. Ibid., 96.

13. Ibid., 134, 138.

14. Schindler, *Mardi Gras Treasures: Invitations,* 19.

15. Arthur Burton LaCour, *New Orleans Masquerade: Chronicles of Carnival* (New Orleans: Pelican Publishing, 1957), 32.

16. Arthur Hardy, *Mardi Gras in New Orleans: An Illustrated History* (New Orleans: Arthur Hardy Enterprises, 2001), 67.

17. Jason Berry, "Behind the Scenes at Carnival," *Louisiana Cultural Vistas* 13, no. 1 (2002): 72.

18. Henri Schindler, "The Grand Tableau," in *Arthur Hardy's Mardi Gras Guide 2002* (New Orleans: Arthur Hardy Enterprises, 2002), 9, 116.

19. Personal observation.

20. David Lee Simons, "Krewe du Few," *Gambit Weekly* 20, no. 5 (2 February 1999): 23.

21. Ibid.

22. Carolyn Kolb, "Waltzing through the Century," *New Orleans Magazine* 29, no. 5 (February 1995): 60.

23. Ibid.

24. Zulu Social Aid and Pleasure Club website, 2002. Zululand, description of characters. http://www .mardigrasneworleans.com/zulu/zululand.html.

25. Jason Berry, Jonathan Foose, and Tad Jones, *Up from the Cradle of Jazz: New Orleans Music since World War II* (Athens: University of Georgia Press, 1986), 211.

26. Jason Berry, "Memories of Carnival Past," *New Orleans Magazine* 29, no. 5 (1995): 57.

27. Berry, Foose, and Jones, *Up from the Cradle of Jazz,* 211.

28. Ibid., 216.

29. Personal observation.

30. Berry, Foose, and Jones, *Up from the Cradle of Jazz,* 234.

31. Personal observation.

32. Personal observation.

33. Gill, *Lords of Misrule,* 88.

34. Henri Schindler, *Mardi Gras New Orleans* (Paris: Flammarion, 1997), 46.

35. Personal observation.

36. Gill, *Lords of Misrule,* 276.

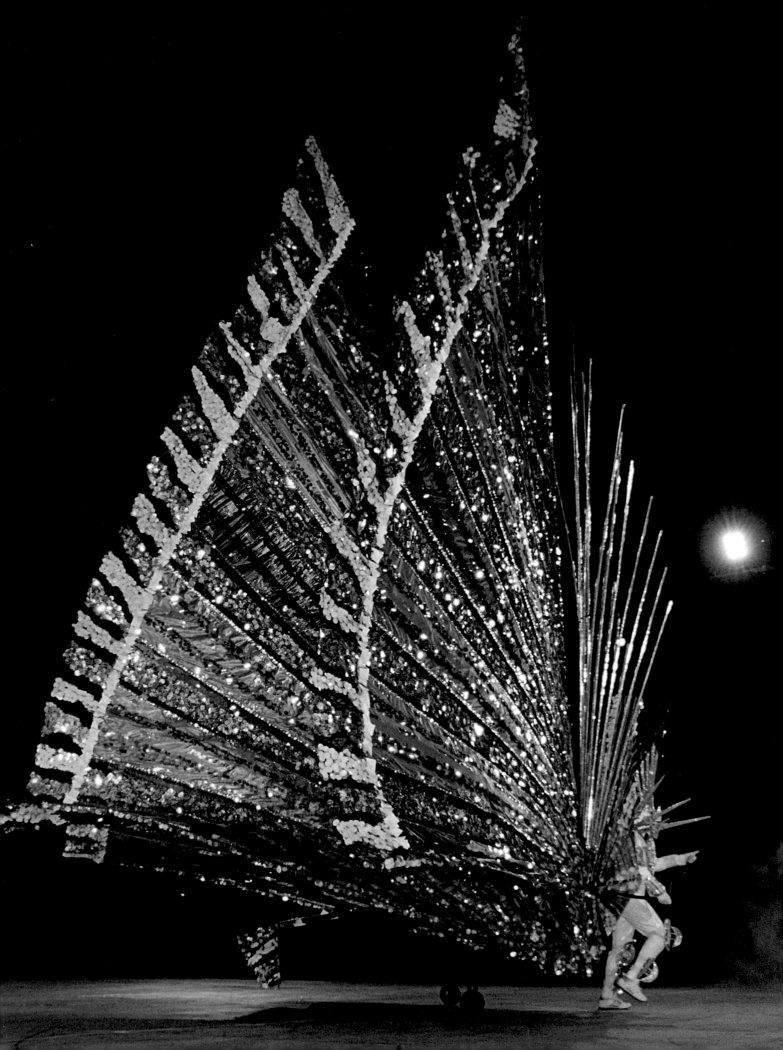

WORKS CITED

Abercrombie, Thomas A. "La Fiesta del carnaval postcolonial en Oruro: Clase, etnicidad y nacionalismo en la danza folklórica." *Revista Andina* 10, no. 2 (1992): 279–352.

———. *Pathways of Memory and Power: Ethnography and History among an Andean People.* Madison: University of Wisconsin Press, 1998.

———. "Q'aqchas and la Plebe in "Rebellion": Carnival vs. Lent in Eighteenth-Century Potosí." *Journal of Latin American Anthropology* 2, no. 1 (1996): 62–111.

Abrahams, Roger D., and Richard Bauman. "Ranges of Festival Behavior." In *The Reversible World: Symbolic Inversion in Art and Society,* edited by Barbara A. Babcock, pp. 193–208. Ithaca: Cornell University Press, 1978.

Adam, Adolf. "Aschermittwoch." In *Lexikon für Theologie und Kirche,* vol. 1, edited by Walter Kasper, pp. 1058–1059. Freiburg im Breisgau: Herder, 1993.

Almeida, Renato. *Inteligência do Folclore.* Rio de Janeiro: Livros de Portugal, 1957.

Alvarez del Villar, José. *Hombres y caballos de México: Historia y práctica de la charrería.* México, DF: Panorama Editorial, 1980.

Amado, Jorge. *O País do Carnaval.* São Paulo: Martins Editôra, 1961 [1931].

Ancelet, Barry Jean. *"Capitaine, voyage ton flag": The Traditional Cajun Country Mardi Gras.* Lafayette: Center for Louisiana Studies, 1989.

———. "Mardi Gras and the Media: Who's Fooling Whom?" *Southern Folklore* 46, no. 3 (1989): 211–219.

Ancelet, Barry Jean, Jay Edwards, and Glen Pitre. *Cajun Country.* Jackson: University Press of Mississippi, 1991.

Angola Maconde, Juan. *Raíces de un pueblo: Cultura afroboliviana.* La Paz: Producciones Cima, 2000.

Anthony, Michael. *Parade of the Carnivals of Trinidad 1839–1989.* Port of Spain: Circle Press, 1989.

Apaza Orozco, Humberto. "La Morenada ENAF reivindica el trabajo de los metalurgistsa." *La Patria* (special Carnival edition), 9 February 2002, p. 10.

Araújo, Rita de Cássia Barbosa. *Festas: Máscaras do Tempo-Entrudo, máscara e frevo no carnaval do Recife.* Recife: Fundação de Cultura Cidade do Recife, 1996.

———. "Festas públicas e carnavais: O Negro e a cultura popular de Pernambuco." In *O Negro e a construção do carnaval no nordeste,* organized by Luis Sávio de Almeida et al., pp. 31–62. Maceió: Universidad Federal de Alagôas, 1996.

Arnaudov, D. *Studies in the Bulgarian Rituals and Legends* (in Bulgarian), vol. 2. Sofia: Publishing House of the Bulgarian Academy of Sciences, 1972.

Arzáns de Orzua y Vela, Bartolomé. *Historia de la villa imperial de Potosí.* 3 vols. Edited by Lewis Hanke and Gunner Mendoza. Providence, RI: Brown University Press, 1965 [1735].

Averill, Gage. *A Day for the Hunter, a Day for the Prey: Popular Music and Power in Haiti.* Chicago: University of Chicago Press, 1997.

Bakhtin, Mikhail. *Rabelais and His World.* Trans. by Helène Iswolsky. Bloomington: Indiana University Press, 1984.

Ballesteros, José Ramon. *Origin y evolución del charro mexicano.* México, DF: Librería de Manuel Porrúa, 1972.

Baltrušaitis, Jurgis. *Le Miroir: Révélations, science fiction et fallacies.* Paris: Le Seuil, 1978.

Barbaro, Paolo. *Venezia la città ritrovata.* Venice: Marsilio, 1998.

Barthes, Roland. *Mythologies.* Paris: Seuil, 1957.

Beltrán Avila, Marcos. *Capítulos de la historia colonial de Oruro.* La Paz: La República, 1925.

Beltrán Heredia, Agusto. "Carnaval de Oruro." In *Carnaval de Oruro, Tarabuco y Fiesta del Gran Poder,* pp. 17–70. La Paz: Editorial los Amigos del Libro, 1977.

Beltrán Heredia, Augusto, and Josermo Murillo Vacarreza.

The 2003 King of Carnival, Curtis Eustace. Port of Spain, Trinidad and Tobago. *Photograph by Noel Norton, 2003.*

"Diablada Ferroviaria." *La Patria* (special Carnival edition), 9 February 2002, p. 4.

Benjamin, Roberto. "Os Ursos: Uma influência européia num carnaval afro-indigena." In *Suplemento Cultural: O Carnaval de Pernambuco,* pp. 3–6. Recife: Diário Oficial, 2001.

Berry, Jason. "African Cultural Memory in New Orleans Music." *Black Music Research Journal* 8, no. 1 (1988): 3–12.

———. "Behind the Scenes at Carnival." *Louisiana Cultural Vistas* 13, no. 1 (2002): 66–73.

———. "Memories of Carnival Past." *New Orleans Magazine* 29, no. 5 (1995): 54–58.

Berry, Jason, Jonathan Foose, and Tad Jones. *Up from the Cradle of Jazz: New Orleans Music since World War II.* Athens: University of Georgia Press, 1986.

Besson, Gerard, and Bridget Brereton. *The Book of Trinidad.* Port-of-Spain: Paria Publishing, 1992.

Bettin, Gianfranco. *Dove volano i leoni.* Milan: Garzanti, 1991.

Blanco Conde, Xesús. *Laza: O Entroido Enxebre.* Ourense: Diputación Provincial de Ourense, 2000.

Boero Rojo, Hugo. *Fiesta boliviana.* La Paz: Editorial los Amigos del Libro, 1991.

Bonald Neto, Olímpio. *Os Gigantes foliões em Pernambuco.* Olinda: Fundação Centro de Preservação dos Sítios Históricos, 1992.

Bonet Correa, Antonio. "La Fiesta Como Metáfora." In *España Festejante: El Siglo XVIII,* edited by Margarita Torrione, pp. 11–14. Málaga: Centro de Ediciones de la Diputación de Málaga, 2000.

Brasseaux, Carl A. *Acadian to Cajun: Transformation of a People, 1803–1877.* Jackson: University Press of Mississippi, 1991.

———. *The Founding of New Acadia: The Beginnings of Acadian Life in Louisiana, 1765–1803.* Baton Rouge: Louisiana State University Press, 1987.

Braudel, Fernand, and Folco Quilici. *Venise.* Paris: Arthaud, 1984.

Brodsky, Joseph. *Watermark.* New York: Farrar, Straus and Giroux, 1992.

Brooks, Francis Joseph. "Parish and Cofradía in Eighteenth-Century Mexico." Ph.D. dissertation, Princeton University, 1976.

Brown, Karen McCarthy. "Art and Resistance: Haiti's Political Murals, October 1994." *African Arts* 29, no. 2 (1996): 46–59.

Brusatin, Manlio, ed. *Venezia e lo spazio scenico.* Venice: Editions La Biennale, 1979.

Buezo, Catalina. *El Carnaval y Otras Procesiones Burlescas del Viejo Madrid.* Madrid: Avapiés, 1992.

Burckhardt-Seebass, Christine, Josef Mooser, Philipp Sarasin, and Martin Schaffner, eds. *Zwischentöne: Fasnacht und städtische Gesellschaft in Basel 1923–1998.* Basel: Buchverlag der Basler Zeitung, 1998.

Bürgi, Thomas. "Geburt der Fasnacht aus dem Geist der Immigration: Die Basler Fastnacht vom Ende des Zunftregiments bis zum Ersten Weltkrieg." In *Zwischentöne: Fasnacht und städtische Gesellschaft in Basel 1923–1998,* edited by Christine Burckhardt-Seebass et al., pp. 13–24. Basel: Buchverlag der Basler Zeitung, 1998.

Burke, Peter. "Le carnaval de Venice: Esquisse pour une histoire de longue durée." In *Les jeux à la Renaissance,* edited by P. Aviès and J. C. Margolin, pp. 55–63. Paris: Vrin, 1982.

———. *Popular Culture in Early Modern Europe.* New York: New York University Press, 1978.

Burkert, W. "Euenios der Seher von Apollonia und Apollon Lykeios: Mythos jenseits der Text." *Kernos* 10 (1997): 73–81.

Burton, Richard E. *Afro-Creole: Power, Opposition, and Play in the Caribbean.* Ithaca, NY: Cornell University Press, 1997.

Cacciari, Massimo. "Memoria sul Carnevale." In *Psicologia storica del Carnevale di Venezia,* by Florens Christian Rang, edited by Franco Desideri, pp. 77–91. Venice: Arsenale, 1983

Cajías, Fernando. "Carnaval de 1783." *Presencia* (special edition: *Oruro Carnaval Historia y Tradición*), 8 February 1997, pp. 5–7.

———. "Los Objectivos de la revolución de 1781: El Caso de Oruro." *Revista Andina* 1, no. 2 (1983): 407–428.

"Calendar." In *The New Encyclopedia Britannica,* vol. 3, pp. 600–603. Chicago: Encyclopedia Britannica, 15th edition, 1974.

Caro Baroja, Julio. *El Carnaval.* Madrid: Taurus Ediciones, 1986.

———. *España primitiva y romana.* Barcelona: Editorial Seix Barral, 1957.

Casanova, Giacomo. *History of My Life.* 12 vols. New York: Harcourt, Brace and World, 1966–1971 [1826–1838].

Cazorla Murillo, Fabrizio y Mauricio. *Gran tradicional auténtica diablada de Oruro.* Oruro: Gran Tradicional Auténtica Diablada de Oruro, 2000.

Cazzola, Piero. "I viaggiatori dell'Est europeo." In *Venezia dei grandi viaggiatori,* edited by Franco Paloscia, pp. 141–169. Rome: Abete, 1989.

Cejas Pabón, Rafael. "Pujllay." *Presencia* (special edition: *Oruro carnaval historia y tradición*), 8 February 1997, pp. 18–19.

Cerulli, Ernesta. *Vestirsi spogliarsi travestirsi.* Palermo: Sellerio, 1981.

Cervantes Saavedra, Miguel de. *The History of the Ingenious Gentleman, Don Quijote de la Mancha.* New York: Norton, 1995 [1605].

Chambers, E. K. *The Mediaeval Stage.* 3 vols. London: Oxford University Press, 1925.

Chamorro, J. Arturo. *La Música popular en Tlaxcala.* Tlahuapan, Puebla: Premiá Editora de Libros, 1983.

Chavero, Alfredo, ed. "Lienzo de Tlaxcala." In *Antigüedades mexicanas publicadas por la junta colombina de México en el cuarto centenario de descubrimiento de América,* Part 6, pp. 1–80. México, DF: Secretaría de Fomento, 1892.

Cheeseman, Tom. *The Shocking Ballad Picture Show: German Popular Literature and Cultural History.* Oxford: Berg, 1994.

Christian, Marcus. *I Am New Orleans: A Poem.* New Orleans: privately printed, 1968.

Cipriani, Arrigo. *The Harry's Bar Cookbook.* New York: Bantam Books, 1991.

"Coca y tradición se combinaron en la Morenda Central Cocanis," *La Patria* (special Carnival edition), 9 February 2002, p. 11.

Cocchiara, Giuseppe. *Il mondo alla rovescia.*

Turin: Boringhieri, 1963.

Cocho, Federico. *O carnaval en Galicia.* Vigo: Edicións Xerais de Galicia, 1992.

Cohen, Henning, and Tristram Potter Coffin, eds. *The Folklore of American Holidays.* Detroit: Gale, 1987.

Cole, Hubert. *Christophe, King of Haiti.* New York: Viking, 1967.

Cole, Toby. *Venice: A Portable Reader.* New York: Frontier Press, 1995.

Collins, Roger. *Early Medieval Spain. Unity and Diversity, 400–1000.* New York: St. Martin's Press, 1983.

Comune di Venezia. *Il carnevale veneziano del Casanova: Passioni enogastronomiche.* Venice: Municipality of Venice, 1998.

Cosentino, Donald. "Returning the Dead." *The World and I* (October 1994): 223–243.

———. *The Sacred Arts of Haitian Vodou.* Los Angeles: UCLA Fowler Museum of Cultural History, 1995.

———. "Titid Mon Amour: Lwas and Saints in the Haitian Heart." *The World and I* (October 1991): 616–625.

———. "Vodou Carnival." *Aperture* 126 (Winter 1992): 22–29.

Cowan, Jane K. "Women, Men, and Pre-Lenten Carnival in Northern Greece: An Anthropological Exploration of Gender Transformation in Symbol and Practice." *Rural History* 5, no. 2 (1994): 195–210.

Crowley, Daniel J. *African Myth and Black Reality in Bahian Carnaval.* Monograph Series, no. 25. Los Angeles: UCLA Museum of Cultural History, 1984.

———. "Carnival as Secular Ritual: a Pan-Portuguese Perspective." In *Folklore and Historical Process,* edited by Auguštin Dunja Rihtman and Maja Povrzanovif, pp. 143–148. Zagreb: Institute of Folklore Research, 1989.

———. "Midnight Robbers." In *Trinidad Carnival,* pp. 164–185. Port of Spain: Paria Publishing Company Limited, 1988. (A re-publication of *Caribbean Quarterly* 4, nos. 3–4, 1956.)

———. "The Traditional Masks of Carnival." In *Trinidad Carnival,* pp. 42–90. Port of Spain: Paria Publishing, 1988. (A republication of *Caribbean Quarterly* 4, nos. 3–4, 1956.)

Curtin, Philip. *The Atlantic Slave Trade: A Census.* Madison: University of Wisconsin Press, 1969.

da Matta, Roberto. *Carnavais, malandros e heróis: Para uma sociologia do dilema brasileiro.* Rio de Janeiro: Jorge Zahar Editores, 1978.

D'Annunzio, Gabriele. *Notturno.* Milan: Garzanti, 1995 [1921].

Dasairas, Xerardo. *O Entroido en Terras de Monterrei.* Vilaboa (Pontevedra): Ediciôns do Cumio, 1990.

Davis, Susan. *Parades and Power: Street Theatre in Nineteenth-Century Philadelphia.* Philadelphia: Temple University Press, 1986.

Dawkins, R. M. "The Modern Carnival in Thrace and the Cult of Dionysus." *Journal of Hellenic Studies* 26 (1906):191–206.

de Brosses, Charles. *Lettres familières écrites d'Italie en 1739 et 1740.* Paris: Librairie Academique, 1869.

Demme, Jonathan, director. *Haiti Dreams of Democracy.* Clinica Estetico, 1987.

Dias Blue, Anthony. "Feeling Groggy." *American Way* (January 2003): 44–45.

Drewal, Henry, and Margaret Thompson Drewal. *Gelede.* Bloomington: Indiana University Press, 1983.

Duchesne, Louis, ed. *Liber pontificalis.* 2 vols. Paris, 1889.

Dürst, Hans. "Das Cliquenwesen und die Basler Fasnacht." *Schweizerisches Archiv für Volkskunde* 69 (1969): 2–24.

Eco, Umberto. *Sugli specchi e altri saggi.* Milan: Bompiani, 1985.

"El Carnaval de Oruro apasiona y atrae a millones de personas." *La Patria* (special Carnival edition), 9 February 2002, p. 1A.

Epstein, Dena J. *Sinful Tunes and Spirituals: Black Folk Music to the Civil War.* Urbana: University of Illinois Press, 1977.

Estensssoro Fuchs, Juan Carlos. "Los Bailes de los indios y el proyecto colonial." *Revista Andina* 10, no. 2 (1992): 353–404.

Eusebietti, Dora. *Piccola storia dei burattini e delle maschere.* Turin: Sei, 1966.

Falassi, Alessandro, ed. *La Festa.* Milan: Electa, 1988.

———. ed. *Time Out of Time: Essays on the Festival.* Albuquerque: University of New Mexico Press, 1987.

Fano, Nicola. *Le maschere italiane.* Bologna: Il Mulino, 2001.

Fellini, Federico, and Bernardino Zapponi. *Il Casanova di Fellini.* Turin: Einaudi, 1976.

Fol, Alexander. *The Thracian Dionysos,* Book 1, *Zagreus* (in German). Sofia: Sofia University Press, 1993.

———. *The Thracian Dionysos,* Book 2, *Sabazius* (in Bulgarian, with abstract in English). Sofia: Sofia University Press, 1994.

———. *The Thracian Dionysos,* Book 3, *Naming and Faith* (in Bulgarian, with abstract in English). Sophia: Sofia University Press, 2002.

———. *The Thracian Orphism* (in Bulgarian, with abstracts in Russian and English). Sofia: Sofia University Press, 1986.

Fol, Valeria. "The Kouker without Mask: The Masquerade Feasts in Southeastern Europe." *Orpheus: Journal of Indoeuropean and Thracian Studies* 7 (1997): 83–99.

———. "Le Loup en Thrace Hyperboréenne." In *I Congreso de mitologia mediterránea: La razón del mito.* Terrasa, Julio de 1998, pp. 110–118. Madrid: Universidad Nacional de Educación a Distancia, 1998.

———. *The Rock, the Horse, and the Fire: Early Thracian Ritual Tradition* (in Bulgarian). Sofia: Arges, 1993.

Fontana, Alesssandro. "La verita delle maschere." In *Venezia e lo spazio scenico,* edited by Manlio Brusatin. Venice: Editions La Biennale, 1979.

Franci, Simonetta. "Carnevale di Venezia (Biennale e Teatro). La socialità come produzione e consumo." Ph.D. dissertation, University of Bologna, 1983.

Frazer, George. *The Golden Bough: A Study in Magic and Religion,* Part 5. 2 vols. New York: St. Martin's, 1990 [1890].

Freyre, Gilberto. *The Mansions and the Shanties: The Making of Modern Brazil.* Translated by Harriet de Onís from the Portuguese *Sobrados e mucambos,* first published in 1936. New York: Alfred A. Knopf, 1963.

———. *The Masters and the Slaves: A Study in the Development of Brazilian Civilization.* Translated by Samuel Putnam from the Portuguese *Casa grande e senzala,* first published in

1933. New York: Alfred A. Knopf, 1964.

Garzoni, Tomaso. *La Piazza Universale di tutte le professioni del mondo.* Venice: Gio. Battista Somascho, 1585.

Gennep, Arnold van. *Manuel de folklore français contemporain,* vol. 1, *Les ceremonies périodiques cycliques et saisonières,* Section 3, *Carnaval/Carême-Pâcques.* Paris: A. et J. Picaud, 1937–1938.

Gibson. Charles. *The Aztecs under Spanish Rule: A History of the Indians in the Valley of Mexico.* Stanford, CA: Stanford University Press, 1964.

———. *Tlaxcala in the Sixteenth Century.* Stanford, CA: Stanford University Press, 1967.

Gill, James. *Lords of Misrule: Mardi Gras and the Politics of Race in New Orleans.* Jackson: University Press of Mississippi, 1997.

Gilmore, David. *Carnival and Culture: Sex, Symbol, and Status in Spain.* New Haven: Yale University Press, 1998.

Giroux, Françoise. *Carnavals et fetes d'hiver.* Paris: Centre Georges Pompidou, 1984.

Glassie, Henry. *All Silver and No Brass: An Irish Christmas Mumming.* Bloomington: Indiana University Press, 1975.

Goldoni, Carlo. *Opere complete di Carlo Goldoni edite dal Municipio di Venezia nel II centenario della nascita.* 34 vols. Venice: Istituto Veneto di Arti Grafiche, 1907–1935.

González Reboredo, José Manuel and José Mariño Ferro. *Entroido: Aproximación a la Fiesta del Carnaval en Galicia.* La Coruña: Editorial Diputación Provincial, 1987.

Gossman, Lionel. *Basel in the Age of Burckhardt: A Study in Unseasonable Ideas.* Chicago: University of Chicago Press, 2000.

Goudar, Ange. *L'espion chinois.* 6 volumes. Cologne, 1764.

Gracián y Morales, Baltasar. *El Criticón.* Madrid: Espasa-Calpe, 1971.

Grevembroch, Giovanni. *Gli abiti de' Veneziani di quasi ogni età con diligenza raccolti, e dipinti nel secolo XVIII.* 4 vols. Venice: Filippi, 1981 (facsimile of a manuscript in the Correr Museum of Venice).

Gruzinski, Serge. *The Conquest of Mexico: The Incorporation of Indian Societies into the Western World, Sixteenth-Eighteenth Centuries.* Translated by Eileen Corrigan. Cambridge: Polity Press, 1993.

Guerra Guiterrez, Alberto. *Diablada Artistica Urus.* Oruro: Diablada Artistica Urus, 2000.

Guillermoprieto, Alma. *Samba.* New York: Vintage Books, Random House, 1991.

Habicht, Peter. *Lifting the Mask: Your Guide to the Basel* Fasnacht. Basel: Bergli Books, 2001.

Hall, Gwendolyn Midlo. *Africans in Colonial Louisiana: The Development of Afro-Creole Culture in the Eighteenth Century.* Baton Rouge: Louisiana State University Press, 1992.

Hardy, Arthur. *Mardi Gras in New Orleans: An Illustrated History.* New Orleans: Arthur Hardy Enterprises, 2001.

Harris, Max. *Carnival and Other Christian Festivals, Folk Theology, and Folk Performance.* Austin: University of Texas Press, 2003.

Herald Wire Services. "Haitians Celebrate in 'Carnival of Hope.'" *Miami Herald,* 28 February 1995, p. 3A.

Hernández Xochitiotzin, Desiderio. "Orígenes del carnaval en Europa, México y Tlaxcala" and "Conclusions." In *Tlaxcala es una fiesta: Mesa redonda sobre el Carnaval Tlaxcala 90,* pp. 15–20, 35–39. Tlaxcala: H. Ayuntamiento de Tlaxcala, 1990.

Herskovits Melville J., and Frances S. Herskovits. *Dahomean Narrative: A Cross-Cultural Analysis.* Evanston, IL: Northwestern University Press, 1958.

Hill, Errol. *The Trinidad Carnival.* London: New Beacon Books, 1997.

Hillgarth, J. N. *The Spanish Kingdoms, 1250–1516.* 2 vols. Oxford: Claredon Press, 1978.

Honour, Hugh, and John Fleming. *Venice and the Grand Tour.* Boston: Bulfinch Press, 1991.

Howells, William Dell. *Venetian Life.* Leipzig: Tauchnitz, 1866.

Hurbon, Laennec. "American Fantasy and Haitian Vodou." In *The Sacred Arts of Haitian Vodou,* edited by Donald J. Cosentino, pp. 181–197. Los Angeles: UCLA Fowler Museum of Cultural History, 1995.

H. Xochitiotzin Ortega, José Guadalupe. "Los Carnavales de Tlaxcala." *México Desconocido* 180 (February 1992): 17–21.

Ingham, John M. *Mary, Michael, and Lucifer: Folk Catholicism in Central Mexico.* Austin: University of Texas Press, 1986.

James, Henry. *Italian Hours.* New York: Grove Press, 1959 [1909].

Jeangardy, Ady. "Carnaval Histoire." *Sourire* 1, no. 3 (February 1995): 18–39.

Johnson, Jerah. "New Orleans's Congo Square: An Urban Setting for Early Afro-American Culture Formation." *Louisiana History* 32, no. 2 (1991): 117–157.

Johnson, Kim. "Introduction." In *Trinidad Carnival,* pp. xi–xxii. Port of Spain: Paria Publishing, 1988. (A re-publication of *Caribbean Quarterly* 4, nos. 3–4, 1956.)

Kakouri, K. *Dionysiaka: Aspects of the Popular Thracian Religion of To-day.* Athens: G. C. Eleftheroudakis, 1965. (Greek edition, 1963).

Karakostov, S. *Bulgarian Theater: Middle Ages, Renaissance, Enlightenment* (in Bulgarian). Sofia: Publishing House of the Bulgarian Academy of Sciences, 1972.

Kinser, Samuel. *Carnival American Style: Mardi Gras at New Orleans and Mobile.* Chicago: University of Chicago Press, 1990.

Klein, Herbert S. *Bolivia: The Evolution of a Multi-Ethnic Society.* New York: Oxford University Press, 1982.

Kmen, Henry A. *Music in New Orleans: The Formative Years, 1791–1841.* Baton Rouge: Louisiana State University Press, 1966.

Knox, Israel. "Towards a Philosophy of Humor." *Journal of Philosophy* 48, no. 18 (1951): 541–548.

Kolb, Carolyn. "Waltzing through the Century." *New Orleans Magazine* 29, no. 5 (February 1995): 59–61.

Koster, Henry. *Travels in Brazil.* 2d ed., 2 vols. London: Longman, Hurst, Rees, Orme & Brown, 1817.

Kraev, G. *Bulgarian Masquerade Games* (in Bulgarian). Sofia: Publishing House "Alice-7," 1996.

Laborde, Errol. *Mardi Gras! A Celebration.* Conception and photography by Mitchell Osborne. New Orleans: Picayune Press, 1981.

LaCour, Arthur Burton. *New Orleans Masquerade: Chronicles of Carnival.* New Orleans: Pelican Publishing, 1957.

Larra y Sanchez de Castro, Mariano José de. "Todo el mundo es mascaras, Todo el año es carnaval." *El Pobrecito Hablador* 14 March, 1833.

Lechtman, Heather. "Andean Value System and the Development of Prehispanic Metallurgy." *Technology and Culture* 25, no. 1 (1984): 1–36.

Lechuga, Ruth. "Carnival in Tlaxcala." In *Behind the Mask in Mexico,* edited by Janet Brody Esser, pp. 142–171. Santa Fe: Museum of New Mexico Press, 1988.

———. *Máscaras traditionales de México.* México, DF: Banco Nacional de Obras y Servicios Publicos, 1991.

"Leo Bussola" Carnevale di Venezia 2001. Special pamphlet of the Venice Tourist Board. Venice: Azienda di Promozione Turistica, 2001.

Le Roy Ladurie, Emmanuel. *The Beggar and the Professor: A Sixteenth-Century Family Saga.* Translated by Arthur Goldhammer. Chicago: University of Chicago Press, 1997.

Lévi-Strauss, Claude. *La Voie des masques.* 2 vols. Geneva: Skira, 1975.

Lindahl, Carl. "Finding the Field through the Discovery of the Self." In *Working the Field: Accounts from French Louisiana,* edited by Jacques Henry and Sara LeMenestral, pp. 33–50. Westport, CN: Praeger, 2003.

———. "One Family's Mardi Gras: The Moreaus of Basile." *Louisiana Cultural Vistas* 9, no. 3 (1998): 46–53.

———. "The Power of Being Outnumbered." *Louisiana Folklore Miscellany* 12 (1997): 43–76.

———. "The Presence of the Past in the Cajun Country Mardi Gras." *Journal of Folklore Research* 33 (1996): 125–153.

———. "Ways Inside the Circle of Mardi Gras." *Journal of American Folklore* 114 (2001): 132–139.

Lindahl, Carl, and Carolyn Ware. *Cajun Mardi Gras Masks.* Jackson: University Press of Mississippi, 1997.

Lisón Tolsana, Carmelo. *Antropología Cultural de Galicia.* Madrid: Akal Universitaria, 1983

Lucena Filho, Severino Alves. *Azulão do BANDEPE: Uma estratégia de comunicação organizacional.* Recife: Author's edition with support from the Banco de Pernambuco, 1998.

MacDermot, Mercia. *Bulgarian Folk Customs.* London: Jessica Kingsley, 1998.

Maertens, Jean-Thierry. *Le masque et le miroir.* Paris: Aubier Montaigne, 1978.

Mangini, Nicola. *I teatri di Venezia.* Milan: Mursia, 1974.

Mann, Thomas. *Der Tod in Venedig.* Berlin: Fischer, 1912. (For a recent critical edition in English see *Death in Venice,* New York: Norton, 1994.)

Matas, Mercedes. "'s goht um d'Wurscht!" Zeitgeschichte im Spiegel von Sujets der Basler Fasnacht 1923–1996, dargestellt am Beispiel der vier Jubiläumscliquen." In *Zwischentöne: Fasnacht und städtische Gesellschaft in Basel 1923–1998,* edited by Christine Burckhardt-Seebass et al., pp. 101–112. Basel: Buchverlag der Basler Zeitung, 1998.

Maurer, Doris, and Arnold E. Maurer. *Literarischer Führer durch Italien.* Frankfurt: Insel Verlag, 1988.

McAlister, Elizabeth. *Rara: Vodou, Power, and Performance in Haiti and Its Diaspora.* Berkeley: University of California Press, 2002.

McCarthy, Mary. "Venice Observed." In *The Stones of Florence and Venice Observed,* pp. 171–281. London: Penguin, 1972 [1956].

McFarren, Peter. Ed. *Mascaras de los Andes bolivianos.* La Paz: Editorial Quipus, 1993.

Meier, Eugen A., ed. *Die Basler Fasnacht: Geschichte und Gegenwart einer lebendigen Tradition.* Basel: Fasnachts-Comité, 1985.

———. "Die Fasnacht im Alten Basel." In *Die Basler Fasnacht: Geschichte und Gegenwart einer lebendigen Tradition,* edited by Eugen A Meier, pp. 23–74. Basel: Fasnachts-Comité, 1985.

Mendoza Salazar, David. "Caporales." *Presencia* (special edition: *Oruro carnaval historia y tradición*), 8 February 1997, p. 4.

Mercado, Melchor María. *Album de paisajes, tipos humanos y costumbres de Bolivia (1841–1869).* Sucre: Archivo y Biblioteca Nacional de Bolivia, 1991.

Mezger, Werner. *Narrenidee und Fastnachtsbrauch: Studien zum Fortleben des Mittelalters in der europäischen Festkultur.* Constance: Universitätsverlag Konstanz, 1991.

Mintz, Sidney, and Michel-Rolph Trouillot. "The Social History of Haitian Vodou." In *The Sacred Arts of Haitian Vodou,* edited by Donald J. Cosentino, pp. 123–147. Los Angeles: UCLA Fowler Museum of Cultural History, 1995.

-minu. *d'Goschdym-Kischte.* Basel: Gissler-Verlag, 1981.

Mire, Pat (director). *Dance for a Chicken: The Cajun Mardi Gras.* 57-min., 1/2-inch video format, color. Eunice, LA: Attakapas Productions, 1993.

Montaño Aragon, Mario. *Raices semíticas en la religiosidad Aymara y Kichua.* La Paz: Biblioteca Popular Boliviana de UH, 1979.

Moraes, Eneida. *História do carnaval carioca.* Rio de Janeiro: Editôra Record, 1987.

Morris, James. *Venice.* London: Faber and Faber, 1974.

Morris, Jan. "Venice en hiver." *GEO* 33 (1981): 132–156.

Muñoz Camargo, Diego. *Historia de Tlaxcala.* Facsimile edition. México, DF: Secretaría de Fomento, 1966 [1892].

Muñoz Carrión, Antonio. "Elementos Comunicacionales en la Parodia Grotesca: Introducción Metodológica." *Revista Internacional de Sociología* 44, no. 1 (1986): 81–103.

Murillo Vacarreza, Josermo. "Un hipotesis sobre el origin del baile de los diablos." *La Patria* (special Carnival edition), 9 February 2002.

Napier, David. *Mask: Transformation and Paradox.* Berkeley: University of California Press, 1985.

Nash, June. *We Eat the Mines and the Mines Eat Us: Dependency and Exploitation in Bolivian Tin Mines.* New York: Columbia University Press, 1993.

"Negritos." *Presencia* (special edition: *Oruro carnaval historia y tradición*), 8 February 1997, p. 19.

Nunley, John. "The Beat Goes On: Recycling and Improvisation in the Music of Trinidad and Tobago." In *Recycling, Reseen: Folk Art from the Global Scrap Heap,* pp. 130–139. New York: Abrams, 1996.

———. "Masquerade Mix-up in Trinidad Carnival: Live Once, Die Forever." In *Caribbean Festival Arts: Each and Every Bit of Difference,* edited by John Nunley and Judith Bettelheim, pp. 85–117. Seattle: University of Washington Press, 1988.

Nunley, John, and Judith Bettelheim, eds. *Caribbean Festival Arts: Each and Every Bit of Difference.* Seattle: University of Washington Press, 1988.

Nunley, John, and Cara McCarthy. *Masks: Faces of Culture.* New York: Abrams, 2000.

Nutini, Hugo G. "Clan Organization in a Nahuatl-Speaking Village of the State of Tlaxcala, Mexico." *American Anthropologist* 63 (1961): 62–78.

———. "An Outline of Tlaxcaltecan Culture, History, Ethnology, and Demography." In *The Tlaxcaltecan Prehistory, Demography, Morphology, and Genetics,* edited by Michael H. Crawford, pp. 24–34. Lawrence: University of Kansas Press, 1976.

———. *San Bernardino Contla: Marriage and Family Structure in a Tlaxcalan Municipio.* Pittsburgh: University of Pittsburgh Press, 1968.

Nutini, Hugo G., and Betty Bell. *Ritual Kinship: The Structure and Historical Development of the Compadrazgo System in Rural Tlaxcala.* 2 vols. Princeton: Princeton University Press, 1980.

Obbink, D. "Cosmology as Initiation vs. The Critique of Orphic Mysteries." In *Studies on the Derveni Papyrus,* edited by A. Lacks and W. Most Glenn, pp. 39–54. Oxford: Clarendon, 1997.

Oliveira, Valdemar de. *Frevo, capoeira e passo.* Recife: Companhia Editôra de Pernambuco, 1971.

Orloff, Alexander. *Carnival: Myth and Cult.* Wörgl, Austria: Perlinger Verlag, 1981.

Orozco, Ramiro, ed. *Caporales centrales.* La Paz: Producciones Gráficas Tauro, 1998.

O'Shea, William James, et al. "Lent." In *New Catholic Encyclopedia,* vol. 7, pp. 468–469. Detroit: Gale, 2003.

Overbeck, Alicia O. "Bolivia, Land of Fiestas." *National Geographic* 66, no. 5 (1934): 645–660.

Page, Joseph A. *The Brazilians.* New York: Addison-Wesley, 1995.

Palazzeschi, Aldo. *Il Doge.* Milan: Mondadori, 1967.

Paredes-Candia, Antonio. *Tradiciones orueñas.* La Paz: Ediciones Ilsa, 1980.

Parkinson, Wenda. *"This Gilded African": Toussaint L'Ouverture.* London: Quartet Books, 1980.

Payne, Stanley G. *Spanish Catholicism: An Historical Overview.* Madison: University of Wisconsin Press, 1984.

Paz, Octavio. *The Labyrinth of Solitude.* New York: Grove Press, 1961.

Pearse, Andrew. "Carnival in Nineteenth-Century Trinidad." In *Trinidad Carnival,* pp. 4–41. Port of Spain: Paria Publishing, 1988. (A re-publication of *Caribbean Quarterly* 4, nos. 3–4, 1956.)

Pierson, Donald. *Negroes in Brazil: A Study of Race Contact at Bahia.* Chicago: University of Chicago Press, 1942.

Pinto, Tiago de Oliveira. "The Pernambuco Carnival and Its Formal Organizations: Music as an Expression of Hierarchies and Power in Brazil." *Yearbook for Traditional Music* 26 (1994): 20–38.

Pizarro Cuenca, Arturo. *La Cultura negra en Bolivia.* La Paz: Ediciones ISLA, 1977.

Poppi, Cesare. "The Other Within: Masks and Masquerades in Europe." In *Masks and the Art of Expression*, edited by John Mack, pp. 190–215. New York: Abrams, 1994.

Portoghesi, Paolo, and Maurizio Scaparro, eds. *Carnevale del Teatro.* Venice: Editions La Biennale, 1980.

Poulter, A. G. *Nicopolis ad Istrum: A Roman to Early Byzantium City.* London: Leicester Universtiy Press, 1999.

Preto, Paolo. *I servizi segreti di Venezia.* Milan: Il Saggiatore, 1994.

Programa de Carnaval Tlaxcala. Tlaxcala: Secretaría de Turismo, 1999, 2002.

Proust, Marcel. "La fugitive." In *A' la recherche du temps perdu,* vol. 3, pp. 417–688. Paris: Gallimard, 1954.

Puchner, W. "Die thrakische Karnevalsszene und die Ursprungstrheorien zum altgriechischen Drama. Ein Beitrag zur wissenschaftsgeschichtlichen Rezeptionsforschung." *Balkan Studies* 24, no. 1 (1983): 107–122.

Puppa, Paolo. "Il carnevale veneziano: La forza e la forma l'energia della piazza." *STILB* 3, nos. 14–15 (1983): 6–7.

Putnam, Helena, and Barry Jean Ancelet. *"Chanson de Mardi Gras* (Basile)." In *Cajun Country Mardi Gras: Variety within a Culture,* pp. 5–6. Program for a performance at the Liberty Theater, Eunice, LA, 18 February. Eunice: Liberty Cultural Association, 1995.

Ramos de Temoltzin, Isaura. "Aspectos históricos de la danza en México." In *Tlaxcala es una fiesta: Mesa redonda sobre el Carnaval Tlaxcala 90,* pp. 21–28. Tlaxcala: H. Ayuntamiento de Tlaxcala, 1990.

———. *Danzas de carnaval en Tlaxcala.* Tlaxcala: H. Ayuntamiento de Tlaxcala, 1997.

Ramos Galicia, Yolanda. *Calendario de ferias y fiestas tradicionales del estado Tlaxcala.* México, DF: Instituto Nacional de Antropología e Historia, 1992.

Rampello, Davide. "Progettare il Carnevale." In *Carnevale di Venezia: Che la festa cominci,* edited by Fulvio Roiter, pp. 13–14. Milan: Electa, 1994.

Ravicz , Marilyn Ekdahl. *Early Colonial Religious Drama in Mexico: From Tzompantli to Golgotha.* Washington, D.C.: Catholic University of America Press, 1970.

Raychevski, S., and Valeria Fol. *The Kouker without Mask* (in Bulgarian). Sofia: "St. Kl. Ochridski" University Press, 1993.

Real, Katarina (Katharine Royal Cate). "The Brazilian Urban Carnaval: A Discussion of its Origins, Nature, and Ethnological Significance." Master's thesis, University of North Carolina, Chapel Hill, 1960.

———. *O Folclore no Carnaval do Recife.* 2d ed. Recife: Editôra Massangana, Fundação Joaquim Nabuco, 1990.

———. "Sobrevivências medievais no carnaval de Pernambuco." In *Anais da I Jornada de Estudos Medievais-1996,* pp. 105–122. Aracaju, Sergipe: Secretaria de Estado da Cultura de Sergipe, 1997.

Reato, Danilo. *Storia del Carnevale di Venezia.* Venice: Filippi, 1988.

———. *Venezia: Una città in maschera.* Venice: Filippi, 1998.

Redford, Bruce. *Venice and the Grand Tour.* New Haven: Yale University Press, 1996.

Regalado, Mariana. "Ounhas Couces do Nabizo (a few kicks from the donkey): Evaluation in the Performance of the Testament of the Donkey." Master's thesis, New York University, 1992.

Reich, H. *Der Mimus.* Berlin: Weidmannsche Buchhandlung, 1903.

Rendón Garcini, Ricardo. "Las Haciendas pulqueras." In *Tlaxcala: Textos de su historia,* vol. 1, edited by Lía García Verástegui and Ma. Esther Pérez Salas C., pp. 74–75. México, DF: Instituto de Investigaciones Dr. José María Luis Mora, 1990.

Renier-Michiel Giustina. *Origine delle feste veneziane.* Venice: Filippi, 1994 [1916] (abridged edition, originally published in five volumes, Venice: Alvisopoli, 1817–1827).

Revelard, Michel. *Musée International du Carnaval et du Masque.* Binche: Crédit Communal, n.d

Revollo Fernández, Antonio. "Tinku." *Presencia* (special edition: *Oruro carnaval historia y tradición*), 8 February 1997, p. 18.

Ribeiro, Pedro, and Maria Lúcia Montes. *Maracatu de baque virado.* São Paulo: Serviços de Imprensa Quatro Imagens, 1998.

Ribeiro, René. *Religião e relações raciais.* Rio de Janeiro: Ministério de Educação e Cultura, 1956.

Riggio, Milla C., ed. "Trinidad and Tobago Carnival." *Drama Review* 42, no. 3 (1998).

Risco, Vicente. "Notas sobre las Fiestas de Carnaval en Galicia." *Revista de Dialectología y Tradiciones Populares* 4, nos. 2–3 (1948): 163–96, 339–68.

Roiter, Fulvio. *Carnevale di Venezia: Che la festa cominci.* Milan: Electa, 1994.

———. *Carnevale di Venezia tra maschera e ragione.* Padua: Dagor, 1981.

Roma Riu, Josefina. *Aragón y el Carnaval.* Zaragoza: Guara Editorial, 1980.

Roshto, Ronnie E. "Georgie and Allen Manuel and Cajun Wire Screen Masks." *Louisiana Folklore Miscellany* 7 (1992): 33–49.

Rossi, Aldo. "Il progetto per Il Teatro del mondo." In *Venezia e lo spazio scenico,* edited by Manlio Brusatin, p. 7. Venice: Editions la Biennale, 1979.

Ruiz, Juan, archpriest of Hita. *El Libro de Buen Amor.* Madrid: Editorial Castalia, 1985.

Rules of the Sacred Orthodox Church (in Bulgarian). Sofia: Union of the Priests' Fraternities in Bulgaria, 1936.

Sá, Hernane Tavares. *The Brazilians: People of Tomorrow.* New York: John Day Company Sales, 1947.

Sahagún, Fray Bernardino de. *Florentine Codex: General History of the Things of New Spain,* Book 2, *The Ceremonies.* Translated and edited by Arthur J. O. Anderson and Charles Dibble. Salt Lake City: University of Utah Press, 1981.

Salvalaggio, Nantas. *Attenzione Caduta Angeli.* Vicenza: Neri Pozza, 1995.

Santagiuliana, Fabio, and Giuliano Scabia. *Venezia i giorni delle maschere.* Udine: Magnus Editions, 1980.

Santana Sandoval, Andrés. "Carnaval, la fiesta colectiva." In *Tlaxcala es una fiesta: Mesa redonda sobre el Carnaval Tlaxcala 90,* pp. 29–34. Tlaxcala: H. Ayuntamiento de Tlaxcala, 1990.

Sartorius, Carl Christian. *Mexico and the Mexicans.* London: Trubner, 1859. Reprint, México, DF: San Angel Ediciones, 1973.

Sawin, Patricia E. "Transparent Masks: The Ideology and Practice of Disguise in Contemporary Cajun Mardi Gras." *Journal of American Folklore* 114 (2001): 175–203.

Scarpa, Tiziano. *Venezia è un pesce.* Milan: Feltrinelli, 2000.

Scarsella, Alessandro. *Le maschere veneziane.* Rome: Newton Compton, 1998.

———. "Proposte per una topica del mito di Venezia." *Ateneo Veneto* 25, nos. 1–2 (1987): 161–176.

Schindler, Henri. "The Grand Tableau." In *Arthur Hardy's Mardi Gras Guide 2002,* pp. 58–63, 114, 116–118. New Orleans: Arthur Hardy Enterprises, 2002.

———. *Mardi Gras New Orleans.* Paris: Flammarion, 1997.

———. *Mardi Gras Treasures: Float Designs of the Golden Age.* Gretna, LA: Pelican Publishing, 2001.

———. *Mardi Gras Treasures: Invitations of the Golden Age.* Gretna, LA: Pelican Publishing, 2000.

Sevilla, Amparo, Hilda Rodriguez, and Elizabeth Camara. *Danzas y bailes tradicionales del estado de Tlaxcala.* Tlahuapan, Puebla: Premiá Editora de Libros, 1983.

Sexton, Rocky L., and Harry Oster. *"Une 'Tite Poule Grass ou la Fille Ainée:* A Comparative Analysis Cajun and Creole Mardi Gras Songs." *Journal of American Folklore* 114 (2001): 204–224.

Sgarbi, Vittorio. "La Marchesa Casati, Dandy." In *Dell'Italia: Uomini e luoghi,* pp. 164–172. Milan: Rizzoli, 1991.

Shacochis, Bob. *The Immaculate Invasion.* New York: Viking, 1999.

Silva, Leonardo Dantas. "A instituição do Rei do Congo e sua presença nos maracatus." In *Estudos sobre a escravidão negra,* vol. 2, edited by L. D. Silva, pp. 1–7. Recife: Editôra Massangana, Fundação Joaquim Nabuco, 1988.

Simoën, Jean-Claude, ed. *Le Voyage à Venise.* Paris: Lattès, 1992.

Simons, David Lee. "Krewe du Few." *Gambit Weekly* 20, no. 5 (2 February 1999): 23–26.

Slavin, J. P. "As Aristide's Support Ebbs, Tensions Grow." *Los Angeles Times,* 3 (March 2003): M3

Solsten, Eric, and Sandra W. Meditz, eds. *Spain: A Country Study.* Washington DC: Library of Congress. 1990.

Spencer, Elaine Glovka. "Regimenting Revelry: Rhenish Carnival in the Early Nineteenth Century." *Central European History* 28, no. 4 (1995): 457–481.

Spoto, Donald. *Marilyn Monroe: The Biography.* New York: HarperCollins, 1993.

Stucchi, Loredana, and Mario Verdone. *Le Maschere Italiane.* Rome: Newton Compton, 1984.

Taboada Chivite, Xesús. "La Cencerrada en Galicia." In *Ritos y creencias gallegas,* pp. 203 -218. A Coruña: Salvora, 1980. (Reprinted from Actas del I Congreso Nacional de Artes y Costumbres Populares, 1969.)

———. "El Entierro de la Sardina: Ritualidad del carnaval gallego." In *Ritos y creencias gallegas,* pp. 47–56. A Coruña: Salvora, 1980. (Reprinted from *Duoro-Litorial* 6, nos. 1–2, n.d.)

———. *Etnografía galega.* Vigo: Editorial Galaxia, 1972.

Tassini, Giuseppe. *Feste Spettacoli Divertimenti Piaceri degli antichi Veneziani.* Venice: Filippi, 1961 [1890].

——— (under the anagrammed pseudonym G. Nissati). *Aneddoti Storici Veneziani.* Venice: Filippi, 1965 [1897].

Templeman, Robert Whitney. "AfroBolivians." In *Encyclopedia of World Cultures,* vol. 7, *South America,* edited by Johannes Wilbert, pp. 7–10. New York: G. K. Hall/ Macmillan, 1994.

———. "We Are People of the *Yungas:* We Are the *Saya* Race." In *Blackness in Latin America and the Caribbean: Social Dynamics and Cultural Transformations,* edited by Norman E. Whitten, Jr., and Arlene Torres, pp. 426–444. Bloomington: Indiana University Press, 1998.

Thompson, E. A. *The Goths in Spain.* Oxford: Caredon Press, 1969.

Thompson, E. P. "Rough Music." In *Customs in Common: Studies in Traditional Popular Culture,* edited by E. P. Thompson, pp. 466–538. New York: New Press, 1993.

Thompson, Robert Farris. *Flash of the Spirit: African and Afro-American Art and Philosophy.* New York: Random House, 1983.

Tokofsky, Peter. "Charivari." In *Folklore: An Encyclopedia of Beliefs, Customs, Tales, Music, and Art,* vol. 1, edited by Thomas A. Green, pp. 120–121. Santa Barbara: ABC-CLIO, 1997.

———. "A Tale of Two Carnivals: Esoteric and Exoteric Performance in the *Fasnet* of Elzach." *Journal of American Folklore* 113 (2000): 357–377.

Toschi, Paolo. *Le Origini del teatro italiano.* Turin: Edizioni Scientifiche Einaudi, 1955.

Trümpy, Hans. "Zur Geschichte der Basler Fasnacht." In *Unsere Fasnacht,* edited by Peter Heman, pp. 17–23. Basel: Verlag, 1971.

Tupkova-Zaimova, V. "Information about Mediaeval Kouker's Games in the Silistra Region." In *Lingual-Ethnographic Studies in Memory of Acad. Stoyan Romanski* (in Bulgarian). Sofia: Publishing House of the Bulgarian Academy of Sciences, 1960.

Turner Victor. *Process, Performance and Pilgrimage. A Study in Comparative Symbology.* New Delhi: Concept Publishing Company, 1979.

Twain, Mark. *The Innocents Abroad.* New York: Oxford University Press, 1996 [1867].

Valeri, Diego. *Fantasie veneziane.* Venice: Neri Pozza, Milan: Mondadori, 1994 [1934].

———. *Guida sentimentale di Venezia.* Florence: Giunti-Martello, 1978 [1942].

———. "Il Mito del Settecento Veneziano." In *Storia della Civiltà Veneziana,* vol. 3, edited by Vittore Branca, pp. 119–129. Florence: Sansoni, 1979.

Vargas, Manuel. "El Carnaval de Oruro." In *Máscaras de los Andes bolivianos,* edited by Peter McFarren, pp. 79–113. La Paz: Editorial Quipus, 1993.

Vargas Luza, Jorge Enrique. *La Diablada de Oruro: Sus máscaras y caretas.* La Paz: Plural Editores, 1998.

Vazquez Santana, Higinio, and J. Ignacio Dávila Garibi. *El Carnaval.* México, DF: Talleres Gráficos de la Nación México, 1931.

Venedikov, Ivan. *The Copper Threshing Floor of the Proto-Bulgarians* (in Bulgarian). Sophia: Nauka I Izkustvo Press, 1983.

Vizyinos, G. M. "The Kalogeroi and the Cult of Dionysos in Thrace" (in Greek). *Hebdomax* 5 (1888): 32–35.

Volli, Ugo. *Teatro o festa: Il Carnevale di Venezia.* Treviso: Arcari, 1980.

Ware, Carolyn E. "'Anything to Act Crazy': Cajun Women and Mardi Gras Disguise." *Journal of American Folklore* 114 (2001): 225–247.

———. "'I Read the Rules Backward': Women, Symbolic Inversion, and the Cajun Mardi Gras Run." *Southern Folklore* 52 (1995): 137–160.

West, M. L. *The Orphic Poems.* Oxford: Clarendon, 1983.

Willeford, William. *The Fool and His Sceptre: A Study in Clowns and Jesters and Their Audience.* Evanston, IL: Northwestern University Press, 1969.

Wunderlin, Dominik. "Die Guggenmusiken in Basel: Die Entwicklung einer fastnächtlichen Bensonderheit." *Schweizer Volkskunde* 6 (1975): 81–94.

Xelhuantzi Ramírez, Alberto. "El Carnaval o carnestolenda en Tlaxcala en el siglo XVIII." *Caceta Cultural del Tlaxcala de Xichténcatl* (10 February 2002): 2A.

Zanzotto, Andrea. "Carnevale di Venezia." In *Sull'altopiano e prose varie,* pp. 183–192. Vicenza: Neri Pozza, 1995.

Zorzi, Alvise. *La Repubblica del Leone (Storia di Venezia).* Milan: Rusconi, 1979.

———. "La Serenissima in festa." In *La Festa,* edited by Alessandro Falassi, pp. 66–70. Milan: Electa, 1988.

———. "Venezia, mito e antimito." In *Venezia dei grandi viaggiatori,* edited by Franco Paloscia, pp. 15–29. Rome: Abete, 1989.

———. *Venezia Austriaca.* Gorizia: Libreria Editrice Goriziana, 2000.

———. *Vita di Marco Polo veneziano.* Milan: Rusconi, 1982.

Zorzi, Lucio Marco. *Fregole no xe fragole: Poesie.* Venice: Editoria Universitaria, 1996.

CONTRIBUTORS

Jason Berry, B.A., a writer and independent producer, is a native of New Orleans. His works as a cultural historian include *The Spirit of Black Hawk: A Mystery of Africans and Indians* and (as a coauthor) *Up from the Cradle of Jazz*. He received a Guggenheim fellowship for a work in progress on jazz funerals. Berry has also written extensively about the Catholic clergy crisis in *Lead Us Not into Temptation* and *Vows of Silence*.

Donald Cosentino, Ph.D., is a professor of world arts and cultures at the University of California, Los Angeles, where he also serves as an editor of the journal *African Arts*. He conducts field research in West Africa and the Caribbean, with a special focus on Black Atlantic myth, art, and religion. He has published widely in scholarly and popular publications and was curator and author of note for the celebrated exhibition *The Sacred Arts of Haitian Vodou,* organized by the UCLA Fowler Museum of Cultural History.

Alessandro Falassi, Ph.D., is a professor of anthropology and folklore at the University for Foreigners in Siena, Italy. His research has concentrated on Italian folklore, with a particular focus on festival and ritual. Some of his publications are *La Terra in Piazza: An Interpretation of the Palio of Siena; Time Out of Time: Essays on Festival; La Festa;* and (as editor) *Les Fêtes du Soleil: Celebrations of the Mediterranean Regions*. He has done extensive research on Venice Carnival and supervised the production of a film on this topic for the Italian Ministry of Culture.

Valeria Fol, Ph.D., is an associate professor of ancient history and culture at the Institute of Thracology in Sofia. A native of Bulgaria, Fol has specialized in the study of ancient history, historical ethnology, and the arts of southeastern Europe. Some of her publications are *The Rock, the Horse and the Fire: Early Thracian Ritualism; The Forgotten Sainte; The Kouker without a Mask;* and *Ancient Thrace: The Silence Talks*. She has also worked as a scriptwriter and consultant for documentaries, including one on Kouker festivals in the rural villages of Bulgaria.

Carl Lindahl, Ph.D., is a professor of English at the University of Houston. He is a noted folklorist specializing in the narrative and festive traditions of medieval England and France as well as twentieth-century America. He co-edited *Swapping Stories: Folktales from Louisiana* (1997), co-authored *Cajun Mardi Gras Masks* (1997), wrote "Finding the Field through the Discovery of the Self" (in *Working the Field: Accounts from French Louisiana,* edited by Jacques Henry and Sara LeMenestrel, 2003), and served as a consultant and narrator for Pat Mire's video *Dance for a Chicken: The Cajun Mardi Gras* (1993).

Barbara Mauldin, Ph.D., has been curator of Latin American Folk Art at the Museum of International Folk

Art (MOIFA) since 1991 and served in other curatorial positions for the Museum of New Mexico prior to that. She has produced or assisted in producing many exhibitions, including *Traditions in Transition: Contemporary Basketweaving of the Southwestern Indians; Familia y Fé; Behind the Mask in Mexico; Folk Art of Brazil's Northeast;* and *Recycled, Re-Seen: Folk Art from the Global Scrap Heap.* Mauldin has a particular interest in festival traditions and costumes of Latin America. Her latest book, *Mexican Masks: Tigers, Devils, and the Dance of Life,* features MOIFA's Mexican mask collection in the context of regional festivals and styles.

Antonio Muñoz Carrión, Ph.D., has graduate degrees from the Faculty of Political Science and Sociology of the Universidad Complutense de Madrid and l'Ecole des Hautes Etudes en Sciences Sociales de París; he holds a doctorate in social anthropology from the Universidad Complutense de Madrid. He began his study of the Entroido of Laza in 1976. In 1985 he received the Premio Nacional de Investigación en Artes y Tradiciones Populares "Marqués de Lozoya" for his study *Las Reglas de la expresión carnavalesca en Laza* (Rules of carnivalesque expression in Laza).

John Nunley, Ph.D., is the Morton D. May Curator of the Arts of Africa, Oceania, and the Americas at the Saint Louis Art Museum. He became interested in masquerades while conducting dissertation research in northern Ghana in 1972–1973, and his later work on festivals and masquerades in Freetown, Sierra Leone, resulted an exhibition and the book *Moving with the Face of the Devil: Art and Politics in Urban West Africa.* Since 1983 Nunley has conducted fieldwork in Caribbean nations on masking and carnivals of the African and European diaspora. His research led directly to his organizing a major traveling exhibition, *Caribbean Festival Arts,* with an accompanying book. Nunley recently oversaw the production of another major exhibition and publication, *Masks: Faces of Culture.*

Katarina Real, M.A., is an anthropologist and folklorist who has devoted most of her forty-year career to studying the popular culture of northeastern Brazil. Among many other teaching and consulting positions,

Real served in Recife as the secretary general for the Pernambuco State Folklore Commission from 1964 to 1968. One of Real's particular interests has been the Carnival of Recife-Olinda, and among her many publications in Portuguese, her book *O Folclore no Carnaval do Recife* is considered to be the most comprehensive work on this topic.

Mariana Regalado, M.A., received her degree in linguistic anthropology at New York University in 1992. Her thesis focused on the Carnival celebration in Laza, Spain, with a linguistic interpretation of the "testament of the donkey" and what it means within the community. In 1989 Regalado worked with Jesús Lozano, an independent documentary video maker, to produce a thirty-minute documentary on Carnival in Laza, sponsored by NYU in Spain.

Cynthia LeCount Samaké, M.A., has spent many years researching the traditional textiles, costumes, and festival traditions of Bolivia, Peru, Thailand, and Laos. She teaches world textiles at the University of California, Davis, and is academic director for the University Research Expeditions Program (UREP). She studied with Daniel J. Crowley at the University of California, Davis, and wrote her master's thesis on tradition and innovation in the Carnival costumes of Oruro. She also curated exhibitions of this material at the San Francisco Craft and Folk Art Museum (1994) and the Bowers Museum of Cultural Art (1996). She curated another exhibit, "¡Viva Carnival! The Daniel J. Crowley Memorial Exhibition," for UC Davis, which highlighted Carnival costumes from the Americas.

Peter Tokofsky, Ph.D., is an associate adjunct professor in the Department of Germanic Languages/World Arts and Cultures at the University of California, Los Angeles. His research interests have focused on German and Swiss folklore and folk life, particularly in the realm of Carnival. His dissertation was titled "The Rules of Fools: Carnival in Southwest Germany." Tokofsky has also published many articles on this topic, including "A Tale of Two Carnivals: Esoteric and Exoteric Performance in the Fasnet of Elzach" and "Masking Gender: A German Carnival Custom in its Social Context."

INDEX

costumes. *See* masks and masquerades
cowbells, 28, 31, 33, 115, 221, 223, 225, 230
cowheads (Carnival character), 278, **279**
Creoles, 123, 139, 175, 243, 247, **316**
criticism, social and political, 9, 14, 25, 29, 40, **108**, **109**, 109–
    13, **110**, **111**, 116, 229
cuadrillas, 145, **146**, 161, 165–66
cuchillos, 163–64

Dance of the Snake, 145, 146, **147**, **148**
dancing, 5, 7, 9, 16, 17, 22, 28, 30, 37, 39, 83, 132, 134, 136,
    138–39, **138-39**, 145–54, 157–69, **165**, 173, 174, 175, 179,
    197, 198, 206, 208, 209–11, 212, 213, 321; and devil groups,
    181; *diablo* group, **182-83**; and square dancing, **166**
Devil (Carnival character), **174**, 179, **180**, 181–84, **182-83**, 194,
    195, **195**, 245, **245**, **279**, 291, **293**, 302
devil groups, 181, 184, 245
Dionysus, 45, 48, 49
distribución da bica, 35–36, **36**
dogs (Carnival characters), 109–10, **110**, 116
Domino (Carnival character), 75
doñas (Carnival characters), 184, **184**, 185
Il Dottore (Carnival character), 75
doubloons, 303–4
drag-queen beauty contests, 309, **313**
dramas, 148, 152, 197; bull, 229; conquest, 174, 175; *diablada*,
    179; folk, **202**, 226–27, **229**; *morenado* dance, 184–85; pro-
    cessional dance, 174, 179, 180, 199
drums, 16, 21, 30, 31, 35, 96, **101**, 106, 114, 115, 117, 163, 175,
    179, 185, **187**, 207, 208, 221, 222, **225**, 227, 230, **230**, 245,
    261, 275; and *batuqueiro* drum corps, 223; and competi-
    tion, 257; conga, 231, 250, 301; outlawing of, 247; snare,
    225, 250; steel, 249–50, **250**, 253; *tamboo-bamboo*, 247,
    250; *tassa*, 239, 250–51
Dummpeter (Carnival character), 103
Duvalier family, 269, 279–81, 283
Dyaddo (Carnival character), 54, 57, 58

Easter, 3, 10
Eastern Orthodox Church, 17, 45, 48; Kouker's Day imperson-
    ation of priest, **56**; opposition to masquerade ritual tradi-
    tion, 49
encabezados, 165
encargados, 165
entierro do entroido, 39–41
entremeses, 25
entroido, 3, 7, 14; in Laza, Spain, 21–42
entrudo, 3, 207–9; efforts to abolish, 208
Ergen (Carnival character), 55, 58
escolas de samba, 221–22
Español (Carnival character), **iv**, 159, **160**, **161**, 165

face painting, 84, **84**, **86**
farandula, 35
farrapada, 37–38
Fasching, 3
Fasnacht, 8–9, 12, 14, 16, 93–119; and cellers, 117; forms of

organization, 105–8; and lanterns, 96, **97**, **100**, 106, 107,
    110–11, **111**, 112; role of clubs, 96; selecting a theme for,
    108–9
Festival of the Marys, 82
flambeau carriers, **302**, 304–5, **305**
floats, 4, 6, 7, 11, 16, 25, 32, 38, 97, 126, 208, 217, 221, 277, 278,
    281, 284, 286, **298**, 303, 308, **316**; in Barcelona Carnival,
    26-27; created by Krewe of Rex, **323**; and social criticism,
    30, **37**
folión, 21, **22**, 33–34
foods, 17, 30, 32, 34, 101, 134, 136, 194, 196, 207, 246, **323**, **324**,
    324; booths for selling, **196**
formigas, 38, 39
frevo, 16, 209–11, **210**
Funkensonntag, 96

Galicia, 7, 21; evolution of Carnival in, 22–30; history of, 22–30
gallerie, 121
Gässle, 108
Gede, **13**, 269, 284–86, 288, 293; paper-mâché figure of, **291**
generals (Carnival characters): Charles Oscar (Chaloskas), 278,
    278, 292, **296**; Gran Van, 278; Kaka, 278; Pet Santi, 278;
    PiTa-PiTris, 278; Plim pa Gouye, 278; Ti-Zozo, 278
giraffes (Carnival characters), **268**
grelos, 21, 34
Guards (Carnival characters), 55, 58, 59, **59**
Guggemusik, 108, 114–15, **115**
guisers, 131, 138
gumbo, **138**, 139, 141; preparation of, 143n.21

Haiti. *See* Carnival in Haiti
Harlequin (Carnival character), 13, **74**, 75, 96, **103**, 208, **208**,
    221, 231, 278, 281. *See also* Arlecchino
Healer (Carnival character), 56, 59
"heart clowns" (Carnival characters), 231, **233**
Hell on a Platter (Carnival character), **312**
horo, 55, 57

Inca emperor (Carnival character), 187
Inca troupes, **188**

jab-jab devils (Carnival characters), 245, **245**, 247
jaraguá (Carnival character), 230
jester. *See* Ueli
jouvay, 259, **260-61**, 262
Junior Carnival, 255, 257, **258**, **259**
Justice (Carnival character), **293**

Kalends, 18n.3, 23
Kiddie Mas, 255, 257, **258**, **259**
king cake, **323**, 324, **324**
King of the Bean, 323
kings (Carnival characters), **252**, 253, **256**, 259, **260**, 278, 291
Knights of Momus, 302
kok kalite, 281, 283, 286
koudyay, 271, 279–81, 284, 286
Koukers (Carnival character), 7–8, **7**, **44-47**, 44–63, **50-61**, 53–

60, **63**; requirements to play, 53

Kouker's Day, 44–62, **260**; chaos and order in, 60–61; and initiatory rituals, 60–61; performers in rituals, 53–56

krewes, 11, 16, 126–27, 301–8; Amon-Ra, 312; Carrollton and Freret, 305; Comus, 301–3, **302**, **306**, **307**, 312, 324; Iris, 305, 308; Lords of Leather, 309; Mwindo, 309; Orpheus, 308, **310-11**; Petronius, 309, **314-15**; Proteus, 302, **306**; Rex, **298**, 302, 304, 312, 314–15; Twelfth Night Revelers, 304, **307**; Yuga, 309; Zulu Social Aid and Pleasure Club, 15, 313, 315, **316**, **317**

Krustnik (Carnival character), 54

lanterns, **9**, 96, **98-99**, 100, **102**, 110, 111, 113; of Alti Dante masqueraders, 102; construction of, 97; and controversy of size of holes in cheese, **111**; depicting dogfight, **111**; in *Fasnacht* processions, 96; with propane pipes, **100**; as standard for piccolo players, **100**; on stationary display in cathedral square, 112, **113**; worn on the head, 97, **97**

larve, 101

Laza, Spain. *See* Carnival in Spain (Laza)

Lent, 3, 4, 8, 9, 10, 12, 17, 24, 28; changes in starting date, 96

licor, 33, 35

liming, 257

lion, 65, **69**, 70

Lucifer (Carnival character), 181, 245

Maälsuppe, 101

Magareta (Carnival character), 57

maracatus nação, **13**, **209**, **222**, 222–24, **223**, **224**, **225**, 321–22

maracatus rurais, **19**, 224–26, **226**

marching bands, 35, 96, **97**, **103**, **104**, 106–108, **107**, **109**, 114–16, **115**, **117**, 185–87, **187**, 192, 194–95, 209–10, **219**, 219, 221, **225**, 225, 227–28, 230, **320**, 320–23, **321**, 321–22, **322**

Mardi Gras, 3, 9, 10–11, 14; and employer-reveler relationships, 132; four meanings of, 126; and gays, 309; and men's wagon, **131**; and protest by Christian fundamentalists, **313**

Mardi Gras associations, 129, 139, 142. *See also* krewes

Mardi Gras Indians (Carnival characters), **16**, 316–20; Goldenstar Hunters Mardi Gras Indian Tribe, **319**, **320**; Wild Tchoupitoulas Mardi Gras Indian Tribe, **318-19**, 321; Yellow Pocahontas Mardi Gras Indian Tribe, **318**

Mardi Gras songs, 125, 129, 136, 138, 142, 142n.13

Mardi Gras suits, 129, 130–31, **139**

Maringuilla (Carnival character), 157

martes de ch'alla, 197

mas, 10, 239, 250–55, 262–63, 265

mas bands and bandleaders, 248, 250–53; Bomparte and Mack Copeland, 248; Breakaway Productions, 253; "Diamond" Jim Harding, 248; D'Midas, **251**, 253; George Bailey, 249, 250–51; Harold Saldina, 248; Hart, 263; Irving McWilliams, 251; Jason Griffith and Old-Fashioned Sailors, 253, 262; Legends, 253, **253**, 263; Peter Minshall, 251, **252**, 265; Poison, 253; Stephen and Elsie Lee Huang, 251; Wayne Berkeley, 251, 263

masks and masquerades, 2, 6, **8**, 12, 13, 14, 15, 24, 25, 28, **28**, 30, 31, 44–62, 107, 147, 154, 164, 212–13, 252; of *achachi*, 179–80; *achachis*, 184; alligator, **289**; Altfrangg, 104, **105**;

Alti Dante, **102**, 103, **114**; American Indians, 245, 248, **249**, 263, **265**, 278, 291, 302, 315–20; and Andean Indian theme groups, 188–89; archangel Michael, 291, **293**; Arlecchino, **74**, 75; Baba Marta, 45; *babau*, 229; Babba, **46**, 54, **55**, 57, 58, **60**; *bakas*, 292; Barber, 55, **56**; in Barcelona Carnival, **26-27**; *baùta*, **66-67**, 75, 77, 83; bears, 181, 227–29, **228**; Beelzebub, 245; Big Shot of Africa, 315; Blâtzlibajass, 103, **103**, **104**; Bookman, **14**, 245, 263, **264**; Brighella, 75; bull, 229, **229**; *burrinhas*, 231, **232**; Capitano, 75; *caporales*, 175, 184, **186**, 186–87, **187**, 199; *catirina*, 229; *catrines*, 158–59, **158-59**, **160**, **166**, **168**; Chaloskas, 278, **278**, 292, **296**; *charros*, 145, **146**, **147**, **154**, **155**, **156**, 156–57; China Supay, 181; *chinas diablas*, **180**, 199; *chivarrudos*, **144**, 161, 163, 164, **164**; *cholitas*, 185; clowns, 229; Columbina, 75, 208, 221, 231; of commedia dell'arte, **74**; condor, 181; cowheads, 278, **279**; demoniacal, 72; Devil, **174**, 179, **180**, **181**, 181–84, **182-83**, 194, **195**, 195, 245, **245**, **279**, 291, **293**, 302; *diablada*, 190; dogs, 109–10, **110**, 116; Domino, 75; *doñas*, 184, **184**, 185; Il Dottore, 75; Dummpeter, 103; Dyaddo, 54, 57, 58; Ergen, 55, 58; *Español*, **iv**, 159, **160**, **161**, 165; and face painting, **84**, 86; in fantasy-style costumes, **76**, **82**, **83**; General Charles Oscar (Chaloskas), 278, **278**, 292, **296**; General Gran Van, 278; General Kaka, 278; General Pet Santi, 278; General PiTa-PiTris, 278; General Plim pa Gouye, 278; General Ti-Zozo, 278; giraffes, **268**; goddess with rooster on head, **20**; Guards, 55, 58, 59, **59**; Harlequin, 13, **74**, 75, 96, **103**, 208, **208**, 221, 231, 278, 281; Healer, 56, 59; heart clowns, 231, **233**; Hell on a Platter, **312**; in historic-style court costumes, **8**, **78**, 79; Inca emperor, 187; *jab-jab* devils, 245, **245**, 247; *jaraguá*, 230; Justice, **293**; kings, **252**, 253, **256**, 259, **260**, 278, 291; Koukers, 7–8, **7**, 43–63, **44-47**, **50-61**, **63**; Krustnik, 54; with lion symbol of St. Mark, **69**; Lucifer, 181, 245; Magareta, 57; Mardi Gras Indians, **16**, 316–20; **318-20**; Maringuilla, 157; Medusa, **71**; Midnight Robber, 248, **249**, 263, **263**; mock priest, 229; *moco jumbies*, 245, 263, **271**; Momma, 55, 57; *morenas*, **28**, 31, 38, **40**, **42**; *morenos*, **12**, 184, 190, **201**; mouse, **112**; Mr. Big Stuff, 315; *nana*, **157**, 157–58; *oso*, 164; outer space alien, **102**; Pantalone, 75; *papangús*, 231, **232**; papier-mâché, 101, **102**, 115; *payasito*, 164; *peliqueiros*, **6**, 7, 13, **25**, 30, 31, **31**, 33–36, **35**, 38–40; penguin, **84**; Pierrot, 13, **75**, 104, 208, 221, 231, 245, 247; pig, **288**; Pizarro, 187; Plague Doctor, 75, **75**; Pop, 56, **56**, 57; Province Prince, 315; Pulcinella, **69**, 75, 208, 245; queens, **209**, 222, **223**, 224, **224**, 253, 259, 278; Ranger, 56; *reyes morenos*, 184; sailors, 245, **248**, 248, **262**, 262–63; Saint Michael, 181, **182-83**; *sauvages*, **vi**, 9, 123, 125, **125**, **128**, **130**, **134**, **135**, 135–36, 140, 141; *Schnitzelbangg*, **116**, 116–18; with seashell theme, **82**; Shoeshine, 56, 57; Soulful Warriors, **316**; stickmen, 245, 247; stilt walkers, **72-73**, 245, 263, **267**, 278; Taino *caciques*, 291, **295**; Three Blind Mice, **312**; *tinkus*, 175, 188, **189**; Tobas, 189, **191**; Tribos groups, 226–27; Tsar, 54, 56, **61**; Tsaritsa, 55, 58; Tsiganin, 55, 57; Tsiganka, 55; Ueli, **92**, **93**, 104; *vasarias/os*, 157, **157**, 163; vicious dog, **110**; *Waggis*, 14, 105, **105**, **106**, **115**; wandering Jew, 291, **295**; werewolves, 278, **279**; whipmasters, 245, **246**; Witch Doctor, 315; *zonbi*, 269, 284, **284**, 285; Zulu king, 291, **294**, 315;